Lecture Notes in Computer Science   11624

Commenced Publication in 1973
Founding and Former Series Editors:
Gerhard Goos, Juris Hartmanis, and Jan van Leeuwen

More information about this series at http://www.springer.com/series/7407

Sanjay Misra · Osvaldo Gervasi ·
Beniamino Murgante · Elena Stankova ·
Vladimir Korkhov · Carmelo Torre ·
Ana Maria A. C. Rocha ·
David Taniar · Bernady O. Apduhan ·
Eufemia Tarantino (Eds.)

Computational Science and Its Applications – ICCSA 2019

19th International Conference
Saint Petersburg, Russia, July 1–4, 2019
Proceedings, Part VI

 Springer

Editors
Sanjay Misra 🄳
Covenant University
Ota, Nigeria

Beniamino Murgante 🄳
University of Basilicata
Potenza, Italy

Vladimir Korkhov 🄳
Saint Petersburg State University
Saint Petersburg, Russia

Ana Maria A. C. Rocha 🄳
University of Minho
Braga, Portugal

Bernady O. Apduhan
Kyushu Sangyo University
Fukuoka, Japan

Osvaldo Gervasi 🄳
University of Perugia
Perugia, Italy

Elena Stankova 🄳
Saint Petersburg State University
Saint Petersburg, Russia

Carmelo Torre 🄳
Polytechnic University of Bari
Bari, Italy

David Taniar 🄳
Monash University
Clayton, VIC, Australia

Eufemia Tarantino 🄳
Polytechnic University of Bari
Bari, Italy

ISSN 0302-9743   ISSN 1611-3349 (electronic)
Lecture Notes in Computer Science
ISBN 978-3-030-24310-4   ISBN 978-3-030-24311-1 (eBook)
https://doi.org/10.1007/978-3-030-24311-1

LNCS Sublibrary: SL1 – Theoretical Computer Science and General Issues

This Springer imprint is published by the registered company Springer Nature Switzerland AG
The registered company address is: Gewerbestrasse 11, 6330 Cham, Switzerland

Preface

These six volumes (LNCS volumes 11619–11624) consist of the peer-reviewed papers from the 2019 International Conference on Computational Science and Its Applications (ICCSA 2019) held in St. Petersburg, Russia during July 1–4, 2019, in collaboration with the St. Petersburg University, St. Petersburg, Russia.

ICCSA 2019 was a successful event in the International Conferences on Computational Science and Its Applications (ICCSA) series, previously held in Melbourne, Australia (2018), Trieste, Italy (2017), Beijing, China (2016), Banff, Canada (2015), Guimaraes, Portugal (2014), Ho Chi Minh City, Vietnam (2013), Salvador, Brazil (2012), Santander, Spain (2011), Fukuoka, Japan (2010), Suwon, South Korea (2009), Perugia, Italy (2008), Kuala Lumpur, Malaysia (2007), Glasgow, UK (2006), Singapore (2005), Assisi, Italy (2004), Montreal, Canada (2003), and (as ICCS) Amsterdam, The Netherlands (2002) and San Francisco, USA (2001).

Computational science is a main pillar of most of the current research, industrial and commercial activities, and plays a unique role in exploiting ICT innovative technologies. The ICCSA conference series have been providing a venue to researchers and industry practitioners to discuss new ideas, to share complex problems and their solutions, and to shape new trends in computational science.

Apart from the general track, ICCSA 2019 also included 33 workshops, in various areas of computational sciences, ranging from computational science technologies, to specific areas of computational sciences, such as software engineering, security, artificial intelligence, and blockchain technologies. We accepted 64 papers distributed in the five general tracks, 259 in workshops and ten short papers. We would like to show our appreciations to the workshop chairs and co-chairs.

The success of the ICCSA conference series, in general, and ICCSA 2019, in particular, is due to the support of many people: authors, presenters, participants, keynote speakers, workshop chairs, Organizing Committee members, student volunteers, Program Committee members, Advisory Committee members, international liaison chairs, reviewers and people in other various roles. We would like to thank them all.

We also thank our publisher, Springer, for accepting to publish the proceedings, for sponsoring part of the best papers awards and for their kind assistance and cooperation during the editing process.

We cordially invite you to visit the ICCSA website http://www.iccsa.org where you can find all relevant information about this interesting and exciting event.

July 2019

Osvaldo Gervasi
Beniamino Murgante
Sanjay Misra

Welcome to St. Petersburg

Welcome to St. Petersburg, the Venice of the North, the city of three revolutions, creation of czar Peter the Great, the most European city in Russia. ICCSA 2019 was hosted by St. Petersburg State University, during July 1–4, 2019.

St. Petersburg is the second largest city in Russia after Moscow. It is the former capital of Russia and has a lot of attractions related to this role in the past: imperial palaces and parks both in the city center and suburbs, respectable buildings of nobles and state institutions, multitude of rivers and canals with more than 300 bridges of various forms and sizes. Extraordinary history and rich cultural traditions of both imperial Russia and the Soviet Union attracted and inspired many examples of world's greatest architecture, literature, music, and visual art, some of which can be found in the famous Hermitage and State Russian Museum located in the heart of the city. Late June and early July is the season of white nights where the sun sets only for a few hours, and the nighttime is covered with mysterious twilight.

What to do in the city:

- Enjoy the white nights, see the open bridges during the night and cargo ships passing by from Ladoga Lake to the Gulf of Finland and back. Dvortsovy bridge is open at about 1am. Be sure to stay on the correct side of the river when the bridges open!
- Visit Hermitage (Winter palace) and State Russian Museum to see great examples of international and Russian art, and the Kunstkammer, the oldest museum of St. Petersburg founded by Peter the Great.
- Travel to St. Petersburg suburbs Peterhof and Tsarskoe Selo to see imperial palaces and splendid parks, famous Peterhof fountains.
- Eat Russian food: borsch (beetroot soup), pelmeni and vareniki (meat and sweet dumplings), bliny (pancakes), vinegret (beetroot salad), drink kvas and maybe some vodka.
- Walk around and inside the Peter and Paul Fortress, the place where the city began in 1703.
- Visit the Mariinsky Theater for famous Russian ballet and opera.
- Have a boat tour along the Neva River and canals to look at the city from the water.
- Walk along Nevsky Prospect, the main street of the city.
- Climb St. Isaac's Cathedral colonnade to enjoy great city views.
- Go down to the Metro, the city's underground train network with some Soviet-style museum-like stations.
- Pay a visit to the recently renovated Summer Garden, the oldest park of St. Petersburg.
- Visit a new modern open space on the New Holland Island to see modern art exhibitions, performances and just to relax and enjoy sitting on the grass with an ice cream or lemonade during a hot summer day.

St. Petersburg State University is the oldest university in Russia, an actively developing, world-class center of research and education. The university dates back to 1724, when Peter the Great founded the Academy of Sciences and Arts as well as the first Academic University and the university preparatory school in Russia. At present there are over 5,000 academic staff members and more than 30,000 students, receiving education in more than 400 educational programs at 25 faculties and institutes.

The venue of ICCSA is the Faculty of Economics located on Tavricheskaya Street, other faculties and university buildings are distributed all over the city with the main campus located on Vasilievsky Island and the natural science faculties (Mathematics and Mechanics, Applied Mathematics and Control Processes, Physics, Chemistry) located on the campus about 40 kilometers away from the city center in Peterhof.

Elena Stankova
Vladimir Korkhov
Nataliia Kulabukhova

Organization

ICCSA 2019 was organized by St. Petersburg University (Russia), University of Perugia (Italy), University of Basilicata (Italy), Monash University (Australia), Kyushu Sangyo University (Japan), University of Minho, (Portugal).

Honorary General Chairs

Antonio Laganà	University of Perugia, Italy
Norio Shiratori	Tohoku University, Japan
Kenneth C. J. Tan	Sardina Systems, Estonia

General Chairs

Osvaldo Gervasi	University of Perugia, Italy
Elena Stankova	St. Petersburg University, Russia
Bernady O. Apduhan	Kyushu Sangyo University, Japan

Program Committee Chairs

Beniamino Murgante	University of Basilicata, Italy
David Taniar	Monash University, Australia
Vladimir Korkov	St. Petersburg University, Russia
Ana Maria A. C. Rocha	University of Minho, Portugal

International Advisory Committee

Jemal Abawajy	Deakin University, Australia
Dharma P. Agarwal	University of Cincinnati, USA
Rajkumar Buyya	Melbourne University, Australia
Claudia Bauzer Medeiros	University of Campinas, Brazil
Manfred M. Fisher	Vienna University of Economics and Business, Austria
Marina L. Gavrilova	University of Calgary, Canada
Yee Leung	Chinese University of Hong Kong, SAR China

International Liaison Chairs

Ana Carla P. Bitencourt	Universidade Federal do Reconcavo da Bahia, Brazil
Giuseppe Borruso	University of Trieste, Italy
Alfredo Cuzzocrea	ICAR-CNR and University of Calabria, Italy
Maria Irene Falcão	University of Minho, Portugal
Robert C. H. Hsu	Chung Hua University, Taiwan
Tai-Hoon Kim	Hannam University, South Korea
Sanjay Misra	Covenant University, Nigeria

Takashi Naka   Kyushu Sangyo University, Japan
Rafael D. C. Santos   National Institute for Space Research, Brazil
Maribel Yasmina Santos University of Minho, Portugal

Workshop and Session Organizing Chairs

Beniamino Murgante   University of Basilicata, Italy
Sanjay Misra   Covenant University, Nigeria
Jorge Gustavo Rocha   University of Minho, Portugal

Award Chair

Wenny Rahayu   La Trobe University, Australia

Publicity Committee Chairs

Elmer Dadios   De La Salle University, Philippines
Hong Quang Nguyen   International University (VNU-HCM), Vietnam
Daisuke Takahashi   Tsukuba University, Japan
Shangwang Wang   Beijing University of Posts and Telecommunications,
                        China

Workshop Organizers

Advanced Transport Tools and Methods (A2TM 2019)

Massimiliano Petri   University of Pisa, Italy
Antonio Pratelli   University of Pisa, Italy

Advanced Computational Approaches in Fractals, Wavelet, Entropy and Data Mining Applications (AAFTWTETDT 2019)

Yeliz Karaca   University of Massachusetts Medical School, USA
Yu-Dong Zhang   University of Leicester, UK
Majaz Moonis   University of Massachusettes Medical School, USA

Advances in Artificial Intelligence Learning Technologies: Blended Learning, STEM, Computational Thinking and Coding (AAILT 2019)

Alfredo Milani   University of Perugia, Italy
Sergio Tasso   University of Perugia, Italy
Valentina Poggioni   University of Perugia, Italy

Affective Computing and Emotion Recognition (ACER-EMORE 2019)

Alfredo Milani   University of Perugia, Italy
Valentina Franzoni   University of Perugia, Italy
Giulio Biondi   University of Florence, Itay

Advances in Information Systems and Technologies for Emergency Management, Risk Assessment and Mitigation Based on the Resilience Concepts (ASTER 2019)

Maurizio Pollino   ENEA, Italy
Marco Vona   University of Basilicata, Italy
Beniamino Murgante   University of Basilicata, Italy

Blockchain and Distributed Ledgers: Technologies and Application (BDLTA 2019)

Vladimir Korkhov   St. Petersburg State University, Russia
Elena Stankova   St. Petersburg State University, Russia

Bio and Neuro-inspired Computing and Applications (BIONCA 2019)

Nadia Nedjah   State University of Rio de Janeiro, Brazil
Luiza de Macedo Mourell State University of Rio de Janeiro, Brazil

Computer Aided Modeling, Simulation, and Analysis (CAMSA 2018)

Jie Shen   University of Michigan, USA
Hao Chen   Shanghai University of Engineering Science, China
Youguo He   Jiangsu University, China

Computational and Applied Statistics (CAS 2019)

Ana Cristina Braga   University of Minho, Portugal

Computational Mathematics, Statistics, and Information Management (CMSIM 2019)

M. Filomena Teodoro   Portuguese Naval Academy and Lisbon University,
                         Portugal

Computational Optimization and Applications (COA 2019)

Ana Maria Rocha   University of Minho, Portugal
Humberto Rocha   University of Coimbra, Portugal

Computational Astrochemistry (CompAstro 2019)

Marzio Rosi   University of Perugia, Italy
Dimitrios Skouteris   Master-up, Perugia, Italy
Fanny Vazart   Université Grenoble Alpes, France
Albert Rimola   Universitat Autònoma de Barcelona, Spain

Cities, Technologies, and Planning (CTP 2019)

Beniamino Murgante   University of Basilicata, Italy
Giuseppe Borruso   University of Trieste, Italy

Econometrics and Multidimensional Evaluation in the Urban Environment (EMEUE 2019)

Carmelo M. Torre	Polytechnic of Bari, Italy
Pierluigi Morano	Polytechnic of Bari, Italy
Maria Cerreta	University of Naples Federico II, Italy
Paola Perchinunno	University of Bari, Italy
Francesco Tajani	University of Rome La Sapienza, Italy

Future Computing System Technologies and Applications (FISTA 2019)

Bernady O. Apduhan	Kyushu Sangyo University, Japan
Rafael Santos	National Institute for Space Research, Brazil

Geographical Analysis, Urban Modeling, Spatial Statistics (GEO-AND-MOD 2019)

Beniamino Murgante	University of Basilicata, Italy
Giuseppe Borruso	University of Trieste, Italy
Hartmut Asche	University of Potsdam, Germany

Geomatics for Resource Monitoring and Control (GRMC 2019)

Eufemia Tarantino	Polytechnic of Bari, Italy
Rosa Lasaponara	Italian Research Council, IMAA-CNR, Italy
Benedetto Figorito	ARPA Puglia, Italy
Umberto Fratino	Polytechnic of Bari, Italy

International Symposium on Software Quality (ISSQ 2019)

Sanjay Misra	Covenant University, Nigeria

Land Use Monitoring for Sustainability (LUMS 2019)

Carmelo M. Torre	Polytechnic of Bari, Italy
Alessandro Bonifazi	Polytechnic of Bari, Italy
Pasquale Balena	Polytechnic of Bari, Italy
Beniamino Murgante	University of Basilicata, Italy
Eric Gielen	Polytechnic University of Valencia, Spain

Machine Learning for Space and Earth Observation Data (ML-SEOD 2019)

Rafael Santos	Brazilian National Institute for Space Research, Brazil
Karine Reis Ferreira	National Institute for Space Research, Brazil

Mobile-Computing, Sensing, and Actuation in Cyber Physical Systems (MSA4CPS 2019)

Saad Qaisar	National University of Sciences and Technology, Pakistan
Moonseong Kim	Seoul Theological University, South Korea

Quantum Chemical Modeling of Solids with Computers: From Plane Waves to Local Structures (QuaCheSol 2019)

Andrei Tchougréeff	Russia Academy of Sciences, Russia
Richard Dronskowski	RWTH Aachen University, Germany
Taku Onishi	Mie University and Tromsoe University, Japan

Scientific Computing Infrastructure (SCI 2019)

Vladimir Korkhov	St. Petersburg State University, Russia
Elena Stankova	St. Petersburg State University, Russia
Nataliia Kulabukhova	St. Petersburg State University, Russia

Computational Studies for Energy and Comfort in Building (SECoB 2019)

Senhorinha Teixeira	University of Minho, Portugal
Angela Silva	Viana do Castelo Polytechnic Institute, Portugal
Ana Maria Rocha	University of Minho, Portugal

Software Engineering Processes and Applications (SEPA 2019)

Sanjay Misra	Covenant University, Nigeria

Smart Factory Convergence (SFC 2019)

Jongpil Jeong	Sungkyunkwan University, South Korea

Smart City and Water. Resource and Risk (Smart_Water 2019)

Giuseppe Borruso	University of Trieste, Italy
Ginevra Balletto	University of Cagliari, Italy
Gianfranco Becciu	Polytechnic University of Milan, Italy
Chiara Garau	University of Cagliari, Italy
Beniamino Murgante	University of Basilicata, Italy
Francesco Viola	University of Cagliari, Italy

Sustainability Performance Assessment: Models, Approaches, and Applications Toward Interdisciplinary and Integrated Solutions (SPA 2019)

Francesco Scorza	University of Basilicata, Italy
Valentin Grecu	Lucia Blaga University on Sibiu, Romania
Jolanta Dvarioniene	Kaunas University, Lithuania
Sabrina Lai	University of Cagliari, Italy

Theoretical and Computational Chemistry and Its Applications (TCCMA 2019)

Noelia Faginas Lago	University of Perugia, Italy
Andrea Lombardi	University of Perugia, Italy

Tools and Techniques in Software Development Processes (TTSDP 2019)

Sanjay Misra	Covenant University, Nigeria

Virtual Reality and Applications (VRA 2019)

Osvaldo Gervasi	University of Perugia, Italy
Sergio Tasso	University of Perugia, Italy

Collective, Massive and Evolutionary Systems (WCES 2019)

Alfredo Milani	University of Perugia, Italy
Valentina Franzoni	University of Rome La Sapienza, Italy
Rajdeep Niyogi	Indian Institute of Technology at Roorkee, India
Stefano Marcugini	University of Perugia, Italy

Parallel and Distributed Data Mining (WPDM 2019)

Massimo Cafaro	University of Salento, Italy
Italo Epicoco	University of Salento, Italy
Marco Pulimeno	University of Salento, Italy
Giovanni Aloisio	University of Salento, Italy

Program Committee

Kenneth Adamson	University of Ulster, UK
Vera Afreixo	University of Aveiro, Portugal
Filipe Alvelos	University of Minho, Portugal
Remadevi Arjun	National Institute of Technology Karnataka, India
Hartmut Asche	University of Potsdam, Germany
Ginevra Balletto	University of Cagliari, Italy
Michela Bertolotto	University College Dublin, Ireland
Sandro Bimonte	CEMAGREF, TSCF, France
Rod Blais	University of Calgary, Canada
Ivan Blečić	University of Sassari, Italy
Giuseppe Borruso	University of Trieste, Italy
Ana Cristina Braga	University of Minho, Portugal
Massimo Cafaro	University of Salento, Italy
Yves Caniou	Lyon University, France
José A. Cardoso e Cunha	Universidade Nova de Lisboa, Portugal
Leocadio G. Casado	University of Almeria, Spain
Carlo Cattani	University of Salerno, Italy
Mete Celik	Erciyes University, Turkey
Hyunseung Choo	Sungkyunkwan University, South Korea
Min Young Chung	Sungkyunkwan University, South Korea
Florbela Maria da Cruz Domingues Correia	Polytechnic Institute of Viana do Castelo, Portugal
Gilberto Corso Pereira	Federal University of Bahia, Brazil
Alessandro Costantini	INFN, Italy
Carla Dal Sasso Freitas	Universidade Federal do Rio Grande do Sul, Brazil
Pradesh Debba	The Council for Scientific and Industrial Research (CSIR), South Africa
Hendrik Decker	Instituto Tecnológico de Informática, Spain

Frank Devai	London South Bank University, UK
Rodolphe Devillers	Memorial University of Newfoundland, Canada
Joana Matos Dias	University of Coimbra, Portugal
Paolino Di Felice	University of L'Aquila, Italy
Prabu Dorairaj	NetApp, India/USA
M. Irene Falcao	University of Minho, Portugal
Cherry Liu Fang	U.S. DOE Ames Laboratory, USA
Florbela P. Fernandes	Polytechnic Institute of Bragança, Portugal
Jose-Jesus Fernandez	National Centre for Biotechnology, CSIS, Spain
Paula Odete Fernandes	Polytechnic Institute of Bragança, Portugal
Adelaide de Fátima Baptista Valente Freitas	University of Aveiro, Portugal
Manuel Carlos Figueiredo	University of Minho, Portugal
Valentina Franzoni	University of Rome La Sapienza, Italy
Maria Celia Furtado Rocha	PRODEB–PósCultura/UFBA, Brazil
Chiara Garau	University of Cagliari, Italy
Paulino Jose Garcia Nieto	University of Oviedo, Spain
Jerome Gensel	LSR-IMAG, France
Maria Giaoutzi	National Technical University, Athens, Greece
Arminda Manuela Andrade Pereira Gonçalves	University of Minho, Portugal
Andrzej M. Goscinski	Deakin University, Australia
Sevin Gümgüm	Izmir University of Economics, Turkey
Alex Hagen-Zanker	University of Cambridge, UK
Shanmugasundaram Hariharan	B.S. Abdur Rahman University, India
Eligius M. T. Hendrix	University of Malaga/Wageningen University, Spain/The Netherlands
Hisamoto Hiyoshi	Gunma University, Japan
Mustafa Inceoglu	EGE University, Turkey
Jongpil Jeong	Sungkyunkwan University, South Korea
Peter Jimack	University of Leeds, UK
Qun Jin	Waseda University, Japan
A. S. M. Kayes	La Trobe University, Australia
Farid Karimipour	Vienna University of Technology, Austria
Baris Kazar	Oracle Corp., USA
Maulana Adhinugraha Kiki	Telkom University, Indonesia
DongSeong Kim	University of Canterbury, New Zealand
Taihoon Kim	Hannam University, South Korea
Ivana Kolingerova	University of West Bohemia, Czech Republic
Nataliia Kulabukhova	St. Petersburg University, Russia
Vladimir Korkhov	St. Petersburg University, Russia
Rosa Lasaponara	National Research Council, Italy
Maurizio Lazzari	National Research Council, Italy
Cheng Siong Lee	Monash University, Australia
Sangyoun Lee	Yonsei University, South Korea

Jongchan Lee	Kunsan National University, South Korea
Chendong Li	University of Connecticut, USA
Gang Li	Deakin University, Australia
Fang Liu	AMES Laboratories, USA
Xin Liu	University of Calgary, Canada
Andrea Lombardi	University of Perugia, Italy
Savino Longo	University of Bari, Italy
Tinghuai Ma	NanJing University of Information Science and Technology, China
Ernesto Marcheggiani	Katholieke Universiteit Leuven, Belgium
Antonino Marvuglia	Research Centre Henri Tudor, Luxembourg
Nicola Masini	National Research Council, Italy
Eric Medvet	University of Trieste, Italy
Nirvana Meratnia	University of Twente, The Netherlands
Noelia Faginas Lago	University of Perugia, Italy
Giuseppe Modica	University of Reggio Calabria, Italy
Josè Luis Montaña	University of Cantabria, Spain
Maria Filipa Mourão	IP from Viana do Castelo, Portugal
Louiza de Macedo Mourelle	State University of Rio de Janeiro, Brazil
Nadia Nedjah	State University of Rio de Janeiro, Brazil
Laszlo Neumann	University of Girona, Spain
Kok-Leong Ong	Deakin University, Australia
Belen Palop	Universidad de Valladolid, Spain
Marcin Paprzycki	Polish Academy of Sciences, Poland
Eric Pardede	La Trobe University, Australia
Kwangjin Park	Wonkwang University, South Korea
Ana Isabel Pereira	Polytechnic Institute of Bragança, Portugal
Massimiliano Petri	University of Pisa, Italy
Maurizio Pollino	Italian National Agency for New Technologies, Energy and Sustainable Economic Development, Italy
Alenka Poplin	University of Hamburg, Germany
Vidyasagar Potdar	Curtin University of Technology, Australia
David C. Prosperi	Florida Atlantic University, USA
Wenny Rahayu	La Trobe University, Australia
Jerzy Respondek	Silesian University of Technology Poland
Humberto Rocha	INESC-Coimbra, Portugal
Jon Rokne	University of Calgary, Canada
Octavio Roncero	CSIC, Spain
Maytham Safar	Kuwait University, Kuwait
Chiara Saracino	A.O. Ospedale Niguarda Ca' Granda - Milano, Italy
Haiduke Sarafian	The Pennsylvania State University, USA
Francesco Scorza	University of Basilicata, Italy
Marco Paulo Seabra dos Reis	University of Coimbra, Portugal
Jie Shen	University of Michigan, USA

Qi Shi	Liverpool John Moores University, UK
Dale Shires	U.S. Army Research Laboratory, USA
Inês Soares	University of Coimbra, Portugal
Elena Stankova	St. Petersburg University, Russia
Takuo Suganuma	Tohoku University, Japan
Eufemia Tarantino	Polytechnic of Bari, Italy
Sergio Tasso	University of Perugia, Italy
Ana Paula Teixeira	University of Trás-os-Montes and Alto Douro, Portugal
Senhorinha Teixeira	University of Minho, Portugal
M. Filomena Teodoro	Portuguese Naval Academy and University of Lisbon, Portugal
Parimala Thulasiraman	University of Manitoba, Canada
Carmelo Torre	Polytechnic of Bari, Italy
Javier Martinez Torres	Centro Universitario de la Defensa Zaragoza, Spain
Giuseppe A. Trunfio	University of Sassari, Italy
Pablo Vanegas	University of Cuenca, Equador
Marco Vizzari	University of Perugia, Italy
Varun Vohra	Merck Inc., USA
Koichi Wada	University of Tsukuba, Japan
Krzysztof Walkowiak	Wroclaw University of Technology, Poland
Zequn Wang	Intelligent Automation Inc., USA
Robert Weibel	University of Zurich, Switzerland
Frank Westad	Norwegian University of Science and Technology, Norway
Roland Wismüller	Universität Siegen, Germany
Mudasser Wyne	SOET National University, USA
Chung-Huang Yang	National Kaohsiung Normal University, Taiwan
Xin-She Yang	National Physical Laboratory, UK
Salim Zabir	France Telecom Japan Co., Japan
Haifeng Zhao	University of California, Davis, USA
Fabiana Zollo	University of Venice Cà Foscari, Italy
Albert Y. Zomaya	University of Sydney, Australia

Additional Reviewers

Adewumi Oluwasegun	Covenant University, Nigeria
Afreixo Vera	University of Aveiro, Portugal
Agrawal Akshat	International Institute of Information Technology Bangalore, India
Aguilar Antonio	University of Barcelona, Spain
Ahmad Rashid	Microwave and Antenna Lab, School of Engineering, South Korea
Ahmed Waseem	Federal University of Technology, Nigeria
Alamri Sultan	Taibah University, Medina, Saudi Arabia
Alfa Abraham	Kogi State College of Education, Nigeria
Alvelos Filipe	University of Minho, Portugal

Amato Federico	University of Basilicata, Italy
Amin Benatia Mohamed	Groupe Cesi, Francia
Andrianov Serge	Institute for Informatics of Tatarstan Academy of Sciences, Russia
Apduhan Bernady	Kyushu Sangyo University, Japan
Aquilanti Vincenzo	University of Perugia, Italy
Arjun Remadevi	National Institute of Technology Karnataka, India
Arogundade Oluwasefunmi	Federal University of Agriculture, Nigeria
Ascenzi Daniela	University of Trento, Italy
Ayeni Foluso	Southern University and A&M College, USA
Azubuike Ezenwoke	Covenant University, Nigeria
Balacco Gabriella	Polytechnic of Bari, Italy
Balena Pasquale	Polytechnic of Bari, Italy
Balletto Ginevra	University of Cagliari, Italy
Barrile Vincenzo	Mediterranean University of Reggio Calabria, Italy
Bartolomei Massimiliano	Spanish National Research Council, Spain
Behera Ranjan Kumar	Indian Institute of Technology Patna, India
Biondi Giulio	University of Florence, Italy
Bist Ankur Singh	KIET Ghaziabad, India
Blecic Ivan	University of Cagliari, Italy
Bogdanov Alexander	St. Petersburg State University, Russia
Borgogno Mondino Enrico Corrado	University of Turin, Italy
Borruso Giuseppe	University of Trieste, Italy
Bostenaru Maria	Ion Mincu University of Architecture and Urbanism, Romania
Braga Ana Cristina	University of Minho, Portugal
Cafaro Massimo	University of Salento, Italy
Capolupo Alessandra	University of Naples Federico II, Italy
Carvalho-Silva Valter	Universidade Estadual de Goiás, Brazil
Cerreta Maria	University Federico II of Naples, Italy
Chan Sheung Wai	Hong Kong Baptist Hospital, SAR China
Cho Chulhee	Seoul Guarantee Insurance Company Ltd., South Korea
Choi Jae-Young	Sungkyunkwan University, South Korea
Correia Anacleto	Base Naval de Lisboa, Portugal
Correia Elisete	University of Trás-Os-Montes e Alto Douro, Portugal
Correia Florbela Maria da Cruz Domingues	Instituto Politécnico de Viana do Castelo, Portugal
Costa e Silva Eliana	Polytechnic of Porto, Portugal
Costa Lino	Universidade do Minho, Portugal
Costantini Alessandro	Istituto Nazionale di Fisica Nucleare, Italy
Crawford Broderick	Pontificia Universidad Católica de Valparaíso, Chile
Cutini Valerio	University of Pisa, Italy
D'Acierno Luca	University of Naples Federico II, Italy
Danese Maria	Italian National Research Council, Italy
Dantas Coutinho Nayara	University of Perugia, Italy
Degtyarev Alexander	St. Petersburg State University, Russia

Dereli Dursun Ahu	UNSW Sydney, Australia
Devai Frank	London South Bank University, UK
Di Bari Gabriele	University of Florence, Italy
Dias Joana	University of Coimbra, Portugal
Diaz Diana	National University of Colombia, Colombia
Elfadaly Abdelaziz	University of Basilicata, Italy
Enriquez Palma Pedro Alberto	Universidad de la Rioja, Spain
Epicoco Italo	University of Salento, Italy
Esposito Giuseppina	Sapienza University of Rome, Italy
Faginas-Lago M. Noelia	University of Perugia, Italy
Fajardo Jorge	Universidad Politécnica Salesiana (UPS), Ecuador
Falcinelli Stefano	University of Perugia, Italy
Farina Alessandro	University of Pisa, Italy
Fattoruso Grazia	ENEA, Italy
Fernandes Florbela	Escola Superior de Tecnologia e Gestão de Bragancca, Portugal
Fernandes Paula	Escola Superior de Tecnologia e Gestão, Portugal
Fernández Ledesma Javier Darío	Universidad Pontificia Bolivariana, Bolivia
Ferreira Ana C.	University of Lisbon, Portugal
Ferrão Maria	Universidade da Beira Interior, Portugal
Figueiredo Manuel Carlos	Universidade do Minho, Portugal
Florez Hector	Universidad Distrital Francisco Jose de Caldas, Colombia
Franzoni Valentina	University of Perugia, Italy
Freitau Adelaide de Fátima Baptista Valente	University of Aveiro, Portugal
Friday Agbo	University of Eastern Finland, Finland
Frunzete Madalin	Polytechnic University of Bucharest, Romania
Fusco Giovanni	Laboratoire ESPACE, CNRS, France
Gabrani Goldie	Bml Munjal University, India
Gankevich Ivan	St. Petersburg State University, Russia
Garau Chiara	University of Cagliari, Italy
Garcia Ernesto	University of the Basque Country, Spain
Gavrilova Marina	University of Calgary, Canada
Gervasi Osvaldo	University of Perugia, Italy
Gilner Ewa	Silesian University of Technology, Poland
Gioia Andrea	University of Bari, Italy
Giorgi Giacomo	University of Perugia, Italy
Gonçalves Arminda Manuela	University of Minho, Portugal
Gorbachev Yuriy	Geolink Technologies, Russia
Gotoh Yusuke	Kyoto University, Japan
Goyal Rinkaj	Guru Gobind Singh Indraprastha University, India
Gümgüm Sevin	Izmir Economy University, Turkey

Osho Oluwafemi	Federal University of Technology Minna, Nigeria
Ozturk Savas	The Scientific and Technological Research Council of Turkey, Turkey
Panetta J. B.	University of Georgia, USA
Pardede Eric	La Trobe University, Australia
Perchinunno Paola	University of Bari, Italy
Pereira Ana	Instituto Politécnico de Bragança, Portugal
Peschechera Giuseppe	University of Bari, Italy
Petri Massimiliano	University of Pisa, Italy
Petrovic Marjana	University of Zagreb, Croatia
Pham Quoc Trung	Ho Chi Minh City University of Technology, Vietnam
Pinto Telmo	University of Minho, Portugal
Plekhanov Evgeny	Russian Academy of Economics, Russia
Poggioni Valentina	University of Perugia, Italy
Polidoro Maria João	University of Lisbon, Portugal
Pollino Maurizio	ENEA, Italy
Popoola Segun	Covenant University, Nigeria
Pratelli Antonio	University of Pisa, Italy
Pulimeno Marco	University of Salento, Italy
Rasool Hamid	National University of Sciences and Technology, Pakistan
Reis Marco	Universidade de Coimbra, Portugal
Respondek Jerzy	Silesian University of Technology, Poland
Riaz Nida	National University of Sciences and Technology, Pakistan
Rimola Albert	Autonomous University of Barcelona, Spain
Rocha Ana Maria	University of Minho, Portugal
Rocha Humberto	University of Coimbra, Portugal
Rosi Marzio	University of Perugia, Italy
Santos Rafael	National Institute for Space Research, Brazil
Santucci Valentino	University Stranieri of Perugia, Italy
Saponaro Mirko	Polytechnic of Bari, Italy
Sarafian Haiduke	Pennsylvania State University, USA
Scorza Francesco	University of Basilicata, Italy
Sedova Olya	St. Petersburg State University, Russia
Semanjski Ivana	Ghent University, Belgium
Sharma Jeetu	Mody University of Science and Technology, India
Sharma Purnima	University of Lucknow, India
Shchegoleva Nadezhda	Petersburg State Electrotechnical University, Russia
Shen Jie	University of Michigan, USA
Shoaib Muhammad	Sungkyunkwan University, South Korea
Shou Huahao	Zhejiang University of Technology, China
Silva-Fortes Carina	ESTeSL-IPL, Portugal
Silva Ângela Maria	Escola Superior de Ciências Empresariais, Portugal
Singh Upasana	The University of Manchester, UK
Singh V. B.	University of Delhi, India

Skouteris Dimitrios	Master-up, Perugia, Italy
Soares Inês	INESCC and IPATIMUP, Portugal
Soares Michel	Universidade Federal de Sergipe, Brazil
Sosnin Petr	Ulyanovsk State Technical University, Russia
Sousa Ines	University of Minho, Portugal
Stankova Elena	St. Petersburg State University, Russia
Stritih Uros	University of Ljubljana, Slovenia
Tanaka Kazuaki	Kyushu Institute of Technology, Japan
Tarantino Eufemia	Polytechnic of Bari, Italy
Tasso Sergio	University of Perugia, Italy
Teixeira Senhorinha	University of Minho, Portugal
Tengku Adil	La Trobe University, Australia
Teodoro M. Filomena	Lisbon University, Portugal
Torre Carmelo Maria	Polytechnic of Bari, Italy
Totaro Vincenzo	Polytechnic of Bari, Italy
Tripathi Aprna	GLA University, India
Vancsics Béla	University of Szeged, Hungary
Vasyunin Dmitry	University of Amsterdam, The Netherlands
Vig Rekha	The Northcap University, India
Walkowiak Krzysztof	Wroclaw University of Technology, Poland
Wanderley Fernando	New University of Lisbon, Portugal
Wang Chao	University of Science and Technology of China, China
Westad Frank	CAMO Software AS, USA
Yamazaki Takeshi	University of Tokyo, Japan
Zahra Noore	University of Guilan, India
Zollo Fabiana	University of Venice Ca' Foscari, Italy
Zullo Francesco	University of L'Aquila, Italy
Žemlička Michal	Charles University in Prague, Czech Republic
Živković Ljiljana	Republic Agency for Spatial Planning, Serbia

Sponsoring Organizations

ICCSA 2019 would not have been possible without tremendous support of many organizations and institutions, for which all organizers and participants of ICCSA 2019 express their sincere gratitude:

Springer Nature Switzerland AG, Germany
(http://www.springer.com)

St. Petersburg University, Russia
(http://english.spbu.ru/)

University of Perugia, Italy
(http://www.unipg.it)

University of Basilicata, Italy
(http://www.unibas.it)

Monash University, Australia
(http://monash.edu)

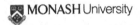

Kyushu Sangyo University, Japan
(www.kyusan-u.ac.jp)

Universidade do Minho, Portugal
(http://www.uminho.pt)

Contents – Part VI

Is a Smart City Really Smart? (Smart Cities 2019)

Smart City and Water. Resource and Risk (Smart Water 2019)

Virtual Reality and Applications (VRA 2019)

Collective, Massive and Evolutionary Systems (WCES 2019)

Parallel and Distributed Data Mining (WPDM 2019)

Computational Studies for Energy and Comfort in Building (SeCoDB 2019)

Engineering Modelling of Building Energy Consumption in Cities: Identifying Key Variables and Their Interactions with the Built Environment

Javier Urquizo[1,3]([✉]), Carlos Calderón[1], and Philip James[2]

[1] School of Architecture Planning and Landscape,
Newcastle University, Newcastle upon Tyne NE1 7RU, UK
carlos.calderon@newcastle.ac.uk
[2] School of Civil Engineering and Geosciences, Newcastle University,
Newcastle upon Tyne NE1 7RU, UK
philip.james@newcastle.ac.uk
[3] Escuela Superior Politécnica del Litoral, ESPOL, FIEC,
Campus Gustavo Galindo Km. 30.5 Vía Perimetral,
P.O. Box 09-01-5863, Guayaquil, Ecuador
jurquizo@espol.edu.ec
http://www.espol.edu.ec, https://www.ncl.ac.uk

Abstract. This paper focuses on a spatial domestic energy framework of sub-city areas in the United Kingdom using Newcastle upon Tyne as a case study. The framework estimates the energy end-use at the single dwelling level on three aggregate scales: district, neighbourhood and community. The framework uses two aggregation approaches, one using an approximated prototype-cluster of similar dwellings at the district scale and the other using a novel, sub-city DEM modelling of building and its micro-cohesive energy structures in neighbourhoods and communities. The validation strategy compare the modelled gas and electricity values in three representative districts against the DECC values in two aggregate hierarchical areas for electricity and gas: the DECC Medium Layer Super Output Area (MLSOA), and the Lower Layer Super Output Area (LLSOA). Our work discusses this framework in key areas: the availability of data, the number of surveyed variables and data processing methods for filling blanks in order to have an individual dwelling's complete energy Standard Assessment Procedure (SAP) profile, methods to provide evidence for finding patterns residing in the data set, methods for estimating the annual composite (gas and electricity) energy consumption for individual and aggregated dwellings, the validation strategy, the uncertainties associated in the data and model, and scaling and replication in other cities.

Keywords: Spatial interpolation · Record imputation ·
Distributed target scenarios · Domestic energy consumption ·
Structure detection · Urban energy modelling

© Springer Nature Switzerland AG 2019
S. Misra et al. (Eds.): ICCSA 2019, LNCS 11624, pp. 3–25, 2019.
https://doi.org/10.1007/978-3-030-24311-1_1

1 Introduction

Swan and Ugursal [1, p. 1828] state that "the bottom-up engineering approach is the only method that can fully develop the energy consumption of the sector without any historical energy consumption information" and that "these techniques have the capability of determining the impact of new technologies" [1, p. 1833] which, in turn, makes the method ideally suited for an area-based delivery approach favoured by local authorities (LAs). This paper discusses a particular spatial bottom-up area-based energy framework, the Newcastle Energy Model Framework (NCRF) [2], using two modelling approaches: clusters in districts and individual Domestic Energy Modelling (DEM) in neighbourhoods and communities. Because of assumptions in the nature of physics-based energy modelling, it is inevitable perhaps that there will be significant discrepancies between energy estimates and actual published UK government consumption figures. However, the energy estimates may still provide useful insights, as they are largely based on the physical parameters of the dwellings. In our research, the results are encouraging in some ways as there is a degree of spatial consistency across the results.

Our work represents a framework to attempt to estimate spatial domestic energy consumption in individual dwellings and aggregated areas using a spatially enabled database to represent local area characteristics. We argue that, as the scale decreases, the local area characteristics are more important. Model estimates in the sub-city DEM are improved in neighbourhoods by taking into consideration more variables. However, assessing the individual dwelling's energy consumption in the sub-city DEM approach requires more than a simple counting of the individual dwellings. Specifically, what must be examined is the role of local structures like micro-cohesive energy supply structures (district and group heating), dwelling in electricity time-of-use tariff (in the UK the Economy 7 tariff E7 i.e. pay normal prices during the day, but cheaper rates for seven hours during the night) and planned permission granted for converting houses to Houses in Multiple Occupations (HMO) and houses and flats having sharing amenities, as a number of researchers have suggested, for instance, [3] and [4]. The reason for having an increased number of data set variables is that this may lead to a better insight into the effect of uncertainties in the aggregated process [5] by generating a more complete representation of the dwelling. In the case of dwellings using the Economy 7 tariff, an increase number of variables is needed to provide a better description of the dwelling (the hot water heating system and the tank insulation are the new variables).

Using the Unique Property Reference Number (UPRN) code of an individual dwelling, it is likely to link secondary sources, either by Topographic Identification (TOID), and/or address to produce a better representation of individual dwelling predictors, instead or adopting archetypes to simplify the complexity of housing stock, e.g. two archetypes in the [6] physical model, 1,000 archetypes in the [7] BREHOMES model, 47 archetypes [8] in the CDEM model, which are difficult to relate to the specific address of a dwelling.

2   Overview of the Newcastle Energy Framework Methodology NCRF

This section reviews the roadmap in terms of data flow, process and milestones to produce estimates of energy in a single dwelling and aggregates in sub-city areas. NCRF [9] is a spatially referenced parameterised per-dwelling domestic energy framework developed with the purpose of estimating the energy consumption in sub-city areas. The design of the framework is sufficiently flexible to scale-up in continuous geographic areas allowing energy estimates (electricity and gas). The roadmap described in Fig. 1 defines four processes that are completed sequentially: the spatially-referenced per-dwelling integration across multiple secondary data sets; the model refinement; the spatially-referenced per-dwelling and sub-city energy aggregates; and the validation strategy.

The per-dwelling integration process uses spatial interpolation and multiple imputation (see Fig. 1) procedures to replace an incomplete, missing, duplicated and inaccurate local 2009 convenience secondary data sources, the Newcastle Carbon Route Model (NCRM) [10] (see Fig. 2) with a set of plausible new data values. The new data values represent valid inferences that properly reflect the uncertainty due to missing values. At the end of this process, a complete set of valid records of the case study areas are ready for refinement.

The model refinement process provides precise data in cohesive structures by identifying at least one neighbour with a known value that can be used as a template for predicting the values in the whole urban structure. The refinement is for two cohesive structures: the first is those that affect the energy aggregation processes like district heating, group heating and Economy 7; and the second is those that provide a physical context to a cohesive community through planning regulations, in particular the change of use for dwelling houses due to the legislation that gives councils the freedom to choose areas where landlords must submit a planning application to rent their properties to unrelated tenants (houses in multiple occupation HMO). At the end of this process, a complete set of records is ready for input in a Building Research Environment Domestic Energy Model (BREDEM). Another refinement assigns a better estimate to floor area (one of the key energy drivers) to houses that are in shared occupancy.

The energy estimation process is the core process, as it estimates the annual electricity and gas consumption using three scales. The first is for individual dwellings (then groups of repeated dwellings to estimate the annual heating gas consumption of multiple repeated per-property types). The second and third are of annual electricity and gas consumption estimates in two levels of detail (sub-city aggregates): Neighbourhoods (Lower Layer Super Output Areas—LLSOAs) and Districts (Medium Layer Super Output Areas—MLSOAs). Because the DECC statistics display aggregates of annual electricity consumption of dwellings using the Economy 7 (E7) tariff, we also aggregate dwellings with households using E7.

In the final process, the per-dwelling property type and sub-city energy estimates (electricity, gas or E7) were validated (compared) against the 2009 Department of Energy and Climate Change (DECC) estimates in three different scales:

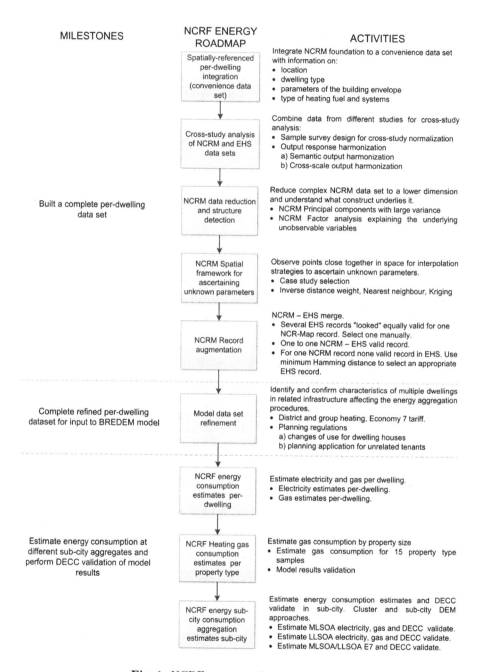

Fig. 1. NCRF energy estimates roadmap

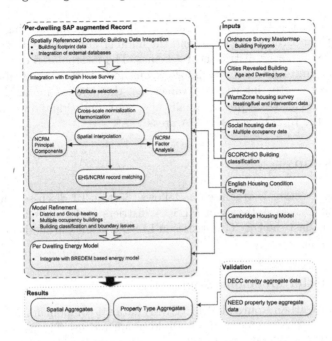

Fig. 2. NCRF data and processes

first the per-dwelling-type heating gas estimates set up by DECC with support from the Energy Saving Trust (EST) and energy suppliers for the National Energy Efficiency Data Framework (NEED) project [11]; and two aggregates of electricity, gas and E7 in the districts (MLSOA) and neighbourhoods (LLSOA) levels.

In the MLSOAs, the cluster model uses six dwelling archetype prototypes in every cluster to capture the mean effects in the interaction between the physical variables as the individual effect will cancel out at this scale. In every cluster prototype there are assumed regional weather characteristics and standard occupancy values. The cluster centre (mean) is the prototype of the cluster. In NCRF we want the centre (mean) in each cluster to be one particular dwelling. This is the reason why the six medoids were utilised to replace the six mean values in each cluster. The cluster energy method estimates the energy in every cluster by multiplying the Cambridge Housing Model (CHM) energy estimate [12] of the full SAP cluster prototype by the number of dwellings in every cluster. The process is repeated for every cluster in the MLSOA. In the LLSOA instead, the sub-city DEM model method uses city records to improve the data quality in the detailed model. The sub-city DEM uses secondary data sets from Arm's Length Management Organizations (ALMO) to gather rented and leased social housing characteristics and specific data on energy systems. The sub-city DEM also utilise the NCRM Registered Social Landlords housing information and HMO licensing from the local authority (LA), and shared housing data from Housing

Associations and the LA, to understand dwellings in group heating schemes, dwellings with an Economy 7 tariff, and the number and characteristics of residential dwellings sharing district heat schemes. The interpolated data are compared with accurate detailed city information, and in the case of discrepancy city records correct the interpolated values, i.e. the detailed model data set is refined. The sub-city DEM process finally aggregates individual dwelling energy estimation in the LLSOA and MLSOA areas.

3   Discussion

The discussion section is organised as follows. Section 3.1 discusses the cluster model against DECC statistics in MLSOA districts and Sect. 3.2 the sub-city DEM model against the DECC statistics in LLSOA neighbourhoods in the three selected case studies.

3.1   The Cluster Modelling Approach

The Newcastle Carbon Route Model (NCRM) data set components are generally available in some form to many, if not all, local authorities. The use of common values for UPRN and TOID (individual and aggregated) has made possible the use of spatial data from different resolutions and their combination with other types of spatial information.

The main NCRM data sets are the Warm Zone Programme and the English Housing Survey (EHS). Warm Zone is a major initiative designed to systematically reduce fuel poverty on a local area basis in cities, and the English Housing Survey is a national initiative for providing accurate information on the type and condition of housing and the people living there. The spatial visualization of NCRM WarmZone records and their further integration with other data sets is achieved through two spatial elements: the national address Gazetteer unique property identifier, the UPRN (the dwelling code) and the Ordnance Survey (OS) MasterMap^{TM} unique topographic identifier, the TOID (the building code). All data sets used in our work (WarmZone, EHS, Gazetteer and Ordnance Survey) are generally available in some form to many if not all local authorities.

The modelling approach of the cluster model is top-down. The top-down method involves patterning dwellings with similar energy profiles in the city, and then disaggregating the patterns [13] based on the MLSOA's proportions. Our work has shown that six key surveyed variables (dwelling size, dwelling age, building form, wall construction, heating and number of floors) perform well in explaining the energy consumption of aggregated dwellings in districts, three of the six variables were composites (building form, wall construction and heating). One of the issues highlighted in integrating these spatial data sets is the definition of what constitutes the floor area. The NCRM dwellings are assigned their building foot print area [10] instead of an individual useable floor area which is required for CHM (and other BREDEM models). Therefore, the very first activity is to find the usable floor area of individual dwellings through computation. In addition, the problem is further exacerbated where we have complex building with Homes in Multiple Occupations (HMOs) or individual rented rooms and mixed-use (commercial and residential) buildings.

Warm Zone Surveys do not have a value of usable floor area recorded for individual dwellings in complex buildings. Our work has provided a solution involving secondary sources that is time consuming and not ideal. It would be better if there were a straightforward method of calculating usable floor area or data were collected in a different manner. Usable floor area is a key variable in understanding energy consumption but, especially for complex or mixed-use buildings, a solution to estimate usable floor area is not obvious. In our work, a painstaking process using a variety of secondary data (described in Sect. 2) was developed. However, more robust solutions need to be developed to facilitate this type of modelling. These could be extensions of the NLPG/LLPG, energy audits or other means of better capturing the detailed usage of buildings from an energy perspective. An interesting development is the use of 3D structures that have both internal and external levels of detail providing a ready means to associate usage with spaces, such as the system developed in Berlin using a CityGML. The CityGML uses an application schema for the Geographic Markup Language (GML). Model for energy diagnostic and urban energy policy support [14,15]. In the UK, the Ordnance Survey is also investigating the addition of 3D products within their portfolio of survey products [19]. In 2014, Ordnance Survey began to release building height attribution with their 2D topography data [16] and additionally it has been enriching the 3D models with generic annotation e.g. from images of buildings [17].

Principal component analysis underpinning the cluster model (see Sect. 2) was used to provide both a method for explaining how many of the surveyed categorical variables are needed to explain the total variance within the reduced data set, and to detect the correlations between the variables. Besides these more obvious uses, our work has shown that there is an additional benefit as the principal component also provides group estimates of EHS 'donor' records before the NCRM nearest neighbour multiple imputations method actually selects the best 'donor' in an augmentation strategy. This shows that the principal component analysis is a worthwhile process; however, it remains to be seen whether the principal component results will be transferable to other cities because regional climates make for different insulation and heating supply requirements. However, other local authorities should consider this type of approach to collate data from existing sources with the requirement that there has to be a large sample so its application will be statistically valid.

One observation from the NCRM data set is that some of the variables are easy to collect, for example building types, because these are easy to see and also it is easy to add building data from other data sets such as the Ordnance Survey or buy it from commercial vendors such as Cities Revealed. However, integrating a number of sources from multiple collections throws up a number of semantic and cross-scale output harmonization issues but on the other hand also provides the ability to cross-check. An illustration of this in our case was the errors in the

Building Age in the NCRM Cities Revealed data set which were easily identified and rectified by NCRM YHN build dates (see Sect. 2). Building age is a difficult variable as it requires expert knowledge to age an individual building correctly. Other variables are difficult because they are hidden, such as wall insulation. Missing data was a real problem because for example 17% of the people surveyed in Warm Zone did not know the insulation type, especially in cavity walls. In these cases, the survey generates 'don't knows' and we decided to disregard the whole record. This will have implications when trying to replicate NCRM in other cities, because physically hidden variables are difficult for surveyors to identify, even to the point that there could be significant bias in the sample because the 'don't knows' are relevant, e.g. in rented properties. One way to avoid this problem is by having a much larger sample than normal, as is the case with NCRM.

Our work has shown that clustering provides evidence to find patterns residing in the NCRM data through partitioning of the six dimensional data vector into subsets based on the closeness or similarity among the data of the same kind. Another innovative approach is the use of the two-step sequential cluster to identify the cluster structure in the NCRM complete data set of observations (hierarchical cluster analysis) and the optimal cluster method to assign observations (k-means cluster analysis), i.e. both the hierarchical and the k-means cluster analysis techniques were used sequentially. Our work has shown that this hybrid approach gave good results, i.e. first, the Ward's method (hierarchical cluster) was used to obtain the possible number of clusters (eight for the NCRM data set) and the way they merge, as seen from the dendrogram, and then the k-means clustering was run with only the chosen optimum number (eight) of clusters in which to place all the observations.

The cluster method shows sensible energy estimate results both citywide and when disaggregating the cluster results over the MLSOAs. This approach, however, requires reasonably good data, in our case even though the NCRM WarmZone data have some variables that are difficult to collect; the sample size is citywide and in each MLSOA, is largely in excess of the minimum and preferable size. Formann recommends a minimum sample size of at least 2^m (where m=6 equals the number of clustering variables) and preferably $5 * 2^m$ [18, p. 4], i.e. in this study between 64 and 320 observations. If the minimum is not reached, the medoid shows weakness to outliers, but that is not the case for the Warm Zone Survey in Newcastle. Also, the high coverage guarantees that if the six variables were to be inputted in a different way (order) they would still produce the same cluster results. This shows the potential of integrating different data sets in energy modelling. However, access to this critical data set was only made possible by signing a non-disclosure agreement as the NCRM WarmZone data are commercially sensitive and potentially valuable. Because this type of data is so important to energy studies, it should be considered part of the open data strategy of the [20] so that other research studies can utilise the data easily.

Also critical in the open data strategy is a definitive single address register not only for local authorities but for the Royal Mail, Ordnance Survey and

DECC. Local authorities are working through the Improvement and Development Agency (I&DeA) for local government to establish the Local Government Information House (LGIH) by forming the GeoPlace Limited Liability Partnership (LLP) to produce a single definitive National Address Gazetteer (NAG). Government is also looking at options to ensure that the Postcode Address File (produced by the Royal Mail and regulated by Ofcom) continue to be a part of the single definitive address (the NAG).

However, the NEED framework data sets are combined using the NLPG unique property reference number (UPRN) as the integrating code in a twofold process. First, the address data from each of the data sets included in NEED is used to assign a UPRN to each record within that data set and then the UPRN is used to link records from one data set to the corresponding record in each of the other data sets. In Newcastle, as in other cities, the address matching in mixed-use buildings is more complicated for two reasons: firstly, the mixed-use building is less likely to be primarily addressed by a number, as is the case with domestic homes, and, secondly, several businesses may occupy the same buildings and it is difficult to identify the domestic dwellings arrangement within the building. Additionally, address information in HEED (which is part of NEED) did not allow a reliable match for individual flats within a building. One possible solution for NEED is replacing the NLPG UPRN with the AddressBase^{TM} UPRN; this should allow better analysis of the impact of measures for flats and increase confidence in the address information. AddressBase^{TM} is actually three data sets from GeoPlace and the Ordnance Survey: Royal Mail Postcode Address File (PAF), NLPG and OS AddressLayer^{TM} with further information from the Valuation Office. A final comment is that all these data sets are well trusted but an open access policy needs to be effective.

The energy model used to estimate the energy end-use of every cluster prototype was the Cambridge Housing Model (CHM). CHM is a national model requiring a full SAP input (115 variables). This study has shown that by combining data from different geographies and sources it is possible to augment limited NCRM WarmZone data with EHS data to create a full SAP input for use in energy models (see Sect. 2). This approach saves a great deal of time and also repurposes the NCRM WarmZone data, which were difficult and expensive to collect, for energy modelling. Moreover, validating (with respect to DECC consumption values) the modelled data at the MLSOA level needs full coverage of the whole district, but cluster data did not have a full coverage in the MLSOAs and did not have the complete SAP input records. To fulfil these requirements, NCRF has proven that record generation (for missing records to achieve complete coverage) and augmentation (for missing fields in every record) algorithms lead to the desired full coverage SAP input in the MLSOAs (see Sect. 2). Spatial interpolation algorithms were used as a record generation strategy and a nearest neighbour multiple imputations algorithm was used as a record augmentation strategy both with a reasonable success given that performing a physical survey for a full SAP data on each and every dwelling in Newcastle is not possible. Spatial interpolation and multiple imputation algorithms are not straightforward implementations because we have to consider the practical problems associated with cohesive structures e.g. shared houses, communal heating structures and district heating as well as regional weather variations, local built types (e.g. the Tyneside flat) and non-standard occupancy [21]. The sources for information about cohesive structures are available in a limited selection of useful websites containing local sources (e.g. HMO licensing) but they require patience and time to link the data to the building databases.

However, urban spaces are not only two dimensional areas; they also have the third dimension that defines the volumetric characteristic of the buildings, i.e. there is a need for a three dimensional (volumetric) patterns to define the physical urban space. [22] argues that the built environment can be seen as a setting for human activities and the volumetric patterns of the residential areas are in three different densities, low, medium and high rise.

NCRF has shown that the volumetric patterns and initial coverage of the survey data could be used to assign an appropriate point-based method for spatial interpolation in the three selected case study areas. For a cluster with low density building patterns, the Inverse Distance Weighting (IDW) deterministic method is commonly used, whereas for a compact building distribution with high coverage the nearest-neighbour (NN) is appropriate. For complex high rise structures of different building and uses-classes, a stochastic method is a sensible choice. The IDW algorithm was applied in Castle because it shows a cluster distribution; the NN was applied to South Heaton because it shows a compact distribution. Westgate is complex because the building classes (including tower block buildings) are diverse in the area; this made appropriate the use of the Kriging stochastic method. Kriging not only considers the distance between surrounding points but also the spatial autocorrelation (dwellings being in the same building) among the observations. In summary, the volumetric patterns and initial coverage of the survey data simple analyses could be used to inform the best strategy for filling-in the gaps, although further work would be needed to fully understand the boundary conditions. Although this seems to be a promising approach to completing the gaps, the link between urban building density patterns and spatial interpolation needs to be fully investigated. However, understanding urban form in this way has the potential to inform LAs and the like about the areas where there is a need to improve the data collection strategy.

To cope with the fields missing in the NCRM record (to obtain a full SAP record); NCRF has shown that an imputed method is an algorithm for record augmentation (see Sect. 2). In our augmentation strategy the two data sets are from different geographies. NCRM cluster prototype (the acceptor) is a local data set and EHS (the donor) is a national data set. Predicted values were then generated for all NCRM cluster prototype records using the following two-step procedure: first, 'donor' records were sorted by the 'acceptor' common fusion variables (CFV) (see Sect. 2), and then the missing values were given by the 'donor' record nearest to the acceptor. Imputed values were used only after establishing the matches, as this preserves the variability in the data as well as the correlations across the NCRM survey [23].

The fact that in the record augmentation strategy (see Sect. 2 for details of the strategy), the 'perfect outcome', there is a single best suitable EHS record with all CFV being equal in both, the NCRM and the EHS data sets—leading to a single EHS 'donor'—is only possible on 11% in South Heaton and 1% in Westgate suggests that one possible solution is to apply the nearest neighbour imputation as a method for handling missing values to acquire a full SAP record input to the energy model. To improve the search effectiveness and reduce the computing time, nearest neighbour multiple imputations require a previous pre-filter stage in which the principal component analysis gives the appropriate (reduced) number of EHS records. This two-stage process suggests that missing values of NCRM were estimated even though EHS covers only 0.073% of the English housing stock and the Warm Zone programme covers approximately 63.69% of Newcastle residential housing stock.

The reader should also consider that these processes can be misleading and cause the user to assume that the NCRM data has more data observations than actually surveyed and may magnify the confidence in the energy estimation results. Realistically, the goal of spatial interpolation, multiple imputation and aggregation strategy are initially to provide completed SAP records for areas where there are DECC statistics (i.e. MLSOA and LLSOA) and to make the validation process possible. Interpolation and imputation are techniques that produce values respectively within the range of NCRM and EHS data values and are not meant to recreate individual missing values by optimal point prediction.

The three case study selection is adequate because they cover a wide range of volumetric patterns in the city. Furthermore, Castle and South Heaton show high concentrations (above city average) of certain energy clusters, making these districts more homogeneous. Westgate, having close to average and low concentration of energy clusters is more diverse. From a policy perspective, it is reasonable to suggest that an increase in the accuracy of the data in places where there are complex mixed-use properties rather than homogeneous areas would be useful to provide better inputs to energy models, and this also has implications for reducing the cost of data collection.

The cluster energy method estimates the energy in every cluster by multiplying the CHM energy estimate of the full SAP cluster prototype by the number of dwellings in every cluster. The process is repeated for every cluster in the MLSOA. The aggregated cluster result suggests that the cluster size and composition not only reflect the energy efficiency of the Newcastle stock, but what was encouraging, the potential impact of applying certain retrofitting measures is possible. What was good from the cluster model district results is that they enable us to model aggregate energy consumption using a reduced number of variables.

NCRF has shown that clustering (or classification of houses into groups) represents a measure of homogeneity in energy consumption. The areas with high concentration of specific energy clusters show a close approximation with the DECC values, whereas areas having close to average and low concentration of energy clusters show a more distant approximation with DECC values. Castle and South Heaton have concentrations of particular clusters which show close approximation to DECC values of 5% and 3%, respectively. The Westgate result shows less close approximation to DECC value (27%). The Westgate result may suggest that the micro-level energy structures in Westgate, planned permission granted for converting houses to HMOs and houses and flats sharing amenities in neighbourhoods play an important role in the overall energy consumption in the case study areas, particularly in complex areas, which has implications for better data collection methods.

The scaling of the cluster model to a city-level is not problematic as the clusters were produced at the city-level, and the number of record guarantees robustness to outliers in all MLSOAs. The main challenge to replicate the cluster model in other cities is bringing the information together in a way that it will be useful for meaningful analysis. Currently, the Warm Zone programme throughout England is grouped into larger area hubs, covering Hull, London/South East, Midlands, North East, and Nottingham/the East Midlands. For other regions, similar surveys have to be implemented to collect the physical characteristics of dwellings.

However, when the cluster model is downscaled to LLSOA (neighbourhood) level the limits of this approach start to appear. Some homogenous areas still showed reasonable comparison with the DECC figures (e.g. Castle LLSOAs 8308 and 8311) but there was little consistency with other values being widely off (e.g. Westgate LLSOAs 8394 and 8399). In Westgate, the increased local building, socio-economic and physical characteristics of the urban area play a more important part in the estimation of dwelling energy consumption, and that is the potential reason for having increased differences.

In the policy arena, the government is leading the spatial information publication and reuse of location-specific data through the [24] UK Location Programme. The programme ensures UK compliance with the EU INSPIRE Directive, of the 900+ data sets published, around 200 are mandated by INSPIRE; however, data quality is still an issue and so is harmonization and scale. NCRF has proven that spatial enabling sub-city scale energy modelling is a potential way forward, and within this scope, the emphasis of the Location Data Programme should be reconsidered and replaced with a more rigorous analysis in which the building is the unit of analysis. If that is possible, then all the methods described in this section can be replicated in every city in the UK to compute district level energy aggregates.

3.2   Sub-city DEM Modelling Approach in Neighbourhoods

The main motivation of creating a sub-city DEM model that allows the estimation of individual dwellings annual energy consumption is that modelling the physical processes in individual dwellings with standard occupancy has the potential to provide LAs with realistic, simulated estimated energy values for buildings that can be aggregated at many scales to provide a baseline for use in retrofit or micro-generation or other energy related planning. The initial variables of the sub-city DEM energy profile are: usable floor area, dwelling type, construction date, number of floors above ground, predominant type of wall structure, cavity wall insulation, main heating fuel, primary heating system, boiler group and tenure. As with the cluster model, the usable floor area of all individual dwellings in the sub-city DEM model were corrected from the initial building footprint area value using secondary sources in the same three-step process detailed earlier in Sect. 3.1.

NCRF uses record generation algorithms with the sub-city DEM NCRM complete ten-variable records data set in the three case study areas (Castle, South Heaton and Westgate) to obtain complete coverage in the corresponding MLSOAs areas. As with the cluster model, the record generation algorithms prove to be a useful tool to obtain full coverage in geographic areas. The Inverse Distance Weighting (IDW) algorithm was used in Castle because dwellings show a cluster distribution, while the nearest neighbour (NN) was used in South Heaton because dwellings show a uniform distribution. Stochastic Kriging was used in Westgate because it has one of the most diverse collections of building classes (including tower blocks buildings) in the Newcastle area.

NCRF has shown that city records can be used to improve the data quality in the sub-city DEM model because of several reasons, first local authorities have extra information to help with the validation process, as an example, YHN council homes have an accurate build date taken from the deeds. This study uses secondary data sets from Arm's Length Management Organizations (ALMO) to gather rented and leased social housing characteristics and specific data on energy systems. The research utilised the NCRM Registered Social Landlords housing information and HMO licensing from the LA, and shared housing data from Housing Associations and the LA, to understand dwellings in group heating schemes, dwellings with an Economy 7 tariff, and the number and characteristics of residential dwellings sharing district heat schemes. The interpolated data are compared with accurate detailed city information, and in the case of discrepancy city records correct the interpolated values, i.e. the sub-city DEM model data set is refined.

Additional procedural refinement is needed when computing the residential consumption load-share in mixed residential/commercial district heating schemes, because is difficult to model and disaggregate each component in the mix. Mixed residential/commercial load sharing in existing district heating data is also problematic because of different time-of-use. There is no individual residential meter (so it is problematic to model individual behaviour and practices) and no charge for the actual domestic energy use and residential energy prices are subsidised. The need for understanding and modelling the load share in shared district heating is becoming increasingly important. The current model for the Newcastle district heating is to focus initially on connecting existing district heating, larger commercial loads, and new commercial and residential developments, and then to extend the network into the existing domestic sector [25, p. 33]. Connecting Byker's existing district heating is the most problematic task because it is by far the biggest (almost 2,000 households) and most complex district heating site in Newcastle. One possible solution is to introduce and manage a transparent charging system and install controls and meters in homes [26]. Better models for Newcastle's future district heating will become a bigger issue because we need better methods to disaggregate and assign domestic energy consumption to individual residential and commercial loads because of different time-of-use; we also need to model individual household behaviour. One further area of procedural refinement concerns interpolating data close to the boundary. Spatial modellers should be aware of the limitations of interpolation boundaries and adjust results accordingly.

NCRF has shown that there are a higher number of data quality refinements in areas with low Warm Zone Survey penetration, complex urban energy supply structures, complex building types and a large number of non-self-contained household properties. Westgate and South Heaton required more adjustments due to the relatively low penetration of survey data in tower blocks, adjustment to the individual dwelling's usable floor area, a significant number of complex load shared energy structures, and rented on room-by-room properties. The refinement was made, respectively, in 69.46% and 24.53% of the complete ten-variable records for a complete coverage. Castle's simple building types (mostly semi-detached and detached houses) and high penetration survey required refinement in only 4% of the complete ten-variable records for a complete coverage. Urban complexity in terms of the built form and usage patterns potentially signpost data collection priority areas [27]. The sub-city DEM model uses the same augmentation algorithm that the cluster model uses. What is different is that the common fusion variables are individual (rather than composite), have increased to ten, and include tenure. The sub-city DEM model also uses the CHM to estimate the energy consumption in individual dwellings.

Tenure is an interesting variable in the case study areas because they show different composition. There are major contributions from owner occupied and council rented properties in Castle, private rented student accommodation, council rented properties and owner occupied in South Heaton, and social housing in Westgate. Private rented properties are inefficient; this perhaps increases the amount of households in fuel poverty [28]. Difficulties arise if the private tenant is poor, because due to the recent government reform [29], the cheapest 30% of private rental properties should be available for those in receipt of housing benefit (HB). The maximum payable HB is also limited to the maximum four-bedroom rate, and there is an age cap for singles living in a shared apartment; this will probably have the end result of encouraging private rented householders to behave in a 'cost-conscious' manner and move to cheaper accommodation if they cannot afford to meet the gap between their Local Housing Allowance (LHA) entitlement and the rent charged by the landlord [29]. However, social housing differs from housing in other tenures in many ways, as social housing occupants are more likely to live in areas of high unemployment [30, p. 8]; also, social tenants enjoy less space per person than other tenures, and because of living in small size dwellings they are more likely to be dissatisfied than others. Moreover, new build social housing is still disproportionately in the most deprived neighbourhoods [31]. However, YHN housing is efficient housing due to the following four reasons: 70% of the houses meet and maintain the decent homes standard [32]; 45% of their housing has efficient heating system installed; 60% has double glazing; and 40% has insulation in loft and walls [33]. However, social tenants are more likely to be in fuel poverty because their income is low, even considering the Housing Benefit due to fuel price rises [34, p. 6], despite the small size and good condition of the social housing. One possible solution is to have a policy that monitors: the housing condition to all tenures, the impact of HB cuts in the residual incomes, their job opportunities (relative to the location) and perhaps supports and increases HB among older home-owners.

The NCRM RSL tenure has a significant share in Westgate. NCRM RSL tenure shows households in a non-standard occupancy and dwellings in shared-ownership. Shared-ownerships are difficult to model due to two reasons: they are both a rented and an owned property, and the household size is small, so occupancy may not be standard. This is indicative of the complexity of the energy modelling when trying to model at the level of the individual dwelling.

NCRF has shown that the validation of NCRF with respect to comparable DECC statistics is problematic. The validation cannot compare the number of meters because DECC statistics use aggregated consumption by Meter Point Administration Number (MPAN) to ensure energy consumption is accurately recorded, whereas in the case of YHN district heating schemes there are no individual heat meters. YHN argues economical and operational reasons for not having individual heat meters. The economic reasons are the cost of billing and renewal of meters and the operational reason is that district heating was originally designed to provide a constant and steady supply of hot water, then metering is likely to change people's use of the system and create high peaks in demand, which could make the heating system less reliable [35, p. 5]. [36, p. 198] argue that as for heating use, there is consistent evidence that metering in combination with consumption-dependent charging can act as an incentive for more sustainable heating behaviours in district heated dwellings, and [37] argue that indoor climate habits relate to experience with valves and meters gained at their workplace. The validation is also problematic because YHN and Newcastle City Council with other councils in the North East England purchase the fuel for district and group heating in bulk, and DECC statistics are on individual MPAN.

NCRF has shown that Economy 7(E7) (the off-peak electricity tariff) mostly uses electric storage heaters although there are also using warm air heating systems. If the heat in the dwelling and water is by electricity, but don't have storage heaters or a hot water tank, E7 probably will not be so cost effective. If the heat in the dwelling is with gas, E7 could still be a good fit, provided the bulk of the electricity use is at night. The E7 model needs two additional variables for the hot water in the energy profile: the hot water heating system and the tank insulation. E7 is used in a variety of tenures and building types. It is prevalent in owner occupied small area properties in the Castle area, while the city owned tower block in South Heaton uses storage heaters, and the housing association properties in Westgate use storage heaters. This also potentially has an impact on fuel poverty policy and strategy given the amount of E7 heating existing in social housing tenures. This again is indicative of the complexity of the model and the difficulty of national data sets and models in properly addressing this type of fuel tariff. These three micro energy structures (HMOs, District Heating and E7 tariff) are difficult to model both from existing data and with current energy models. As an example, [26] argues that "approximately 2/3 of all tenants in the community heating schemes receive housing benefits. Currently housing benefits can be claimed for infrastructure and communal heating charges, but not for energy charges. Therefore any changes in energy charges have a profound effect on all tenants, while a modification in infrastructure or communal heating charges will only benefit or disadvantage tenants who do not receive housing benefits." Understanding their spatial distribution and potential impact is a first step to address shortcomings in current national energy models and demonstrates the importance of a detailed understanding of local physical characteristics of the building stock.

NCRF has shown that the sub-city DEM energy model allows estimation of energy consumption aggregates in a bottom-up approach. The aggregating strategy is as follows: by building, by block, by building classes and by LLSOAs; a further aggregation was made to the MLSOA level for comparison purposes with the cluster approach. Bottom-up is a sensible approach because it allows for ad-hoc energy retrofit planning scenarios and seeing patterns of base line energy consumption. NCRF are energy estimates using the physical properties of the building which would still be useful for retrofit evaluation or evidence based comparison of different strategies at an area level. It would even provide the means of implementing different energy efficient strategies with a great impact at the local level, rather than the more general approach made at citywide levels.

In summary, NCRF has integrated a number of data sets in a way that we were able to integrate with well-respected national level energy models such as the CHM, so every individual building has their own energy SAP profile. There are many uncertainties in extending the coverage and getting full SAP records to compare to DECC statistics in aggregated areas. However, this approach highlights an interesting way to move forward in energy modelling and it has set-out different ways of reducing the uncertainties using secondary sources. There are also issues in the way the data are being collected and restrictions on the distribution.

Given the uncertainties, it is not surprising perhaps that aggregated sub-city DEM model building totals are some way from DECC aggregates. Perhaps the biggest influence here is the lack of real occupancy data which becomes more important in a per-building analysis. This highlights a potential research avenue for a per-building approach to area energy modelling through the integration of better socio-economic data. In addition, the issues facing the city with respect to the physical characteristics of the building stock and current energy efficiency measures are highlighted through the detailed analysis, both spatial and aspatial, of individual buildings. Even the collation and integration of data sets without an accompanying energy model has potential to provide insights into the make-up of a city's residential building stock.

NCRF (and therefore CHM) does not take into account the microclimate, however, at the scale of the individual buildings detailed models exist, such as EnergyPlus^{TM}. Urban microclimate effects on energy demand were analysed by [38], who used an urban microclimate model and the building energy software EnergyPlus^{TM} [39]. These models have to be supplied with suitable boundary conditions, which represent the urban microclimate. However, in order to consider interactions between energy demand and the urban microclimate, more complex tools are needed. The interactions between buildings and the landscape in low density Castle presumably create a real increase in energy consumption because there is an increase in the mean daily heat output from the heating system due to smaller increases in the outdoor air temperature due to heat island effects. One possible way to improve the weather data would be to spatially merge NCRM data with detailed weather data that is readily available. Urban microclimate is a key element during the design stages of sustainable and comfortable urban spaces, although the physics underlying the interaction of urban microclimate with buildings is complex to model.

The NCRF and DECC statistics show different aggregated counts in the same geographic areas because DECC statistics shows unallocated loads (where the address information within the Gemserv database is incomplete, invalid or missing); therefore, this underestimates the aggregated energy in neighbourhoods. However, it is unclear whether such incidental reductions (or implicit bias) of energy consumption in some neighbourhoods will last over a period of time or whether DECC is intentionally implementing strategies in a long-term goal to reduce this implicit bias.

The NCRF number of thermal zones is not well defined in several building types: rented on room-by-room accommodation, linear terraces and tower blocks. For example, a separate thermal zone for each heated room in rented on room-by-room properties would require information (e.g. which windows affect the space) that is difficult if not impossible to automatically extract, but important for estimating the internal temperatures for each room or space. The NCRF probably underestimates the energy consumption because a reduced number of thermal zones in areas of South Heaton with linear terraces, tower blocks in Westgate, HMOs and social housing shared accommodation. A way forward is to have statistics for space per person in the EPC and SAP. However, there are several practical and policy issues to address. First, HMOs with shared essential facilities have no individual tenancy agreement and there is no need to provide an EPC in the housing market in the UK. Secondly, the EPC methodology considers the number of habitable rooms but what constitutes a room is not well defined (the energy rating is adjusted for the floor area of a building). Meanwhile, [40, pp. 90–121] does consider the number of habitable rooms and the number heated habitable rooms, but as all SAP and BREDEM models do not consider occupancy in the heated rooms, this made it less possible to compute the space per person.

DECC underestimate the energy consumption in LLSOAs with district heating because it only considers individualized energy consumption and YHN purchases energy in blocks for households in District Heating. These bulk consumptions do not appear in individualized DECC statistics. More complete statistics on district heating networks are presumably about to be published in accordance with the Energy Efficiency [41, Article 11].

There is no clear cut-off for residential and small commercial premises so DECC underestimates the energy consumption due to the fact that the ground floor part of a building has, for example, been converted to a small shop. Domestic cut-off is based on arbitrary consumption figures used by industry; DECC uses the gas industry cut off threshold of 73,200 kWh. This means a number of smaller commercial/industrial consumers were wrongly allocated as domestic, i.e. DECC underestimates the energy consumption in this LLSOA. This is an issue in South Heaton; however, the use and integration of secondary sources into sub-city DEM energy modelling databases as demonstrated in this study does enable this level of fine-grained building-use modelling.

There is no definitive source for the number of households 'not on the gas grid.' The energy use of individual households in multi-tenanted commercial/residential buildings is difficult to estimate if there is no agreed measure or sub-metering system. With this type of building, it can also be difficult to build a clear picture of energy use in the building because landlords use energy to provide services in the shared parts of the building (e.g. lifts and pumps), plus the use in the tenanted areas. Additional issues are when some tenants pay for their own metered electricity supply or purchase other fuel directly. One possible solution for delivering sub-metering is through the incentives on the Carbon Reduction Commitment (CRC), announced in the Energy White Paper 2007.

NCRF does not consider the inter-building effect created by surrounding buildings. The energy consumption is underestimated in aggregated buildings because of the reduced solar radiance. However, this effect is complex and requires the modelling of a network of buildings. The South Heaton case study shows that the LLSOAs energy consumption may have modelling inaccuracies created by the nearby buildings. Physical building models would need detailed topological information (as provided by NCRM) in order to model inter-building effects effectively. For densifying urban environments, this is likely to be a relatively significant effect. Specifically, the role of inter-building effects must be examined as a number of researchers have suggested (e.g. [38, 42, 43]). Also, urban form from the point of view of environmental performance in cities as addressed in [44]; and, energy use and density as the results of [45] seem to suggest.

Weather correction methodologies in DECC/NEED and CHM lead to discrepancies, the main reason being that the exact methodology for weather correction for NEED/DECC is not fully disclosed. In order to be confident in the use of DECC/NEED statistics for validation purposes, clear and unambiguous information needs to be provided on weather corrections as these can have significant impact on estimated values.

In summary, there are some discrepancies in the sub-city DEM model results partly because of the uncertainties in the way national models model individual occupancy, but also because there are no individual consumption data to calibrate with the dwelling energy estimations. However, having this sub-city DEM model opens-up the development of low-carbon energy technologies at the community and neighbourhood levels through providing a physically-based energy consumption estimate at the building level that provides realistic energy consumption patterns and detailed spatial information based on the physical characteristics of the building and the outputs from a national energy model.

4   Conclusions

The aim of the research was fulfilled as the spatially enabled model and rich thematic database facilitates, first and foremost, integrated mapping practices, i.e. a NCRM data set accessible by a digital computer including a set of maps in the grid reference system used in Great Britain; a NCRF framework of varying and selectable scale from an individual dwelling to streets, communities, neighbourhoods and districts, and capable of presentation individual and aggregated domestic energy consumption on a computer display; tools for calculating, delineating, and displaying building dimensions in an orthographic projection; and means for coupling the computer to other computers for data exchange.

Previous modelling approaches adopted a number of house archetypes which together represent all dwellings in the stock. This study identifies individual dwellings' energy profiles to estimate individual and aggregated energy consumption. The cluster model uses six categorical variables (dwelling age, wall construction, building form, dwelling size, heating and number of storeys) to capture the mean effects in the interaction between the physical variables in districts as the individual effect will cancel out at this scale. The framework estimates in the sub-city DEM model are improved in neighbourhoods by taking into consideration ten variables (usable floor area, dwelling type, construction date, number of floors above ground, predominant type of wall structure, cavity wall insulation, main heating fuel, primary heating system, boiler group and tenure) and local micro-cohesive structures. The reason for the increased number of variables is to obtain a better insight into the effect of uncertainties of the aggregated process by generating a more complete representation of the dwelling.

Acknowledgement. We would also like to acknowledge the help we received from Newcastle City Council, who permitted me to use their data sets (especially Adrian McLoughlin). This proved to be unique and invaluable for this paper.

References

1. Swan, L.G., Ugursal, V.I.: Modeling of end-use energy consumption in the residential sector: a review of modeling techniques. Renew. Sustain. Energy Rev. **13**(8), 1819–1835 (2009)
2. Urquizo, J., Calderon, C., James, P.: Understanding the complexities of domestic energy reductions in cities: integrating data sets generally available in the United Kingdom's local authorities. Cities **74**, 292–309 (2018a)
3. Weber, C., Keirstead, J., Samsatli, N., Shah, N., Fisk, D.: Trade-offs between layout of cities and design of district energy systems. In: Efficiency, Cost, Optimization, Simulation and Environmental Impact, ECOS 2010 (2010). https://workspace.imperial.ac.uk/urbanenergysystems/Public/ecos2010_weber.pdf
4. Cheng, V., Steemers, K.: Modelling domestic energy consumption at district scale: a tool to support national and local energy policies. Environ. Model. Softw. **26**(10), 1186–1198 (2011)
5. Urquizo, J., Calderon, C., James, P.: Using a local framework combining principal component regression and monte carlo simulation for uncertainty and sensitivity analysis of a domestic energy model in sub-city areas. Energies **10**(12), 1–22 (2017b)
6. Johnston, D.: A physically-based energy and carbon dioxide emission model of the UK housing stock. Ph.D. thesis, Leeds Metropolitan University (2003). http://www.leedsmet.ac.uk/as/cebe/team/johnston_thesis.pdf
7. Shorrock, L., Dunster, J., (1997). The physically-based model brehomes and its use in deriving scenarios for the energy use and carbon dioxide emissions of the UK housing stock. Energy Policy **25**(12), 1027–1037 (2003). http://www.sciencedirect.com/science/article/pii/S0301421597001304
8. Firth, S., Lomas, K., Wright, A.: Targeting household energy-efficiency measures using sensitivity analysis. Build. Res. Inf. **38**, 25–41 (2010)
9. Calderon, C., James, P., Urquizo, J., McLoughlin, A.: A GIS domestic building framework to estimate energy end-use demand in UK sub-city areas. Energy Build. **96**, 236–250 (2015). URL http://www.sciencedirect.com/science/article/pii/S0378778815002212
10. Calderon, C., James, P., Alderson, D., McLoughlin, A., Wagner, T.: Data availability and repeatability for urban carbon modelling: a CarbonRouteMap for Newcastle upon Tyne. In: Retrofit 2012, Manchester England (2012). http://www.energy.salford.ac.uk/page/day_2_papers
11. DECC: National energy efficient data need framework - report on the development of the data-framework and initial analysis. Technical report, Department of Energy and Climate Change (2011). http://www.cewales.org.uk/cew/wp-content/uploads/National-Energy-Efficiency-Data-Framework.pdf
12. Hughes, M.: A guide to the Cambridge housing model. Technical report, Department of Energy and Climate Change (2011). https://www.gov.uk/government/statistics/cambridge-housing-model-and-user-guide
13. Urquizo, J., Calderon, C., James, P.: Modelling household spatial energy intensity consumption patterns for building envelopes, heating systems and temperature controls in cities. Appl. Energy **226**, 670–681 (2018b)
14. Kolbe, T.: Representing and exchanging 3D city models with CityGML. In: Lee, J., Zlatanova, S. (eds.) 3D Geo-Information Sciences. LNGC, pp. 15–31. Springer, Heidelberg (2009). https://doi.org/10.1007/978-3-540-87395-2_2

15. Nouvel, R., Schulte, C., Eicker, U., Pietruschka, D., Coors, V.: Urban energy analysis based on 3D city model for national scale. In: International Building Performance Simulation Association IBPSA (2013). http://www.ibpsa.org/proceedings/BS2013/p_989.pdf

16. Sargent, I., Harding, J., Freeman, M., Holland, D.: The building blocks of user-focused 3D building data. In: Efficient Capturing of 3D Objects at a National Level: With A Focus on Buildings and Infrastructure, EUROSDR/ISPRS Workshop (2014). http://www.eurosdr.net/workshops/eurosdrisprs-workshop-efficient-capturing-3d-objects-national-level-focus-buildings-and

17. Jones, C., Rosin, P., Slate, J.: Semantic and geometric enrichment of 3D geo-spatial models with captioned photos and labelled illustrations. In: 25th International Conference on Computational Linguistics, Coling 2014, Workshop on Vision and Language (2014). https://vision.cs.bath.ac.uk/VL_2014/programme.html

18. Dolnicar, S.: A review of unquestioned standards in using cluster analysis for data-driven market segmentation. In: CD Conference Proceedings of the Australian and New Zealand Marketing Academy Conference 2002 (ANZMAC 2002). Deakin University, Melbourne (2002). http://ro.uow.edu.au/commpapers/273/

19. Capstick, D., Heathcote, G.: Moving towards 3D from a national mapping agency perspective. In: Abdul-Rahman, A., Zlatanova, S., Coors, V. (eds.) Innovations in 3D GeoInformation Systems. LNGC, pp. 491–500. Springer, Heidelberg (2006). https://doi.org/10.1007/978-3-540-36998-1_38

20. HM Government: Open Data White Paper: Unleashing the Potential (CM 8353). TSO@Blackwell and other accredited agents, London (2012). ISBN 9780101835329. https://www.gov.uk/government/publications/open-data-white-paper-unleashing-the-potential

21. Urquizo, J., Calderon, C., James, P.: 2016 IEEE Ecuador Technical Chapters Meeting (ETCM), 12–14 October 2016 (2016)

22. Rapoport, A.: CHAPTER 1 - Urban design as the organization of space, time, meaning and communication. In: Rapoport, A. (ed.) Human Aspects of Urban Form, Pergamon, pp. 8–47 (1977)

23. Rubin, D.B.: Multiple imputation after 18+ years. J. Am. Stat. Assoc. **91**, 473–489 (1996). http://www.tandfonline.com/doi/abs/10.1080/01621459.1996.10476908

24. DEFRA: Defra open data strategy. Technical report (PB13785), Department for Environment, Food and Rural Affairs, London (2012). https://www.gov.uk/government/publications/defra-open-data-strategy Directive 2012/27/EU, 2012. of the European Parliament and of the Council of 25 October 2012 on Energy Efficiency, Amending Directives 2009/125/ec and 2010/30/eu and repealing directives 2004/8/ec and 2006/32/ec (text with EEA relevance). Technical report (L 315/1-56), Off. J. Eur. Union Brussels. http://eur-lex.europa.eu/LexUriServ/LexUriServ.do?uri=OJ:L:2012:315:0001:0056:EN:PDF

25. NAREC: Newcastle City Council energy masterplan. Technical report, NAREC Distributed Energy, Blyth Northumberland (2012). https://www.newcastle.gov.uk/sites/drupalncc.newcastle.gov.uk/files/wwwfileroot/environment/energy/ncc_energy_masterplan_may_2012.pdf

26. French, C., Joyce, S., Gorton, I., Heppenstall, T.: Critical friend report on district & group heating. Technical report, Newcastle upon Tyne: YHN and IRES: Newcastle University, Newcastle upon Tyne (2007). http://www.yhn.org.uk/pdf/MainBoard22May07DistrictandGroupHeatingTLCItem11.pdf

27. Urquizo, J., Calderon, C., James, P.: Metrics of urban morphology and their impact on energy consumption: a case study in the United Kingdom. Energy Res. Soc. Sci. **32**, 196–212 (2017a)

28. DECC: Private rented sector energy efficiency regulations (domestic) (England and Wales): consultation on implementation of the energy act 2011 provision for energy efficiency regulation of the domestic private rented sector. Technical report (URN 14D/228), Department of Energy and Climate Change, London (2014). https://www.gov.uk/government/ploads/system/uploads/attachment_data/file/346767/Domestic_PRS_Regulations_Consultation_Draft_v1_6_No_tracks_final_version.pdf

29. DWP: The impact of recent reforms to local housing allowances: summary of key findings. Technical report, Department for Work and Pensions, London (2014). ISBN 978-1-910219-31-7. https://www.gov.uk/government/uploads/system/uploads/attachment_data/file/329902/rr874-lha-impact-of-recent-reforms-summary.pdf

30. Lupton, R., et al.: Growing up in social housing in Britain. A profile of four generations, 1946 to the present day. Technical report, Tenant Service Authority, London (2009). http://www.jrf.org.uk/sites/files/jrf/social-housing-britain-FULL.pdf

31. Hills, J.: Ends and means: the future roles of social housing in England (casereport 34). Technical report, The London School of Economics and Political Science, London (2007). ISSN 1465-3001. http://eprints.lse.ac.uk/5568/1/Ends_and_Means_The_future_roles_of_social_housing_in_England_1.pdf

32. DCLG: A decent home: definition and guidance for implementation. Technical report (06HC03962), Department for Communities and Local Government, London (2006). https://www.gov.uk/government/uploads/system/uploads/attachment_data/file/7812/138355.pdf

33. Gallagher, I., Langhorne, D.: Environmental sustainability strategy. Technical report, Your Homes Newcastle, Newcastle Upon Tyne (2011). http://www.yhn.org.uk/pdf/EnvironmentalSustainabilityStrategy.pdf

34. Palmer, G., MacInnes, T., Kenway, P.: Cold and poor: an analysis of the link between fuel poverty and low income. Technical report, New Policy Institute, London (2008). ISBN 978-1-902080-24-6. http://www.poverty.org.uk/reports/fuelpoverty.pdf

35. YHN: District and group heating - a guide for tenants. Technical report, Your Homes Newcastle, Newcastle upon Tyne (2014). http://www.yhn.org.uk/pdf/Districtandgroupheatingtenants.PDF

36. Morgenstern, P., Lowe, R., Chiu, L.: Heat metering: sociotechnical challenges in district-heated social housing. Build. Res. Inf. **43**(2), 197–209 (2015)

37. Gram-Hanssen, K.: Residential heat comfort practices: understanding users. Build. Res. Inf. **38**(2), 175–186 (2010)

38. Yang, X., Zhao, L., Bruse, M., Meng, Q.: An integrated simulation method for building energy performance assessment in urban environments. Energy Build. **54**, 243–251 (2012)

39. Crawley, D., et al.: EnergyPlus: new, capable, and linked. J. Arch. Plan. Res. **21**(4), 292–302 (2004)

40. BRE: The governments standard assessment procedure for energy rating of dwellings. Technical report, Building Research Establishment (2009). http://www.bre.co.uk/filelibrary/SAP/2009/SAP-2009_9-90.pdf

41. Directive 2012/27/EU (2012) of the European Parliament and of the Council of 25 October 2012 on energy efficiency, amending Directives 2009/125/EC and 2010/30/EU and repealing Directives 2004/8/EC and 2006/32/EC (Text with EEA relevance) (L 315/1-56). Brussels: OJ. http://eur-lex.europa.eu/LexUriServ/LexUriServ.do?uri=OJ:L:2012:315:0001:0056:EN:PDF. Accessed 12 Aug 2014

42. Pisello, A., Taylor, J., Xu, X., Cotana, F.: Inter-building effect: simulating the impact of a network of buildings on the accuracy of building energy performance predictions. Build. Environ. **58**, 37–45 (2012)
43. Bueno, B., Norford, L., Pigeon, G., Britter, R.: A resistance capacitance network model for the analysis of the interactions between the energy performance of buildings and the urban climate. Build. Environ. **54**, 116–125 (2012)
44. Adolphe, L.: A simplified model of urban morphology: application to an analysis of the environmental performance of cities. Environ. Plan. B: Plan. Des. **28**(2), 183–200 (2001)
45. Steemers, K.: Energy and the city: density, buildings and transport. Energy Build. **35**(1), 3–14 (2003)

Multi-objective Optimization of Solar Thermal Systems Applied to Residential Building in Portugal

Ana Cristina Ferreira[1,2($\boxtimes$)] (ID), Ângela Silva[1,3,4] (ID), and Senhorinha Teixeira[1] (ID)

[1] ALGORITMI Centre, University of Minho, Guimarães, Portugal
acferreira@dps.uminho.pt
[2] Mechanical Engineering and Resource Sustainability Center (MEtRICs), University of Minho, Guimarães, Portugal
[3] Centro de Investigação em Organizações, Mercados e Gestão Industrial (COMEGI), Universidade Lusíada Norte, Vila Nova de Famalicão, Portugal
[4] Escola Superior de Ciências Empresariais, Instituto Politécnico de Viana do Castelo, Valença, Portugal

Abstract. Thermal-economic evaluation represents an effective tool to optimize thermal systems. This study presents a mathematical model that encloses the physical variable equations and a set of equations that define the purchase cost of the main system components. The main objective of this study is the thermo-economic optimisation of solar thermal systems for residential building applications, considering a multi-objective approach. The simulations were performed through a MatLab code, by implementing an elitist variant of NASGA-II. The numerical model disclosed a Pareto front considering the optimal trade-off solutions for the minimum investment cost and the maximum solar collection efficiency. The optimal solutions disclose a set of optimal solutions for which the solar collection efficiency vary 28.3% and 77.0% and the investment costs vary between 2,099€ and 3,308€. Results show that gains in solar collection efficiency above 70% imply a great increase in the total purchase cost, implying a bump of almost 1,000€, from a total investment cost of 2,200€ to 3,200€. As a conclusion, the solar collector area is one of the most important decision variables in the multi-objective optimization of thermal-economic analysis of solar thermal systems.

Keywords: Solar thermal systems · Multi-objective optimisation · NSGA-II

1 Introduction

All over the world, the implementation of solar thermal systems to suppress the domestic hot water needs has been increasing over the years, mostly, as a way to increase the energy efficiency in the residential sector [1]. The greatest advantage of solar energy is that it is clean and can be supplied without any environmental pollution. However, the proper sizing of the components of a solar energy system is a complex

S. Misra et al. (Eds.): ICCSA 2019, LNCS 11624, pp. 26–39, 2019.
https://doi.org/10.1007/978-3-030-24311-1_2

problem, which includes both predictable (collector and other components' performance characteristics) and unpredictable (weather) data [2].

Important factors that affect the solar heat market are the costs of the plant components, the characteristics of the infrastructures and the local conditions regarding the solar irradiation and the energy consumption. In fact, and despite all the technological considerations, the cost of a solar-thermal system may vary by up to 20% from the average, depending on the collector design and building exposure to the sunlight. Solar collectors typically supply 60% to 80% of the hot water needs, whereas the remaining 20–40% is provided by another heat source, usually electricity or gas [3]. Kalogirou presented a review referring several types of solar thermal collectors and applications, such as flat-plate, parabolic trough, evacuated tube, Fresnel lens, parabolic dish and helio stat field collectors which are used in this system [4]. The solar collectors can be used for domestic, commercial and industrial purposes. Ong and Tong present in their study a system composed of solar water heaters depending upon collector and storage tank design and sizing and weather conditions (solar radiation intensity and ambient temperature) [5].

In recent years, studying the optimum performance of energy systems with thermodynamic models have been an attractive option for researchers [5–9]. Ust, Sahin and Kodal [6] introduced a new thermo-economic performance analysis based on an objective function defined as the power output per unit of total cost. It is of utmost importance to integrate costs and physical variables to simultaneously optimize the economic and physical output. Thermal-economics combines thermodynamic analysis and economic principles to evaluate the costs of energy production in each of the power plant components [7, 8]. These costs can be useful to disclose the most cost-effective configuration of the components and, then, improving the overall system design the components and, then, improving the overall system design [9]. Assaf and Shabani [10] developed a sizing multi-objective optimisation using the genetic algorithm on a solar-hydrogen combined heat and power system integrated with solar-thermal collectors to supply both power and heat (i.e. hot water demand) to an application. Lin et al. [11] also presented a multi-objective optimisation strategy for thermal energy storage using phase change materials for solar air systems, in which two performance indicators of average heat transfer effectiveness and effective phase change materials charging time were used as the conflicting objectives. In [12], a building integrated solar thermal system with seasonal storage was optimized with the use of TRNSYS modelling software in order to evaluate different integration options of the solar collector array. The model calculates the space heating needs during the heating period as well as the annual domestic hot-water needs of a typical single-family detached home in the city of Thessaloniki. More recently, Yılmaz [13], proposed a novel methodology for determining the optimum orientation and sizing of water-in-glass evacuated tube solar water heating systems, for residential usage. A transient model was conducted for the prediction of a full year's system performance via the System Advisor Model. Asadi *et al.* [14] presented a combination of thermo-economic analysis and multi-objective optimization of a 10 kW single-effect ammonia-water solar absorption cooling system. A thermodynamic model is derived, and energy-exergy analyses are conducted. Also, the effects of various solar collector types including a flat plate, evacuated tube, compound parabolic, and parabolic trough collectors on the system performance are examined at different ambient temperatures.

The studies available in the literature are mostly focused in the analysis of either a solar thermal system with a single fixed technology where the goal is to optimise a single component and its operational conditions or find the best option and size for a specific application [5, 10–12, 15]. The purpose of the present work is distinct from those perspectives: the main objective is the development of a simplified optimisation model that reveals the optimal values for the physical variables (e.g. solar collector area, storage tank volume) that will lead to lowest investment cost without compromising the solar collection efficiency. A set of equations, modelling the thermodynamics of a solar thermal system, was defined to calculate the physical system variables. Based on a costing methodology, the investment cost equations for the thermal system are also defined. Each cost equation is formulated considering the most relevant physical parameter that influences the cost of a certain component. The numerical solution was obtained using NSGA-II, through MatLab® software. A Pareto front was determined, disclosing the best solutions considering the investment cost minimization and the maximization of solar collection efficiency as objective functions.

2 System Description and Physical Model

2.1 System Description

The solar radiation is converted directly into thermal energy and it is absorbed and transferred to a fluid stream. Most commercial and domestic applications are built-in at low and medium-temperature ranges (40 °C to 80 °C), which in fact corresponds to the largest share of heat consumption, mainly Domestic Hot Water (DHW) and space heating [3, 4]. The most important components of a solar thermal system are the solar collector, the pump and a controller (in the case of active systems), the storage tank to accumulate heat from the working fluid and the circuit of pipes (see the representative scheme at Fig. 1). These are the most important components when sizing solar thermal systems considering energy production and storage.

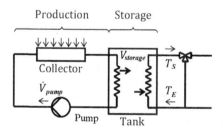

Fig. 1. Scheme of the main circuit of the solar thermal system.

The solar collector is the main component of solar thermal systems. The sunlight is absorbed by a material, converted to heat and transferred to a fluid stream. The heated fluid (generally air, water, or antifreeze liquid) can be used for several purposes such as space heating, hot-water heating, process heating, and even cooling.

Several designs of flat solar collectors are available, including with or without single or multiple glass covers, or with a vacuum for reducing the heat losses in so-called unglazed, glazed or evacuated collector designs, respectively. The presence of a glass layer or vacuum allows operation with higher efficiencies at higher temperatures over an extended temperature range. For domestic use, the temperature at the point of supply is, usually, of about 45 °C. To reach that temperature, the heated water temperature should be accumulated at a temperature of 60 °C.

2.2   Mathematical Modelling

The useful power collected by the thermal fluid (see Eq. (1)), can be estimated by the correlation between the solar collection area (A_{solar}), solar irradiation (I_g), collector absorbance (α), collector aperture transmittance (τ), the global losses coefficient (U_L) and the temperature variation between the mean temperature of the thermal fluid (15 °C $\leq t_f \leq$ 180 °C) and the ambient temperature (assumed to be a fixed temperature, t_a = 15 °C). When using directly the mean temperature of the fluid, it is necessary to introduce a corrector factor, the irrigation factor, F', which reduces the useful power and takes the value of 0.789.

$$P = A_{solar} \cdot F' \cdot \left[I_g \cdot \tau \cdot \alpha - U_L \left(t_f - t_a \right) \right] \tag{1}$$

The solar collection efficiency is defined by the ratio between the captured and the received energy. The efficiency of the collection ($\eta_{collection}$) of the solar collection might be calculated as the Eq. (2) for a certain mass flow of thermal fluid.

$$\eta_{collection} = F'(\tau\alpha) - (F'U_L) T^* - (F'U_L) I_g T^{*2} \tag{2}$$

The linear losses coefficient $F'U_L$ was assumed to be 3.6844 W/m^2 K. The term T^* represents the maximum temperature that the collector can reach for certain ambient temperature and solar irradiation, as defined as in Eq. (3).

$$T^* = \frac{\left(t_f - t_a \right)}{I_g} \tag{3}$$

Based on the data from several commercial models, the solar collection efficiency can be approximated to a second-degree polynomial function as presented in Fig. 2.

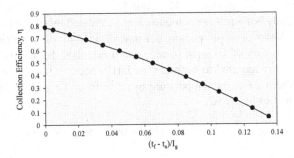

Fig. 2. Characteristic curve of solar collection efficiency, as a function of the maximum temperature that the collector can reach for certain ambient temperature and irradiation.

When solar energy is enough to increase the thermal fluid temperature and the heat transfer process is ensured, water circulates from storage to the collector. Then, the heated water returns to the storage tank, where it is stored until it is needed. As a pump circulates the water, the collectors can be mounted either above or below the storage tank.

Direct circulation systems often use a single storage tank equipped with an auxiliary water heater, but two-tank storage systems can also be used [4, 15]. The mass flow that is pumped in the primary circuit depends on the collection aperture area and the thermal properties of the thermal fluid that is used in the system, the specific heat (c_p) and the density (ρ_{tfluid}), as presented in the Eq. (4). The thermal fluid used in the primary circuit is a mixture of antifreeze with water in appropriate concentrations to the minimum temperature of a certain location.

$$\dot{V}_{pump} = \left(\frac{10F'U_{L0}}{c_{p\,tfluid}} \cdot A_{solar} \cdot 3600 \right) \cdot \frac{1}{\rho_{tfluid}} \qquad (4)$$

The need for energy does not always coincide with the time of production, so it is necessary to have an accumulation system to meet the demand in times of low radiation or no consumption. The use of vertical tanks has the advantage of favouring water stratification. Thus, it is ensured that the hottest water is in the upper part of the accumulator, which is precisely where it is extracted. There is a correlation between the percentage of incident solar energy use and the optimum volume of the deposit per unit area of the solar collector, as presented by the Eq. (5). According to [16], the optimal storage volume per unit of solar collection area is 0.070 m^3/m^2. Higher values do not lead to greater use of incident solar energy, but only contribute to the increase in the storage tank volume and its cost [16].

$$0.060\,m^3/m^2 < \frac{V_{storage}}{A_{solar}} < 0.090\,m^3/m^2 \qquad (5)$$

2.3 Energy Requirements to Suppress DHW of a Reference Building

Considering a residential building, located in Lisbon, with an occupation of 4 people with a need of 40 L of water per person and per day at 60 °C, the daily hot water consumption correspond to 160 L day^{-1}. The solar panel is optimally oriented, 45° South, and set with an inclination of 51° angle [17].

The specific daily hot water consumption was calculated by taking into account the ratio between the water need per person, per day, divided by the number of residents. Table 1 gives a summary of all input parameters to calculate the thermal requirements for DHW. The energy required to suppress the DHW needs (Q_{DHW}) can be calculated by the Eq. (6), where ΔT is the temperature increase from the grid water temperature, which was assumed to be 35 °C.

$$Q_{DHW} = Cons_{dhw} \cdot (4.187/3600) \cdot \Delta T \cdot 365\,days \qquad (6)$$

Table 1 Input parameters to calculate the thermal requirements for DHW

Parameter	Value
Daily hot water consumption, C_{onsDHW}	160 L day^{-1}
Hot water temperature	60 °C
Panel direction	South (45°)
Yearly sum of global irradiation (Lisbon)	1,890 kWh/m^2
Q$_{DHW}$	**2,377 kWh.year^{-1}**

For this reference scenario, the energy required to suppress the DHW needs is approximately 2 377 kWh year^{-1}. According to [16], at least, an equivalent area of 1 m^2 of solar collection is required to suppress a demand of 500 kWh year^{-1}.

3 Economic Model of Solar Thermal Components

The costing methodology, based on the approach developed by [18], consists on the derivation of a cost expression for each component by integrating thermodynamic and cost coefficients, adjusted for this kind of technology, and also taking into account real market data. Each cost equation was defined considering physical variables, which can be classified as size and quality variables. In terms of methodology, the equations are defined considering that the cost of each component is based on a reference case and includes a cost coefficient, a reference size factor, F_{ref}, which scales the component and, for some system components, a quality factor. The basic formulation is presented in the Eq. (7):

$$C_i = C_{ref,i}\ F_{ref} \cdot \left(\frac{F_i}{F_{ref}}\right)^b \tag{7}$$

where the term C_{ref} is the reference cost coefficient that corresponds to a cost per unit of (one or more) physical parameter, F_{ref} and F_i are the reference and the physical variable value and b is the sizing exponent.

3.1 Solar Collector Cost Equation

The purchase cost of the solar collector (C_{solar}) is affected by two main variables: the solar collector area and the collection efficiency. The variable with the highest weight is the area (A_{solar}) [in m^2]. The collector cost equation is given by Eq. (8):

$$C_{solar} = C_{ref,\ solar} \cdot A_{ref,\ solar} \cdot \left(\frac{A_{solar}}{A_{ref,\ solar}}\right)^{b_{solar}} \cdot \left(\frac{1}{1 - \eta_{collection}}\right)^c \tag{8}$$

where, the reference cost coefficient, $C_{ref,\ solar}$, is 298.54€/m^2; the reference collector area, $A_{ref,\ solar}$, is assumed to be 2.5 m^2; the area sizing factor (b_{solar}) is assumed to be

0.5, and the efficiency exponent is fixed at $c = 0.1$. The value for the collection efficiency is obtained from the Eq. (2) considering a specific climate condition.

3.2 Pump Cost Equation

The purchase cost equation of the circulation pump, (C_{pump}) is defined considering the flow rate ($\dot{V}_{pump}$) as the main operational variable affecting the cost of this component (Eq. (9)). The term $C_{ref,\ pump}$ corresponds to the constant reference cost of the pump cost, $\dot{V}_{ref,\ pump}$ [in m³/h] is the reference pump flow rate and b_{pump} is the sizing exponent. The reference cost coefficient is equal to 322.45€/(m³/h), the reference flow rate was assumed as 0.98 m³/h and the sizing factor was set at 0.3.

$$C_{pump} = C_{ref,pump} \cdot \dot{V}_{ref,pump} \left(\frac{\dot{V}_{pump}}{\dot{V}_{ref,pump}} \right)^{b_{pump}} \tag{9}$$

3.3 Storage Tank Cost Equation

Regarding the storage tank cost equation, the physical variable that mostly affects its price is the storage volume ($V_{storage}$) [in m³] as presented in Eq. (10), where the reference cost coefficient is $C_{ref,\ storage}$= 3,647.45€/m³; the reference storage volume is assumed to be $V_{ref,\ storage} = 0.32$ m³; and the sizing factor is equal to $b_{storage}$ 0.3.

$$C_{storage} = C_{ref,storage} \cdot V_{ref,storage} \left(\frac{V_{storage}}{V_{ref,storage}} \right)^{b_{storage}} \tag{10}$$

3.4 Total Investment Costs

The capital investment of the components corresponds to the sum of the purchase cost of the pump cost, the storage tank cost and the solar collector cost. The estimated cost regarding the engineering expenses with the installation ($C_{installation}$) usually represents a variable percentage of the investment of the main components. Thus, the total investment costs are calculated by the Eq. (11):

$$C_{inv} = C_{pump} + C_{storage} + C_{solar} + C_{installation} + C_{circulation} \tag{11}$$

where the $C_{installation}$ was assumed to be 10% of the total cost of collector, the storage tank and the circulation pump. The circulation costs ($C_{circulation}$) were defined as a fixed value (500€), since, for the range of individual domestic applications, the prices do not vary significantly [4].

4 Optimization Modelling

Real-world optimization problems are complex to implement in terms of a number of variables, nature of the objective function or even because of the existence of many local optimal. As the one presented herein, some of the optimization problems consider more than one conflicting objective functions to be optimized, resulting in multi-objective optimization problems. A unique solution that simultaneously optimizes all the objective function does not exist and, therefore, different solutions will produce trade-offs between different objectives values. The set of solutions create a multi-dimensional function space, typically represented by Pareto curves [10].

4.1 Objective Functions, Decision Variables and Constraints

In the present study, two key objective functions were defined for optimization: the minimization of the total investment cost of the solar thermal system and the maximization of the solar collection efficiency as defined in Eq. (12):

$$Minimize \quad F_m(x), \quad m = 1 \ and \ 2;$$
$$F_1(x) = C_{inv} \tag{12}$$
$$F_2(x) = -\eta_{collection}$$

The definition of the decision variables is one of the most important steps in formulating an optimization problem. The variable bounds of an optimization problem restrict each decision variable to a lower and upper limit which institutes a space called decision variable space. Based on preliminary tests to the physical model, three explicit decision variables were defined in the numerical model. The selected decision variables include the maximum temperature variation that the collector can reach for certain ambient temperature and as a function of solar irradiation (T^*), the solar collection area (A_{solar}) and the tank storage volume ($V_{storage}$). The three decision variables were lower and upper bounded as presented by the Eqs. (13), (14) and (15).

$$0.005 \leq T* \leq 0.140 \quad [°C/(W/m^2)] \tag{13}$$

$$2.0 \leq A_{solar} \leq 8.0 \quad [m^2] \tag{14}$$

$$0.060 \leq V_{Storage} \leq 0.540 \quad [m^3] \tag{15}$$

Few linear constraints were considered regarding the significance of physical variables of the model. Table 2 identifies the linear constraints assumed in the model and depicts the reason for its consideration. These constraints aim to limit the operational parameters that give significance to the thermal model: (1) guarantee that there is a temperature difference that promotes the heat transfer between the thermal fluid and the water; (2) define the temperature limits for the thermal fluid, which is characteristically a solution of water and of propilenoglicol; (3) set a range for solar irradiation.

Table 2. Definition of linear constraints and the reason for its consideration

Linear constraint	Reason
$t_f - t_a > 10\ °C$	Ensure the heat transfer process between the thermal fluid and the water
$15\ °C \leq t_f \leq 180\ °C$	Simple limits of thermal fluid temperature
$950\ W/m^2 \leq I_g \leq 1,000\ W/m^2$	Limit the solar irradiation to characteristic values for direct radiation

4.2   Optimization Algorithm: NSGA-II

In this work, a variant of NSGA-II was implemented (Fig. 3). This algorithm is a non-dominant and elitist GA that favours individuals with better fitness value (rank) and that can help to increase the diversity of the population [19]. This approach was chosen due to the convergence reduced time, the capability of solving a mathematical model with non-linear functions of a complex physical and economic model, when compared with gradient-based methods [20].

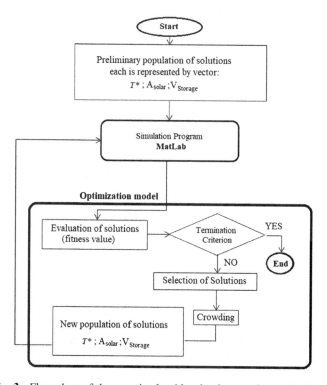

Fig. 3. Flow chart of the genetic algorithm implementation at MatLab®.

The elitist selection mechanism picks the current best solutions of each generation without applying any operators to them. However, since it uses a controlled elitist genetic algorithm, there is a balance between exploitation and exploration of the objective functions space. The algorithm creates a population that is feasible with respect to bounds and linear constraints. Each solution is denoted by the vector $[T^*, A_{solar}, V_{Storage,}]$, where its elements represent the decision variables (e.g. size of the system's components). Then the algorithm evaluates the objective function and constraints for the population and it uses those values to create scores for the population through the comparison of fitness function values. The population and the offspring are combined into one matrix to extend the population, by computing the rank and crowding distance. Then, the Pareto optimal solutions are tabulated, considering that the trade-off between competing objectives is resolved. The optimization problem was solved with "*gamultiobj*" MatLab® routine, considering a population size of 60 and a Pareto fraction of 0.35. All other parameters were set according to the default values of the MatLab® routine.

5 Results and Discussion

In multi-objective optimization, each of the points in the Pareto curve represents a point where one objective function value may not be improved without worsening others. Therefore, decision-makers select one of them based on the best interest conditions. The multi-objective optimization results are expressed as a two dimensional Pareto front in Fig. 4. The optimization converged when the average change in the spread of Pareto solutions was less than the minimum distance between objective function values. The objective function was evaluated a total of 6,601 times and 109 generations were generated, minimizing the equipment purchase investment cost while the solar collection efficiency is being maximized.

As shown in Fig. 4, a set of optimal solutions for which the solar collection efficiency varies from 28.3% to 78.0% and the investment costs vary between 2,099.5€ and 3,308.3€ can be observed. From the analysis of the Pareto curve, it is shown that gains in overall efficiency above 70% imply a great increase in the total purchase cost,

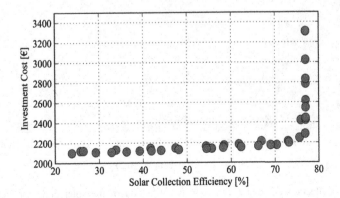

Fig. 4. Pareto optimal frontiers in objectives' solution space.

i.e., varying from a total investment cost of 2,200€ (with an efficiency of 70%) to an investment cost of 3,200€ (with an efficiency of 78%).

Table 3 presents the maximum and minimum values for the decision variables within the optimal frontiers in objectives' space. Due to the importance of the physical values such as the solar collection area and the storage volume tank in the total investment cost, both decision variables are closer to the lower bound that was considered. By the other hand, the maximum temperature that the collector can reach is affected by the solar irradiation, which has a direct and positive influence in the collection efficiency. In fact, when the fluid mean temperature is equal to the ambient temperature, the efficiency is referred as the optical one, representing its maximum value. Considering the changeability of the decision variables, a sensitivity analysis of the sizing factors in the purchase cost equations should be performed in order to better adjust the weight of the physical variables in the respective component cost.

Table 3. Maximum and minimum values for the decision variables within the optimal frontiers in objectives' solution space

Decision variable	Minimum value	Maximum value
Temperature Parameter, T^* [°C/(W/m^2)]	0.0052	0.1062
Solar Collection Area, A_{solar} [m^2]	2.032	4.260
Storage Tank Volume, $V_{storage}$ [m^3]	0.062	0.682

Figure 5 discloses a contour surface showing the variation of solar collection efficiency as a function of the solar collector area and the solar irradiation, using the optimal population results. As expected, higher solar collection areas and high values of irradiation lead to increased collection efficiencies. Thus, the sizing coefficient of the collector area in the solar collector has a great influence on problem modelling.

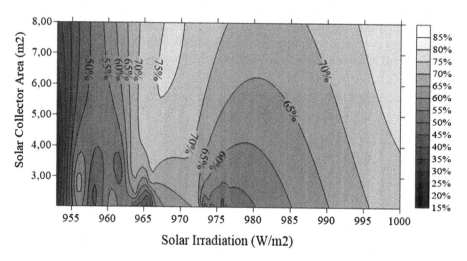

Fig. 5. Solar collection efficiency variation as a function of the solar collector area and the irradiation for the optimal solution.

Figure 6 depicts a contour surface showing the variation of the total purchase cost of the thermal system as a function of the solar collector area and the storage tank volume, using the optimal solution population results. Results a positive correlation between the increase of system cost with the solar collector area. In fact, this decision variable directly affects the sizing of all the components, and consequently the cost of all of the subcomponents.

For a combination of lower values of solar collector area and storage volumes, the variation of the total investment cost is not linear, showing that the storage volume has a greater impact on the investment.

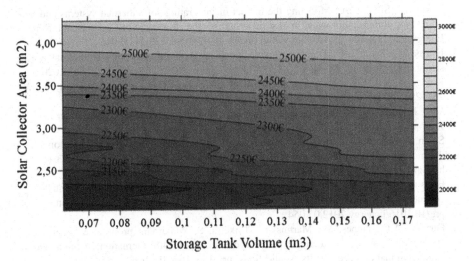

Fig. 6. Total investment cost of the thermal system as a function of the optimal solution for the solar collector area and the irradiation for the optimal solution.

6   Conclusions

In this paper, thermo-economic modelling and multi-objective optimization of a thermal solar system have been done. A multi-objective optimization was performed by defining as objective functions the maximization of solar collection efficiency and the minimization of the total purchase cost of the system. Pareto curves were obtained and analysed. According to the obtained Pareto front, the optimal solution discloses a set of function value's for which the solar collection efficiency vary 28.3% and 78.0% and the investment costs vary between 2,099.5€ and 3,308.3€. The most important decision variable is the solar collector area since this physical variable affects the sizing of the remaining subcomponents of the solar thermal system and, therefore, it deeply affects the total investment cost of the system. A sensitivity analysis of the sizing factors of the cost equations should be performed in order to improve the model accuracy in determining the relative cost of each component.

Acknowledgements. The first author would like to express her gratitude for the support given by the Portuguese Foundation for Science and Technology (FCT) through the Post-Doc Research Grant SFRH/BPD/121446/2016. This work has been supported by FCT within the Project Scope UID/CEC/00319/2019 (ALGORITMI) and Project Scope UID/EMS/04077/2019 (METRICS).

References

1. da Graça, G.C., Augusto, A., Lerer, M.M.: Solar powered net zero energy houses for southern Europe: feasibility study. Sol. Energy. **86**, 634–646 (2012). https://doi.org/10.1016/j.solener.2011.11.008
2. Neves, D., Silva, C.A.: Modeling the impact of integrating solar thermal systems and heat pumps for domestic hot water in electric systems – the case study of Corvo Island. Renew. Energy **72**, 113–124 (2014). https://doi.org/10.1016/j.renene.2014.06.046
3. Evarts, J.C., Swan, L.G.: Domestic hot water consumption estimates for solar thermal system sizing. Energy Build. **58**, 58–65 (2013). https://doi.org/10.1016/j.enbuild.2012.11.020
4. Kalogirou, S.A.: Solar thermal collectors and applications. Prog. Energy Combust. Sci. **30**, 231–295 (2004). https://doi.org/10.1016/j.pecs.2004.02.001
5. Ong, K.S., Tong, W.L.: System performance of U-Tube and heat pipe solar water heaters. J. Appl. Sci. Eng. **15**, 105–110 (2012)
6. Sahin, B., Kodal, A.: Performance analysis of an endoreversible heat engine based on a new thermoeconomic optimization criterion. Energy Convers. Manag. **42**, 1085–1093 (2001). https://doi.org/10.1016/S0196-8904(00)00120-5
7. Ferreira, A.C.M., et al.: An economic perspective on the optimisation of a small-scale cogeneration system for the Portuguese scenario. Energy **45**, 436–444 (2012). https://doi.org/10.1016/j.energy.2012.05.054
8. Ferreira, A.C., Nunes, M., Martins, L., Teixeira, S.: Maximum profit of a cogeneration system based on stirling thermodynamic cycle. In: 2014 14th International Conference on Computational Science and Its Applications, pp. 156–160. IEEE (2014)
9. Bejan, A., Tsatsaronis, G., Moran, M.: Thermal Design and Optimization. Wiley, New York (1996)
10. Assaf, J., Shabani, B.: Multi-objective sizing optimisation of a solar-thermal system integrated with a solar-hydrogen combined heat and power system, using genetic algorithm. Energy Convers. Manag. **164**, 518–532 (2018). https://doi.org/10.1016/j.enconman.2018.03.026
11. Lin, W., Ma, Z., Ren, H., Gschwander, S., Wang, S.: Multi-objective optimisation of thermal energy storage using phase change materials for solar air systems. Renew. Energy **130**, 1116–1129 (2019). https://doi.org/10.1016/j.renene.2018.08.071
12. Antoniadis, C.N., Martinopoulos, G.: Optimization of a building integrated solar thermal system with seasonal storage using TRNSYS. Renew. Energy **137**, 56–66 (2019). https://doi.org/10.1016/j.renene.2018.03.074
13. Yılmaz, İ.H.: Residential use of solar water heating in Turkey: a novel thermo-economic optimization for energy savings, cost benefit and ecology. J. Clean. Prod. **204**, 511–524 (2018). https://doi.org/10.1016/j.jclepro.2018.09.060
14. Asadi, J., Amani, P., Amani, M., Kasaeian, A., Bahiraei, M.: Thermo-economic analysis and multi-objective optimization of absorption cooling system driven by various solar collectors. Energy Convers. Manag. **173**, 715–727 (2018). https://doi.org/10.1016/j.enconman.2018.08.013

15. Tian, Y., Zhao, C.Y.: A review of solar collectors and thermal energy storage in solar thermal applications. Appl. Energy **104**, 538–553 (2013). https://doi.org/10.1016/j.apenergy.2012.11.051
16. Lebeña, E.P., Costa, J.C.: Installers of thermal solar equipment. In: INETI/DGEG (ed.) Conversão Térmica da Energia Solar, pp. 1–89. INETI/DGEG, Lisboa (2008)
17. Greenstream Publishing: Solar Electricity Handbook. http://www.solarelectricityhandbook.com/solar-irradiance.html
18. Ferreira, A.C., Nunes, M.L., Teixeira, J.C.F., Martins, L.A.S.B., Teixeira, S.F.C.F.: Thermodynamic and economic optimization of a solar-powered Stirling engine for micro-cogeneration purposes. Energy **111**, 1–17 (2016). https://doi.org/10.1016/j.energy.2016.05.091
19. MathWorks, M.: gaoptimset: Create genetic algorithm options structure (2014). https://www.mathworks.com/help/gads/gamultiobj.html
20. Ferreira, A.C.M., Rocha, A.M.A.C., Teixeira, S.F.C.F., Nunes, M.L., Martins, L.B.: On solving the profit maximization of small cogeneration systems. In: Murgante, B., et al. (eds.) ICCSA 2012. LNCS, vol. 7335, pp. 147–158. Springer, Heidelberg (2012). https://doi.org/10.1007/978-3-642-31137-6_11

Assessment of Indoor Thermal Conditions in a Cinema Room Using CFD Simulation: A Case Study

Nelson Rodrigues[1,2]([⊠]) [iD], João Silva[1,2] [iD], José Teixeira[2] [iD], and Senhorinha Teixeira[1] [iD]

[1] ALGORITMI Center, University of Minho, Guimarães, Portugal
nelson.rodrigues@dps.uminho.pt
[2] Mechanical Engineering and Resource Sustainability Center (MEtRICs),
University of Minho, Guimarães, Portugal

Abstract. This work aims to characterize the experience lived by a user of a movie theater in the dimension related to the thermal environment. An exhaustive survey of information was made in order to allow the characterization of a set of variables that can affect the user experience in this type of contexts. The collection of information included: a checklist for characterization of space and its use; the experimental measurement of the variables related to the thermal environment and the calculation of thermal comfort indexes and a subjective analysis of the thermal comfort of the users of the space, result of the implementation of two questionnaires to analyze the perception of the users against the conditions of a movie theater. Furthermore, the space was modeled using ANSYS software, which allowed the subsequent simulation of the flow inside the Cinema in order to also study the thermal comfort.

In order to obtain solid bases for a better understanding of the parameters that affect the well-being of the user, the values obtained with the calculation of the thermal comfort indexes and the experimental measurements were compared with those referenced in ISO 7330:2005, the values that resulted from the subjective evaluation and with the results obtained with the CFD simulation. Both results provided a prediction of thermal comfort near thermal neutrality, though with a small difference of 0.6 points in the thermal sensation scale. The simulation provided further insight of the localized thermal environment and about the influence of people's presence.

Keywords: Thermal comfort · Cinema · CFD simulation

1 Introduction

Thermal environment plays a fundamental role in decision making from the point of view of comfort and performance of individuals. It is a complex field that attracts the interest of several researchers, since a long time [1]. The thermal environment is interconnected with a set of thermal variables that influence the heat exchanges between the individual and the environment in which it is inserted [2]. The environmental variables are the average radiant temperature, air temperature, air velocity, and

© Springer Nature Switzerland AG 2019
S. Misra et al. (Eds.): ICCSA 2019, LNCS 11624, pp. 40–51, 2019.
https://doi.org/10.1007/978-3-030-24311-1_3

air humidity [3, 4]. Additionally, thermal comfort is also influenced by personal variables, namely, metabolic rate and clothing insulation, as well as personal factors such as stress and medication among others [5, 6].

People spend much of their time indoors and many of those spaces are air-conditioned, whose equipment programming must be properly regulated, taking into account the health, comfort, and the productivity of its occupants [7, 8]. When the thermal environment is not the most appropriate, individuals tend to change their behavior and expectations in order to adapt to the environment. This change leads to a lower tolerance regarding the inadequacy of the thermal environment in air-conditioned spaces when compared with naturally ventilated spaces [9]. The physical effects caused by uncomfortable environments, induce agitation, which can reduce attention and concentration, and lead to fatigue and drowsiness. Physiologically, an individual needs to maintain its internal temperature within very narrow limits, at approximately 37 °C, which requires a constant search for thermal equilibrium, namely, homeothermy. Homeothermy is ensured whenever the heat produced by the organism equals the net heat flow to the environment so that the temperature remains constant [10].

Thermal neutrality is attributed to the state of thermal comfort [11], provided there is no local thermal discomfort [12]. ASHRAE Standard-55 (2004) defines thermal comfort as the mental state that expresses a man's satisfaction with the thermal environment that surrounds him, and ISO 7730:2005 defines it as an expression of satisfaction with the environment that surrounds the individual. According to Parsons [5], the environmental variables combined with the indexes of metabolism and clothing (designated by individual parameters), form the basic elements that define thermal comfort. There are several thermal comfort evaluation equations, however, the mostly used method in design guides and standards is the one developed by Fanger [6]. This method is based on the theory of thermo-regulation and thermal equilibrium and defines two complementary indexes, PMV - Predicted Mean Vote and PPD - Predicted Percentage of Dissatisfied People or Predictable Percentage of Dissatisfied.

As of 31 December 2016, there were 549 cinema screens in Portugal, 192 of them in Multiplex venues (8 or more cinemas), with a total of 103,583 seats, of which 35,758 seats in venues with eight or more cinemas. In the year 2016 650,011 cinema sessions were shown, for a total of 14,890,813 spectators[13]. The rooms had an average of 188.67 seats, with an average occupancy rate of approximately 12%. Considering the average duration of TOP 10 of the movies most seen in 2016, 117 min, the sum of hours that the spectators spent inside the Portuguese cinemas will be around 29,037,085 h. The specific case of a cinema experience requires an environment technically prepared for a relaxing and thus comfortable environment. The experience of watching a movie in a movie theater results from a sensory experience, where the inadequacy of the thermal environment or another element such as; the sound, the lighting, and others, may provoke interference and break the established tune between the spectator and the narrative.

Particularly in the matter of the thermal environment, the environmental variables should be adjusted through the air conditioning systems according to the occupancy rate and the outside temperature, considering that individuals they will be at rest, seated and quiet, with the clothing in accordance with the outside temperature.

In recent years, the study of optimum performance and the influence of these set of parameters with numerical models has been an attractive option for researchers [14–20]. Results showed that CFD simulations are an important tool to support experimental campaigns due to their ability to evaluate thermal comfort. Aryal [14] with CFD experiments showed that the thermal comfort level is deteriorated in some specific regions with the installation of partition and can be improved by adjusting air parameters at the supply diffuser and location of extract grilles. Buratti et al. [15] used a CFD tool for thermal comfort evaluation in natural convection and in transient conditions in a room. Results showed that the thermal sensation is uniform in the absence of the direct component of solar radiation. Aste et al. [16] analyzed the performance of an innovative local heating solution in terms of thermal comfort. For this, a 3D CFD model was developed to estimate the effects of set variables on human thermal comfort. It was verified that the air temperature in the room is not significantly influenced by the heating system, but the heat is directly radiated to people, ensuring comfortable conditions and contributing to artworks preservation. Shahzad [17] investigated the application and performance of an advanced personal comfort system, a thermal chair, using CFD. With CFD analysis it was improved by 20% the overall comfort. Alizadeh [18] performed an investigation of the effect of placing ceiling fan on thermal comfort level inside a room using CFD simulation. With this study, it was possible to provide an insightful understanding of the thermal comfort in a room and to perform a parametric study to enhance thermal comfort inside the room. Abdeen et al. [19] developed a CFD model to optimize solar chimney design to maximize indoor air velocity induced by natural convection, with a particular emphasis on thermal comfort. Ahmed et al. [20] carried out a CFD analysis to obtain velocity and temperature profiles inside a room in order to calculate the air diffusion performance index.

The objective of this study is to characterize the thermal environment, trying to obtain solid bases for a better understanding of the parameters that affect the experience lived by the users of these spaces. Afterward, the characterization of PPD-PMV as a method of Thermal Comfort evaluation and the importance of the use of questionnaires as a tool for the subjective evaluation of thermal comfort is made.

2   Methodology

2.1   Cinema Description

The space under study is a room of a cinema complex. The choice of this room is due to the fact that this is the largest room of this cinema complex, with 170 seats and its capacity to be the closest to the average capacity of the National Rooms, 188 seats. The room does not have the means that allow the natural renovation of the air during the sessions of cinema, being the renovation is forced through air conditioning equipment. Air insufflation is done through six points located on the ceiling of the room, and the extraction through holes under the seats of the chairs.

The HVAC system is made up of an MCQUAY Model 75 19 equipment, which is installed next to the facade on the exterior of the building. This equipment does not have a reuse or air recirculation system, so the air in the room is always new air coming from the outside. The room temperature is set at 22 °C, for an upper capacity of approximately 25%, and the equipment is only activated approximately 10 to 15 min from the beginning of the session. The control that controls the equipment is outside the room, inside the projection booth.

2.2 Field Measurements

Occupancy. In order to select the measurement points, the distribution of occupancy per seat was calculated based on 6,041 tickets sold in the period between December 1, 2016, and January 31, 2017, for the study room. Due to material limitations, for this study only the following measurement points were chosen: B8, place with the highest occupancy rate (2.56%); K14, place with the lowest occupancy rate (0.08%) and G12, a place with the sample median (0.40%). Figure 1 represents the distribution of occupancy in the living room floor plan.

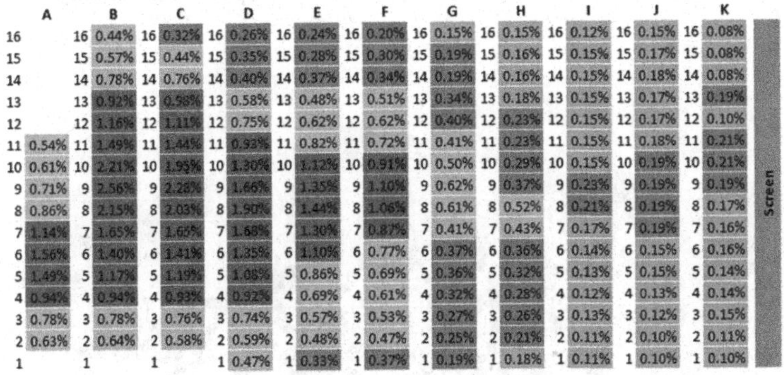

	A	B	C	D	E	F	G	H	I	J	K
16		0.44%	0.32%	0.26%	0.24%	0.20%	0.15%	0.15%	0.12%	0.15%	0.08%
15		0.57%	0.44%	0.35%	0.28%	0.30%	0.19%	0.16%	0.15%	0.17%	0.08%
14		0.78%	0.76%	0.40%	0.37%	0.34%	0.19%	0.16%	0.15%	0.15%	0.08%
13		0.92%	0.58%	0.58%	0.48%	0.51%	0.34%	0.18%	0.15%	0.17%	0.19%
12		1.16%	1.11%	0.75%	0.62%	0.62%	0.40%	0.23%	0.15%	0.17%	0.10%
11	0.54%	1.49%	1.44%	0.93%	0.82%	0.72%	0.41%	0.23%	0.15%	0.18%	0.21%
10	0.61%	2.21%	1.95%	1.30%	1.12%	0.91%	0.50%	0.29%	0.15%	0.19%	0.21%
9	0.71%	2.56%	2.28%	1.66%	1.35%	1.10%	0.62%	0.37%	0.28%	0.19%	0.19%
8	0.86%	2.15%	2.03%	1.90%	1.44%	1.06%	0.61%	0.52%	0.21%	0.19%	0.17%
7	1.14%	1.65%	1.65%	1.68%	1.30%	0.87%	0.41%	0.43%	0.17%	0.19%	0.16%
6	1.56%	1.40%	1.41%	1.35%	1.10%	0.77%	0.37%	0.36%	0.14%	0.15%	0.16%
5	1.49%	1.17%	1.19%	1.08%	0.86%	0.69%	0.36%	0.32%	0.13%	0.15%	0.14%
4	0.94%	0.94%	0.93%	0.92%	0.69%	0.61%	0.32%	0.28%	0.12%	0.13%	0.14%
3	0.78%	0.78%	0.76%	0.74%	0.57%	0.53%	0.27%	0.26%	0.13%	0.12%	0.15%
2	0.63%	0.64%	0.58%	0.59%	0.48%	0.47%	0.25%	0.21%	0.11%	0.10%	0.11%
1				0.47%	0.33%	0.37%	0.19%	0.18%	0.11%	0.10%	0.10%

Fig. 1. Occupation and distribution in the cinema room. (Color figure online)

Environmental Characterization. The characterization of the thermal environment of the study space was done by means of experimental measurements in April 2017, at the previously selected points and in randomly chosen sessions. For the measurement of variables in real time, it is necessary to use some instruments simultaneously, and its calibration has much relevance in the accuracy of the data obtained. For this study, the instruments were assigned by the Department of Production and Systems of the University of Minho, and there were no changes in their calibration.

For the experimental measurements, the following instruments were used:

- A Casella brand globe thermometer model RS2842:1992, to measure individual exposure to radiant heat. This was placed at chest level on a tripod to remain stable, and a stabilization period of about 30 min;
- An anemometer TSI Velocicheck Model 8330 anemometer to measure air velocity, also placed at chest level on a tripod and had a stabilization period of 5 min;

- Three USB Data loggers from Elcar, model EL-USB, to measure the temperature, relative humidity of the air and calculate the dew point. They were also placed on a tripod at chest level.

The temperature and relative humidity of the outdoor air at the time of the different measurements were registered by consulting the website of the Portuguese Institute of the Sea and Atmosphere since these two variables can affect the interior thermal environment and its perception [21].

2.3   Simulation Study

Modelation of the 3D Environment. The first phase of a computational fluid dynamics (CFD) simulation consists in the definition of the study domain. To that purpose, a modelation program, such as DesignModeler® was used. Through the cinema schematics and with local observation, a 3D model of the cinema room was created. Additionally, the full definition of the domain needs the inclusion of boundary conditions. Figure 2 represents the domain with the respective boundary conditions identified.

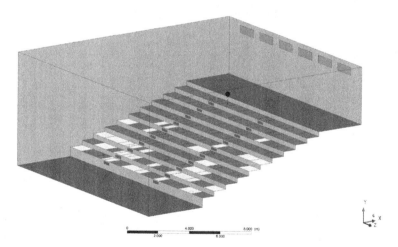

Fig. 2. Representation of the modelated cinema room and its boundary conditions. The black point represents the location of the experimental measurements. (Color figure online)

Each boundary condition is represented by a scheme of colors where: the walls are represented in grey, the air inlets are represented by orange, the dark blue represents the cinema floor, the color purple represents the outlets, the red represents the seats occupied by people and the light blue areas represent the unoccupied seats.

The conditions simulated were based on the conditions verified on April 19, where the cinema had a bigger attendance. As such, the inlets were defined according to the specifications of the HVAC systems and the Portuguese regulations [22], as such, a velocity input of 0.25 m/s was applied. The cinema is within a building and, as such, for simplification, the walls were considered adiabatic. Similarly, the same is true to the cinema floor. The air outlets of the cinema were defined as passive, using pressure outlet boundaries with a relative pressure of 0 Pa.

Regarding the temperatures within the cinema, people are the main heat source of the domain, which makes their presence in the simulation important. On April 19, the attendance in the cinema was of 76% of its full capacity. However, people do not spread evenly over the cinema seats, there is a preference for certain seats (Fig. 1). This preference creates a concentration of people and heat that may influence the temperature distribution and affect the localized thermal comfort. Considering this, the seats in the cinema were selected through a distribution that accounted for the probability of a seat to be occupied. The selection mechanism was accomplished through a Python® script. The basic concept consisted of three main steps: The first step was to export the table contained the relative frequencies occupation for each seat in a CSV file that was later imported into a NumPy data structure. The second step consisted in transforming the relative frequencies in integer values to create a list of frequencies. As such, each frequency was multiplied by 100 and rounded to an integer value. This step allowed keeping the relative probability of the seats and the information of the low-frequency values. For example, in the seats where the occupation was only 0.08%, this information would be lost if rounded directly. The third step consisted in the creation of a list of frequencies. The list contained a unique identifier and a reference to a seat, repeated the number of times that matched its frequency. Once the list was created, a random number comprised between the size of the list was generated, giving an index of a seat. After a seat is taken, all its references are removed from the list. This last step is repeated until all people are placed. For the occupied places, the wall temperature was defined as 33 °C as this is the average skin temperature for people in comfort [23].

The resolution of the differential equations that define a CFD problem implies the use of discrete volume methodology in order to discretize the domain. This method consists in dividing the global volume into smaller elements until it is considered that the fluid properties within the small volumes are not significant. The mesh generation was focused on reducing the element deformation, thus keeping a good quality to reduce the computation time and facilitate the numeric convergence. For this purpose, the domain was divided into smaller regular geometries to better accommodate the mesh blocks. In total, the domain was divided into 3604 bodies. To guarantee a good definition of the boundary layer, it is important to obtain a good representation of the near wall phenomena such as heat transfer, each wall had a mesh refinement with elements of reduced size near it, followed by a growing gradient. In total, the final mesh as represented in Fig. 3 had a total of 1,254,690 elements.

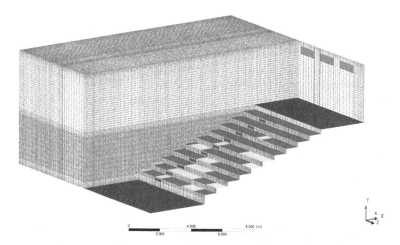

Fig. 3. Representation of the mesh used in the simulation of the cinema room. (Color figure online)

Since a good mesh positively affects the numerical solution and the simulation speed, it is important to determine its quality through different quality indices, such as the "Element Quality", "Orthogonal Quality" and "Skewness". The former two indices vary between the values of 0 and 1, where 0 is an element of bad quality and 1 presents a good quality. The average value for the Element quality and Orthogonal Quality are 0.48 and 1 respectively. As for the latter index, 0 represents a good element which is not distorted and, at the limit, the value 1 represents a completely distorted element. The average value for this index is 0.

Once the domain is discretized, follows the definition of the variables to study. To include the temperature and heat transfer, the energy equation was activated. Additionally, to correctly model the transfer and its mechanisms, the radiation model "Surface to Surface" was included, allowing accounting the thermal radiant fluxes. To account for the turbulence in the flow, the model k-ω was selected since it accounts for flows with low Reynolds numbers [24, 25].

3   Results and Discussion

3.1   Experimental Results

Experimental measurements were performed at a measurement point inside the room at the B8 site, starting at 15:00 and ending at 20:30 on April 19, 2017. During this period there were two sessions of cinema, the first one began at 15:30 and the end at 18:00, with an occupancy rate of 76.4% and the second one starting at 18:50 and ending at 21:00, occupancy rate of 34.7%.

Table 1 summarizes the results of the calculated indexes, identifying the maximum, minimum, mean values and standard deviations of the obtained values for the first session.

Table 1. Experimental measurements results

	Max.	Min.	Avg.	Std.
Temperature (°C)	24.5	20.0	22.2	0.9
Dew point (°C)	15.5	8.9	14	1.2
Relative humidity (%)	65	37	59.9	4.2

For the calculation of PPD and PMV indexes, the average metabolic value of a 70 kg man with a skin surface of 1.8 m^2 was used as a reference, sitting in a comfortable environment, met = 1, and thermal insulation, which represents a typical indoor clothing combination during the winter. The values of the environmental parameters used to calculate the indexes were those recorded during the periods of the cinema sessions, with an interval of 15 min.

Table 2 summarizes the results of the calculated indexes, identifying the maximum, minimum, mean values and standard deviations of the obtained values.

Table 2. PMV and PPD values

	PMV	PPD (%)
Avg.	−0.30	6.89
Max.	0.05	5.05
Min.	−0.80	18.59
Std.	0.25	6.31

3.2   Numerical Results

Temperature, Velocity and PMV Fields. The results for the computed velocity fields are represented in Fig. 4, which is composed of four orthogonal planes – one parallel to the YZ plane, one to the XY plane and two planes parallel to the ZX plane at different heights, to capture the details of the velocity near the inlets and near the zone occupied by the people. The results allow us to understand how the air moves throughout the cinema, with the greatest air velocities located at the height of the air inlets. This behavior is expected as the boundary conditions in the inlets was defined as 0.25 m/s providing the air with its highest kinetic energy. Besides, this promotes the renovation of the hot air that tends to accumulate near the ceiling due to stratification. Additionally, the results show that there are few regions where the air is stagnant (with zero velocity), adding to the effectiveness and quality of the ventilation. The zones near the cinema seats presented an average velocity near 0.05 m/s, a value which makes the air movement imperceptible.

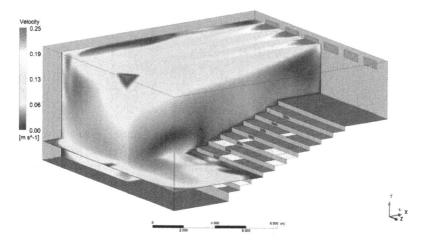

Fig. 4. Simulated velocity fields in the cinema room. (Color figure online)

In order to get a better comparison between different results, the same representation was applied to the temperature field in the cinema, represented by Fig. 5. The air provided by the ventilation system was defined as having 22 °C. In the present case, the ventilation has a lower temperature than the average room temperature, providing a cooling effect. This is visible by the darker blue color near the air inlets representing the lowest temperature. As previously referred, people are the main source of heat in the cinema and their contribution is enough to change the thermal environment. In Fig. 5 is possible to verify this behavior with greater temperatures near the seats and the consequent gradient along the cinema height. Overall, the volume averaged simulated temperature was near 24 °C.

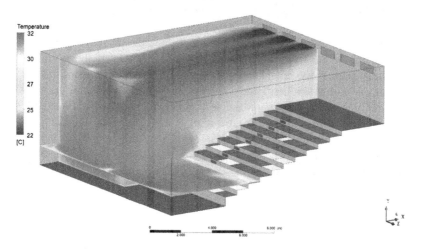

Fig. 5. Simulated temperature fields in the cinema room. (Color figure online)

After taking into account the temperature and velocities variations of an occupied cinema, it was possible to determine a field of local PMV values. For the calculation, there were constant variables, taken from the measurements in the field, namely, the relative humidity with a value of 60%, the metabolic rate of 1 Met and the clothing insulation of 1 clo. The variations occurred in the velocities, air temperature, and radiant temperature. The former variables where the result of the simulation as previously described. As for the latter parameter, since there was not a main source of radiant temperature, in the calculation its value was equal to the air temperature. The local PMV fields were calculated using a Python® script that iterated through the temperature and velocity values of each mesh cell and, together with the other thermal environment parameters calculated the PMV value for that cell. The resulting field is represented in Fig. 6. The simulations performed predicted an average PMV value for the room of 0.3, which is a little above of the ±0.2 limit for the Class A category as described in ISO 7730:2005. The simulation also adds the advantage of being able to verify local discomfort zones. Figure 6 shows that the temperature provided by the people is enough to alter the comfort perception, increasing the PMV value to 1.5.

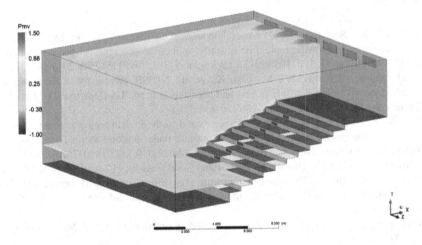

Fig. 6. Simulated PMV fields in the cinema room. (Color figure online)

4 Conclusions

Through field measurements, it was possible to verify that the thermal environment in the cinema room was near thermal neutrality with a predicted mean vote of −0.3. This value predicts that only about 6.89% of the people frequenting the cinema would be dissatisfied regarding the thermal environment.

The simulations were able to provide a better insight into the ventilation system in the cinema, especially regarding localized details. In terms of the ventilation, there were few zones with stagnant air and the temperature was mostly uniform. Comparing with the measured data, there still was a difference of 2 °C from 22 °C measured, to 24 °C calculated.

However, since thermal comfort depends on other parameters, local PMV values were calculated. These fields allowed a better understanding of the predicted thermal sensation throughout the cinema and the verification that the people in the cinema alter the prediction values, thus this energy addition should be included when applying the PMV calculation. In this regard, the difference was of 0.6 from −0.3, local measured, to 0.3 when simulated. This difference changes the direction of comfort prediction towards a hot sensation. Still, both values are near thermal comfort and the Class A region. The CFD methodology also proved to be a valuable tool for the study and improvement of the comfort parameters since they can be easily changed, and the effect known. To better evaluate the simulation performed, further comparison points should be added, as well as a better study of the inlet and outlet conditions.

Acknowledgments. The authors would like to express their gratitude for the support given by FCT within the Project Scope UID/CEC/00319/2019 (ALGORITMI) and Project Scope UID/EMS/04077/2019 (METRICS).

References

1. Pantavou, K., Santamouris, M., Asimakopoulos, D., Theoharatos, G.: Evaluating the performance of bioclimatic indices on quantifying thermal sensation for pedestrians. Adv. Build. Energy Res. **7**, 170–185 (2013). https://doi.org/10.1080/17512549.2013.865557
2. Jacklitsch, B., Williams, W., Musolin, K., et al.: NIOSH criteria for a recommended standard: occupational exposure to heat and hot environments. US Department of Health & Human Services Publication 2016-106 (2016)
3. Yao, Y., Lian, Z., Liu, W., Shen, Q.: Experimental study on skin temperature and thermal comfort of the human body in a recumbent posture under uniform thermal environments. Indoor Built Environ. **16**, 505–518 (2007). https://doi.org/10.1177/1420326X07084291
4. ASHRAE Standard 55: Thermal Environmental Conditions for Human Occupancy (2004)
5. Parsons, K.C.: Human Thermal Environments: The Effects of Hot, Moderate, and Cold Environments on Human Health, Comfort, and Performance, 3rd edn. Taylor & Francis, London (2014)
6. Fanger, P.: Assessment of man's thermal comfort in practice. Br. J. Ind. Med. **1**, 313–324 (1973)
7. Rai, A.C., Lin, C.-H., Chen, Q.: Numerical modeling of particle generation from ozone reactions with human-worn clothing in indoor environments. Atmos. Environ. **102**, 145–155 (2015). https://doi.org/10.1016/J.ATMOSENV.2014.11.058
8. Richardson, G., Eick, S., Jones, R.: How is the indoor environment related to asthma?: literature review. J. Adv. Nurs. **52**, 328–339 (2005). https://doi.org/10.1111/j.1365-2648.2005.03591.x
9. Brager, G., Dedear, R.: Thermal adaptation in the built environment: a literature review. Energy Build. **27**, 83–96 (1998). https://doi.org/10.1016/S0378-7788(97)00053-4
10. Rodrigues, C.: Higiene e Segurança do Trabalho – Manual Técnico do Formando, 13th edn (2014)
11. Frontczak, M., Wargocki, P.: Literature survey on how different factors influence human comfort in indoor environments. Build. Environ. **46**, 922–937 (2011). https://doi.org/10.1016/J.BUILDENV.2010.10.021

12. ISO 7730: Ergonomics of the thermal environment – analytical determination and interpretation of thermal comfort using calculation of the PMV and PPD indices and local thermal comfort criteria (2005)
13. ICA: ICA - Instituto do Cinema e do Audiovisual (2016)
14. Aryal, P., Leephakpreeda, T.: CFD analysis on thermal comfort and energy consumption effected by partitions in air-conditioned building. Energy Procedia **79**, 183–188 (2015). https://doi.org/10.1016/J.EGYPRO.2015.11.459
15. Buratti, C., Palladino, D., Moretti, E.: Prediction Of indoor conditions and thermal comfort using CFD simulations: a case study based on experimental data. Energy Procedia **126**, 115–122 (2017). https://doi.org/10.1016/J.EGYPRO.2017.08.130
16. Aste, N., Della, Torre S., Adhikari, R.S., et al.: CFD comfort analysis of a sustainable solution for church heating. Energy Procedia **105**, 2797–2802 (2017). https://doi.org/10.1016/J.EGYPRO.2017.03.603
17. Shahzad, S., Calautit, J.K., Calautit, K., et al.: Advanced personal comfort system (APCS) for the workplace: a review and case study. Energy Build. **173**, 689–709 (2018). https://doi.org/10.1016/J.ENBUILD.2018.02.008
18. Alizadeh, M., Sadrameli, S.M.: Numerical modeling and optimization of thermal comfort in building: central composite design and CFD simulation. Energy Build. **164**, 187–202 (2018). https://doi.org/10.1016/J.ENBUILD.2018.01.006
19. Abdeen, A., Serageldin, A.A., Ibrahim, M.G.E., et al.: Solar chimney optimization for enhancing thermal comfort in Egypt: an experimental and numerical study. Sol. Energy **180**, 524–536 (2019). https://doi.org/10.1016/J.SOLENER.2019.01.063
20. Ahmed, A.F., Mina, E.M., AbdelMessih, R.N., Younan, G.W.: Studying comfort and energy usage for different room arrangements using a simplified flow pattern for highly-cooled and conventional operations. Ain Shams Eng. J. **10**, 83–91 (2019). https://doi.org/10.1016/J.ASEJ.2018.12.002
21. Charles, K.E.: Fanger's Thermal Comfort and Draught Models (2003)
22. Portaria n.º 353-A/2013: Regulamento de desempenho energético dos edifícios de comércio e serviços (recs) requisitos de ventilação e qualidade do ar interior (2013)
23. Liu, W., Lian, Z., Deng, Q.: Use of mean skin temperature in evaluation of individual thermal comfort for a person in a sleeping posture under steady thermal environment. Indoor Built Environ. **24**, 489–499 (2015). https://doi.org/10.1177/1420326X14527975
24. Zhai, Z.J., Zhang, Z., Zhang, W., Chen, Q.Y.: Evaluation of various turbulence models in predicting airflow and turbulence in enclosed environments by CFD: part 1—summary of prevalent turbulence models. HVAC&R Res. **13**, 853–870 (2007). https://doi.org/10.1080/10789669.2007.10391459
25. Rodrigues, N.J.O., Oliveira, R.F., Teixeira, S.F.C.F., et al.: Thermal comfort assessment of a surgical room through computational fluid dynamics using local PMV index. Work **51**, 445–456 (2015). https://doi.org/10.3233/WOR-141882

Simulation of PMV and PPD Thermal Comfort Using EnergyPlus

Diogo Esteves[1,2] (iD), João Silva[1,2] (iD), Nelson Rodrigues[1,2] (iD),
Luís Martins[2] (iD), José Teixeira[2] (iD), and Senhorinha Teixeira[1(✉)] (iD)

[1] ALGORITMI Center, University of Minho, Guimarães, Portugal
st@dps.uminho.pt
[2] Mechanical Engineering and Resource Sustainability Center (MEtRICs),
University of Minho, Guimarães, Portugal

Abstract. This work aims to simulate the thermal comfort for the user of a movie theater in the dimension related to considering the thermal environment parameters by the using EnergyPlus software. The results from simulation are then compared with the experimental ones. In order to calculate and model the thermal comfort, it was necessary a proper characterization of the space that included the measured occupancy, thermal environment variables, distinct electric equipment and lights. To compute the Predicted Mean Vote (PMV) and the Predictable Percentage of Dissatisfied (PPD) in EnergyPlus, the metabolic rate, air velocity and clothing insulation were defined according to the cinema specifications.

The results obtained from EnergyPlus were then compared with the experimentally measured ones. Minor differences were observed regarding the comfort sensation. Despite the differences, the variation in the percentage of dissatisfied people is smaller than 2%. Furthermore, this work also allowed verifying that the occupancy rate is a determining factor in the thermal comfort sensation and, in this case, people provided the necessary energy to heat the cinema room in the second session that occurred at night.

Keywords: Thermal comfort · Energy performance of buildings · Cinema · EnergyPlus

1 Introduction

The energy performance of a building and its relationship with the thermal environment plays a fundamental role in decision making from the point of view of the individual's comfort. It is a complex field that has been attracting the interest of many researchers [1]. The thermal environment represents a set of thermal variables that influence the heat exchanges between the individual and the environment in which it is inserted [2]. Yao et al. [3] mentioned that the thermal environment results from the complex interaction between the average radiant temperature, air temperature, air velocity and air humidity, referred to as environmental parameters.

People spend much of their time indoors, where many of these environments are air-conditioned and the equipment programming must be properly regulated, taking

© Springer Nature Switzerland AG 2019
S. Misra et al. (Eds.): ICCSA 2019, LNCS 11624, pp. 52–65, 2019.
https://doi.org/10.1007/978-3-030-24311-1_4

into account the health, comfort and productivity of its occupants [4, 5]. When the thermal environment is not the most appropriate, individuals tend to adapt their behavior and expectations in order to adapt to that environment. They usually have a lower tolerance for the inadequacy of the thermal environment in air-conditioned spaces compared with naturally ventilated ones [6]. The physical effects caused by uncomfortable environments induce agitation, which can reduce attention and concentration, and lead to fatigue and drowsiness. The individual needs to maintain its internal temperature within very narrow limits at a temperature of approximately 37 ° C, which necessitates a constant search for thermal equilibrium, called homeothermy. This equilibrium is ensured whenever the heat produced by the organism is equal to the heat flow to the environment so that the temperature remains constant [7], ensuring the optimal operation of the main functions of the particular organism, the central nervous system.

Thermal neutrality can be attributed to the state of thermal comfort [8], provided that there is no local thermal discomfort (ISO 7330:2005), as this can be felt as a whole or in part of the body, as a result of asymmetries of radiant temperature, vertical temperature, air velocity, soil temperature and others. ASHRAE (2004) [9] defines thermal comfort as the mental state that expresses a man's satisfaction with the thermal environment that surrounds him; and whereas the ISO 7730:2005 defines it as an expression of satisfaction with the environment that surrounds the individual. According to Parsons [10], the environmental variables combined with the indexes of metabolic rate and clothing (designated by individual parameters), form the basic elements that define thermal comfort. There are numerous thermal comfort evaluation indices, however, a method developed by Fanger is, indeed, the most used in designing guides and standards [11]. The method is based on the theory of thermo-regulation and thermal equilibrium in 2 indexes, which are: PMV - Predicted Mean Vote; PPD - Predicted Percentage of Dissatisfied People or predictable percentage of dissatisfied. The PMV index represents the predicted mean vote in a 7-point thermal sensation scale, ranging from −3 (Very cold) to +3 (Very hot). The value of 0 represents a neutral sensation towards the thermal environment and thus a comfortable sensation. The PPD index is a complementary index to the PMV, indicating the predicted percentage of dissatisfied people. For a value of 0 for the PMV, the PPD takes its lowest value of 5% dissatisfied people. When the PMV values deviate from 0 (comfort position) either positively or negatively, the PPD value increases indicating a higher percentage of dissatisfied people.

In order to provide a good cinema experience, it is essential to guarantee the thermal comfort of the users. As of 31 December 2016, there were 549 cinema screens in Portugal, 192 of them in Multiplex venues (8 or more cinemas), with a total of 103,583 seats, of which 35,758 seats in venues with eight or more cinemas. In the year 2016 650,011 cinema sessions were shown, for a total of 14,890,813 spectators [12]. The rooms had an average of 187 seats, with an average occupancy rate of approximately 12%. Considering the average duration of TOP 10 movies most seen in 2016, 117 min, the sum of hours that the spectators spent inside the Portuguese cinemas will be around 29,037,085 h.

The cinema experience requires an environment technically prepared for this purpose, capable of providing the user with a surrounding that the latter cannot replicate in other spaces. Watching a film in a movie theater results in the temporary occupation of an air-conditioned space for a certain period of time. A sensory experience, where the inadequacy of the thermal environment or another element such as; the sound, the lighting and others, can provoke interference and break the established tune between the spectator and the narrative.

In recent years, studying the optimum performance and understanding the energy consumption using numerical models has been an attractive option for researchers [13–20].

Yu et al. [13] developed a building energy consumption simulation through EnergyPlus. With this study, it was possible to understand and analyze the impact of the envelope heat consumption for different thermal performances and energy savings potentials.

Zhao et al. [14] optimized the energy consumption of a heating, ventilation and air conditioning system (HVAC) using an occupant-oriented mixed-mode EnergyPlus predictive control system, without forgetting the individual thermal comfort preference. With this work, it was possible to reduce the active HVAC energy consumption.

Pombeiro et al. [15] presented the formulation for three models that optimize the control of an HVAC system in an experimental room, which are coupled with two thermal models for the indoor temperature. Their results show that both the dynamic programming and genetic algorithms are capable of optimizing the usage of the HVAC.

Yun et al. [16] explored the role of occupants' perceived control in their subjective evaluation of thermal environments and its effects on cooling energy consumption in air-conditioned buildings. To do this, dynamic building energy simulations were conducted using EnergyPlus to examine the influence of perceived control on building energy consumption. With this study, it was possible to reduce the cooling energy consumption by 9% without sacrificing the thermal comfort of the occupants.

Cetin et al. [17] presented the development and validation of an on/off controller for residential applications in EnergyPlus using a custom EMS (energy management system). This on/off controller improves the HVAC energy use by around 19% in terms of the Normalized Mean Bias Error (NMBE) at the one-minute level compared to the results without the application of the on/off controller.

Ashrafian et al. [18] simulated two classrooms in order two understand the impact of different transparency ratios and window combinations in two critical orientations (west and east) on occupants' comfort and the energy demands of the classrooms. The referred authors concluded that reductions of 15-18% in electricity consumption can be obtained through appropriate design and the energy required for heating can be reduced by 8.5%.

Rincón et al. [19] examined an alternative low-cost earthen construction system using EnergyPlus. Results showed that the combination of night ventilation and roof solar protection in the high-inertia earthbag building leads to almost a total elimination of thermal discomfort during the year.

Escandón et al. [20] developed a surrogate model to speed up the thermal comfort prediction for any member of a building category, ensuring high reliability by testing the entire simulation process with real data measured in-situ. The model with high reliability reduced the computational times by 98% which is very useful to plan the energy retrofit of large housing stocks, by optimizing as quickly as possible.

The objective of this study is to calculate PMV and PPD using EnergyPlus simulation software and compare it with experimental results.

2   Methodology

2.1   Cinema Description

Room. The space under study is Room 2, presented in Fig. 1, of a cinema complex in Penafiel and began its activity in April 2014. The complex is composed by 3 cinema rooms with a total of 366 places. For the present study, the focus is in the largest room of this cinema complex, containing 170 seats; its capacity is the closest to the average capacity of 188 seats for the National Rooms.

The room does not have the means to allow the natural renovation of the air during the sessions of cinema, the air renovation is thus forced through the air conditioning equipment. The air supply is done through six points located on the ceiling of the room, and the extraction through holes under the chairs.

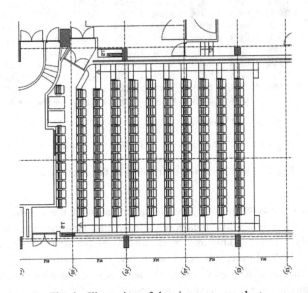

Fig. 1. Illustration of the cinema room plant.

HVAC System. The HVAC system is composed by an MCQUAY Model 75 19 equipment, which is installed next to the facade on the exterior of the building. This equipment does not have a system of air recirculation, thus all the air that enters the room is new air coming from the outside.

When the room occupancy surpasses, approximately, 25% of its capacity, the HVAC system is activated 10 to 15 min after the beginning of the session at a temperature of 22 °C. The equipment control unit is located outside the room, within the projection booth.

2.2 Field Measurements

Occupancy. In order to select the measurement points, the distribution of occupancy per seat was calculated based on the seats preference of the 6,041 tickets sold in the period between December 1, 2016, and January 31, 2017, for the study room. Due to material limitations, for this study only the following measurement points were chosen: B8, place with the highest occupancy rate (2.56%); K14, place with the lowest occupancy rate (0.08%) and G12, a place with the sample median (0.40%). Figure 2 represents the distribution of occupancy in the room floor plan.

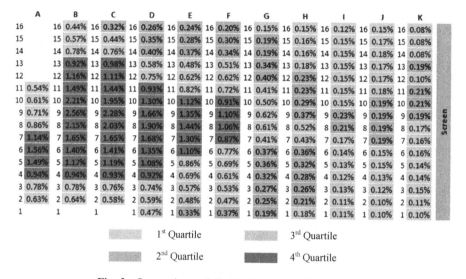

Fig. 2. Occupation and distribution in the cinema room.

Environmental Characterization. The characterization of the thermal environment of the studied space was done by means of experimental measurements in April 2017, in the previously selected points and in randomly chosen sessions. To measure the different variables in real time, it is necessary to use some instruments simultaneously, and its calibration has much relevance in the accuracy of the data obtained. For this study, the instruments were assigned by the Department of Production and Systems of the University of Minho, and there were no changes in their calibration.

For the experimental measurements, the following instruments were used:

- A globe thermometer, namely, a Casella model RS2842:1992, was used to measure the individual exposure to radiant heat. The device was placed at the chest level, on a tripod, to remain stable. A waiting period of about 30 min preceding the first measurement was necessary for stabilizing the device readings and assure data reliability. Results were collected every 15 min. The globe thermometer was also used to track down possible sources of radiant heat mentioned above;

- A TSI Velocicheck Model 8330 anemometer was used to measure air velocity. It was placed at chest level on a tripod so as to remain stable and not oscillated, waiting about 5 min before the first measurement was performed and results were collected every 15 min;
- Three USB Datalogger from Elcar, model EL-USB, to measure the temperature, relative humidity of the air and calculate the dew point. They were placed on a tripod at chest level and remained stable at that location during the measurement period. The equipment has been programmed in the "Easy Log" software to collect data every minute. Due to material limitations, it was not possible to place the instruments in more than one height level.

In the course of this study, it was important to record the temperature and relative humidity of the outdoor air at the time of the different measurements, since these two variables can affect the interior thermal environment and its perception [21]. For this purpose, the website of the Portuguese Institute of the Sea and Atmosphere was used since it registers the daily average temperature (°C) and relative humidity (%), as well as the minimum and maximum values for several climatological stations, measured at 1.5 m height. The data consulted were provided by the Climatological Station of Porto S. Gens and regarded the 19th of April 2017, when this study took place.

2.3   Simulation Study

The EnergyPlus is a powerful energy simulation software with a high potential for space analysis and improvement when compared with other software.

The types of energy analysis software like the EnergyPlus have wide application prospects. Many conclusions can be obtained through the simulation of the building energy consumption under different thermomechanical conditions.

The EnergyPlus is a simulation tool for modern buildings approved by the Portuguese Department of Energy. It is based on two tools developed during the 70s after the oil crisis: BLAST and DOE-2. The EnergyPlus is an Open Source code used worldwide. The software can model with excellent precision radiant and convection heat fluxes between indoor and outdoor, HVAC systems performance, heat exchanges with the ground, thermal comfort, natural, artificial and hybrid systems. Additionally, it can simulate ventilation, airflows and allows dynamic transient simulations with a time interval range between 1 h and 1 min, using an hourly representative year.

3D Model. The definition of the 3D model was based on the elements collected at the time of characterization of the space.

The geometry was modeled with Sketchupro2016 software associated with OpenStudio. The room was designed in two blocks. The first represents the upper part of the room where the occupation is made. The second block is the lower part of the room, through which the air is extracted and is an empty space (Fig. 3).

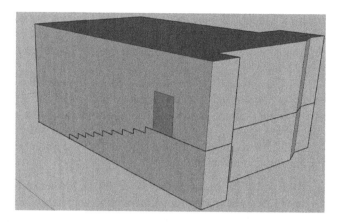

Fig. 3. Geometry of the movie theater.

The next step was the characterization of the surfaces of the model, according to exposure and location and boundary conditions. The South and East walls were considered as being exterior while the rest were defined as interior and considered as adiabatic surfaces. In Fig. 4 the exterior walls are in blue and the interior walls are in pink.

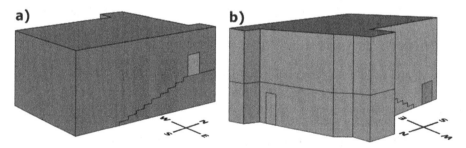

Fig. 4. Representation of the exterior walls at blue, (a) and the interior walls at pink (b). (Color figure online)

Although two different spaces were defined, they were assumed to belong to the same thermal zone in order to facilitate the simulation.

After the definition of the 3D model with the characteristics of the surfaces and the thermal zone, the model was extracted to the OpenStudio plugin that is connected to the EnergyPlus. It was decided to use OpenStudio because it has a friendlier and simpler interface than working directly with the EnergyPlus.

Climate Data. To obtain the values of PMV and PPD it is necessary to choose a climate file for the location where the cinema is located. The Climas-SCE1.05 software was used to obtain the reference Meteorological Year and the corresponding weather statistics. The software prepares the climate file for the format ".epw" (ESP-r/ EnergyPlus Weather format) (Fig. 5).

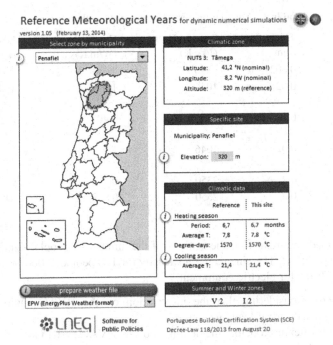

Fig. 5. Climas-SCE1.05 software.

Schedules. The schedules were defined for the whole year. The profiles of occupancy, air infiltration, activity level, ventilation and heating and cooling thermostat, lighting, electric equipment were thus constructed. First, daily profiles were built for weekdays, Saturday and Sunday. Then went on to build a weekly and monthly profile ending in the construction of the annual profile.

In the case of the activity level, taking into consideration that in the cinema people are in a sitting and resting state, the basal metabolic rate was assumed, namely, 105 W. Once that this situation does not vary, this value remained constant throughout the year.

In order to calculate the PMV and the PPD, work efficiency, air velocity and clothing schedules were also created. Taking into account the Air Changes per Hour required for the cinema occupation, a value of 0.25 m/s was assumed for air velocity. Regarding the clothing insulation, a value of 1 clo was chosen since it represented the standard clothing insulation for that time of the year. For the work efficiency, it was assumed a value of 0 since there was almost no mechanical activity and is safe to assume that almost all the metabolic energy was released as heat.

Materials and Constructions. In order to define the constructive elements, the constituent materials were defined in terms of roughness, thickness, conductivity, density and specific heat. Next, the layered constructions were created from the exterior surface to the interior surface and the ground contact surface. Table 1 presents the material properties considered in the EnergyPlus software.

Table 1. Material properties of the surface elements.

	Thickness (mm)	Specific Heat (J/kg.K)	Conductivity (W/m.K)	Density (kg/m³)
Exterior wall	0.002	890	230	2700
Interior wall (layer 1)	0.02	1046	1.3	1900
Interior wall (layer 2)	0.11	960	0.407	875.5
Interior wall (layer 3)	0.02	1046	1.3	1900
Exterior roof	0.2	2350	0.818	940
Ground	0.2	2350	0.818	940

Loads. The loads are related to the settings of the number of people, lighting power and electric equipment. The cinema has a capacity for 170 people, 2,000 W of lighting power and 2 W/m^2 for electric equipment.

HVAC System. Considering that the information on the HVAC equipment was scarce, a system with ideal loads was used.

This mode is often used before the definition of the HVAC system to be installed. It has been defined that the system is 100% available from the moment the room is opened until the end of the last session.

Cooling and Heating Thermostat Schedule. For the normal daily profiles, the maximum temperature was considered as 28 °C and whenever the room opens at about 15:00, the cooling is set to a temperature of 23 °C.

For the normal operating period, a minimum temperature of 18 °C has been set while the room is closed, which is changed to 21 °C when opening the room.

Output Variables. Finally, the outputs of interest were defined, namely, Zone Thermal Confort Fanger Model PMV, Zone Thermal Confort Fanger Model PPD and Zone Mean Air Temperature.

3   Results and Discussion

3.1   Experimental Results

Experimental measurements were performed at a measurement point inside the room at the B8 seat, starting at 15:00 and ending at 20:30 on April 19, 2017. During this period there were two sessions of cinema, the first one began at 15:30 and the ended at 18:00, with an occupancy rate of 76.4%. The second one started at 18:50 and ended at 21.00, with an occupancy rate of 34.7%.

Table 2 summarizes the results for the measured variables, identifying the maximum, minimum, mean values and standard deviations of the obtained values for the first session.

Table 2. Experimental measurements results.

	Max.	Min.	Avg.	Std.
Temperature (°C)	24.5	20.0	22.2	0.9
Dew point (°C)	15.5	8.9	14	1.2
Relative humidity (%)	65	37	59.9	4.2

For the calculation of PPD and PMV indexes, the average metabolic value of a 70 kg man with a skin surface of 1.8 m^2 was used as a reference, sitting in a comfortable environment with 1 met ($\approx$58.2 W/m^2), and 1 clo, which represents a typical indoor clothing combination during the winter. The values of the environmental parameters used to calculate the indexes were those recorded during the periods of the cinema sessions, with an interval of 15 min.

Table 3 summarizes the results for the calculated indexes, identifying the maximum, minimum and mean values.

Table 3. PMV and PPD values calculated using the experimental results.

	PMV	PPD (%)
Max.	0.05	19.0
Min.	−0.80	5.0
Avg.	−0.30	8.2

3.2 Numerical Results

In order to compare the experimental measurements with the EnergyPlus simulations, the latter were made with the same experimental conditions on April 19, 2017. Figure 6 shows the average indoor temperature in the movie theater on April 19. The first increment of temperature starts with first session. The initial observed behavior, with a rapid increase in the temperature from 19.8 °C to 22.2 °C, is related to the heat released by the cinema theater users, alongside with the HVAC system being in the heating mode for a while, as the initial temperature was below the setpoint of 21 °C. However, when the average temperature reaches 23 °C, it is possible to verify a stabilization trend of the temperature that corresponds to the cooling setpoint of the HVAC system. Afterwards, a decrease of temperature occurs when the first session ends. This behavior is expected since at this moment people leave the room and, therefore, that heat source is removed and the outside temperature was lower. Then, the temperature increase again due to the beginning of the second session. Meanwhile, the second increase is not as sudden since there is a lower occupation rate and the exterior temperature in this time, from 18:50 to 21:00, is lower, increasing the heat losses to the exterior, and the HVAC system is in neutral mode as the temperature is bellow the 23 °C.

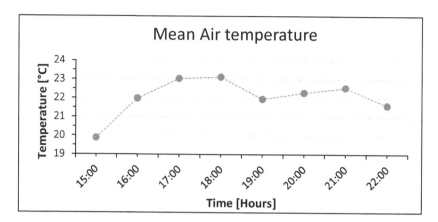

Fig. 6. Indoor air temperature.

Since the temperature is not the only determining factor of thermal comfort, it was necessary to compute the PMV and PPD indexes. The results are presented in Fig. 7.

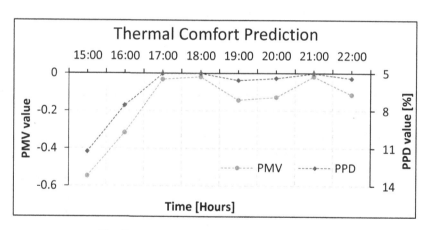

Fig. 7. PMV and PPV results from EnergyPlus.

In the present work, the remaining thermal variables (relative humidity and radiant temperature) do not change considerably and the comfort indexes follow the temperature pattern. While at the beginning, the thermal sensation trends to a cold sensation, due to initial HVAC heating mode condition and to the room occupancy, the PMV value quickly becomes close to zero, corresponding to a neutral/comfortable sensation.

Table 4 summarizes the results of the calculated comfort indexes, identifying the maximum, minimum, and mean values of the obtained indexes, alongside their differences with the experimental data. Through the comparison, it is possible to verify that the differences are small where the average PPD value does not surpass 2%.

These small differences may be related to the inherent error associated to the numerical methods, or even to the approximations considered in the problem definition. As for example, the thermal insulation values and the ventilation parameters measurements are susceptible to acquisition uncertainty and may even vary during the considered period, also, the HVAC system in the simulations was considered ideal with an initial heating mode and a rapid increasing temperature towards the setting point of 23 °C, which wouldn't probably occur with a normal HVAC system. Furthermore, EnergyPlus software calculates the thermal comfort indexes assuming the values in a middle point of the room while the experimental point (seat B8) had a different location, near the top back of the room.

Table 4. PMV and PPD values calculated within the EnergyPlus software and their respective difference with the experimental data.

	PMV		PPD (%)		Temp. (°C)	
	Calculated	Difference	Calculated	Difference	Calculated	Difference
Max.	−0.02	−0.07	11.3	−7.7	23.1	−1.4
Min.	−0.55	0.25	5.0	0.0	19.9	−0.1
Avg.	−0.16	0.14	6.3	−1.9	22.0	−0.2

4 Conclusions

The objective of calculating the PMV and PPD by using the EnergyPlus was successfully met. The second objective was to verify if these results were similar to those obtained experimentally and it is concluded that despite some differences, they are similar. In the simulations, the cinema room has a thermal comfort between the neutral and the slightly cold with a low percentage of people dissatisfied. This result is also verified in the experimental data, although the PMV value is slighting more negative, probably due to the initial cold conditions. Despite this difference, the variation in the percentage of dissatisfied people is smaller than 2%. Usually, in HVAC systems, the setpoint temperature for cooling conditions is 25 °C instead of the defined 23 °C which explains the obtained cold sensations. Furthermore, this work allowed confirm that the occupancy rate is a determining factor to obtain a thermal comfort sensation. During most of the time, people do not provide the necessary energy to heat the cinema room. However, in the second session, this heat was enough. Additionally, the HVAC system is also an important factor to stabilize the temperature. As an improvement measure, the simulation should be repeated without considering an ideal HVAC system and the results checked, and experimental measurements should be made again in other cinema sessions and times of the year.

Acknowledgments. The authors would like to express their gratitude for the support given by FCT within the Project Scope UID/CEC/00319/2019 (ALGORITMI) and Project Scope UID/EMS/04077/2019 (METRICS).

References

1. Pantavou, K., Santamouris, M., Asimakopoulos, D., Theoharatos, G.: Evaluating the performance of bioclimatic indices on quantifying thermal sensation for pedestrians. Adv. Build Energy Res. **7**, 170–185 (2013). https://doi.org/10.1080/17512549.2013.865557
2. Dias, A.: Avaliação da perceção da influência do conforto térmico na produtividade. University of Minho (2013)
3. Yao, Y., Lian, Z., Liu, W., Shen, Q.: Experimental Study on skin temperature and thermal comfort of the human body in a recumbent posture under uniform thermal environments. Indoor Built Environ. **16**, 505–518 (2007). https://doi.org/10.1177/1420326X07084291
4. Rai, A.C., Lin, C.-H., Chen, Q.: Numerical modeling of particle generation from ozone reactions with human-worn clothing in indoor environments. Atmos. Environ. **102**, 145–155 (2015). https://doi.org/10.1016/J.ATMOSENV.2014.11.058
5. Richardson, G., Eick, S., Jones, R.: How is the indoor environment related to asthma?: literature review. J. Adv. Nurs. **52**, 328–339 (2005). https://doi.org/10.1111/j.1365-2648.2005.03591.x
6. Brager, G.S., de Dear, R.J.: Thermal adaptation in the built environment: a literature review. Energy Build. **27**, 83–96 (1998). https://doi.org/10.1016/S0378-7788(97)00053-4
7. Rodrigues, C.: Higiene e Segurança do Trabalho – Manual Técnico do Formando, 13th edn (2014)
8. Frontczak, M., Wargocki, P.: Literature survey on how different factors influence human comfort in indoor environments. Build. Environ. **46**, 922–937 (2011). https://doi.org/10.1016/J.BUILDENV.2010.10.021
9. ASHRAE Standard 55-2004: Thermal environmental conditions for human occupancy. Ashrae Stand (2004)
10. Parsons, K.: Human Thermal Environments: The Effects of Hot, Moderate, and Cold Environments on Human Health, Comfort, and Performance, 2nd edn. Taylor & Francis, Abingdon (2003)
11. Fanger, P.: Assessment of man's thermal comfort in practice. Br. J. Ind. Med. **1**, 313–324 (1973)
12. ICA: ICA - Instituto do Cinema e do Audiovisual (2016)
13. Yu, S., Cui, Y., Xu, X., Feng, G.: Impact of civil envelope on energy consumption based on EnergyPlus. Procedia Eng. **121**, 1528–1534 (2015). https://doi.org/10.1016/J.PROENG.2015.09.130
14. Zhao, J., Lam, K.P., Ydstie, B.E., Loftness, V.: Occupant-oriented mixed-mode EnergyPlus predictive control simulation. Energy Build. **117**, 362–371 (2016). https://doi.org/10.1016/J.ENBUILD.2015.09.027
15. Pombeiro, H., Machado, M.J., Silva, C.: Dynamic programming and genetic algorithms to control an HVAC system: maximizing thermal comfort and minimizing cost with PV production and storage. Sustain. Cities Soc. **34**, 228–238 (2017). https://doi.org/10.1016/J.SCS.2017.05.021
16. Yun, G.Y.: Influences of perceived control on thermal comfort and energy use in buildings. Energy Build. **158**, 822–830 (2018). https://doi.org/10.1016/J.ENBUILD.2017.10.044
17. Cetin, K.S., Fathollahzadeh, M.H., Kunwar, N., et al.: Development and validation of an HVAC on/off controller in EnergyPlus for energy simulation of residential and small commercial buildings. Energy Build. **183**, 467–483 (2019). https://doi.org/10.1016/J.ENBUILD.2018.11.005

18. Ashrafian, T., Moazzen, N.: The impact of glazing ratio and window configuration on occupants' comfort and energy demand: the case study of a school building in Eskisehir, Turkey. Sustain. Cities Soc **47**, 101483 (2019). https://doi.org/10.1016/J.SCS.2019.101483
19. Rincón, L., Carrobé, A., Martorell, I., Medrano, M.: Improving thermal comfort of earthen dwellings in sub-Saharan Africa with passive design. J. Build. Eng. **24**, 100732 (2019). https://doi.org/10.1016/J.JOBE.2019.100732
20. Escandón, R., Ascione, F., Bianco, N., et al.: Thermal comfort prediction in a building category: artificial neural network generation from calibrated models for a social housing stock in southern Europe. Appl. Therm. Eng. **150**, 492–505 (2019). https://doi.org/10.1016/J.APPLTHERMALENG.2019.01.013
21. Charles, K.E.: Fanger's Thermal Comfort and Draught Models (2003)

Smart Factory Convergence (SFC 2019)

Under Sampling Adaboosting Shapelet Transformation for Time Series Feature Extraction

Yohan Joo and Jongpil Jeong[✉]

Department of Smart Factory Convergence, Sungkyunkwan University,
Suwon, Gyeonggi-do 16419, Republic of Korea
{yahoo4903,jpjeong}@skku.edu

Abstract. To predict for machine defects, a classifier is required to classify the time series data collected from the sensors into the fault state and the normal state. In many cases, the data collected by sensors is time series data collected at various frequencies. Excessive computer load is required to handle this as it is. Therefore, there has been a lot of research being done on the process of extracting features that are highly classified from time series data. In particular, data generated at real-world is unbalanced and noisy, requiring time series classifiers to minimize their impact. Shapelet transformation is generally effectively known for classifying time series data. This paper proposes a process of feature extraction that is strong for noise and over-fitting to be applicable in practice. We can extract the feature from the time series data through the proposed algorithm and expect it to be used in various fields such as smart factory.

Keywords: Shapelet · Adaboosting · Under Sampling ·
Time series classification

1 Introduction

There has been a variety of studies on the use of sensors and big data analysis for the purpose of preserving the prediction of machine defects. Studies have been conducted to effectively classify time series datasets sampled at certain frequencies in normal and fault conditions on sensors in order to maintain the machine's preventive. Specially, a variety of methods have been proposed to extract features that best represent the characteristics of a time series in order to effectively handle a variety of sampling data. The simplest method, most commonly used to extract characteristics from time series data, is a statistical technique that extracts means, standard deviations, curvature, etc. from time series data. In the framework proposed by Helwig et al. [1], high dimensional time series data of 100 Hz were simplified by calculating means, variances, and curvature. Zhu et al. [2] also introduced the Shapelet transform based classification framework to determine short term voltage stability, which is a highly categorised transformation technique that uses information acquisition to record high titled decision boundaries.

© Springer Nature Switzerland AG 2019
S. Misra et al. (Eds.): ICCSA 2019, LNCS 11624, pp. 69–80, 2019.
https://doi.org/10.1007/978-3-030-24311-1_5

Shapelet transformation is a technique that converts data into distance data so that it can generate decision boundaries that are highly classified based on information gain. It has a high classification performance through the process of extracting partial time series that can best represent it from a single time series. Recently, a method was proposed for converting multivariate time series data into distance data by applying a shapelet separately to each set.

This paper proposes an effective feature approach to binary classification of time series datasets. The proposed feature extraction technique is an ensemble combining Random Under Sampling and Adaboosting techniques. The results of each classification shall be evaluated so that the results are reflected in the next sampling. Finally, adaptive learning is repeated and converted into distance data that can produce high classification results. The transformed distance data is classified through the classification phase and can be recorded for high classification results.

This paper is organized as follows. In Sect. 1, the necessity of the algorithm proposed in this paper is explained in connection with the industrial field. Section 2 explains the methodology of the proposed algorithm, and Sect. 3 explains the structure of the proposed algorithm. Section 4 experiments the performance evaluation of the proposed algorithm. Finally, conclusion and future works are presented in Sect. 5.

2   Related Work

2.1   Time Series Shapelet Classification

Shapelet means the part sequence that best represents this for the Time series data [3]. The Time Series Shapelet Classification method extracts a partial sequence from a time series, obtains the Euclidean distance from sub sequence and the existing time series data and converts the time series data into distance data. It is then a method of classifying the data by finding a sub sequence that provides a clear decision boundary with high information gain for converted distance data. Instead of requiring complex computations and therefore having to spend a lot of time on them, it is a way of recording high classification performance. For a more detailed description of the Shapelet, see [4] of Ye et al. and [5] of Zhu et al. Figure 1 shows the method of Shapelet Transformation.

2.2   Sampling Method

Under sampling technique is a technique that samples only part of a sample used from data. In contrast, the technique of synthesize new data or creating samples that are larger than traditional datasets by randomly add traditional data is called over sampling technology. These techniques are an effective way to reduce the impact of noisy data and overfitting or underfitting in the data. Randomly reducing or duplicating data on existing datasets is called random sampling. It is known that this is simple but can be more effective in many

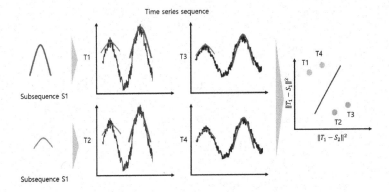

Fig. 1. Shapelet transformation

cases compared to other complex algorithms [14]. However, overfitting can occur if the same data are duplicated or under-fitting can occur if critical data are removed. A representative method of oversampling proposed to address this is the SMOTE (Synthetic Minority Oversampling Technique) algorithm proposed by Chawla et al. [6]. SMOTE algorithms have reduced the risk of overfitting by synthesizing existing data and are commonly used in many studies. Han et al. [7] proposed Borderline-SMOTE, which clarifies the classification boundary by applying the SMOTE algorithm only to the decision boundary portion of the class. Under sampling techniques are representative of NCL (Neighborhood Cleaning Rule) algorithms that remove data based on ENN (Edited Nearest Neighbor) algorithms [9]. Figure 2 show the under sampling which is the representative sampling method.

2.3   Ensemble Method

Ensemble in classification method means the way for reducing the risk of noise and overfitting and recording high classification performance by several iterative processes. A simple form of ensemble technique is the Bagging algorithm. The Bagging algorithm is a method of generating multiple samples of boot straps, and then applying the weak classifier to each sample to aggregate the results obtained to produce the final classification results according to the principle of majority decision. As with bagging, the Boosting algorithm generates multiple bootstrap samples and applies weak classifier to each one. And then, it evaluates the performance of each classification's results to provide further feedback to next sampling so that better results can be obtained. The Boosting method representatively includes the adaboost algorithm [11], SMOTEBoosting [12], and the Random Forest algorithm [13]. Figure 3 show the random forest algorithm which is the representative ensemble method.

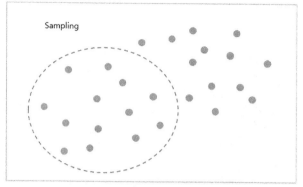

Fig. 2. Example of sampling method: under sampling

3   Under Sampling Adaboosting Feature Extraction

3.1   Overall Process

This paper proposes a feature extraction method that minimizes the risk of noisy data and overfitting. The process is expressed:

1. Initialize the sample's weights.
2. Based on the weight of the sample, sample it through under sampling.
3. After applying the shapelet classification to the generated data set, evaluate the performance and apply the shapelet transformation. Multiply the weight of the model by the weight of the corresponding distance data according to performance.
4. The sample weights are adjusted so that data with poor performance can be reflected in the next sampling by adding the weight of the sample.
5. After repeating the steps from 2 to 4 add all the distance data that was finally obtained and normalize it.

3.2   Feature Extraction

The feature extraction technique proposed in this paper is based on the adaboost algorithm and combined with the Shapelet Transformation. The adaboost algorithm is one of the ensemble techniques, which increases accuracy by repeatedly learning samples that are misclassified by allowing classification results to be reflected in the next sampling process. For under sampled dataset, apply the shapelet classification and shapelet transformation respectively, and evaluate the classification results to set the weights for the model and each sample. The weight of the sample is reflected in the next sampling process, and repeated learning gradually produces a highly accurate classifier. Finally, aggregate the

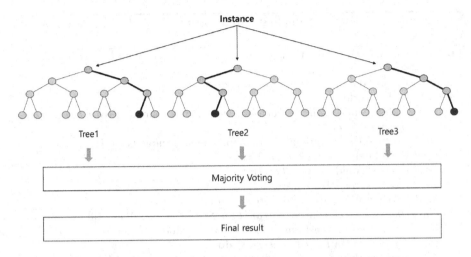

Fig. 3. Example of ensemble method: random forest

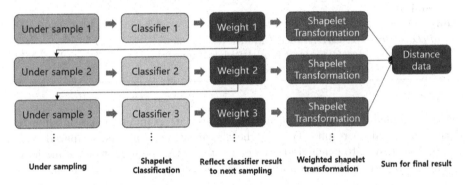

Fig. 4. Overall schematic of under sampling AdaBoosting algorithm

distances converted data according to the majority decision principle reflecting the weight of the model. The algorithm and its schematic are shown in Fig. 4.

The structure of the algorithm can be found in the following Algorithm 1:

The algorithm first receives training data, training data labels, test data, and parameter values as input. The parameter n means the number of repetitions of the ensemble, and l means the length of the shapelet. In this algorithm, training is performed on train data, and the transformation results is output to the test data. As a result, this experimental algorithm can compare the characteristics of the output test data with the actual *testLabel*.

The start of the algorithm begins by operating the for statement for the number of number of input parameter n. It execute the following command for each number of times of the for statement. First, under sampling is performed by inputting *trainTimeSeries* data and *trainLabel* to the random under sampling function. Second, we design the shapelet classification classifier by learn-

Algorithm 1 . Under Sampling Adaboosting Shapelet Transformation Algorithm

---

Input: Single time series training data $trainTimeseries$, $trainLabel$, $testTimeseries$, $parameter\{n, l\}$
Output: Distance data $trainDistance$, $testDistance$
    for all $i \leftarrow 1$ to n **do**
        under_sample, under_sample_label $\leftarrow$ RandomUnderSampling($trainTimeseries$, $trainLabel$, sample_weight)
        clf $\leftarrow$ ShapeletClassification(under_sample, under_sample_label, l)
        valid $\leftarrow$ clf.prediction($trainTimeSeries$)
        error $\leftarrow$ count(valid != $trainLabel$)
        error_rate $\leftarrow$ error / len($trainLabel$)
        Model_Weight[i] = log((1-error_rate) / error_rate)
        $trainDistance \leftarrow$ clf.transform($trainTimeSeries$)*Model_Weight[i]
        $testDistance \leftarrow$ clf.transform($testTimeSeries$)*Model_Weight[i]
        for all $j \leftarrow 1$ to len($trainTimeseries$) **do**
            sample_weight[j] *= exp((-1)*Model_weight[i]*$trainLabel$[j]*clf[j])
            sample_weight[j] = sample_weight[j] / Z (Z : normalization factor)
        end for
    end for
    $trainDistance \leftarrow trainDistance$ / Model_Weight.sum()
    $testDistance \leftarrow testDistance$ / Model_Weight.sum()
    return $trainDistance$, $testDistance$

---

ing the sampled data. Third, $trainTimeSeries$ data is input to the classifier to derive classification results. Fourth, the classification results is compared with the correct answer to calculated the error rate. Fifth, the weight of the model is calculated based on the error rate. The model weight are calculated as follows:

$$Model\_Weight = \frac{1}{2} \ln \frac{1 - \epsilon_m}{\epsilon_m}$$

The ϵ means error rate. Sixth, the feature of the sample is extracted by multiplying the result of $trainDistance$ and model shapelet transformation based on the weight of the model and the model learned by the corresponding sample. In the seventh, the weight of the sample to be reflected in the next sampling is calculated. The equation for the sample weights follows:

$$sample\_weight = \frac{sample\_weight * exp((-1) * MW * trainLabel * clf)}{Z}$$

where MW is Model_Weight and Z is normalization factor. The weights of the calculated samples are reflected in the random under sampling process during the ensemble process, and the learning is repeated. It is possible to continuously repeat the learning of samples whose classification performance is lacking due to lack of learning thereby enabling more complicated and precise learning. As a result, the final feature is returned by synthesizing repeated features.

This process is based on the principle of the adaboost algorithm. The adaboost algorithm evaluates the samples that were learned before in the ensemble process and reflects them in the next sampling process. Through this, it is possible to perform repeated learning for samples whose classification performance is poor due to lack of learning. Therefore, as the number of iterations increases, it is possible to design a precise classifier by repeating learning on data with a low learning rate. The finally designed classifier capable of recording high classification performance through repeated learning. Figure 5 show how adaboosting method can create effective classifier.

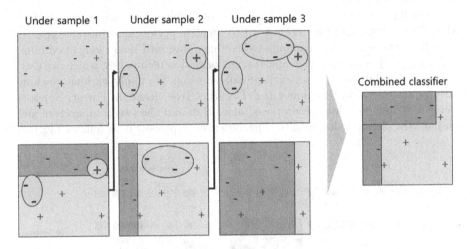

Fig. 5. Working process of adaboosting algorithm

In summary, this algorithm performs a shapelet classification on a partial sample made by Random Under Sampling. The performance of the classified results is then assessed to obtain the weight of the model according to its performance. Depending on the weight, time series data is converted to distance data through shapelet transformation. Depending on the results of the classification, the weight of the sample is reset and the weight is reflected in the next sample. This process is repeated n times so that the results are combined to return the final distance data.

Such under sampling and adaboosting techniques are known to have the effect of minimizing the influence of noise and overfitting according to the prior research [11]. In addition, it has been used in various studies because it can design strong classifiers through repeated learning and has excellent classification performance. Shapelet Transformation technique is also known to record excellent performance in classification of time series data. The algorithm proposed in this paper proposes feature extraction technique of time series data by combining algorithms that have been verified with excellent performance according to these previous studies. Therefore, it is expected that the performance of the proposed algorithm will be improved to better performance than the existing methods.

4   Experimental Design and Implementation

In this paper, we focus the experimental design of our proposed algorithm rather than performance evaluation. To do this, we construct an experiment to test the performance of the proposed algorithm. The purpose of this experiment is to test whether the performance of this algorithm is superior to that of other algorithms for real time series data.

We design an experiment to verify the performance of the proposed algorithm. First, control groups are set up to identify performance advantages. As controls group, statistical techniques (average, standard deviation, maximum, minimum, etc.) and common shapelet transformation techniques, which are used in time series data feature extraction can be used. We apply various machine learning classification techniques (ex. Decision Tree, Random Forest, Support Vector Machine etc.) for the proposed algorithm and the two comparators and compare the classification results. The experiment process is as follows Fig. 6.

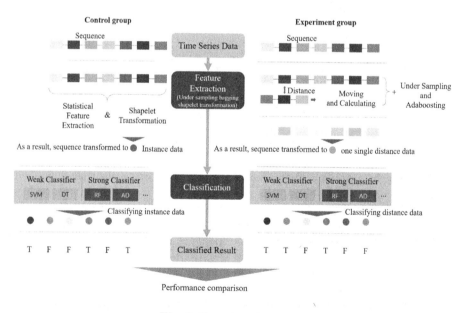

Fig. 6. Experiment process

4.1   Experiment Environment

We can use various time series data from open source to test our experiment. In this paper, we design an experiment using hydraulic system data including various time series data among several open source data. In this data, various time series data collected from various kinds of sensors are included and classification experiments can be performed. By using this, time series data collected at various sampling rates can be used. Among them, 5 kinds of data (temperature, vibration, cooling power, etc.) are collected at 1 Hz. All data are labeled with stability 0 or 1, 0 means steady state, and 1 means non-steady state. The PC to be used for the experiment will be i7-8700K, and 16 GB of DDR4 RAM.

In general, evaluation results are confirmed by applying various evaluation indexes used in evaluation of classification algorithms. In the data classification problem, it is better to avoid using the accuracy because the imbalance between the data can cause the bias. In the designed experiments, performance is evaluated using G-mean and F-measure rather than accuracy. Here, the normal data labeled as "0" is referred to as "Negative", and the defect data labeled as "1" is referred to as "Positive". True Positive(TP) and True Negative(TN) are defined as when normal data is classified as normal and when the defect data are classified as defective. On the other hand, False Positive (FP) and False Negative (FN) are referred to when the defect data is classified as normal and when the normal data is classified as the defect, respectively. At this time, TP rate (TPR, Precision) and TN rate (TNR, Recall) can be calculated as follows.

$$TPR = TP/(TP + FN)$$

$$TNR = TP/(TP + FP)$$

G-mean is the geometric mean of TPR and TNR. Generally, it has a range of $[0, 1]$, and the higher the score, the higher the performance. F-measure means the harmonic mean of precision and recall. Likewise, the higher the score, the higher the performance Through TPR and TNR, G-mean and F-measure are defined as follows:

$$G\text{-}mean = \sqrt{TPR \times TNR}$$

$$F\text{-}measure = 2 \times \frac{Recall \times Precision}{Recall + Precision}$$

4.2   Configuration for Training and Test Data Set

We should distinguish five 1 Hz data from the hydraulic system mentioned above. 70% of the total data is classified as train, and 30% as test. At this time, cross-validation is performed to test the performance of the learning model. In general, there is a risk of overfitting in the case of classification and prediction models through machine learning techniques. While overfitting can result in high performance for a particular dataset, there is a risk that performance may drop dramatically if the test data changes. In order to prevent such a risk, we perform multiple cross validation by dividing the train data and the test data in the dataset. It is considered that the problem caused by overfitting is minimized when the same good performance is recorded in repeated cross validation. In this experiment, five(train, test) sets configurations are proposed by dividing each division criterion. This allows us to configure a set of data to apply multiple cross validation test. Figure 7 shows the data partitioning technique for cross validation.

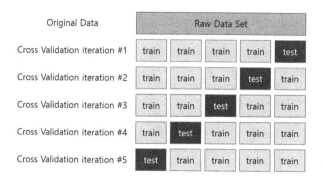

Fig. 7. Cross validation

4.3 Feature Extraction

The main contribution of this paper is the proposal of a new feature extraction algorithm. To verify the performance of the proposed algorithm, a control group and an experimental group are selected. As experimental group, the feature extracted through the algorithm described in this paper is specified. For the control group, feature extracted from 'statistical feature extraction' and 'shapelet transformation' are selected.

In this experiment, two techniques are used as a control group. The first is statistical feature extraction technique which is generally used in industrial field. The statistical feature extraction technique refers to a technique in which mean, standard deviation, and kurtosis are extracted as a feature of sampled signals. It is t he most commonly used technique because it is sample, computationally simple, and does not require high computing resources. As another control group, the shapelet transformation, which is the idea based on this paper, is selected. By comparing the performance with the shapelet transformation, we experiment to see how the proposed algorithm improves performance. Figure 8 shows the feature extraction technique of the control group and the feature extraction technique of the experimental group.

Fig. 8. Comparison of feature extraction methods

4.4 Classification

After applying various classification algorithms to the extracted results, the results are evaluated. This process is repeatedly applied to various classification algorithms, and it is confirmed whether the proposed algorithm has effective superiority. Classification algorithm can confirm performance by applying both weak classifier and strong classifier. We can use SVM (Supporter Vector Machine, RBF-SVM, Linear SVM), and DT (Decision Tree) which are commonly used in simple classification problem. The strong classifier is a classifier with a more sophisticated classification algorithm than the weak classifier. Typically, algorithms such as a random forest, adaboosting, and gradient boosting can be used, Each of the algorithms is evaluated as results of recording the optimum performance through parameter optimization. The classification results are evaluated according to the evaluation criteria described above, and it is judged whether the performance of the proposed algorithm is superior to the feature extraction technique selected as the control group.

This algorithm is thought to be able to prove its performance through experiments in *Python* environment. With the *tslearn* library provided by Python, we can implement the shapelet and the proposed algorithm, Under Sampling Adaboosting Shapelet Transformation. The various machine learning algorithms used for classification can also be used with the *sklearn* library.

5 Conclusion

Data from sensors such as mechanical equipment are far from ideal shapes. Factory data sets are basically very unbalanced because they are not prone to defects in a refined environment. Also, because of the variety of noise environments, the data includes a lot of noise. Therefore, using these acquired data requires time series processing techniques that are resistant to over-fitting and noise in the process. This paper proposes a feature extraction technique that has been developed by adding ensembles and sampling methods to a shapelet transformation that can produce a high classification effect for time series data. For the proposed Under Sampling Adaboosting Shapelet transformation, repeated ensemble techniques are expected to be added to the normal shapelet to produce more effective results for noise and overfitting. However, the adaboost technique has the disadvantage of spending a lot of time on the operation because parallel processing is not supported compared to the one that requires a lot of computations. In the following studies, to address this problem, a dataset is divided and algorithms are redesigned to allow partial parallelism.

Acknowledgments. This research was supported by the MSIT (Ministry of Science and ICT), Korea, under the ITRC (Information Technology Research Center) support program (IITP-2019-2018-0-01417) supervised by the IITP (Institute for Information & communications Technology Promotion). This work has supported by the Gyeonggi Techno Park grant funded by the Gyeonggi-Do government (No. Y181802).

References

1. Helwig, N., Pignanelli, E., Schutze, A.: Condition monitoring of a complex hydraulic system using multivariate statistics. In: Proceedings of IEEE Instrumentation and Measurement Technology Conference (I2MTC), pp. 210–215, July 2015
2. Zhu, L., Lu, C., Dong, Z.Y., Hong, C.: Imbalance learning machine based power system short term voltage stability assessment. IEEE Trans. Ind. Inform. **13**, 2533–2543 (2017)
3. Ye, L., Keogh, E.: Time series shapelets: a new primitive for data mining. In: Proceedings of 15th ACM SIGKDD International Conference on Knowledge Discovery Data Mining, pp. 947–955, June 2009
4. Lines, J., Davis, L.M., Hills, J., et al.: A shapelet transform for time series classification. In: Proceedings of 18th ACM SIGKDD International Conference on Knowledge Discovery Data Mining, pp. 289–297, August 2012
5. Zhu, L., Lu, C., Sun, Y.: Time series shapelet classification based online short term voltage stability assessment. IEEE Trans. Power Syst. **31**(2), 1430–1439 (2016)
6. Chawla, N.V., Bowyer, K.W., Hall, L.O., Kegelmeyer, W.P.: SMOTE: synthetic minority over sampling technique. J. Artif. Intell. Res. **16**, 321–357 (2002)
7. Han, H., Wang, W.-Y., Mao, B.-H.: Borderline-SMOTE: a new over-sampling method in imbalanced data sets learning. In: Huang, D.-S., Zhang, X.-P., Huang, G.-B. (eds.) ICIC 2005. LNCS, vol. 3644, pp. 878–887. Springer, Heidelberg (2005). https://doi.org/10.1007/11538059_91
8. He, H., Yai, B., Garcia, E., Li, S.: ADASYN: adaptive synthetic sampling approach for imbalanced learning. In: Proceedings of IEEE International Joint Conference on Neural Networks, pp. 1322–1328, June 2008
9. Laurikkala, J.: Improving identification of difficult small classes by balancing class distribution. In: Quaglini, S., Barahona, P., Andreassen, S. (eds.) AIME 2001. LNCS (LNAI), vol. 2101, pp. 63–66. Springer, Heidelberg (2001). https://doi.org/10.1007/3-540-48229-6_9
10. Breiman, L.: Bagging predictors. Mach. Learn. **24**(2), 123–140 (1996)
11. Freund, Y., Schapire, R.E.: A decision theoretic generalization of online learning and an application to boosting. J. Comput. Syst. Sci. **55**(1), 119–139 (1997)
12. Chawla, N.V., Lazarevic, A., Hall, L.O., Bowyer, K.W.: SMOTEBoost: improving prediction of the minority class in boosting. In: Lavrač, N., Gamberger, D., Todorovski, L., Blockeel, H. (eds.) PKDD 2003. LNCS (LNAI), vol. 2838, pp. 107–119. Springer, Heidelberg (2003). https://doi.org/10.1007/978-3-540-39804-2_12
13. Breiman, L.: Random forest. Mach. Learn. **45**(1), 5–32 (2001)
14. Lee, T., Lee, K., Kim, C.: Performance of machine learning algorithms for classimbalanced process fault detection problems. IEEE Trans. Seminocuctor Manuf. **29**(4), 436–445 (2016)

Knowledge-Based Multi-agent System for Smart Factory of Small-Sized Manufacturing Enterprises in Korea

Byungjun Park and Jongpil Jeong[✉]

Department of smart Factory convergence, Sungkyunkwan University,
Suwon, Gyeonggi-do 16419, Republic of Korea
{bjunpark,jpjeong}@skku.edu

Abstract. This paper focuses on the development of practical application prototype of information and communication model that can be applied in the field in order to solve the problems of SME manufacturing and manufacturing companies in each manufacturing industry. We are trying to establish a process to implement a smart factory by adding a specialist network through problem-solving data management based on the cases of bad people in the manufacturing process including field workers. It also has the implication of supporting field work by providing Manufacturing Problem Solving (MPS) processes to shop floor workers.

Keywords: SME manufacturing ·
MPS (Manufacturing Problem Solving) process ·
KBM (Knowledge-based multi-agent system)

1 Introduction

Large companies can build large-scale smart factories from scratch, but for small and medium-sized enterprises, it is common to expect high cost-effectiveness in addition to existing manufacturing facilities at low cost and in a short period of time. Toyota's production system is a major methodology that enables large corporations to continue to grow. It is a production philosophy that aims for a bigger target condition through continuous improvement [1,2]. Whether it is building a large-scale smart factory or adding it to, existing facilities, the basics of the way in which the project is implemented are the same. It has a purpose, a budget, and a deadline. It sets the scope of execution within it, and makes it clear that the system and the schedule are clear [3].

Fault diagnosis of the manufacturing system is a problem that causes continuous difficulty for the operator at the manufacturing site [4]. IoT technology and manufacturing facilities require investment in developing advanced sensors, connecting software platforms and building equipment. This technological improvement possibility and the method of establishing linking with the existing information database in the manufacturing industry field are meaningful studies in that it is possible to execute efficiently in the investment sector.

© Springer Nature Switzerland AG 2019
S. Misra et al. (Eds.): ICCSA 2019, LNCS 11624, pp. 81–93, 2019.
https://doi.org/10.1007/978-3-030-24311-1_6

This paper is organized as follows. In Sect. 2, it is composed the 16 fields of industry related to this work, the area of process automation, and smart factories in Korea are classified as basic level, intermediate level, and advanced level. Provides literature review of key topics in manufacturing issues, knowledge representation, PLM (Product lifecycle management) and CBR (Case-Based Reasoning). Section 3 discusses the generated model, which is the basis of the conceptual approach adopted to define the data structures needed to manage manufacturing problem knowledge. Section 4 describes the prototype application developed. This paper concludes with conclusions and future studies.

2   Related Work

The establishment of smart factories in Korean SMEs is more appropriate than the system approach, unlike large corporations, where the factory level diagnosis and the smart factory uptake approach are appropriate. Therefore, in this paper, we will diagnose the smart factory basic level, intermediate level and advanced level according to the field level diagnosis, and propose a plan to build the smart factory at the target level.

2.1   CBR Based Kepner-Tregoe Problem Solving Method

In general, about 6 problem solving methods are used for problem solving method such as defect in manufacturing site [5]. Their common feature is the definition of the problem and the process of problem solving through root cause and various cause analysis [6]. Among them, DMAIC (Define - Measure - Analyze - Improve - Control) method and Shainin method (Define the Project - Establishment effective Measuring System - Generate Clues - List suspect Variables - Statistically designed Experiments - Interaction realistic Tolerances - Irreversible Corrective Decision Analysis - Statistical Process Control-Monitoring Results-Leverage lessons learned) will have similarities in defining the problem or project to be solved in the process and determining and starting the process at the earliest [7–9]. A failure is when part of the manufacturing system does not meet the outage specifications. As a result, production may be discontinued and production goals may not be reached. The gap between the result state and the intended state is defined as the problem. If you see a production problem, you need a detailed process of analyzing the problem and creating a solution [10]. In this paper, Kepner-Tregoe problem solving method and Eight Disciplines (8D) are applied to solving manufacturing problems in order to solve bad problems and to build a smart factory. Kepner–Tregoe problem solving method is composed 4 steps [11]. First is situation analysis. Second is problem Analysis. Third is decision analysis. And the last is potential problem and potential opportunity analysis. Figure 1 represents the definition of manufacturing problem solving definition.

These methods are based on Continuous Improvement Process (CIP) and Manufacturing Problem Solving (MPS) [12]. Obviously, 8D is a problem-solving

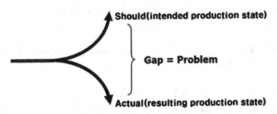

Fig. 1. Kepner-Tregoe MPS (Manufacturing Problem Solving) definition

method that focuses more on solving production problems [13]. In order to support suppliers in the troubleshooting activities developed by Ford Motor in the early 1990s, 8D consists of eight main steps: (1) team definition, (2) problem description, (3) containment actions (4) root cause analysis, (5) definition of potential corrective action and validation, (6) introduction of corrective action, (7) definition of lesson, (8) team celebration. Sharing team members' knowledge and experience is a key element in implementing all troubleshooting methods [14]. These methods provide a structured process that facilitates improvement and discovery of the solution. Nonetheless, training is generally provided to team members, but these methods are only successful when driven by experienced and knowledgeable workers (e.g., provided by software tools). The literature shows that industrial applications of PFMEA (Potential Failure Mode and Effects Analysis) are complex, time consuming and ineffective [15–17]. Also, results are low and results are not corrected in regular improvement activities, and there is a problem maintaining effective feedback. Some of the problems with PFMEA relate to the fact that they are based on a spreadsheet approach that makes reusing results and identifying similarities difficult.

2.2 Knowledge Management System

What is important in smart factory is the accumulation of all manufacturing data and the databaseization of their relevance [18]. Here, we can present a standard model for the establishment of an up-level smart factory through process automation and IoT work in accordance with the problems presented by field workers in order to build a smart factory in Korea. Here we propose a knowledge management (KM) approach [19–21].: • Promoting reuse of PFMEA analysis results • Facilitates the collection and reuse of data and knowledge of the manufacturing level at the factory level or manufacturing process during daily MPS activities related to improving over-all equipment efficiency (OEE). Focuses on product and process quality issues (i.e., quality claims and scrap), unusual production speeds and failures among the various topics considered by OEE • Provide problem solving software tools based on 8D methods to actors in the workplace. This tool can also be used by users with very low knowledge of the manufacturing system in which they are working. • Supports manufacturing knowledge sharing and integration across multiple manufacturing factories.

2.3   Smart Factory Construction Plan and Process Automation Area Check by Industry

The establishment of a smart factory in Korea starts with selecting which industry in the manufacturing and production factories. The process automation area is checked through the level check according to the screening to determine the level of the smart factory to be completed. In the case of manufacturing industry, smart factory is divided into 1 casting, 2 forging, 3 mold, 4 injection molding, 5 press, 6 welding, 7 precision machining, 8 heat treatment, 9 plating, 10 coating, 11 machine parts assembly, 12 cosmetics, 13 pharmaceuticals, 14 enterprise resource management, 15 product development, and 16 supply chain management.

Table 1. 5 levels for SME smart factory in Korea.

Implementation phase	Automation	Plant operation	Business
Advancement	Automation combined with control automation and digitalidentification	Self-diagnosis and control using CPS,IoT, BigData	Real-time customized service through value chain linkage
Intermediate level	Automation of facility control	Real-time decision making and equipment control	Real-time decision making and control actively responding to market and customer needs
Medium level	Real-time collection of plant data	Performance-oriented factory operating analysis from facilities	Real-time information exchange such as information management based process operation
Foundation level	Barcode and RFID-based basic logistics information collection	Process logistics center performance management	Performance and quality-oriented functions
No ICT	handwork	Handwork	Phone and e-mail collaboration

According to the target stage of SME manufacturing companies in smart factory, SME Smart Factory in Korea is generally composed of 5 levels as shown in Table 1.

- Level 1: Factory level of manual ICT unemployed
- Level 2: Factory level of barcode and RFID-based basic logistics information gathering stage at Foundation level
- Level 3: Factory level of collecting plant data in real time with medium level

- Level 4: Factory level of facility control automation phase with real-time decision making and facility control at intermediate level
- Level 5: At the advanced level, real-time customer service is available at the factory level.

Currently, most of SME factories in Korea are in the level 1 or level 2.

3 Knowledge-Based Multi-agent System

In this paper, the knowledge-based multi-agent system is a solution process for networking of related problem experts by expanding the solution to manufacturing defect and process-related problems occurring in manufacturing factories in Korea at the level of manufacturing workers in factories [19]. At present, the smart factory level of most SMEs in Korea is level 1 or level 2, which is the level of the problem-solving manual in the factory, or sensor information acquisition with RFID. Figure 2 illustrates a knowledge-based MPS for manufacturing failure problems.

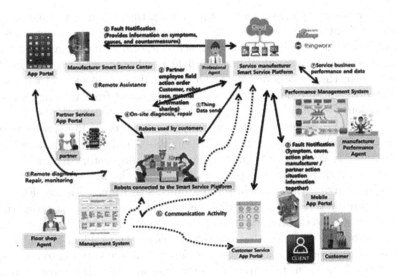

Fig. 2. Knowledge-based MPS model

1. Thing Data send: Step 1 is the step of sending signal data of the manufacturing site from the sensor attached device such as fault report data.
2. Fault Notification (Provides information on symptoms, causes, and countermeasures): In step 2, the failure signal judged by the field worker is transmitted to the failure report as to the failure symptom, the cause of failure, and the corresponding countermeasure.

3. Partner employee field action order (Customer, robot, case, material information sharing): The second stage is also the stage where the partner agent sends the site information at the same time. And share information about the robot, the bad case, and equipment information.
4. Fault Notification (Symptom, cause, action plan, manufacturer/partner action situation information together): Step 2 sends the failure information, which includes information about the failure, the cause of the failure, the action plan, and the situation that the manufacturer and the partner must cope with.
5. Remote Assistance: Step 3 is the Remote Assistance phase.
6. On-site diagnosis, repair: Step 4 is the diagnosis and repair phase at the fault site.
7. Remote diagnosis, Repair, monitoring: Step 5 is the remote diagnosis, maintenance, and monitoring.
8. Communication activity: Step 6 is a step to communicate the solution of the expert on the fault situation and to proceed with the work.
9. Service business performance and data: Step 7 is the step of accumulating and maintaining this data.

First, when a faulty case occurs at the manufacturing site, it is classified into 16 manufacturing sectors (such as welding, manufacturing, supply chain and so on), and the consumer side determines which field of manufacturing expert networking should be connected. When the field is selected, whether the problem is a problem in the process or whether it is a facility problem, and whether it can be used as an automation field, will be understood from the supplier side. In the problem recognition stage, the problem type posted by the field worker is categorized as a problem of the existing type, new type, improvement type through the database search of the CBR method, and if the problem of the product defect is detected, the product manufacturing history management of the PLM system [22]. Once the problem is defined, the process of resolving it is solved by applying the problem-solving process of Kepner-Tregoe. First, the problem definition is defined as the difference between as is and to be, describing the current state and defining the target state. Root cause analysis is performed through the process of presenting various causes of the problem and analyzing it. In the solution presentation stage, the solution is suggested through agent-based networking. Then, it is applied to the field and then it is processed as a process to accumulate it on a case-by-case basis. The characteristic aspect of the proposed system is that it provides a solution through expert networking in solving all the problems presented by the manufacturing worker, so that the whole manufacturing process and efficient process construction.

4 Use Cases

4.1 Manufacturing Problem-Solving Process

Manufacturing problem-solving process is configured as follows:

- Equipment/Logistics Automation
- Infra aspect for smart factory implementation, facility/logistics automation is required together with standardized two-way communication system
- Based on this, smart factory is realized by system intelligence.

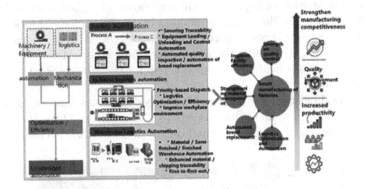

Fig. 3. Equipment/Logistics automation

Figure 3 shows an example of the implementation of a company's equipment and logistics automation system in Korea. It is a top priority to deliver goods to consumers quickly and safely using any means, such as shipping, air, rail or road. Logistics automation systems have fields such as logistics facilities, logistics information systems. The automation system for the logistics facilities is composed of automation warehouses (three-dimensional automatic warehouses, semi-automated warehouses, float rack automation, etc.) and unmanned conveying systems (rail guided vehicles, automatic palletizer systems, conveyors). Logistics information system is composed of automation control system, inventory management system, wireless management system (RFID), automatic classification system, dispatch system, order management system (OMS). Logistics automation is also urgent in terms of efficiency and cost reduction. In logistics warehouse, robotization and ITization are promoted in each of these areas such as admission, storage, inventory management, picking, packing (packaging), shipping, saving and unmanned. In the equipment automation production facility, a flexible conveying system that replaces the conveying line by the fixed facility centering on the conveying line conveyer which supplies parts and materials is being carried out, and the case of using the AGV is increasing. Due to the compactness of the AGV (Automatic Guided Vehicle), the AGV can travel at a maximum driving speed of 120 m/min in a production facility or in a narrow space below. Since the body (driving part) and the turntable for moving are independent from each other and rotated 360°, it can be introduced into various devices, and is easy to carry. Equipped with a safety scanner that detects obstacles, it is safe to drive multiple vehicles in a narrow passage.

In the case of multiple AGV operations, the entire operation control system such as the optimum allocation is performed, so that it is possible to increase the production capacity and flexibly cope with it. It is a new solution that is used in various production sites and logistics sites with flexible pallet transport system, replacing fixed equipment such as pallet conveying parts and conveyors. Normally, a person walks around and picks up or finds a shelf product, picks out, packages, ships and shuts out the necessary goods. This is a revolution that shipped from the stock to the computer in stock. In the latest automatic warehouse, automation of logistics in the warehouse of logistics bases (logistics centers, warehouses) is also being automated by the technology of forks, traveling cargo conveyors, robots and computer control. As a new movement, the automatic conveying truck lifts the picking shelf up to the designated place, and automation in various fields that does not require the movement of the worker is also performed.

Equipment/Logistics Automation - Process Logistics Automation. AGV means an unmanned vehicle that travels to a destination along the route by installing a necessary induction method on the floor, wall, and ceiling.

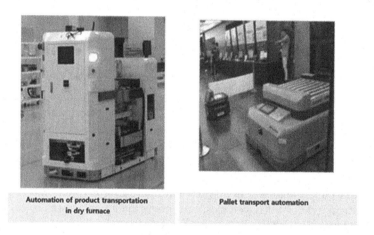

Automation of product transportation
in dry furnace

Pallet transport automation

Fig. 4. Equipment/Logistics automation - process logistics automation (AGV)

Figure 4 is an example of automated unmanned vehicle and pallet logistics operation operated by a company in Korea. Unmanned vehicle means a vehicle equipped with an induction system including an electro magnetic system, an optical system, and an anti-collision system, which are mainly used for manufacturing facilities and warehouses. Unmanned transportation system is used for material transportation in warehouse, container and semi-conductor LCD process. It is part of automation production system and carries out parts process of each process and movement of logistics between production lines. It is used to ensure flexibility. In the industrial field, the unmanned vehicle carries the role of material transfer between the processes, and is manufactured in various forms according to the process used. Unmanned vehicles are often called laser-guided vehicles (LGVs) or self-guided vehicles (SGVs). In recent years, the development of a smart digital transfer device replacing a forklift in the logistics center has been active. This transfer robot, which is called an unmanned transfer robot, is designed as an intelligent robot system. It is designed as an intelligent robot system. It is equipped with control technology of driving device using Omni wheel, terrain sensing technology using 3D laser scanner, robot autonomous driving technology and evasion technology, And system integration control technology, it can be used in various fields in the production site. The resulting productivity effect is significant.

Automation of pallet logistics operations. Pallet Logistics automation or pallet transportation system is a unit type automatic warehouse (automatic rack system) that automatically transports pallet unit products or parts and stores them in high-tier racks. It is possible to effectively use the high direction to increase the storage efficiency. Since the input and output instructions of the cargo are computerized, it is easy to manage the first-in, first-out, and leads to quality improvement. Pallets designed in the form of a hand lift. The automated logistics robot is a logistics automation robot for unmanned transportation and is particularly suitable for sites where pallets are frequently transported. In the meantime, people have transported goods on pallets directly to factories and warehouses. More specifically, this operation of pumping the hand lift and transferring the weight of the worker to transfer the heavy weight of the workload imposes a burden on the worker's body, while the work speed is also slow, and it is necessary to calibrate the position several times.

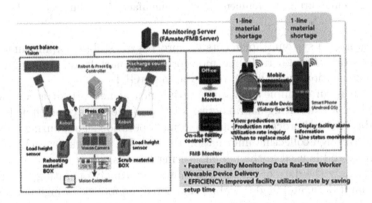

Fig. 5. Communications in smart factory

Figure 5 represents an example of a two-way communication case, in a case where a worker establishes a real-time monitoring system by automatically notifying the wearable device of facility monitoring data (production status, facility alarm information, etc). It represents manufacturing environment and safety. It is composed of some items. System item is press process product. Application field presents pressing process automobile parts. Robot specifications are 6 axis multi joint type IP67. Gripper item is chunk gripping.

4.2   Manufacturing Neural Networks

Figure 6 represents Visualization and Informatization of Manufacturing Environment/Safety - Manufacturing Neural Networks. By efficiently operating the main utilities of the factory, it is possible to realize cost reduction, quality assurance, and equipment pre-shutdown by precise analysis of major environmental factors (particle, power, vibration, temperature/humidity, etc.)

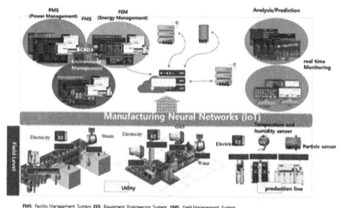

Fig. 6. Manufacturing environment/safety - manufacturing neural networks (IoT)

The proposed system implements the process of establishing manufacturing neural network through real-time monitoring of smart factory manufacturing process information by region through the main GUI.

Figure 6 is an example of manufacturing neural network of a company in Korea. The manufacturing neural network is one of the types of machine learning that enables normal process through abnormal operation signal during abnormal operation through collecting information through IoT sensors for each device in the process, and is used in the manufacturing process.

We use only the data of the devices that are normally operating, i.e., do not need the fault data, and made an abnormal detection model through non-teacher learning. In addition, it is possible to detect anomalies by using a combination of multiple sensors, which may be different from each other in the correlation between the sensors and the types of the sensors. Fault data is required to actually predict the time at which the fault will occur.

It is important to cope with the preventive preservation function because the failure of the work robot stops the production line and lowers the operation rate. It is characterized by the use of the deep learning in the manufacturing factory [20], So that it can be introduced while reducing the burden on the user.

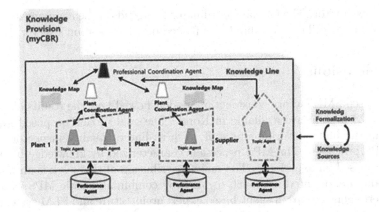

Fig. 7. Manufacturing Troubleshooting System

4.3   Manufacturing Troubleshooting System

Figure 7 represents Manufacturing Troubleshooting System. From the IT perspective, the proposed process model is based on a multi-agent architecture. Figure 7 shows the application to the proposed MPS system. The proposed MPS system architecture supports the deployment of multiple agents in different manufactur-ing factories in the company [21]. It supports the placement of the entire area in various manufacturing processes or production units at each location. In this way, each agent hosted in a specific production unit at a specific location can exchange information with all other agents hosted at different production units and locations through the company's intranet. The multi-agent architecture has been simplified using only the parts that are relevant to this smart factory system. The three agent types include the following in a multi-agent architecture:

- The field agent is extended to include the collection of context information from the PLM system at the plant site to complete the definition of the problem. This type of agent is as many as an MPS system user.
- Manufacturing Performance Management Agent calculates similarities through past cases and similar cases of bad problems that have occurred through the company's bad troubleshooting database and suggests the best solutions based on specific cases. There are as many agents of this type as production units, and each production unit is hosted in the central unit of that production unit.
- Expert Agent coordinates communication among agents and is responsible for selecting the best solution among the solutions proposed by the performance management agent. There are two types. The global reconciliation agent acts as a global reconciliation of the architecture at all connected locations. Coordination agents perform coordination of a single location. Get help from a topic agent in a known location. There is one global coordinator and one fac-

tory coordinator. The Global Coordinator is hosted on the company's central server and the Plant Coordinator is hosted on each location's server.

5 Conclusions

The proposed SME factory construction model showed how the results obtained by the MPS system are available in Korea. The goal of this proposed system is to help the manufacturing site staff, such as line or quality inspectors, perform MPS processes. The MPS process is characterized by knowledge-intensive activities based on experience. The main contribution of this work is an innovative production-oriented approach to MPS by combining classic MPS methods and expert agent groups in agent-based expert architecture and PLM systems. In addition, it is also characterized by the use of agent-based expert group and manufacturing neural network environment in the step-by-step approach for establishing smart factory in Korea. Future research and development work can be summarized as follows.

- It is necessary to develop global best practice by expanding development system by connecting to MES (Manufacturing Execution System) built in Korea.
- A cloud-based, universal platform must be developed to automatically apply the proposed solution to the specific context of each manufacturing process, for example, in a facility or logistics process.
- Development of a database that meets public interest through open source based application data sets with manufacturing facility and process data information through systematic data management of manufacturing system problems in developed systems.

Acknowledge. This research was supported by Basic Science Research Program through the National Research Foundation of Korea (NRF) funded by the Ministry of Education (NRF-2017R1A6A3A11035613).

References

1. Bhuiyan, N., Baghel, A.: An overview of continuous improvement: from the past to the present. Manag. Decis. **43**(5), 761–771 (2015)
2. Rother, M.: Toyota Kata: Managing People for Improvement, Adaptiveness, and Superior Results. McGraw-Hill Professional, New York (2010)
3. Yang, Y.B.: MES technology analysis and optimization for electronic manufacturing industry. In: International Conference on Robots Intelligent System (ICRIS), pp. 202–205 (2017)
4. Xiong, J.: Fault diagnosis method based on improved evidence reasoning. Math. Probl. Eng. **3**(4), 1–9 (2019)
5. Camarillo, A., Rios, J., Althoff, K.: CBR and PLM applied to diagnosis and technical support during problem solving in the Continuous Improvement Process of manufacturing plants. Procedia Manuf. **13**, 987–994 (2017)

6. Chigurupati, A., Lassar, N.: Root cause analysis using artificial intelligence. In: Reliability and Maintainability Symposium (RAMS), pp. 1–5 (2017)
7. De Mast, J., Lokkerbol, J.: An analysis of the Six Sigma DMAIC method from the perspective of problem solving. Int. J. Prod. Econ. **139**, 604–614 (2012)
8. Shainin, R.D.: Statistical engineering six decades of improved process and systems performance. Qual. Eng. **24**(2), 171–183 (2012)
9. Prashar, A.: Adoption of Six Sigma DMAIC to reduce cost of poor quality. J. Prod. Perform. Manag. **63**(1), 103–126 (2014)
10. Miltenburg, J.: Production planning problem where products have alternative routings and bills-of-material. Int. J. Prod. Res. **39**, 1755–1775 (2001)
11. Kepner, C.H., Tregoe, B.B.: The New Rational Manager - An Updated Edition for a New World. Princeton Research Press, Princeton (2008)
12. Ham, W., Park, S.: A framework for the continuous performance improvement of manned assembly lines. Int. J. Prod. Res. **52**(18), 5432–5450 (2014)
13. Riesenberger, C.A., Sousa, S.D.: The 8D methodology: an effective way to reduce recurrence of customer complaints. World Congr. Eng. **3**, 2225–2230 (2010)
14. Marjanca, K.: With 8D method to excellent quality. Revija za Univerzalno Odličnost **1**(3), 118–129 (2012)
15. Liu, D.R., Ke, C.K.: Knowledge support for problem-solving in a production process: a hybrid of knowledge discovery and case-based reasoning. Expert Syst. Appl. **33**, 147–61 (2007)
16. Richter, M.M., Weber, R.O.: Case-Based Reasoning: A Textbook. Springer, Heidelberg (2013). https://doi.org/10.1007/978-3-642-40167-1
17. Camarillo, A., Rios, J., Althoff, K.: Product lifecycle management as data repository for manufacturing problem solving. MDPI Mater. **11**(8), 1469–1487 (2018)
18. Putri, N., Mustafa, K., Norlida, B.: Knowledge management system in industries. In: 4th International Conference on Electronics and System Engineering (ICEESE), pp. 107–111 (2018)
19. Bach, K.: Knowledge acquisition for case-based reasoning systems. Ph.D. thesis. University of Hildesheim (2012)
20. Walker, A.J.: An artificial neural network driven decision-making system for manufacturing disturbance mitigation in reconfigurable systems. In: 13th IEEE International Conference on Control & Automation (ICCA), pp. 695–700 (2017)
21. Camarillo, A., Ríos, J., Althoff, K.: Knowledge-based multi-agent system for manufacturing problem solving process in production plants. J. Manuf. Syst. **47**, 115–127 (2018)
22. Glushchenko, F., Fedotova, A.: Developing automotive production with using product lifecycle management system. In: 2nd School on DCNAR, pp. 38–40 (2018)

Design and Performance Analysis of Docker-Based Smart Manufacturing Platform Based on Deep Learning Model

Soonsung Hwang, Jaehyoung Lee, Dongyeon Kim, and Jongpil Jeong$^{(\boxtimes)}$

Department of Smart Factory Convergence, Sungkyunkwan University,
Suwon, Gyeonggi-do 16419, Republic of Korea
{suns303,objective,kdy5958,jpjeong}@skku.edu

Abstract. Breakdown of equipment causes very large damage to the factory. Research is continuously being conducted to prevent break down of equipment by detecting abnormal signs before equipment failure. This paper proposes an anomaly detection for system architecture based on a docker container. A docker is a virtualized container with many performance and scalability advantages. We have used the deep learning model of Autoencoder to effectively anomaly detection and its performance has been proven through experiments.

Keywords: Anomaly detection · Autoencoder · Docker · Smart Manufacturing · RMSE

1 Introduction

Docker, a container-based virtualization technology, provides an environment in which all containers can run applications on the same system. Developers can easily customize and package their runtime environment from a set of files called Docker Images. Once the Docker Image is created, the user can run the image on any host computer using the Docker Engine. The ability to build a single image of the docker and run it from anywhere greatly simplifies the development, delivery, and deployment of applications [1]. More and more companies are now building container-based platforms using Docker. The docker is very easy to develop and extensible [2].

We propose a system architecture for manufacturing using a docker. We demonstrate the process of anomaly detection in equipment through system architecture [3,4]. In this paper is based on case studies applied to actual factories. Our manufacturing plant is a PCB gold plating process. If equipment failure occurs breakdown during production, this will lead to a large loss of the plant. Equipment can be divided into normal section, abnormal symptom section, breakdown. Before the breakdown, abnormality symptom interval always occurs. Unlike the normal section, there are several different symptoms in the abnormal symptom section. If an abnormal symptom is caught in the abnormal symptom section and the action is taken, the equipment can be prevented from breakdown. We aim to anomaly detection in the anomaly section before equipment failure [5]. We propose system architecture that From the sensor data collection stage attached to the facility, to the process of alarming the operator after anomaly detection using artificial intelligence. We use Autoencoder model for anomaly detection [6,7].

The composition of our paper is as follows. In Sect. 2, related work describe the Docker platform and the Autoencoder model. In Sect. 3, we proposed system architecture. Section 4 shows the experiment results. Finally, our conclusion is drawn in Sect. 5.

2   Relate Work

2.1   Docker-Based Platform

Docker is the world's leading software container platform. Containers are a single object that contains all the necessary components for the software to run, and each container operates in an isolated environment. Therefore, containerized software runs the same way regardless of the operating system environment. This looks similar to a virtual machine, but unlike a VM, the Docker virtualizes the operating system, not the hardware. Thus, the container can share the OS kernel with other containers, and each container runs as an isolated process in user space. Therefore, containers are more portable and efficient than VMs.

However, containers are not necessarily better than VMs. First, containers can be more vulnerable to security. If a user has superuser privileges in a container, theoretically, that user may have problems with the superuser's privileges to the underlying OS underneath the container. It is therefore recommended that containers be handled in the same way as other server applications. Containers also make it easy for developers to develop applications because they make the application-driven environment a safe that does not need to be opened, but conversely developers are more difficult to understand the contents of the safe. This means you can easily distribute your app, but your app will be more likely to be deployed on the wrong container. Finally, it's a good idea to divide the system to be distributed into smaller parts, but on the contrary, there are more parts to manage. For the above reasons, Docker supports VM, so container and VM can coexist and it is recommended to use containers and VM appropriately according to the situation. If you do not know when and how you will use it, it is better to use the VM in situations where you need to run a container on a system that needs to run multiple copies of the same application and run multiple applications on a single system.

If you use a docker in the right environment, the docker makes it easier to build a virtualized environment based on the container. The docker consists of an image and a container, and the set value can be composed into an image and executed in a container. Compared to virtual machines, they run at a much faster speed and do not virtualize hardware, which improves memory access and file system performance.

2.2   Autoencoder Model

We use Autoencoders as anomalous detection models. An Autoencoder is a neural network that copies inputs to outputs [8]. Figure 1 shows the structure of Autoencoder. The Autoencoder consists of an encoder and a decoder. The encoder is called the recognition network and translates the input into an internal representation. The decoder is called generative network and converts its internal representation to output [9]. Because the auto-encoder reconstructs the input, the output is called reconstruction, and the loss function is computed with the difference between input and reconstruction [10].

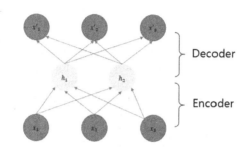

Fig. 1. Autoencoder model architecture.

The Autoencoder can only be compressed with data similar to the trained data. In addition, Autoencoder automatically learns from data, which is a useful property. Learning from data automatically means that you can easily train a particular type of algorithm that works well for certain types of input values. It is only necessary to properly train the data without the need for new engineering measures. Encoders and decoders are chosen as parametric functions and differentiated in terms of distance functions, so the parameters of the encoding/decoding function can be optimized using a stochastic gradient descent to minimize reconstruction loss.

The formula of Autoencoder is as follows.

$$Encoder : h = f'_\theta(x) = s(Wx + b') \tag{1}$$

$$Decoder : x' = g'_\theta(h) = s(W'h + b') \tag{2}$$

In 2012, a way to apply Autoencoder has been found in greedy layer-wise pretraining of deep convolutional neural networks [11]. However, as the random weight initialization schemes were found to be sufficient to train deep networks from scratch, the Autoencoder quickly disappeared from fashion. In 2014, batch normalization [12] began to allow much deeper networks, and by the end of 2015 it was possible to arbitrarily train deep networks using residual learning [13].

3 Docker-Based Smart Manufacturing Platform Based on Deep Learning Model

We propose a Docker-based Smart Manufacturing Platform based on Deep Learning Model as shown in Fig. 2. Our platform runs DAQ, Database, Kafka, Web application, Predictor, and Model Training containers on the docker engine. The docker-based platform provided function that Application Scheduling, Container Scheduling, Service Discovery, Container Cluster Management, and Container Networking.

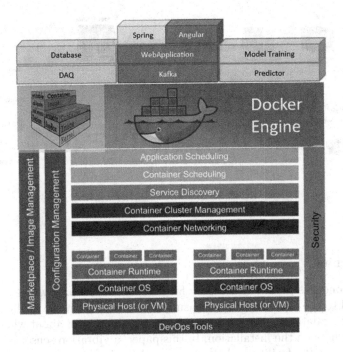

Fig. 2. Docker-based Smart Manufacturing Platform.

This section describes the architecture of the Autoencoder based anomaly detection and monitoring system proposed in this paper. As shown in Fig. 3, the structure of our system is as follows.

Step 1: Attach vibration sensor from equipment and collect data.
Step 2: Send PLC data and sensor data of the equipment collected from DAQ to database.
Step 3: Send the data stored in the database to create a learning model.
Step 4: Generate normal data learning model using auto-encoder model.
Step 5: Create a normal data learning model and load the learning model into edge computing.

Step 6: Send the data collected by DAQ to Predictor in real time.

Step 7: Normal data When the normal data is entered into the learning model, the RMSE becomes low, and when the untrained data enters the data, the RMSE becomes high.

Step 8: Monitor the RMSE value in real time and pay attention to whether abnormalities occur periodically.

Step 9: Periodically, if the RMSE value is high, it is recognized as an abnormal symptom and an alarm is sent to the user.

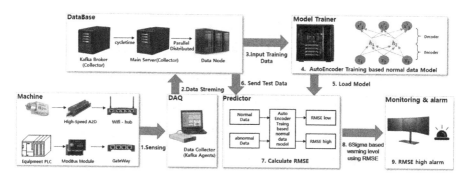

Fig. 3. System architecture.

3.1 Machine

This component is part of the factory facility. This is the part where the sensor is attached to the part where the measurement is desired in the facility and the corresponding data is collected. Here, you have to be careful about what data to attach to where on the installation. In this paper, a vibration sensor is attached to the crane of the facility and the motor and the bearing to collect data. The crane moves horizontal, vertical, and pitch. Horizontal has 3 sensors, Vertical has 2, Peach has 1 sensor, and 6 sensors per crane.

3.2 DAQ: Data Acquisition

This component is the part that collects facility data. We collect sensor data and PLC data from the machine and stream data using Apache Kafka which is Hadoop ecosystem. Apache Kafka is a distributed messaging system that outperforms traditional messaging systems through an architectural design that specializes in high-volume real-time log processing. It is based on the Pub-Sub model and consists of Producer, Consumer, and Broker. The Broker manages the message based on the topic, and the Producer generates a message for the topic and forwards the message to the Broker. When a Broker categorizes and stacks messages received by a topic, Consumers who subscribe to the topic process the message. The difference with existing messaging systems is that they are designed based on distributed systems, which makes it easier to configure distribution and replication over existing messaging systems. In addition, TCP - based protocol with simple message header reduces the overhead, and it can reduce the number of TCP/IP roundtrips by sending a large number of messages to the broker at once.

Figure 4 is the process of data collection process used in this paper. Figure 4 shows Sensor Data Collector and PLC Event Collector. The sensor data in this paper is collected by attaching a vibration sensor to the motor and the bearing to collect the vibration data generated during the movement of the equipment. The sensor data collects 2096 data per 0.5 s. The PLC event data is data indicating the start and end of the facility. The Sensor Data Collector collects data from the process, and the PLC Event Collector collects events from the start and end of the PLC. These two collectors are collected by SensorData Collector through Kafka Broker, stored in parallel by HBase, periodically send data to Kafka Broker in PLC Event Collector, and receive data by PLC Data Collector.

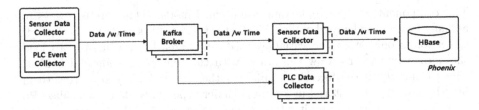

Fig. 4. Data gathering process.

3.3   DataBase

This component is a database. Our system uses two kinds of database. First, the sensor data received from the DAQ component is stored in parallel to the Hadoop ecosystem NoSQL Hbase. We use NoSQL because we have a lot of sensor data. The second database uses postgres, an RDB that simply queries the data results in a web application. The reason for using two databases is that it is efficient to save the data that does not modify the value like sensor data in Nosql and to build the system by saving the data that needs CRUD in RDB to the web application.

3.4   Model Trainer

This component generates a normal data learning model using an Autoencoder model. Figure 5 shows the Trainer process of the model. We created a learning model using the Python library Tensor flow using the PLC data collector from the DAQ component and the sensor data from HBase of the DataBase component. We train only normal data with Autoencoder model.

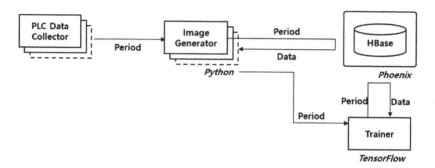

Fig. 5. Model training process.

3.5 Predictor

This component predicts by loading the learned model. There are two ways to actually predict the learned model. The first is to use a file saved as a checkpoint. Checkpoints only store the variables used when creating the model. To load the data, you have to draw the graph with the tensorflow code and load it. The second way is to store the graphs together rather than just storing them like checkpoints. It is stored in Protocol Buffer type. This file is also called Pb and can be used by loading it into the tensor flow service. We built the model server using the latter Tensorflow Serving. Our system only trains normal data. When abnormal data comes in as input data, it uses RMSE and recognizes it as abnormal data when RMSE is high.

3.6 Monitoring Alarm

This component alerts the user when an anomaly data detected. Figure 6 is our alert alarm web application process. Autoencoder model was trained by using PLC data from DAQ component and sensor data stored in HBase. It is a process that judges the abnormality of the data collected in real time using the Predictor component and confirms the abnormality in the web application. This component is a web application. The frontend uses the angular framework and the backend framework uses the spring boot.

3.7 RMSE-Based Warning Level

The following is a structure that notifies the user when the RMSE becomes high and recognized as an abnormal symptom. RMSE is often used as a measure to evaluate the model by obtaining the difference between the predicted value and actual value of the model with the mean square root error.

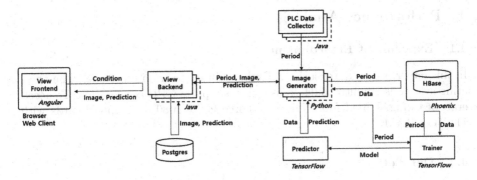

Fig. 6. Monitoring alarm process.

The formula of RMSE is as follows.

$$RMSE = \sqrt{\frac{1}{n}\sum_{i=1}^{n}(y_i - \hat{y}_i)^2} \tag{3}$$

The RMSE generated using the Autoencoder model is the error value obtained by subtracting the actual sensor data from the predicted value of the actual sensor data in the learning model. We applied the 6 sigma technique after finding the normal distribution of RMSE. Figure 7 structure is a structure that gives warning alarm to the user by using RMSE. First, if the RMSE value is higher than the level1 value, it goes to State A. If it continues to exceed the warning level line, it goes to State B and alarms the user. If there is no value beyond the warning level in State A, it goes to State C and the alarm will not sound to the user. In case of exceeding warning level value again in State C, it goes to State D and goes to State B again and gives alarm to the user.

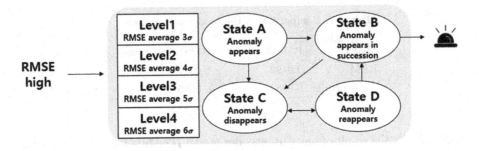

Fig. 7. Alarm process.

4   Performance Analysis

4.1   Experiment Environment

In this paper, we used TensorFlow Python library to train the model. The operating system is Ubuntu 16.04. Tensor flow supports GPU acceleration. To accelerate learning, I used four Nvidia GeForce GTX 1080 Ti graphics cards with 11 GB of RAM.

4.2   DataSet

The data set used in this paper was obtained by attaching a vibration sensor to the bearing, motor, and body of the equipment in the gold plating process of D Company. There are five facilities, and there are three types of equipment movement. Horizontal, Vertical, and Pitch. The sensor is measured in bearings, motors, and body for each movement of each facility. The learning unit learns the cycle unit of the equipment from the time when the equipment starts moving to the time when the equipment stops. The vibration sensor data generated in this process is analyzed by T-F spectrum which is a time-frequency domain by converting fast Fourier transform.

4.3   Model Result

In this paper, we compare the model performance using Restricted Boltzmann machine and Autoencoder algorithm as shown in Table 1. The model train the unit of the cycle from equipment the start to end as one input value. The input cycle value of the next time distinguishes between normal and abnormal through the difference from the reconstruction value predicted by model. The same parameters used for each model were learning rate = 0.01, Batch = 128, Epoch = 1000, and Hidden Dimension = 512.

Table 1. Comparison of the model performance.

Model	RMSE (normal)	RMSE (abnormal)
RBM	0.0192	0.0321
Autoencoder	0.0084	0.0395

Figure 8 is the result of our Autoencoder model. The first figure is the actual value of the model, and the second figure is the result of the model. The last figure is the RMSE result minus the actual value and the predicted result.

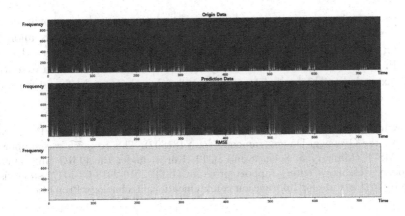

Fig. 8. Autoencoder model result.

4.4 Monitoring Result

This section is the result of using our model to alert the user. Figure 9 shows the user's current facility status using the bar chart. It is bar chart screen before actual equipment breakdown. One bar represents the 6 min RMSE value, which is the cycle time of the facility. It is a system that warns the user when the RMSE value exceeds the warning level that we set. The alarm continues to be given to the user since the level value is continuously exceeded every cycle.

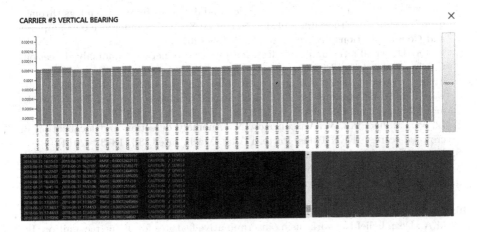

Fig. 9. Monitoring using bar chart.

5   Conclusion

In this paper, we propose a new architecture based on artificial intelligence. A platform based on a docker can be easily extended because it has good scalability.

While there are many services available on the platform, we have shown results for services related to anomaly detection. Autoencoder was used as anomaly detection model indications and anomaly indications could be detected effectively. In the next study, if the anomaly data is collected to a certain extent, it will be extended to the fault detection classification that can be found from the anomaly detection to the cause.

Acknowledgement. This work has supported by the Gyeonggi Techno Park grant funded by the Gyeonggi-Do government (No. Y181802). This research was supported by the MSIT (Ministry of Science and ICT), Korea, under the ITRC (Information Technology Research Center) support program (IITP-2019-2018-0-01417) supervised by the IITP (Institute for Information communications Technology Promotion).

References

1. Ismail, B.I., et al.: Evaluation of docker as edge computing platform. In: 2015 IEEE Conference on Open Systems (ICOS), pp. 130–135 (2015)
2. Shah, J., Dubaria, D.: Building modern clouds: using docker, kubernetes & Google cloud platform. In: 2019 IEEE 9th Annual Computing and Communication Workshop and Conference (CCWC), pp. 184–189 (2019)
3. Javaid, A., et al.: A deep learning approach for network intrusion detection system. In: Proceedings of the 9th EAI International Conference on Bio-inspired Information and Communications Technologies (formerly BIONETICS), pp. 21–26. ICST (Institute for Computer Sciences, Social-Informatics and Telecommunications Engineering) (2016)
4. Du, M., et al.: Deeplog: anomaly detection and diagnosis from system logs through deep learning. In: Proceedings of the 2017 ACM SIGSAC Conference on Computer and Communications Security, pp. 1285–1298 (2017)
5. Kwon, D., et al.: A survey of deep learning-based network anomaly detection. Cluster Comput. 1–13 (2017)
6. Tang, T.A., et al.: Deep learning approach for network intrusion detection in software defined networking. In: 2016 International Conference on Wireless Networks and Mobile Communications (WINCOM), pp. 258–263 (2016)
7. Li, W., Mahadevan, V., Vasconcelos, N.: Anomaly detection and localization in crowded scenes. IEEE Trans. Pattern Anal. Mach. Intell. **36**, 18–32 (2014)
8. Ngiam, J., et al.: Multimodal deep learning. In: Proceedings of the 28th International Conference on Machine Learning (ICML-11), pp. 689–696 (2011)
9. Andrew, G., et al.: Deep canonical correlation analysis. In: International Conference on Machine Learning, pp. 1247–1255 (2013)
10. Mohamed, A., Sainath, T.N., Dahl, G.E., Ramabhadran, B., Hinton, G.E., Picheny, M.A.: Deep belief Networks using discriminative features for phone recognition. In: ICASSP, pp. 5060–5063 (2011)
11. Erhan, D., et al.: Why does unsupervised pre-training help deep learning? J. Mach. Learn. Res. **11**, 625–660 (2010)
12. Ioffe, S., Szegedy, C.: Batch normalization: accelerating deep network training by reducing internal covariate shift. arXiv preprint arXiv:1502.03167 (2015)
13. He, K., et al.: Deep residual learning for image recognition. In: Proceedings of the IEEE Conference on Computer Vision and Pattern Recognition, pp. 770–778 (2016)

Open Source Based Industrial IoT Platforms for Smart Factory: Concept, Comparison and Challenges

Myungsoo Kim, Jaehyeong Lee, and Jongpil Jeong[✉]

Department of Smart Factory Convergence, Sungkyunkwan University,
Suwon, Gyeonggi-do 16419, Republic of Korea
{sioals,objective,jpjeong}@skku.edu

Abstract. As Internet of Things (IoT) and Services are applied to manufacturing industries, Industry 4.0 is evolving. For Industry 4.0 to be
realized in the factory, it is essential to implement horizontal integration
of cross enterprise value networks, vertical integration within the factory.
As interest in IoT has increased, number of platforms that are designed
to support it has increased greatly. Because of the different approaches,
standards, use cases, and the types of Industrial IoT platforms are very
complex and diverse. Therefore, it is difficult to understand, choose and
apply the appropriate platform. In this study, we examine the function,
effectiveness and cautions for open source based platforms that can be
applied to IoT based smart manufacturing. In addition, the architecture
of five open source IIoT platforms are analyzed by our reference architecture and clean up all in Table. Finally, we present the use cases of
Industrial IoT environment and analyze its effects.

Keywords: Smart factory · IIoT platform · Open source ·
Edge computing

1 Introduction

Most of initial implementation of IoT was a special project rather than a standard solution so system integrators or service providers had to designate scope
of implementation, design and manage it. As industrial IoT is becoming more
common, employees in industries expect that business system will perform completely and automated tasks. In other words, it is expected that IoT should be
available to existing systems and that it can be connected to the Internet and
generate business value using data collected and analyzed from manufacturing
facilities. Based on these demands, a number of suppliers have developed components that enable them to deploy industrial IoT platforms or applications,
often relying on the ecosystem of partners to provide solutions. In most cases,
partners provide IoT devices, cloud storage, edge computing, enterprise applications, overall project management or system integration. Industrial IoT, which

S. Misra et al. (Eds.): ICCSA 2019, LNCS 11624, pp. 105–120, 2019.
https://doi.org/10.1007/978-3-030-24311-1_8

is based on automated robots and data, can help businesses innovate so that businesses are fully computerized, highly automated, and autonomously operate in certain areas [1, 2].

IoT nowadays promotes the adoption of different open source technologies, standards and protocols that help devices communicate with one another. The following are the drivers that prompt organisations to adopt open source technologies for IoT.

- Cost: Adoption of open source IoT frameworks involves no costs at all, as these are free for use. This encourages the community and organisations to implement IoT without any hesitation.
- Innovation: Open source code from the community helps in building newer applications, leading to more innovation and agility. The developers are able to build different products, which will be interoperable across different OSs such as Android, Windows, iOS (iPhone OS) and Linux.
- Open APIs (Application Programming Interface): Use of open source APIs for the IoT framework offers a common gateway for different software, hardware and the systems to communicate with one another.
- Libraries: An open source IoT framework offers a wide range of libraries, SDKs (Software Development Kit) and open source hardware like Raspberry Pi and Arduino, ensuring that companies remain on the cutting edge of technology by using different open sourced tools to customise IoT platforms.
- Security: Open source software can protect individual data by implementing really strong encryption for the use of the general public, and hence supply the building blocks for mobile security and the protection of data.
- Interoperability: Adoption of open source solves the problem of interoperability.

Today's global market has at least 49 IoT platforms to meet the needs of diverse user and application groups such as enterprise, government, farmer, healthcare, and manufacturing. However, because of the lack of overall knowledge of the IoT platform, researchers and enthusiasts can hardly choose a specific IoT platform when they are in the product or solution development phase that leverages IoT support technology [3]. Savaglio et al. [4] Investigated and compared the most relevant autonomic and cognitive structure for the IoT. They investigated architectural style management and other applications with self management and cognitive abilities. These architectures strive to minimize human intervention and protect the heterogeneity of the device, which is an interesting research topic and deserves further study in the future. Palade et al. [5] studied the evaluation criteria of IoT middleware by calculating the weights of other standards using Analytic Hierarchy Process (AHP) method. They analyzed and compared middleware performance in service registration and service configuration. Finally, they compared the application development process of four middleware through four different scenarios. Kim et al. [6] examined various IoT applications and abstracted the general platform model. They introduce the concept of things, which is closely related to the devices presented in this paper. The gateway provides connectivity to the platform when things can not communicate directly with the platform. Service users as well as services and software providers are connected to the platform by RESTful APIs. If complex data processing is not required on the platform, service usage may be directly connected to the device to collect metrology data. Thus, the most important thing in implementing a smart factory is data.

This paper consists of the following: In Sect. 2, we define four key functions of the IIoT platform and derived reference alignment through them. In Sect. 3, we compare and analyze features of the five representative open source platforms based on reference architecture of IIoT platform and clean up all in Table. Finally, In Sect. 4, we present use case of industrial environment and analyze its effects.

2 Concept of Open Source Based IIoT Platforms

IoT platform of users can remotely collect data and manage all IoT devices from a single system [7]. Although there are many IoT platforms that are available online, all of them are based on IoT platform host and quality of support. As a result, IoT platform performs a major function of converting its factories to Smart Factories. Overall, the IoT platform should have the following functions: Extract data from equipment, sensors, and devices, Connect and analyze edge devices, Store large amounts of data, analyze, and lastly Control data in real time [8].

2.1 Support for Device Management and Integration

Device management is one of the most important functions that can be expected from any IoT software platform. The IoT platform should maintain a list of connected devices, track their operational status, be able to handle configuration, firmware (or other software) updates, and provide device level error reporting and processing. Ultimately, device users should be able to obtain individual device level statistics. Integrated support is another important function that can be expected from IoT software platforms. The API should provide access to critical operations and data that should be exposed on the IoT platform. It is common to use REST APIs to achieve this objective.

2.2 Securing Information

Information security measures that are needed to operate IoT software platforms are much higher than normal software applications and services. Millions of devices that connect to IoT platforms need to predict a proportional number of vulnerabilities. Generally, network connectivity between IoT devices and IoT software platforms needs to be encrypted with a strong encryption mechanism to avoid the possibility of eavesdropping. However, most low cost, low power devices included in modern IoT software platforms cannot support these advanced access control measures. Thus, the IoT software platform itself needs to implement an alternative means of dealing with these device level problems. For example, the level can be improved by how to separate IoT traffic into a private network, secure strong information at the cloud application level, and updating the firmware through authentication [9].

2.3 Data Acquisition Protocol

Another important aspect to note is the type of protocol used to communicate data between components of the IoT software platform. IoT platform needs to be expanded to millions or billions of devices (nodes). Lightweight communication protocols should be used to enable low energy use and low network bandwidth functions. The protocols used for data collection can be classified according to several categories, such as applications, payload containers, messaging, and legacy protocols [10].

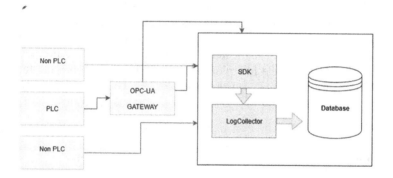

Fig. 1. Edge data flow

In the meantime, the manufacturing industry has been able to achieve productivity enhancement through process specific automation based on Programmable Logic Controller (PLC) and embedded PC. This automation consists of vertically integrated optimization systems through PLC vendors' specialized industrial Ethernet protocols EtherNet/IP, Profinet, CC-Link, POWERLINK and EtherCAT. In Fig. 1, data from various protocols generated by PLC Devices are directed to SDK via OPC UA(Open platform Communications Unified Architecture) protocol. Data will then be stored in the database via LogCollector. The database can be divided as five data types. This can be largely divided into PLC device data, Data from Non PLC devices (through SDK), Data from Non PLC devices (through TCP), Security Data from OPC UA gateways, log data. This data becomes target data for machine learning techniques for efficient process control.

2.4   Data Analysis

Data collected from sensors connected to IoT platforms should be analyzed intelligently in order to gain meaningful insight. There are four main types of analysis available for IoT data: realtime, batch, prediction and interactive analysis. Realtime analysis performs an online analysis of streaming data. Batch analysis executes actions against accumulated data sets. Therefore, the deployment task runs at a scheduled time and can last for hours or days. Predictive analysis focuses on predictions based on various statistics and machine learning techniques. Interactive analytics perform multiple navigation analyses on streaming and batch data. Lastly, this is a realtime analysis that is weighted on all IoT software platforms.

2.5   Reference Architecture of IIoT Platform

Based on the concept of the above four IoT platforms, we have derived reference architecture. In the case of Fig. 2, the function of the IIoT platform is drawn in reference architecture focusing on data processing. First, sensors and actuators are connected to IoT devices. In the IoT gateway and IoT devices, the data flow is not significantly preprocessed, and in the cloud, there is a way to move up to the cloud, or to pre the data before it is stored in the cloud through edge computing, or to extract only the necessary data from the edge device, and store it in the cloud. In other words, devices have processors and storage capacities that can run software and connect to IoT integrated middleware. If the device cannot connect directly to the additional system, it is connected to the gateway. A gateway provides the skills and mechanisms necessary to transform different protocols, communication technologies, and payload formats. IoT Integration Middleware serves as an integrated layer for various types of sensors, actuators, IoT devices and applications. IoT integration middleware is not limited to functions described above. With numerous IIoT open source

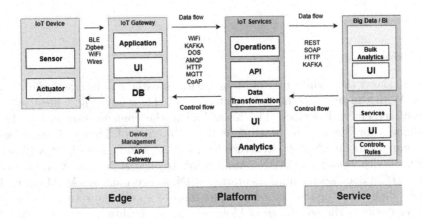

Fig. 2. Reference architecture of IIoT platform

platforms, tools and open stack to add functions, the combination method is endless. Application refers to software that uses IoT Integration Middleware to gain insight into the physical environment and to manipulate the physical environment.

3   Comparison of Open Source Based IIoT Platforms

In this section, five open source based IoT platforms that can be used at industrial sites are compared and analyzed based on their respective open structure. The open source platforms analyzed here are Kaa, Sitewere, DeviceHive, and Fiware. Describes the strengths and weaknesses of each platform, focusing on the data flow of the IIoT reference architecture, and compares the functions that are considered important at the industrial site. Lastly, clean up all in Table 1.

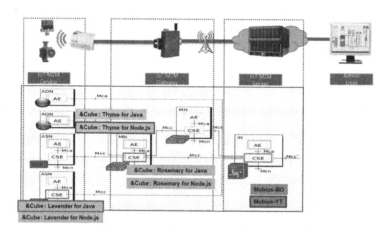

Fig. 3. Mobius IoT platform structure [11]

3.1   Mobius

Figure 3 shows the architecture of Mobius with essential and interaction of functions. With the reference of the architecture of this study, Fig. 3 illustrates a map of servers and devices. The lower half is the configuration of oneM2M (Standards for Machine to Machine and the Internet of Things) system, and the components are IN (Infrastructure Node), MN (Middle Node), ASN (Application Service Node) and ADN (Application Dedicated Node). As described, Mobius is an open source implementation of IN, a server side oneM2M entity. It gathers data from the device and provides data to applications and other gateways or devices. The advantage of Mobius is that it faithfully follows oneM2M. The IoT application communicates with the field domain IoT gateway/device via Mobius. To connect to Cube through TAS (Ting Adaptation Software) to activate the Internet, Cube communicates with Mobius via oneM2M standard API. In addition, IoT applications use the oneM2M standard API.

And then, MobiusYT is a middleware server platform that connects various IoT devices through physical communication media and creates virtual representation (oneM2M resources) for each IoT device, enabling communication between devices and IoT applications. In this way, MobiusYT provides an open environment and API for users to build their IoT ecosystem by interconnecting their devices and developing userspecific IoT services. Mobius implements IN-CSE, a cloud server in the infrastructure domain. It also supports protocol bindings include HTTP (HyperText Transfer Protocol), CoAP (Constrained Application Protocol), MQTT (Message Queuing Telemetry Transport), and Web sockets.

3.2 Kaa

Figure 4 shows the architecture of Kaa essential and interaction of functions. With the reference of the architecture of this study, the SDK collects data end points, communicates configuration profiles, and enables messaging at the end points. It supports REST communication with the server and can distribute SDK to devices. It is a middleware platform for building IoT end-to-end applications that can be used as a gateway or application server. Supports device management, device interaction, remote device configuration and distributed remote device firmware updates, cloud service creation, data collection and analysis, user behavior analysis, targeted event notification, and big data-based data storage. As IIoT platform of Kaa, It has quite many function as follows: Remote factory floor monitoring, Unified factory wide interconnectivity, Predictive maintenance, Gateway apps and edge analytics, cloud based data storage and analytics. The disadvantage of Kaa (personal server deployment) is that it is not possible to look up data stored through REST APIs on the server, which means that users must develop other develop other applications for this function [12].

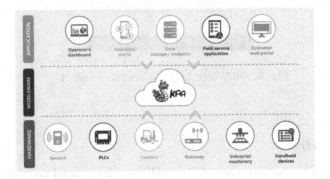

Fig. 4. Kaa IoT platform structure [13]

3.3   SiteWhere

Figure 5 shows the architecture of SiteWhere with essential and interaction of functions. With the reference of the architecture of this study, data from devices and commands to device components is organized by device components. Moreover, they also represent sensor and actuator components. This is because they are not explicitly described within an architecture. Users can connect devices with MQTT, AMQP (Advanced Message Queuing Protocol), Stomp, and other devices via self registration, REST service, or batch. Because devices can communicate through platforms and various protocols, a gateway concept exists between devices and platforms, but is not depicted as a separate component. It supports MQTT, AMQP, and REST communication with the server.

It is an open source middleware platform created and maintained licensed under common public attributes license. The main functions of the platform are provided by the SiteWhereTenant engine, including the device management and communication engine. Therefore, these components consist of IoT integration middleware in the reference architecture. The REST APIs and Integration component enables additional applications to be connected to the platform. It aggregates with third party integration frameworks such as Module AnyPoint.

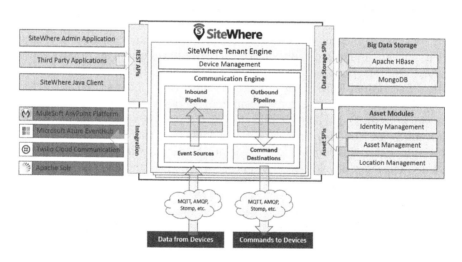

Fig. 5. SiteWhere IoT platform structure [14]

3.4   DeviceHive

Figure 6 shows the architecture of DeviceHive with essential and interaction of functions. With the reference of the architecture of this study, devices communicates and passes it to the gateway. DeviceHive is a micro service based system, built with high scalability and availability in mind. Looking at the architecture for subsequent data processing, the RESTful and Websocket APIs were provided to enhance user convenience. Finally, various plugin services are left optically to preserve the scalability features of open source platform.

To sum it up, DeviceHive is an open source IoT platform that is rich in functions distributed under Apache 2.0 license. DeviceHive is free to use and change. Even though it is an open source, online versions can be used as PaaS, free trial versions can be provided, or they can be expanded to paid versions. Further function is that Docker and Kubenets placement options are provided. Users can download and use both public and private clouds, and can scale a single virtual machine to an enterprise class cluster. Users can connect to a device or hacker board via REST API, WebSockets, or MQTT. To successfully deploy the solution, users must install PostgreSQL, Apache Kafka, and Java 8 or later. Devicehive's disadvantage is that measurement data on the device (when deploying a personal server) is cached. This means that if user restarts the server or run out of memory, user loses all of your data. If users want this function, they should create additional connectors or modify the back end logic [17].

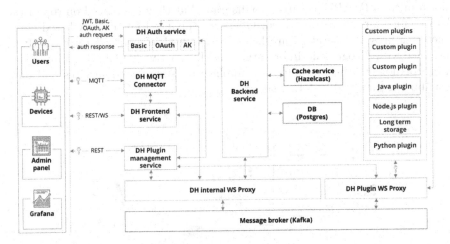

Fig. 6. DeviceHive IoT platform structure [15]

3.5   FIWARE

Figure 7 shows the architecture of FIWARE with essential and interaction of functions. With the reference of the architecture of this study, the implementation of FIWARE IoT architecture ranges from simple scenarios that connect several devices to a data field backend Context Broker using standard IoT communication protocols to scenarios that distribute to large IoT networks and platforms to provide advanced configuration. [16] FIWARE is funded by the

114   M. Kim et al.

European Union and the European Commission. The FIWARE catalog contains a Generic Enabler (GE) that represents a rich library of components. The architecture in Fig. 6 shows only GE in the IoT segment. FIWARE distinguishes only devices from NGSI13 devices. Since the FIWARE manual explains that the device may have integrated sensors and actuators, all device components consist of device, sensor, and actuator components. Devices can communicate directly with IoT backend or through gateways located within IoT Edge. Both IoT gateway and IoT NGSI gateway will activate and manage device communication with IoT backend.

Thus, IoT Edge represents the gateway of the IoT reference architecture. FIWARE is a Pub/Sub Implementationation of NGSI-9 and NGSI-10 Open RESTful API specifications and only support REST communication with the server. The IoT BackEnd and Data Context Broker provide the main functions of FIWARE, so they are encapsulated by IoT Integration Middleware. FIWARE's documentation describes how additional applications are connected to the platform through a data context broker. It provides platform and standardized API aggregation for variable fields. Application components are not shown in the FIWARE architecture diagram, but they are placed on top of the data context broker as described. Offers an enhanced OpenStack based cloud where features and catalogs are hosted. Advanced Web based User Interface: Interface with Geographic Information and Interactive 3D Chart. Components and tools for creating mashups and application store based services and data distribution that enable data visualization.

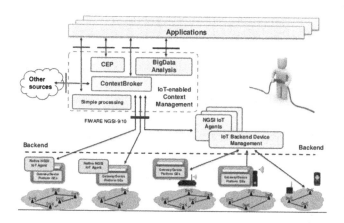

Fig. 7. FIWARE IoT platform structure [16]

Table 1. Comparison of Opensource based IoT platform

Open source platform	Kaa	FIWARE	Device Hive	Sitewhere	Mobius
Protocol	MQTT, CoAP, XMPP, HTTP	HTTP, MQTT	REST API, WebSockets, MQTT	AMQP, Stomp, MQTT, WebSocket	MQTT, CoAP, HTTP, WebSocket
Encryption	RSA, AES, SSL	Basic Authentication	JWT	SSL, Spring Security	Basic Authentication
GUI/Dash Board	✓	✓	✓	✓	✓
Database	MogoDB, Casandra, Hadoop, NoSQL	MySQL	PogreSQL, SAP Hana	MongoDB, HBase, InfluxDB	MySQL
Data analytics	Apache Cassandra, Apache Zappelin	Apache Spark, Apache Flink	Apache Spark	Apache Spark	Apache Spark
Language	C, C++ Java	C, C++ Java, Python	Java script	C++	node.js
Integration	Rest APIs	Rest APIs	Rest APIs MQTT APIs	Rest APIs Any point, and more	Rest APIs

4   Challenges of Open Source Based IIoT Platforms

So far, we analyze and research of the IIoT platform concepts, and application method with practical guide. Also, we compare five open source IoT perform through reference architecture for actual site application. Based on the above research, this section presents IIoT platform use case and analyzes its effects.

4.1   Right Choosing of IIoT Platform for Smart Factory

The first priority is to select suppliers who provide all three previously described IoT functions (application execution, data aggregation and storage and connection management). It is important that these elements are placed in place and fully integrated. When a company purchases or applies a platform that does not have one or more of these layers, it creates unnecessary complexity and costs because the platform must be imported from another layer. Adjacent functions, such as analysis and machine learning, are also becoming increasingly important in realizing the value of IoT. Second, the extent to which the platform is coordinated with the developer's technology should be reviewed. Businesses should ensure that the core IoT platform complies with the technology of the development team and keep in mind that implementation work is required even if it is a comprehensive platform product. The IoT platform may need to be proficient in certain programming languages. If a developer is a professional Java programmer but needs to use Python in a new IoT platform, difference in technologies will slow down and implementation will be delayed. Finally, openness and ease of integration should be considered. Businesses should choose IoT platforms that meet business requirements and allow distribution while minimizing impact on current systems. Purchaser should first consider whether IoT platform features openness and ease of integration. It is also important to see whether IoT platforms can converge properly between open frameworks (open source). An open framework is modularized using easy to use APIs, and is easily integrated and fits seamlessly into existing IT architectures. This is particularly important for companies with enterprise service buses or complex event handling architectures. This is because a link with the IT environment in the field can seamlessly integrate the new framework with existing systems. In particular, companies should look for vendors that provide a comprehensive platform that meets risks and business models for the IoT. And the platform provider must have a clear understanding of how it differs from its competitors.

4.2   Design of Open Source Based IIoT Platform for Smart Factory

Smart factory is to implement a manufacturing system consisting of intelligent autonomous systems that respond immediately to productivity, efficiency, energy savings, increase in efficiency and energy. Data communication between the process systems and interworking with the higher systems are essential. To this end, the OPC Foundation standardizes OPC UA, an industrial protocol for data integration, and implements standard extensions for realtime data communication and security (Fig. 8).

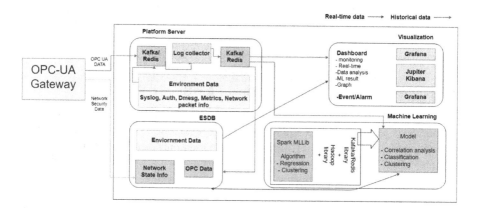

Fig. 8. Open source based IIoT platform for smart factory

Figure 7 describes the Industrial IoT platform architecture proposed in this paper, which shows the overall flow from the edge mentioned in the section above to the platform server and to the area of service where final machine learning techniques are utilized and visualized. It supports a standard protocol (OPC UA) for communication with various industrial equipment operating independently and on a limited basis at industrial sites, and supports real time event storage and streaming at the same time. In addition to PLC, it provides flexible data pipelines for communication with IoT devices such as embedded devices and schema sensors, and has various database interlocking functions for data exchange and storage with external systems. It also supports the analysis of forecast through big data and machine learning and the visualization of real time day sites and analysis data such as tea trees, graphs, tables, and reactive SVG animations, enabling easy implementation of factory specific smart factory in a short period of time. As shown here, the essential part is to integrate data collected from the IIoT platform, process and analyze meaningful information from the data, and provide services that can be used by operators and managers in decision making [17].

4.3   Use Case and Implementation of IIoT Platform

With the introduction of smart factory into manufacturing processes, the optimal manufacturing process can be derived to suit the environment of each demand manufacturing company through the editor of the existing manufacturing process that is difficult to change organically. In addition, it provides sample processes for each type of manufacturer for smart factory learning and supports hands on practices for understanding processes and optimizing process design. By creating these OPC UA training kits, workers at industrial sites help integrate protocols and use control through Opc UA. In addition, it can help understand the flow of data and eventually create OPC UA Gateway for Industrial IoT Platforms [18]. The detailed functions are as follows (Fig. 9).

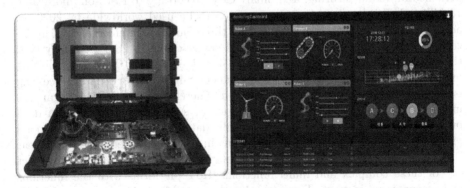

Fig. 9. Use case and implementation of IIoT platform

- Modeling through OPC UA protocol.
- It Reflects into real time address space after modeling
- GUI makes modeling easy and simple.
- Automatically correct references for easy modeling editing.
- XML extraction allows manual insertion of any OPC server.
- It can be modeled by drag and drop without the need to remodel nodes already registered in the address space.

OPC UA has limitations in systems that require quick response or systems that require high-speed control. High-speed data communication is supported, but we cannot guarantee high-speed responsiveness. TimeSensitive Network (TSN) has emerged as an alternative to the high speed control limits of OPC UA. TSN is a feature set that is added to standard Ethernet to support applications that require deterministic characteristics for data transmission of data. It is similar to real-time communication by reserving traffic lanes for communication packets to eliminate latency for critical data. TSN, which is an extension standard for Ethernet, is under the leadership of CISCO. In addition, in older plants that do not support OPC UA, separate devices that support OPC UA should be additionally installed to work with existing facilities. However, despite the restrictions, 450 companies worldwide are working with OPC Foundation, among them with industrial protocol companies related to smart factory, and standardization is underway. Smart Factory is sometimes called a data factory. This means that the acquisition and integration of data are the most important features in smart factory construction. Applications are being carried out in various research and industries and are challenging in smart manufacturing as well as smooth construction of IIoT platform.

5   Conclusion

IoT shows huge potential that can affect many industries such as automotive, agricultural, manufacturing, and Smart City. According to Ericsson, more than 18 billion IoT related devices are expected to be used worldwide by 2022. In addition, device growth is accelerated by three factors: the emergence of applications for IoT, new business models, and device costs [19]. Smart factory is at the center of the rapid increase in the use of IoT equipment. When establishing industrial IoT platform in order to implement Smart Factory, data processing is the most difficult part for those involved. Therefore, many IoT platforms are making a lot of investments and strategies to secure technical skills in data processing. In terms of the IIoT platform, data processing is involved in all processes with a heart like role, and it has huge competitive edge if it is clear that data processing is done with IoT platform. It is very difficult to select one of these complex and multi functional IIoT platforms with the functions and resources users want. Thus, to solve these problems, the structure of each open source IIoT platform was replaced by a reference architecture. This effect helps people quickly understand structure through communication and data flow between each element. Section 3 research major functions of using IoT platform and presents the necessary guide from the user's perspective. Based on all of the above, Sect. 4 introduced five open source structures, which are widely used in the field, based on Fig. 1, and researched various features. And then, Table 1, which features five open source IIoT platforms, will be of great help to IoT developers and entrepreneurs who wish to apply them. Finally, we presents Industrial IoT platform Architecture that is proposed and explains that data flow, integration, information processing and service are implemented from edge area to IIoT platform to service area that becomes visualization. Through this paper, users of the IIoT platform, IT developers and researcher can get help when choosing the appropriate IIoT platform and broaden their understanding of the IIoT platform. In the following research, it is possible to implement services and evaluate performance by utilizing two or more open source platforms that are appropriate for the IIoT platform presented above.

Acknowledgement. This research was supported by the MSIT (Ministry of Science and ICT), Korea, under the ITRC (Information Technology Research Center) support program (IITP-2019-2018-0-01417) supervised by the IITP (Institute for Information & communications Technology Promotion).

This research was supported by Basic Science Research Program through the National Research Foundation of Korea (NRF) funded by the Ministry of Education (NRF-2016R1D1A1B03933828).

This work has supported by the Gyeonggi Techno Park grant funded by the Gyeonggi-Do government (No. Y181802).

References

1. Chen, B., et al.: Smart factory of industry 4.0: key technologies, application case, and challenges. IEEE Access **3**(6), 6505–6519 (2017)
2. Atzori, L., et al.: The internet of things: a survey. Comput. Netw. **54**, 2787–2805 (2010)
3. Top 49 tools internet of things. https://www.profitbricks.com/. Accessed 4 May 2019
4. Savaglio, C., Fortino, G.: Autonomic and cognitive architectures for the internet of things. In: Di Fatta, G., Fortino, G., Li, W., Pathan, M., Stahl, F., Guerrieri, A. (eds.) IDCS 2015. LNCS, vol. 9258, pp. 39–47. Springer, Cham (2015). https://doi.org/10.1007/978-3-319-23237-9_5
5. Abdur Razzaque, M., et al.: Middleware for internet of things: a survey. IEEE Internet Things J. **3**(1), 70–95 (2016)
6. Kim, J., et al.: M2M service platforms: survey, issues, and enabling technologies. IEEE Commun. Surv. Tutorials **16**(1), 61–76 (2013)
7. Ngu, A., et al.: IoT middleware: a survey on issues and enabling technologies. IEEE Internet Things J. **3**(4), 1–20 (2017)
8. Cruz, D., et al.: A reference model for internet of things middleware. IEEE Internet Things J. **5**(2), 871–883 (2018)
9. Singh, M., et al.: Secure MQTT for internet of things. In: Tomar, G. (ed.) 5th International Conference on Communication Systems and Network Technologies, pp. 746–751. IEEE, Gwalior (2015). https://doi.org/10.1109/CSNT.2015.16

10. Zhu, Q., et al.: IoT gateway: bridging wireless sensor networks into Internet of things. In: IEEE/IFIP International Conference on Embedded and Ubiquitous Computing, pp. 347–352. IEEE, Hong kong (2010). https://doi.org/10.1109/EUC.2010.58

11. Mobius Architecture. http://developers.iotocean.org/archives/module/mobius. Accessed 4 May 2019

12. Key Capability of the Kaa IoT platform. https://www.kaaproject.org/platform/. Accessed 4 May 2019

13. Kaa Architecture. https://kaaproject.github.io/kaa/docs/v0.10.0/Architecture-overview/. Accessed 4 May 2019

14. Sitewhere Architecture. https://github.com/sitewhere/sitewhere. Accessed 4 May 2019

15. DeviceHive Architecture. https://devicehive.com/. Accessed 4 May 2019

16. Fiware Architecture. https://www.fiware.org/. Accessed 4 May 2019

17. Um, C., et al.: Industrial device monitoring and control system based on oneM2M for edge computing. In: Pal, N.R. (ed.) 2018 IEEE Symposium Series on Computational Intelligence, pp. 1528–1533. IEEE, Bangalore (2018). https://doi.org/10.1109/SSCI.2018.8628736

18. Cho, H., et al.: Implementation and performance analysis of power and cost-reduced OPC UA gateway for industrial IoT platforms. In: 2018 28th International Telecommunication Networks and Applications Conference (ITNAC), pp. 1–3. IEEE, Sydney (2018). https://doi.org/10.1109/atnac.2018.8615377

19. Ericsson, A.B.: The Internet of Things forecast. https://www.ericsson.com/en/mobilityreport/internet-of-things-forecast/. Accessed 15 Mar 2019

Container-Based Multi-purpose IoT Architecture for User-Friendly Applications with Cloud Chatbot Agent

Jaehyeong Lee, Changyong Um, Soonsung Hwang, and Jongpil Jeong[✉]

Department of Smart Factory Convergence,
Sungkyunkwan University, Suwon, Gyeonggi-do 16419, Republic of Korea
{objective,e7217,suns303,jpjeong}@skku.edu

Abstract. IoT is a new era technology that can be used by end users because of its functionality and necessity. Most of IoT devices are aimed at versatile smart devices, and these features need to be conveniently provided to users, such as for use in mobile. In addition, these devices must be able to tailor various functions and purposes to the needs of the user. Currently, open source platform provides flexibility in perspective of the developers in order to enable multi-purpose as a single device in terms of requirements for end users. However, this flexibility should be reconsidered from the end users, too. In this paper, we propose the cloud based multi-purpose IoT and provide convenience to the end user through the chatbot agent for end user friendliness. In addition, container technology is applied for versatility and flexibility of devices. These researches can be useful in multi-purpose robot pendants, protocol conversion genders in factory area, and motor boxes that can convert gears in smart toys situations where change flexibility and affinity are required according to the request of users.

Keywords: Internet of Things · User-Friendly Applications ·
Chatbot agent · Docker

1 Introduction

IoT is creating a new digital age as a mega-trend. IoT, which is different from existing web technology, has new value by connecting objects and interacting and interacting with the Internet [1,2]. In the IoT environment, the intelligent 'Things' have the purpose of being able to clearly recognize the state of the surroundings by continuously providing their own state, making it easy to make the decision making [2]. IoT is not just a field, it is changing the whole daily life and it is being applied and developed all over the industry. According to the Gartner report and Cisco's announcement, more than 2 billion connected products and over 50 billion smart objects are expected to emerge by 2020, and this is realizing [3].

© Springer Nature Switzerland AG 2019
S. Misra et al. (Eds.): ICCSA 2019, LNCS 11624, pp. 121–134, 2019.
https://doi.org/10.1007/978-3-030-24311-1_9

For using IoT more clearly, it is necessary to study about user-friendly human to machine interface (HMI) [4]. Historically, the most effective HMI is smart phone. Most modern people have a smart phone and this personalized end device, is being used to connect people and people. For human-to-human communication, voice transmission, e-mail, and instance message service applications are commonly used, which can be a good model for IoT. According to this necessity, in the IoT environment, it has been developed to use chatbot of instance message application [5]. The chatbots in the IoT environment are similar to the agent concept. Agent generally means "self-contained, interactive, and simultaneously running object" that has internal state and communication functions [6].

Docker, a Linux-based container technology, has a platform for both distributors and developers, making it easy to deploy and develop. In addition, it is possible to execute an application in an environment independent manner, and it is possible that these applications do not influence each other [7].

As mentioned above, chatbot can perform enough role as an agent for end users in IoT environment, and it is possible to customize IoT affinity through them. Also, using Docker as a the container technology, one device can be used for multi purpose according to the needs of the end user. Therefore, the use category of chatbot for multi-purpose device in IoT environment can be broadened when using Docker, and the affinity of platform can be improved. For example, robot control pendants commonly used in smart factories are all provided as dedicated controllers for the robot itself. However, the IoT environment can present a model through a multi-purpose IoT, such as a single stand-alone model and connecting through an application in it.

User-friendliness in software and architecture is very important. User friendliness is a broad representation of a user's experience and can be measured in terms of usability in terms of software and architecture. This is a key indicator of how easy it is for users to use the software and adapt to the user's various requirements. The existing models for usability measurements are represented by the Nelson model and the ISO 9261 model, which is sufficient to evaluate the architecture and software quality. Therefore, we can discuss the user-friendly application of Cloud based IoT.

In this paper, we propose a new method to improve the end user affinity of cloud based multi-purpose IoT by combining chatbot and container technology. This paper has contributed by convergence of parts and presenting a new type of architecture and device. Also, by evaluating each model as user friendliness, we express the advantage of this system.

This paper is configured as follows: In Sect. 2, we discuss the multi-purpose IoT, chatbot, Docker, and model for evaluating user-friendliness. In Sect. 3, we combine the Docker and chatbot agent for cloud based multi-purpose IoT and describe the overall architecture. In Sect. 4, we evaluate this architecture through a model for implementing the entire system and evaluating user-friendliness. In Sect. 5, we discuss the contribution of this paper and future research.

2   Related Work

2.1   Cloud Based Multi-purpose IoT

IoT is a global infrastructure for the information society, providing improved services by interconnecting things based on existing evolving, interoperable information and communication technologies (ICT) [8]. The environment with numerous devices and information objects is connected through the network. The vision of IoT is a smart environment that is all connected by smart devices. Using IoT, you can seamlessly integrate physical objects with Internet-like systems, allowing you to interact with physical objects and connect to cyber agents to achieve mission-critical goals [9,10].

Cloud computing is a computing paradigm that provides users with an on demand ICT infrastructure. This includes servers and networks where users can access information, which can be connected anytime and anywhere at the request of the user. This model eliminates the need to physically store and process data in the same space by providing the virtual space in which data of user is stored and processed [11,12].

Cloud-based IoT is a model that improves the efficiency of work by solving tasks that require complex computation or high computing power in the cloud in order to solve resource constraints of devices that can generally perform limited computing. Cloud-based multi-purpose IoT performs data storage and processing in the virtual space of the cloud. In addition, it can sensitively respond to user requests and actively change its functionality within limited device resources. Therefore, user friendliness and agility to changes become essential requirements.

2.2   Chatbot Agent

Chatbot is also called messenger bot because it is based on text messages that user and bot exchange in the chat space. The user enters a text message in the virtual space, and the software analyzes the message, creates an appropriate response, and sends the message back to the user. Therefore, the user can communicate with the soft-agent-bot through the interaction with the soft-agent-bot and confirm that the soft-agent-bot has performed the correct operation. In general, chatbot is a system that send corresponding messages according to the rules that are already defined as needed. In the early developed version, a method of confirming simple matching of keywords and returning a value has been performed. However, due to recent developments of various technologies, a natural language entered by a user is grasped and analyzed to define requirements. Chatbot can perform the requirements and respond to the results [13].

The function of such a chatbot means that the chatbot can operate as an agent as mentioned above. Agent is an abstract object in terms of software engineering, and has the same domain as methods, functions, and modules, but differs in that it performs autonomous operations instead of simple functions [6,14]. The chatbot agent will have the key technologies listed in Table 1.

Table 1. Chatbot agent technology.

Function	Description
Natural Language Processing	Ability to recognize and process human language Features such as search, query, and translation
Semantic Response	Responsive technique that can perform logical estimation and action using recognized meanings
Text Mining	Ability to acquire new data from unstructured text data
Context-aware Computing	Technology that provides user-centered intelligent service that informs current situation

2.3   Docker: Linux Light-Weight Container

Light-weight virtualization technology can reduce the amount of computing resources required to run guest OS compared to virtual machine (VM). During the past hour, server virtualization and isolation have been implemented using hypervisor-based virtualization technology in general [15]. Customize virtual hardware and virtual applications to create a virtual machine that is independent of the underlying host. The operating system is installed and works on each VM instance. Container virtualization is different from other virtualization technologies in terms of virtualization and quarantine, but it can be implemented functionally close. This can be considered a viable alternative to hypervisor-based virtualization [16].

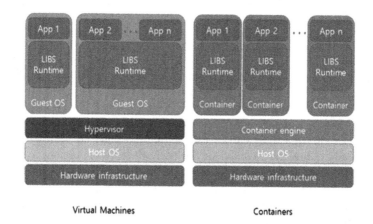

Fig. 1. Virtual machine and container.

Figure 1 shows the types of virtual machines and container-based structures. Unlike hypervisor-based virtual machines, container-based virtualization implements processes through container engines. OS-level process isolation does not require hardware and driver virtualization [16]. In particular, containers share the same OS kernel as the underlying host system and provide independent characteristics of the virtual network interface, process space, and file system. These shared kernel features enable containers to reduce image volume and enable more efficient virtualization systems.

It is the Docker platform that makes container concepts more widely used. Docker leverages the underlying container for engines and provides the ability to efficiently create, run, manage and remove containerized applications. A Docker container is created based on a base image stored in a particular private or public registry. The Docker can add a read/write layer on top of the image and store the image in a hierarchical form. Also, Docker has a fast implementation process. Lightweight properties of containers can be utilized in various networking areas. For example, an under-processing device, such as a single-board computer, can efficiently run container-based applications based on container images associated with IoT edge computing. Virtualization technologies such as VMs, containers, and Unicorns have been actively studied as an important element of the architecture for implementing IoT services [17,18].

2.4   User-Friendliness: Usability Model

User friendliness is a factor that can express the user's experience and can be measured by usability. Usability is a conceptual indicator to confirm convenience, ease in using software products. Since software has begun to be used, this factor has been valued as a very important value. In this area, Nelson model and ISO model are mainly used [19]. Software in the Nielsen model has been studied as an attribute that influences software acceptability as a single product. He has divided this acceptability into practical or social acceptance and has come up with an assessment of usability through the provision of five sub-attributes: learnability, efficiency, memorability, errors, and satisfaction. Another model that is often used is the ISO 9216 model(2001). The International Standardization

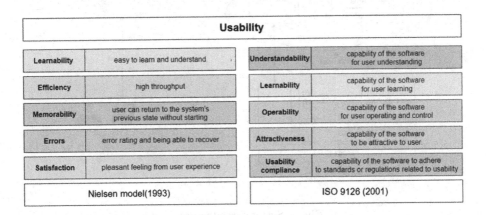

Fig. 2. Usability models.

Organization defined sub-attributes of usability as understandability, learnability, operability, attractiveness, usability compliance. The definitions of these two models are shown in the following Fig. 2.

3   Container-Based Multi-purpose IoT Architecture for User-Friendly Applications

We propose a user-friendly application for multi-purpose IoT, which is the main aim of this paper. To this section, we propose a new system architecture, demonstrate the user-friendliness, agility, and flexibility that this model can have by experimenting with connecting Docker and Telegram chatbot to actual IoT.

3.1   System Architecture

Figure 3 shows the architecture for rapidly changing the multi-purpose IoT according to the user's request while using the user-friendly chatbot. Multi-purpose IoT has a lot of applications that are being held for versatility. Also, it has contained client to connect with cloud and to operate Docker agent. The client will connect to the chatbot server by connecting to the Internet after confirming the network at the first operation. You can also launch and delete the contained application in the future and download the Docker image from the cloud. In the cloud area, a chatbot server exists to provide virtual space to connect with IoT and Telegram users. Through this, an authentication function for mutual authentication and a database function for storing data generated

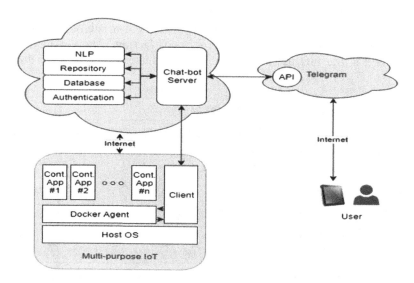

Fig. 3. System architecture.

in IoT and telegram should be provided. In addition, you should have a repository for linking Docker application images and a Natural Language Processing (NLP) processor that can process your language from Telegram messenger. The user can instruct the work through the process of transmitting text data to the chatbot through the telegram app. The job can be provided with a report on the current status of the device, the current status of the current Docker images, and the number of current Docker images. You can also interrupt the execution of the image of the locker to change the state of the device or command the download of the Docker image to run a new image of the Docker.

3.2   Application of Chatbot Agent

The chatbot agent uses the data received from the Telegram API and the data received from the IoT device to determine the state of the device. Assuming all available apps are Docker images, you can run the device by running this Docker image at your request. Under this assumption, the user can request the following requirements from the device.

- User requests authentication to use IoT device
  The user enters the serial number of device into the chatbot to register IoT device. If the device has been previously registered via the Internet, the user is granted the privilege through the serial number inquiry. In the telegram, since the user is identified with the telephone number, compliance status of the user is already secured. Therefore, there is no need for a different security for using IoT, and if possible, the IoT device and the user smart phone can be mutually authenticated through a device serial number and phone number exchange process at a short distance
- User inquires current device status and application behavior and status
  The user sends a status inquiry message to the chatbot through the Telegram. The chatbot agent processes the message in a natural language through the NLP and recognizes the request of user based on the message. The chatbot agent transmits the current device status inquiry to the client that has finally transmitted the data according to the request of the proper user registered, and the client transmits the status data to the client. The status data should include not only the status of the device but also whether or not the application is operating, whether it is present or not, and whether it operates normally. The chatbot agent transmits the inquired data through the Telegram API so that the user can check the status of the device and the operation of the application.
- The user can inquire the application which can be installed on the device or already installed, and download new one
  User can use the Telegram, server, NLP as mentioned above to query the currently possible installing and already installed applications. The chatbot agent introduces the application that exists in the repository (in Docker registry) based on the message, and inquires and delivers the installed app based on the data received from the client. If user want to install a new Docker

image according to the request, the chatbot server will send the address of the repository to the client and IoT will download the Docker image from the repository via the connected Internet.

- User want to delete, disable, and launch other apps
  If you want to delete the already installed Docker image according to the user's request, the chatbot server requests the client to stop and delete the image. This makes it easy to delete apps that users have already installed. Also, since it is already contained image, it has no effect on other operations of IoT. If the user is asked to stop the running app and run another app, the chatbot agent will also send the request to the client and run it.

4 Experimental Results

4.1 Experimental Environment and Method

We can see this by connecting the client applied to IoT and the chatbot agent in the public cloud area. In this experiment, NLP was excluded for the simplicity of the experiment. Raspberry pi 3B+ was used as an end device. Chatbot server was implemented in Ubuntu 18.04 LTS version, which is a laptop VM instance. In this experiment, we proposed an IoT device as a temperature and humidity gauging unit and used AM2315 sensor. The entire process of using the Docker and chatbot was very flexible and efficient because it used the existing open-source platform. In order to perform the operation of chatbot agent mentioned above, operation options of chatbot are specified as shown in the following Table 2.

Table 2. Chatbot command.

Command	Description
/status	Report current operation status of Docker image, existence of image and status of device
/run d-img 'name'	Docker image with name will be executed
/stop d-img 'name'	Docker image with name will be stopped
/delete d-img 'name'	Docker image with name will be deleted

Raspberry Pi, an end device for operation, has also prepared the following Docker image to assume that various modules can be combined. In order for the Docker image to be executed, the Docker image is configured so that a run Docker agent is executed through the client and at the same time a specific file of the image is started. The configured Docker image is shown in Table 3.

The experimental procedure is as follows. Step 1. Docker image does not exist and current status inquiry, Step 2. After Img I download, executing Img I automatically, Step 3. Current status inquiry again, Step 4. Delete downloaded Img I, Step 5. After downloading Img II, executing Img II, and step 6. Stop Img II

Table 3. Docker images.

Image name	Description
Img I	Temperature measurement
Img II	Humidity measurement

When Step 1 is executed, we can see through the Telegram API that the server receives the message sent by the user and reports the current application status of IoT. The IoT client inquires its status according to the request of the server and transmits its status to the server again. Figure 4a and b show IoT status and return data in Telegram.

(b) Step 1 in IoT

(a) Step 1 in Telegram

Fig. 4. Experimental Step 1.

When Step 2 is executed, the IoT client was asked to run a specific image but did not have the image. Therefore, the IoT client automatically downloads and runs an image that it holds in the cloud repository. This automatic action is one of the main functions of the proposed system and the chatbot agent and shows that the end user can conveniently use it without any new connection or control of the developer. Figure 5a and b show the results.

Due to the result of Step 2 of the experiment, the 'Img1' Docker image was present in the IoT, and it was verified through the Telegram with Step 3. Figure 6a show these results. Also, by allowing the image to be deleted through the Telegram, the management of the IoT application with Step 4 was able to confirm the user friendliness through the Figs. 6b and 7a.

By performing the tests in Step 5 and Step 6, we can confirm that the process can be held in a halt state and that the application can be run again. Everything was done through Telegram and cloud-based IoT systems without downloading

(b) Step 2 in IoT

(a) Step 2 in Telegram

Fig. 5. Experimental Step 2.

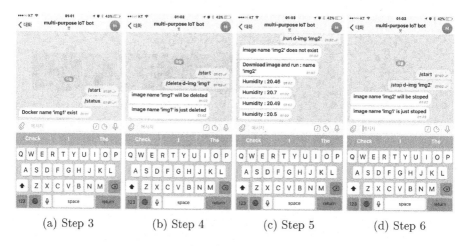

(a) Step 3   (b) Step 4   (c) Step 5   (d) Step 6

Fig. 6. Experimental Step 3, 4, 5 and 6 in Telegram.

new mobile applications. Figures 6c and 7b show the results of Step 5, while Figs. 6d and 7c show the results of Step 6.

Through these experimental results, we were able to guarantee a user friendly connection between the server and the IoT client that handles the message through the Telegram API. In addition, this method is possible to secure the multi-purpose IoT by running and downloading the image of the Docker and controlling the installed application.

(a) Step 4

(b) Step 5

(c) Step 6

Fig. 7. Experimental Step 4, 5 and 6 in IoT.

4.2 Evaluation of User-Friendliness

As already mentioned in Sect. 2.4, the model that evaluates the usability of the software generally use the Nelson model and the ISO model. We can evaluate the quality of the architecture by comparing the cases using the proposed architecture, using only the chatbot, and using only the Docker.

Evaluating the case that only the chatbot is used by the Nelson model and ISO increases the ease of handling by user and efficiency of the application of the IoT device through the chatbot and IoT server. However, if the application is downloaded through the server, It will be downloaded directly to the main OS system. There is a disadvantage in that it is fundamentally overlapping with other applications and can lead to errors. This exists as a factor that decreases the error in the Nelson model and the usability compliance in the ISO model. In addition, it is difficult to retrieve the state of the library already installed, and it is difficult to delete the libraries.

When evaluating the case where only the Docker is used, the user must meet the unfamiliar application user interface (UI) or without the UI like developers. In addition, there is a disadvantage in understanding or using it because it is inconvenient for recognizing the user's natural language.

When evaluating the use of a chatbot with Docker, ordinary users can control their own devices through familiar and familiar UI screens that they use every day, have. Moreover, the method of recognizing natural language through chatbot as well as the way through UI is progressing continuously. Also, even if you delete the program you are using, it does not affect the main OS because it is already containerized per application. In case of an error, it is easy to modify the Docker image, so there is ease of use and error management.

The overall evaluation of these assessments can be shown in the following three graphs through the Fig. 8.

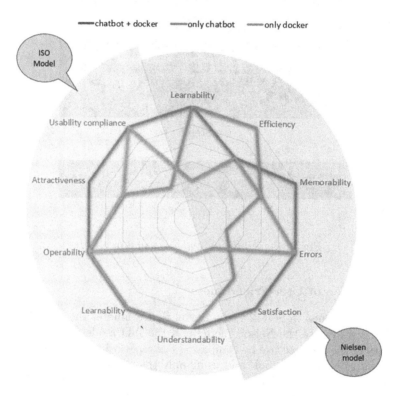

Fig. 8. Evaluation of User-friendliness.

5   Conclusion

In summary, this research is shown that it is possible to use a Docker image to control a multi-purpose device from a conventional research that controls a cloud based IoT through a message using a chatbot, and it is possible to change the device purpose according to a user request. We also confirmed that this whole process has a user friendness that developers do not need. Using these solutions, universal pendants for in-plant industrial robots can be produced independently for multiple vendors and can be used for protocol conversion genders that need to be changed according to the situation. Future research will focus on user-friendly industrial platforms or user-friendly robot pendant using large-capacity text natural language processing using 5G.

Acknowledgment. This work has supported by the Gyeonggi Techno Park grant funded by the Gyeonggi-Do government (No. Y181802). This research was supported by the MSIT (Ministry of Science and ICT), Korea, under the ITRC (Information Technology Research Center) support program (IITP-2019-2018-0-01417) supervised by the IITP (Institute for Information & communications Technology Promotion).

References

1. Gubbi, J., Buyya, R., Marusic, S., Palaniswami, M.: Internet of Things (IoT): a vision, architectural elements, and future directions. Future Gen. Comput. Syst. **29**(7), 1645–1660 (2013)
2. Evans, D.: The Internet of Things How the Next Evolution of the Internet is Changing Everything. Cisco Internet Business Solutions Group (IBSG), pp. 346–360 (2011)
3. van der Meulen, R.: Gartner Says 6.4 Billion Connected 'Things' Will Be in Use in 2016, Up 30 Percent From 2015. Stamford, Connecticut (2016)
4. Ungurean, I., Gaitan, N.C., Gaitan, V.G.: An IoT architecture for things from industrial environment. In: 2014 10th International Conference on Communications (COMM), pp. 1–4 (2014)
5. Kar, R., Haldar, R.: Applying chatbots to the internet of things: opportunities and architectural elements. Int. J. Adv. Comput. Sci. Appl. **7**(11), 147–154 (2016)
6. Nwana, H.S.: Software agents: an overview. Knowl. Eng. Rev. **11**(3), 205–244 (1996)
7. Merkel, D.: Docker: lightweight Linux containers for consistent development and deployment. Linux J. **239**, 2 (2014)
8. Bandyopadhyay, D., Sen, J.: Internet of things: applications and challenges in technology and standardization. Wirel. Pers. Commun. **58**(1), 49–69 (2011)
9. Stankovic, J.A.: Research directions for the internet of things. IEEE Internet Things J. **1**(1), 3–7 (2014)
10. Santucci, G.: Internet of the future and internet of things: what is at stake and how are we getting prepared for them. In: eMatch Conference, Oslo (2009)
11. Rimal, B.P., Choi, E., Lumb, I.: A taxonomy and survey of cloud computing systems. In: 5th International Joint Conference on INC, IMS, and IDC, NCM 2009, pp. 44–51 (2009)
12. Duan, Y., Fu, G., Zhou, N., Sun, X., Narendra, N.C., Hu, B.: Everything as a service (XaaS) on the cloud: origins, current and future trends. In: 2015 IEEE 8th International Conference on Cloud Computing (CLOUD), pp. 621–628 (2015)
13. Noguera-Arnaldos, J.Á., Paredes-Valverde, M.A., Salas-Zárate, M.P., Rodríguez-García, M.Á., Valencia-García, R., Ochoa, J.L.: im4Things: an ontology-based natural language interface for controlling devices in the Internet of Things. In: Alor-Hernández, G., Valencia-García, R. (eds.) Current Trends on Knowledge-Based Systems, vol. 120, pp. 3–22. Springer, Cham (2017). https://doi.org/10.1007/978-3-319-51905-0_1

14. Huang, J., Zhou, M., Yang, D.: Extracting chatbot knowledge from online discussion forums. In: IJCAI, vol. 7, pp. 423–428 (2007)
15. Desai, A., Oza, R., Sharma, P., Patel, B.: Hypervisor: a survey on concepts and taxonomy. Int. J. Innov. Technol. Exploring Eng. 2(3), 222–225 (2013)
16. Morabito, R., Kjällman, J., Komu, M.: Hypervisors vs. lightweight virtualization: a performance comparison. In: 2015 IEEE International Conference on Cloud Engineering (IC2E), pp. 386–393 (2015)
17. Celesti, A., Mulfari, D., Fazio, M., Villari, M., Puliafito, A.: Exploring container virtualization in IoT clouds. In: 2016 IEEE International Conference on Smart Computing (SMARTCOMP), pp. 1–6 (2016)
18. Bernstein, D.: Containers and cloud: from LXC to docker to kubernetes. IEEE Cloud Comput. 3, 81–84 (2014)
19. Madan, A., Dubey, S.K.: Usability evaluation methods: a literature review. Int. J. Eng. Sci. Technol. 4(2), 590–599 (2012)

Is a Smart City Really Smart? (Smart Cities 2019)

Smart Islands: A Systematic Review on Urban Policies and Smart Governance

Giulia Desogus, Pasquale Mistretta, and Chiara Garau[✉]

DICAAR – Department of Civil and Environmental Engineering
and Architecture, University of Cagliari, Cagliari, Italy
{g.desogus, p.mistretta, cgarau}@unica.it

Abstract. The purpose of the article is to identify a key analysis able to combine smart governance with urban and place-based dynamics in island contexts. To this end, authors schematize types, classifications, levels of smart performance and also the most common issues and resolutions in island contexts, starting from a systematic review of the terminology studied in the last 11 years. This literature review proposes a systematic approach by analyzing the most well-known databases in scientific research (Google Scholar, Scopus and Science Direct) in order to catalog and systematize the most optimal methodologies and approaches in the study of island contexts. This article shows a first phase of a broader research, and it provides a bibliographic basis to understand how the Smart paradigm can change the normal management perspective of the island territory.

Keywords: Smart island · Systematic literature review ·
Smart Island definitions · Smart Cities

1 Introduction

Although today the attention to smart island is growing [1–4], the features of island territories need a deepening in urban planning and place-based governance field. Starting from the analysis of smart island definitions, this article wants to understand how urban policy and smart governance are applied and studied in the island territories, in order to find useful guidelines for the definition of optimal standards for the development of the same island contexts. This need emerged because during this study, authors found difficult to find a single definition of the term smart island. In addition, *"the island regions suffer from structural handicaps linked to their island status, the permanence of which impairs their economic and social development"* [5:136]. However, it must be underlined that, although the literature has not yet defined a common criterion for the analysis of a smart island, the European Union has introduced

---

This paper is the result of the joint work of the authors. In particular, Sects. 2, 3, and 4 have been jointly written by Giulia Desogus and Chiara Garau. Giulia Desogus has written Sect. 1. Chiara Garau has written Sect. 5 and revised the whole paper and checked for its comprehensive consistency. Pasquale Mistretta supervised the article.

S. Misra et al. (Eds.): ICCSA 2019, LNCS 11624, pp. 137–151, 2019.
https://doi.org/10.1007/978-3-030-24311-1_10

in the EU legislation two fundamental indications reserved to the island regions, as highlighted by Garau and Desogus in a recent article [6]. They are:

[a] the "Declaration on Island Regions" annexed to the Treaty of Amsterdam of 1997 [5], in which the structural disadvantages of island contexts are recognized and the application of specific measures are encouraged to further integrate them into the internal market with fair conditions; [b] "Guidelines for integrated actions on the island regions of the European Union" published in 2002 [5], in which the structural indications to undertake an evaluation of the policies to be implemented are highlighted and some characteristics of the structural problems, common to the island regions, are listed.

With these premises, the paper is organized as follows: Sect. 2 reviews the scientific literature on the definition of smart island. Section 3 combined these concepts in order to define a unique main topic on this field. In Sect. 4, the aggregation of all concepts founded, defined in the previous sections, is aggregated for identifying which are the terms that can connect the smart island field to urban policies and smart governance. Finally, the paper concludes by analyzing the obtained results.

2 The Attempt to Frame the Smart Island Definitions

In the light of the emerged information, Table 1 shows a schematic framework of the different definitions of smart island, existing in the scientific community.

The comparison of the different definitions (Table 1) led the authors to define a smart island as a place in which the peculiarities of insularity are valued through the good practices to preserve the sustainable development, with the aim of creating sustainable local economic development and high quality of life, mitigating the negative effects of insularity through the use of information and communications technology (ICT). In other words, a smart island develops the entire territory through the management of infrastructures, the natural resources and the culture heritage; the climate change mitigation and adaptation efforts; finally, the enhancement of tourism and coastal-marine resources that represent the main source of income.

In addition, this comparison allows to find not only the key words best suited to the concept of smart island, but also common issues and solutions. Table 2 shows the outcome of the research and a first schematization of the main components that characterize the most widely used terminology associated with the smart islands concept. They are: "Sustainability Island", "Insular Territories", "Smartness and Island", "Smart City and Insular", "Island Urban Planning", "ICT Island", "E-government Island". From the comparative analysis of the definitions (Table 2) three fundamental points emerge:

[a] although there are several projects under the smart island paradigm, a standardized definition - that describes its relationship with urban policies and governance - does not yet exist;

[b] the six dimensions typical of the smart city (economy, mobility, governance, environment, living and society) are respected and used. However, new questions are imagined in order to implement the six pillars with issues closely related to insularity (for example, coastal and marine resources, tourism);

Table 1. Definitions of smart island

Author	Definition
(2013) SMILEGOV Project Multi-level Governance [7]	"An insular area […] creates sustainable local economic development and high quality of life by excelling in multiple key areas of sustainability" [7]
(2015) Opinion of the European Economic and Social Committee [8] TEN/558 Smart Island [9]	"With the term « smart islands » , the EESC is specifically referring to an insular area that creates sustainable local economic development and a high quality of life by excelling in multiple key areas of sustainability" [8:3] [9:3]
(2015) EE-Spanish government project [10]	"The objective is to finance initiatives that integrate smart island strategies, contribute to the improvement of public services in the territory, and are aimed at mitigating the negative effects of insularity through the use of information and communications technology (ITC)". [11]
(2016) Smart islands projects and strategies [12]	"The definition of an island as smart relates to its ability to implement integrated solutions to the management of infrastructures and natural resources, namely energy, transport and mobility, waste and water, all while promoting the use of innovative and socially inclusive governance and financing scheme" [12:11]
(2016) Smart islands declaration [13] Smart island initiative [14]	"Define a smart island as an insular territory that embarks on a climate resilient pathway, combining climate change mitigation and adaptation efforts, in order to create sustainable local economic development and a high quality of life for the local population by implementing smart and integrated solutions" [13:2, 14]
(2017) Pantazis et al. [15]	"The term smart sustainable island […] has the same meaning with the term smart sustainable city, but in addition: (1) it refers to the entire region of an island and not to a specific city (2) the term "sustainable" means that the entire island follows all the good practices to preserve the sustainable development and the protection of the environment, natural and urban, including the culture heritage in a holistic and integrated manner" [15:47]
(2017) Dominguez et al. [16]	"An island is an ecologically isolated self-contained territory with a principal and network of smaller cities and villages. In many islands, in recent decades, tourism has formed the main source of income" [16:236]
(2018) Herrera Priano et al. [17]	"The main scientific contribution of The Model for the Smart Development of Island Territories is to define an initial model that considers the significance of the

(continued)

Table 1. (*continued*)

Author	Definition
(2018) Garau et al. [6]	Smart effect for both governments and cities as part of a regional/territorial development scheme" [17:23] A "smart island is […] a territory capable of responding to structural problems related to insularity, also through a network of relationships that have as main points the structural characteristics of the place" [6]

Table 2. Overview of terms used in smart island definitions

	Local Development	Quality of life	Instruction	Human capital	Culture heritage	Tourism	Public services	Governance	Protection landscape	Coastal marine resources	Sustainable Development	Climate	Mobility	Economy	Energy	Environment	Water	Waste	ICT	Smart city comparison
[10]	X	X		X				X				X	X	X	X					
[11] [12]	X	X	X	X				X			X	X	X	X	X		X	X		
[13] [14]					X	X		X											X	
[15]								X	X	X		X	X	X	X	X	X	X		
[16] [17]	X	X						X				X	X	X		X			X	
[18]		X		X	X			X	X			X	X							X
[19]		X												X			X			
[20]	X						X													X
[7]	X		X					X		X	X	X	X	X	X	X	X	X		

[c] most of the analyzed projects highlight a strong use of e-governance and its application through Information and Communication Technologies (ICTs), by promoting the Islands' competitive development [18–20].

The terms derived from the smart island definitions (Table 2) allowed to identify some key words that integrate the smart island concept, such as smart governance and urban policies. Therefore, authors decided to extend the search for a terminology that links these three terms, through a literature revision that has already used these keywords: Smart Island, Sustainability Island, Insular Territories, Smartness and Island, Smart City and Insular, Island Urban Planning, ICT Island, E-government Island. The purpose of this research was in fact to determine if a suitable terminology exists in literature, capable of encompassing the three terms just mentioned (smart island, smart governance and urban policies).

2.1   Literature Review Methodology

In the review of the scientific literature a systematic approach is adopted [20]. The keywords, summarized and identified in Table 3, were searched in the main databases (Google Scholar, Scopus, Science Direct) through a time filter from 2007 (because it is the year in which the smart cities term started to be used in the current meaning [21]) to 2018. Table 3 shows the results of the research, where, after a preliminary analysis and after having eliminated the repeated items, 203 articles were obtained. Of these, 90 articles were open access.

Table 3. Result of the search from Google Scholar, Scopus and Science Direct databases

Termini	Articles for each database			Total number	Total number (excluding duplicates)
	Google Scholar	Scopus	Science Direct		
Smart Island	16	22	8	46	43
Sustainability Island	100	25	3	127	121
insularTerritories	2	2	0	4	3
Smartness and Island	0	0	0	0	0
Smart City and Insular	1	0	0	1	1
Island Urban Planning	10	4	1	15	15
ICT Island	6	1	1	8	8
E-government Island	11	2	0	13	12

Then, titles and keywords are evaluated in order to understand which documents faced the smart island paradigm in relation to the sought concepts (Sustainability Island, Insular Territories, Smartness and Island, Smart City and Insular, Island Urban Planning, ICT Island, E-government Island). In this way, 33 articles were selected.

A further selection was made after reading the abstracts, thus arriving at 16 documents, totally reviewed in full. This work allowed to put together information on the tools and performances adopted in the smart islands. Nine papers were selected. Table 4 summarizes these nine papers selected and for each one identifies the purpose, the methodology adopted, the tools used and how the urban performance was analyzed.

The literature study highlights that 4 articles [15, 16, 23, 27] present methods and tools able to connect insular contexts with smart governance and urban policies. This shows how the three terms (smart island, smart governance and urban policies) are linked through the objectives and methodologies expressed in Table 4 despite their

Table 4. A literature review of the concept of smart island

Papers	Aim	Methodology	Tools	How the Urban performance is analyzed
1. [22]	After identifying the main sustainability issues of EU islands, authors argue for a stronger awareness of islands issues in EU policy processes. In particular, they identified three issues: (a) many islands are excluded from the definition of EU Islands; (b) many islands do not fit into categories provided in the EU's impact assessment guidelines; (c) there is no statistical data for monitoring sustainable development in EU insular regions	**SENSOR protocol** it is based on surveys in the 4 SENSOR sensitive regions, that can be summarised as follows: coastal, post-industrial, mountainous and islands	Sustainability Impact Assessment Tools (SIAT) to support decision-making on policies related to land use (European FP6 funded project SENSOR3)	It identifies the location of EU islands based on a spatial dataset, and elaborates a set of European island sustainability issues that are identified through expert interviews
2. [23]	The objective is the urban sustainability, in order to improve the quality of life. From this investigation and strategies, authors analysed best practice	Q METHODOLOGY It is organised as follows: (1) semi-structured interviews (2) The data collected are then processed through the Principal Component Analysis (PCA), (3) their results are translated in factors as groups of opinion or social perspectives	(1) semi-structured interviews (2) PCA (see methodology section)	The authors chose different indicators of urban sustainability (they are: 1. the city's current development level; 2. public security; 3. environment; 4. culture and education; 5. economy; 6. funding; 7. governance; 8. migration; 9. public 10. participation and poverty)

(*continued*)

Table 4. (*continued*)

Papers	Aim	Methodology	Tools	How the Urban performance is analyzed
3. [24]	The main objectives are: (i) the analysis of the ICT developments in Samoa, (ii) how implementing these ICT developments (iii) which strategies are necessary for Samoa	QUALITATIVE METHODS through interviews of key stakeholders in the ICT sector in Samoa	(1) semi-structured interviews	The interviews are compared (a) with the World Bank Infodev framework (2005) and also (b) with the Regional framework for action on ICT
4. [25]	The main objectives are: (i) developing an integral model which incorporates the factors and key processes of a socio-ecological system, (ii) defining the most relevant sustainability indicators in the case study of El Hierro	FUERTEVENTURA SUSTAINABILITY MODEL (FSM) The methodology is an integral dynamic model, combined with other methods (indicators, policy and scenario analysis)	The FSM was constructed following the system dynamics methodology and using the Vensim software	A set of sustainability indicators is integrated in the sustainability island model. FSM is constituted by nine macro variables
5. [26]	The aim of this study is to investigate patterns of landscape changes in small islands (such as Gili Matra Islands, Lombok, Indonesia)	PATTERNS OF LAND USE/LAND COVER (LU/LC) Authors use different images in different years (from 2010 to 2014) in order to understand landscape change pattern	(1) Satellite images QuickBird in 2010 and GeoEye in 2014 (2) Geographic Position System (GPS) (3) ArcGIS 10.2.2	The authors layered different satellite images
6. [27]	The aim of this study is to estimate the effects of e-government (e-G) development on environmental sustainability in Small island developing states (SIDS)	THREE EMPIRICAL MODELS 1. model estimates the impact of (e-G) development on government effectiveness 2. model for estimate the impact of e-G on	Authors examined every model with the Wooldridge test for autocorrelation, with the Breusch-Pagan test and White's test for heteroscedasticity. They detected autocorrelation and	Performance is assessed throught e-government development index. Authors established the equation to estimate the effects of e-government on government effectiveness and a

(*continued*)

Table 4. (*continued*)

Papers	Aim	Methodology	Tools	How the Urban performance is analyzed
		environmental sustainability; 3. model for estimate the impact of e-G development on environmental sustainability	heteroscedasticity in any models, in order to apply feasible generalized least squares to correct the autocorrelation and heteroskedasticity	second equation estimates the effects of e-government on environmental sustainability
7. [16]	The aim is to create a theoretical and practical conceptualization of smart island, using the case study of El Hierro (Canary Islands, Spain)	THEORETICAL AND PRACTICAL CONCEPTUALIZATION The methodology is	Authors used the case study as a research method. This study considers as smart prototype the Hierro Island. The used tool is (a) literature review and (b) the European Smart Cities indicators	Authors considered a set of indicators as a result of the analysis of the different strategies of development of cities and destinations. They define3 groups of 12 key indicators (Smart Gov; Smart Tech, Smart Experience)
8. [15]	The aim of this work is to: (a) have a new concept of "smart sustainable cities" and "smart sustainable islands" (b) have a methodological framework of concepts and actions	ISLAND SMARTIFICATION AND SUSTAINABILITY (S2I2) INDEX The S2I2 index is used to measure the efficiency of the local authorities	(1) The major part of the ITU index system (ITU 2016) is adopted. (2) The typical used indices or indicators is Key Performance Index (KPI) for Smart Sustainable (green) Cities	Authors create an island smartification and a sustainability index called S2I2. They consider diferent parameters
9. [28]	The aim is considering the complex dynamics of insular territories/regions	CORINE LAND COVER (CLC) The CLC maps homogeneous landscape patterns (areas smaller than 25 ha are considered and a set of generalization rules were defined)	(1) GIS tools (2) CLC, (3) literature review	Performance is assessed trought three-level hierarchical classification system and trought 44 classes at the third and most detailed level

connection is not explicit. Moreover, none of the articles presented the same tool and it is necessary to underline that 2 of the 9 articles use a series of Smart factors already applied to the now consolidated representation of smart cities through the six classics dimensions: economy, mobility, governance, environment, living, and society [21] to describe the smart islands. These are:

1. Theoretical and practical conceptualization model in [16]: The smart island is divided into indicators by European Smart City and then 12 criteria, inserted in three sets, are identified. These are: (a) Smart Gov (1. The government investments cover the visitors 'needs; 2. Local societies benefit from tourism suppliers; 3. Internet facilities 4. E-Government); (b) Smart Tech (1. Technology for data management; 2. Broadband networks infrastructure; 3. Tourism products and services platform; 4. Sharing Data); (c) (1. Tourism experience exchange; 2. Corporate Citizenship; 3. Improved Smart Management in innovation and participation; 4. ICT services for Smart experience). These criteria were tested through the case study of the Island of El Hierro (Canary Islands, Spain). This appears effective because the article, extending the Smart City paradigms, focuses on the typical characteristics of the island territories. This is important for building a set of easily operational criteria to define a smart island.

2. Island smartification and sustainability (S2I2) index model in [15]: the transition from the concept of smart sustainable cities to smart sustainable islands, led the authors to develop an index for the smartification and sustainability of the islands. Subsequently, a review of the literature on Smart Cities defined 5 main dimensions of smartification that contain different sub-dimensions. These are: (a) ICT and economics (Network Facilities, Information Facilities, Innovation & Opportunities, Economic sustainability, Island Productivity, Tourism); (b) Sustainability of resources (Energy, Water Natural Resources, Environmental monitoring & sustainability); (c) Infrastructure (Building, Transport, Sanitation, Municipal pipe networks, Recycling infrastructures); (d) Quality of life (Convenience & Comfort, Security & Safety, Health care, Education); (e) Company (Openness & public participation, Social sustainability & equity, Governance sustainability).

3   Results: Main Topics on Smart Island Definitions

This analysis shows that the aforementioned articles [15, 16] are the most theoretical ones. This underlines how the search for an optimal definition of smart island leads to a more all-encompassing fragmentation of the same term into indicators. However, in the literature the study of the terms used to analyze the urban policies and the smart governance of the islands is less investigated, even if in these articles the connection of these three terms is not explicit. In other words, what are the terms that can create a comparison between urban governance, urban policies of the smart island territories?

To this end, authors defined the main topics on smart islands, through an in-depth analysis of the 9 revised articles (Table 5).

All articles reviewed contained information on sustainable development and on the environment. The social analysis - that includes "local development", "quality of life",

Table 5. Smart island definitions and the main topics of the revised articles

	Local Development	Quality of life	Instruction	Human capital	Culture heritage	Tourism	Public services	Governance	Protection landscape	Coastal marine resources	Sustainable Development	Climate	Mobility	Economy	Energy	Environment	Water	Waste	ICT	Smart city comparison
[26]		X	X		X		X	X	X	X		X	X	X	X	X				
[27]	X	X	X	X		X	X				X	X	X	X	X					
[28]	X		X				X				X					X				X
[29]	X		X		X		X				X	X		X	X	X	X			
[30]							X	X	X		X					X	X			
[31]				X			X	X			X	X	X	X	X	X	X	X		
[32]	X	X	X	X		X		X			X	X	X	X	X	X	X	X	X	X
[33]		X	X		X	X	X	X	X	X	X	X	X	X	X	X	X	X	X	X
[34]	X	X					X				X					X	X			

"instruction", "human capital" - is included in 7 articles: all 4 topics are present in the articles [23] and [16] that show the growth and progress of the cities of Angra do Heroísmo (Terceira island, Azores) and of El Hierro (Canary Islands, Spain).

In summary, the most discussed issues are local development [16, 23–25, 28], quality of life [15, 16, 23, 28], education [15, 16, 22–24] and of human capital [16, 22, 23, 25]. Cultural heritage is also an important topic [15, 16, 22, 23, 25, 26], highlighting several island correlations related to case studies [16, 23, 25] and to the relationship between Insularity and European policies [22].

The environmental analysis (which includes the terms "protection landscape", "coastal marine resources", "climate", "mobility", "economy", "energy", "water", "waste") is, in a different way, included in all articles except in one [24]. It focuses on the use and application of digital technologies. The use of ICT is a predominant theme [15, 16, 24, 27] from the theoretical to the practical conceptualization in terms of e-government and use of digital technology [24, 27], and also in term of theoretical critical analysis on "smartification" [15] and of application to a case study [16]. While a comparison between smart island and smart city was not so a common topic [15, 16].

This analysis led authors to try to understand the possible connections between the keywords of the 9 revised articles and the most used terminologies within them, summarized in Table 2. Figure 1 shows the keywords of the 9 articles, summarized in Table 4 and represented in 8 groups.

The six groups represented with dashed lines show the terms emerged from the analysis of the definitions shown in Table 2. The two groups represented with a

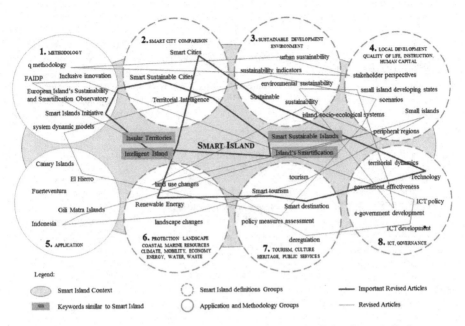

Fig. 1. Smart island definitions and keyword analysis (Color figure online)

continuous line represent the keywords that describe a methodology and the case studies analyzed in the articles. While the keywords that are more similar to smart island terminology are included in the green rectangle, the keywords are joined by green lines representing 8 revised articles, and only an article has no keywords [22]. It is interesting to note that only one article mentions in its key words "Smart Island" [16], and only one article approaches the concept [15], these articles are represented in Fig. 1 by red lines. Even if the other articles [16, 23–28] do not use the specific term "Smart Island" the keywords are all referable to the terms used in Smart Island (Table 2).

4 Discussions: Smart Island Definition Through Urban Performances Analysis

The analysis conducted revealed that there are no keywords, able to identify urban policies and a smart governance of a smart island. For this reason, authors found these keywords through the analysis of the urban performance indicators of the 9 revised articles outlined in Table 4. This is because the authors noted that most of the revised articles analyze the urban performance, through a set of sustainability indicators that, although they consider different parameters, identify insular territorial development strategies.

The objective of this analysis was to determine how the performance indicators of the different articles may highlight one or more terminologies capable of synthesizing and connecting the terms described in Sect. 2 (smart island, governance and urban

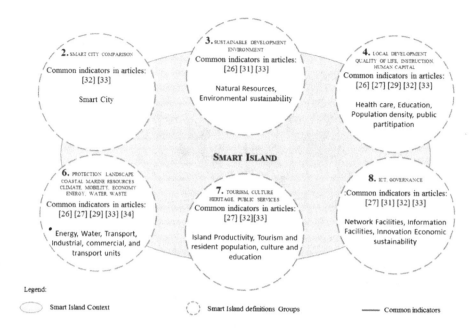

Fig. 2. Smart island definitions and urban performances analysis

policies). In order to achieve this, the authors analyzed which indicators used in the articles can be traced back to the terms derived from the Smart Island definitions (Table 2).

In this regard, Fig. 2 shows that 7 of 9 articles [15, 16, 22, 23, 25, 27, 28] use indicators to define the smart island. Social indicators including "local development", "quality of life", "instruction", "human capital" are used in 5 of 7 articles [15, 16, 22, 23, 25]. Environmental indicators include terms such as "protection landscape", "coastal marine resources", "climate", "mobility", "economy", "energy" and "water", "waste" and they are described in 6 of 7 articles [15, 22, 23, 25, 27, 28].

The other groups have fewer indicators. In summary, terms similar to "sustainable development" and "environment" are used as indicators in 3 articles [15, 22, 27]. "Tourism", "culture heritage", "public services" are used in [15, 16, 23] and terms similar to "ITC" and "governance" become indicators in [15, 16, 22, 27].

The analysis shows that indicators used in [15] are the only ones that include all the terms derived from the definitions. While, as underlined in Sect. 2, a comparison between smart island and smart city is made only in [15, 16]. Furthermore, it is important to underline that in all 9 articles no indicator has been found that cannot be included in one of these groups.

Figure 2 shows the indicators used in the analyzed articles. Figure 2 also shows three distinct sub-categories (territory, governance and environment) in relation to the terms study in relation of the typical features of the islands.

5 Conclusions

This paper presented a detailed review of the terminology, through the analysis of smart island definitions and the literature. The concept of smart island, extensively analyzed in this paper, is therefore represented by the definitions described in Table 1 and by the terms that characterize the urban performance of the projects described in the revised articles (Fig. 2).

In a nutshell, the study of smart island definitions - related to (1) the main topics of the revised articles (Table 5) and to (2) keyword analysis (Fig. 1) - constituted an important basis of analysis to identify which are the terms that create a comparison between the urban performances of the smart island territories. In fact, these last concepts shown that in the revised articles there is, although this is not explicitly, the connection between the urban policies and a smart governance of a smart island.

In this context, authors found that, considering the previous analyzes, it could be possible to have a synthetic indicator of smart island.

Smart Island = Smart city and Smart Territory paradigms (economy, mobility, governance, environment, living, society) + Peculiarities of Islands (insularity, island productivity, tourism, island culture, Coastal marine resources).

Therefore, on the basis of the analysis described, the authors propose 6 keywords that identify the urban policies and smart governance of the smart islands. These are:

(1) Smart island territory and smart insular territories.
(2) Smart island government and smart island local development.
(3) Island Sustainable Development and Island Environment.

The condition of insularity must be the basis of each term because it serves to identify the typical characteristics of the islands. The used terms represent a schematization of how a territory, through a smart paradigm, is able to respond to the common problems related to insularity.

In other words, these allow to identify issues related to the territory, governance and sustainability for an intelligent insular context.

Moreover, this paper established the basis for a future comparison of the maturity of the smart island and the identification of the synthetic indicator above-mentioned.

In fact, considering that all the revised articles make quantitative analysis, the performance measurement and the identification of a synthetic indicator are necessary preconditions to study the smart island.

Acknowledgments. This study was supported by the MIUR (Ministry of Education, Universities and Research [Italy]) through a project entitled *Governing tHe smart city: a governance-centred approach to SmarT urbanism - GHOST* (Project code: RBSI14FDPF; CUP Code: F22I15000070008), financed with the SIR (Scientific Independence of Young Researchers) programme. We authorize the MIUR to reproduce and distribute reprints for Governmental purposes, notwithstanding any copyright notations thereon. Any opinions, findings and conclusions or recommendations expressed in this material are those of the authors, and do not necessarily reflect the views of the MIUR.

References

1. Smart Island World Congress - SIWC (Calvià, Maiorca) (2018). http://www.smartisland congress.com/en/home. Accessed 17 Dec 2018
2. The Attica Islands Network. https://atticaislandsnetwork.gr/. Accessed 17 Dec 2018
3. La Possession.re, institutional site of the city of "La Possession" (Réunion). http://www. lapossession-coeurdeville.re/ma-smart-city.html. Accessed 17 Dec 2018
4. Cozumel island intelligent. Cozumel ISLA Intelligent. https://islacozumel.gob.mx/ayunt amiento/sala-de-prensa/comunicados/cozumel-entre-los-mejores-destinos-inteligentes-en-el-mundo-considerado-punto-de-referencia-por-sus-trabajos-de-sustentabilidad. Accessed 17 Dec 2018
5. European Union: Treaty of Amsterdam (1997). http://www.europarl.europa.eu/topics/treaty/ pdf/amst-en.pdf. Accessed 17 Dec 2018
6. Garau, C., Desogus, G.: A preliminary analysis for the development of Smart Island contexts. In: Proceedings of the 2nd International Forum on architecture and urbanism. Pescara, December 2018
7. Chatzimpiros, A., et al.: SMILEGOV Project Multilevel Governance. Enhancing effective implementation of sustainable energy action plans in European islands through reinforcement of smart multilevel governance. Final Report (2013). https://www.sustainableislands. eu/BlockImages/InLibraryData/GalleryData/D1.3%20Result-Oriented%20publishable% 20Report.pdf. Accessed 17 Dec 2018
8. European Union: Opinion of the European Economic and Social Committee on Smart islands (2015). https://eur-lex.europa.eu/legal-content/EN/TXT/?uri=CELEX%3A52014IE 5752. Accessed 17 Dec 2018
9. European Union, TEN/558 Smart island (2015). https://www.eesc.europa.eu/en/our-work/ opinions-information-reports/opinions/smart-islands. Accessed 17 Dec 2018
10. EE-Spanish government project, Ministerio de Industria, Energía Y Turismo (2015). https:// www.boe.es/boe/dias/2015/08/01/pdfs/BOE-A-2015-8704.pdf. Accessed 17 Dec 2018
11. Deign, J.: First Smart Cities and now Smart Islands. Cisco network, January 2016. https:// newsroom.cisco.com/feature-content?articleId=1735451. Accessed 17 Dec 2018
12. Smart Islands Projects and Strategies. Issued from the 1st European Smart Islands Forum, June 2016, Athens, Greece (2016). https://library.fes.de/pdf-files/bueros/athen/12860.pdf. Accessed 17 Dec 2018
13. Smart Islands Declaration (2016). http://www.smartislandsinitiative.eu/pdf/Smart_Islands_ Declaration.pdf. Accessed 17 Dec 2018
14. Smart Island Initiative (2016). http://www.smartislandsinitiative.eu/en/index.php. Accessed 17 Dec 2018
15. Pantazis, D.N., et al.: Smart sustainable islands vs smart sustainable cities. In: ISPRS Annals of the Photogrammetry, Remote Sensing and Spatial Information Sciences, vol. IV-4/W3, 2017 2nd International Conference on Smart Data and Smart Cities, 4–6 October, Puebla, Mexico (2017)
16. Dominguez, C.D., Hernández, M.R., Talavera, A.S., López, E.P.: Smart island tourism and strategic marketing: the case of the island of El Hierro. In: Act as del Seminario Internacional Destinos Turísticos Inteligentes: nuevos horizontes en la investigación y gestión del turismo, Alicante, p. 236 (2017)
17. Herrera, P.F., Armas, R.L., Guerra, C.F.: Developing smart regions: proposal and application of a model for island territories. Int. J. E-Planning Res. (IJEPR) 7(2), 26 (2018)
18. Baum, S., Van Gellecum, Y., Yigitcanlar, T.: Wired communities in the city: Sydney, Australia. Geogr. Res. 42, 2 (2004)

19. Caragliu, A., Del Bo, C., Nijkamp, P.: Smart cities in Europe. J. Urban Technol. 18(2), 65–82 (2011)
20. Trindade, E.P., Hinnig, M.P.F., Da Costa, E.M., Marques, J.S., Bastos, R.C., Yigitcanlar, T.: Sustainable development of smart cities: a systematic review of the literature. J. Open Innov.: Technol. Mark. Complexity 3, 11 (2017)
21. Giffinger, R.: Smart cities – Ranking of European medium-sized cities (2007). http://www.smart-cities.eu/download/smart_cities_final_report.pdf. Accessed 22 Dec 2018
22. Moncada, S., Camilleri, M., Formosa, S., Galea, R.: Islands at the Periphery: integrating the challenges of Island sustainability into European Policy. European FP6 project SENSOR (2009)
23. Sánchez A.F., Gil F.S., Sabater L.A., Dentinho T.P.: AQ Methodology approach to define urban sustainability challenges in a small insular city. In: Proceedings of the 51st European Congress of the Regional Association International, 30 August to 3 September, Barcelona (2011)
24. Tuugalei, I., Mow, C.: Issues and challenges, strategies and recommendations, in the development of ICT in a Small Island Developing State: the case of Samoa. EJISDC 63(2), 1–24 (2014)
25. Banos-González, I., Martínez-Fernández, J., Esteve, M.A.: Tools for sustainability assessment in island socio-ecological systems: an application to the Canary Islands. Island Stud. J. 11(1), 9–34 (2016)
26. Kurniawan, F., Adrianto, L., Bengen, D.G., Prasetyo, L.B.: Patterns of landscape change on small islands: a case of Gili Matra Islands, Marine Tourism Park, Indonesia. In: Proceedings of the International Conference, Intelligent Planning Towards Smart Cities, 3–4 November, Surabaya, Indonesia (2015)
27. Lee, Y.B.: Exploring the relationship between e-government development and environmental sustainability: a study of small island developing states. Sustainability 9, 732 (2017)
28. Castanho, R.A.: Dynamics of the Land Use Changes and the Associated Barriers and Opportunities for Sustainable Development on Peripheral and Insular Territories: The Madeira Island (Portugal). Provisional chapter (2018). https://www.intechopen.com/online-first/dynamics-of-the-land-use-changes-and-the-associated-barriers-and-opportunities-for-su stainable-devel

Smart City Governance and Children's Rights: Perspectives and Findings from Literature on Natural Elements Influencing Children's Activities Within Public Spaces

Chiara Garau[1(✉)], Alfonso Annunziata[1], and David Vale[2]

[1] Department of Civil and Environmental Engineering and Architecture,
University of Cagliari, 09129 Cagliari, Italy
cgarau@unica.it, annunziata.alfonso@yahoo.it
[2] Faculty of Architecture, University of Lisbon, 1349-055 Lisbon, Portugal
dvale@fa.ulisboa.pt

Abstract. This paper shows a comprehensive literature review based on a comparative method that investigates a set of 25 papers from different disciplinary fields. The articles are retrieved from the Web of Science and SCOPUS databases and individuated through queries containing the key terms child, play, city, neighbourhood, outdoor space, public space, urban space, mobility. The timeframe considered spans from 2004 to present. The analysis focuses on three related aspects: (i) methodology; (ii) conceptual apparatus describing children's experience of spaces; (iii) green spaces and natural elements incorporated in public space design considered as determinant of children's outdoor activities. This paper provides detailed information on the relationship between the availability of natural settings and elements and children's outdoor practices and activities. Retrieving from previous studies the concept of practicability the authors reflect on significance of natural elements in reinforcing the potential of the built environment to promote children's independent playful practices. This study is instrumental in structuring an analytic methodology for determining a synthetic index of the practicability of public spaces. The relevance of a methodology for assessing practicability relies on its potential to enable a better understanding of conditions conducive to children's independent playful practices and to support governance by assisting the implementation of strategies of urban regeneration within the smart city paradigm.

Keywords: Smart cities governance · Systematic literature review ·
Children's independent activities · Built environment

This paper is the result of the joint work of the authors. 'Methodology' 'The conceptual apparatus' and 'Conclusions' were written jointly by the authors. Chiara Garau wrote the 'Literature review on children's activities within the public space'. Alfonso Annunziata wrote the 'Natural settings correlates of children's independent activities'. David Vale wrote the 'Introduction'.

© Springer Nature Switzerland AG 2019
S. Misra et al. (Eds.): ICCSA 2019, LNCS 11624, pp. 152–168, 2019.
https://doi.org/10.1007/978-3-030-24311-1_11

1 Introduction

This paper investigates the potential of natural spaces and elements integrated into the public space to enable children's independent functional, recreational and social activities, through a comprehensive review of the literature concerning the built environment correlates of children's activities within the public space [1].

This study is part of a broader research aimed at developing a synthetic index and an assessment tool for investigating the potential of the built environment to promote children's outdoor independent and playful activities. This potential is encompassed in the concept of practicability. This study aims to address two aspects: (i) the definition of a conceptual apparatus for describing the enabling conditions and developmental effects of children's independent outdoor activities (CIAs); (ii) identifying features of blue/green infrastructures, integrated in the public space, that enable children's outdoor practices and activities.

This paper focuses on children's independent activities (CIAs) as a fundamental actualisation of what Henry Lefebvre calls "the right to the city" [1–3]. Outdoor independent activities include independent mobility and agency and thus incorporate the complex of practices producing the meaningful engagement with the material environment: exploration, occupation and transformation of spaces, intra-active play, structured group activities, imaginative and creative games.

The issue of children's independent activities leads to investigate whether the contemporary city incorporate in its socio-spatial and symbolic structures a "place for children" [4].

The research on children's outdoor activities reflects a shift in the conception of children and the recognition of their right to "a life of their own" [5] and to health - intended as a state of complete physical, mental and social well-being [6]. Studies involving concepts and methodologies from different disciplines, such as urban planning, social sciences, environmental psychology, geography, medicine, consistently relate children's outdoor play, as well as their independent spatial mobility and physical activity to positive effects on their physical well-being, on their emotional, cognitive and social development, on the acquisition of spatial and environmental skills, on the construction of their social and individual identity.

In particular, outdoor activities are related to bodily health, healthier weight and more stable body mass index [7, 8], to better motor coordination and balance and to reducing incidence of obesity and of cardio-vascular diseases [6, 9–12]. Involvement in outdoor practices is also associated to positive effects in sense of ownership, emotion regulation, intellectual and creative development, socialisation, development of language and collaborative competences, sensitivity and sympathy towards other species, independence, autonomy, sense of confidence and of self-esteem and in supporting the development of tactics [13–17].

In general terms, positive effects of outdoor activities on children's health can be re-conceptualised through the capability approach, as effects on children's fundamental capability to develop. This, in turn, incorporates ten central capabilities: life; bodily health; bodily integrity; affiliation; practical reason; play; senses, imagination, and thought; emotions; connection to nature and other species; control over one's environment [6, 18, 19].

Therefore, the questions of childhood and of its place within the contemporary city [4] emerge as a central issue within the global processes of growing urbanization: the construction of a built environment that ensures children's right to the city involves both the conceptualization of children as political becomings [17] – whose tactics and agency have future salience, being mobilized and informing adult practices – and the awareness of children's right to the city as a component of their right to well-being and as a pre-condition of their integral development. Moreover, an accessible and usable public space can determine better conditions of access to public spaces and urban opportunities for all city-users. Thus, children can be regarded as city-users whose well-being, independence and satisfactory engagement with urban spaces are an indicator of the sustainability and inclusivity of the contemporary city [20].

This study is, in fact, instrumental in structuring the conceptual and theoretical framework of the analytic methodology for assessing the practicability of the public space, in organising the layout of the evaluation tool and in offering a preliminary insight into the built environment aspects relevant for enabling children's practices.

Considering these premises, the paper is organised in four sections: the first section illustrates a summary of the most relevant perspectives informing the research on children's experience and perception of the public space; in the second one the methodology adopted for this study is clarified; then the results are presented and in the fourth one, a discussion of the results is presented. The paper concludes by considering the limitations of the study and by illustrating its relevance for the development of an analytic methodology for assessing the practicability of public spaces.

2   Methodology

A set of 195 papers from different disciplinary fields (Education, Educational Research, Environmental Sciences, Geography, Environmental Studies, Urban Studies, Transportation, Planning Development, Civil Engineering, Environmental Engineering, Architecture) is retrieved from the Web of Science and SCOPUS databases and individuated via queries containing the key terms child, play, city, neighbourhood, outdoor space, public space, urban space, mobility. The time frame considered spans from 1990 to present (see Fig. 1). In a second stage, a sample of 25 journal articles is selected and is investigated via a comparative content analysis.

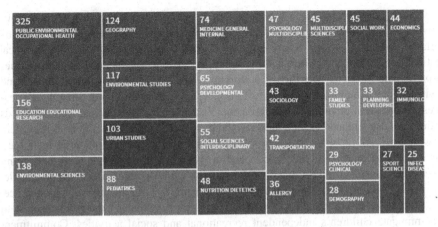

Fig. 1. Distribution of articles among different disciplinary fields. Results obtained frome the Web of Science database by entering the query [(child AND ("play" OR "mobility") AND ("city" OR "neighbourhood" OR "outdoor space" OR "urban space" OR "public space")]. Timespan: 1990–2019.

The final sample is selected through an analysis of the abstracts. The criteria are: (i) articles considering a sample of children whose age is included, at least partially, within the range 5–13 years: this is the range of age considered by the authors in previous studies on the practicability and inclusivity of the public space [2, 3] (ii) articles considering as dependent variable either children's independent mobility, autonomy or exploration and experimentation and as correlates, or independent variables, built environment spatial and material factors; (iii) a reduced timeframe spanning from 2004 to present. The analysis focuses on 7 related aspects: (i) Area of the study, sample size and methods; (ii) impacts of the discussed research; (iii) the dependent variable, i.e. which aspect of outdoor activities is considered; (iv) developmental effects associated to children's engagement in outdoor activities; (v) Categories for describing children's experience of spaces and elements of the environment related to children's perceptions and practices; (vi) Categories of the public space considered as places of children's practices; (vii) elements of the public space considered as positive or negative related to children's CIAs.

For each functional, material, spatial or social BE factor considered as an independent variable it is specified the direction of the relation, discerning positive, negative and ambiguous relations, and cases in which the direction of the relation is not specified. The content comparative analysis is developed through the utilisation of a matrix, whose layout is derived from the SCOPE tool [3] and from the IAAPE tool [21]. In particular, the correlates of children's activities are organised into 11 categories, reflecting 11 dimensions including the BE spatial, functional, cultural, socioeconomic factors and individual socio-demographic characteristics influencing levels and patterns of children's outdoor activities. These dimensions include Connectivity, Convenience, Comfort, Conviviality, Conspicuousness, Coexistence, Commitment, Socio/cultural factors, individual children's factors, individual Parents' factors, Dwelling factors.

Connectivity refers to the integration of a public open space into a continuous network of walkable surfaces and into the arterial network of the collective transportation routes. Convenience refers to the conditions of access to different local destinations, formal and informal sites of play, and of density, intended as opportunities to participate in social activities. Comfort measures the effects of microclimatic and environmental conditions, treatment of surfaces, and geometric and constructive features of pedestrian facilities to increase people's sense of wellbeing, and fulfil the needs of different users related to their abilities and purposes. Conviviality refers to the extent to which the public space promotes interactions with social and material resources, enabling functional, optional, and social activities, and activating self-reinforcing processes. Conspicuousness reflects the extent to which public spaces are imageable, interesting, and inviting, in terms of spatial legibility, complexity, and coherence. Coexistence refers to the impact of traffic on the potential of the public space to accommodate children's independent recreational and social activities. Commitment refers to factors indicative of the engagement, responsibility, and liability of local agencies toward the promotion of children's independent mobility and activities across public spaces.

Socio-economic and cultural factors refer to environmental social and cultural structures and economic conditions determining whether children's independence is regarded as a goal, a necessity, or a condition to be prevented [4]. Children's individual factors include their specific socio-demographic attributes and refer to the impacts of gender, age, ethnicity, perceptions of self-efficacy and capacity constraints on their likelihood to engage independently in outdoor activities. Parental individual factors include parents' socio-demographic characteristics and account for the influence of their socio-economic status, education, age, ethnicity on parental styles and on propensity to support children's independence. Finally, Dwelling factors considers to what extent the typological characters of the housing, presence of semi-private transition spaces, and the setting influence children's propensity and opportunities to independently participate in outdoor activities.

3 Literature Review on Children's Activities Within the Public Space

3.1 Aspects of Children's Experience of the Public Space

Existing studies consider specific aspects or dimensions of children's outdoor activities: physical activity, defined as any bodily movement produced by skeletal muscles that results in energy expenditure [22]; children's independent mobility, defined as the freedom and/or ability of children to travel across the urban space without adult supervision; and outdoor play, conceptualised as a cheap, informal, and easily accessible vector to physical activity [23] and as a creative act of spatial appropriation and of meaningful engagement with spaces and objects, fostering dwelling with and enchantment [24].

3.2 Socio-Cultural Determinants of Outdoor Children's Activities

The existing literature shows that the levels of children's engagement in outdoor activities are affected by different factors: children's individual characteristics, parental styles, cultural constructs and socio-physical environment of the contemporary city. In particular, children's characteristics include their ability, wish and willing to be independent and issues related to their developmental stage or to their health [4].

Age and school stage are frequently considered as positively related to children's independent mobility (CIM) and phisical activity (PA), and they are associated to changes in patterns of activity, and in the definition of important places, thus of spaces that enable purposive behaviours [25]. Parental styles refer to parents' propensity and willingness to enable children to independently engage in outdoor activities within the public space. This aspect reflects parents' socio-economic status, familiar condition, education, ethnicity: in particular confidence in child's spatial competence, perception of social cohesion and connection, concerns related to the characteristics of traffic flows and to the presence of strangers strongly affect the degree to which children are afforded independence. Cultural constructs emerge as a central factor in influencing levels of outdoor practices, according to conceptualisations of childhood, of gender and of parental roles [4]. The presence of other children in the neighbourhood is positively associated to outdoor activities, particularly if associated with other enabling resources: quality of buildings, enabling materials, social cohesion, eyes on the street, available spaces [17]. The socio-economic status of neighbourhood emerge as a positive correlate of children's mobility and activity, particularly by affecting perceptions of the social *milieu* [9]. Finally, fragilities of the social *milieu*, including exposure to violent incidents, consumption of narcotics and alcoholics, segregation, poverty, bullying are negatively associated to levels of children's activities. Nevertheless, the literature identifies the perception of these phenomena, more than their actual significance, as a relevant determinant of limitations on parental propensity to support children's independence as well as on children's willing to engage in outdoor activities.

3.3 Built Environment Factors

Material, spatial and functional elements of the built environment associated to children's levels and patterns of activities refer to different levels of scale, from the configuration of the urban structure to material, compositional properties of specific pedestrian surfaces. BE factors include the configuration of the street network, distances from specific destinations, residential density, land-use patterns, the availability of informal or formal sites for play, the household settings. In particular path directness, the grid configuration of the road network, the continuity of the pedestrian network and its accessibility, intended as the absence of physical barriers are positively related to children's mobility and activities.

Density [6, 7, 9, 26–31], conceptualised as residential density, building density or population density, emerges as a significant correlate of children's independent mobility or leisure activities. Nevertheless, the direction of the relation between density and children's outdoor activities is ambiguous. Broberg et al. [32] individuate residential and population density as positively related to children's mobility to affordances and to the number of actualized affordances, but observed a negative relation between building density, operationalised as Floor Area Ratio, and children's mobility. Furthermore, Sharmin and Kamruzzaman [26] observe a negative association between CIM and residential density, yet underlining its insignificant effect and the heterogeneity of the results across the studies analysed. We raise the hypothesis that density might exert a non-linear relationship with CIM, which further complicates the generalization of results from different urban contexts.

Further ambiguity emerges in relation to the effect of land-use mix on children's activities: Despite being identified by Jane Jacobs [33] as central to increasing diversity and vitality of the urban realm, and being positively related to children's mobility by the Committee on Environmental Health [28] and by Whitzman and Mizrachi [16] a negative association with CIM is found by Sharmin and Kamruzzaman [26]: yet underlining the heterogeneity of results across the studies. Furthermore, positive associations to children's activity are found for availability, accessibility and proximity of local destinations, formal sites of play and informal sites of play. Local destinations include local shops [29], kindergarten, child-centre-based-care, family support service, child health clinic and playgroup [31] or cinemas, libraries and shopping centres [5, 16, 34]. Formal sites of play include the specialised spaces of playgrounds, Swimming pool, Swimming club, Tennis clubs, playfields and school grounds and the structured spaces of parks, community gardens and pocket parks [5, 25, 31]. Informal sites of play include thresholds spaces and transition spaces, such as woods, wastelands, alleyways, overgrown edges, vacant lots, construction sites and wild lands [5, 6, 35]. The identification of informal sites as important places enabling children's activities incorporates the relevance of spaces not subject to adults' restrictions and practices and the significance of loose, available spaces and elements as material resources enabling multiple purposive, intentional, social and creative activities. These factors emerge as pre-conditions for children's spatial appropriation, territoriality and satisfactory engagement with the public space.

Micro-scale elements and composition of the road space and of its spatial boundaries are often related to concerns about safety. In particular, the separation of pedestrian surfaces and passable lanes, the design of cross-roads, and the width as well as the function of streets are identified as determinants of perceptions related to traffic danger. Moreover, the presence of commercial activities and services along a street, the functional and spatial continuity between street space and buildings, the percentage of windows facing the street enable the natural surveillance of pedestrian spaces. On the other hand, the presence of elements regarded by users as signs of disorderliness, neglect and abandonment determine the perception of social milieu fragilities associated to social dangers. The concepts of eyes on the street and "broken window", incorporate these antithetic characteristics of spaces and refer to the nexus between built environment factors and social milieu attributes, which constitute the children's experience of the public space. Finally, adults' control on children's activities, including authority constraints [36], interferences, and physical manicuring of the landscape which communicates adults' ownership [6] are related to restrictions on children's activities and spatial appropriations [16, 25].

4   Findings and Discussion: The Conceptual Apparatus

Witten et al. [17] observe that research on children's practices within public spaces focus on determinants of children's independent mobility identified and described through statistical modelling techniques within a socio-ecological framework. A fundamental yet neglected issue is how everyday practices of walking, cycling or scootering are experienced by different children and how relational or material aspects of diverse places may shape children's sensory and affective experiences of the public space. These observations lead to focusing of research on environmental resources effective for enabling behaviors directly contributing to changes in children's psychological experience.

The definition of place is a first fundamental element: places are intended as favoured or important settings. A place is imbued with both use value and conceptional value. Thus, it is a setting perceived as useful, and in particular, as a setting that supports purposive and intentional activities and meaningful psychological experience. The importance of a setting results from a combination of spatial, material and social affordances related to accessibility and spatial connections with other relevant settings, play opportunities and functional capabilities, sense of privacy and territoriality, opportunities to meet friends and peers (sense fo belonging and togetherness), exposure to environmental and social danger [25].

The concept of affective atmosphere underlines how the combination and overlapping of sensory - social, material, olfactory – and symbolic stimuli, determine the felt experience of a place and shape tactics to claim and use spaces. Tactics, intended as acts of interpretation and negotiation of use of space, articulate children's agency and patterns of activity within the public space [17].

Pyyry [24] observes that the interaction with material and social resources, including exploration, experimentation and/or manipulation of loose elements, can produce a joyful and meaningful engagement with the public space. This intense involvement, defined as *dwelling with,* implies the acts of claiming, interpreting and appropriating spaces that determines the unusual experience of enchantment. Enchantment refers to a sense of wonder and as a moment of simultaneous disconnect and immersion. Thus, the concept of affordance emerges as central to the definitions of enabling conditions of children's activities. Affordances can be defined as the functional properties of the environment that offer a child opportunities to interact actively with the environment [9, 26, 32, 37, 38]. Affordances include also the emotional and social opportunities and restrictions incorporated into an environment. Affordances can be potential or actualised through action. The concept of affordance overcomes the subject-object dichotomy. It refers to properties of the environment that are perceived by the user as opportunities, but this perception emerges only when children's characteristics, including abilities, physical attributes, social needs or personal intentions correspond to environmental features.

On the other hand, the developmental effect of children's CIAs is better understood by referring to the concept of capability. Capability is described as a valuable state of being or a condition that a person can access [6, 18, 19]. In particular, for children the foundational capability is the "capability to develop" [6].

These concepts constitute the theoretical framework for defining the concept of practicability and contextualising the findings of the comparative content analysis, which are discussed in the following sections. Building on notions of child-friendliness, walkability, affordance, functioning and capability, Practicability can be defined as the potential of the built environment to enable children's mobility, agency and experience of the public space, by increasing their possibilities to engage in independent functional, optional, recreational and social outdoor activities. Practicability is thus determined by the functional, emotional and social affordances incorporated in the built environment, by their availability, usefulness, usability and perceivability [9, 35].

5 Findings and Discussion: Natural Settings Correlates of Children's Independent Activities

Richard Louv [39] introduces the notion of "nature deficit disorder" to describe the loss of the opportunity for children to explore "wild lands" and Chawla [6] underlines the significance of landscaping as an essential a part of the basic infrastructure of a settlement as electricity, water, sewers, and paving. In particular, within the landscape urbanism and the landscape as infrastructure paradigms, the two networks strategy focuses on the design of blue/green networks as carrying structures that organize the contemporary city at different scales while facilitating the synergy of ecology, economy and social processes [40]. A trans-scalar mosaic of patches of natural spaces can constitute the framework of a multi-functional system that serves water purification, drainage, retention and biodiversity while incorporating a capillary network of public spaces and direct pedestrian and cycling paths [6, 40]. The comparative content analysis of the selected articles underlines that natural settings, landscaping and natural elements significantly increase the practicability of the public space and its conductivity to children's independent activities, by affecting built environment characteristics related to the dimensions of convenience, comfort, conviviality and conspicuousness (Table 1).

Table 1. Results of the Comparative content analysis for the most relevant selected articles

Article	Methodology	Conceptual apparatus	Correlates of children's CIAs related to natural settings
Min and Lee [25]	Data collection: Field interviews and place-centered behavioral observations; Data analysis: Chi-squared tests; t-tests; measure of inter-rater reliabilities	Place; Space; psycological realm; behavorial realms;	Availability of informal sites for play (vacant and undeveloped natural areas); Vegetation coverage; Variety of microclimatic conditions; Availability of loose spaces; Size and morphological regularity of available spaces; Privacy; Variety of spatial conditions; Articulation of edges; Availability of enabling materials;
Chawla [6]	Literature review;	Capabilities; self-construction of places; continuity with natural processes; Environmental congruence;	Distance to green areas; Availability of formal/informal sites for play; Presence of vegetation; Biodiversity; Presence of water features; Cleanliness of water features; Availability of enabling materials; Variety of spatial conditions; Imageability; Complexity; Management of planted areas (cleanliness; use of pesticides); Access to green areas affected by ethnicity and SES;
Villanueva et al. [30]	Literature review;	Ecology of childhood; exposure; resource;	Availability of formal and informal sites for play; Availability of enabling materials; Imageability, Human scale; complexity;
Witten et al. [17]	Quantitative data collection: GPS; Travel diaries; Accelerometers; Individual interviews, Group discussion, School based focus groups;	Hyperdiversity; Enabling places; Third places; Tactics; Affective atmosphere;	Access to formal sites for play; Availability of loose spaces; Availability of enabling materials for imaginative/creative/intra-active play;

(continued)

Table 1. (*continued*)

Article	Methodology	Conceptual apparatus	Correlates of children's CIAs related to natural settings
Chaudhury et al. [41]	Qualitative study: go-along neighbourhood walking interviews and homebased interviews. Deductive thematic analysis;	Potential, perceived, utilised and shaped affordances;	Distance to Public open spaces; Availability of Public open spaces; Meeting places; Availability of loose spaces; Variety of spatial conditions; Availability of enabling materials;
Garau et al. [3]	Data collection: Focus groups; Urban exploration; Secondary data. Determination of the I_{SCOPE} Index of practicability	Autonomy; Affordance; Capability	Vegetation density; Urban water features incorporated in public space design; Availability of regions (clusters) of space for play; Imageability; Complexity; Management of planted areas

5.1 Convenience

The literature review underlines the function of natural settings as formal and informal sites of play. Natural settings can incorporate different "third places", including destination spaces, threshold spaces and transition spaces relevant for children's socialisation and community life. In particular, green areas, parks, nature/conservation areas, woods, wastelands, vacant lots, river banks, beaches, ponds and construction sites are identified as places enabling experimentation, exploration, manipulation, including making constructions with loose parts, quietly resting, watching or dabbling in sand or water, climbing, sliding down slopes, sitting and talking with other children, or playing non competitive games like 'hide and seek' and 'tiggy' [6, 15, 23, 28, 29, 35].

The availability, accessibility and sense of territoriality emerge as fundamental characters of these spaces, for enabling children's spatial appropriation, and for determining the conceptional and use value of a natural setting. At a different scale, pockets of nature, integrated in the design of the public space, incorporate loose, available spaces for children's independent activities. This condition is identified as a correlate of children's recreational and social practices [9, 15–17, 25, 35, 40–43] as opposed to the manufactured, rigidly designed tight space of the playground [24]. In particular, the openness, undeterminedness of loose surfaces enable sense of territoriality, appropriation, thus allowing for children to engage in intra-active play with spaces and things, and with other living materials. In other words, loose spaces are a fundamental condition for increasing the child-friendliness of cities. Min and Lee [25] and Garau et al. [3] identify size and morphological regularity as a fundamental condition for increasing the openness of a space to diverse informal and structured recreational and social practices. A further positive effect on children's outdoor independent activities is determined by the function of natural settings as meeting places [30, 34, 41, 43]. A meeting place can be defined as an available and accessible place for social interactions and developing networks of support.

5.2 Comfort

The integration of natural elements in the public space is related also to improved conditions of comfort and well-being, resulting from the control of micro-climatic conditions and from the emotional affordances incorporated in natural elements and settings. Jamme, Bahl, and Banerjee [9] and Nordström [34] observe that the presence of vegetation and green spaces determines a sense of belonging and positive perceptions on the child-friendliness of spaces. Min and Lee [25] underline that the presence of natural elements is conducive to the identification of a setting as an important place. The integration of water features in the public space, water cleanliness and opportunities to sit in proximity of the water features incorporate functional and contextual/emotional affordances that positively affect children's perceptions of the public space and their propensity to engage in recreational and social activities [6, 16].

Broberg et al. [32] observe a positive association between the proportion of green structure, defined as the proportion of fields, forests, parks, and water out of the total grid cell area with emotional and action level functional affordances. Yet, this factor is negatively related to the amount of leisure-time, activity-level functional affordances and social affordances and to the number of actualised affordances. This finding seems to indicate the potential of dense built environment to incorporate a greater number and variety of social, functional and emotional opportunities: this assumption recalls Jane Jacobs's recognition of variety of primary and secondary function as a pre-codition for diversity and vitality [33]. Nevertheless, Witten et al. [17] underline that the identification of a setting as an important or enabling places results from the combination of material, social and symbolic stimuli. Consequently, similar spatial conditions, including similar natural settings, can be characterized by different affective atmospheres, producing different felt experiences. Furthermore, vegetation and bio-diversity are related to positive effects on physical health. According to Rook [44], the great variety and number of microbiota that coexist with diverse vegetation, animal species, and fertile soils is associated with the development of a well-regulated immune system.

Contact with natural spaces is related with benefits in terms of cognitive functioning and self-control. The frequent view of natural settings is associated by Faber, Taylor, Kuo, and Sullivan [45] with better performances on tests of concentration, control of impulsivity, and delay of gratification.

Finally, Ferré, Guitart, and Ferret [42] and Min and Lee [25] observe a positive association between levels of independent activities and variety of microclimatic conditions. This aspect emphasises the complex relationship between perceptions of thermal comfort and macro and micro-climatic conditions, individual activity, physiology, adaptation – including clothing, change in metabolic heath, posture and position – as well as personal choice, memory and expectation [46]. Vegetation, depending on its position, orientation, extent, density, physiology, acts as a versatile, self-regulating element of control of conditions of ventilation and irradiation [47].

5.3 Conviviality

The functional affordances incorporated in natural settings affect the conviviality dimension of public open spaces, by increasing the opportunities for children's functional, optional, and social activities. The diversity of spatial conditions is a further positive attribute of public open spaces, and of natural settings, associated with children's possibilities to engage in independent activities. The diversity of landscape elements and topography (slopes, steps, terraces, level changes) are positively associated with children's independent activities by Chaudhury et al. [41] and by Min and Lee [25]. The minimal geometry designed by variations in the morphology of surfaces thus incorporates potential functional affordances for different informal or structured recreational and social activities: a shaded area incorporates a repaired space for resting, a sloped lawn a surface for playing sliding, a hill encloses an obstacle to climb on, a partition can be re-signified and transformed in a springboard for jumping or in a balance beam [2]. Finally, vegetation, grass, dirt surfaces, water features, loose elements incorporating affordances for contacts, exploration and manipulation, are identified as significant correlates of children's independent outdoor activities. Chawla [6] and Chaudhury et al. [41] underline the relevance of a tree, as well as of lawns, sand banks, of a brook, or bushes as enabling materials for physical activity, for retreating and resting, for play activities; patches of dirt or loose parts (earth, water, stones, grass, and branches) are resources for creative and imaginative play, including manipulation and construction. Vilanueva et al. observe that natural play environments, incorporating natural elements and vegetation appear more conducive to children's cognitive and physical development than physical man-made play areas [30]. Opportunities for contact with insects and small animals habitats, vegetation, sand, stone as well as water, are found to be positively related to adults' and children's perceptions of natural play spaces. Witten et al. [17] observe in which ways vegetation incorporate enabling resources, and thus constitute a material condition for determining the affective atmosphere of enabling places: a tree, located in a threshold space lying between and within view of surrounding buildings, is appropriated by a group of children and imbued with meaning.

The tree is identified as a material resource and is transformed in a place of inclusion and belonging through frequent practices. The materiality of the tree and the sociability it generates produce an affective atmosphere, reflected in the act of naming a tree the "family tree"; the affective atmosphere, incorporated in the materiality of the tree, is both the product and the constitutive condition of the relational bonds among the children [17]. This process of appropriation and transformation of a space through social activities is a manifestation of childhood tactics. Kyttä et al. [35] and McGlone [43] underline the opportunities to interact with small animals. McGlone [43] also observes that garden beds constitute opportunities for gardening and for semi-structured activities, including hiding, chatting, sitting and observing insects. Furniture can be perceived by children as an affordance for semi-structured, informal activities: a seat bench is thus appropriated and transformed through play, in open, adaptable, versatile object for jumping and climbing. In general terms, the availability of temporary, adaptable features is positively associated to children's propensity and possibility to engage in independent activities. Finally, Pyyry [24], observes that the manipulation, experimentation and appropriation of spatial elements and loose objects, can result in intra-active play and can generate a meaningful, affectual engagement with a specific setting or place. Reflecting on two children climbing up a stone wall with the help of a tree, Pyyry [24] observes that the children were invited to exploration by the diverting and fascinating character of the setting. This can be referred to as things powers: the potential of material elements to affect human bodies.

Finally, natural elements, including plants, mature trees, landscaping, major landscape elements, affect the conspicuosness of the public space by reinforcing its complexity, human scale and imageability [5, 16, 35, 43].

6 Conclusion

This extensive review aims to contribute to the academic research on child-friendly cities, to the governance processes within the smart-city paradigm [2, 3] and to the urban-planning practice, by supporting the understanding and the re-shaping of the relationship between green/blue infrastructure, grey infrastructure, built environment and children's functional, optional and social practices. The contribution of the literature review involves two aspects: (i) structuring a conceptual apparatus for describing children's experience of the public space, and the enabling conditions of their independent activities; (ii) clarifying how and to what extent natural settings and elements integrated in the public space affect children's practices. The first aspect is articulated by the introduction and definition of the concepts of important place, of enabling place, of capability, and of affordance. The latter, in particular, emphasizes the relation among the characters of the public space that incorporate functional, emotional and social opportunities, the individual abilities, competences and tactics, and the resulting spatial practices and perceptions.

The concept of practicability is introduced to broaden the notion of child-friendliness, and to highlight the material, spatial, functional and social conditions of the public space that affect children's mobility, agency and experience by maximizing their propensity and possibilities to engage in independent outdoor activities. The notion of independent activities itself implies a shift from the concepts of independent mobility and physical activity, emphasizing both the aspect of the independence and of the multiplicity of activities, including exploration and spatial appropriation. These are regarded as conditions for a meaningful experience of the public space that restores children's right to the city and significantly affects their physical, cognitive, social and emotional development.

The third aspect focuses on the significance of natural settings and elements as affordances and spatial focus of children's independent activities. The literature review emphasizes that natural settings, including destination, threshold and transitory spaces, emerge in children's accounts as behavior settings, and as spaces imbued with meaning and use and symbolic value. Natural settings are identified as important places. Hence, children identify natural settings as spaces both useful and conducive to purposive behavior. It is the variety of emotional, social and functional opportunities, the sense of territoriality and of belonging that determine the potential of natural settings to support practices respondent to children's multiple purposes and needs. Thus, the characters of looseness, vagueness and availability of natural settings and elements integrated in the built environment emerge from this literature review as instrumental to maximizing children's possibilities of choice among different social and recreational activities, including physical activity, imaginative, creative and intra-active play and structured group activities.

These findings produce an image of green/blue infrastructure as a transcalar and continuous mosaic of natural settings, including both formalized spaces and vague, thresholds and transitory spaces, connected to the networks of public space, pedestrian paths and services and amenities relevant for children. The future development of this research will focus on the definition of indicators for the operationalization of the characters of natural settings identified as correlates of children's activities. The definition of indicators, of use-value function and quality thresholds, will be instrumental to the improvement of the synthetic index of practicability and of Survey on Conditions of Practicable Environments [3]. The structuring of a methodological framework for the assessment of the public space is aimed at supporting the implementation of governance practices, policies and strategies, within the smart-city paradigm, for designing and building networks of safe, stimulating, vibrant public spaces to promote equality and inclusivity.

Acknowledgments. This study was supported by the MIUR (Ministry of Education, Universities and Research [Italy] through a project entitled *Governing tHe smart city: a gOvernance-centred approach to SmarT urbanism - GHOST* (Project code: RBSI14FDPF; CUP Code: F22I15000070008), financed with the SIR (Scientific Independence of Young Researchers) programme. We authorize the MIUR to reproduce and distribute reprints for Governmental purposes, notwithstanding any copyright notations thereon. Any opinions, findings and conclusions or recommendations expressed in this material are those of the authors, and do not necessarily reflect the views of the MIUR.

This study was also supported by the project 'Healthy Cities and Smart Territories', founded by the Foundation of Sardinia and Autonomous Region of Sardinia (Fondazione di Sardegna – Convenzione triennale tra la Fondazione di Sardegna e gli Atenei Sardi Regione Sardegna 2016).

References

1. Lefebvre, H.: The right to the city. In: Kofman, E., Lebas, E. (eds.) Writings on Cities, pp. 63–184. Blackwell, Cambridge (1995)
2. Annunziata, A., Garau, C.: Understanding kid-friendly urban space for a more inclusive smart city: the case study of Cagliari (Italy). In: Gervasi, O., et al. (eds.) ICCSA 2018. LNCS, vol. 10962, pp. 589–605. Springer, Cham (2018). https://doi.org/10.1007/978-3-319-95168-3_40
3. Garau, C., Annunziata, A., Coni, M.: A methodological framework for assessing practicability of the urban space: the survey on conditions of practicable environments (SCOPE) procedure applied in the case study of Cagliari (Italy). Sustainability **10**(11), 4189 (2018)

4. Churchman, A.: Is there a place for children in the city? J. Urban Des. **8**(2), 99–111 (2003)
5. O'brien, M., Jones, D., Sloan, D., Rustin, M.: Children's independent spatial mobility in the urban public realm. Childhood **7**(3), 257–277 (2000)
6. Chawla, L.: Benefits of nature contact for children. J. Plan. Lit. **30**(4), 433–452 (2015)
7. Galvez, M.P., et al.: Associations between neighborhood resources and physical activity in inner-city minority children. Acad. Pediatr. **13**(1), 20–26 (2013)
8. Burdette, H.L., Whitaker, R.C.: A national study of neighborhood safety, outdoor play, television viewing, and obesity in preschool children. Pediatrics **116**(3), 657–662 (2005)
9. Jamme, H.T.W., Bahl, D., Banerjee, T.: Between "broken windows" and the "eyes on the street:" Walking to school in inner city San Diego. J. Environ. Psychol. **55**, 121–138 (2018)
10. Lopes, F., Cordovil, R., Neto, C.: Children's independent mobility in Portugal: effects of urbanization degree and motorized modes of travel. J. Transp. Geogr. **41**, 210–219 (2014)
11. Christian, H., et al.: The influence of the neighborhood physical environment on early child health and development: a review and call for research. Health Place **33**, 25–36 (2015)
12. Kyttä, A.M., Broberg, A.K., Kahila, M.H.: Urban environment and children's active lifestyle: SoftGIS revealing children's behavioral patterns and meaningful places. Am. J. Health Promot. **26**(5), e137–e148 (2012)
13. Goltsman, S., Kelly, L., McKay, S., Algara, P., Wight, L.: Raising "free range kids": creating neighborhood parks that promote environmental stewardship. J. Green Build. **4**(2), 90–106 (2009)
14. Lin, E.Y., et al.: Social and built-environment factors related to children's independent mobility: the importance of neighbourhood cohesion and connectedness. Health Place **46**, 107–113 (2017)
15. Furneaux, A., Manaugh, K.: Eyes on the alley: children's appropriation of alley space in Riverdale, Toronto. Child. Geographies **17**, 204–216 (2018)
16. Whitzman, C., Mizrachi, D.: Creating child-friendly high-rise environments: beyond wastelands and glasshouses. Urban Policy Res. **30**(3), 233–249 (2012)
17. Witten, K., Kearns, R., Carroll, P., Asiasiga, L.: Children's everyday encounters and affective relations with place: experiences of hyperdiversity in Auckland neighbourhoods. Soc. Cult. Geogr. **9365**, 1–18 (2017)
18. Sen, A.: Capability and well-being. In: Nussbaum, M., Sen, A. (eds.) The Quality of Life, pp. 30–53. Clarendon Press, Oxford, UK (1993)
19. Nussbaum, M.C.: Creating Capabilities, p. 2011. Harvard University Press, Cambridge (2011)
20. Carroll, P., Witten, K., Kearns, R., Donovan, P.: Kids in the city: children's use and experiences of urban neighbourhoods in Auckland, New Zealand. J. Urban Des. **20**(4), 417–436 (2015)
21. Moura, F., Cambra, P., Gonçalves, A.B.: Measuring walkability for distinct pedestrian groups with a participatory assessment method: a case study in Lisbon. Landscape Urban Plan. **157**, 282–296 (2017)
22. Caspersen, C.J., Powell, K.E., Christenson, G.M.: Physical activity, exercise, and physical fitness: definitions and distinctions for health-related research. Public Health Rep. **100**(2), 126 (1985)
23. Aarts, M.J., Wendel-Vos, W., van Oers, H.A., van de Goor, I.A., Schuit, A.J.: Environmental determinants of outdoor play in children: a large-scale cross-sectional study. Am. J. Prev. Med. **39**(3), 212–219 (2010)
24. Pyyry, N.: Thinking with broken glass: making pedagogical spaces of enchantment in the city. Environ. Educ. Res. **23**(10), 1391–1401 (2017)
25. Min, B., Lee, J.: Children's neighborhood place as a psychological and behavioral domain. J. Environ. Psychol. **26**(1), 51–71 (2006)

26. Sharmin, S., Kamruzzaman, M.: Association between the built environment and children's independent mobility: a meta-analytic review. J. Transp. Geogr. **61**(2017), 104–117 (2017)

27. Gillespie, J.: Being and becoming: writing children into planning theory. Plan. Theory **12**(1), 64–80 (2013)

28. Committee on Environmental Health: The built environment: designing communities to promote physical activity in children. Pediatrics **123**(6), 1591–1598 (2009)

29. Oliver, M., et al.: Associations between the neighbourhood built environment and out of school physical activity and active travel: an examination from the Kids in the City study. Health Place **36**, 57–64 (2015)

30. Villanueva, K., et al.: Can the neighborhood built environment make a difference in children's development? Building the research agenda to create evidence for place-based children's policy. Acad. Pediatr. **16**(1), 10–19 (2016)

31. Christian, H., et al.: Relationship between the neighbourhood built environment and early child development. Health Place **48**, 90–101 (2017)

32. Broberg, A., Kyttä, M., Fagerholm, N.: Child-friendly urban structures: bullerby revisited. J. Environ. Psychol. **35**, 110–120 (2013)

33. Jacobs, J.: The Death and Life of Great American Cities. Random House, New York (1961)

34. Nordström, M.: Children's views on child-friendly environments in different geographical, cultural and social neighbourhoods. Urban Stud. **47**(3), 514–528 (2010)

35. Kyttä, M., Oliver, M., Ikeda, E., Ahmadi, E., Omiya, I., Laatikainen, T.: Children as urbanites: mapping the affordances and behavior settings of urban environments for Finnish and Japanese children. Child. Geogr. **16**(3), 319–332 (2018)

36. Davis, A., Jones, L.J.: Children in the urban environment: an issue for the new public health agenda. Health Place **2**(2), 107–113 (1996)

37. Kyttä, M.: Children in Outdoor Contexts. Affordances and Independent Mobility in the Assessment of Environmental Child Friendliness. VDM Verlag Dr. Müller, Saarbröcken (2008)

38. Gibson, J.J.: The Ecological Approach to Visual Perception, p. 1986. Lawrence Erlbaum, Hillsdale (1979)

39. Louv, R.: Last Child in the Woods. Algonquin Books, Chapel Hill (2005)

40. Tjallingii, S.: Planning with water and traffic networks - carrying structures of the urban landscape. In: Nijhuis, S., Jauslin, D., Van Der Hoeven, F. (eds.) Flowscapes – Designing infrastructure as landscape, pp. 57–80. Delft University of Technology, Delft (2015)

41. Chaudhury, M., Hinckson, E., Badland, H., Oliver, M.: Children's independence and affordances experienced in the context of public open spaces: a study of diverse inner-city and suburban neighbourhoods in Auckland, New Zealand. Child. Geogr. **17**, 49–63 (2017)

42. Ferré, M.B., Guitart, A.O., Ferret, M.P.: Children and playgrounds in Mediterranean cities. Child. Geogr. **4**(2), 173–183 (2006)

43. McGlone, N.: Pop-Up kids: exploring children's experience of temporary public space. Aust. Planner **53**(2), 117–126 (2016)

44. Rook, G.: Regulation of the Immune System by Biodiversity from the Natural Environment. PNAS Proc. Natl. Acad. Sci. USA **110**(46), 18360–18367 (2013)

45. Taylor, A.F., Kuo, F.E., Sullivan, W.C.: Views of nature and self-discipline: evidence from inner-city children. J. Environ. Psychol. **22**, 49–63 (2002)

46. Nikolopoulou, M., Baker, N., Steemers, K.: Thermal comfort in outdoor urban spaces: understanding the human parameter. Sol. Energy **70**(3), 227–235 (2001)

47. Klemm, W., Heusinkveld, B.G., Lenzholzer, S., Van Hove, B.: Street greenery and its physical and psychological impact on thermal comfort. Landscape Urban Plan. **138**, 87–98 (2015)

The Concept of the Deviant Behavior Detection System via Surveillance Cameras

Nikolay Teslya[1,2] ⓘ, Igor Ryabchikov[2(✉)], and Evgeniy Lipkin[2]

[1] SPIIRAS, 14th Line 39, 199178 St. Petersburg, Russia
teslya@iias.spb.su
[2] ITMO University, Kronverksky pr. 49, 197101 St. Petersburg, Russia
i.a.ryabchikov@gmail.com, eugenejsm@mail.ru

Abstract. One of the tasks of a Smart City is an ensuring the safety of its residents. Dangerous situations are often caused by deviant behavior of people: robbery, fight, kidnapping, attack, etc. Nowadays all cities are equipped with video surveillance systems that are used to monitor city life. They also can be used to detect potentially dangerous situation in a real-time and to inform emergency services to taking actions that will help to eliminate them. Due to the huge amount of video material, to solve the problem of detecting dangerous situations, it is necessary to use modern intelligent technologies that allow their automatic analysis. This paper proposes a review of modern technologies, and concept of the deviant behavior detection system based on the reviewed technologies.

Keywords: Deviant behavior · Surveillance · Computer vision · Smart city · Neural network · 3D skeleton · Markov logic networks

1 Introduction

Nowadays many cities are increasingly introducing the concept of a smart city to ensure sustainable development. Within the scope of this concept, the use of various sensors and data accumulation and processing systems for the analysis and formation of decisions and recommendations on the management of the city is considered. Also, gathered information in a smart city can be used to provide services for the city citizens, making life in the city more comfortable.

One of the important part of smart city system is a Closed-circuit television (CCTV) or video surveillance system. For example there are more than 500000 CCTV cameras only in London. The CCTV is mostly used now for ensuring the safety of smart city residents. Until recently, it was used mainly as evidences sources and for analyzing incidents after their completion. But it has much greater potential, which can be revealed through the use of modern computer vision technologies, which allow automatic analysis of a huge amount of video in real time. An example of the

This work was partly supported by the grant of ITMO University (Project № 618268).

successful application of such technologies is the face recognition system which was used at the 2018 World Cup and helped to identify over 180 wanted offenders [1].

But computer vision technologies are not limited to face recognition – they can provide the detection of complex scenes, thereby providing real-time awareness of the dangerous situations occurring in the city and allowing timely actions to eliminate them. Often a dangerous situation is caused by the deviant behavior of people: robbery, assault, fighting, placing suspicious objects in public places, etc.

The complexity of the task of deviant behavior detection lies in the strong variability of scenes of interest: they can run for a variable amount of time and contain a variable number of people performing a wide range of interactions. At the same time, the amount of data that can be utilized by machine learning techniques (examples of scenes of interest) is relatively small, taking into account the variability. For example, in accordance with recent burglary published in UK Police Department web site [2], after getting money from ATM, a victim was followed by two individuals, and then stopped with threatening and demanding cash. The victim managed to run off but the men caught up with him and subjected him to a prolonged violent attack during which he was punched and kicked repeatedly and threatened with knives. His attackers then ran off.

The paper presents an overview of the existing intelligent technologies that can be used to develop a system for detecting complex scenes of deviant behavior via the city's video surveillance cameras, and the concept of such a system. Section 2 presents adopted systems of dangerous situations detection in smart cities. Section 3 describes the early approaches of solving the problem of deviant behavior detection. Section 4 presents an overview of modern computer vision technologies, which make it possible to obtain a compact set of sufficiently representative features of the scene. Section 5 presents examples of scenes of deviant behavior and their distinguishing features that can be detected. Section 6 describes the proposed concept of a deviant behavior detection system.

2 Dangerous Situations Detection in Smart Cities

Timely detection of dangerous situations will make it possible to provide immediate help to victims, prevent further escalation and detain the perpetrators. The use of sensors and application of intelligent technologies for this purpose falls into the concept of smart city. At the moment there are a number of successful projects aimed at detecting dangerous situations:

- Detection and localization of gunfire using sound sensors. The technology allows not only to respond quickly to the incident, but also to provide the police with a vision of the situation and develop a strategy for action. An example of its implementation is the ShotSpotter project [3], adopted in more than 90 cities of USA.
- Wanted criminals detection with face recognition technologies. An example of the implementation is the FindFace Public Safety system [4], which was used at the 2018 World Cup and helped to identify over 180 wanted offenders.

- Smoke detection via surveillance cameras. An example is the SmokeCatcher system [5], mainly used on industrial sites.
- Detection of abandoned objects in public places via surveillance cameras. An example is the Reco3.26 system [6].

But so far no finished system has been introduced for detecting deviant behavior of people that is ready for use in a real environment. A review of existing approaches is presented below.

3   Early Solutions for Deviant Behavior Detection

In earlier works, the task of classifying people's activities was mainly divided into three stages: segmentation of regions of interest in frames based on simple hypotheses (for example, by the presence of motion); handcrafted features calculation for the selected regions; and video clips classification according to these features using machine learning, for example, the Support Vector Machines (SVM) classifier. For instance, in [7], an approach for people's activities classification based on optical flow analysis, histograms of oriented gradients and the Bag-of-Words (BoF) model utilization is presented. First, the points of interest are detected by the scale-invariant features transformation (SIFT) algorithm. Then, histograms of oriented gradients and histograms of optical flow, which are used as words in the Bag-of-Words model, are calculated in the surrounding regions of the points. Finally, SVM is used for the classification of activities in the frame.

The disadvantage of this approach in relation to the task of deviant behavior detection is the focus on detecting only activities that have distinctive signs of movement (speed, acceleration). But in complex scenes of deviant behavior, there may be no obvious differences in speed and acceleration (for example, a robbery without a fight or a confrontation scene preceding a fight). In addition, the handcrafted features often have poor interpretability and reflect actions of people only indirectly, due to which the behavior of such classifiers can be unpredictable when used in a real diverse environment. But despite the fact that at the moment there are more advanced computer vision technologies that allow for a more in-depth analysis of videos, such approaches are still emerging, improving the results of earlier work. The main motivation is the fact that these solutions are often less computationally expensive.

In [8], a fight detection approach is proposed that is largely similar to [7] but differs by the method of region segmentation - segmentation is based on the optical flow instead of SIFT algorithm, also there are differences in histograms of oriented gradients and optical flow calculation. Similarly, the Bag-of-Words model is applied to histograms and the classification is performed using SVM. The approach was tested on a dataset containing scenes of hockey fights [9] and archived 95% accuracy.

In [10], an approach of violent behavior detection in crowds based on the analysis of changes in textural properties of the Gray Level Co-occurrence Matrix (GLCM) over time is proposed. First, each frame of the video is divided by the grid into multiple sub-frames of equal size. Further processing and classification are performed individually for each sub-frame. To remove the effect of the background, the difference of the

GLCM matrices for adjacent frames is calculated. Then, based on the resulting matrix, various statistical properties are calculated: energy, contrast, homogeneity, correlation, and dissimilarity. According to the properties obtained for each time frame of the video, the final properties are calculated: mean, standard deviation, skewness, interframe uniformity. Then the classification is performed using Random Forests. The method was tested on the Violent Flow dataset [11] and showed 86% accuracy (for comparison, MoSIFT [7] showed 89% accuracy).

With the development of convolutional neural networks, a host of computer vision technologies have emerged that allows the estimation of various features of a video content giving a glance on what is happening. But so far no solution has been proposed that uses their full potential. An example is the Eye in the Sky project, which proposes the use of drones for observing areas and detecting fights based on a 2D skeleton (key points of the body) of a person [12]. For fights classification, SVM is used, which consumes angles between the limbs of a body of a single person. The proposed approach achieved 88.8% accuracy on the data set proposed by the developers. The main shortcomings of the approach is that the system takes into account only a single person pose, and does not consider a movement in time.

4 Related Modern Computer Vision Technologies

The main difficulty in detecting scenes of deviant behavior of people lies in the strong variability of such scenes. To reduce variability, it is necessary to form a small but representative set of properties describing the observing scene for further analyses. Below are the technologies that allows the extraction of such properties from plain RGB videos.

4.1 Detection of People

Detection of people is one of the first tasks that must be solved for the purpose of deviant behavior classification. Detection refers to the evaluation of bounding boxes for each person present in the frame.

The best results for the detection of pedestrians within the MOT17Det Challenge (https://motchallenge.net/data/MOT17Det/) were achieved in works [13–15]. All of them offer variations of convolutional neural networks with modifications to solve the multi-scale problem.

4.2 Tracking and Re-identifying People on Video

Another vital task for people's actions analyzation is matching of people detected on individual frames. To solve it, various properties of appearance and behavior (colors, speed, etc.) are used, as well as the assumption of smooth movements of people in adjacent frames, manifested in a slow change in their position and posture. The difficulty this task acquires in crowded scenes with a significant overlap of people. The popular challenges for tracking people on video are Multi-Person PoseTrack 2018 (https://posetrack.net/workshops/ecc201201/) and VOT2018 (http://www.votchallenge. net/vot2018/). In Multi-Person PoseTrack, in addition to short-term tracking of people, there is the task of two-dimensional poses evaluation. In VOT2018, the task is to assess the bounding boxes of people during the short-term and long-term tracking (when a person can disappear from view for a long period of time). The best results on Multi-Person PoseTrack were obtained in [16], which proposes the propagation of poses from previous frames using optical flow, and their comparison with the detected ones. In [17], the results of the VOT2018 Challenge and description of the participants' approaches are presented.

4.3   Three-Dimensional Human Skeleton Evaluation

Probably the most representative properties of the scene are three-dimensional human skeletons (Fig. 1) - sets of key points of bodies (head, torso, shoulders, elbows, palms, pelvis, knees, feet, etc.). On their basis, a large range of actions and interactions of people can be classified, for example, punches, kicks, transfer of an object, search of pockets, etc.

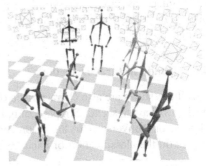

Fig. 1. Example of three-dimensional skeletons evaluation from the CMU Panoptic dataset [16].

One of the most popular data sets for training and validating human actions detection models is Human3.6M [19], associated with the prestigious challenge ECCV 18 (https://posetrack.net/workshops/eccv2018/). This challenge proposes a subset of images of Human3.6M and sets the task of detecting the three coordinates of each joint in the 3D space of the camera. The best results were achieved in [20–23]. A survey of human actions classification approaches using skeletons is presented in [24].

4.4   Objects Segmentation and Classification

A scene of deviant behavior is characterized by the interaction of people with each other and surrounding objects. Such objects can be bags, shop windows, ATMs, vehicles, tools, etc. Thus, a classifier of objects is an important component for understanding the scene. At the same time, the segmentation of objects is necessary to determine the exact relative position of objects and people, as well as the dimensions of objects. In this case, segmentation refers to the evaluation of areas directly occupied by objects. The task of segmentation and classification rises in the popular challenge COCO Detection 2018 (http://cocodataset.org/#detection-2018). Best segmentation results were achieved using Mask R-CNN [25]. A review of modern approaches for the classification of objects is presented in [26].

4.5   Surfaces Segmentation and Determination of Their Orientation

The landscape determination (surrounding obstacles, walls, roads, etc.) can help in analyzing the actions of people on a scene. For example, determining the location of the walls and correlating it with the location of the alleged victim and deviants, it can be concluded whether the victim could retreat or was blocked, which in turn increases the likelihood of a deviant behavior.

In [27, 28], approaches are proposed for segmentation of surfaces (planes) and determination of their orientation using a single RGB image. The approaches are based on the use of neural networks, trained end-to-end. For training, data sets containing RGB-D images are used, allowing to segment and estimate the parameters of the presented three-dimensional planes with simple calculations. Neural networks take an RGB image as input and provide segmentation maps (probabilities of each pixel belonging to one or another plane) and parameters of these planes (three-dimensional normal vectors) as output.

4.6   Hand Gestures Detection

Specific gestures are also characteristic of various participants (victims, aggressors) in a deviant behavior scene. Simple examples are clenched hands, grabbing a person by clothes, or, conversely, trying to prevent an attack with an open palm. A review of papers on the classification of hand gestures is presented in article [29].

4.7   Face Detection

Currently, there are numerous technologies for face detection and individuals identification, for example, the popular open source system OpenFace [30]. In video surveillance, an example of the use of such technologies is the identification of wanted criminals. For the purpose of deviant behavior detection, it is proposed to use these technologies to determine whether the face of the suspect is open (and it is possible to use the image for person identification in future). If the face of the suspect is covered with a mask or helmet, this increases suspiciousness and may testify in favor of the deviant behavior manifestation.

4.8   Gender Recognition

Gender can increase confidence in the classification of ambiguous cases, given the statistics of manifestations of deviant behavior (for example, the likelihood of a woman being a robber may be less than a man [31]). In paper [32], the Faster-RCNN convolutional neural network for gender classification, pre-trained for human detection, is proposed. The work [33] proposes the use of SVM for gender classification by features of color and texture—Hue-Saturation-Value (HSV) and Local Binary Patterns (LBP).

4.9 Determination of Clothing

Clothing can also be used as an additional feature when classifying ambiguous scenes, reflecting the "aggressiveness" of the scene participants. For that purpose, the color range and type of clothing may be considered. The work [34] proposes the calculation of color (HSV) and textural (HOG, MB-LBP) features of clothing items, and the subsequent classification of the type of clothing using Gentle AdaBoost [35] and color using KNN. The work [36] also proposes the calculation of various color (histograms of colors) and textural features (HOG, Bag of dense SIFT Features, DCT responses). SVM is used for clothing classification. In [37] the use of a convolutional neural network (based on AlexNet) for classifying the type of clothing and defining various attributes (color, sleeve length, neckline, etc.) is proposed.

5 Examples of Deviant Behavior Scenes

Using the computer vision technologies described above, a lot of features of observing scenes can be extracted: the position and appearance of people, the surrounding objects, the landscape, the interaction of people with each other and with objects. We assume that these features are sufficient for detecting a large spectrum of deviant behavior scenes. For example, consider the scenes presented in the UCF-Crime [38] and I-LIDS [39] data sets. UCF-Crime contains 1900 videos (128 h in total), which depict 13 types of scenes of abnormal incidents and deviant behavior of people recorded by surveillance cameras: abuse, arrest, arson, assault, road accident, burglary, explosion, fighting, robbery, shooting, stealing, shoplifting, vandalism. Videos were collected from YouTube and LiveLeaks. I-LIDS is provided by the UK government to benchmark Video Analytics systems. It focuses on several tasks, in particular, the detection of abandoned packages, the observation of doorways (detection of all incoming/outgoing people) and tracking of people through several intersecting and non-intersecting video surveillance cameras. For each scenario, there is approximately 24 h of video.

Most of the fight scenes from the UCF-Crime set correlate with the presence of simple intrinsic actions (in particular, punches and kicks) performed towards a near person, falls and specific poses (Fig. 2 left and middle). These actions are short in time, highly discriminative, and can be distinguished observing a three-dimensional human skeleton. But of particular interest is the task of fights detection before their escalation, when timely intervention can prevent them. In that case, individual actions performed by people are less expressive, but when considering actions of all the participants in the scene for a sufficiently long period of time, it is possible to distinguish suspicious activity. For example, in Fig. 2, the right represents a frame of a confrontation scene without a clear manifestation of violence. Deviant behavior is manifested in the following actions: the advance and retreat of the parties of the conflict, the pursuit while keeping each other in sight, accompanied by grasping and specific gestures. For the detection of such scenes, the following technologies can be used: tracking of people, three-dimensional skeletons evaluation and hand gestures classification.

Fig. 2. Fight scenes from the UCF-Crime dataset.

The important task is the detection of abandoned packages left in public places (Fig. 3). For that purpose, we need to track people and objects carried by them (in the hands, on the back, etc.) and detect when the carrier moves away from the object (while taking into account special cases, such as transfer of the object to another carrier). We can also detect the sudden absence of the object in a person (if the fact of placing the object did not get on the video) and the presence of a placed object, near which there is no permanent person. For that task, we can use technologies for objects segmentation and classification, tracking and re-identification of people and objects, three-dimensional skeletons evaluation.

Fig. 3. The scene of leaving the bag in a public place from the I-LIDS dataset.

Another type of deviant behavior is a burglary of ATMs (as well as cars, shop windows, etc.) (Fig. 4). Its characterizing signs can be the presence of people near ATMs in non-standard positions (bent, in a squat, etc.) or performing some "active" movements in relation to the ATM (strikes, using a lever, etc.). Increases the likelihood of deviant behavior the presence of objects in hands of suspects. To avoid false positive detections during regular maintenance, we can classify the appearance (form) of the employee, as well as check the scheduled service time. Technologies for people tracking, three-dimensional skeleton evaluation, segmentation and classification of objects (in the hands of people, ATMs, etc.) and clothing classification can be used.

Fig. 4. The ATM robbery scene from the UCF-Crime dataset.

Many types of robbery can be recognized by detecting the pose of the threat of a weapon against a nearby person (Fig. 5), in which a robber is in for a sufficiently long period of time. To detect the pose, technologies for three-dimensional skeletons evaluation, objects segmentation and classification (in the hands of an intruder) can be used. Increase confidence in the correct classification of the threat can the hidden face of the attacker (face detection technology).

Fig. 5. Scenes of robbery with the threat of a weapon from the UCF-Crime data set.

A popular method of robbery is that one or several people drive up to a victim, search/retrieve items (bags, wallets, etc.) and quickly drive away from the crime scene (Fig. 6). Sometimes a robbery is accompanied by the threat of a weapon. To detect this type of robbery, we can track the approaching of strangers, the transfer of objects to them (or the search of pockets) and their escape. As well as additional characteristic actions of alleged victims and robbers (did the victim try to retreat, were there any signs of resistance). To detect such scenes we can utilize technologies for tracking of people and objects, three-dimensional skeleton evaluation, segmentation and classification of objects, as well as technologies for detecting surfaces and their orientations (for correlating the actions of participants of the scene with the terrain, for example, whether the victim could retreat or was behind the wall).

Fig. 6. Scenes of the robbery by people on vehicles from the UCF-Crime dataset.

6   The Concept of the Deviant Behavior Detection System

For deviant behavior scenes classification it is tempting to use machine learning to automatically build a model. But, although the computer vision technologies described above can significantly reduce the variability of the original set of features (RGB frame sequences), the scenes of interest still have strong variability, since they can last a variable amount of time and contain a variable number of interacting people and objects. In addition, it's difficult to get a sufficient number of realistic examples of deviant behavior sequences to train the model. The solution is the utilization of crime experts knowledge. Based on the gathered knowledge, descriptions of scenes of interest will be formed in a formal language that supports inference (for instance, first-order logic). The elementary units (atoms) will be individual simple actions of people in time (sit down, take an object, get closer to a person or an object, etc.), features of people's appearance (gender, clothes), features of objects (type, size) and features of the terrain (wall positions, time of a day, terrain type) calculated on the basis of the computer vision components outputs and the provided background knowledge. With this approach, the decisions taken by the detection system can be explained. In [40], the application of first-order logic for scene recognition by smart agents in smart homes is considered. In the proposed approach, first, various qualitative features of objects in the room are detected (shape, color, topology and location) as well as the presence of special target objects that the agent can classify (TV, printer, table, etc.). Features are detected by low-level perception components and are represented as predicates used during reasoning in accordance with the agent's domain knowledge. As a result of the reasoning, the observed picture can be supplemented, and conclusions can be made about the condition of the room and the necessity of intervention (for example, spilled water in a room near an open window when it rains may indicate the need to shut the window and wipe the floor).

As an example, let's consider a possible description of the scene of the robbery presented in Fig. 6 in a first order logic (Table 1). For simplicity, this description of the scene does not take into account the time or sequence of events, but it's taken into account in atoms formed on the basis of the outputs of the perception components at a lower level (in particular, DistanceReducedBetween (Drives, Vict) and DistanceIncreasedBetween (Drives, Vict)). It should be noted that confidence in detecting deviant behavior can be increased by considering additional signs, in addition to the rules presented in Table 1. Among such signs are weapons threatening, victim's attempt to retreat, signs of struggle, gender of participants, the presence of masks on intruders, etc. Moreover, almost all basic features can be detected only with a certain confidence due to the specificity of the machine perception components and the fuzziness of certain features. Thus, the use of a probabilistic model suggests itself.

Table 1. Description of a street robbery scene in a first order logic.

№	Knowledge base rules
1	$\forall$Vehic.$\forall$Vict. $\forall$Crim. DistanceReducedBetween(Vehic, Vict) $\wedge$ (GotOutOfA(Crim,Vehic) $\vee$ WasOnA(Crim,Vehic)) $\wedge$ WereClose(Crim, Vict) $\rightarrow$ DroveUpTo(Crim, Vict)
2	$\forall$Crim. $\forall$Vict. $\forall$Bag. ReachedForAPocket(Crim, Vict) $\vee$ ReachedForABag(Crim, Bag) $\wedge$ HoldABag(Vict, Bag) $\rightarrow$ SearchedA(Crim, Vict)
3	$\forall$Vict. $\forall$Item. $\forall$Crim. HoldedA(Vict, Item) $\wedge$ HoldedA(Vict, Item) $\vee$ WereInHandingPose(Vict) $\rightarrow$ TookAnItem(Crim, Vict)
4	$\forall$Vehic. $\forall$Vict. $\forall$Crim. DistanceIncreasedBetween(Vehic, Vict) $\wedge$ (GotInA(Crim,Vehic) v WasOnA(Crim,Vehic)) $\wedge$ WereClose(Crim, Vict) $\rightarrow$ DoveAwayFrom(Crim, Vict)
5	$\forall$Vehic.$\forall$Vict. $\forall$Crim. DroveUpTo(Crim, Vict) $\wedge$ (SearchedA(Crim, Vehic) $\vee$ TookAnItem(Crim, Vict)) $\wedge$ DroveAwayFrom(Crim, Vict) $\rightarrow$ RoberryHappend(Crime, Vict)

The integration of probabilistic models and relational structures is the main topic of Statistical Relational Learning (SRL) discipline. It provides the formation of complex knowledge structures, while taking into account the various uncertainties of the real world. One of the most popular representational formalisms of SRL is the Markov Logic Network (MLN) [41], combining first-order logic and probabilistic graphical models (Markov networks). MLN is a first-order knowledge base with weights associated with each formula and reflecting their veracity. Through the grounding of the formulas of the knowledge base, a Markov network is formed that contains nodes for each ground atom and edges between the nodes if the corresponding ground atoms are found together in at least one ground formula. Inference is carried out on the formed Markov network. The disadvantage of MLN is the computational complexity of training and inference in Markov Networks, but there are approaches that allow you to get closer to the solution with reasonable computational costs. An example of the use of MLN in computer vision is presented in [42], which poses the task of matching people and their cars in parking lots via surveillance cameras.

The concept of the deviant behavior detection system proposed in this paper is presented in Fig. 7. It is proposed to form an initial set of features of the observed scene based on the technologies for people detection and tracking, three-dimensional skeleton evaluation, segmentation and classification of objects, segmentation and orientation evaluation of surfaces, gestures classification, face detection, gender and clothing classification. Further, the high-level scene properties are formed in the form of predicates of first-order logic. To classify the actions and postures of people, it is proposed to use approaches based on machine learning, for example, [43], most of the other properties can be hand-crafted. For example, to determine the predicate DistanceReducedBetween (Vehic, Vict), we can track the change in the distance between each pair of people and vehicles in the scene. For the classification of deviant behavior, scenes of interest will be modelled in a first order logic language based on the crime experts knowledge. When classifying complex scenes (containing many interrelated factors), MLN is suggested. The weights of the formulas will also be set by experts, and the weights of atomic predicates will be formed based on the detection confidence.

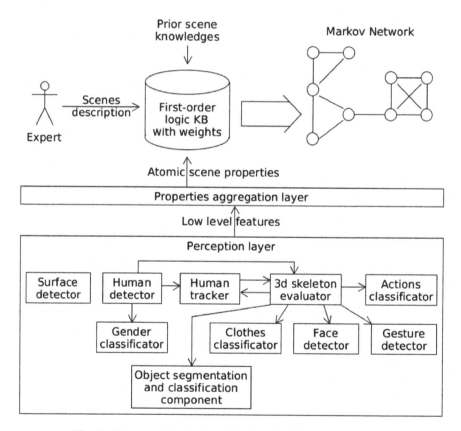

Fig. 7. Diagram of the deviant behavior detection system concept.

7 Conclusion

In this paper, the concept of a deviant behavior detection system via the city's video surveillance cameras was presented. Such a system can increase the awareness of the city administration about the events taking place in it, promptly react to problem situations and, as a result, increase the safety of residents. A brief overview of modern computer vision technologies providing a set of representative features of the observed scene to be formed was presented. To solve the problem of the strong variability of the scenes of interest, it is proposed to utilize the experts' knowledge representing the description of scenes in a first-order logic. To account for real life uncertainties, MLN utilization is proposed. Also, examples of real deviant behavior scenes were presented, and a possible formal description of the street robbery scene was proposed.

References

1. Rostec: NtechLab Face Recognition System Prevents Sponsor's Trophy Theft at the 2018 FIFA World Cup. https://rostec.ru/en/news/ntechlab-face-recognition-system-prevents-spon sor-s-trophy-theft-at-the-2018-fifa-world-cup-/. Accessed 10 Mar 2019
2. West Yorkshire Police. Appeal Over Violent Street Robbery, Armley, Leeds. https://www. westyorkshire.police.uk/news-appeals/appeal-over-violent-street-robbery-armley-leeds. Accessed 10 Mar 2019
3. ShotSpotter. https://www.shotspotter.com/. Accessed 5 May 2019
4. FindFace Public Safety. https://findface.pro/ru/face-recognition-public-safety.html. Accessed 5 May 2019
5. SmokeCatcher, Video Smoke Detection for critical environments. http://www.araani.com/ en/smokecatcher/. Accessed 5 May 2019
6. Smart Recognition System Reco3.26. https://www.reco326.com/index.php/en/. Accessed 5 May 2019
7. Chen, M., Hauptmann, A.: Mosift: Recognizing human actions in surveillance videos. Pittsburgh (2009). http://www.cs.cmu.edu/~mychen/publication/ChenMoSIFTCMU09.pdf. Accessed 10 Mar 2019
8. Zhou, P., Ding, Q., Luo, H., Hou, X.: Violence detection in surveillance video using low-level features. PLoS One 13(10) (2018). https://doi.org/10.1371/journal.pone.0203668
9. Bermejo Nievas, E., Deniz Suarez, O., Bueno García, G., Sukthankar, R.: Violence detection in video using computer vision techniques. In: Real, P., Diaz-Pernil, D., Molina-Abril, H., Berciano, A., Kropatsch, W. (eds.) CAIP 2011. LNCS, vol. 6855, pp. 332–339. Springer, Heidelberg (2011). https://doi.org/10.1007/978-3-642-23678-5_39
10. Lloyd, K., Rosin, P.L., Marshall, D., Moore, S.C.: Detecting violent and abnormal crowd activity using temporal analysis of grey level co-occurrence matrix (GLCM)-based texture measures. Mach. Vis. Appl. 28(3–4), 361–371 (2017). https://doi.org/10.1007/s00138-017-0830-x
11. Hassner, T., Itcher, Y., Kliper-Gross, O.: Violent flows: real-time detection of violent crowd behavior. In: Computer Society Conference on Computer Vision and Pattern Recognition Workshops, pp. 1–6. IEEE (2012). https://doi.org/10.1109/cvprw.2012.6239348
12. Singh, A., Patil, D., Omkar, S.N.: Eye in the sky: real-time drone surveillance system (DSS) for violent individuals identification using scatternet hybrid deep learning network. In: Proceedings of the IEEE Conference on Computer Vision and Pattern Recognition Workshops, pp. 1629–1637 (2018)

13. Cai, Z., Fan, Q., Feris, Rogerio S., Vasconcelos, N.: A Unified Multi-scale Deep Convolutional Neural Network for Fast Object Detection. In: Leibe, B., Matas, J., Sebe, N., Welling, M. (eds.) ECCV 2016. LNCS, vol. 9908, pp. 354–370. Springer, Cham (2016). https://doi.org/10.1007/978-3-319-46493-0_22

14. Yu, F., Li, W., Li, Q., Liu, Yu., Shi, X., Yan, J.: POI: multiple object tracking with high performance detection and appearance feature. In: Hua, G., Jégou, H. (eds.) ECCV 2016. LNCS, vol. 9914, pp. 36–42. Springer, Cham (2016). https://doi.org/10.1007/978-3-319-48881-3_3

15. Lin, C., Lu, J., Wang, G., Zhou, J.: Graininess-aware deep feature learning for pedestrian detection. In: Ferrari, V., Hebert, M., Sminchisescu, C., Weiss, Y. (eds.) ECCV 2018. LNCS, vol. 11213, pp. 745–761. Springer, Cham (2018). https://doi.org/10.1007/978-3-030-01240-3_45

16. Xiao, B., Wu, H., Wei, Y.: Simple baselines for human pose estimation and tracking. In: Ferrari, V., Hebert, M., Sminchisescu, C., Weiss, Y. (eds.) ECCV 2018. LNCS, vol. 11210, pp. 472–487. Springer, Cham (2018). https://doi.org/10.1007/978-3-030-01231-1_29

17. Kristan, M., et al.: The sixth visual object tracking VOT2018 challenge results. In: Leal-Taixé, L., Roth, S. (eds.) ECCV 2018. LNCS, vol. 11129, pp. 3–53. Springer, Cham (2019). https://doi.org/10.1007/978-3-030-11009-3_1

18. Joo, H., et al.: Panoptic studio: a massively multiview system for social motion capture. In: IEEE International Conference on Computer Vision, pp. 3334–3342. IEEE (2015). https://doi.org/10.1109/iccv.2015.381

19. Ionescu, C., Papava, D., Olaru, V., Sminchisescu, C.: Human3. 6 m: large scale datasets and predictive methods for 3D human sensing in natural environments. IEEE Trans. Pattern Anal. Mach. Intell. 36(7), 1325–1339 (2014). https://doi.org/10.1109/tpami.2013.248

20. Sárándi, I., Linder, T., Arras, K.O., Leibe, B.: Synthetic occlusion augmentation with volumetric heatmaps for the 2018 ECCV posetrack challenge on 3D human pose estimation (2018). https://arxiv.org/pdf/1809.04987.pdf. Accessed 10 Mar 2019

21. Sun, X., Li, C., Lin, S.: An Integral Pose Regression System for the ECCV 2018 PoseTrack Challenge. (2018). https://arxiv.org/pdf/1805.04095.pdf. Accessed 10 Mar 2019

22. Pavlakos, G., Zhou, X., Daniilidis, K.: Ordinal depth supervision for 3D human pose estimation. In: IEEE Conference on Computer Vision and Pattern Recognition, pp. 7307–7316. IEEE (2018). https://doi.org/10.1109/cvpr.2018.00763

23. Park, S., Kwak, N.: 3D Human Pose Estimation with Relational Networks (2018). http://bmvc2018.org/contents/papers/0530.pdf. Accessed 10 Mar 2019

24. Wang, P., Li, W., Ogunbona, P., Wan, J., Escalera, S.: RGB-D-based human motion recognition with deep learning: A survey. Comput. Vis. Image Underst. 171, 118–139 (2018). https://doi.org/10.1016/j.cviu.2018.04.007

25. He, K., Gkioxari, G., Dollár, P., Girshick, R.: Mask R-CNN. In: IEEE International Conference on Computer Vision, pp. 2961–2969). IEEE (2017). https://doi.org/10.1109/iccv.2017.322

26. Liu, L., et al.: Deep learning for generic object detection: A survey. (2018). https://arxiv.org/abs/1809.02165. Accessed 10 Mar 2019

27. Yang, F., Zhou, Z.: Recovering 3D planes from a single image via convolutional neural networks. In: Ferrari, V., Hebert, M., Sminchisescu, C., Weiss, Y. (eds.) ECCV 2018. LNCS, vol. 11214, pp. 87–103. Springer, Cham (2018). https://doi.org/10.1007/978-3-030-01249-6_6

28. Liu, C., Yang, J., Ceylan, D., Yumer, E., Furukawa, Y.: PlaneNet: piece-wise planar reconstruction from a single RGB image. In: IEEE Conference on Computer Vision and Pattern Recognition, pp. 2579–2588. IEEE (2018). https://doi.org/10.1109/cvpr.2018.00273

29. Nandwana, B., Tazi, S., Trivedi, S., Kumar, D., Vipparthi, S.K.: A survey paper on hand gesture recognition. In: 7th International Conference on Communication Systems and Network Technologies (CSNT), pp. 147–152. IEEE (2017). https://doi.org/10.1109/csnt.2017.8418527

30. Baltrušaitis, T., Robinson, P., Morency, L.P.: Openface: an open source facial behavior analysis toolkit. In: IEEE Winter Conference on Applications of Computer Vision (WACV), pp. 1–10. IEEE (2016). https://doi.org/10.1109/wacv.2016.7477553

31. Rennison, C.M., Melde, C.: Gender and robbery: a national test. Deviant Behav. 35(4), 275–296 (2014). https://doi.org/10.1080/01639625.2013.848104

32. Chahyati, D., Fanany, M.I., Arymurthy, A.M.: Man woman detection in surveillance images. In: 5th International Conference on Information and Communication Technology (IColC7), pp. 1–4. IEEE (2017). https://doi.org/10.1109/icoict.2017.8074682

33. Geelen, C.D., Wijnhoven, R.G., Dubbelman, G.: Gender classification in low-resolution surveillance video: in-depth comparison of random forests and SVMs. In: Video Surveillance and Transportation Imaging Applications 2015, vol. 9407, p. 94070 M. International Society for Optics and Photonics. SPIE, San Francisco (2015). https://doi.org/10.1117/12.2077079

34. Zhu, J., Liao, S., Lei, Z., Yi, D., Li, S.: Pedestrian attribute classification in surveillance: database and evaluation. In: IEEE International Conference on Computer Vision Workshops, pp. 331–338. IEEE (2013). https://doi.org/10.1109/iccvw.2013.51

35. Friedman, J., Hastie, T., Tibshirani, R.: Additive logistic regression: a statistical view of boosting (with discussion and a rejoinder by the authors). In: The Annals of Statistics, vol. 28, № 2, pp. 337–407. Stanford (2000). http://statweb.stanford.edu/~jhf/ftp/boost.ps. Accessed 10 Mar 2019

36. Yang, M., Yu, K.: Real-time clothing recognition in surveillance videos. In: 18th IEEE International Conference on Image Processing, pp. 2937–2940. IEEE (2011). https://doi.org/10.1109/icip.2011.6116276

37. Lao, B., Jagadeesh, K.: Convolutional neural networks for fashion classification and object detection. In: Computer Vision, CCCV 2015, pp. 120–129 (2016). http://cs231n.stanford.edu/reports/2015/pdfs/BLAO_KJAG_CS231N_FinalPaperFashionClassification.pdf. Accessed 10 Mar 2019

38. Sultani, W., Chen, C., Shah, M.: Real-world anomaly detection in surveillance videos. In: IEEE Conference on Computer Vision and Pattern Recognition, pp. 6479–6488. IEEE (2018). https://doi.org/10.1109/cvpr.2018.00678

39. Branch, H.O.S.D.: Imagery library for intelligent detection systems (i-LIDS). In: IET Conference on Crime and Security, pp. 445–448. IET (2006). https://assets.publishing.service.gov.uk/government/uploads/system/uploads/attachment_data/file/143870/ilids-brochure.pdf. Accessed 10 Mar 2019

40. Falomir, Z., Olteţeanu, A.M.: Logics based on qualitative descriptors for scene understanding. Neurocomputing 161, 3–16 (2015). https://doi.org/10.1016/j.neucom.2015.01.074

41. Richardson, M., Domingos, P.: Markov logic networks. Mach. Learn. 62(1–2), 107–136 (2006). https://doi.org/10.1007/s10994-006-5833-1

42. Tran, S.D., Davis, L.S.: Event modeling and recognition using Markov logic networks. In: Forsyth, D., Torr, P., Zisserman, A. (eds.) ECCV 2008. LNCS, vol. 5303, pp. 610–623. Springer, Heidelberg (2008). https://doi.org/10.1007/978-3-540-88688-4_45

43. Du, Y., Fu, Y., Wang, L.: Skeleton based action recognition with convolutional neural network. In: 3rd IAPR Asian Conference on Pattern Recognition (ACPR), pp. 579–583. IEEE (2015). https://doi.org/10.1109/acpr.2015.7486569

Slow Tourism and Smart Community.
The Case of Sulcis - Iglesiente (Sardinia -Italy)

Ginevra Balletto[1,3(✉)], Alessandra Milesi[1,3], Silvia Battino[2,3],
Giuseppe Borruso[2,3], and Luigi Mundula[1,3]

[1] DICAAR – Department of Civil and Environmental Engineering and Architecture,
University of Cagliari, Via Marengo 2, Cagliari, Italy
{balletto,mundulaluigi}@unica.it,
alessandramilesi.unica@gmail.com
[2] DISEA – Economics and Business, University of Sassari,
Via Muroni 25, Sassari, Italy
sbattino@uniss.it
[3] DEAMS – Department of Economics, Business,
Mathematics and Statistical Sciences "Bruno de Finetti",
University of Trieste, Trieste, Italy
giuseppe.borruso@deams.units.it

Abstract. In the last few years the term resilience has entered into force in the policies and practices concerning the territorial development. The paper, interpreting the territory through the paradigm of systemic complexity, aim to read the territorial resilience in a dynamic and procedural sense that is as the response to change not simply according to adaptive (passive) modalities, but through a reaction, that is by implementing a "regenerative" response from the territory and, therefore, from its communities. In other words, there is a community resilience that shows itself through the capacity of human groups to resist environmental changes, which involves upheavals not only of a natural, but also of a social nature. It resists, even not restoring the previous balance, but preserving identity through the change and adaptation to new situations. In this framework the aim of the paper is to represent the slow network of the Sulcis Iglesiente area in the Sardinia region - a vulnerable area due to it has been affected by an intense mining activity and more recently hit by flooding events and socio-economic stress - and the role of the smart community in relaunching its touristic image. Here, in fact, started in 2016 a slow tourism experience in the shape of a way practicable on foot, by bicycle or on horseback, that retraces the ancient mining routes of the Sulcis Iglesiente - Guspinese, developing a ring of about 400 km length.

Keywords: Slow tourism · Sustainable tourism · Ecological tourism

This study is supported by RE-MINE - Restoration and rehabilitation of abandoned mining sites, funded by the Foundation of Sardinia (Grant CUP F72F16003160002) and TSULKI - Tourism and Sustainability in the Sulcis (Sardinia- Italy) SULCIS-821319, funded by Region of Sardinia. This paper is the result of the joint work of the authors. Section 1 was been written by S. Battino; Sect. 2 by L Mundula and A. Milesi; Sect. 3 by G Borruso; Sect. 4 by G. Balletto and G Borruso; Sect. 5 by G. Balletto, A. Milesi and L Mundula; Sect. 6 was jointly written by G. Balletto and G. Borruso. The imeges were processed by A. Milesi and G. Cosseddu.

© Springer Nature Switzerland AG 2019
S. Misra et al. (Eds.): ICCSA 2019, LNCS 11624, pp. 184–199, 2019.
https://doi.org/10.1007/978-3-030-24311-1_13

1 Slow Tourism Social Network

In Italy and in other European countries the local communities, the public and private bodies have been joining forces for some time now to plan, according to the guidelines of sustainable development, the tourist offer of the destinations. Specifically, the places most involved in these actions are the marginal areas, too often cut off from the international tourist circuits, where the enhancement of the landscape and the use of the same become the main object of interest. The natural and cultural heritage and the different local specificities are increasingly organized in the form of thematic itineraries (religious, culinary, etc.) capable of stimulating new forms of slow and outdoor tourism [1–5]. Religious paths, eno-gastronomic itineraries, old routes taken by miners are all of cultural importance. This importance has been confirmed since 1987 by the Council of Europe (CoE) which, through the "European Cultural Routes" program, considers the cultural routes to be useful instruments for strengthening European identity. A useful program for promoting the socio-economic development of territories, for encouraging motivated cultural tourism respectful of places and for promoting the protection and enhancement of natural and cultural heritage [6, 7]. The Cultural Routes, both those best known by the public of travelers, such as the Pilgrim's Way to Santiago or the Via Francigena, and those that in a less sensational way are practiced in different European regions, strengthen the spirit of cohesion and inclusion, giving value to small villages and encourage more intense connections between rural and urban areas. The initiative recently undertaken in Italy, under the direction of the Ministry of Cultural Heritage and Activities and Tourism (MiBACT), seems to be moving in this direction. It consists in the enhancement of the identity of places and characteristics of Italian landscapes with the express desire to create a structured system of routes capable of connecting the resources present in the different regions. It is in this framework that the MiBACT "Digital Atlas of the Paths of Italy" takes shape (http://www.turismo. beniculturali.it/cammini/). This is an innovative tool through which it is possible to benefit, in digitized form, from an informative heritage consisting of the maps of 42 recognized Italian Routes (out of 113 passed to the coordination committee) divided into historical, naturalistic, religious and cultural that meet international standards. The cartographic representation of each path is associated with information on distances, accessibility and signs, for a total length of over 6,500 km.

The "Digital Atlas of the Paths of Italy", with a mobile friendly interface, represents a useful tool for the promotion of large areas of the Italian territory that are not well known, but rich in landscape goods. A tool that satisfies in an innovative way even before the trip, through the use of modern devices, the needs of a responsible, alternative and slow tourism. The routes tracks show the points of interest, the stages, the junctions, the deviations as well as the variants that can be practiced; each of them is then associated with a technical sheet with signs, accessibility, seasonality and length. Equally useful is the presence of links to the websites of each itinerary and the photographic and multimedia equipment accessible from the "multimedia" section, as well as various links to social networks, now essential to convey information and communicate specific offers of use. The evolution of digital tools and Information and Communications Technology (ICT) can in this case improve the conditions of competitiveness and attractiveness of the territories involved and enrich the local tourist experience [8]. An integrated system of innovative services, available to tourists on mobile devices, which simplify their access to information and landscape resources that fall into the area affected by the cultural routes.

This represents a different approach to the use of the territory, made even more innovative thanks to the possibility of interaction and sharing of the tourist experience between the different actors. In this sense the Sulcis Iglesiente offers a multitude of contexts with multiple possibilities of use (wave, walk, bike,..) characterized by the landscape pruning of abandoned mines and which finds its synthesis in the Way of Santa Barbara.

2 The Santa Barbara Walk: Slow Network of the Sulcis Iglesiente

The Santa Barbara walk retraces the ancient mining routes of the Sulcis Iglesiente - Guspinese, developing as a ring for a length of about 400 km [9]. Since 2013 it has been included in the regional register of historical-religious paths of Sardinia and in 2017 the Ministry of Cultural Heritage and Activities and Tourism has included it in the first Atlas of the Paths of Italy.

It is accessible on foot, by bicycle or by horse and its altitude spans from zero at the sea level to an altitude of 900 m. The route consists of 24 stages in the Sulcis area defined on the basis of the following parameters: length in km, difficulty traveling and availability of accommodation facilities. The walk crosses a territory characterized by a complex mining basin, which constitutes the Geomineral Historical Environmental Park of Sardinia [10–12, 18, 19].

The area of Sulcis Iglesiente has been for millennia interested from a complex mining activity, such as to be considered the main extractive basin not only of the Island but of the whole Mediterranean. This territory was the most important district for national and international mining due to its large production of lead and zinc (Fig. 1).

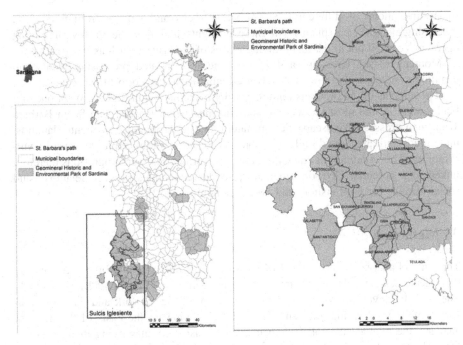

Fig. 1. Territorial framework of the Santa Barbara Path - Sulcis Iglesiente

The crisis in the mining sector and the subsequent closure of the mines in the 1990s left a rich heritage of industrial archeology and infrastructure, as well as a unique landscape.

The landscape of the path is characterized by a complex geological heritage and industrial archeology - mineral deposits, excavations and mine dumps and buildings - from an important ancient archeological heritage - domus de janas, nuraghi, sacred wells, etc. - and significant heritage natural (beaches, cliffs, lagoons, etc.).

The context of South-Western Sardinia, where most of the route is located, is geologically set on Cambrian-early Ordovician rocks, dating back to about 550 million years ago. Starting from the bottom, the geological succession shows the terrigenous sediments (mostly sandstones) of the Nebida Formation, followed upwards by the thick carbonate successions (dolomites and limestones) of the Gonnesa Formation, up to the fine-grained slates of the Cabitza Formation, which in the whole region are unconformably covered by the conglomerates and other coarse-grained siliciclastic sediments of the middle-late Ordovician Monte Argentu Formation ("Puddinga" Auct.) [11].

These rocks shaped the landscapes of the Iglesiente and Sulcis, where the sea and the mountains merge, and where, for millennia, men have fought against the adversities of nature to extract a large underground wealth of ore deposits, profoundly modifying the morphological aspect of the territory.

The landscapes of South West Sardinia are in fact deeply marked by the consequences of mining activities, with the presence of large open-air and underground excavations, mine adits, tunnels and numerous mine wastes. These latter are constituted

188 G. Balletto et al.

by accumulations of different types of waste rocks and tailings from mines and processing/metallurgical plants. All these elements highlight the vastity of mining operations carried out in the main mining places of the district, such as the great mines of Monteponi, San Giovanni and Masua, and their related processing plants and handling systems, as the historical Laveria Lamarmora and Porto Flavia plants.

The remains of the previous mining activity make the Santa Barbara Walk one of a kind among all the most known national and international paths. The Santa Barbara Walk then crosses a landscape rich in natural and anthropogenic elements (landfills, mine muds and abandoned buildings), but at the same time mutable, because its vulnerability. This condition of changing landscape (or landscape in progress) is therefore linked to a potential GeoTourism that "provides economic, cultural, relational and social benefits for both visitors and host communities" [12].

3 Methodology

The authors analyzed the behavior of the smart community (walk, bike and wave) in the Sulcis Iglesiente, also in relation to the recent definition of the Santa Barbara's Path. The analysis developed was based on the concept of the network and on the examination of its fundamental elements [13]. In fact, taking up the basis of the network analysis, the relevant territorial elements were considered, classifying them in points (or nodes) and lines (or arcs), zones (or areas) according to their punctual, georeferenced nature and the connections between these elements [14].

The analysis of network structures has, in fact, the advantage of understanding the organization of the territory in an "oriented" manner, independent from hypotheses of homogeneity of space. In the case in question, the movements of people for the reasons related to tourism in the area take place along paths, the linear elements of the network, and the connectors between these act as privileged places such as origin, destination and flow interchange. As part of this work, the network analysis focused on the classification and representation of nodes, arcs and areas; proceeding with a first analysis on the spatial distribution of these and trying to highlight the more "dense" areas - in the present research following a 'visual' approach - as regards the various ways of using the territory.

Following a lack of official data concerning the number of people accessing the path in its different segments and on preferences about ways of enjoying it, the authors decided to rely on a 'smart community' of users, as in "Neogeography" approach [15], relying on the user-generated contents by means of GPS - enable portable devices. In particular, the authors have investigated the traces left freely on the web by walk and bike tourists who have visited the Sulcis Iglesiente. These data currently represent the only data available regarding the Santa Barbara path.

At the same time we proceeded to construct the information layers attributable to the elements characterizing the landscape of the Sulcis Iglesiente, and to the evaluation of the main hospitality typologies present in Sulcis Iglesiente. We use the following categories:

1. **Santa Barbara's path** (arcs): Santa Barbara path consists of 24 stages that can be downloaded from the official web site of Foundation of Santa Barbara's Path [9].

2. **GPS walk and bike tracks** (arcs): the digital application used for data collection was Wikiloc, which allows the user to record in real time, save and share GPS tracks related to their itineraries [16]. In addition to the track it is possible to save and georeference the photographs as well as comment, evaluate and report particularities along the route. The Wikiloc community is made up of over 4 million users who share about 11 million tracks and 20 million photos. The search for traces was limited to the area of Sulcis Iglesiente, selecting only the tracks that intersect the official St. Barbara's path. The final result was the downloading of 460 useful tracks divided as follows: 230 walk tracks (downloaded between 20 and 29 January 2019) and 230 bike tracks (downloaded between 21 January and 3 February 2019). In particular, the data download was performed manually, using the geographic search option made available by the website, applying search filters. Following the identification of all the tracks, we proceeded with the homogenization of the data, transforming the paths into shape files and implementing the database with some fields obtained directly from the user data registration (path length, name of path, upload date, number of views, number of downloads, category of user, sex and origin). The data were processed by means of an open source GIS platform (QGIS 3.4).

3. **Raster wave, run and bike tracks** (arcs): the WMTS service (web map tile service) of STRAVA was used to display and download in raster format data relating to run, bike and wave tracks classified according to travel intensity.

4. **Points of interest historical and landscape (POI),** (nodes): the points of interest, related to historical and cultural sites, and to sites of environmental and landscape interest, have been overlaid on the map in order to analyze the relationships between the position of these elements and the paths taken by users.

5. **Maritime state concessions** (nodes): It was used the official data relating to maritime state concession for recreational tourism activities. It has been hypothesized that the state concessions represent nodes both for walk and bike users and for traditional users.

6. **Abandoned mines** (areas): the mining sites of Sulcis-Iglesiente and Guspinese districts have been for a long time the real economic and cultural driving force of their territories. Indeed, many of the existing urban centers in these areas were created to support mining. The activities initiated from the II millennium BC and carried out until the late 1990's left positive and negative inheritances. While the mining industry has brought economic prosperity and cultural growth, it has certainly left a hard legacy of environmental degradation, geomorphological instability and widespread pollution [17].

7. **Geomorphological and hydraulic hazards** (areas): data on geomorphological and hydraulic hazard published in the RAS Geoportal were downloaded and overlaid. The data have been shaped on the area of interest and thematized on the basis of hazard and risk classes. This phase evidenced the incompleteness of the available data, as the territories of Sulcis-Iglesiente and Guspinese have been only partially studied, regarding the aspects of hydraulic and geomorphological risks. However, the presence of instability phenomena, both natural and deriving from human

activities, is marked and evident throughout the territory. In the study area, these phenomena include physical and mechanical instability of mine wastes and excavations and phenomena related to the sinking of the soil better known as Sinkholes, studied with increasing attention over the last few years [20].

8. **Sinkholes** (areas): Data about these phenomena, linked to sudden land collapses, have not yet been made public in vector format, therefore it was not possible to proceed with the precise identification and location of related sites. As described by Mureddu [21], the general setting of these phenomena refers both to large outcrops of Paleozoic limestones in Sulcis Iglesiente, subject to natural sinking of the overlying alluvial detrital covers, (e.g. Cixerri, Narcao-Nuxis and S. Anna Arresi plains), and to areas of past mining affected by sinkhole-type landslides and collapses. These latter are generated by sudden failure of roofs due to the decrease of geomechanical properties of rocks at the sides of deep mining voids. A comparison with the Hydrogeological Planning Plan (PAI) of the Sardinia Region highlighted that out of 247 measured subsidence phenomena 214 (85%) occur in areas outside the PAI boundaries and may not be classified as landslide risk sites. From a comparison with the Landslide Phenomena Inventory in Italy (I.F.F.I. Project), it emerges that 175 sites among those surveyed (71%) by the technical table have not been inventoried. In many areas of the territories of South-West Sardinia, particularly those lacking adequate vegetation and soil cover, past mining activities greatly enhanced the rock stability problems deriving from the natural presence of steeply sloping slopes set on fractured rocks [22].

9. **Hospitality** (nodes): the main hospitality typologies present in Sulcis Iglesiente: hotel, extra hotel (B&B, landlords, holiday homes, camping), home sharing. The data relating to the hotel and extra-hotel equipment were taken from Region of Sardinia open data[1], while data on home sharing were taken from the Airbnb site (downloaded between 4 and 12 February 2019).

Table 1. Information layers.

Information layer	Code	Description	Source	Ref. date
Network	NW01	St. Barbara's path	https://www.camminominerariodisantabarbara.org/	2019
	NW02	walk tracks	https://it.wikiloc.com/	2019
	NW03	bike tracks	https://it.wikiloc.com/	2019
	NW04	wave tracks	https://github.com/bertt/wmts	2019
	NW05	run tracks	https://github.com/bertt/wmts	2019
	NW06	bike tracks	https://github.com/bertt/wmts	2019

(continued)

---

[1] http://opendata.sardegnaturismocloud.it/IT/turismo/offerta/ricettivita/(2017).

Table 1. (*continued*)

Information layer	Code	Description	Source	Ref. date
Point of interest	POI01	historical and cultural point of interest	http://webgis2.regione.sardegna.it	2015
	POI02	points of landscape interest	http://webgis2.regione.sardegna.it	2015
	POI03	maritime state concessions	http://dati.mit.gov.it/catalog/dataset/ concessioni-demaniali-marittime	2018
Mining areas	MA01	Abandoned mining areas	http://webgis2.regione.sardegna.it	2015
Risk areas	RA01	Hydraulic hazard	http://www.sardegnageoportale.it	2018
	RA02	Geomorphological hazard	http://www.sardegnageoportale.it	2018
Receptions nodes	N01	hotel	http://opendata.sardegnaturismocloud.it/IT/ turismo/offerta/ricettivita/	2017
	N02	non hotel	http://dati.regione.sardegna.it/dataset/ registro-regionale-degli-identificativi- univoci-iun-delle-strutture-ricettive-extra- alberghiere	2017
	N03	home sharing	https://www.airbnb.it/	2019

4 Slow Network Analysis

The evaluation of the spatial distribution of the tracks (wave, walk and bike) and the relative density (n. Downloads from Wikiloc) and the correlation of the attributes of the environmental information system (Table 1) allows to represent the slow network of Sulcis Iglesiente. In particular, the interpretation of the information layers took place associating for each network (NW01, NW02, NW03, NW05, NW06) the different wave (NW04, N01), environmental (MA01, MA02, RA01, RA02) and receptivity (N04, N05, N06) nodes. The authors then selected the main cartographic representations of the information layer associations, Fig. 2(a–b).

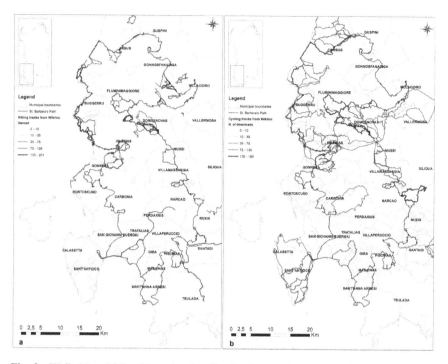

Fig. 2. Walk (a) and bike (b) tracks classification by number of downloads from Wikiloc

In particular, the bike tracks have a diffused layout compared to the localized ones. About the density of the tracks is found:

– the density of the walk tracks (Fig. 2a) is prevalent in the northernmost area, between Iglesias - Domusnovas and along the Iglesias Arbus coast;
– the density tracks bike (Fig. 2b) is prevalent to the north and south of the Sulcis Iglesiente. To the north in the inland areas of Iglesias Domusnovas up to the Iglesias coast - Arbus. To the south instead of the island of Sant'Antioco.

The authors then interpreted of the information layers took place associating for each network (all NW) the points of interest (all POI), the mining areas (MA01), the areas at risk (all RA) and the receptivity nodes (all N). The overlapping of all these information layers show the distribution and concentration in the abandoned mining areas (MA01) and therefore identify the risk areas. From the comparative analysis of the Wikiloc walk tracks and Strava tracks (Fig. 3), we can highlight some significant aspects: to the north, where the concentration of POI01 and POI02 points of interest is greater than the mines abandoned sites (MA01) are also concentrated and dense footpaths. Furthermore, the walking tracks follow the path of Santa Barbara. From the comparative analysis of the Wikiloc bike tracks and Strava (Fig. 4) we can see a slow diffused and uniform network in the Sulcis Iglesiente area. However, even in this case there is a greater concentration in the North, with circular traces that partly follow the path of Santa Barbara. To the South the traces are distributed and concentrated on the island of Sant'Antioco along the coast in correspondence with points of natural and landscape interest.

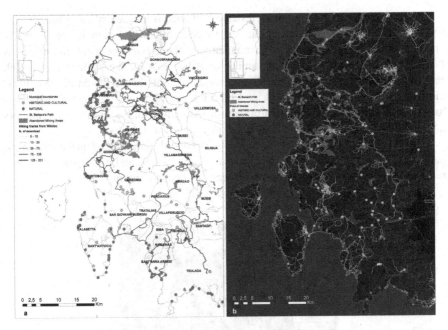

Fig. 3. Walk tracks from Wikiloc (a) and Strava run heatmap (b) with POI01, POI02, MA01

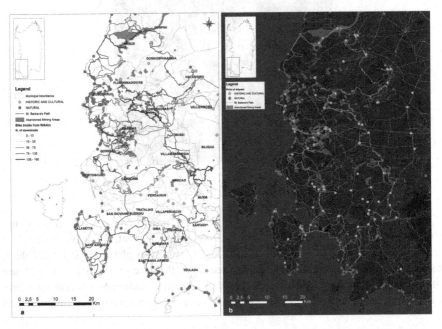

Fig. 4. Wikiloc Bike path (a) and Strava bike heatmap (b) with POI01, POI02, MA01

The slow network in the Sulcis Iglesiente, obtained from the walk and bike tracks, shows diversities, both in distribution and in concentration, within the territory. In particular the walk tracks are in correspondence of the greater concentration of points of interest of the mining landscape, unlike what happens for the cycle tracks, which seem to follow sporting and competitive motivations, not always linked to the context landmarks. However, both the walk and bike tracks highlight that the Santa Barbara Path constitutes an important infrastructure for slow tourism. Furthermore, the authors analyzed the distribution and concentration of Strava wave traces.

These wave tracks are distributed and concentrated the correspondence of the safest coasts (Buggerru - Masua, north; Isola di San Pietro, south) and of the state maritime concessions which constitute the main services of beach tourism (Fig. 5).

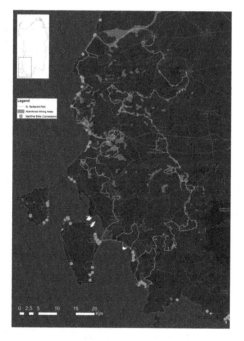

Fig. 5. Strava wave heatmap with NW01, P01, P02, MA01

In summary, the comparative evaluation show the walk tracks are located and dense in the north of the Sulcis Iglesiente and that are correlated with the wave tracks.

In fact, from the traces of the Wikiloc and Strava web platforms it's possible to observe how the cycle paths present intersections with wave traces in correspondence with the maritime state concessions. The environmental information layers then provide contextual elements (mining landscape and environmental risks, natural and anthropic points of interest) which, associated with the distribution and concentration of the tracks, allow highlighting as the walk and bike tracks are in sensitive and in morphological evolution contexts.

5   Slow Tourism and Accomodation in Sulcis Iglesiente

The Sulcis Iglesiente, because of its strong mineral characterization, presents a young - about 20 years old - tourism. The accommodation offer varies from traditional hotels to extra-hotel accommodations such as B&B, guest houses, camping, etc., up to home sharing. However, offer is variable throughout the year depending on the type of structure. In fact, while the hotel offer is greater in the summer period, like that of home sharing, the non-hotel accommodation offer is instead constant throughout the year [11]. Slow tourism is less and less linked to seasonality and more tied to the territory and to the local community and therefore prefers extra-hotel [12].

The objective was to assess the density by type of accommodation in the Sulcis Iglesiente, to understand the degree of territorial response in relation to the slow network. This analysis shows how the territory responds in a different way: the typology of home sharing shows a greater concentration in coastal municipalities (Fig. 6C), the non-hotel hotel offer is instead more evenly distributed over the territory (Fig. 6A and B). However, offer is variable throughout the year depending on the type of structure. In fact, while the hotel offer is greater in the summer period, like that of home sharing, the non-hotel accommodation offer is instead constant throughout the year [13]. Slow tourism is less and less linked to seasonality and more tied to the territory and to the local community and therefore prefers extra-hotel [23].

The spatial analysis developed by overlapping the information layers relating to the punctual position of the hotel and extra hotel facilities (N01 and N02) with the Santa Barbara path (NW01), the walk tracks (NW02) and the bike tracks (NW03) of Wikiloc and disused mining areas (MA01). The information layer relating to home sharing (N03) was selected not as a point-in-point data, in order not to burden the representation, but as an attribute relating to density by municipality. This is also because home sharing has a 'variable form' linked to seasonal seaside tourism in competition with with hotels [24]. Because the distribution of Strava's run and bike tracks confirms what was shown by the Wikiloc walk and bike tracks, it was not considered relevant to overlap these layers too. Through the Figs. 6, and 7 the authors represented the tourist offer and the slow network of Sulcis Iglesiente. In particular Fig. 6 shows how the concentration of the accommodation offer is unbalanced towards the coastal municipalities.

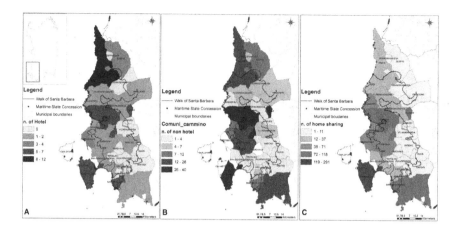

Fig. 6. Distribution of accommodation facilities in the Sulcis area: A. Hotels, B. Extra hotel, C. Home sharing

The hotel and home sharing facilities supply is mainly concentrated in the summer period and in coastal area, demonstrating that tourism in Sardinia is still highly seasonal and linked to seaside tourism. Otherwise, the extra-hotel type of accommodation offer is constant throughout the year, resulting unrelated to seaside tourism. Moreover, the extra-hotel offer is more evenly distributed throughout the territory and localized near the points of historical, cultural and natural interest. Figure 7 instead shows how the set of hotels and extra-hotel structures of Iglesias, Guspini, Arbus, Fluminimaggiore, Buggerru, Guspini are located near the abandoned mining sites.

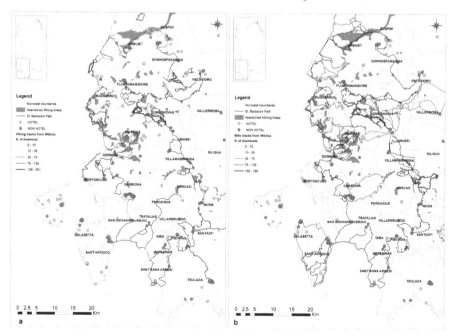

Fig. 7. Wikiloc walk path (a) and run path (b) with N01, N02

This confirms that the home sharing also in the Sulcis is strongly in competition with the hotel supply. On the other hand, the extra-hotel offer, also located in the more internal territory of the Sulcis Iglesiente area, represents an important response to slow tourism, both because it is highly contextualized and because it is free from summer seasonality [14]. In this research framework, also based on voluntary data, which certainly still deserves developments and insights, the territory of Sulcis Iglesiente proves to be a territory suitable for slow tourism. Furthermore, the slow network shown is consistent with the abandoned mining context from which it draws appeal and motivation together with the marine context.

6 Conclusions

The natural and historical emergencies, above all the anthropic emergencies deriving from the mining remains, constitute the landscape background of the Sulcis Iglesiente, on which the slow network is rooted. The representation of the slow network (on foot and by bicycle) of the Sulcis Iglesiente is attributable to the tourism of the paths, which presents similarities with the new forms of national and international tourism. It is a tourism deeply linked to the context, from the landscape to local knowledge and traditions. Slow tourism intercepts a tourist demand more oriented towards non-hotel accommodation, which in the case of Sulcis Iglesiente requires strengthening interventions. Furthermore, the organization and image of the non-hotel structure is the basis for the promotion of the slow network. The analysis of the spatial distribution of the elements of the slow network of the Sulcis Iglesiente, make possible also to observe how the walk community mainly crosses the abandoned mining sites, highlighting a cultural motivation, while the bike community is distributed over the whole territory of the Sulcis Iglesiente, according to a sporting motivation.

The evolution of the mining landscape of the Sulcis Iglesiente is correlated to the danger deriving from the ordinary and extraordinary geological instability connected to the abandonment of the mines. In this sense, the smart community plays and can play an important role also in reporting dangerous situations to allow an immediate knowledge of the most significant environmental changes. For this particular evolutionary condition of the landscape, the authors in agreement with the National Research and Innovation Roadmap on Smart Communities (2016), aim to promote and consolidate the slow network in the Sulcis Iglesiente, even with the recent Santa Barbara Walk, considering that the management of risks based on voluntary information is of particular importance. Following these guidelines and ideas, further step of the present work will be the development of an application that allows to register the dangerousness of the places and at the same time to update the information layers related to the hydrogeological risks, to better govern the danger of the evolving landscape of the Sulcis and of the path of Santa Barbara in particular. More in detail, the idea is to propose the creation of a sort of 'digital hub' able to collect the information deriving from the different already existing social networks to share not only the available information but even the request of information, among the smart community users of the Santa Barbara Walk. In the same vein, the Santa Barbara path have to evolve also towards a more structured and integrated typologies of management (i.e. quality certification for all the infrastructures and facilities of the network) in order to promote the transition from seasonal tourism towards more sustainable and resilient forms in time and space. Finally, the present research, under the agreement protocol between the Universities of Cagliari and Sassari, the Regional Centre for Planning and the Santa Barbara Walk Foundation (signed in December 2018), intends to develop further analysis to define governance actions and to favor the diversification and integration between new and traditional forms of tourism.

References

1. Greffe, X.: Is rural tourism a lever for economic and social development? J. Sustain. Tourism **2**, 23–40 (1994)
2. Olsen, M.: Tourism themed routes: a Queensland perspective. J. Vacation Mark. **9**, 331–341 (2003)
3. Meyer, D.: Tourism routes and gateways: key issues for the development of tourism routes and gateways and their potential for pro-poor tourism. Overseas Development Institute, London (2004)
4. Csapo, J., Berki, M.: Existing and future tourism potential and geographical basis of thematic routes in South Transdanubia, Hungary. In: International Conference of Territorial Intelligence, Besançon 2008, Besançon, France, October 2008, p. 10 (2009)
5. Battino, S., Balletto, G., Borruso, G., Donato, C.: Internal areas and smart tourism. Promoting territories in Sardinia Island. In: Gervasi, O., et al. (eds.) ICCSA 2018. LNCS, vol. 10964, pp. 44–57. Springer, Cham (2018). https://doi.org/10.1007/978-3-319-95174-4_4
6. Majdoub, W.: Analizing cultural routes from a multidimensional perspective. Almatourism **2**, 29–37 (2010)
7. Corinto, G.L.: Food and gastronomic tourism for developing rural areas around the via Francigena in Tuscany. Almatourism **7**, 106–122 (2017)
8. Katsoni, V., Dologlou, N.: ICT applications in smart ecotourism environments. In: Stratigea, A., Kyriakides, E., Nicolaides, C. (eds.) Smart Cities in the Mediterranean. PI, pp. 225–244. Springer, Cham (2017). https://doi.org/10.1007/978-3-319-54558-5_11
9. Pinna, G.: Il cammino minerario di Santa Barbara. A piedi in Sardegna tra storia e natura. Terre di mezzo editore, Milano (2017)
10. Balletto, G., Michele, P., Giuseppe, B., Naitza, S.: Sardinia Geopark and smart tourism network. The project of the 'pilgrim way' of Santa Barbara. In: TICCIH CHILE 2018 CONGRESS Patrimonio Industrial: Entendiendo el Pasado, Haciendo el Futuro Sostenible, CHL, June 2018
11. Servizio Geologico d'Italia: Carta geologica d'Italia in scala 1:50000. Foglio 555 "Iglesias" (2015)
12. Gordon, J.E.: Geotourism and Cultural Heritage. Edward Elgar Publishing, Cheltenham (2018)
13. Del Chiappa, G.: La sostenibilità del turismo: prospettive di analisi e casi concreti. FrancoAngeli, Milano (2018)
14. Caffyn, A.: 16 slow tourism. In: Agarwal, S., Busby, G., Huang, R. (eds.) Special Interest Tourism: Concepts, Contexts and Cases, p. 183. Cabi, Boston (2018)
15. Turner, A.J.: Introduction to Neogeography. O'Reilly Media, Sebastopol (2006)
16. Battino, S., Lampreu S.: La carta a portata di click: web mapping, itinerari e condivisione. In: ASITA 2018, pp. 103–112. Federazione ASITA, Milano (2018)

17. Todde, E.: The evolution of the mining village of Montevecchio from archival sources to museum reconversion. RiMe. Rivista dell'Istituto di Storia dell'Europa Mediterranea, 83–100 (2018)
18. Salvatore, R., Chiodo, E.: Non Più e non ancora. Le aree fragili tra conservazione ambientale, cambiamento sociale e sviluppo turistico. Franco Angeli, Milano (2017)
19. Mossa, A., Camúñez-Ruiz, J.A., Morandi, F.: Current state of the first Unesco Global Geopark: a case study of the geological and mining park of Sardinia, Italy. GeoJ. Tourism Geosites 22(2), 403–418 (2018)
20. Bollati, I., Coratza, P., Panizza, V., Pelfini, M.: Lithological and structural control on Italian mountain geoheritage: opportunities for tourism, outdoor and educational activities. Quaestiones Geographicae 37(3), 53–73 (2018)
21. Mureddu, A.: Research and data processing activities preparatory to the drafting of the Sinkholes Map of the regional territory, on a geological basis at a scale of 1: 250,000. Mem. Desc. MapGeol. D'It.XCIX, pp. 385–400 (2015)
22. Caredda, P., Mariolu, E., Nisio, S.: I sinkholes in Sardegna meridionale. Alcuni esempi dal Sulcis-Iglesiente e possibili correlazioni con le attività antropiche. In: 2 Workshop internazionale: I sinkholes. Gli sprofondamenti catastrofici nell'ambiente naturale ed in quello antropizzato. ISPRA, Roma, 3–4 dicembre 2009 (2009)
23. Destination of Sardinia 2018–2021: Strategic Development and Marketing Tourism Plan of Sardinia. http://www.regione.sardegna.it/documenti/1_231_20181221121007.pdf
24. Yang, Y., Tan, K.P.S., Li, X.R.: Antecedents and consequences of home-sharing stays: Evidence from a nationwide household tourism survey. Tourism Manag. 70, 15–28 (2019)

Sport and Smart Communities. Assessing the Sporting Attractiveness and Community Perceptions of Cagliari (Sardinia, Italy)

Mara Ladu[1(✉)], Ginevra Balletto[1], and Giuseppe Borruso[2]

[1] DICAAR - Department of Civil Environmental Engineering and Architecture, University of Cagliari, Cagliari, Italy
{maraladu,balletto}@unica.it
[2] DEAMS - Department of Economics, Business, Mathematics and Statistics Sciences "Bruno de Finetti", University of Trieste, 34127 Trieste, Italy
giuseppe.borruso@deams.units.it

Abstract. Sport has always played a very important role in civil society, becoming a clear expression of different cultures and lifestyles throughout history. Nowadays, it is considered an essential enabler in pursuing sustainable development of our cities and regions. A prerequisite for improvement of sporting attractiveness of our contemporary cities is to integrate sport into broader urban transformation and regeneration processes. As a matter of fact, more and more people prefer to play sport in different places and at different times, understanding the city as an ideal palimpsest for sports activities. In this regard, the Smart Community has gradually become an extraordinary source of information useful for policy makers. A wide range of ICT tools allows to develop Community Maps which reveal needs and aspirations of people, thus informing sports policies and a community-based participatory planning. The study aims to assess the sporting attraction of Cagliari through the analysis of different evidences drawn from the community perception of sports activities and initiatives. It focused on material and immaterial actions carried out to promote sport in the city, smart community sport behaviours, community perceptions on benefits that sport provides for human well-being and for city development through the administration of a questionnaire. The outcome highlights the role of Smart community in understanding sport behaviours of local people and in defining shared strategies to strengthen the sport-city link in the sustainable development of Cagliari.

Keywords: Smart Communities · Sport governance · Sustainable development

This study is endorsed by Sportiumscrl (Milan), a specialized design consortium that has signed (10 September 2018) a memorandum of understanding with the University of Cagliari for all the design phases the new stadium of Cagliari.
This paper is the result of the joint work of the authors. In particular: Sect. 1 by G. Balletto; Sect. 2 by M. Ladu, Sect. 3 by G Borruso; Sect. 4 has been jointly written by M. Ladu and G Balletto; Sect. 5 by G Balletto; Sect. 6 by G. Borruso; Sect. 7 has been jointly written by M. Ladu and G. Balletto.

© Springer Nature Switzerland AG 2019
S. Misra et al. (Eds.): ICCSA 2019, LNCS 11624, pp. 200–215, 2019.
https://doi.org/10.1007/978-3-030-24311-1_14

1   Introduction

Sport has always played a very important role in civil society, becoming a clear expression of different cultures and communities' lifestyles throughout history. It has been conceived as a strategic means to exploit the nature of political ideologies and aspirations since ancient times [1]. Sometimes, it proved to be useful for achieving positive and negative political goals. As a matter of fact, sport has been assumed as an educational and population control practice, but also as a vehicle for propaganda and amplification of differences between ethnic groups [2]. Several dictatorships have often promoted and sustained the realization of sports facilities and the organization of sporting events for their self-celebration [3], reaching the maximum epilogue during the Fascist era, up until the Cold War [4].

Nowadays, sport is a fundamental element of the health and well-being of people, a trigger for economic and social regeneration of our cities and regions [5] and, more generally, an essential enabler in pursuing sustainable development. The 2030 Agenda for Sustainable Development [6], which represents the primary reference point for guiding the human use of our planet, states that: «37. *Sport is also an important enabler of sustainable development. We recognize the growing contribution of sport to the realization of development and peace in its promotion of tolerance and respect and the contributions it makes to the empowerment of women and of young people, individuals and communities as well as to health, education and social inclusion objectives*».

This is a crucial principle which requires to integrate sport into society and peace [7], economic and environmental urban policies, as well as into urban governance and planning.

Most cultural principles and approaches reached at the international level to strengthen the relationship between Sport and the City and to highlight the role of sport in pursuing sustainable development of our cities and regions have been introduced in Italy to inform the political agenda. Over the past years, the Italian Government and the CONI (*Italian National Olympic Committee*) have promoted policies to sustain a comprehensive regeneration of existing sports facilities in peripheral areas establishing a special fund ("*Sport and peripheries*" Fund - Law No 9 of 22 January 2016). Their aim is to face the economic and social imbalances as well as the urban security issues in deprived areas through specific material and immaterial actions capable of increasing sports activities and spreading a healthy lifestyle in the urban environment.

Anyway, a condition for improving the sporting attractiveness of our contemporary cities is to consider a field of investigation that no longer corresponds only with the system of existing sports facilities but rather with the broader - and sometimes fragmented - network of open spaces and green areas that characterizes each urban context [8]. As a matter of fact, nowadays more and more people prefer playing sport according to their personal needs and interests, in different places and at different times, understanding the city as an ideal palimpsest for sports activities [9].

In Italy as well, in addition to the traditional competitive sport - based on the cultural models of Olympic sports - it is certainly on the rise sport activity intended as a loisir and as a search for physical well-being in close relationship with nature [10].

The contemporary ways of using urban spaces constitute a real challenge for urban governance and planning because demand to integrate sport into comprehensive urban regeneration and sustainable development strategies [11]. More specifically, urban transformation and regeneration programs, from those required by the Mega Events to those needed at local and neighbourhood scale, should guarantee a network of spaces and sport facilities able to embrace the new phenomenon called "street sport" [12], which stimulates virtuous behaviours and healthy lifestyles [13] thus generating a widespread sense of belonging, cohesion and social inclusion [14].

In this regard, the introduction of electronic technologies and digital data capture supports decision-makers in understanding needs and aspirations of local communities and, as a consequence, in implementing effective urban policies.

Indeed, although the citizens participation has long been declared as a fundamental component in political decision-making processes to guarantee the environmental and social quality of urban governance and planning [15], this cultural assumption can be effectively implemented in the era of ICT. A wide range of innovative tools and applications are available to save and share the data requested to build a deep knowledge of different lifestyles existing in our contemporary society [16].

In this sense, the Smart Communities movement, developed over the 1990 s to increase the number of users involved in IT [17], has become essential to understand sport experiences and behaviours, as well as to build smart, inclusive [18] and sustainable [19] cities.

2 Smart Community and Sport Urban Planning

In the information age, the Smart Community represents a significant part of our contemporary society that makes use or extensive use of available technological tools, services and devices to promote organization and efficiency, to improve the quality of life but also to share personal knowledge, opinions and interests [20].

California Institute for Smart Communities states that a Smart Community is «a community in which government, business, and residents understand the potential of information technology, and make a conscious decision to use that technology to transform life and work in their region in significant and positive ways» [21].

With reference to the present research objective, it is necessary to recognize that the Smart community has gradually become an extraordinary source of data for policy makers. Thanks to the rapid progress of information and communication technologies (ICT), the Smart Community shares different types of geo-referenced information on the territory, to reveal the daily life styles and sports behavior and in the events of people in the city [22].

The most innovative sport-health apps that track our mobility such as Strava, Runtastic and Endomondo - just to mention some of the most popular ones - allow people to upload data referred to personal sport trainings and performances into specific web services [23]. De facto, the numerous users involved contribute to develop interesting "Community Maps" which describes a still unknown image of the city consisting of different nodes and networks, with places marked by high crossing densities. All the signs and traces impressed in these operating systems make the

Community Map a strategic knowledge tool useful in interpreting social phenomena and in recognizing future trends, thus informing visions undertaken through sport city planning [24].

For this reason, the information provided by the Smart Community contribute to establish a new community-based model of governance [25], while collaborative mapping may be assumed as a strategic means for community-based participatory planning [26]. A smart community initiative is an integrated communication approach between communities: local governments, schools, businesses, citizens and health and social services useful for identifying shared governance strategies.

Nowadays, public authorities can directly consult citizens, through the administration of specific questionnaires aimed at assessing their needs and aspirations with greater efficiency due to the community maps, which constitute the first element of territorial representation of the behavior of the smart community [27].

In this sense, managing the heterogeneous information provided by the smart community allow policy makers to define measures for more inclusive and livable urban environments, in line with the greater attention that people give to health and well-being from a young age.

3 Data and Methods

In line with the above-mentioned theoretical aspects and following the target of paper, we addressed the issues concerned with sport and smart participation following different approaches. Three main methods have been followed, responding to different focuses on the sport aspects of the city.

- A first set of research involved the analysis of the material and immaterial actions carried on to promote the city at national and international level, this resulting into the inserting into Cagliari into the European City of Sport competition. So, a first set of analysis was based on a desk research of all the documents relevant for understanding such framework. The two candidature dossiers drawn up respectively for the European City of Sport 2017 competition [28] and for hosting the sailing regattas of the 2024 Olympic Games in Rome [29] were fundamental to understanding the political approach adopted by the local administration for sports government, as well as the most significant material and immaterial actions carried on over the past years (urban renewal and redevelopment schemes; public events and bottom-up initiatives).
- Geographical analysis of the 'bottom up' approach towards sport, by the analysis of the 'Community Maps' deriving from sport amateurs and professionals using sport apps, which results can be visually and geographically represented. That was possible using the Strava Heat Maps showing the concentration of lines where sport activities concentrate in the world, and with a particular reference to the city of Cagliari. This was possible by using such maps and integrating them into a desktop GIS in order to integrate it with other data sources relevant for understanding the geographical location and spatial distribution of sport facilities, locations and areas of interest. The outcome is the result of an overlapping of the sport facilities -

shapefile provided by the Sardinia Region, while the main urban parks in Cagliari have been selected and geo-referenced by the authors.

- Community perceptions on benefits that sport provides for human well-being and for city development through the distribution of a specific questionnaire[1] for analysing the mood of citizens on sport activities and opportunities. The questionnaire has been targeted towards more than 300 people and organizations involved in sport activities, both as professionals and amateurs, as well as public administrators.

The specific case of the metropolitan city of Cagliari, with its complex system of nodes of various ranks and specializations, connected to the networks of urban parks, squares, boulevard and promenade [30], appears particularly attractive to the "street sport" [4]. This is a favourable condition where the values of sport are disseminated throughout the city and sport itself becomes a "common good" [31].

In this context, the Municipality of Cagliari recognized the role of sport on the political agenda, promoting and supporting policies with numerous initiatives, materials (sports facilities, urban trail and environmental paths) and intangible (events), in order to improve its sporting attractiveness.

4 Material and Immaterial Actions for Cagliari-Street Sport

Over the last years, Cagliari City Council have promoted a significant program of interventions and initiatives to establish sport as an essential enabler in pursuing sustainable development goals. The political agenda has been defined according to the cultural awareness that sport, played in all its forms and modalities, encourages healthy habits and spreads civic values, thus becoming an essential activity for the personal growth of people. Moreover, the local government strategy is based on a deep acknowledgement of the peculiar environmental, geographical and climatic features of the City, which make it an attractive place to play different types of sport and outdoor activities for more than 300 days a year [28].

Thanks to these favourable conditions, Cagliari has been designated European City of Sport 2017 by ACES Europe (European Capitals and Cities of Sport Federation). In addition, Cagliari was a candidate for hosting the sailing regattas of the 2024 Olympic Games in Rome - candidature resumed [29].

However, it should be acknowledged that Cagliari has been elected "European City of Sport" also by virtue of the several measures and interventions carried out by the Local Administration, together with private investors, voluntary sports organizations and other associations and sports clubs. Cagliari offers a rich and widespread system of outdoor and indoor sports facilities (over 150), from the centre to the periphery, where people can play a variety of activities, including team sports, gymnastics, popular sports such as football, volleyball, basketball, up to niche sports [28]. About half (74) of the aforementioned sports facilities are owned by the Municipality, which still today represents the main public institution involved in the local sports governance.

---

[1] Proposed by the two authors G. Balletto and G. Borruso (April 2018).

The growing awareness of the key role played by public authorities in stimulating healthy lifestyles, also promoting a sustainable urban planning and governance, has led the City to integrate sport into important urban transformation and regeneration processes, both at a local and territorial scale [32]. The following are the main strategic strategies implemented or in progress (see Fig. 1):

(a) The recent seafront (LungomarePoetto), which gave a renewed meaning to the coastal landscape, through the dunes and green layout with new ways of using the space (walk, run and bicycle).

(b) The important operation - on going - of refurbishment and reconstruction of the new Stadium of Cagliari, which will have approximately 30,000 seat capacity. This great investment will provide the City with a smart sports arena close to the sea and well-connected with the existing system of urban centralities and networks of different ranks and specializations (green and blue network)

(c) The redevelopment scheme of a large green space in the Sant'Elia district, which has recently become a new urban park (Parco degliAnelli). It includes areas for sports and leisure activities, equipped green spaces, pedestrian and cycle paths.

(d) Redevelopment project of the pedestrian promenade from historic port (d1) to SuSiccu zone (d2), connected to the new promenade on the seafront (near the new stadium and Parco degliAnelli), connecting the city to its environmental system

(e) The installation of the Luna Rossa' headquarter in the historic port (Molo Ichnusa). Luna Rossa crew, in preparation for the 36th edition of the America's Cup, has selected Cagliari by virtue of their exceptional weather conditions for sailing sports, which allow to sail more than 200 days a year.

Among the intangible shares promoted by the Municipality of Cagliari there are sports events that have progressively involved more and more people. We can mention:

- "*AteneiKa*", the event that every year involves most of the university students in sports competitions, seminars, games and musical entertainments for ten days in the university campus "Sa Duchessa";

- "*Cagliari respira*", the half marathon (about 20 km) organized by the Asd Cagliari Marathon Club to involve people in a day dedicated to sport, health, ecology and fun;

- "*SoloWomenRun*", the event with which Cagliari has joined the national women's race circuit, encouraging more than 13,000 women to take part in the 5th edition (10 March 2019). It consists of two routes, the Open (about 4 km) and the Challenge (about 9 km) route.

The significant program of material and immaterial actions carried out by the Local Administration, together with private investors, voluntary sports organizations and other associations and sports clubs, led ACES to designate Cagliari as the "Best European City of Sport 2017" [33].

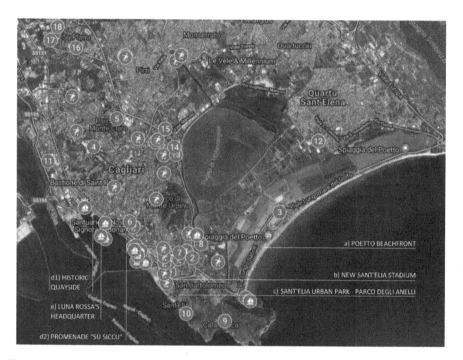

Fig. 1. AThe system of sports facilities in Cagliari and the main strategic projects. Source: Elaboration of the authors G. Balletto and G Borruso (2018).

The selection has been made with reference to a set of specific indicators concerning popular and competitive sports activities, as well as inclusive sports initiatives and innovative proposals, taking into account their media and economic impact, especially with regard to the investments made by the City to promote sports activities.

This constant commitment has been recently confirmed by the Il Sole 24 Ore survey - *Sportiness index 2018* [34] - aimed to assign a Sportiness index to each of the 107 Italian provinces. Cagliari has reached the third place in the top 20 ranking.

According to the criteria established by the survey, which consists of different categories and sub-categories, Cagliari is:

- the 2nd in the Category *"Sports performance index"* (Indice di sportività) by virtue of the high number of people which are members of sports bodies, clubs and associations.
- the 1st in the Category *"Team Sport"* (Sport di squadra), especially with regard to the sub-categories of Professional Football, Basketball, Amateur, Sport Clubs and the territory;
- only the 24th in the Category *"Individual Sports"* (Sport individuali), even if should be acknowledged that the City proves to be more attractive to play swimming, tennis, water sports and other indoor sports;
- the 5th in the Category *"Sport and Society"* (Sport e Società), reaching good performances in the sub-categories of sports and children, sports media and women's

sports, while could do something more to improve its position for sport and nature and sport and tourism.

In summary the material and immaterial actions related to sport offer multiple benefits to the city of Cagliari, from health to new forms of tourism, between local and global [32].

5 Cagliari: Sport and Smart Community

To evaluate the sport attractiveness of the City of Cagliari, authors chose to analyze also the ways in which citizens use urban space. The growing interest from local communities towards individual and non-structured sport activities implies inviting local decision and policy makers to configure the overall city as an ideal framework for sport and defining policies aimed at enhancing the street sport phenomenon.

In the city of Cagliari, such a phenomenon is ongoing long since and developing between land and sea. It interests the open spaces of the consolidated city, parks and gardens, walks along the historical waterfront and the seaside, beaches, sea, capes, humid zones and those having a high naturalistic and environmental value, to be extended to the borders of the municipality, to reach a metropolitan dimension.

Observing carefully the Strava Global Heatmap, based on the traces of open-air activities, a different Cagliari appears, made of networks stepped and lived in different ways and with different frequencies by a Smart Community willing – more or less knowingly – to share its personal sport experience by mean of fitted for purpose apps. The Strava Global Heatmaps allow to evaluate the spatial distribution of traces marked on space by the Smart Community, particularly those related to the three open-air sport activities, as running, biking and swimming. (see Fig. 2a, b, c).

Running is particularly practiced in all the parts of the city. It is practiced at margins of the street and road lines in the flat space, along the tree-lined streets walks and the pedestrian pathways in the historical city, the public gardens, the promenade of the historical waterfront and the Poetto seaside, around and inside the main urban parks (Monte Urpinu, Monte Claro, San Michele, Terramaini, Molentargius – Salt flats).

Furthermore, traces are highly visible also in the retail high streets and in the neighborhoods, in areas with higher residential density, intersecting squares, places and intersections.

With reference to biking, the traces coincide with the main road axis, with those fitted with dedicated pedestrian/bike pathways, and with streets around hills and neighborhoods of the city. Differently from running, biking is practiced also in the street and urban networks at sovra-local and metropolitan level, at the margins of urban centres.

Swimming – as the third open-air sport – concentrates in the initial part of the coast, where best meteo-marine conditions are present and, in general, higher levels of security and safety. Furthermore, this part of the beach is fitted with direct and indirect services for sport activities, and it is well connected with the rest of the city by means of local public transport and the bike network.

(a)

(b)

(c)

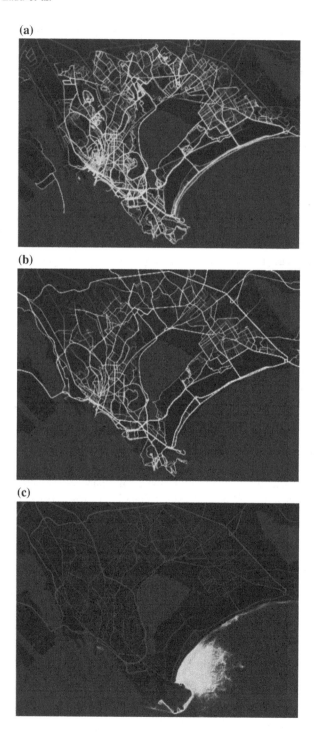

Fig. 2. a, b, c. The three heatmap show respectively the density of running and cycling routes of users, as well as their swimming activity. Source: Strava Global Heatmap, 2019 [35].

With the Fig. 3 the authors have evidenced how the street sport of Cagliari has a territorial metropolitan distribution. This metropolitan layout gives the sports theme a strategic importance especially for the management of parks, squares and waterfronts, places that are by definition suitable for the practice of street sport.

Moreover, thanks to street sport it is possible to identify new itineraries useful for pedestrian cycle mobility far from vehicular traffic flows.

In other words, the sports smart community has highlighted the dimension of the street sport theme, offering useful insights for subsequent in-depth research on the public city, from wellness to pedestrian cycle transport.

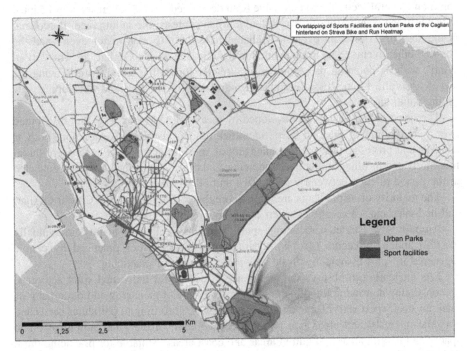

Fig. 3. A first recognition of the existing urban facilities and the most important urban parks in the city to develop future policies aimed to reinforce their relationship with running and cycling routes traced by the Smart Community. Source: Elaboration of the authors (2019) on Strava Global Heatmap [35] and on Gis data from OpendataSardegna [36].

6   Cagliari Is a Sports City? A Questionnaire to Measure Community Perceptions

A research has been carried on by means of a questionnaire, targeted towards people and organizations involved in sport activities, both as professionals and amateurs, as well as public administrators. This has been done in order to better understand the role played by sport in the City of Cagliari, both referred to the lifestyles of the population and to the awareness that the population itself developed about the importance of playing sport and having an active attitude to improve the quality of life and at the same time boost economic and social development of a territory.

The choice of developing a questionnaire (april 2018) on a theme as 'city and sport', aimed at understanding the relationship between city and sport in the perception of big events - as well as ordinary ones - as possible means of urban transformation and regeneration.

The research has been developed following a parallel approach, preparing two questionnaires for the two cities of Cagliari and Trieste. The two questionnaires share a common, general section, and then have been developed with different sections adapted to better fit the peculiarities of two different urban contests: the sailing race 'Barcolana' in the case of Trieste, an event that characterize the city as a major event, and the possible other events to be implemented in the city; the city of Cagliari as 'The City of Wind', with its potential of becoming an attractor for sailing activities, following the fact it hosts the Luna Rossa Team as a main hub for training and developing new sailing solutions.

The questionnaire has been developed by means of a Google Form and distributed over a community of selected users, identified among people active in sport, both as amateur and professionals, and as managers of sporting activities. People were therefore motivated in filling in the questionnaires, and other 300 forms have been collected in the period of time between 9 May 2018 and 30 October 2018.

The majority of respondents are male (more than 60%), born in the City of Cagliari and its hinterland, of an age between 26 and 60 years.

Around 80% started practicing sport activities regularly, mainly individually (67,6%) and as amateurs (48,4%). Team sports and activities practiced by people registered in sport associations follow as preferred way of practicing.

It is interesting to observe the preference of people for individual sport activities, demonstrating a growing trend in contemporary society of managing and organizing its own physical, sport activities in an autonomous way, according to particular needs and personal interests, and also, as a possible consequence of the good supply of urban spaces and natural areas - as humid areas and coast areas - suitable for practicing these activities: all elements that the city of Cagliari seem to be quite fitted with. That seems to be confirmed by analysing the main sports practiced (see Fig. 4), as Sailing// Windsurf/Kitesurf, Running and similar, following by Bike (road and mountain), Swimming and Soccer. Low percentages have been registered for Body building, Tennis, other water sports, martial arts and Beach tennis.

The questionnaire reveals also the weight that sport has in the life of people in terms of time and costs. The time dedicated to sport during the week is on average 2 to 3 h (31,4%) and among 4 and 5 (34,2%), to reach a timeframe bigger than 6 h (22,6%). Only 11,8% of interviewees dedicate less than 1 h per week to sport.

About costs, 37,4% spends more than 500 euro per year, nonetheless a certain number of people seem spending less than 100 euros per year (21,3%).

Again, another suggestion to confirm the capacity offered by the city to practice open air sports - namely street sports - and not necessarily in dedicated infrastructures.

If you practice sport activities regularly, sign the modality and the main sports practiced (multiple answers are possible).

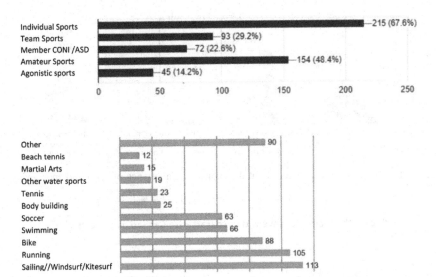

Fig. 4. People's sporting behaviours and personal interests. The main sports practiced in Cagliari.

The parts of the city more directly interested by sport activities and by the related ones have been identified in the Poetto area, in the urban seaside promenàde and in the parks (Molentargius, Monte Urpinu, etc.).

A part from the stress on the favourable conditions of the city, due to the environmental, geographical and climate characters and to the good set of facilities, infrastructure, services and sport functions, the questionnaire highlighted also the widespread awareness of the benefits coming from sport events at different scales. The 96% of interviewees declares that sport events are particularly important for the well-being of people and for enhancing the image of the city. Furthermore, more than 80% agrees on the fact that sport plays a relevant role for the economic development of the city.

Many respondents agree on the need to extend sport events in time, involving also other parts of the city, other than those favoured and already widely used (see Fig. 5).

The interviews highlight the A-League football championship as the main sport event in the city (42,3%), followed by the sailing race and other water sports (32,2%) and, to a minor extent, the Marathon and Half Marathon (9%) (see Fig. 6).

Over 90% of the interviewees agrees on the fact that it would be preferable to develop an international sport event. Most of the respondents think the city should develop sail events (49%), and particularly water sports (10%), run & triathlon (9%), as well as university/olympic games (8%) (see Fig. 7).

To what extent do you agree or disagree with the following statements?

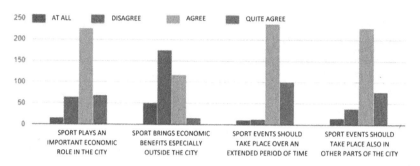

Fig. 5. Perception of interviewees about the economic importance of sport and sport events.

Which is the main sport event that characterize Cagliari as a Sports City?

Fig. 6. Perception of interviewees about the main sport event in Cagliari.

95% of interviewees agrees also on the need to promote also other specific activities, as cultural, enogastronomic, traditional events, as well as scientific and divulgative events, other than other sport events.

These first results appear quite significant and should be considered by decision makers, as citizens' involvement is of major importance to activate processes of urban development responding to real needs and aims of a population. In such sense, the results of the questionnaire could provide an important contribution to confirm Cagliari as the City of Sport also in the future.

Do you think would be important to organize an international event in Cagliari?

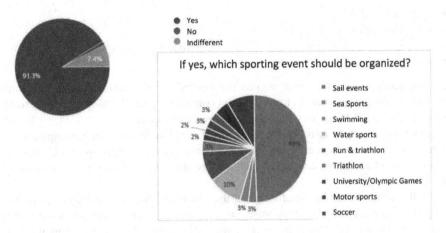

Fig. 7. Perception of interviewees about the importance to develop an international sport event in Cagliari.

7   Conclusions

The present study has assessed the sporting attractiveness of the city of Cagliari.

The authors analyzed urban interventions and popular initiatives for the diffusion of sport. Furthermore, the perception of citizens among sport, quality of life, socio-economic development was evaluated.

The results of the questionnaire have on the whole confirmed the findings of the Il Sole 24 Ore survey - *Sportiness index 2018* of Cagliari, that is a place that is highly suitable for welcoming the phenomenon of street sport. The challenge is to make the city of Cagliari more sustainable and "fit for sport". Specifically, some interviewees of the questionnaire presented interesting proposals for the future.

First of all, smart community is fully aware of the main geographical, environmental and climatic characteristics of Cagliari, which allow practicing outdoor sports almost all year round. The suggestions made by the interviewed community highlighted possible actions, such as:

- marketing activities at national and international level, to enhance the sports offer in a very favorable urban and landscape context;
- integrate the policies for the promotion of sport with those of areas of natural and environmental interest, as part of a sustainable transport vision.

This is also in line with the national survey of the Sole 24 ore, in particular with the sub-categories Sport and Nature and Sport and Tourism, where Cagliari ranked respectively 10th and 16th.

This confirms the maturity of the sports smart community. It is aware of the context and prepared to make a contribution to future prospects.

Other interviewees have highlighted the need for actions to improve the benefits deriving from the correlation between sport, wellness and social inclusion, such as:

- sports and suburbs
- redevelop before building new sports facilities;
- expanding the local community aware of the importance of sport;
- internationalization of sporting events.

This study shows that new actions are needed for the future starting from the interesting indications coming from the local community, which has shown itself to be attentive and loyal to the city through sport and street sport.

Furthermore, the results offer new and important suggestions for the implementation of the program of material and immaterial actions necessary to confirm Cagliari as a city of sport in the near future, which will be the object of a subsequent research development.

In this sense, it can be concluded that the role of the Smart Community gives this study an important contribution to managing and strengthening the connection between sport and the city and, therefore, in defining a shared model of social, economic and environmental development, as indicated by Agenda 2030.

References

1. Turner, D., Carnicelli, S.: Lifestyle Sports and Public Policy. Routledge, London (2017)
2. Balletto, G., Borruso, G.: Sport & the City: Forma ed effetti territoriali. In: Atti della XXII Conferenza Nazionale ASITA, Bolzano, 27–29 November 2018, pp. 67–74. ASITA (2018)
3. Strazzeri, I.: Introduzione alla Sociologia dello Sport. Lampi di stampa, Milano (2018)
4. Balletto, G., Borruso, G.: Sport and City. The case of Cagliari's new stadium (Sardinia – Italy). In: Proceedings of the 22nd IPSAPA/ISPALEM International Scientific Conference Aversa/Caserta (Italy), 2–3 July 2018 (2018, in print)
5. Gratton, C., Henry, I. (eds.): Sport in the City: The Role of Sport in Economic and Social Regeneration. Routledge, London (2001)
6. UNGA (United Nations General Assembly): Transforming our world: the 2030 Agenda for Sustainable Development. Resolution adopted by the General Assembly on 25 September 2015. A/RES/70/1 (2015)
7. Harrison, V.S., Boehmer, J.: Sport for development and peace: framing the global conversation. Commun. Sport. SAGE J. (2019)
8. Lindsey, I., Darby, P.: Sport and the sustainable development goals: where is the policy coherence? Int. Rev. Sociol. Sport. SAGE J. (2018)
9. Vargas-Hernández, J.G., Pallagst, K., Zdunek-Wielgołaska, J.A.: Urban green spaces for sustainable community development: a strategic management approach. In: Benna, U. (ed.) Optimizing Regional Development Through Transformative Urbanization, pp. 271–287. IGI Global (2019)
10. ISTAT (Istituto Nazionale di Statistica): Lo sport che cambia. I comportamenti emergenti e le nuove tendenze nella pratica sportiva in Italia (2005)
11. CNAPPC (Consiglio Nazionale Architetti, Pianificatori, Paesaggisti e Conservatori): Il Piano Nazionale per la Rigenerazione Urbana Sostenibile (2015)
12. Koch, N.: Sports and the city. Geogr. Compass **12**(3), e12360 (2018)

13. Eigenschenk, B., et al.: Benefits of outdoor sports for society. A systematic literature review and reflections on evidence. Int. J. Environ. Res. Public Health **16**(6), 937 (2019)
14. Kiuppis, F.: Inclusion in sport: Disability and participation. Sport Soc. **21**, 4–21 (2018)
15. Burini, F. (ed.): Partecipazione e governance territoriale. Dall'Europaall'Italia. FrancoAngeli, Milano (2013)
16. Anttiroiko, A.V.: Wellness City: Health and Well-being in Urban Economic Development. Palgrave Pivot, Cham (2018)
17. Pérez-delHoyo, R., Mora, H., Paredes, J.F.: Using social network data to improve planning and design of smart cities. Urban Growth Circ. Econ. **179**, 171–178 (2018)
18. Agergaard, S.: Rethinking Sports and Integration: Developing a Transnational Perspective on Migrants and Descendants in Sports. Routledge, Abingdon (2018)
19. Taks, M.: Social sustainability of non-mega sport events in a global world. Eur. J. Sport Soc. **10**(2), 121–141 (2013)
20. Nisar, T.M., Prabhakar, G., Strakova, L.: Social media information benefits, knowledge management and smart organizations. J. Bus. Res. **94**, 264–272 (2019)
21. California Institute for Smart Communities: Smart Communities Guide Book (2001)
22. Langdon, J., Marsden-Heathcote, J.: Community sport event management. In: Wilson, R., Platts, C. (eds.) Managing and Developing Community Sport, pp. 109–125. Routledge (2018)
23. Fister, I., Fister Jr., I., Fister, D.: Computational intelligence in sports. Vol 22. Springer Nature Switzerland AG (2019)
24. Herrera, F.: Pedestrian malls of Southern California, the present, the past, and the future, Doctoral dissertation, California State Polytechnic University, Pomona (2018)
25. Preite, G., Epifani, F.: Agenda Digitale. Nuovi modelli di governance territoriale. In: Pollice F. (ed.) Ricerche sul Salento. Il Contributo del Dipartimento di Storia, Società e Studi sull'Uomo alla conoscenza del territorio. Rapporto 2018, pp. 451–458, Placetelling. Collana di Studi Geografici sui luoghi e sulle loro rappresentazioni, 1/ 2018 (2018)
26. Mac Gillavry, E.: Collaborative mapping and gis: an alternative geographic information framework. In: Dragicevic, S., Balram, S. (eds.) Collaborative Geographic Information Systems, pp. 103–120. Idea Group, Hershey (2006)
27. Rizzi, F.: Smart city, smart community, smart specialization per il management dellasostenibilità. FrancoAngeli (2014)
28. Municipality of Cagliari: Cagliari Sporting Environment. Dossier candidacy European City of Sport (2017)
29. Municipality of Cagliari: Cagliari Dossier candidacy for hosting the sailing regattas
30. Clark, P., Niemi, M., Niemelä, J.: Sport, Recreation and Green Space in the European City, vol. 16. BoD-Books on Demand (2018)
31. Angrilli, M.: Piano Progetto Paesaggio: Urbanistica e recupero del bene comune. FrancoAngeli (2018)
32. Gibson, H.J., Lamont, M., Kennelly, M., Buning, R.J.: Introduction to the special issue active sport tourism. J. Sport Tourism **22**, 83–91 (2018)
33. Municipality of Cagliari: Cagliari European City of Sport 2017. Activity Report January-September (2017)
34. Il Sole 24 Ore: Le classifiche del Sole 24 Ore. Indice di sportività (2018). http://lab24.ilsole24ore.com/indiceSportivita/
35. Strava Global Heatmap (2019). https://www.strava.com/heatmap#7.00/-120.90000/38.36000/hot/all
36. Opendata Sardegna (2019). http://www.sardegnageoportale.it/index.php?xsl=2425&s=325563&v=2&c=14414&t=1&tb=14401

Smart City and Water. Resource and Risk (Smart Water 2019)

Water Resources for a Sustainable, Smart and Resilient Urban Development: The Case of Italy

Luigi Mundula$^{(\boxtimes)}$ and Ginevra Balletto

Department of Civil and Environmental Engineering and Architecture
(DICAAR), University of Cagliari, Cagliari, Italy
{luigimundula,balletto}@unica.it

Abstract. Water is a common good indispensable for the survival of living beings, it is a finite resource that increasingly conditions human economic and social development. The minimum biological need per capita for human survival is 5 L of water in 24 h. Without food you can live a month. Without water you do not exceed a week. In order to be able to talk about acceptable living conditions, no less than 50 L of water are required per day for every human being. Over 1 billion people drink "unsafe" water and 3.4 million people each year (5,000 children a day) die from waterborne diseases. The water emergency does not only concern developing countries but also the advanced Europe. Water governance affects both developing and all other countries. The complex supply and distribution and purification situation imposes universal strategies to guarantee socio-economic development in this delicate phase of climate change. The aim of the work is to present the main characteristics of the water management, including risks and opportunities, in the Italian case.

Keywords: Water · Smart cities and territories · Sustainable development

1 Introduction

Water is a common good indispensable for the survival of living beings, it is a finite resource that increasingly conditions human economic and social development [1].

71% of the earth's surface is covered with water but 97.5% is salty. Of the remaining 2.5% only 1% is usable for human activities (the remaining part is mainly in the form of ice). Of this 1%, 93% is used for agricultural purposes. The minimum biological need per capita for human survival is 5 L of water in 24 h. Without food you can live a month. Without water you do not survive longer than a week. In order to be able to talk about acceptable living conditions, no less than 50 L of water are required per day for every human being. The problem is that, according to data released by the World Health Organization (WHO) [2], currently 2.1 billion people live without safe

---

This paper is the result of the joint work of the authors. In particular: Sect. 1, has been jointly written by L. Mundula and G. Balletto; Sect. 2, by G. Balletto; Sect. 3, by L. Mundula; Sect. 4, by L. Mundula and G. Balletto.

© Springer Nature Switzerland AG 2019
S. Misra et al. (Eds.): ICCSA 2019, LNCS 11624, pp. 219–232, 2019.
https://doi.org/10.1007/978-3-030-24311-1_15

water at home and more than 700 children under five years of age die every day from diarrhea or diseases linked to unsafe water and poor sanitation [3]. According to the 2018 World Report on the development of water resources [4], currently, around 4 billion people live in areas where water is scarce for at least a month a year, and this amount is set to rise, with a world population that could reach 10.2 billion units by mid-century. Today we use a total of about 4,600 km^2 of water: 70% goes for agriculture, 20% for industrial activities and 10% for household consumption. However, the demand is destined to grow: in the last 100 years it has increased by six times, and each year rises by 1%.

The water emergency does not only concern developing countries but also the advanced Europe. According to the WHO [5], "in 2015 more than 62 million out of 912 million people, lack access to an adequate sanitation facility and 14 million do not use a basic drinking-water source. While access has increased in the last decades, there are notable disparities between rural and urban areas. [Moreover] 14 diarrhea deaths a day are estimated attributable to inadequate water, sanitation and hygiene".

The need for an adequate availability of the water resource brings to the fore the role of the infrastructures that guarantee its use. A role amplified by the rapid technological restructuring that has produced important effects on urban-territorial economies: greater access to the global market, intensification of local competition, the decline of traditional production processes, the emergence of a second process of "deindustrialization" in urban areas.

From the analysis of community and global policies, infrastructures, in its various characterizations, increasingly emerge as a growth factor.

The reference development models, used in particular by international organizations such as the World Bank, focus on the availability of infrastructures in the sectors considered strategic, and current EU policies are addressed, for relaunching economy and growth, towards more sustained investments in infrastructures.

This approach is particularly evident in those analyses [6] that relate the presence of infrastructures in the territory and the per capita income levels: where the levels of infrastructure are higher than the national average, there are often fewer inequalities among the per capita income levels.

Infrastructures are increasingly becoming a measure of competitiveness, especially if we look at the new European scenario resulting from the integration process which, involving the removal of barriers to labor and asset mobility, and greater capital mobility, is characterized by more competitive conditions compared to the past.

In this new context, every regional economy in the EU is exposed to greater competition, not only for what concerns the supply of products, but also in the offer of location factors for productive activities. For the economically weaker European regions and in particular for those most disadvantaged due to the lack of infrastructure and services (such as Southern Italy), the risk of succumbing to the competition for the attraction of Foreign Direct Investment (FDI) increases. It also increases the risk of losing a part of its entrepreneurial and investment resources to the benefit of more advanced areas, favored by the presence of external economies connected to agglomeration factors, or to benefit other regions capable of ensuring companies obtain a better relationship between benefits and costs.

Although the infrastructural endowment represents a necessary condition, it is not a sufficient condition for starting a sustainable development path. Only an efficient (smart) management of resources and of its infrastructures makes it possible to obtain such a result. In this framework will be analyzed the case of water resources for civil use in Italy.

2   The Withdrawal of Water Resources in Italy

Water has unique properties, including being the only chemical compound that can be found in the three phases (liquid, gaseous and solid) and for this reason it is also the main element with spatial distribution that varies over time [7].

In particular, the largest reservoir of fresh water in the world consists of groundwater, which amounts to more than 97% of all fresh water available on earth (excluding glaciers and polar ice caps). The remaining 3% is mainly composed of surface waters (lakes, rivers, wetlands) and soil humidity.

Given competing pressures it is estimated that by 2030 global water demand can exceed actual availability by 40% [8]. The need for water is, in fact, closely linked to various sectors: we use water, as well as for civil uses, to generate and sustain economic activities and agriculture, commercial fishing, energy production, industry manufacturing, transport and tourism.

The amount of resource available is conditioned as much by orogenetic factors as by climatic factors. The climate factor is central as the out-flows are mainly closely related to the influxes. In most regions the predominantly impermeable soil structure and the absence of natural reservoirs of significant capacity do not allow an effective time lag of the two phenomena. The historical seasonal variations that characterize the meteorological situations of the individual regions have recently been associated with global events that tend to exalt their extreme values.

Climate change in progress, together with the increase in rainfall and the increase in atmospheric temperature are the main phenomena that modify the geographical distribution of water [9].

The set of climate change, places of precipitation and collection of natural water resources and concentration of water demand for personal and productive uses (management and distribution) constitute the local and global scenario [10].

In this context, also the imbalances related to the quantity of water available between populations increase (USA, 580 L/day; Italy 380 L/day; Germany, 200 L/day; China, 90 L/day; Cambodia, Haiti and Uganda, 10 L/day), increasing also the gap between health, well-being and social status [4], boosting tensions and conflicts [11].

In particular, on a global scale there has been a noticeable increase in temperature, the effects of which can change the circulation of air masses in the atmosphere. The forecast models provide significant indications, which in Italian latitudes highlight a more accentuated space-time concentration of precipitation, a decrease in snowfall and an increase in evaporation volumes with a consequent decrease in outflows. Italy is included in a climate transition zone between the European continental area and the Mediterranean one. The virtual separation line between the two areas can be approximated in correspondence with the regions of Tuscany, Emilia Romagna and Sardinia. South of this hypothetical climate dividing line there is a lower general rainfall with a tendency to establish long periods of drought. In the area to the north of this line, the annual amount of rainfall remains almost unchanged, but rainfall tends to be concentrated in high intensity cyclonic events. The fact that these climatic conditions recur in the short term accentuates the imbalance between the availability and demand of the water resource, as not only is availability reduced, but the time lag between availability and demand increases. The quality of water resources is also constantly threatened by pollution and by hydro-morphological changes due to the man activity, which cause tangible alterations, even in quantitative terms, of aquatic eco-systems.

Looking at the water for civil use (that covers 20% of the plurality of use)[1], in Italy the total amount of water withdrawal from environment in 2012 was about 9.5 billion of cubic meter (Table 1) according to an articulated framework of sources (Table 1) - 48% from groundwater (water well), 10.37% from lakes and reservoirs, 4.7% from watercourses, 37% from spring water, 0.1% from desalted waters.

Table 1. Total amount of water withdrawal from environment (2012) - thousands of cubic meters[a]

District	Spring	Well	Stream	Lakes/artificial basin	Marine/brackish water	Total
Po River	666,703	1,769,610	97,558	86,083	0	2.619,954
E. Alps	426,823	601,754	67,952	1,054	0	1,097,583
N. AM	166,169	459,814	210,773	84,765	1,094	922,615
Serchio River	8,084	23,787	0	0	0	31,871
C. AM	957,947	340,523	13,153	24,126	0	1,335,749
S. AM	1,055,561	871,440	49,058	425,342	0	2,401,401
Sicily	169,735	419,456	4,631	113,350	6,853	714,025
Sardinia	39,655	40,818	3,521	246,026	0	330,020
Other	5,075	352	0	0	0	5,427
Total	3,495,752	4,527,554	446,646	980,746	7,947	9,458,645

[a]E. Alps = Eastern Alps; N. AM = Northern Apennine Mountains; C. AM = Central Apennine Mountains; S. AM = Southern Apennine Mountains

In Italy the lack of water is a national emergency: in the summer of 2017, 10 regions have declared the state of calamity. It should be noted that climate change (increase in temperatures, concentration of rainfall - increasingly short and violent - in some months of the year alternating with long periods of drought, contraction in

---

[1] The use of water in Italy is distributed as following: civil – drinking water (20%), industrial (21%), energy (5%), agricultural (51%), zootechnical (3%).

volumes of glaciers) is leading to a decrease in availability in the main river basins - Po, Adige, Arno and Tevere - and the consequent reduction in water outflows. In particular, in 2017 there was an exceptional lack of available water resources: in all four major river basins, the average annual flows recorded a decrease compared to the average of the reference period 1981–2010, with an average overall reduction of 39.6%).

The classic response to the lack of water resources is the use of dams. In Italy there are 534 Great Dams (Table 2): about 72% in regular operation (of which 57% for hydroelectric use), about 21% in experimental operation, 5% out of service, while the remaining 2% is still under construction; and about 10,000 littles reservoirs. The authorized volume of the Great Dams is about 11% less than the potential reservoir volume. This difference is substantially due to the tests still in progress which contribute with a 7.5% volume less than the potential reservoir volume.

Table 2. Summary at national level of the state of operation of the Great Dams (June 2017)[a]

Status	Dams		Capacity (millions m^3)		Difference
	N	%	Potential	Authorized	%
Under construction	666,703	1,769,610	97,558	86,083	0
In testing	426,823	601,754	67,952	1,054	0
In exercise	166,169	459,814	210,773	84,765	1,094
Limited capacity	8,084	23,787	0	0	0
Temporary out of order	957,947	340,523	13,153	24,126	0
Total Great Dams[b]	3,495,752	4,527,554	446,646	980,746	7,947

[a]Source: Ministry of Infrastructure and Transport - General Directorate for Dams and Water and Electricity Infrastructures (ex RID).
[b]Including 3 billion cubic meters determined by regulatory barriers of the large pre-alpine natural lakes (Garda, Maggiore, Iseo, Orta, Varese)

Looking at the regional data (Table 3) it is evident that this criticality particularly affects the southern regions (besides the case of Umbria) which see an average of 20% in terms of non-used volume.

The total potential volume of large Italian dams is 13.748 billion m^3, which however is not evenly distributed: 28% in the north, 15% in the center and the remaining 57% in the south and on the islands. It should also be noted that 58% of the volume is for irrigation use.

Despite the presence of numerous dams, a particularly critical water emergency occurs cyclically in Southern Italy. This situation follows a series of years of increasingly low thunderstorm rainfall, which occurred in the last decade due to a high level of network losses, as shown in the next paragraph.

Table 3. Regional distribution of the state Great Dams (June 2017).[a]

Region	Dams	Potential volume	Authorized volume	Difference
	n.	Millions of m^3		%
Piedmont	59	374,46	368,11	1,70%
Aosta Valley	8	142,48	130	8,76%
Lombardy	77	3876,17	3838,04	0,98%
Trentino-South Tyrol	37	647,68	630,68	2,62%
Veneto	18	237,97	234,97	1,26%
Friuli-Venezia Giulia	12	190,86	181,55	4,88%
Liguria	13	60,69	59,4	2,13%
Emilia-Romagna	24	158,91	153,42	3,45%
Tuscany	51	321,11	312,18	2,78%
Umbria	10	430,4	236,61	45,03%
Marche	16	119,07	114,07	4,20%
Lazio	21	519,06	518,15	0,18%
Abruzzo	14	370,38	370,38	0,00%
Molise	7	202,91	170,66	15,89%
Campania	17	293,1	249,78	14,78%
Apulia	9	541,42	464,03	14,29%
Basilicata	14	910,41	786,24	13,64%
Calabria	22	586,44	422,04	28,03%
Sicily	46	1104,98	850,93	22,99%
Sardinia	59	2505,49	2012,72	19,67%
ITALY[b]	**534**	**13.593,99**	**12.103,96**	**10,96%**

[a]Source: Ministry of Infrastructure and Transport - General Directorate for Dams and Water and Electricity Infrastructures (ex RID).
[b]Including 3 billion cubic meters determined by regulatory barriers of the large pre-alpine natural lakes (Garda, Maggiore, Iseo, Orta, Varese)

3 Management and Use of Water for Civil Use

The availability of the water resource for civil use is affected by different losses during its management cycle: purification treatment (part of the water is used in the purification process, whereby the output volume from the implant is less than the incoming), losses of the municipal networks of distribution, inattentive use of end-users, inefficiency in the treatment of waste water (sewerage and purification) [12].

Water treatment technologies (fresh and waste) have improved over the last 20 years, however climate change and the growing demand for water require particular attention in the policy and conservation management of eco-systems (rivers, lakes, ponds and lagoons), both as sources and both as receivers [13].

In 2015, the total volume of water withdrawn for drinking use in Italy from the over 1,800 supply source management bodies amount to 8.32 billion cubic meters (Table 4)[2].

Comparing this data with that of the 28 countries of the European Union [14], Italy with 156 cubic meters per inhabitant (427 L per day) is the country with the largest withdrawal, followed by Ireland (135 m^3 per inhabitant) and Greece (131 m^3 per inhabitant). By contrast, Malta is the country where the value of the indicator reaches the minimum (31 m^3 per inhabitant). Rather low drinking water withdrawals are made in most Eastern European countries (Fig. 1).

Table 4. Water introduced into the municipal networks for the distribution of drinking water - thousands of cubic meters (2015): Source: Istat - Atlante statistico dei comuni (http://asc.istat.it/asc_BL/)

Region	2015	2012	Diff.%
Piedmont	584067	600420	-2,80%
Aosta Valley	26086	27430	-5,15%
Lombardy	1391876	1434135	-3,04%
Trentino-South Tyrol	159809	146909	8,07%
Veneto	647582	633857	2,12%
Friuli-Venezia Giulia	195590	204302	-4,45%
Liguria	238693	241338	-1,11%
Emilia-Romagna	469602	482537	-2,75%
Tuscany	426724	425579	0,27%
Umbria	101978	105473	-3,43%
Marche	168585	166550	1,21%
Lazio	972537	942144	3,13%
Abruzzo	230777	231353	-0,25%
Molise	53493	54329	-1,56%
Campania	820103	827502	-0,90%
Apulia	426648	448165	-5,04%
Basilicata	97754	70591	27,79%
Calabria	350038	327652	6,40%
Sicily	683149	693419	-1,50%
Sardinia	275000	293171	-6,61%
ITALY	8320091	8356856	-0,44%

The comparison between the volumes of water injected and dispensed makes it possible to assess the network water losses that represent an important criticality in the management of water resources [15].

The total water losses percentage, the rate of water supplied that does not reach end users, amounted to 41.4% nationally, equal to 3.45 billion cubic meters, in 2015 (was

---

[2] 76.3% of this volume, amounting to just over seven billion cubic meters, was measured using suitable measuring instruments while the remaining 23.7% was estimated by the source managers. In the absence of meters, it is common to use the maximum concession flow rate as an estimate parameter, although it does not correspond to the actual withdrawal value.

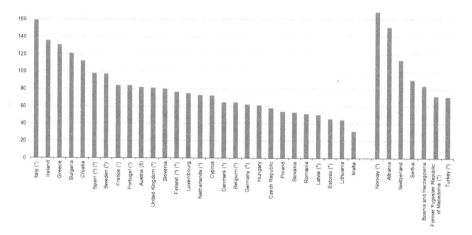

Fig. 1. Withdrawals of drinking water in 28 EU countries. Year 2015 or last year available, cubic meters per inhabitant. (Source: https://ec.europa.eu/eurostat/statistics-explained/index.php?title=File:Total_freshwater_abstraction_for_public_water_supply,_2015_(m³_per_inhabitant)_V4.png)

38% in 2012). In detail the real water losses, due to corrosion or deterioration of the pipes, breaks in the pipes or faulty joints and inefficiencies, amount to 38.3%; while apparent water losses, attributable to unauthorized consumption and measurement errors, are 3.1% of the water introduced into the network [16].

Utilitalia (the association of water, energy and environmental Italian companies), analyzed 54 companies that serve over 30 million people discovering that the average dispersion rate in the North is 26%, in the Center and in the South by 46%. Old pipes often run underground and maintenance is scarce. 60% of the infrastructures were laid over 30 years ago (70% in large urban centers) and 25% have over half a century of life (40% in large cities) [17].

These high dispersion and losses levels (Table 5), that are increasing in almost all the municipalities [14], are explained by the age of the pipelines (36% are between the ages of 31 and 50, and 22% have over 50) and by the very low average price of water in Italy. A cubic meter (1000 L) of water in Italy costs 1.43 euro, compared to the European average value of 4.01 euro [18].

Particular attention should also be paid to the treatment of wastewater, which, if not properly treated, is a potential source of pollution of groundwater [19]. In Italy the situation, from this point of view, is rather critical (so much so as to be subject to sanctions by the EU), high-lighting at national level in 2015 an average value of about 40% of untreated wastewater[3] (Fig. 2).

---

[3] For non-compliance in the implementation of Directive 91/271/EEC, implemented by Italy with Legislative Decree 152/2006, on the treatment of wastewater, Italy has already suffered two sentences by the European Court of Justice, the C565-10 (Procedure 2004-2034) and C85-13 (Procedure 2009–2034) and the launch of a new infringement procedure (Procedure 2014–2059).

Table 5. Network dispersions in Italy by Regions and Province

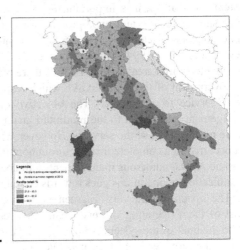

Region	2012	2015	Difference 2015-2012
Piedmont	38	35,2	-2,8
Aosta Valley	21,9	18,7	-3,2
Lombardy	26,5	28,7	2,2
Trentino-South Tyrol	25,6	29,8	4,2
Veneto	35,6	40	4,4
Friuli-Venezia Giulia	44,9	47,8	2,9
Liguria	31,2	32,8	1,6
Emilia-Romagna	25,6	30,7	5,1
Tuscany	38,6	43,4	4,8
Umbria	38,5	46,8	8,3
Marche	28,9	34,1	5,2
Lazio	45,1	52,9	7,8
Abruzzo	42,3	47,9	5,6
Molise	47,2	47,4	0,2
Campania	45,8	46,7	0,9
Apulia	34,6	45,9	11,3
Basilicata	38,5	56,3	17,8
Calabria	35,4	41,1	5,7
Sicily	45,6	50	4,4
Sardinia	54,8	55,6	0,8

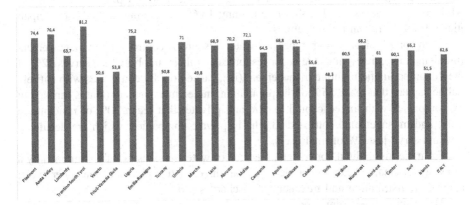

Fig. 2. % treated waste water compared to the total urban loads – 2015

In this context it is to be noted that in 342 municipalities, in which about 1.4 million inhabitants reside (equal to 2.4% of the total population), this service is absent, i.e., urban wastewater is not collected in public plants in operation. The most critical situations are recorded in Sicily, where there are 75 municipalities without purification (12.9% of the regional population), in Calabria with 57 municipalities (7% of the population) and in Campania, with 55 municipalities (3.9% of the population). With reference to the macro-regions, the highest purification rate is recorded in the North-West, where 68.2% of all the potentially generated load is treated. The least suitable is, instead, the purification system of the Islands, which guarantees a treatment of 51.5% compared to the potential generated.

A further element of reflection is provided by the water resources management system. First of all, it is important to point out that according to the Italian law the ownership of surface and underground water resources is always public. Its management, conversely, can be public, private or mixed. From the administrative point of view, based on a 1994 law then revised in 2006, Italy was divided into 64 ATOs (optimal territorial areas), while in 2011 there were 94. For each ATO there is an Entity of Government of the Area (EGA), which responds to the Region, which entrusts the water service to a manager. The objective of the legislation was to optimize the management reducing it to the minimum, making sure that for each ATO there was a single management of the services. However, assignments to single managers have not yet occurred in a complete manner throughout the national territory and for this reason, in some ATOs, numerous managements still coexist, although it is true that the process of unification of operations goes towards completion and has reached 82% of operators.

The system is still very fragmented, with over two thousand operators surveyed, most of them operating in very small local realities, perhaps lost in the mountains, while the bulk of the system is now consolidated around some main operators. Almost half of the turnover is, in fact, generated by 5% of the operators.

More in detail [14], the municipal water networks are managed by a total of 2,306 bodies (331 specialized bodies manage 86.4% of the volumes put on the network, while 1,975 managers deal with the remaining 13.6%) operating in 8,024 municipalities (99.7% of Italian municipalities).

There are basically four types of water resources control: direct management (municipalities directly manage water resources and their supply) which serves 12% of the Italian population; public management (i.e., carried out by companies with entirely public capital) that reach 55% of the population; mixed management (that is carried out by companies with mixed capital, public and private) that reach 30% of residents in Italy, and managements entrusted to wholly private companies, which are decidedly few and serve just 3% of total users.

From the highlighted above data, the state of water services in Italy, burdened by a growing demand, appears rather lacking in all three relative phases of the water cycle: adduction, distribution and treatment of discharges [20].

The main critical points are:

- the insufficient drinking supply that concerns 35% of the population;
- the high percentage of water dispersed in the phase that goes from the adduction to the supply to the end-users;
- the limited territorial coverage of sewerage and purification services;
- the high number of irregularities found in the treatment of dis-charges;
- the failure to adapt the purification service to the EU regulations both in terms of service coverage and type of treatment.

These deficiencies are particularly serious in some areas of the country: the regions of the South and the two major islands suffer from serious infrastructural deficits, an aqueduct and sewerage network in very bad conditions (see the volume of water dispersed), as well as a structural underneath - equipment for sewage treatment plants.

4   A Possible Way

The data shown in the previous paragraph testify both a high shortage of water infrastructure, the lack of adaptation of existing ones and a lack of ordinary and extraordinary maintenance, as well as important managerial inefficiencies.

If it is true, however, that the improvement of the infrastructures contributes to the improvement of quality, only the synergistic action of management efficiency and adequate infrastructure is such as to guarantee a real improvement in the offer and consequently in the territorial development and growth.

It can be noted that at the political level development and growth are mostly treated as synonyms, not considering the various studies that, focusing on the role of the territory, define sustainable, resilient and smart development models, that overcome the concepts of growth, that is at the increase in production (GDP) and income. Looking solely at the quantitative progress (growth) of GDP (or GNP) means indeed to-tally denying its qualitative dimension. Today the word development cannot refer only to a process of an economic nature, but must be interpreted as a multidimensional process, the result of which is the general improvement of the living conditions of the current and future population through the most appropriate technologies. This means not only higher levels of education, good health and reduction of social inequalities [21].

It also means protecting the environment, stable institutions, guarantees of freedom and protection of essential rights. This regards too, the water, as stated by the SDG' 6th goal.

In this perspective, a correct infrastructural endowment (specifically the water supply) is a necessary but not sufficient condition for development, especially in a context that has become increasingly international and competitive.

If we should use an approach based on growth, the "simple" construction of new reservoirs, pipelines or the replacement of old and deteriorated pipelines would be the ideal solution. But such a solution, however useful, would not solve the problem. We need to move on to a smart approach, based on the efficiency in resource management and therefore on the determination and identification of what the demand of individual territories actually is; on the "sustainable" use of the available resources oriented to a reduction in waste and to an intelligent consumption, as well as the resilience of the infrastructures themselves, so that they can withstand the stresses and shocks they will inevitably face.

The actions to be taken should so concern:

- increasing the availability of the water resource, if there is no possibility of tapping into underground aquifers or natural reservoirs (either because they do not exist or are almost completely used, and thus counter the negative effects of drought), by proceeding to a rational planning of resource with the creation of interconnections between different hydraulic systems, thus redistributing the resource not only in a temporal sense but also in a spatial one, channeling water where there is greater demand;
- contracting consumption through reducing the losses in the adduction and distribution networks, a prudent regulation of the network pressure and a tariff policy that disincentives too high consumption;

- managing efficiently the resource through a careful verification of the quantity of water supplied to the users through the installation of counters in correspondence of the single derivations;
- diversification of the water networks according to the specific needs of the use of the water supplied. For civil needs water with drinking characteristics is required, while lower quality water can be reserved for improper use (washing of cars, vehicles, garden irrigation, rinsing of sanitary appliances). Differentiation of the service based on the intended use of water can be achieved by adopting dual networks, which find favorable conditions of use when new plants are built;
- - the adoption of smart metering systems in homes. There are still too many cases in which citizens pay for water not on the basis of what they consume (or waste) but rather on the square meters of their home (a measure sometimes weighted according to the number of residents in the apartment);
- the use of natural techniques for the valorization of water built in close relationship with the landscape, such as structures for collecting rainwater[4] or traditional land preservation practices, rather than resorting only to man-made infrastructures, such as artificial water basins, irrigation canals or water treatment plants.

Starting from these considerations, the need to redefine the so-called "correct infrastructural endowment" emerges. This is a necessary condition for the realization of forms of sustainable, resilient and smart development especially in the European context, where the process of economic integration has exposed the regional economies to a constant comparison, not only for what concerns the offer of products but also regarding the offer of location factors for production activities. The main traditional indicators of the correct basic infrastructural endowment (the regional supply per capita, the dedicated financial resources, the services offered, the management, the costs of use) must therefore be integrated with territorial indicators based on the demand in relation to the different regional contexts.

The model that appears more appropriate, following the triple helix of Etzkovitz [23] and starting from the concept of territorial governance, places institutions, management bodies and citizens in a virtuous relationship and uses new technologies not as a new technological wave to be compared or as a tool of static analysis, but as a real design philosophy. The possibilities of overcoming the constraints represented by the scarcity of individual resources are thus made evident by exploiting the agglomerative advantages, identifiable in cooperation ties, in terms of exchange of experiences and sharing of resources, and above all in the formation of external economies of scale, represented by the significant reduction in asset management costs, thanks to the joint use of a series of services and infrastructures aimed at mitigating or eliminating impacts on the environment [24].

Preventing impacts on the reference ecosystem is related to the need to create forms of sustainable, resilient and smart development. The objective is a general improvement in the exploitation of resources based on a series of constraints and opportunities

---

[4] An example comes from China where the government has planned the creation of 16 sponge-cities, which by 2020 should be able to recycle 70% of rainwater thanks to better permeability of the soil and the restoration of adjacent marshes, as well as counteract floods and droughts [22].

represented by the elements of the reference context. This is the direction of the rules and (voluntary) tools operating in the context of the European Union and international, which propose restructuring models of processes focused on minimizing waste and production disadvantages for the continuous improvement of territorial performance [25].

Hence the need for an adequate methodology for forecasting and calculating the social, economic and environmental effects and implications, in order to overcome the constraint posed by a typically quantitative approach to the feasibility assessments, which arises from having applied partial techniques and purely economic cuts (i.e., the Analysis of preferences and sensitivity). By inserting the environmental variable, this last approach would show indeed all its limitations, because the vastness of the scales involved would assign to the environmental component a role limited to the simple minimization of the negative effects (the "externalities") of the territorial development strategies. Then it raises the need to develop an analytical method capable of identifying all the direct and indirect relations existing between the economic system and the social and environmental systems [26].

The answer can only be found in a multidisciplinary approach that allows for the complete integration of the various aspects and the different needs related to sustainability, resilience and smartness of a specific territorial area, aiming at maximizing the environmental quality and the quality of life (of its inhabitants).

This approach must therefore be transformed into an endogenous model of socioeconomic development, through the application of adequate tools to face the logic of the qualitative approach of local and global environmental complexity, in analogy with the ancient Rome's approach to 'Curator aquarum' [27]; unique and highest authority of water policies related to the ancient known world. The interdisciplinary and global approach are therefore the only viable way for the responsible management of water understood as a universally recognized common good [28].

References

1. United Nations: Johannesburg Summit 2002 Facts Sheets: Facts About Water (2002). http://www.johannesburgsummit.org/html/media_info/pressreleases_factsheets/wssd4_water.pdf
2. WHO/UNICEF: Progress on drinking water, sanitation and hygiene (2017). https://www.who.int/water_sanitation_health/publications/jmp-2017/en/. Accessed 29 Mar 2019
3. UNICEF. https://data.unicef.org/topic/child-health/diarrhoeal-disease/. Accessed 29 Mar 2019
4. World Water Development Report (2018). https://unesdoc.unesco.org/ark:/48223/pf0000261424. Accessed 29 Mar 2019
5. World Health Organization. http://www.euro.who.int/en/health-topics/environment-and-health/water-and-sanitation. Accessed 29 Mar 2019
6. Deloitte-Luiss "Gli investimenti in infrastrutture" (2018). http://ediliziainrete.it/attualita/investimenti-in-infrastrutture-i-risultati-del-3-degrees-studio-deloitte-slash-luiss. Accessed 29 Mar 2019
7. Perry, J., Vanderklein, E.L.: Water Quality: Management of a Natural Resource. Wiley, Hoboken (2009)
8. The 2030 Water Resources Group: Charting our water future (2009). https://www.mckinsey.com/~/media/mckinsey/dotcom/client_service/sustainability/pdfs/charting%20our%20water%20future/charting_our_water_future_full_report_.ashx. Accessed 29 Mar 2019

9. McNabb, D.E.: The global need for water sustainability. In: McNabb, D.E. (ed.) Global Pathways to Water Sustainability, pp. 31–50. Palgrave Macmillan, Cham (2019). https://doi. org/10.1007/978-3-030-04085-7_3

10. Endo, T., Kakinuma, K., Yoshikawa, S., Kanae, S.: Are water markets globally applicable? Environ. Res. Lett. **13**(3), 034032 (2018)

11. Lonergan, S.C.: Water and conflict: rhetoric and reality. In: Environmental Conflict, pp. 109–124. Routledge (2018)

12. Roccaro, P., Verlicchi, P.: Wastewater and Reuse: Wastewater or simply water? (2018). https://www.sciencedirect.com/science/article/pii/S2468584418300308

13. Letcher, T.M., Vallero, D.A. (eds.): Waste: A Handbook for Management. Academic Press (2019)

14. ISTAT: Censimento delle acque per uso civile (2017). https://www.istat.it/it/files//2017/12/ Report-Censimento-acque.pdf. Accessed 29 Mar 2019

15. Landriani, L., Lepore, L., D'Amore, G., Pozzoli, S., Alvino, F.: Decorporatization of a municipal water utility: a case study from Italy. Util. Policy **57**, 43–47 (2019)

16. Baldino, N., Pujol, D.S.: Characterizing the recent decline of water consumption in Italian cities. Investigaciones geográficas **69**, 9–21 (2018)

17. Fondazione Utilitatis a Cassa Depositi e Prestiti: Blue Book 2017. I dati sul servizio idrico integrato in Italia. Utilitatis (2017)

18. 11ème édition du baromètre NUS Consulting sur les prix des services d'eau et d'assainissement en Europe, http://www.fp2e.org/userfiles/files/DOSSIER%20DE%20PRESSE_NUS_Consul ting_2017_FP2E_Prix_services_eau_baromètre_européen.pdf. Accessed 29 Mar 2019

19. Tang, J., Zhang, C., Shi, X., Sun, J., Cunningham, J.A.: Municipal wastewater treatment plants coupled with electrochemical, biological and bio-electrochemical technologies: opportunities and challenge toward energy self-sufficiency. J. Environ. Manag. **234**, 396–403 (2019)

20. Bonoli, A., Di Fusco, E., Zanni, S., Lauriola, I., Ciriello, V., Di Federico, V.: Green smart technology for water (GST4Water): life cycle analysis of urban water consumption. Water **11**(2), 389 (2019)

21. Sistach, L.M.: Laudato si' e grandi città. Libreria Editrice Vaticana, Città del Vaticano (2018)

22. Chan, F.K.S., Griffiths, J.A., Higgitt, D., Xu, S., Zhu, F., Tang, Y., Xu, Y., Thorne, C.R.: "Sponge City" in China—a breakthrough of planning and flood risk management in the urban context. Land Use Policy **76**, 772–778 (2018)

23. Etzkowitz, H., Leydesdorff, L.: The Triple Helix – University-industry-government relations: a laboratory for knowledge based economic development. EASST Rev. **14**(1), 14–19 (1995)

24. Barbero, S., Pallaro, A.: Relation between man and water (2019). https://iris.polito.it/ retrieve/handle/11583/2646134/114450/Barbero_Pallaro_Relation%20between%20man%2 0and%20water_The%20awareness%20of%20living%20water%20for%20sustainable%20de sign.pdf

25. Rey, D., Pérez-Blanco, C.D., Escriva-Bou, A., Girard, C., Veldkamp, T.I.: Role of economic instruments in water allocation reform: lessons from Europe. Int. J. Water Resour. Dev. **35**(2), 206–239 (2019)

26. Koundouri, P., Akinsete, E., Tsani, S.: Socio-economic and policy implications of multi-stressed rivers: a European perspective. In: Multiple Stressors in River Ecosystems, pp. 335–351. Elsevier (2019)

27. Pace, P.: Acquedotti di Roma e il De aquaeductu di Frontino, B&T Multimedia (2010)

28. Schulz, C.: Governance-related values as dimensions of good water governance. Wiley Interdiscip. Rev.: Water **6**(1), e1322 (2019)

A Pilot Plant for Energy Harvesting from Falling Water in Drainpipes. Technical and Economic Analysis

Giacomo Viccione$^{(\boxtimes)}$ ⓘ, Antonio Nesticò ⓘ, Federica Vernieri, and Maurizio Cimmino

Department of Civil Engineering, University of Salerno, 84084 Fisciano, SA, Italy
gviccion@unisa.it

Abstract. Renewable energy sources are currently object of great attention from the scientific community involved on the matter, in the general context of the ongoing climate change and related implications. In this work, we investigate the costs needed to implement a technical solution to harvest energy from drainpipes. To this aim, a pilot plant was built at the Laboratory of Environmental and Maritime Hydraulics (LIDAM), University of Salerno, Italy.

The driving idea consists in the possibility of collecting rainwater at the roof of a building, storing it in tanks. In this way, the established hydraulic head can be converted into kinetic energy at the bottom of the building as can be easily explained by applying the Bernoulli's principle. Here, a water jet of mean velocity of up to tens of m/s is formed at the pipe outlet as it is provided with a nozzle. The stream is directed against a Pelton turbine where the rotational kinetic energy is finally converted into electrical energy by means of a DC brushed motor turned as generator.

The analysis of the investment and management costs of the pilot plant provides useful economic parameters for implementing the project in practice.

Keywords: Hydropower · Pelton · Drainpipes · Cost analysis

1 Introduction

The presence of water in the form of water bodies, aquifers, glaciers, rainfalls and runoff is the result of state changes, i.e. evapotranspiration, condensation, sublimation/desublimation, ice melting, thanks to the energy transferred by the sun on the atmosphere and the earth's surface. Solar irradiation, highest at the equator and lowest at the poles, determines non-equilibrium thermal conditions, yielding air masses which originate spatial and temporal meteorological events. The result is the water cycle, also called hydrologic cycle, involving the continuous circulation of water in the Earth-atmosphere system making its presence continually changing from one form to another [1–3].

Every year sun irradiation takes away from the oceans the equivalent of un meter of water depth, that is 875 km^3 equivalent in volume. Others 160 km^3 evaporate from the continents. Water evaporation varies depending mainly on the season and geographic latitude.

© Springer Nature Switzerland AG 2019
S. Misra et al. (Eds.): ICCSA 2019, LNCS 11624, pp. 233–242, 2019.
https://doi.org/10.1007/978-3-030-24311-1_16

Precipitations vary as well, with annual average values of 1140 mm and 720 mm for oceans and continents, respectively. Globally, the average annual rainfall is 1020 mm, 970 mm for the Italian peninsula. Italy is the first country for water consumption in Europe, the third worldwide, after Canada and United States. The water resource is not equally distributed among the Regions. The availability decrease from North to South with Puglia, Sicilia and Sardegna Regions receiving only 40 to 50% less precipitations than the ones falling in the North.

The exploitation of water as a source of energy has its origins back in time, when Greeks and Romans used watermills for irrigation, grind corns for bread or olives for olive oil [4, 5]. Today, hydropower is among the first renewable source to be produced, attaining a percentage of 18% worldwide [6]. The energy is harvested thanks to the existence of a difference in height through which water gains pressure and kinetic energy or by means of run-of-the-river generation plants. Anyway, the power output is generated by connecting the turbine axis to an alternator, according to an energy conversion efficiency η being the ratio between the useful output of an energy conversion machine and the input, in energy terms. Actually, the tendency is toward the creation of small (SHPs) or micro (MHPs) or pico-hydropower (PHPs) plants due the availability of water flowing, providing power to isolated homes or to small communities [7–9].

The experimental study carried out at the Laboratory of Environmental and Maritime Hydraulics (LIDAM), University of Salerno, Italy, consisting of a pilot plant for energy harvesting from falling water in drainpipes, is the basis for technical and economic analysis next presented.

2 Materials and Methods

The pilot plant (Fig. 1a) consists of a steel tank, 100 l of capacity, placed at 4,90 m above ground to reproduce a single level building. At its bottom, a vertical pvc pipe is bolted, reproducing a drainpipe of 0,09 m of inner diameter with an hydraulic capacity of 8,1 l/s. The tank is fed with the local water supply to the aim of reproduce the recharge as a consequence of a meteoric event. A solenoid valve connected to a float prevents the inlet of water once the tank reaches 60% of its capacity, that is 60 l. A Pelton micro-turbine connected to a 36 V generator is placed at the lower end where an adjustable nozzle, that is a reduction of two consecutive truncated cones, see Fig. 1b, produces a water jet. The hydroelectric energy produced is then stored in a 2–12 V, 250 A/h battery. Two nozzles have been tested with lower diameters of 3 mm and 5 mm, respectively.

In order to fix the Pelton turbine to the generator, the horizontal shaft was turned on a lathe and a central hole was performed on the runner wheel (Fig. 2a), shaped the axis (Fig. 2b) and finally two holes are pierced to ensure the generator-turbine connection by means of tightened screws (Fig. 3).

An off-the shelf DC brushed motor (Fig. 3) was turned as generator to produce electricity. As the expected output voltage is of the order of 10^0 V, a 36 V model is taken into account to prevent power failures. In the Table 1 are given the related technical specifications.

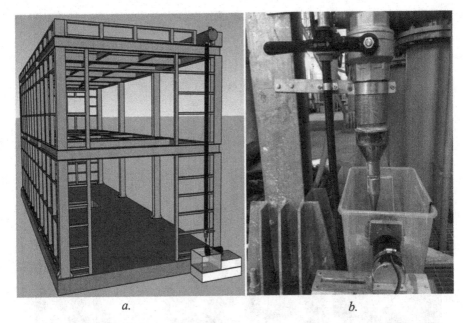

a.   *b.*

Fig. 1. *a.* Sketch of the pilot plant built at the Laboratory of Environmental and Maritime Hydraulics (LIDAM), University of Salerno, Italy. *b.* A particular of the adopted nozzles assisted with the shut-off valve.

a.   *b.*

Fig. 2. *a.* Execution of the central slot on the runner wheel with a precision drill. *b.* Axis shaping.

Fig. 3. Final assembling of the Pelton turbine on the generator axis.

Table 1. Technical specification of the adopted brushed motor.

DC motor type	Brushed
Length	135 mm
Shaft diameter	90 mm
Current rating	9.8 A
Dimensions	157 mm
Maximum output torque	0.68 Nm
Output speed	2,800 RPM
Supply voltage	36 V

In the following the pilot plant is analysed both from a technical and financial point of view, taking into account the investment and maintenance costs. The results, next presented in Sects. 3 and 4, are derived following the fundamentals of orifices for the technical analysis, whereas financial aspects are tackled with the Appraisal method-ology. Latter elaborations are the result of the studies carried out at the Project Evaluation Laboratory (PEL) at the Department of Civil Engineering of the University of Salerno.

3   Results of the Technical Analysis

The operating height $H_a = 4.45$ m is obtained by considering the vertical distance between the nozzle outlet and the lower end of the tank. In the definition of the expected flow rate Q two aspects are therefore not taken into account, specifically:

- the maximum water depth $h_t = 0.24$ m reached at the tank is neglected, in order to obtain a conservative estimate of the outflow discharge Q (see Table 2);
- the vertical distance between the nozzle outlet and the contracted section is neglected as it is of order of 10^{-2} m or less.

Two nozzles are taken into account, with outlet diameters $d_u = 5 \ 10^{-3}$ m and $d_u = 3 \ 10^{-3}$ respectively. The efflux of water from the orifice can be evaluated with the following:

$$Q = \mu\sigma\sqrt{2g \, H_a} \tag{1}$$

being $\mu \in [0.6, 0.99]$ the efflux coefficient. Here, $\mu = 0.8$, nearly coincident with the contraction coefficient C_c, because of the particular configuration of the adopted nozzle.

$$\sigma = \frac{\pi d_u^2}{4} \tag{2}$$

The expected flow rate Q is compared with the measured flow rate Q_m derived with the bucket method [10]. A bucket of known volume (Vol = 10 l) is taken as reference for the measure of Q_m. The time to fill the bucket is 57 s and 152 s for $d_u = 5 \ 10^{-3}$ m and $d_u = 3 \ 10^{-3}$ respectively. In the following Table 2, the expected volume flow rate Q, the corresponding velocity at the contraction section V_c and the measured flow rate Q_m are given, showing a good agreement under the hypotheses above stated.

Table 2. Expected $Q(d_u)$ and measured $Q_m(d_u)$ volume flow rates. The mean velocity at the contraction section V_c is derived for Q.

d_u [mm]	Q [cl/s]	V_c [m/s]	Q_m [cl/s]
3	5.3	10.61	6.6
5	14.68	10.19	17

3.1   Measurement of Output Voltage V and Intensity I with the Brushed Motor

Measurements of the output voltage V and current intensity I are taken with the 2460 High Current SourceMeter® Source Measure Unit (SMU) Keithley Instrument (Fig. 4). The developed output power P_{out} is then derived by the following:

$$P = \frac{V^2}{R} \tag{3}$$

since there is no phase shift between voltage and intensity signals, that is the adopted generator is of direct current type.

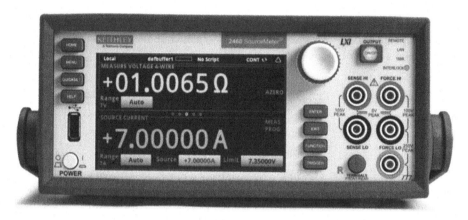

Fig. 4. The 2460 Keithley 100 V, 7 A, 100 W high current SourceMeter® unit (SMU) instrument

Since the theoretical power is given by

$$P_t = \gamma Q H_a \tag{4}$$

the efficiency η is calculated as:

$$\eta = \frac{P_{out}}{P_t} \tag{5}$$

In the Table 3 are given V, P_{out}, P_t and η.

Table 3. Output Voltage V, power P_{out}, theoretical power P_t and efficiency η.

d_u [mm]	V [V]	P_{out} [mW]	P_t [mW]	η [-]
3	2.3	384	2,970	13%
5	6.5	3,420	7,670	45%

4   Estimate of the Pilot Plant Costs

With reference to the pilot plant for energy harvesting from falling water in drainpipes, technically described in the previous paragraphs, market surveys are carried out aimed at estimating investment and management costs [11, 12]. The retrieval of merchant information from specialized magazines and directly from operators in the sector makes it possible to apply the direct procedure to pass forecast judgments.

The investment cost, to be sustained for the concrete implementation of the intervention in the Campania Region (Italy), depends on the expenditure items for the purchase and installation of the plant components:

- 100 l cylindrical container in stainless steel;
- 2 V–12 V 250 A/h battery;
- brushed motor;
- Pelton turbine,
- inverter,
- connection elements.

The evaluations results are detailed in Table 4. The total investment cost, equal to € 1,563.49, is the sum of the expenditure for the plant components purchase (€ 1,341.13) and the installation works cost (€ 222.36). It should be noted that the monetary amounts relating to purchases are gross of Value Added Tax (VAT), assuming that private individuals make the investment.

For the installation works, concerning the adaptation of the system to the downpipe and the assembly, the data are taken from price lists, also confirmed in the light of the direct information.

Table 4. Pilot plant investment costs.

Expenditure items		Amount
100 litre cylindrical container in stainless steel		200.00 €
2V-12V 250A/h battery		735.00 €
Brushed motor		215.13 €
Pelton turbine		74.00 €
Inverter		17.00 €
Connection elements		100.00 €
	(a)	1,341.13 €
Installation work		
- worker (4h × 23,59 €/h)		94.36 €
- electrician (4h × 32,00 €/h)		128.00 €
	(b)	222.36 €
	TOT. (a)+(b)	1,563.49 €

The management costs of the pilot plant relate to ordinary and extraordinary maintenance. Routine maintenance consists of checking the battery and mechanical components wear. The photovoltaic battery used at 2 V continuously has a cycle of 20 years; for the study system it lasts about 30 years.

The turbine is made of PVC and is tested for a cycle of 5 years of continuous work. In the plant, in relation to the use of about 1 month each year, the turbine has a cycle of about 60 years.

The inverter, which rectifies and redistributes the energy from the motor to the battery, lasts about 15 years, after which it shall be replaced.

Starting from the technical information on the parts of the pilot plant, even considering the reliability levels, the annual ordinary and extraordinary maintenance takes place in verification operations, therefore of cleaning/replacing the filter of the container and cleaning the mechanical system, for average total cost of € 30/year.

5 Discussion and Future Perspectives

The experimental campaign, here presented, shed light on some aspects of technical nature. First of all, it is evident that the developed output power strongly depends on the adopted nozzle, changing from $P_t = 384$ mW to $P_t = 3420$ mW when the output diameter passes from $d_u = 3 \ 10^{-3}$ m to $d_u = 5 \ 10^{-3}$. Consequently, the global efficiency undergoes to a variation from 13% al 45%. The limited number of the used nozzles suggest the use of new ones of different output diameter d_u, with the aim of identifying an optimum point in terms of efficiency. The system can be optimized by varying the geometry of the Pelton turbine as well. In particular, the number and shape of the buckets has shown to sensibly influence the results [7]. In addition, it is of interest to investigate the use of generators of brushless type. Preliminary results, not included in the present memory, have shown that higher efficiencies could be reached. It is, however, worth nothing that if one considers an operating height doubled (i.e. $H_a = 9.00$ m) and a nozzle with an output diameter one order of magnitude greater (let's say $d_u = 4 \ 10^{-2}$ m), flow rates of up two order of magnitudes can be attained, that is tens of litres per second.

From an economic point of view, it appears that the cost of the intervention is limited. This both in terms of initial investment, in total of € 1,563.49, and with regard to the management cost, on average equal to € 30/year. This leads to the prospect of the real feasibility of the plant. The need to extend the research by implementing the Cost-Benefit Analysis and perhaps also employing a multi-criteria economic assessment technique should be considered where it is intended to estimate not only the strictly monetary effects of the project, but also those social and environmental [13–17].

6 Conclusions

In this work, we have discussed about the possibility of harvest energy from drainpipes. To this aim, a pilot plant was built at the Laboratory of Environmental and Maritime Hydraulics (LIDAM), University of Salerno, Italy. Production depends on several factors, namely the random nature of rainfall precipitations, spatially and temporally varying over the globe, geometry of the nozzle and Pelton turbine, available hydraulic heads. Anyway in a social context in marked by a strong focus for the environment, the rational use of available energy along with the production of clean forms is fundamental in terms of energy saving and environmental protection. The residential sector can contribute in a significant way with the realization of micro-production at a diffuse scale with the possibility of use the energy harvested locally. In this regard, the economic analysis shows a low cost of the intervention, both in terms of initial investment (€ 1,563.49) and with regard to the management cost (€ 30/year). Which shows the real feasibility of the plant. Furthermore, the studies in progress within the Project Evaluation Laboratory (PEL) at the Department of Civil Engineering of the University of Salerno provide for an extension of this research through the implementation of both Cost-Benefit Analysis, both of multi-criteria economic evaluation techniques. The aim is to estimate not only the closely monetary effects but also the social and environmental impacts of the hydraulic system.

(*) **Author Contributions.** Antonio Nesticò and Giacomo Viccione have conceived and structured the article. Giacomo Viccione and Federica Vernieri have deepened the theoretical questions and the technical problems of Hydraulics. Antonio Nesticò and Maurizio Cimmino have deepened the economic analysis.

References

1. Stricker, J.N.M., Kim, C.R., Feddes, R.A., van Dam, J.C., Droogers, P., de Rooij, G.H.: The terrestrial hydrological cycle. In: Raschke E., Jacob D. (eds.) Energy and Water Cycles in the Climate System. NATO ASI Series (Series I: Global Environmental Change), vol. 5, pp. 419–444 (1993). https://doi.org/10.1007/978-3-642-76957-3_15
2. Bosilovich, M.G., Schubert, S.D., Walker, G.K.: Global changes of the water cycle intensity. J. Clim. **18**, 1591–1608 (2005). https://doi.org/10.1175/JCLI3357.1
3. "The Water Cycle summary": USGS Water Science School. https://water.usgs.gov/edu/watercyclesummary.html. Accessed 25 Mar 2019
4. Grano, M.C., Del Monte, M., Lazzari, M., Bishop, P.: Fluvial dynamics and watermills location in basilicata (southern Italy). Geografia Fisica e Dinamica Quaternaria **39**(2), 149–160 (2016)
5. Germanidou, S.: Watermills in Byzantine Greece (fifth-twelfth centuries) a preliminary approach to the archaeology of Byzantine hydraulic milling technology. Byzantion: Revue Internationale des Etudes Byzantines **84**, 185–201 (2014)
6. "Renewables 2018 global status report". http://www.ren21.net/gsr-2018/. Accessed 25 Mar 2019
7. Viccione, G., Immediata, N., Cimmino, M., Evangelista, S.: A laboratory investigation of a domestic hydropower model. In: Proceedings, vol. 2, no. 11, p. 686 (2018). https://doi.org/10.3390/proceedings2110686
8. Viccione, G., Amato, R., Martucciello, M.: Hydropower potential from the AUSINO drinking water system. In: Proceedings, vol. 2, no. 11, p. 688 (2018). https://doi.org/10.3390/proceedings2110688
9. Fiore, P., Viccione, G., Ippolito, L.: The sustainable refunctionalisation of watermills. Analysis and proposals in a case-study. In: 42nd IAHS World Congress on Housing, Napoli (Italy), 10–13 April 2018, pp. 270–282 (2018)
10. Viccione, G., Evangelista, S., de Marinis, G.: Experimental analysis of the hydraulic performance of wire-wound filter cartridges in domestic plants. Water **10**, 309 (2018). https://doi.org/10.3390/w10030309

11. Napoli, G., Gabrielli, L., Barbaro, S.: The efficiency of the incentives for the public buildings energy retrofit. The case of the Italian regions of the "objective convergence". Valori e Valutazioni (18), 25–39 (2017)

12. Nesticò, A., He, S., De Mare, G., Benintendi, R., Maselli, G.: The ALARP principle in the cost-benefit analysis for the acceptability of investment risk. Sustainability **10**(12), 4668 (2018). https://doi.org/10.3390/su10124668

13. Bottero, M., Ferretti, V., Mondini, G.: Constructing multi-attribute value functions for sustainability assessment of urban projects. In: Murgante, B., et al. (eds.) ICCSA 2014. LNCS, vol. 8581, pp. 51–64. Springer, Cham (2014). https://doi.org/10.1007/978-3-319-09150-1_5

14. Nesticò, A., Pipolo, O.: A protocol for sustainable building interventions: financial analysis and environmental effects. Int. J. Bus. Intell. Data Min. **10**(3), 199–212 (2015). https://doi.org/10.1504/IJBIDM.2015.071325

15. Del Giudice, V., De Paola, P., Forte, F.: Valuation of historical, cultural and environmental resources, between traditional approaches and future perspectives. In: Green Energy and Technology, pp. 177–186 (2018). https://doi.org/10.1007/978-3-319-78271-3_14

16. Della Spina, L., Calabrò, F.: Decision support model for conservation, reuse and valorization of the historic cultural heritage. In: Gervasi, O., et al. (eds.) ICCSA 2018. LNCS, vol. 10962, pp. 3–17. Springer, Cham (2018). https://doi.org/10.1007/978-3-319-95168-3_1

17. Nesticò, A., Guarini, M.R., Morano, P., Sica, F.: An economic analysis algorithm for urban forestry projects. Sustainability **11**(2), 314 (2019). https://doi.org/10.3390/su11020314

An Ontology Based Approach for Data Model Construction Supporting the Management and Planning of the Integrated Water Service

Michele Grimaldi[1], Monica Sebillo[1(✉)], Giuliana Vitiello[1], and Vincenzo Pellecchia[2]

[1] University of Salerno, 84084 Fisciano, SA, Italy
{migrimaldi,msebillo,gvitiello}@unisa.it
[2] Water Management Authority AATO-1, Campania, Italy
vpellecchia@enteidricocampano.it

Abstract. The Italian Ministry of Infrastructures and Transport has started the implementation of SINFI, the National Federated Infrastructure Information Service, whose goal is both to share information about infrastructures and underground utilities, and offer a single dashboard that efficiently manages and monitors all interventions. Although the data model underlying SINFI has been designed with a general-purpose approach, it doesn't result in line with the actual needs of the operators of the Integrated Water Service that instead has to be compliant with the updating of the plans of intervention according to the macro-indicators of technical quality referred to in the ARERA resolution.

The aim of this paper is to propose a data model that allows measuring such macro-indicators and generating interoperable datasets. An ontological approach has been used that has produced a data storage model as implemented in the Semantic Web.

Keywords: Integrated Water Service · Ontology · SINFI · Indicators RQTI

1 Introduction

The Authorities responsible for the regulation and control of the Integrated Water Service (Servizio Idrico Integrato - SII) have matured the awareness of the need to significantly improve the level of knowledge about the infrastructures distributed on the Italian territory. This attentiveness has both stimulated further investigation conceived to define methodologies capable to support data modelling, and motivated new actions addressed to put into practice such metodologies.

The initial analysis, already underway for several years, has highlighted a series of critical issues. Italian water services are suffering from a significant infrastructural deficit, in terms of both quality and quantity of supply, and of sewerage systems and water treatments. Even in the field of management, measurement systems and controlling computer systems require urgent investments needed for both the recovery of operational efficiency and saving of water and energy in systems and networks to combine safety, quality, and continuity of service, environmental protection, and sustainable use of the resource itself [1].

© Springer Nature Switzerland AG 2019
S. Misra et al. (Eds.): ICCSA 2019, LNCS 11624, pp. 243–252, 2019.
https://doi.org/10.1007/978-3-030-24311-1_17

At international level, the attention to the knowledge of infrastructures is recognized by the recently published *Underground Infrastructure Concept Development Study (UICDS) Engineering Report*, which has examined the state of information of the American underground infrastructure, costs and benefits, as well as future opportunities for an improvement of the current status. The report describes a number of candidate models for describing information, and recommends a series of related activities, including the development of an integration model prototype for information related to underground infrastructures, namely "Model for Underground Data Definition and Integration" (MUDDI) [2, 3].

The study presented in the report demonstrates that the development of interoperable underground infrastructure data standards is extremely important to support a series of essential business processes for the economy and society, now and in the future. In particular, the geospatial community and the wider one of engineers and property developers have long understood the value of standardized and interoperable infrastructure data. However, there have been important obstacles to the creation of this data, among the others, the absence of standardized models useful for guiding the storage and development of existing databases.

A factor that inhibits the development of standardized infrastructure data is the perception, by both public and private utilities, that development costs are too high and far outweigh the benefits that could be brought to the system. However, it emerged from the report that there are strong indications on the possibility of being able to derive significant benefits from achieving the standardization and interoperability of infrastructure data.

In Italy, the Ministry of Infrastructures and Transport (Ministero delle Infrastrutture e dei Trasporti) has started implementing the National Federated Infrastructure Information Service (Sistema Informativo Nazionale Federato delle Infrastrutture - SINFI) [4–7]. However, the data model proposed in SINFI is not fully responsive to the needs of today companies that manage SII. As a matter of fact, the update of the "investment plan", developed according to the macro indicators of the technical quality referred to the Regulation of the technical quality of the Integrated Water Service (RQTI) resolution by ARERA [8], is one of the mandatory activities requested by the Service Operators, which would benefit from a standardization of the database of water infrastructure.

In summary, the picture that emerges highlights the presence of two needs by public and private utilities, as follows:

- the need to comply with the obligation to populate the SINFI database, and
- the need to monitor the infrastructures of the water system according to the technical quality requirements by implementing the performance indicators.

The research carried out along this line is meant to define models and develop methods for an effective monitoring of the existing infrastructures and of plan investment for SII. In particular, the present paper describes how the basic specifications provided by SINFI can be adopted and adapted for this system by expanding the parameters to measure the macro indicators of performance. A set of schemas is then described to embed a catalog of spatial reference metadata addressed to the SII census and empowerment.

The rest of the paper is organized as follows. Section 2 briefly describes the SINFI specifications and the regulation of technical quality for SII and for each service within it (RQTI). In Sect. 3, the spatial catalog is built starting from a (non) functional requirements analysis. Conclusions are drawn in Sect. 4.

2 Method and Material

In order to define the data model underlying SII monitoring activities, a case-based approach has been followed, aimed at characterizing in a more representative manner the different categories in which SII has been broken down. The general purpose being to simulate its operating characteristics and evaluate results in terms of decision-making support.

In the following Subsections, specifications underlying SINFI are summarized and an excerpt of RQTI is presented.

2.1 National Federated Infrastructure Information Service

SINFI was established by a Decreto 11 maggio 2016 (GU Serie Generale n.139 del 16-06-2016). It represents the instrument identified for coordination and transparency for the new broadband and ultra-broadband strategy. Its general purpose is to share information about infrastructures and underground utilities, and offer a single dashboard that efficiently manages and monitors all interventions.

The SINFI case studies represent the first application examples of the coordination action carried out by AgID in order to convey the competent administrations to the use and sharing of thematic data models compliant with the national Database Geotopografici (DBGT – Topographic geodatabases) specifications [9].

The SINFI technical specifications represent an extension of the contents of the "07 - underground networks" layer of the DBGT specifications shown in Fig. 1.

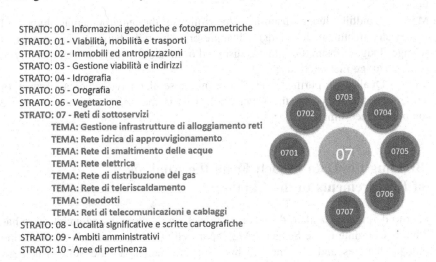

STRATO: 00 - Informazioni geodetiche e fotogrammetriche
STRATO: 01 - Viabilità, mobilità e trasporti
STRATO: 02 - Immobili ed antropizzazioni
STRATO: 03 - Gestione viabilità e indirizzi
STRATO: 04 - Idrografia
STRATO: 05 - Orografia
STRATO: 06 - Vegetazione
STRATO: 07 - Reti di sottoservizi
    TEMA: Gestione infrastrutture di alloggiamento reti
    TEMA: Rete idrica di approvvigionamento
    TEMA: Rete di smaltimento delle acque
    TEMA: Rete elettrica
    TEMA: Rete di distribuzione del gas
    TEMA: Rete di teleriscaldamento
    TEMA: Oleodotti
    TEMA: Reti di telecomunicazioni e cablaggi
STRATO: 08 - Località significative e scritte cartografiche
STRATO: 09 - Ambiti amministrativi
STRATO: 10 - Aree di pertinenza

Fig. 1. Contents of the DBGT specific to SINFI

2.2   Regulation of the Technical Quality of the Integrated Water Service

By the Resolution 917/2017/R/IDR, the Regulatory Authority for Electricity, Gas and Water defines the SII technical quality with an asymmetric and innovative approach. The regulation model especially develops the selectivity, correlation, effectiveness, reward, progression and stability in order to identify correct and effective incentives to promote benefits for users of the different services in specific contexts.

This model results from an extensive consultation (dco 562/2017/R/IDR and 748/2017/R/IDR) and is based on the following indicators:

- prerequisites - the conditions necessary for admission to the incentive mechanism associated with the general standards;
- specific standards - performance parameters to be guaranteed for services provided to individual users where non-compliance requires automatic indemnities;
- general standards - these parameters are broken down into macro-indicators and simple indicators that describe technical conditions for providing a service with an incentive mechanism. The macro-indicators are:

M1 – "Water losses" (to minimise losses, with effective monitoring of water infrastructure), taking into account both actual and percentage water losses;

M2 – "Service interruptions" (to maintain service continuity, also through a suitable configuration of supply sources). It represents the ratio between the total length of interruptions in a year and the number of end users served by the supplier;

M3 – "Quality of water supplied" (to ensure adequate quality of the resource for human consumption). It uses multi-stage logic, considering: (i) the incidence of non-potability orders; (ii) the rate of non-compliant internal samples; (iii) the level of parameters from non-compliant internal controls;

M4 – "Adequacy of the sewage system" (to minimise environmental impact from waste water). It uses multi-stage logic - considering: (i) the frequency of flooding and/or spills from sewers; (ii) the legal adequacy of flood drains; (iii) the control of flood drains;

M5 – "Landfill sludge disposal" (to minimise the environmental impact of wastewater treatment, for sludge). It represents the ratio between the amount of sewage sludge measured dry that is disposed of in landfills and the total quantity of sewage sludge measured dry;

M6 – "Quality of purified water" (to minimise the environmental impact of wastewater treatment, for the water line). This is the rate wastewater discharge samples exceed limits.

3   Building the Data Model: From the Analysis of Requirements to the Catalog

In order to define the standard data storage model, an ontology-based architecture has been used, according to the Semantic Web approach [10–16]. In order to simulate the operational features and test the reliability of the model, a case study has been developed concerning the water system of the Municipality of Solofra (Southern Italy), as part of the "Programma degli Interventi" ranging (2016–2019). Figure 2 shows the water network of this town.

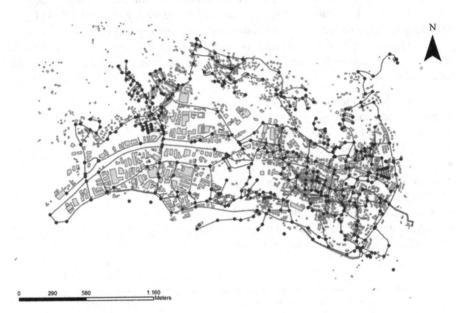

Fig. 2. Water network of municipality of Solofra (Italy)

By adopting a multistep methodology, the identification of the ontology elements has been first performed. Starting from the content specifications of the SINFI tables, SII has been associated to the information layer "07", which is divided into two themes (macro-classes), namely water supply network and water disposal network. Each theme consists of 3 classes as shown in Table 1, namely line, node and network. The first two refer to the geographic elementary units that schematize the network, the network class is related to concepts referring to the network as a whole.

Table 1. Classes: line, node and network

theme 01: Water supply network (0701)	class 01: Section of the water supply network (TR_AAC-070101)
	class 02: Node of the water supply network (TR_AAC-070102)
	class 03: Water supply network (TR_AAC-070103)
theme 02: Water disposal network (0702)	class 01: Section of the water disposal network (TR_AAC-070201)
	class 02: Node of the water disposal network (TR_AAC-070202)
	class 03: Water disposal network (TR_AAC-070203)

Subsequently, for each class, the attributes able to characterize the SII structure have been identified by analyzing the reference manuals of water infrastructure engineering. In conformity with SINFI, each attribute has been assigned an alphanumeric coding that represents its unique and distinctive semantic number, such as ND_AAC_TY that indicates the type of water supply network node, and TR_SAC_TY indicating the type of section of the disposal network of water (Fig. 3).

In addition to the geometric aspects, specific attributes have been introduced in accordance with the performance indexes and with the 6 macro indicators of th technical quality:

- responsible for the operation of the network,
- position and localization,
- typology and function of nodes and traits,
- environmental conditions,
- year of construction,
- operating status and physical conditions,
- survey date,
- type of user connected to the network,
- state of the elements to be maintained or replaced,
- length and working pressure of the pipes.

07010106	TR_AAC_MAT	Materiale [1…n]	Enum (Materiale)	aTratti su	Tracciato
		Tipologia di materiale			

07010108	TR_AAC_PRO	Profondità [0..1]	Enum (Range di profondità)	aTratti su	Tracciato
		Range di profondità cui è posato l'oggetto			

07010104	TR_AAC_DIA	Diametro	Integer	aTratti su	Tracciato
		Diametro nominale/diagonale della sezione [mm]			

07010131	TR_AAC_LUN	Lunghezza tratto	Real
		Indica la lunghezza del tratto in km	·

07010132	TR_AAC_ABI	N°abitanti	String(50)
	Indica il numero di abitanti servito dal tratto		

Fig. 3. Example of alphanumeric coding for attributes according to SINFI content specifications

The basic ontological model depicted in Fig. 4 has been created by using Protégé [17, 18] program. For both the water supply network and the water disposal network, the model has been further expanded with a new class named "Technical Quality". In these new classes, the concepts related to all parameters necessary for computing the macro indicators have been transferred.

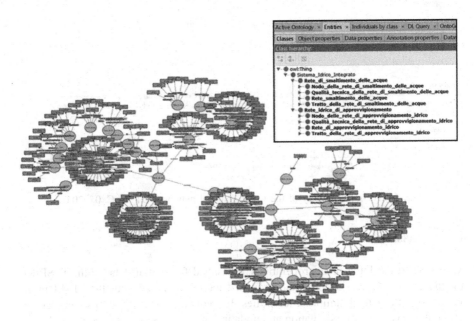

Fig. 4. Data model visualization and Class hierarchy

The cognitive map shown in Fig. 4 has been generated in order to verify the consistency of the concepts. The result has been translated into a catalog expressed in terms of a data storage model organized in compliance with SINFI. In particular, the additional classes shown in Figs. 5 and 6 are:

- Class 04: Technical quality of the water supply network (QT_AAC-070104)
- Class 04: Technical quality of the water disposal network (QT_SAC_070204).

CLASSE: Qualità tecnica della rete di approvvigionamento idrico   (QT_AAC - 070104)

	SINFI
Popolamento della classe	

Definizione
Individua tutti i parametri per il calcolo degli indici di performance e dei macro indicatori come disposto dal programma degli interventi e dal programma di controllo per la Qualità tecnica della rete e delle acque. Per ogni caratteristica è prima riportato l' ID del tratto corrispondente, richiamato dal nome e tipo della rispettiva classe del tratto.

Attributi				
Attributi della classe				SINFI
07010401	QT_AAC_DAT	Anno di riferimento dati	Date	P

Fig. 5. Technical quality of the water supply network (QT_AAC-070104)

CLASSE: Qualità tecnica della rete di smaltimento delle acque (QT_SAC - 070204)

	SINFI
Popolamento della classe	

Definizione
Individua tutti i parametri per il calcolo degli indici di performance e dei macro indicatori come disposto dal programma degli interventi e dal programma di controllo per la Qualità tecnica della rete e delle acque. Per ogni caratteristica è prima riportato l' ID del tratto corrispondente, richiamato dal nome e tipo della rispettiva classe del tratto.

Attributi			
Attributi della classe			SINFI
07010401 QT_SAC_DAT	Anno di riferimento dati	Date	P

Fig. 6. Technical quality of the water disposal network (QT_SAC_070204)

4 Discussion

According to the logic of interoperability envisaged for spatial data by the INSPIRE directive, most of data used by the proposed model is shared with the SINFI information system. This assumption simplifies, by reducing time and cost of implementation, the development, population and updating of the two systems, also through both the reuse of IT components already implemented by Infratel Italia for SINFI, and the shared use (without duplication) of spatial data common to the two systems. In particular, as regards the implementation phase, the model produces significant effects both on the operator side and on the controller side.

In the first case, it allows the monitoring of all the critical issues related to SII management, the optimization of the planning of interventions and the operational support for the preparation of the investment plan, globally improving the performance of the service.

In the second case, the system will allow ARERA to implement the incentive mechanism, which provides for the application of bonuses and penalties for system operators through a multi-criteria comparative system in accordance with the TOPSIS methodology, on a homogeneous and comparable data base among the various operators. In fact, to date, since such a method is not envisaged and the evaluation criteria are codified, the different operators measure the macro-indicators according to their own modalities, strongly influenced by the degree of knowledge of their own system. This will inevitably produce measures that are not perfectly comparable and will influence the outcome of the evaluation. The outcome of the assessment, in fact, if negative, will lead to an increase in the level of investments with consequential rises in the service tariff for the user. In particular, as for the implementation phase, the model produces significant effects, both for to face various critical issues related to the SII management, creating the prerequisites for the provision of other types of value-added services.

5 Conclusions

The present paper intends to underline the need of extending the field of application of DBGTs to the different themes that imply in-depth knowledge of the territory, in order to produce innovative services for the improvement of the SII efficiency and effectiveness.

The proposed model responds to the SINFI specifications in terms of interoperability and then it allows ARERA implementing the bonus-penalty mechanism envisaged by the abovementioned determination.

It should be pointed out that, according to the logic of interoperability envisaged for spatial data by the INSPIRE directive, most of data used by the proposed model is shared with the SINFI information system. This assumption simplifies, by reducing time and cost of implementation, the development, population and updating of the two systems, also through both the reuse of IT components already implemented by Infratel Italia for SINFI, and the shared use (without duplication) of spatial data common to the two systems. In particular, as for the implementation phase, the model could produce significant effects to face various critical issues related to the SII management, creating the prerequisites for the provision of other types of value-added services [19, 20].

However, the emerged limits reside in the lack of capability of intervention by the managers of the service, in structural way on the knowledge of the networks. In fact, the lack of data and tools invalidates the calculation of macro-indicators, making technical quality a mere bureaucratic exercise and not an effective tool for orienting the contents of the "investment plan" towards excellent and performing solutions.

References

1. Grimaldi, M., Fasolino, F., Pellecchia, V.: Urban plan and water infrastructures planning: a methodology based on spatial ANP. Sustainability 9(5), 1–23 (2017)
2. Lieberman, J.: Introduction to MUDDI: Model for Underground Data Definition and Integration, OGC (2018)
3. Model for Underground Data Definition Integration (MUDDI), Engineering Report (2018)
4. Agenzia per l'italia Digitale: Specifiche di contenuto di riferimento per i DataBase delle Reti di sottoservizi e per il SINFI - Versione 3.0 (2016)
5. Agenzia per l'italia Digitale: Specifiche di contenuto di riferimento per i DataBase delle Reti di sottoservizi e per il SINFI - Versione 3.0 (2017)
6. Ministero dello sviluppo econominco: Manuale operativo di prima consegna dei dati per il SINFI, https://www.sinfi.it/portal/index.php/conferimento-dati-sinfi/documentazione. Accessed 21 Feb 2019
7. INFRATEL, AgID, Linee guida per la produzione dati del SINFI. http://www.infratelitalia.it/piani-nazionali-e-regionali/catasto-delle-infrastrutture. Accessed 21 Feb 2019
8. 917/2017/R/IDR: Regulation of the technical quality of the Integrated Water Service or of each of the individual services that compose it (RQTI) (2017)
9. Agenzia per l'italia Digitale: Modifiche introdotte nella versione 3.0 delle Specifiche di contenuto di riferimento per i DataBase delle Reti di sottoservizi e per il SINFI (2017)
10. Hitzler, P., Krotzsch, M., Rudolph, S.: Foundations of Semantic Web Technologies. Chapman & HALL/CRC, Boca Raton (2009)

11. Métral, C., Falquet, G., Vonlanthen, M.: An Ontology-based Model for Urban Planning Communication. In: Teller, J., Lee, J.R., Roussey, C. (eds.) Ontologies for Urban Development. SCI, vol. 61. Springer, Heidelberg (2007). https://doi.org/10.1007/978-3-540-71976-2_6
12. Fox, M.: A Foundation Ontology for Global City Indicators. Global Cities institute, University of Toronto, Toronto (2013)
13. Oulidi, H.J: Spatial Data on Water, Geospatial Technologies and Data Management. ISTE Press – Elsevier, London (2018). Loukis, E.: An ontology for G2G collaboration in public policy making, implementation and evaluation. Artif. Intell. Law 15(1), 19–48 (2007)
14. Bouyerbou, H., Bechkoum, K., Lepage, R.: Geographic ontology for major disasters: methodology and implementation. Int. J. Disaster Risk Reduct. 34, 232–242 (2019)
15. Gil, Y., Blythe, J.: PLANET: a shareable and reusable ontology for representing plans. In: AAAI Workshop on Representational Issues for Real-World Planning Systems (2000)
16. Pundt, H.: Domain ontologies for data sharing—an example from environmental monitoring using field GIS. Comput. Geosci. 28(1), 95–102 (2002). https://doi.org/10.1016/S0098-3004(01)00018-8
17. Tudorache, T., Csongor, N., Natalya, F., Mark, A.: WebProtégé: a collaborative ontology editor and knowledge acquisition tool for the web.". Semant. Web 4(1), 89–99 (2013)
18. Protégé 5.5.0. www.protege.stanford.edu. Accessed 10 Mar 2019
19. Ginige, A., Paolino, L., Romano, M., Sebillo, M., Tortora, G., Vitiello, G.: Information sharing among disaster responders - an interactive spreadsheet-based collaboration approach. Comput. Supported Coop. Work (CSCW) 23(4–6), pp. 547–583 (2014). ISSN 0925-9724
20. Sebillo, M., Vitiello, G., Paolino, L., Ginige, A.: Training emergency responders through augmented reality mobile interfaces. Multimedia Tools Appl. 75(16), 9609–9622 (2016). Springer, New York (2015). https://doi.org/10.1007/s11042-015-2955-0

The 'Dark Side' of the Smartness

Luigi Mundula[1], Ginevra Balletto[1], and Giuseppe Borruso[2(✉)]

[1] DICAAR – Department of Civil and Environmental Engineering
and Architecture, University of Cagliari, Cagliari, Italy
{luigimundula,balletto}@unica.it
[2] DEAMS – Department of Economics, Business,
Mathematics and Statistical Sciences "Bruno de Finetti",
University of Trieste, Trieste, Italy
giuseppe.borruso@deams.units.it

Abstract. Even if there is not a universally shared definition, the term "Smart City" recalls a sustainable, hyper-technological city that is self-sufficient in terms of energy; this type of city uses communication systems between the various technologies to optimize the efficiency of services and to better connect all citizens. Its huge acceptance, both by the scientific community and the urban governance institutions, highlights how the time of reinterpretation of the city had arrived. The smart city, correlated by the transition of the old to the new economy, is based on innovation aimed at achieving maximum efficiency in the urban system through the synergy between traditional functions attributable to the tangible part of the city (residences, services, infrastructures, etc.) and new functions attributable to the intangible one (IoT, virtual and augmented reality, etc.). Reaching these goals drives cities into a circle of continuous evolution, which implies, like all changes, both positive aspects, and side effects, i.e., a 'dark side'. Aim of the paper is to highlight this aspect and its implications. This is found in economic-social dynamics, such as gentrification, filtering and sprawl, environmental and geo-political dynamics, related to finding the resources needed to support digital urban technological innovation and to guarantee high standards of quality of life, and governance dynamics, linked to the capacity of changing the ways of administrate the change and changing radically - thanks to technology - the way of addressing the daily - as well as the strategic - problems and challenges of the city.

Keywords: Smart city · Innovation impacts · Technology effects

1 Introduction

Apart from the - rare - cases of newly founded cities – as Masdar city or Songdo - the implementation of a "smart" logic within a city always implies an operation of transformation of the existing urban fabric.

This paper is the result of the joint work of the authors. In particular: Sect. 1 have been jointly written by L. Mundula, G. Balletto and G. Borruso; Sect. 2 have been written by L. Mundula; Sect. 3 have been written by G. Balletto; Sect. 4 have been written by G. Borruso; and Sect. 5 have been jointly written by L. Mundula, G. Balletto and G. Borruso.

© Springer Nature Switzerland AG 2019
S. Misra et al. (Eds.): ICCSA 2019, LNCS 11624, pp. 253–268, 2019.
https://doi.org/10.1007/978-3-030-24311-1_18

In general, any public investment decision and, in particular, the decision to transform a land or building by local territorial bodies, concerns the present use of economic resources, susceptible to alternative allocations, in view of future benefits [1]. Throughout the process by which the project is identified, the primary objective remains to evaluate the best alternative that ensures the best use of limited resources. The alternative is realized through the comparison of the analysis of the situation that will be determined "with the project" with the analysis of the situation "without the project", i.e., without the specific interventions promoted by the transformation project of a specific urban area [2].

It is easy to understand that the situations that are determined "with" or "without" the project are different from those "before" and "after" the project.

In the first of these situations, in fact, a change and an evolution will be determined regardless of whether or not a project is implemented. In the second situation, on the other hand, attention is mainly focused on change and evolution, which can undergo different aspects and variables, such as real estate or land gains after the introduction of the project itself [3].

Moreover, the project cannot exist if its objectives have not previously been established in coherence with the superordinate ones. The project therefore becomes the technical-economic tool with the characteristic of being evaluated in terms of public interest and economic policy objectives.

The project consequently assumes the role of a tool to intervene, to control and to unite the programmatic objectives of the national plan and the territorial plans with the possible achievements and investments in a specific territory to be developed [4].

Evidently, a transformation project of a territorial area can have both positive and negative consequences that are also connected to other sectors (for example, the agricultural or industrial market). For this reason, the relationships between the various sectors (both upstream and downstream) and the one involved in the project must be considered. The importance of indirect effects is the reason why the system of market prices may not reflect the real value that the community attributes to the project, thus resulting in the system less suitable for the evaluation of benefits and costs. In the case of "smart" transformations of parts of the city this is even more true because of the general consensus towards these transformations that, to date, do not take into due account the collateral effects determined on the economy and on society. These, as will be deepened in the following paragraphs, concern both economic and social effects that, through modifications of the real estate value, determine processes of gentrification, sprawl and crowding out to the detriment of the weaker sections of the population. They imply also environmental and geo-political effects, attributable to the retrieval and disposal of - rare - resources necessary to support the digital urban technological innovation [5] - i.e., cadmium, tungsten, etc., or all those materials that become indispensable for the proper functioning of all the devices related to to-date technological hunger, as well as effects on governance, linked to the risks of hacking the management systems of public services or smart homes, and problems related to the world of information _ fake news, improper use of information deriving from big data of social networks to obtain entrepreneurial advantages, theft of digital identities, etc.

2 Socio-Economic Effects

The transformation of parts of the city according to a "smart" logic makes the latter similar to central areas in the "traditional" meaning of the term, with all the consequences of the case. Residential choices in favor of these locations which involve positive externalities (such as high quality of the settlement fabric, proximity to high-ranking public services - health, education, training, availability of communication infrastructures - physical and digital - at high speed, etc.), compete with the demand expressed by many production activities, increasing the price. Add to this the continuous search for a balance between the cost of housing, which tends to decrease as the distance from the center increases and the cost of mobility, to be understood both in terms of the monetary cost of the transport service and in terms of cost opportunity of the time spent in the move, which, on the contrary, tend to increase as the distance from it increases [6].

The potential effects of this process for the central areas are evident: the congestion and commuting, due to insufficient transport infrastructures and a mobility anchored to the car as the main means of movement, generating both higher economic costs for individuals and families, and lower quality of life.

The competition between the various economic subjects for access to this new kind of central areas and the price that each of them is willing to pay consequently determines both the territorial distribution of the land values and the urban settlement structure. The impacts of these phenomena translate into different phenomena, such as gentrification, filtering and sprawl.

Gentrification has been one of the main themes in the field of urban studies for at least three decades. Its relevance is particularly evident today in the case of urban renewal operations in a smart key, where a change in revenue values is generated.

The gentrification represents that process that sees a part of the population with a higher income "replace" another, with lower income, within low-income neighborhoods. This expulsion of the economically weaker groups, occurs because the acquisition of the properties deriving from a greater income offered, motivated by the attraction for the cultural climate and the informal, convivial and creative atmosphere that is breathed in these neighborhoods, generates conversely an increase in effective income that leads to changes in the social composition of the neighborhood.

Starting from the fundamental contributions of Ricardo and Von Thünen, the urban economy considered the rent generated substantially by the demand for accessibility. The proximity to the urban center, therefore, maximizing the "position value" [7] and minimizing transport costs [8], would represent a certain advantage able to guarantee the stability or growth of real estate values over time. The rent would thus take on the characteristic conical shape, variable in height and width depending on the "city demand" and the consequent dynamics of urbanization of inhabitants and activity [9], but stable in form. It is assumed that rent measures the demand for inhabitants and activities that benefit from proximity, a necessary and sufficient condition to determine its value.

However, the classical theory is not able to explain the presence of deteriorated neighborhoods in central areas of the city [10], nor the fluctuations of rent values in comparative terms between the various parts of the city having the same distance from the center. The slow changes in the physical quality of the building and the consequent population changes in the various urban districts are out of phase in time and of a contrasting sign in space.

In various cities there are found in central areas highly degraded neighborhoods both from a social and economic/environmental point of view. The obsolescent buildings welcome increasingly poor and marginal inhabitants; commercial services close or move; public places (green spaces, social services and open spaces) enter a phase of growing neglect and abandonment due to the high levels of crime and vandalism. Real estate values go down [11].

After a certain time, however, gradual signs of improvement may appear suddenly obsolete production volumes are transformed into original spaces for innovative activities, such as artists and architects' studios, photographic laboratories, fashion, art galleries. Gradually the renovations of housing and buildings and the conversion of technical spaces and industrial areas multiply. The growing building and urban quality initiates a demographic turnover attracting a younger, cultured and dynamic population able to pay prices in continuous growth.

The phenomenon does not occur sporadically at the level of the individual building or of the individual block, but rather concerns entire urban districts. The whole process can be the result of the interaction of so many individual decisions that mutually influence each other in a certain spatial "neighborhood", or the consequence of public administration decisions about the creation of new public goods and/or services premises (parks, squares, infrastructures for accessibility, etc.).

Among these, the mechanism for creating the phenomenon has divided scholars over the last thirty years. Is it a process driven by demand or supply? The rich scientific production on the subject is polarized around two positions. Sociological studies, mainly believe [12–14] that this is a cultural phenomenon driven by demand: the return of middle-high class from the pretty but isolated villas of the suburban residential areas to the lively and varied city life.

The supporters of the supply mechanism, starting from Smith [15], affirm that it is the capital that, under the right conditions, can find it convenient to invest in the degraded neighborhoods of the city and to promote a supply of housing and urban quality, such as to determine population turnover towards the top of the social scale due to the gap that is generated between the current rent, depreciated by the degradation, and the potential rent that is expressed after the realization of the intervention. If this last explanation is convincing in relation to "smart" transformation interventions that require important investments and infrastructural modifications, the former seems better to respond to those cases in which the creation of "smart communities" revitalizes the neighborhood and makes it attractive for middle-high income classes.

Regardless of what the trigger factor is, the life cycle of the urban neighborhood, characterized by an initial phase of construction, a subsequent use and maintenance regime, and therefore degradation, is restarted with renewal interventions due to the gap it creates between the expected rent and the current rent, that is between capitalized rent and potential income. This is the summary of the Rent Gap Theory (RGT) [13, 16–20].

Similarly, the filtering theory[1], aiming to identify the variables that influence the residential choices of the population in an urban environment, is based on the characteristics of the supply. It shows, as the qualitative characteristics of the real estate in the territorial context, can attract the localization of families, thus triggering processes of social polarization or decline. The mechanism is substantiated on the one hand by a demand for quality expressed by "proprietary" and therefore more affluent families that replaces its own assets to move towards a higher quality (filtering up) and on the other by a primary demand (single income families, for rent, students, etc.) that prefers the lower quality homes available, but characterized by lower rent values (filtering down). In other words, filtering is the process in which a home or neighborhood changes real estate values relative to those of the city as a whole.

The mechanisms of substitution of the weaker "social" fabric, no longer able to sustain the new prices, in favor of more affluent classes and, in a complementary way, of poorer classes that go to occupy the areas left free by the wealthier classes which have moved, however, are not a zero-sum game because the weakest part of the population is numerically larger than the more affluent one. This gap determines the need for new areas at affordable prices, which inevitably, due to the dynamics described above, will be located on the margins or outside the existing fabric.

Thus, the so-called phenomenon of urban sprawl is formed, that is to say the spread of cities far beyond the administrative boundaries and towards the smaller centers of urban belts that supply good services and in which the cost of housing is lower. This element must also be crossed with the growing demand by families for a greater housing quality, both with reference to the house itself and to the external environment - greener, less traffic, less parking problems, conditions more easily found outside the big urban concentrations. All this must be placed in a general process of settlement diffusion that has affected the metropolitan territory and the growth of medium-small centers, and that has crossed with suburbanization. The economic-productive organization that favored large industrial concentrations towards more flexible and dispersed settlement patterns throughout the territory has changed, also thanks to technological innovations in telecommunications. The public infrastructure policy has extended the positive externalities for production and residential settlements, joining the spontaneous processes of the market, and making sure that even in the urban suburbs and in the medium-small centers located at short-medium distance from the urban centers there is an infrastructural endowment and public and private services such as to attract economic activities and population. Concerns about urban expansion are no new. In a 1958 essay entitled "Urban Sprawl" that appeared in Fortune, Whyte [40] warned Americans that their propensity for using five hectares to do one's job was not just "bad looks" but even in a "bad economy". In the following years, the movement to contain or reduce sprawl grew in fits and starts following loosely correlated cycles with the economy and the administrations in power. Often, the momentum is renewed by

---

[1] The first version of this theory was developed in the 1920s by Burgess, a member of the Chicago school. In those years Chicago was in its phase of maximum expansion and with this theory Burgess tried to explain its localization model.

finding new slogans. Those who once supported growth control later sided with New Urbanism, sustainable development and smart growth.

A typical concept of American literature on urban development, smart growth, which in the smart city is one of the theoretical referents [21], is a development model "*that serves the economy, the community, and the environment. It changes the terms of the development debate away from the traditional growth/no growth question to how and where should new development be accommodated*" [22]. Even if the origins of the term are not clear, the rapid growth of smart growth can be traced back to three key documents published in the late 90s [23]: *Growing Smart Legislative Guidebook: Model Statutes for Planning and the Management of Change*; *The Tool Kit for Smart Growth* (published by the Natural Resources Defense Council and the Surface Transportation Policy Project); *The Smart Growth and Neighborhood Conservation Act* (issued by the State of Maryland). Although there are no two organizations that define smart growth in exactly the same terms, the logic of a smart growth is based on four propositions:

- whatever the causes (economic forces, consumer preferences or wrong public policies) the dominant form of urban development in the post-war period has the character of an urban sprawl;
- urban sprawl can be defined as a low-density, unplanned, car-dependent development, homogeneous and aesthetically unpleasant;
- urban sprawl has negative effects on environmental quality, social cohesion, public finance and human health.
- urban sprawl, and its associated ills, can be mitigated by policies that promote compact urban growth, a mixed use of the territory, the creation of urban cycling and pedestrian contexts, a shift based primarily on public transport, urban redevelopment policies and of conservation of agricultural land.

The principles resulting from this perspective, which have gained wide recognition, are:

- create a wide range of housing opportunities and choices;
- create walkable neighborhoods;
- encourage a sense of community and collaboration among stakeholders;
- promote, attractive and distinctive places with a strong sense of place;
- make predictable, fair and affordable development decisions;
- encourage mixed use zoning;
- preserve open spaces, agricultural fields, natural beauty and areas characterized by environmental problems;
- provide a wide variety of transportation choices;
- strengthen and direct development towards existing communities;
- promote a higher density of land use.

Research has shown that these principles save money and promote economic growth. Mark and Puentes [24] highlighted three significant ways in which the adoption of this approach is able to improve the local and regional economy. First, by focusing development around existing infrastructures, the costs of public services can be significantly reduced. Fewer roads and sewers will be required, public transport and public service journeys (waste collection, police patrols, etc.) will be shorter, and so on. Second, it has been noted as denser labor markets, healthier city centers, less congestion and greater concentrations of communities contribute to improving worker productivity and increasing average personal income in a region over time. Finally, they found that when a city's economic image improves and its poverty rate declines, the surrounding periphery experiences an increase in income, house prices, and population. Particularly interesting in this regard is a study on the fiscal impacts of alternative development models which compared the relative costs of sprawl and smart growth in New England and the Mid Atlantic. The study found that, given the same increase in the number of users over a 25-year period, a development model based on the logic of "smart growth", focusing on urban centers, on smaller lots, on mixed uses and higher densities would preserve over half a million acres of land compared to a sprawl-based development model. Furthermore, a smart growth development would significantly reduce the kilometers of new roads and sewers needed. Overall, using a "smart growth" development model, the total cost savings would be nearly nine billion dollars for local governments and three billion for state governments.

It is therefore evident that the transformation into "smart city" of parts of the city, driven in particular by the large telecommunications companies [25], involves a dynamic based on the variation of prices [26, 27], centripetal on one side and centrifugal on the other. The first refers to the attractor capacity for the wealthier classes developed by that part of the city once it has been transformed, becoming in fact a centrality. The second refers instead to the effects of expulsion of the weaker classes that will move to areas with lower value of rent, farther from the center, thus fueling urban diffusion and land consumption. Paradoxically, this dynamic in turn recalls the transformation of these areas into a "smart growth" logic that, with the addition of the digital and creative components [21], leads to the request of a "smart" urban transformation of such marginal (or peripheral) areas and therefore the process at its original starting point. It therefore seems that the "smart" urban transformation does not take into due account the effects on the sustainability of the process, with particular reference to the effects on land consumption and social impacts.

To avoid this type of dynamic, which can be traced back to the so-called "market failures", solutions are often proposed linked to the intervention of the State through processes of imposition of maximum price ceilings (such as the agreed fee), which however lead to further negative effects on the demand and supply mechanism, on the quality of the building fabric and on the transparency of transactions. More effective, however more burdensome, it appears instead to be an approach that privileges an action on the whole city system rather than on a single part, thus annulling the relative modifications in the rent values.

3   The Environmental and Geopolitical Effects

The smart city is also the place and result of interactions between anthropic and physical-environmental elements. These elements play an important and growing role in the smart city, defining its essence as technological means for exploiting its potential, at the same time producing a brand new set of waste not yet fully understood on its post-life ending, as well as in accompanying the increase in terms of rent linked to the smart city.

The coexistence of these elements, however, is believed to become sustainable in the smart city thanks to the preponderant technological factor [28], which overcomes the traditional mediation function of planning between these contexts and which becomes a central element. In the smart city, the sustainable management of resources. raw materials, energy and waste, in environmental, economic and social terms, is one of the main objectives. However, the management of resources supply and consumption appears critical even in the smart version of the city. In fact, in the smart city, although the aim is to achieve better levels of energy efficiency and performance to cope with broader environmental aspects, those related to geo-resources are neglected, due to the growing demand arising from the technological market. From the point of view of the management of mineral raw materials, within the smart city' needs, it must be necessarily included not only the "classic" raw materials, always indispensable for the physical development of the city (such as cements, lime, aggregates, steels, aluminum, ceramics, ornamental and building stones), but above all include a long list of "new" and "high-tech" raw materials [29], essential for the technological network that supports the smart city: REE (Rare Earth Elements: Yttrium, Lanthanum, Cerium, Praseodymium, Neodymium, Promezio, Samario, Europio, Gadolinium, Terbium, Dysprosium, Olmium, Erbium, Tulio, Itterbium, Lutetium), Scandio, Gallium, Indium, Germanium, essential for electronics, LED lighting, communication systems, cellular networks and LCD systems; Tungsten, Tin, Niobium and Tantalum, fundamental for alloys, superconductors and permanent magnets; Lithium, graphite, Cobalt and Nickel, essential components for the new accumulators on which the transition from internal combustion to electric transport is based [30].

In most of the "classic" building and ceramics raw materials, the wide geological availability of the EU and Italian territory in particular, guarantee a centuries-old, constant and satisfactory supply of urban areas. This is also true in the cases of iron for steel and aluminum, raw materials whose origin is largely from non-EU areas, and for which there are currently no concerns, given their great availability in contexts characterized by good stability geopolitics and excellent relations with EU markets [31].

The main problems in the exploitation of the most common building raw materials are those inherent to the tensions generated by the whole mining activity in the European territory. Concerns over land use present in Europe since the dawn of time (agriculture or mine?) have overlapped concerns over the environmental impact of mineral extraction, which has been strongly opposed by public opinion in recent years, more and more directed towards ideas of environmental management that results in the so-called "NIMBY syndrome" [32]. If the historical European mining laws already set precise limits to the conflicts over land use, the activity of quarries and mines is currently subject to numerous and stringent regulations, implemented at several levels (EU, national states, regions), aimed at guaranteeing the sustainability of mineral raw material extraction, in terms of landscape and environmental impacts. According to EU indications, for example, these activities tend to be increasingly centralized, compatibly with the geological availability of materials, in districts circumscribed with clusters of mining centers, in order to minimize the consumption of the soil, and possibly near to urban and processing centers - cement plants, ceramic districts, etc., in order to limit energy costs and CO2 emissions.

This work of rationalization and resolution of economic and social conflicts is currently extended only to the European continental sphere and does not concern that in a very limited way the raw materials related to new technologies.

Indeed, the transformation and development of urban areas, from energy-intensive to smart, changing the materials on which it depends, results in a delocalization and an increase in scale, qualitative and quantitative, of conflicts [33]. The raw materials related to electronics, new materials and new energy production and storage systems, in addition to being "strategic", are also "critical" for two main reasons: the presence of the main depots in territorial contexts unrelated to the EU area, characterized by very ancient geological features or peculiar geological units; and the presence in areas characterized by complex geopolitical relations or problems with EU countries, or, often, in areas of high geopolitical instability and characterized by armed conflicts. It is precisely in these last territories, mostly located in sub-Saharan Africa, central and western, that the impact of the transformations in progress has been discharged; the peak in demand for strategic and technological minerals has worked as a detonator of conflicts in newly formed countries, entering weak political and economic contexts, characterized by endemic poverty, corruption of the ruling classes, latent or declared ethnic conflicts. A further factor of social and economic degradation was then experienced in these countries with the recovery and spread of artisanal mining, characterized by unsustainable environmental practices, wild extraction of resources and heavy forms of exploitation, even forced labor, of workers. In these situations, it is not infrequent to see armed groups financing their activities by selling minerals extracted from areas under their control.

Tackling all these issues certainly requires the action of supranational entities. An attempt to intervene on the part of the EU has taken place with the recent "Conflict Minerals Regulation", promulgated in 2017, which follows a similar legislation in force in the USA and which should come fully into force starting from 2021. The mineral correlation is recognized war conflicts, the new law intends to make illegal mining activities in the countries in conflict more difficult. The first objective is therefore to break the link between illegal mining of minerals, their marketing on European markets, financing for conflicts and their extension. The minerals subject to this law are cassiterite (Stagno mineral), coltan - columbo-tantalite: Niobium and Tantalum mineral, wolframite - Tungsten mineral - and gold. These are some of the raw materials that, in recent times, have fed the so-called "four minerals war" in central Africa - Democratic Republic of the Congo, Rwanda, Burundi, supported by the "hunger for universal technology", which ultimately finds in the smart city its maximum expression.

This is the unpublished and little-known face of the smart city, with an ecological footprint no vaster than in the recent past, but increasingly polarized in fragile places both in environmental and in human rights terms [34]. The smart city, although tends to contain energy consumption [35] compared to past city models, requires materials for new purposes, in particular for energy storage in batteries - Lithium, Cobalt, Graphite, Nickel, Aluminum, Manganese and Copper. In other words, the smart city consumes energy differently from the past, through materials that are not exactly energy, of the third and fourth world and produces new types of waste, i.e. e-waste.

The re-use of such waste requires a real epochal change and is substantiated in the passage from the linear - neoclassical - economy to the circular economy, with the awareness that the return will always be less than one due to technological progress, and it will be much lower with each reuse. In other words, e-waste can be considered a potential raw material - second, but with a deadline. Although the aforementioned law is a good start, it immediately shows its flaws. Apart from the limited list of raw materials - which at present should be added at least Cobalt minerals, the text provides for a "responsible market" clause, according to which European industrial groups that import and use "conflict minerals" must control yourself to avoid purchases in war zones and self-certify the origin of the minerals. The disciplinary measures are internal to the multinational firms, which are advised not to import into the European market raw and semi-finished minerals coming from war zones. In this framework the role of the European States and Magistrates who are not authorized to punish crimes is completely absent. Despite its obvious limitations, the "Conflict Minerals Regulation" [36] appears to be a fundamental step towards the sustainability of mining and therefore of cities, in view of the technological transition that characterizes smart cities, alongside the set of indications that guide the current EU policies towards "Critical Raw Materials". After all, the English, French and Italian colonies that have marked the history of the last two centuries, were nothing more than the substantial part and under everyone's eyes, of the ecological footprint of a "city or an entire state" [37]. Today, instead, we are witnessing new forms of hidden colonial exploitation that generate an ecological footprint "of more cities and states". It seems almost paradoxical that, to remind ourselves of the new exploitative colonies, we arrive through creativity.

4   The Effects on the Governance

The main issue related to smart city appears to be the governance, as set of methods, procedures, decisions enclosed within a vision of the city as a while, and not just as a techy 'Black box' where a further layer is added upon the existing set of components of the city.

In general, the term 'smart cities' should be extended, to consider communities - as it is, already, the case, as this term is often accompanying cities in the declinations of smartness - and, furthermore, concepts as 'territorial' and 'peripheries'.

If it is true that cities represent now the most typical way of thinking about human settlements, it is also true that cities, as dense and central places, are no more the only places where attention has to be put. Less dense environments as peri-urban, rur-urban areas and peripheries, where urban characters are present but with lower levels of accessibility and services, represent the real places where the major challenges arise: the discomfort in fact is growing in these areas, the most vulnerable ones, from where explosions, riots and protest are born: yellow gilet, Brexit, US elections, generalized fear of immigration and violence, even if crimes are diminishing, are deeply influenced by the fears and unmet expectations arising from these areas.

Recalling an image referred to the pillars of the Smart City [38], the governance was considered as the 'invisible hand' capable of keeping the different elements or - as said - pillars of the city tightened together. The idea was that of recalling the need to move from 'government' to 'governance', therefore allowing setting up some kind of 'traffic laws' to allow the interaction between people, the physical and the ICT infrastructures.

The pillars sustaining the Smart City are Connections, Data and Sensors, these referring to the different elements that constitute a city in its 'smart' conceiving.

Connections referred to the physical - as well as the immaterial - sets of networks present in the city. On one side the physical dotation of the infrastructure connecting the different parts of a city. In this case the digital backbone of stations, wires, hubs where the digital data flow. On the other side, it implies the presence of the flows and sets of connections along the network. That is the amount of interaction that individuals and groups can set on the network.

Data represent another one of the pillars. The ICT revolution is producing data at an unprecedented pace, both voluntarily and involuntarily, often with a non-complete awareness by producers. Organizations produce massive amounts of data, now mostly becoming available on open platforms, following movements referring to freedom of information and allowing citizens to have free access to such infrastructure. On the other side, big data play a major role in providing - ideally and theoretically - a wide amount of information and - after all - knowledge on the behavior of groups and individuals, as well as of inanimate devices.

This latter point is still an unexplored realm. More than 50% of data is to-date created unmannerly, by devices or automated data generators, this contributing to the traffic along the network. With the increasing number of IoT - Internet of Things - and smart devices connected, the 'automatic' city is more and more feeding itself of traffic flows.

About the user-created data, feeding the so-called big data, here it is important to separate the role of voluntary actions, where users actually create data and disseminate them. This is the case of the so-called "citizen science" in which people contribute in an active way to produce data helping scientists, city planners, decision makers, to gather bottom up data on the ground, de facto helping in integrating platforms of data that a single organization would find time consuming and costly to fill. However, most of user-related data are taken from the traces left by every action done on-line, from a Facebook post to a credit card transaction, to the point and path data taken and used in platforms as Google dashboards with the chronology of our movements - used into applications for traffic estimate - as well as for market research and profiling. Big data on users are also taken quite regularly by organizations for planning solutions: i.e., Transport for London acquiring the Tube Oyster's data on O/Ds or Singapore tracking movements of cars and users.

Sensors - as evident from above - can be from automatic devices, as well as from 'citizens as sensors' as described above. However, apart from these creating data feeding the big data, citizens-sensors mean also involvement in public activities and participations, as open platforms, social networks and media and active city hacking.

The pillars sustaining the Smart City are bounded by a ring of regulation/ governance, that to-date seems to be the hard task, the difficult element to define and correctly channel in order to implement correctly a smart city evolutionary path. The period spanning from the beginning of the years 2000 through to the '10s of the present century has witnessed changes in the interpretation of the Smart City meaning.

In the initial stage of the years 2000, the attention was mainly drawn on the hardware component, that is the smartness of the city represented by the realization of the physical infrastructure on which the Internet connections and data were able to be set and flow. That is the conception of the smartness as the realization of a 'new' utility, after water, energy, basic communication, a smart city, relying on an infrastructure as well, was thought to be the necessary step for keeping a city techy and intelligent, or smart. Some years later, in the mid 2000s, the attention was drawn on apps, or on the software solutions, giving for granted and acquired the hardware component. This is also the period of the social networks and media arising and therefore shifting the attention towards the capacity of social - or the like - platform in enabling the capacities of bottom-up participation of citizens to the decision process. The evolution in the years '10s is towards the integration of hardware and software, and the 'smartness' is perceived on other, different concepts, as the increase of the quality of life. Such aspect appears to be an interesting one in the evolution of the concept and posing serious challenges and expectations on the governance of the technological change imposed to smart cities.

Up to present days, smartness has been considered only as urban, and as a techy element, forgetting a couple of concepts. On one side the consideration that urban environments are spreading, not just creating cities and new urban areas, but dis-tributing the characters of the urban to non-strictly urban environments. That means that sparse contexts are characterized by urban characters of buildings, costumes and activities, without the density, concentration and accessibility of the proper central, urban locations, where the provision of services, and particularly the techy, ICT ones, become easier and more efficient - if compared to countryside (or better: suburbs, peripheries, rur-urban and peri-urban areas) - to set up and to work properly, serving a wide amount of citizens and city-users.

On the other side there is the 'techy' drunkenness, or the idea that a city is 'smart' because it embraces the most recent ICT technologies and supply the widest amount of them to citizens and users, therefore assigning the intelligence and smartness just to some contemporary cities. If it is true that the pace and impact of ICT is unprecedented in time and space, it is still and undoubtedly true that new technologies have always been adopted in cities to enhance its way of functioning: from the energy and water distribution, to innovations as electricity, innovations in mobility in transport, these have always been novelties in urban environment, than spreading to other contexts. And generally, innovations in these sectors have also been coupled with changes in the policies and governance of the cities. The impacting innovation characterized by pri-vate cars had several consequences not only on industry but also on society and, namely, from the time of car mass production and diffusion, profound changes occurred also in the different policies, let alone urban ones, with the obligation, in many cases, of extra spaces to be allowed and dedicated to a particular users' niche - expanding - of car owners, who is generally and implicitly granted an extra-portion of public space just for the fact of owning or using a car.

At present time, the 'smartness' of the Smart City does not seem to be - yet - fully exploited into the paradigm changes in governance as other innovations did in the past. The ICT innovations, devices and tools, as well as applications, seem mainly painted over the city, or a digital conversion of analogical procedures, more like a glittering layer of paint rather than as a substantial, cutting edge revolution in the ways of conceiving and planning the city. In fact, generally, 'smart' applications seem more to be working to solve current needs or problems, in a way translated from the 'business as usual' very often created by the very same 'smart' technology, rather than boosting a change in the procedures underneath the same process. The problem in addressing so appear to be - in the writer's opinion - not in the technology but oh humans, particularly in the capacity of changing the ways of administrate the change and changing radically - thanks to technology - the way of addressing the daily - as well as the strategic - problems and challenges of the city.

In few words, and recalling what Green [39] stated, technology does not mean innovation, particularly in the smart city debate. Several voices are rising underlining that innovation and technology is headed towards integration of technology into bureaucracy and political choices. In Green's words "Today's age of seemingly endless data, theory matters more than ever. In the past, when they collected minimal data and had little capacity for analytics, cities had few choices about how to utilize data… The key barrier to data science is good questions… Cities are not technology problems, and technology cannot solve many of today's most pressing urban challenges. Cities don't need fancy new technology—they need us to ask the right questions, understand the issues that residents face, and think creatively about how to address those problems. Sometimes technology can aid these efforts, but technology cannot provide solutions on its own." [39].

The Dark Side of the Governance appears therefore the excess of available technology and data from different aspects of the city, following profound investments in users' education and on devices, but without a parallel profound rethinking of the process in the light of new technologies and opportunities, actually more as a translation and replication of existing procedures, with the consequence of losing the true benefit of the technological investment and losing sight of the true main character of the (smart) city itself, the people.

5 Conclusions

In the present paper we tried to express some doubts on the, often enthusiastic, evaluations expressed in terms of the potential of ICT in enhancing the city performances in producing urban environments that can be defined as smart in heading towards the utopian targets of the full sustainability.

In particular, the transformation of parts of the city according to a "smart" logic makes the latter similar to central areas in the "traditional" meaning of the term, with all the consequences of the case: modifications of the real estate value, processes of gentrification, sprawl and crowding out to the detriment of the weaker sections of the population. It is therefore evident that the transformation into "smart city" of parts of the city, involves both the attraction of the wealthier classes and the expulsion of the weaker classes that will move to areas with lower value of rent, farther from the center, thus fueling urban diffusion and land consumption. Paradoxically, this dynamic in turn leads to the request of a "smart" urban transformation of such marginal (or peripheral) areas in a vicious cycle. In other words, seems that the "smart" urban transformation does not take into due account the effects on the sustainability of the process.

Moreover, ICT is a large consumer of rare materials. The short life cycle of intelligent systems has made it possible to highlight the need for new materials for the city, not only construction materials, but above all new and rare materials, contributing to increasing social different and political tensions in developing countries.

On the contrary, with reference to the governance, there are at least two elements that put a threat in fully exploiting a 'revolution' of a smart city. On one side there is a strong difficulty of considering the ICT-related components and particularly their implications into real planning and organizational processes. In one sentence, there is a strong difficulty in innovate with the available - and, perspectively, with the incoming - technologies in the processes governing the cities. At present the attention is drawn on some aspects of the problem, as how technology can help us in tackling the effect of malfunctioning of the systems, not trying the propose a true and permanent solution. As a matter of examples, solutions are more addressed towards monitoring, recycling, eliminating, gathering data on waste, rather than on searching for a solution on how to avoid - or limit - them. Similarly, in a certain stage, the 'smartness' was drawn towards app for managing queuing in public offices, while a more effective attention on the process of creating queues - as changing paper documents into properly digital or dematerialised ones - should produce better result on top of the process (leaving the eliminating-queues app the role of managing the residuals). That is particularly difficult because technology is quite easy to change, while procedures, that depend on human culture and habits, are longer to be eradicated or changed from the inside, at their root.

On the other side a conceptual 'dark side' lays into the difficulty - or incapacity - of representing the Smart City in a proper iconography. The ICT revolution in the city at present did not present a visible footprint, as other revolutions that took place in the city did: the revolutions of railway systems, electric lights, private car diffusion in cities had deep influences on the urban forms and also on the policies. New railway stations, energy power plants could and can be opened, inaugurated and attributed to one or another administration. On the contrary, the Smart City holds an iconographic framework that is a virtual one, painted more as a commercial than as a plan for new 'ideal city', as the Renaissance taught us. This is true for the different 'techy' applications, as the hardware component - cables, wi-fi hot spots, etc. - as well as for the software ones - i.e., apps, particularly their attribution to an image of the city. But still they can be part of a political agenda and represent something visible and 'tangible' on smartphone's screen. On the other side, the 'proper' application of the technological side, that is the 'true' innovation of planning and political decision making process, changing things under the bonnet, is something yet too important but at the same time not representable as an image of the city or expendable towards the public. 'A good news is not a news', and the implementation of an ideal dramatic procedural change in the municipal process - i.e., the elimination of paper procedures for citizens - could not have the same effect of a new 'hard' infrastructure or physical component of the city.

As a consequence, the full exploitation of the Smart City, or what will be the name of the new 'Ideal City' of the years to come, will be not complete until it will reach the level of graphical representation and perception and it will be hosted into programmatic and planning actions as a building block of the city.

References

1. Khan, Z., Peters-Anders, J.: Big data in smart cities. In: Sakr, S., Zomaya, A. (eds.) Encyclopedia of Big Data Technologies. Springer, Cham (2018)
2. Aapo, H., Bosch, P., Airaksinen, M.: Comparative analysis of standardized indicators for Smart sustainable cities: what indicators and standards to use and when? Cities **89**, 141–153 (2019)
3. Lecomte, P.: New boundaries: conceptual framework for the analysis of commercial real estate in smart cities. J. Property Invest. Financ. **37**(1), 118–135 (2019)
4. Cronemberger, F., Gil-Garcia, J.R.: Big data and analytics as strategies to generate public value in smart cities: proposing an integrative framework. In: Rodriguez Bolivar, M.P. (ed.) Setting Foundations for the Creation of Public Value in Smart Cities. PAIT, vol. 35, pp. 247–267. Springer, Cham (2019). https://doi.org/10.1007/978-3-319-98953-2_10
5. Park, R.E., Burgess, E.W.: The City. University of Chicago Press, Chicago (2019)
6. Beretta, I.: The social effects of eco-innovations in Italian smart cities. Cities **72**, 115–121 (2018)
7. Marshall, A.: Principles of Economics, 9th variorum edn, vol. 1. Macmillan, London (1961)
8. Alonso, W.: Location and Land Use: Towards a General Theory of Land Rent. Harward University Press, Cambridge (1964)
9. Camagni, R.: Economia urbana: principi e modelli teorici. Nuova Italia Scientifica, Roma (1992)
10. Hoyt, H.: One Hundred Years of Land Values in Chicago. University of Chicago Press, Chicago (1933)
11. Wyly, E.: The Evolving State of Gentrification. Tijdschrift voor economische en sociale geografie **110**(1), 12–25 (2019)
12. Ley, D.: The New Middle Class and the Remaking of Central City. Oxford University Press, Oxford (1996)
13. Ley, D.: Reply: the rent gap revisited. Ann. Assoc. Am. Geogr. **77**, 465–468 (1987)
14. Lipton, S.G.: Evidence of central city revival. J. Am. Inst. Plan. **43**, 136–147 (1977)
15. Smith, N.: Toward a theory of gentrification: a back to the city movement by capital, not people. J. Am. Plan. Assoc. **45**(4), 538–548 (1979)
16. Smith, N.: The New Urban Frontier: Gentrification and the Revanchist City. Routledge, London (1996)
17. Smith, N.: Gentrification and the rent gap. Ann. Assoc. Am. Geogr. **77**(3), 462–465 (1987)
18. Badcock, B.: On the non existence of the rent gap: a reply. Ann. Assoc. Am. Geogr. **80**, 459–461 (1990)
19. Hamnett, C.: The blind men and the elephant: the explanation of gentrification. Trans. Inst. Br. Geogr. **16**, 173–189 (1991)
20. Clark, E.: The rent gap re-examined. Urban Stud. **32**(9), 1489–1503 (1995)
21. Nesti, G.: Città intelligenti, città di genere. Governance e politiche. Carocci editore, Rome (2016)
22. Environmental Protection Agency: About smart growth. http://www.epa.gov/livability/about_sg.htm#what_is_sg. Accessed 14 May 2019

23. Burchell, R., Listokin, D., Galley, C.C.: Smart growth: less than a ghost of urban policy past, less than a bold new horizon. Hous. Policy Debate **44**, 821–879 (2000)
24. Mark, M., Puentes P.: Investing in a better future: a review of the fiscal and competitive advantages of smarter growth development patterns, Discussion Paper, Brookings Institution Center on Urban and Metropolitan Policy, March 2004
25. Hollands, R.: Critical interventions into the corporate smart city. Cambridge J. Regions Econ. Soc. **8**, 61–77 (2015)
26. Neirotti, P., De Marco, A., Cagliano, A.C., Mangano, G., Scorrano, F.: Current trends in smart city initiatives: some stylised facts. Cities **38**, 25–36 (2014)
27. Chang, A., Kalawsky, R.S: European transport sector interventions for smart city. In: 7th International Conference on Power Electronics Systems and Applications, Hong Kong (2019). https://www.researchgate.net/publication/322505416_European_Transport_Sector_Interventions_for_Smart_City. Accessed 14 May 2019
28. Zanella, A., Bui, N., Castellani, A., Vangelista, L., Zorzi, M.: Internet of things for smart cities. IEEE Internet Things J. **1**(1), 22–32 (2014)
29. European Commission: Comunicazione della Commissione al Parlamento Europeo, al Consiglio, al Comitato Economico e Sociale Europeo e al Comitato delle Regioni concernente l'elenco 2017 delle Materie Prime Essenziali per L'UE. COM, p. 490 (2017)
30. Hofmann-Amtenbrink, M., et al.: Towards a system approach for materials research, development and innovation for Europe. http://www.matsearch.ch/wp-content/uploads/2019/02/2019-Towards-a-System-Approach-for-Materials-Research-Development-and-Innovation-for-Europe-.pdf. Accessed 16 May 2019
31. European Union Ad Hoc Working Group on Critical Raw Materials. Report on Critical Raw Materials for the EU. Ref. Ares (2015)1819503 - 29/04/2015, European Commission (2015)
32. European Commission: L'iniziativa "Materie Prime"—Rispondere ai nostri bisogni fondamentali per garantire la crescita e creare posti di lavoro in Europa. COM, p. 699 (2008)
33. Garavaglia, L.: Città dei flussi. I corridoi territoriali in Italia, vol. 4. goWare & Edizioni Guerini e Associati (2017)
34. Le Billon, P.: Fuelling War: Natural Resources and Armed Conflicts. Routledge, London (2013)
35. Saad, M.M., Ibrahim, M.A., El Sayad, Z.M.: Eco-city as approach for sustainable development. Am. Sci. Res. J. Eng. Technol. Sci. (ASRJETS) **28**(1), 54–74 (2017)
36. European Commission: The EU's new conflict mineral regulation. https://eur-lex.europa.eu/legal-content/EN/TXT/?uri=OJ:L:2017:130:TOC. Accessed 16 May 2019
37. Colding, J., Barthel, S.: An urban ecology critique on the "smart city" model. J. Clean. Prod. **164**, 95–101 (2017)
38. Murgante, B., Borruso, G.: Smart cities in a smart world. In: Rassia, S., Pardalos, P. (eds.) Future City Architecture for Optimal Living. Springer, Berlin (2015). https://doi.org/10.1007/978-3-319-15030-7_2
39. Green, B.: The Smart Enough City. MIT Press, Cambridge (2019)
40. Whyte Jr., W.H.: Urban Sprawl, Fortune, pp. 103–109 (1959)

Integrated Assessment of the Anthropic Pressure Level on Natural Water Bodies: The Case Study of the Noce River (Basilicata, Italy)

Stefano Savalli, Lucia Saganeiti[✉], Michele Greco, and Beniamino Murgante

School of Engineering, University of Basilicata,
Viale dell'Ateneo Lucano 10, 85100 Potenza, Italy
48685@studenti.unibas.it, {lucia.saganeiti,
michele.greco,beniamino.murgante}@unibas.it

Abstract. Fragmentation is a phenomenon that involves the transformation of large patches of natural habitats into smaller ones (fragments) that tend to be isolated from the originals. In this case, the degree of environmental fragmentation of the Noce River in the Basilicata region (Italy) will be analysed. Following the installation of hydroelectric plants, the river has undergone such alterations that it has been classified as a Heavily Modified Water Body (HMWB). Environmental fragmentation is caused not only by soil sealing, which causes the loss and subsequent fragmentation of natural patches, but can also be caused by major changes in natural patches. In the case of a territory crossed by a watercourse, these patches may be subject to changes in the natural course of the river or in the vegetation present close to it. The aim of this work is to calculate, through GIS applications, the level of fragmentation of the adjacent area surrounding the water body along which there are several hydroelectric plants. Through a change detection in 2006, 2013 and 2018, metric and biodiversity indicators will be calculated to define the level of anthropic pressure of the water body. The results reveal that the variation of the calculated indices, both for landscape metrics and diversity indices, concerned "natural" land use classes, whose variation caused fragmentation of natural patches by changing the shape of the water body.

Keywords: Fragmentation · River · Diversity index · Natural soil · Environmental health

1 Introduction

Anthropic action has always been a double-faced medal. On the one hand, there are benefits related to the development of buildings and infrastructure to increase the quality of life and the amount of services for the population. On the other hand, the negative effects that have an impact in different areas emerge: economic - energy, hydro-geo-pedological, physical-climatic, ecological-biological, landscape-cultural [1–4]. These

© Springer Nature Switzerland AG 2019
S. Misra et al. (Eds.): ICCSA 2019, LNCS 11624, pp. 269–278, 2019.
https://doi.org/10.1007/978-3-030-24311-1_19

negative effects therefore produce land take, soil sealing, fragmentation and degradation of natural habitats [5, 6]. In terms of soil sealing, human action has been strong enough to cause the natural soil to progressively reduce, speeding up the fragmentation process [7, 8]. Fragmentation is a phenomenon that involves the transformation of large patches of natural habitats into smaller ones (fragments) that tend to be isolated from the originals [9–11]. The environmental fragmentation process, in addition to being caused by soil sealing that causes the loss and subsequent fragmentation of natural patches, can also be caused by major modifications of natural patches. If we take into account a territory crossed by a waterway, these patches may undergo changes related to the natural course of the river or to the vegetation present near the waterway. Alterations caused by excessive use of water for industrial purposes, the development of hydro-electric plants and water purification treatment tanks.

The case study focuses on a section of the Noce river in the Basilicata region (Italy). Previous studies carried out by Environmental Observatory Foundation of Basilicata Region (FARBAS) [12] have shown that several sections of this river have characteristics such as to be classified as Heavily Modified Water Bodies (HMWB) under the European water directives [13, 14]. The level of environmental fragmentation of the Noce River following the recent construction of hydropower plants will be analysed through landscape metrics and diversity indexes. The analyses will be carried out in three time phases: 2006-2013-2018.

2 Materials and Methods

2.1 Study Area

The study area concerns the Noce river in the south of Italy. Originating from the Pincipe of Murge, Noce River covers a total length of 45 km, with a total surface area of 351 km^2 and flows into the Tyrrhenian Sea, in the Castrocucco Plain (about 8 km south of Maratea). The river-bed crosses three provinces in three different regions: the province of Salerno in Camapnia region, the province of Potenza in Basilicata region and the province of Cosenza in Calabria region. Noce river has a hydrological regime characterized by varied flows altered by the significant slopes of the hydro-graphic network and the small size of the basin. In terms of overall impluvium, there are sub-basins with fairly good importance and different shapes and characteristics, dictated by the tributaries of the main course. This paper will only analyse the section of the Noce river falling within the territory of the Basilicata region (Fig. 1).

Along the Noce river there are 11 hydroelectric plants and several installations of transversal works (bridles) that aim at altering the hydrological regime of the watercourse.

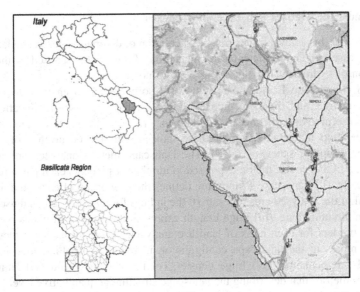

Fig. 1. Study area with indication of the stretch of the Noce river analyzed and the location of the 11 hydroelectric plants.

2.2 Data Acquisition

In order to construct spatial data sets describing the evolution of land use in the study area, several sources of information were considered. (i) The regional technical map - RTC (scale 1:5000) of the Basilicata Region at 2013, available as open data on RSDI regional map portal. (ii) The coordinates of the hydro-electric plants of the regional agency for the protection of the environment. (iii) Dataset for the sewage plants provided by the Basilicata region.

The RTC information layer has been used as a starting point for analysing the soil changes evolution as of 2006-2013-2018. From the CTR of 2013 they have built: the 2006 land use by comparison and digitalization of the 2006 ortho-photo and the 2018 land use by comparison and digitalization with Google earth satellite images.

Three layers of vector information were created on which eighteen classes of land use were identified: (a) uncultivated area, (b) green area, (c) hydroelectric base, (d) bridle, (e) urban centre, (f) crops, (g) sewage treatment plant, (h) river Noce, (i) plant, (j) hydroelectric plant, (k) industrial settlement, (l) urban settlement, (m) beach, (n) roads, (o) vegetation mixed with sand and rock, (p) scarce vegetation, (q) discontinuous vegetation, (r) industrial area, (s) street.

The vector information layers were subsequently rasterized with a pixel size of 3 × 3 m.

2.3   Landscape Metrics and Diversity Indexes

The purpose of this analysis concerns the calculation of diversity indexes and landscape metrics to assess the environmental fragmentation of the territory caused by the recent installation of hydroelectric plants from 2006 to nowadays.

LecoS (Landscape Ecology Statistics) [15] software has been used to calculate landscape metrics and diversity indexes, based on the land use classification. This analysis is useful to describe the structural characteristics of the landscape, to document the changes and the relationship of these indices with the occurrence of different species or groups of species [16–19]. The landscape metrics analyzed are specified following. (i) Land cover: metric expressed in number of pixels in each patch for every land use class. (ii) Landscape Proportion: defines the proportion of each land use class to the total of the analysed area; the sum of the indices for all identified land use classes will return the unit value. (iii) Edge Length expresses the number of pixels present on the patch borders for each class of land use analyzed, a sort of patch perimeter. It is useful to represent the landscape configuration in relation to habitat loss and environmental fragmentation. (iv) Edge density, (v) Patch density and (vi) Number of patches are metrics that describing the landscape structure at quantitative level [20–22].

A diversity index can be defined as the probability that two randomly taken organisms in a given community are not of the same species [23].

The Shannon-Wiener Diversity Index (H_{SH}) is a statistical index based on information theory. It represents the amount of "information" per individual or type of patch, in this specific case [24]. The SH index is expressed by formula:

$$H_{SH} = -\sum_{i=1}^{S} p_i \log_2 p_i$$

Where:

pi is the proportion of the landscape occupied by the patch type (class) i. Shannon's diversity index returns the sum of the proportions of each class over the total. The SH index is a type of diversity index often applied to the assessment of specific diversity and used extensively in the field of landscape ecology [25]. It has a range of values from 0 to ∞. A high value of SH indicates an equal proportion of the categories, while a low value expresses the strong dominance of one category, combined with a poor representativeness of the others.

Simpson's index [26] (H_{SI}) is expressed by the following formula:

$$H_{SI} = 1 - \sum_{i=1}^{S} p_i^2$$

Where:

$\sum_{i=1}^{S} p_i^2$ represents the probability (p) of randomly choosing two organisms of the same species (i) (any of the available S species). The maximum value is reached at $p_i = \frac{1}{S}$ for every i. Simpson's index varies between 0 and 1. The higher the index, the more likely it is that every two randomly designed cells will be different types of patches.

The Evenness index (E_V) - also called uniformity or equitability - describes how equal are the specific abundances between them, that is, how uniformly the individuals of a population are distributed among the species [27]. E_V is obtained from the ratio between the calculated value of H_{SH} and its maximum value with respect to the number of species present in the data sample.

Landscape metrics and diversity indexes were calculated in the study area by first considering the entire study area and then the 500-m buffers around each hydro-electric plant. This has been useful to understand how the landscape has changed following the installation of these plants.

3   Results and Discussions

The study area concerns the main course of the Noce river for a section that extends for about 45 linear km. The 500 m to the right and left of the river bed have been categorized, totalling an area of approximately 54 km^2.

The vector files of the land use to the years 2006, 2013 and 2018 were created, which were subsequently rasterized with pixels of size 3 × 3 m. Through the global area categorization it emerged that, following the recent installation of several hydro-electric plants, land use from 2006 to 2018, does not show significant changes. Analysing the variation of the various classes surfaces, it is highlighted the greatest peak near the spaces that have seen the construction of hydroelectric plants between one year of reference and the other. Between 2006 and 2013, the percentage change in the surface area of the hydro-electric plants class was +47.99%. At the same time as this increase, there was a decrease of the land use class concerning Noce river and discontinuous vegetation in the areas that were most affected by the implementation of hydro-electric plants. In fact, the class of land use concerning the Noce river, has the largest decrease in surface area on both intervals, 2006–2013 and 2013–2018, with a negative variation of 8.20%. This results in a shrinkage of the river bed.

Figure 2 shows the data concerning the landscape metrics at the three time intervals considered. The variation of landscape metrics and diversity indexes in the time intervals considered, over the whole area, does not give useful results to define if and how the construction of new plants has caused environmental fragmentation. The three diversity indexes show a negligible increase (Table 1).

274   S. Savalli et al.

Class	Land cover 2006 km²	2013 km²	2018 km²	Landscape Proportion 2006	2013	2018
Area Incolta	17,686431	17,686431	17,684568	0,03804487	0,038041622	0,037976163
Area Verde	308,615346	308,03895	305,388387	0,663855291	0,662558852	0,6579658
Base Idroelettrica	0,192456	0,192456	0,248427	0,000413988	0,000413952	0,000533477
Briglia	0,000165375	0,000158625	0,000158625	8,54E-06	8,19E-06	8,18E-06
Centro Urbano	24,834033	24,834033	24,825123	0,053419911	0,05341535	0,053309921
Colture	34,755561	34,721703	34,860294	0,074761879	0,074682671	0,07485963
Depuratore	0,001299375	0,001299375	0,001296	6,71E-05	6,71E-05	6,68E-05
Fiume Noce	6,305526	5,788179	6,052482	0,01356367	0,012449754	0,01299721
Impianto Idroelettrico	0,000921375	0,0013635	0,00131625	4,76E-05	7,04E-05	6,78E-05
Insediamento Industriale	2,893239	2,9484	2,98242	0,006223579	0,006341693	0,006404503
Insediamento Urbano	11,44935	11,44935	11,569959	0,02462843	0,024626328	0,024845541
Spiaggia	1,968705	1,968138	2,677455	0,004234836	0,004233254	0,005749616
Strade	11,546793	11,546793	11,546793	0,024838038	0,024835917	0,024795793
Vegetazione mista a Sabb	10,908918	12,356145	15,287697	0,02346592	0,026576747	0,032829079
Vegetazione pressoché as	2,416959	2,416959	2,416959	0,005199064	0,00519862	0,005190222
Vegetazione Sporadica	29,272266	28,917	28,10133	0,06296689	0,062197376	0,060345307
Zona Industriale	1,980612	1,975752	1,952181	0,004260448	0,004249631	0,004192149
Impianto		0,000631125	0,000621		3,26E-05	3,20E-05

	Edge length 2006	2013	2018	Edge density 2006	2013	2018
Area Incolta	35100	35100	35100	0,000679525	0,000679467	0,000678369
Area Verde	435516	436968	422670	0,008431455	0,008458843	0,008168843
Base Idroelettrica	1680	1680	2202	3,252428025	3,252150368	4,255753384
Briglia	324	306	306	6,272539762	5,923559599	5,913989717
Centro Urbano	96480	96480	96414	0,001867823	0,001867663	0,001863371
Colture	135900	135798	135690	0,002630982	0,002628783	0,002622449
Depuratore	540	540	540	1,04542	1,045334047	1,043645244
Fiume Noce	112578	117156	115056	0,002179475	0,00226791	0,00222366
Impianto Idroelettrico	708	1020	984	1,37067	1,974519866	1,901753556
Insediamento Industriale	16596	17322	17148	0,000321293	0,00033532	0,000331415
Insediamento Urbano	82182	82182	83478	0,001591018	0,001590882	0,00161336
Spiaggia	6522	6522	10662	0,000126264	0,000126253	0,000206062
Strade	371700	371700	371700	0,007195997	0,007195383	0,007183758
Vegetazione mista a Sabb	85878	91014	92988	0,001662572	0,001761852	0,001797157
Vegetazione pressoché as	8802	8802	8802	0,000170404	0,000170389	0,000170114
Vegetazione Sporadica	95544	94506	90906	0,001849702	0,001829451	0,001756919
Zona Industriale	5412	5412	5364	0,000104775	0,000104766	0,000103669
Impianto		528	528		1,022104401	1,020453128

	Number of Patches 2006	2013	2018	Patch density 2006	2013	2018
Area Incolta	15	15	15	2,903953593	2,903705686	2,899014567
Area Verde	118	118	112	2,284443493	2,284248473	2,164597543
Base Idroelettrica	4	4	5	7,743876249	7,743215163	9,66338189
Briglia	1	1	1	1,935969062	1,935803791	1,932676378
Centro Urbano	69	69	68	1,335818653	1,335704616	1,314219937
Colture	143	145	143	2,768435759	2,806915496	2,763727221
Depuratore	3	3	3	5,807907187	5,807411372	5,798029134
Fiume Noce	639	727	587	1,23708	1,407329356	1,134481034
Impianto Idroelettrico	6	7	8	1,161581437	1,355062653	1,546141102
Insediamento Industriale	26	27	28	5,033519562	5,226670235	5,411493858
Insediamento Urbano	189	189	191	3,658981528	3,658669164	3,691411882
Spiaggia	2	2	3	3,871938125	3,871607581	5,798029134
Strade	325	325	325	6,29136232	6,29136232	6,281198228
Vegetazione mista a Sabb	82	81	91	1,587494631	1,56800107	1,758735504
Vegetazione pressoché as	5	5	5	9,679845311	9,679018953	9,66338189
Vegetazione Sporadica	82	81	80	1,587494631	1,56800107	1,546141102
Zona Industriale	5	5	5	9,679845311	9,679018953	9,66338189
Impianto		2	2		3,871607581	3,865352756

Fig. 2.   Landscape metrics of total study area in every temporal interval considered.

In order to investigate the issue in more detail, 500-m buffers were created from hydro-electric plants. In this way, 8 areas (Buffer) around the plants along the Noce river were analysed in detail. A sample case is reported for which a variation in the diversity indexes was recorded in the time phases analysed (Hydro-electric power plant n.6 – Buffer n.6 - see Fig. 3).

Table 1. Variation of diversity indexes for total study area and single buffer areas.

Area	Year	I_{SH}	E_V	I_{SI}
Total area	2006	0.48	0.56	0.70
	2013	0.48	0.57	0.70
	2018	0.49	0.57	0.71
Buffer 1 (Hydro-electric plants n.11)	2006	0.42	0.26	0.18
	2013	0.43	0.27	0.19
	2018	0.64	0.40	0.33
Buffer 2 (Hydro-electric plants n.9)	2006	0.60	0.36	0.26
	2013	0.60	0.37	0.26
	2018	0.66	0.37	0.30
Buffer 3 (Hydro-electric plants n.4)	2006	1.42	0.52	0.64
	2013	1.45	0.56	0.66
	2018	1.34	0.57	0.67
Buffer 4 (Hydro-electric plants n.5-10-7)	2006	1.77	0.71	0.76
	2013	1.77	0.71	0.76
	2018	1.80	0.76	0.76
Buffer 5 (Hydro-electric plants n.8-3)	2006	1.49	0.65	0.70
	2013	1.49	0.65	0.70
	2018	1.49	0.65	0.70
Buffer 6 (Hydro-electric plants n.6)	2006	0.87	0.40	0.38
	2013	0.87	0.40	0.38
	2018	0.94	0.43	0.42
Buffer 7 (Hydro-electric plants n.2)	2006	1.30	0.54	0.64
	2013	1.31	0.54	0.64
	2018	1.31	0.54	0.64
Buffer 8 (Hydro-electric plants n.1)	2006	0.88	0.55	0.51
	2013	0.88	0.55	0.51
	2018	0.88	0.55	0.51

Between the two extreme time phases (2006 and 2018), the land use class corresponding to vegetation mixed with sand and rock increased at the cost of the land use class corresponding to the green area. Figure 3 show the variation of the diversity indexes in the area around the hydro-electric plant N. 6 (Buffer 6). The change in the indexes is reflected in an increase of fragmentation degree in the study area.

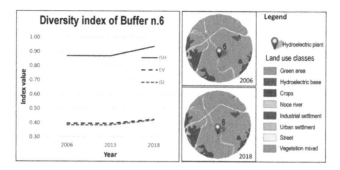

Fig. 3. The image on the left shows the graph of the indexes change and on the right the detail of hydroelectric plant n.6 to 2006 and 2018.

A particular case is that of a multi buffer (Buffer 4) in which the hydroelectric plants n.5-10-7 are concentrated. In this area, despite the concentration of three plants, there was no change in the diversity indexes, which remained stable (see Table 1). In this case, the emergence of new hydro electric plants has not led to environmental fragmentation.

4   Conclusions

No significant land-use change was identified from the analysis of the entire study area. This result can be easily related to 2 factors: (1) the hydroelectric plants on the main course of the Noce river are recent and, therefore, have not significantly influenced an area of about 50 km^2, in the time interval analyzed; (2) the plants are small, the power of the hydroelectric plants varies from a minimum of 50 kW to a maximum of 580 kW. This observation is valid when analyzing the entire area, but it varies when analyzing the area surrounding the hydroelectric plants. indeed, in certain cases, it is evident as the soil transformation undergoes fragmentation in a quickly manner in the proximity of the hydroelectric plant. However, areas with the highest concentration of installations do not necessarily correspond to those most subject to fragmentation and waterproofing. It should be noted that in all cases analyzed the variation of the calculated indexes, both with regard to landscape metrics and diversity indexes mainly concerned classes of natural land use ie. those concerning the "Noce river", "green areas" or "vegetation mixed with sand and rock". Their variation caused fragmentation of natural patches. Human activity, on the other hand, was almost inexistent. This means that, beyond the construction of the plants along the bed of the Noce River, human activity has been limited in compliance with the landscape regulations for the river buffer zones.

The results obtained are in accordance with the preventive study carried out by FARBAS [12] in which it was demonstrated that different sections of the Noce river have characteristics such as to result as Heavily Modified Water Bodies (HMWB).

Acknowledgements. This research has been supported by the Environmental Observatory Foundation of Basilicata Region (FARBAS).

References

1. Romano, B., Zullo, F., Ciabò, S., Fiorini, L., Marucci, A.: Geografie e modelli di 50 anni di consumo di suolo in Italia **5**, 17–28 (2015)
2. Marchetti, M., et al.: Consumo di suolo, dinamiche territoriali e servizi ecosistemici. In: Edizione 2018 (2018)
3. Mazzariello, A., Pilogallo, A., Scorza, F., Murgante, B., Las Casas, G.: Carbon Stock as an Indicator for the Estimation of Anthropic Pressure on Territorial Components, 2 May 2018
4. Pilogallo, A., Saganeiti, L., Scorza, F., Las Casas, G.: Tourism Attractiveness: Main Components for a Spacial Appraisal of Major Destinations According with Ecosystem Services Approach. 2 May 2018
5. Martellozzo, F., Amato, F., Murgante, B., Clarke, K.C.: Modelling the impact of urban growth on agriculture and natural land in Italy to 2030. Appl. Geogr. **91**, 156–167 (2018)
6. Cosentino, C., Amato, F., Murgante, B., Cosentino, C., Amato, F., Murgante, B.: Population-based simulation of urban growth: the Italian case study. Sustainability **10**, 4838 (2018)
7. Saganeiti, L., Pilogallo, A., Scorza, F., Mussuto, G., Murgante, B.: Spatial indicators to evaluate urban fragmentation in Basilicata region (2018)
8. De Montis, A., Martín, B., Ortega, E., Ledda, A., Serra, V.: Landscape fragmentation in Mediterranean Europe: a comparative approach. Land use policy. **64**, 83–94 (2017)
9. Jaeger, J.A.G., Bertiller, R., Schwick, C., Kienast, F.: Suitability criteria for measures of urban sprawl. Ecol. Indic. **10**, 397–406 (2010)
10. Saganeiti, L., et al.: Assessing urban fragmentation at regional scale using sprinkling indexes. Sustainability **10**, 3274 (2018)
11. Saganeiti, L., Pilogallo, A., Scorza, F., Mussuto, G., Murgante, B.: Spatial Indicators to Evaluate Urban Fragmentation in Basilicata Region. 2 May 2018
12. Michele, G., Giovanni, M., Salvatore, G., Anatrone, A.: Analisi degli indicatori di alterazione idrologica nella valutazione preliminare del flusso ecologico per i fiumi della basilicata - Idrotecnica (2017). https://www.idrotecnicaitaliana.it/sommari/analisi-degli-indicatori-di-alterazione-idrologica-nella-valutazione-preliminare-del-flusso-ecologico-per-i-fiumi-della-basilicata/
13. ISPRA: Implementazione della Direttiva 2000/60/CE. Analisi e valutazione degli aspetti idromorfologici. Versione 1.1. Istituto Superiore per la Protezione e la Ricerca Ambientale, Roma (2011)
14. ICRAM: Criteri generali per la definizione delle condizioni di riferimento dei corpi idrici di transizione ai sensi della direttiva 2000/60/ce (2007)
15. Jung, M.: LecoS—a Python plugin for automated landscape ecology analysis. Ecol. Inform. **31**, 18–21 (2016)
16. Turner, M.G., Gardner, R.H.: Landscape Ecology in Theory and Practice. Springer, New York (2015). https://doi.org/10.1007/978-1-4939-2794-4
17. Olsen, L.M., Dale, V.H., Foster, T.: Landscape patterns as indicators of ecological change at Fort Benning, Georgia, USA. Landsc. Urban Plan. **79**, 137–149 (2007)
18. Fidalgo, B., Salas, R., Gaspar, J., Morais, P.: Estimation of plant diversity in a forested mosaic landscape: the role of landscape, habitat and patch features. Rev. Latinoam. Recur. Nat. **5**, 65–73 (2009)

19. Viana, H., Aranha, J.: Estudo da alteração da cobertura do solo no Parque Nacional da Peneda Gerês (1995 e 2007). Análise temporal dos padrões espaciais e avaliação quantitativa da estrutura da paisagem. ESIG 2008 • X Encontro Util. Informação Geográfica, pp. 1–14 (2008)

20. McGarial, K., Marks, B.: FRAGSTAT: spatial pattern analysis program for quantifying landscape structure. United States Dep. Agric. Pacific Northwest Res. Station, 120 p. (1995)

21. Forman, R.T.T.: Some general principles of landscape and regional ecology. Landsc. Ecol. **10**, 133–142 (1995)

22. Bender, D.J., Contreras, T.A., Fahrig, L.: Habitat loss and population decline: a meta-analysis of the patch size effect. Ecology **79**, 517–533 (1998)

23. Keylock, C.J.: Simpson diversity and the Shannon-Wiener index as special cases of a generalized entropy. Oikos **109**, 203–207 (2005)

24. Fedor, P.J., Spellerberg, I.F.: Shannon–Wiener Index. Reference Module in Earth Systems and Environmental Sciences, Encyclopedia of Ecology, pp. 3249–3325 (2008)

25. Gorelick, R.: Combining richness and abundance into a single diversity index using matrix analogues of Shannon's and Simpson's indices. Ecography (Cop.) **29**, 525–530 (2006)

26. Simpson, E.H.: Measurement of diversity. Nature **163**, 688 (1949)

27. Allegro, G., Sciaky, R.: Assessing the potential role of ground beetles (Coleoptera, Carabidae) as bioindicators in poplar stands, with a newly proposed ecological index (FAI). For. Ecol. Manag. **175**, 275–284 (2003)

Sustainability Performance Assessment: Models, Approaches and Applications Toward Interdisciplinary and Integrated Solutions (SPA 2019)

Ecosystem Services Approach to Evaluate Renewable Energy Plants Effects

Angela Pilogallo$^{(\boxtimes)}$, Lucia Saganeiti, Francesco Scorza,
and Beniamino Murgante

Laboratory of Urban and Regional Systems Engineering (LISUT),
School of Engineering, University of Basilicata, Viale dell'Ateneo Lucano 10,
85100 Potenza, Italy
{angela.pilogallo,lucia.saganeiti,francesco.scorza,
beniamino.murgante}@unibas.it

Abstract. Economic, social and environmental aspects have led local, regional and national governments to promote policies to increase the spread of renewable energy (especially wind energy). The transformation into an energy system based on renewable sources is therefore already underway. In this context, the effects of renewable energy sources on ecosystems are to be analyzed. In this regard, the 2005 Millennium Ecosystem Assessment (MA), promoted by the United Nations, is an international reference for the development of a global environmental assessment approach. One of its most innovative contributions is to promote a structured approach in which the value of the ecosystem in the decision-making process should be based on the idea of the services it provides to humans.

This work presents the results of an ex-post analysis carried out to assess the effects of rapid growth of renewable energy plants in a low-density area with a strong agricultural vocation, characterized by an important industrial center and areas of high natural values. The approach used is that of ecosystem services through the use of the most significant INVEST tools in the context: carbon stock and storage, crop production, crop pollination and habitat quality. A spatial combination has been performed in order to assess ecosystem services cumulative loss.

Keywords: RES · Ecosystem services · Carbon stock · Habitat quality ·
Crop production · Crop pollination

1 Introduction

The transition to renewable energy sources (RES) is considered one of the main component to pursue sustainable development goals [1]. From our observatory we have to point out that, especially in the South of Italy, at a regional level, this instance has been implemented by simplified authorisation procedures for the installation of RES plants based on the European incentive policies. This transformation process took place in the absence of a sufficiently robust scoreboard [2]. RES plants impact, indeed, can be critical since they involve land use change e land take, alter landscape perception, are responsible for the fragmentation of ecosystems in which they are located and they lead

S. Misra et al. (Eds.): ICCSA 2019, LNCS 11624, pp. 281–290, 2019.
https://doi.org/10.1007/978-3-030-24311-1_20

to alterations in habitats quality. Essentially, they affect the capacity to deliver ecosystem services (ES).

This approach, promoted by the United Nations through the Millennium Ecosystem Assessment [3], is a useful toolkit to support the decision-making process, to conduct adequate and effective scenario analysis, to build a robust and spatial-explicit assessment scoreboard for all-scale territorial transformations [4–6].

Within this methodological framework, the present work aims to describe the effects of a widespread and scattered growth in RES plants in terms of cumulative ES loss in a context characterized by a low population density and a fragmentation degree ranging between medium and high [7–9].

The study area, representative of the reality of several municipalities located between Basilicata, Campania and Puglia, is characterized by a strong and deep-rooted agricultural vocation, components of naturalistic-environmental value and the prominent presence of a very large industrial center.

Four ecosystem services have been selected to assess specific features of this case study: Carbon Storage and Sequestration, Crop pollination, Crop production and Habitat Quality.

The analytical model used to assess and to represent ES is the InVEST (Integrated Valuation of Ecosystem service and trade-offs) suite [10]; further analyses carried out in GIS environment were then produced in order to obtain a representation of the spatial distribution of the overall cumulative impacts on ecosystem and its capacity to provide ES.

Finally the assessment of cumulative effects was carried out by a spatial combination of effects obtained for each of considered ES.

Our results show that on the basis of the results obtained from the proposed methodology, it is possible to formulate policies that effectively consider local territorial features and values in order to better understand the impacts deriving territorial transformation process.

2   Materials and Methods

2.1   Study Area

Melfi municipality is located in the northern part of the Basilicata region (Italy) on a territorial area of about 205 km^2 and totals 17.878 inhabitants at 2017 [11]. It is characterized by a settlement structure based on two main components: the historic town surrounded by the post second world war residential expansion, and a huge industrial area where the most important Italian Fiat Chrysler Automobiles group (FCA) production plant was established. The rest of the municipal territory is characterized by a strong agricultural vocation and widespread areas of high natural and environmental value that are already fragmented by three railway lines and a high-speed suburban road that serves as the main link with the regional capital, Potenza.

Since 2010, the year of adoption of the Regional Environmental Energy Guideline Plan (PIEAR), this territory has been affected by an intense installation of RES plants, attracting numerous and significant investments from large operators in the sector. By 2018, the number of RES plants in the study area had been set at about 200, including wind turbines and photovoltaic fields, with an installed electricity production capacity close to 200 MW.

2.2 Dataset

Informative layers considered are: (1) TRC land use (Regional technical cartography produced by the Basilicata Region and distributed through OGC standards in RSDI [12]) at 2013; (2) the dataset of RES plants including the most significant dates of the authorization and construction cycle, and attributes concerning the installed generation capacity [Kw] or [Mw] of individual wind turbines.

Concerning land use, we referred to the following LCC: (a) Residential buildings in compact urban centres; (b) Residential buildings in dispersed urban centres; (c) Buildings for industrial and commercial use; (d) Roads and railways; (e) Caves and dumps; (f) Gardens and urban green areas; (g) Orchards; (h) Gardens; (i) Arable land; (j) Olive groves; (k) Vineyards; (l) Pasture or uncultivated areas; (m) Mixed forests; (n) Conifer woods; (o) Broadleaf forests; (p) Watercourses.

The RES plants datasets comes instead from the integration of TRC and GSE (National Energy Services Manager) [13] layers and further plants derived from aerial photogrammetric survey different dates.

In order to carry out an overall assessment of the land take connected to plants construction, a buffer with a radius proportional to the installed power has been created for each wind turbine (see Table 1).

Table 1. Wind plant classification

	Power output	Radius of influence
Micro-mini turbines	0–200 Kw	15 m
Medium sized turbines	200–999 Kw	25 m
Big sized turbines	>1 Mw	50 m

In addition, in order to consider the reduction in the capacity to provide ecosystem services in all the areas included between different turbines, individual installations have been aggregated using as a reference a limit distance of 250 m. With the same purpose, for photovoltaic fields a 25 m belt of pertinence from the perimeter was considered (Fig. 1).

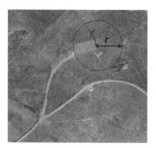 

Fig. 1. Aggregates construction.

2.3   Methods

Global policies since Kyoto [14] have strongly promoted the transition to a low-carbon economy stimulating actions involving local authorities, SMEs and citizens [15–17]. A significant component of this development process is related to the installation of RES plants (in particular wind turbines and photovoltaic fields). Nevertheless these processes of technological settlement generate significant territorial impacts.

The aim of this work is to assess these effects within a low-density settlement context by considering the cumulative impact as a loss of ecosystem service provision.

For this reason, the methodology is essentially composed of two successive steps: the first consists of the evaluation of individual ecosystem services on the two dates considered (2013–2018). To this end, the INVEST modules considered most suitable to describe the peculiarities of the study area were used: Carbon Storage and Sequestration, Habitat quality, Crop Production and Crop Pollination.

The second step was instead aimed at considering the cumulative effects by a weighted combination of the results of the previous step.

Carbon Storage and Sequestration
INVEST Carbon Storage and Sequestration tool requires as input data a land use/land cover (LULC) map and a corresponding table with values of each of the following carbon pool:

- Aboveground biomass including carbon stored in foliage and wood but not in herbaceous cover;
- Belowground biomass including carbon stored in root system;
- Soil, defined as organic carbon (SOC) because stored just in the mineral layer;
- Dead organic matter including carbon present within litter and dry biomass.

It gives as result a raster maintaining the same resolution as the input cover map.

For this work, a pixel size of 5 m was considered in order to include the contribution from urban green areas.

In the lack of data at regional level (as already stated in previous works [18]), values relating to the four carbon tanks have been obtained considering as reference the Guidelines for national greenhouse gas inventories published by the Intergovernmental Panel on Climate Change (IPCC) in 2006 [19].

Our working hypothesis was to assimilate areas affected by RES plants to the urban environment or, more generally, to a process of "land take" that cancels the contribution of these surfaces in terms of ecosystem services.

Crop Production

By using "Crop production" tool, it is possible to make productivity estimates of 175 kinds of crops on the basis of a global scale climate model derived on the base of FAO database supplemented by national and regional datasets.

Developed with the aim of assessing trade-offs between an increase in agricultural profitability and expected ES losses, this tool makes it possible to predict the productivity of an area in relation to different kind.

In our work this tool finds a different application that is an evaluation of policies and territorial changes effects on agricultural productivity with regard to the case study area.

Required input data consist of a land use map, a table of crops and a further summary table containing the values in kg/ha of the nitrogen, phosphorus and potassium compounds on average used throughout the study area. Concerning this work, values indicated in the Integrated Production Specifications of Basilicata Region for wheat have been adopted (Table 2).

Table 2. Summary table of fertilizers compounds values used for the study area

Crop name	Nitrogen rate	Phosphorus rate	Potassium rate
Wheat	110.0	35.0	30.0

Not having detailed information regarding type of crops actually present, analyses were carried out considering all the arable crops cultivated with wheat.

Crop Pollination

"Crop pollination" tool of INVEST allows to map cell by cell potential presence based on a model that evaluates the presence of appropriate environmental conditions or suitable places for pollinators nesting and food availability. Required are:

- a LULC map;
- a table reporting indicators of suitability for nesting and/or for hosting floristic species that serve as food sources for pollinators for each LULC code;
- a summary table about main characteristics of each pollinator species (maximum flight range, seasonality, food preferences).

Results are two maps for each pollinator species and for each season of the year: the first represents "pollinator supply" index that is a measure of pollinator species availability considering both accessibility to food resources and usability of nesting sites; the second map represent "pollinator abundance" map that explicitly shows spatial distribution of pollinators' potential presence.

In this work, the model was applied by considering a generic pollinator and assigning the maximum values for the availability of suitable nesting sites and food resources to wooded areas and uncultivated pastures. Intermediate values were considered for agricultural use while minimum values were assigned to riparian strips and within urban gardens and green areas. Seasonality has not been taken into account.

Habitat Quality

Combining and crossing information from Land Use/Land Cover (LULC) and threats to biodiversity, "Habitat Quality" tool returns two complementary raster maps, one related to the habitats quality and the second that represents habitats degradation. This tool allows indeed to show both positive and negative interactions between the natural environment and anthropic activities further considering distances between the each habitat and degradation sources. It estimates effects of each threat and indirect effects induced by a considered combination of all other threats.

Finally, the model assesses the sensitivity of each land cover class considered as habitat to each individual threat, with a different weight.

Data required are: (1) LULC Map; (2) Summary table of all threats ranging between 0 and 1 and the related impact distance (in km); (3) Threat maps that are binary type raster maps (1 = max threat; 0 = no threat); (4) Sensitivity matrix including values about the suitability of each land use to be a habitat and its own sensitivity to each threat.

Habitat quality literature [20–22] was our data source for compiling threats table while the sensitivity matrix was filled in considering forests and watercourses as most high naturality classes. Zero values were assigned to artificial covers (i.e. urban and settlement and RES plants, as well). Sensitivity values were derived from scientific literature [23–25].

3   Results

The above mentioned elaborations were carried out with reference to two dates: 2013, the year in which the regional cartography was carried out, and 2018. For each of the ecosystem services analysed, the loss over the last 5 years has been calculated considering the territorial transformations induced by RES installations (Fig. 2).

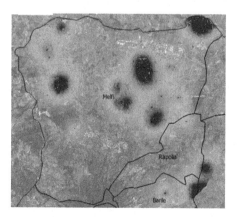

Fig. 2. Loss of ES related to carbon storage in the period 2013–2018.

Losses thus calculated were subsequently normalized in order to work with comparable scale of quantitative outputs. The aim of the work was in fact to obtain a spatial distribution within the study area of the cumulative effects due to ecosystems degradation induced by the presence of photovoltaic systems and wind turbines.

The spatial combination of the individual losses has allowed to obtain a map that represents, by means of gradual color ranges, areas most affected by the coexistence of impacts deriving from each ES included in the analysis.

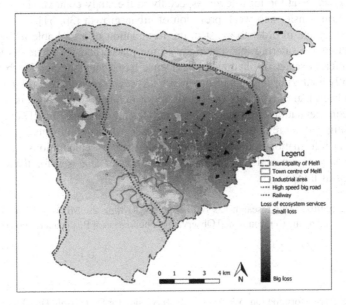

Fig. 3. Cumulative ES losses in the period 2013–2018

As can be seen from Fig. 3, areas suffering maximum degree of cumulative loss coincide perfectly with the aggregates of the installations.

In addition, it is significant that the most compromised area is the one between the city center and the industrial area, where the highest turbines density is recorded.

On the opposite, plants located in the north-west of Melfi municipality do not seem to have caused a marked change in the capacity to provide ES.

4 Conclusions

This work represents a first effort to establish an effective evaluation framework of territorial transformations depending from the evolution of 'energy landscapes'.

If we consider the normative framework developed by Basilicata Region in order to manage such process of energy production transition toward a low carbon model we identifies a simplified authoritative procedures. It is the case in which a lack of integration between sectorial policies (the Energy Plan) and territorial management tools (urban and regional plans) didn't allowed to monitor the effective consequence of the spread development of RES installation on other territorial components. In Basilicata, the approach to identify only a target for RES production without comparing it with suitability criteria of territorial transformation represented a critical weaknesses of decision making process. Our research contributes to demonstrate the result of such approach in term of ex-post assessment and could also be considered as a base-line for future policy development as a mean of the territorial planning toolkit [26–29].

Conspicuous and widespread growth of RES installations, however, has led to significant changes at the local level, especially in the study context, characterized by low population density and weak prevision of urban growth [30, 31].

In this research, in order to assist in the formulation of a tool able to assess these transformations considering the specificity of the places and the instances that come from the different scales of planning, an evidence based methodology has been tested.

By jointly analyzing impacts of different ecosystem services loss, the most critical effects had been identified where the proximity of numbers of RES plants occurred. It suggest recommendations to include maximum density threshold in RES regulations.

As highlighted in previous work [18], future research developments could be aimed at improving information sources possibly by drawing on elaborations carried out in the same study region and testing multi-criteria spatial analyses for the cumulative combination of impacts.

Acknowledgements. This research has been developed within the MEVCSU and INDICARE projects supported by the Environmental Observatory Foundation of Basilicata Region (FARBAS).

References

1. Org, S.U.: Transforming Our World: The 2030 Agenda for Sustainable Development United Nations
2. Attolico, A., Smaldone, R., Scorza, F., De Marco, E., Pilogallo, A.: Investigating good practices for low carbon development perspectives in Basilicata. 2 May 2018. https://doi.org/10.1007/978-3-319-95174-4_58
3. Alcamo, J., Bennett, E.M., Millennium Ecosystem Assessment (Program): Ecosystems and Human Well-Being: A Framework for Assessment. Island Press, Washington D.C. (2003)
4. Scorza, F., Murgante, B., Las Casas, G., Fortino, Y., Pilogallo, A.: Investigating territorial specialization in tourism sector by ecosystem services approach (2019). https://doi.org/10.1007/978-3-319-99444-4_7
5. Scorza, F., Pilogallo, A., Las Casas, G.: Investigating tourism attractiveness in inland areas: ecosystem services, open data and smart specializations (2019). https://doi.org/10.1007/978-3-319-92099-3_4
6. Pilogallo, A., Saganeiti, L., Scorza, F., Las Casas, G.: Tourism attractiveness: main components for a spacial appraisal of major destinations according with ecosystem services approach, 2 May 2018. https://doi.org/10.1007/978-3-319-95174-4_54
7. Saganeiti, L., et al.: Assessing urban fragmentation at regional scale using sprinkling indexes. Sustainability **10**, 3274 (2018). https://doi.org/10.3390/SU10093274

8. Saganeiti, L., Pilogallo, A., Scorza, F., Mussuto, G., Murgante, B.: Spatial indicators to evaluate urban fragmentation in Basilicata Region 2018. https://doi.org/10.1007/978-3-319-95174-4_8

9. Fiorini, L., Marucci, A., Zullo, F., Romano, B.: Indicator engineering for land take control and settlement sustainability. WIT Trans. Ecol. Environ. **217**, 437–446 (2018). WIT Press. https://doi.org/10.2495/SDP180391

10. Nelson, E., et al.: InVEST 3.6.0 User's Guide. The Natural Capital Project (2018)

11. Istat. http://dati.istat.it/

12. RSDI – Geoportale Basilicata. https://rsdi.regione.basilicata.it/

13. GSE. https://www.gse.it/

14. Kyoto Protocol to the United Nations Framework Convention on Climate Change United Nations (1998)

15. Attolico, A., Scorza, F.: A transnational cooperation perspective for "low carbon economy". In: Gervasi, O., et al. (eds.) ICCSA 2016. LNCS, vol. 9786, pp. 636–641. Springer, Cham (2016). https://doi.org/10.1007/978-3-319-42085-1_54

16. Scorza, F., Attolico, A.: Innovations in promoting sustainable development: the local implementation plan designed by the Province of Potenza. In: Gervasi, O., et al. (eds.) ICCSA 2015. LNCS, vol. 9156, pp. 756–766. Springer, Cham (2015). https://doi.org/10.1007/978-3-319-21407-8_54

17. Scorza, F., Attolico, A., Moretti, V., Smaldone, R., Donofrio, D., Laguardia, G.: Growing sustainable behaviors in local communities through smart monitoring systems for energy efficiency: RENERGY outcomes. In: Murgante, B., et al. (eds.) ICCSA 2014. LNCS, vol. 8580, pp. 787–793. Springer, Cham (2014). https://doi.org/10.1007/978-3-319-09129-7_57

18. Mazzariello, A., Pilogallo, A., Scorza, F., Murgante, B., Las Casas, G.: Carbon stock as an indicator for the estimation of anthropic pressure on territorial components. In: Gervasi, O., et al. (eds.) ICCSA 2018. LNCS, vol. 10964, pp. 697–711. Springer, Cham (2018). https://doi.org/10.1007/978-3-319-95174-4_53

19. Chapter 2: Generic Methodologies Applicable to Multiple Land-Use Categories 2006 IPCC Guidelines for National Greenhouse Gas Inventories 2.1

20. Chu, L., et al.: Evolution and prediction of landscape pattern and habitat quality based on CA-Markov and InVEST model in Hubei section of Three Gorges Reservoir Area (TGRA). Sustainability **10**, 3854 (2018). https://doi.org/10.3390/su10113854

21. Sharma, R., et al.: modeling land use and land cover changes and their effects on biodiversity in Central Kalimantan, Indonesia. Land **7**, 57 (2018). https://doi.org/10.3390/land7020057

22. Salata, S., Ronchi, S., Arcidiacono, A., Ghirardelli, F.: Mapping habitat quality in the Lombardy Region, Italy (2017). oneecosystem.pensoft.net

23. Terrado, M., Sabater, S., Chaplin-Kramer, B., Mandle, L., Ziv, G., Acuña, V.: Model development for the assessment of terrestrial and aquatic habitat quality in conservation planning. Sci. Total Environ. **540**, 63–70 (2016). https://doi.org/10.1016/J.SCITOTENV.2015.03.064

24. Sallustio, L., et al.: Assessing habitat quality in relation to the spatial distribution of protected areas in Italy. J. Environ. Manag. **201**, 129–137 (2017). https://doi.org/10.1016/J.JENVMAN.2017.06.031

25. Polasky, S., Nelson, E., Pennington, D., Johnson, K.A.: The impact of land-use change on ecosystem services, biodiversity and returns to landowners: a case study in the State of Minnesota. Environ. Resour. Econ. **48**, 219–242 (2011). https://doi.org/10.1007/s10640-010-9407-0

26. Casas, G.L., Scorza, F.: Sustainable planning: a methodological toolkit. In: Gervasi, O., et al. (eds.) ICCSA 2016. LNCS, vol. 9786, pp. 627–635. Springer, Cham (2016). https://doi.org/10.1007/978-3-319-42085-1_53

27. Las Casas, G.B., Scorza, F., Murgante, B.: From the rules to the models and vice-versa for a new planning rationality. In: Leone, A., Gargiulo, C. (eds.) Environmental and Territorial Modelling for Planning and Design, pp. 499–508. FedOApress (2018). https://doi.org/10. 6093/978-88-6887-048-5
28. Las Casas, G., Scorza, F.: A renewed rational approach from liquid society towards anti-fragile planning (2017). https://doi.org/10.1007/978-3-319-62407-5_36
29. Dvarioniene, J., Grecu, V., Lai, S., Scorza, F.: Four perspectives of applied sustainability: research implications and possible integrations. In: Gervasi, O., et al. (eds.) ICCSA 2017. LNCS, vol. 10409, pp. 554–563. Springer, Cham (2017). https://doi.org/10.1007/978-3-319-62407-5_39
30. Amato, F., Pontrandolfi, P., Murgante, B.: Supporting planning activities with the assessment and the prediction of urban sprawl using spatio-temporal analysis. Ecol. Inform. **30**, 365–378 (2015). https://doi.org/10.1016/j.ecoinf.2015.07.004
31. Amato, F., Maimone, B.A., Martellozzo, F., Nolè, G., Murgante, B.: The effects of urban policies on the development of urban areas. Sustainability **8**, 297 (2016). https://doi.org/10. 3390/su8040297

Cyclable City: A Territorial Assessment Procedure for Disruptive Policy-Making on Urban Mobility

Giovanni Fortunato$^{(\boxtimes)}$, Francesco Scorza, and Beniamino Murgante

Laboratory of Urban and Regional Systems Engineering, School of Engineering,
University of Basilicata, 10, Viale dell'Ateneo Lucano, 85100 Potenza, Italy
giovanni.fortunato88@libero.it,
{francesco.scorza,beniamino.murgante}@unibas.it

Abstract. Urban cycling is one of the main references for the development of sustainable mobility models [1]. Cycling is an active transport mode that is alternative to the use of public and private means of travel. At city scale it collects high levels of users satisfaction. Urban policies encouraging this transport mode are compared with modal split solutions that must take into account the morphological characteristics of the context as well as the organizational dimensions of urban transport. In this work, after highlighting good practices related to traffic moderation, the promotion of soft active mobility (Living street) and the widespread cycling in the urban context, we propose an intervention scenario for the development of an urban cycling infrastructure scheme that integrates current transport infrastructures (mechanized pedestrian mobility) according to a multimodal approach. The sample context is the city of Potenza (Basilicata - Italy). The focus on slow mobility is part of urban mobility strategies. The contribution described in this paper aims at the integration of mechanized pedestrian mobility and local public transport, by road and rail, with active cycle mobility. The aim is to demonstrate how the proposed scheme is feasible with respect to the steepness and integrates infrastructural solutions and reorganization of driveway mobility for widespread use of the bicycle (both traditional and the most innovative forms e-bike and pedelec).

Keywords: Cyclability · Sustainable transport ·
Sustainable urban development

1 Smart (Sustainable) Mobility and Urban Development

Urban mobility is at the center of national and international interest as it represents one of the sectors that can have a significant impact on sustainable development in the future. This is still true if we consider the fact that the world population residing in urban areas will reach 70% of the total in 2050 [2]. The transportation sector is energy-intensive as it has significant implications for energy consumption and polluting emissions. Urban mobility is responsible for 40% of the CO_2 emissions of the transportation sector which, as a whole, produces 25% of greenhouse gas emissions in the European Union's countries [3].

© Springer Nature Switzerland AG 2019
S. Misra et al. (Eds.): ICCSA 2019, LNCS 11624, pp. 291–307, 2019.
https://doi.org/10.1007/978-3-030-24311-1_21

A series of European Union initiatives [4–11] shows that the implementation of sustainable transport policies is at the heart of the European strategy aimed at promoting sustainable development. Faced with the current negative scenario whose data have been mentioned previously and the growing sustainability worries, smart mobility "could also be seen as a set of coordinated actions addressed at improving the efficiency, the effectiveness and the environmental sustainability of cities" [12].

Pinna et al. [13] state that: "mobility cannot be considered smart if it is not sustainable, the most substantial difference between sustainable mobility and smart mobility is that smart mobility is an integrated system comprised of several projects and actions all aimed at sustainability". This highlights that the paradigms of "smart" and "sustainable" are closely connected within the framework of sustainable urban development. Furthermore connectivity is the main element that characterizes smart mobility. This is also confirmed by Lyons [14] who, comparing his conceptual framework with many authors [15–17], provides the following definition of smart urban mobility: "*connectivity in towns and cities that is affordable, effective, attractive and sustainable*". Connectivity is not just about how people and goods move in urban areas but also "*the land use system, transport system and the telecommunications system*" [18].

Many studies show that the use of active travel modes (non-automobile modes such as bicycle ridership) increases when urban neighborhoods are characterized by land use diversity, proximity to retail stores, presence and distribution of transit stations [19–22]. A relevant example is the city of Berlin which has an urban poly-centric structure based on towns that have functional autonomy in the city [23–25].

Urban street design can help make sustainable modes of transport (walking and cycling) more attractive, thus increasing their use in urban travel and reducing the negative externalities on social environmental and economic basis [26–28]. Urban planning should promote compact urban patterns in order to make trips shorter. "*Ensuring enhanced permeability for pedestrians and cyclists can enrich the urban realm and influence how people connect in urban environments*" [14]. Furthermore, there is a connection between people's travel choices and urban form as demonstrated by the definition of 5 environment built variables in the field of urban planning: design, density, diversity, distance to the public transit and destination accessibility [29].

In light of this, the study presented aims to verify the possibility of integrating a system of cycle routes with related infrastructural interventions in the city of Potenza. Within the framework of sustainable mobility, the bicycle is a mean of transport that can contribute to urban sustainability thanks to its social, environmental and economic advantages. This study focuses on design measures aimed at promoting bicycle use, almost completely absent in the city of Potenza, and a consequent modal split from motor vehicles to cycling. In order to design a network of bicycle paths technical requirements for the bicycle facilities based on the review of state of the art manuals and national and international technical guidelines have been considered.

This paper proposes a GIS-based method to design bike facilities, to define the characteristics (such as provenance and distribution in urban area) of the demand of the daily commuters (workers and students) and to assess the bike accessibility to urban attractors.

2 The Global Framework Promoting Urban Cyclability and the Case Study

According to the European Parliament resolution of 27 September 2011 on European road safety 2011–2020 [1], there is a need to promote road safety in order to pursue the "Vision Zero" [30] in terms of accidents through regulatory and design measures which overcome the logic of the separation of road traffic flows between the different means of transport and encourage a shared use of the road as a public space, based on the type of road and the context. An International Transport Forum (ITF) research report shows that road crashes are the ninth main cause of death globally and the main cause of death worldwide for young people aged between 15 and 29 years [31]. Specifically vulnerable road users including pedestrians, cyclists represent 26% of all road traffic deaths [32]. From a safety point-of-view, a considerable lack of safe riding space that characterizes the cycling infrastructure discourages cycling as transport mode for urban trips.

So in the last decade road safety is considered a central issue by international community in the field of sustainable development, as demonstrated by the Decade of Action for Road Safety 2011–2020 [33]. The 2030 Agenda for Sustainable Development, which sets 17 Sustainable Development Goals (SDGs) and their 169 targets, includes 2 targets on the subject of Road Safety policy: one in Goal 3 (Health) and one in Goal 11 (Sustainable cities and communities) [34].

Goal target 3.6 calls for halving in the number of road traffic deaths by 2020 [34]. This is unlikely to be achieved. Sustainable Development Goal (SDG) target 11.2 highlights the importance on implementation of road safety measures in order to effectively create sustainable cities and communities: *"By 2030, provide access to safe, affordable, accessible and sustainable transport systems for all, improving road safety, notably by expanding public transport, with special attention to the needs of those in vulnerable situations, women, children, persons with disabilities and older persons"*.

Many studies show how the installation of bicycle lanes promotes not only the use of the bicycle but also the increase in roadway safety, being in fact an effective and low-cost design street measure that allows the reduction of the risk of accidents for cyclists in a city (cfr. [34–38]). A study conducted by Kondo et al. [39] found that a significant reduction in the probability of bicycle accidents (more than 40%) occurred following the inclusion of bicycle lane in the streets. Jacobsen found that the probability of an accident between a weaker street user (pedestrian or cyclist) and a motor vehicle is inversely related to the pedestrian or bicycle traffic volume [40].

This is an opportunity to redefine the dimensions of mobility at urban level, encouraging a significant transition towards active forms of urban mobility. To achieve sustainable mobility, it is necessary to implement measures aimed at: reducing the need to travel, encouraging modal shift, reducing trip distances (through land-use policy measures) and increasing transport system efficiency [16]. In Europe there are examples of cities that, through their sustainable urban plans, are willing to return the roads intended as "public spaces" to the citizens: the Barcelona "Superblock" model [41, 42], the increase of 30 zones in Paris (at the end of 2017, 45% of the Parisian roads had a speed limit of 30 km/h [43] with the objective of reaching 85% in 2020 [44] and the application of the speed limit of 30 km/h to 87% of the roads in Bilbao as established by its Plan de Movilidad Urbana Sostenible (PMUS) 2015-2030 (the remaining 13% will have a limit of 50 km/h) so that it can be defined as "30 City" [45, 46].

The case study, which is characterized by morphological limits to the diffusion of an extensive network of active mobility, required the experimentation of territorial analysis models in Geographic Information System (GIS) environment for the evaluation of the territory and the road network, the estimation of the journey times, the integration with mechanized transport infrastructures such as escalators, elevators. In a city with considerable slopes such as Potenza these mechanical means support walking, providing a great contribution to improving the quality of pedestrian mobility while reducing pedestrians' physical wear, travel times and discomfort. The city of Potenza can count on the presence of 4 escalators infrastructures.

In light of this, the research allowed to propose a new cycle infrastructure design to increase the use of the bicycle in combination with the public transport system and to increase the extent of the areas served (Buffer Zone) by urban mobility infrastructures [47]. Thus cycling can also be used for medium-long journeys: a part(s) of the trip travelled by bicycle and the rest with public transport. In this scenario, cycling could be used on trips to cover the first and last mile.

The present study assessing the feasibility of creating an urban cycle infrastructure within the city of Potenza is strongly coherent with the policy framework proposed by the Basilicata Region 2016–2026 Transport Plan which encourages forms of active and sustainable mobility both at regional and local level [48]. Moreover urban planning instruments and policy strategies developed in the context of the city of Potenza to promote active and sustainable transport mode have been taken into consideration: the Urban Plan of Potenza [49], the Urban Mobility Plan [50], the ITI Urban Development Program of the city of Potenza [51] and the Italian Highway Code [52].

The city of Potenza, with more than 67,000 inhabitants, has a value of 0 km/10,000 inhabitants of cycle paths, does not have a bike sharing service, but it is the fourth Italian city for "Index of car motorization" with 73,93 vehicles/100 inhabitants. However, Potenza is the Italian Regional County Seat with the largest number of green spaces per inhabitant of 371.6 mq/inh. compared to an average national value of 32.2 mq/inh [51].

Potenza is a city with high steepness: from the study of its orography it emerged that more than 80% of the urban territory has a terrain slope of more than 11%, about 45% of the urban area has a slope of more than 20%; just over 26% of the urban streets have a gradient less than 5% (Fig. 1).

References to national and European experiences allowed the construction of evaluation frameworks of the territorial context in the light of specific design solutions. The results can be transferred to other similar contexts for the construction of sustainable urban mobility projects and policies based on urban cycling.

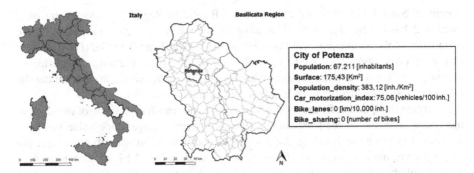

Fig. 1. Location of Basilicata Region in Italy on the left, location of the city of Potenza (red perimeter) in Basilicata Region on the center and data on the city of Potenza on the right. (Color figure online)

3 Cycling and Innovative Solutions for Smart Urban Mobility: The Case of Potenza

The first phase of the study began with the observation and collection of data relating to the urban context in order to verify the possibility of integrating a network of cycle infrastructures for daily journeys for study and work within urban area of the city of Potenza. In this study the indispensable knowledge of the urban cycling environment is obtained through the construction of a specific spatial data model, a territorial database built by GIS software.

In this paragraph, we discuss the approach to territorial analysis aimed at evaluating the city of Potenza's terrain and streets slope, in order to define a network of cycle routes in urban areas. The identification process of the main traffic generators/attractors (urban facilities such as public services and equipment) is described, the urban mobility infrastructures are represented, the demand analysis and the evaluation of the accessibility to public services and equipment are carried out through the realization of isochrones. In this work we followed the example of the Lisboa Horizontal project aimed at planning a network of cycle paths that involves roads with a slope of less than 4%. A group of developers in Lisbon designed an app that tells the cyclist the best routes to use. The Lisbon Horizontal app has also been used in other cities with different orographic profiles such as Madrid, Berlin, Brussels and Zurich [52]. We also followed "Bicipolitana" scheme in the city of Pesaro, whose scheme is created with reference to the model of the subway network.

Existing geographical data, available in the Geoportal of the Basilicata Region (RSDI Basilicata Region) and others resources freely accessible, such as Open Street Map, do not provide no geographical information concerning the morphological features of the land and the streets. The slope of each street segment, in addition to the width of the latter, is taken as a fundamental value for choosing a route more appropriate to accommodate a cycle infrastructure.

The first step consisted in the evaluation of the slope of the streets (length = 810.272 km) of the city of Potenza. From the geo-topographic regional database

(Regional Spatial Data Infrastructure (RSDI) Basilicata Region), vector layers on a municipal basis were downloaded, relating to the urban viability and administrative boundaries of the Municipality of Potenza and the Digital Terrain Model (DTM) blocks with a high resolution (cell size = 5 m) affecting the portion of the territory considered in order to perform a geomorphological analysis on the raster aimed at determining the urban territory and streets' slope expressed in percent terms (%).

Through the QGIS software tools it was possible to transfer the value of the slope to the vector layer of the road network. In this way each average slope value has been associated to the corresponding street segment and it was thus possible to select the arches of the road network by slope classes: less than 5% (12% of the entire road network of the city of Potenza); with a slope of less than 10% (35% of the road network). In the urban area more than 26% of the roads have a slope less than 5%, so these streets are absolutely suitable for cycling for urban trips. Slopes less than 5% are suitable for relatively low-stress cycling [53, 54]. Moreover the American Association of State Highway and Transportation Officials provides desirable uphill gradients for cyclists and respective acceptable lengths (for example, a max length of 240 m corresponds to a gradient of 5–6% while a max length of 60 m corresponds to a gradient of 9%).

As shown in Figs. 2 and 3 the roads with a slope less than 5% are located mostly in the inhabited center of the town and in the Southern part, along the Basento River Park.

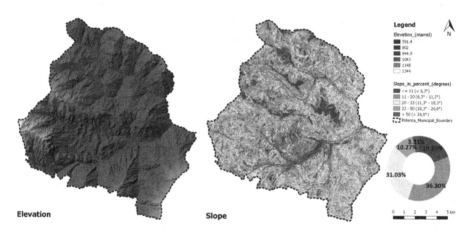

Fig. 2. City of Potenza: terrain elevation and slope

The next step consisted in determining the width of the road section. However these data are important for the purpose of a correct planning of an efficient urban cycle network, as this affects the opportunity to build cycle tracks or bike lanes or integrate traffic calming strategies in shared use paths and areas with other means of transport.

In particular 50% of the roads in the urban area of the city of Potenza has a width greater than 10 m. The width of the road section is considered as a primary design parameter for the realization of safe cycle facilities, especially in the presence of roads with legal speed limits and high operating speed values (Fig. 4).

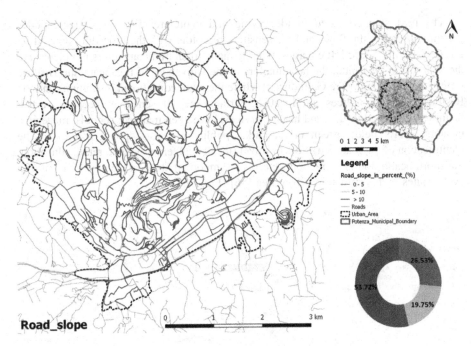

Fig. 3. City of Potenza: road slope in urban area

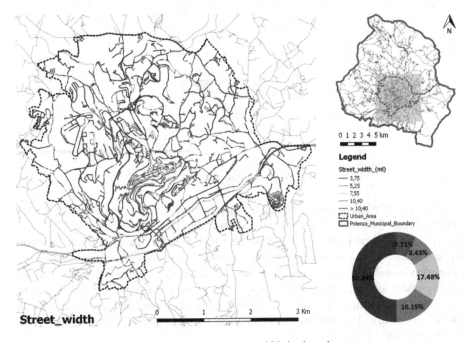

Fig. 4. City of Potenza: street width in the urban area

The next step consisted in identifying and georeferencing the strategic nodes generating road traffic flows and the sensitive receptors with the procedure defined by Las Casas et al. [54, 55]. It emerges, that the main urban traffic attractors in Potenza are the "San Carlo" Hospital, the headquarters of the University of Basilicata, the Historic Center and the Poggio Tre Galli district where the main educational institutions and the Basilicata Region Offices are located. Furthermore all sensitive receptors, urban facilities such as education and health services, have been mapped: schools, museums, theaters, sports fields, green urban parks, public offices, shopping activities. The identification of the main attractors of travel (residential, employment, retail, education, transport, health, tourist attractions, etc.) is an important stage in the development of a cycle routes' network within urban area [56] (Fig. 5).

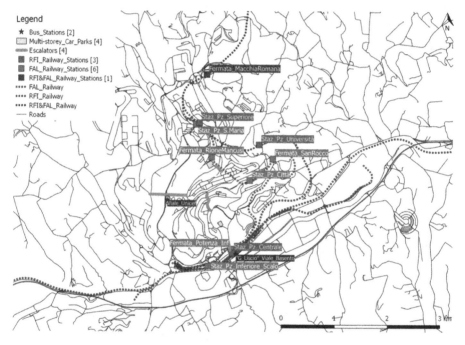

Fig. 5. City of Potenza: urban transport infrastructures

After identifying the main urban traffic attractors, we mapped the infrastructures for urban mobility (road, rail transport) and pedestrian mechanized systems (escalators and elevators): the single-track railway lines, Rete Ferroviaria Italiana (RFI) and Ferrovie Appulo Lucane (FAL), with the relative stations and stops, the four mechanized pedestrian mobility systems (escalator and lift integrated system), the bus stations serving urban and suburban public transport, the four multi-storey car parks, two of which are interchange mechanized connections ("via_Armellini" escalator, "Santa Lucia" escalator). The parking areas may encourage cycling, thus increasing the multimodal transportation.

To assess bicycle accessibility to public services and equipment, from mechanized pedestrian facilities and public transport railway and bus stations, the OpenRouteService website (ORS) was used. It is based on Open Standards and Open Geodata

(OpenStreetMap) and provides different Location Based Services, made by HeiGIT - Heidelberg Institute for Geoinformation Technology, including the "Isochrones Service". This service consists in the realization of isochrones, concentric curves that describe the place of the points having the same characteristics of time from a determined origin. The isochrones also allow to quantify the population and the extension of the land area affected by the curves. Specifically a period of 30 min and a range between the different curves of 5 min were considered (from 5 to 30 min, every 5 min). In order to assess the accessibility to urban facilities, the values are set in the hypothesis of travel by bicycle. Furthermore the accessibility map for urban facilities shows the amount of land area that is covered in 5, 10, 15, 20, 25, 30 min of cycle riding distance. It is also possible to determine the amount of population that can receive services in definite time distance values, mentioned above.

The origin of the isochrones has been placed in correspondence with the facilities of mechanized pedestrian mobility and the stop-stations of local public transport, by road and rail in order to encourage a multimodal and integrated approach to urban mobility. To gain users' availability for cycling the distance between multimodal nodes and the origins/destinations of trips should be small.

Specifically, it was considered:

- railway interchange point "Potenza Superiore Station" on the RFI network – "Potenza S. Maria Station" on the FAL network;
- escalators in "Via Tammone" – "Educational Centre" in Potenza (Poggio Tre Galli district);
- via Armellini, where there is a escalator-lift system, a multi-storey car park, the "Fermata Rione Mancusi" on the FAL network;
- "Potenza Centrale Station" on the RFI network, where you will find the "G. Liscio" bus station, escalators, the "Rione Mancusi Stop" on the FAL network (Fig. 6).

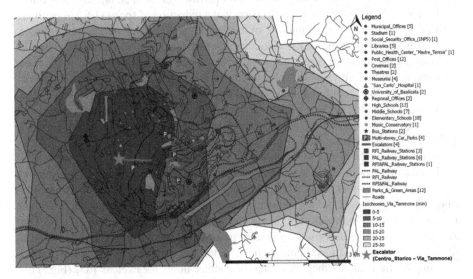

Fig. 6. City of Potenza: isochrones for travel by bicycle from escalator (Centro_Storico – Via_Tammone) to public services and schools in Poggio Tre Galli

4 Intervention Typologies and a Strategic Hypothesis for Potenza Cyclable Network

The Institute of Transport Engineers (ITE) defines Traffic Calming (TC) as "*the combination of mainly physical measures that reduce the negative effects of motor vehicle use, alter driver behavior and improve conditions for non-motorized street users*" [57]. These strategies should ensure that non-motorized users are the first to benefit from street space. An important objective of these measures that affect urban street design is improving the street environment due to the reduction local air pollution and noise caused by motor vehicles and to the increase in the non-motorized users' (cyclists and pedestrians) safety. Traffic calming can be used in street design and it involves design and implementation of physical measures in order to control the speed and/or traffic volume of motor vehicles. Reducing vehicles' speed, cut-through traffic volume and accident frequency and severity in residential streets are the main goals of traffic calming [58].

The Traffic Calming philosophy was introduced at the end of the 60s in the Netherlands first and then in the other Northern European countries in contrast with the dominant principle of the 70s which included the separation of vehicular flows, motorized and not. However this principle required high economic investments and considerable land consumption to create new transport infrastructures [59].

According to Pardon et al. [60] an element that guarantees success in the designing and implementation of the measures is the stakeholders' participation.

In urban areas the traffic calming measures can be implemented to affect speed or volume of motorized vehicle or both. The main purpose of volume control devices (half and full street closures, forced turn islands) is to discourage/eliminate cut-through traffic. The main purpose of speed control measures (speed tables, raised intersections, realigned intersections, chicanes, centre island narrowings) is to physically slow traffic.

Taylor et al. [61] came to the conclusion that a reduction of speed (1.6 km per hour) can lead to a reduction in the number of road accidents by a rate of 5%. According to van Schagen [62] the percentage reduction of road accidents depends on the type of considered road, reaching the highest value for urban roads with low average speed (6%) and the minimum value (3%) for urban roads characterized by the highest speeds.

A measure that could encourage the diffusion of a widespread cycling in urban areas is the realization of contra-flow bike lanes. "*Contra-flow bicycle lanes are bicycle lanes designed to allow bicyclists to ride in the opposite direction of motor vehicle traffic. They convert a oneway traffic street into a two-way street: one direction for motor vehicles and bikes, and the other for bikes only*" [63].

Thanks to these street design strategies continuity and connectivity of cycle routes is guaranteed in a street context characterized by a high degree of safety for all users especially for cyclists. Looking at cyclist travel behaviour, a continuous path, without deviations, makes the bicycle not only a sustainable transport mode but also the most competitive for street users who generally make small-medium movements within 5-10 km distance [64]. In addition to the shortest routes eye contact when passing incoming traffic is an another advantage of counter-flows for cyclists [65] (Fig. 7).

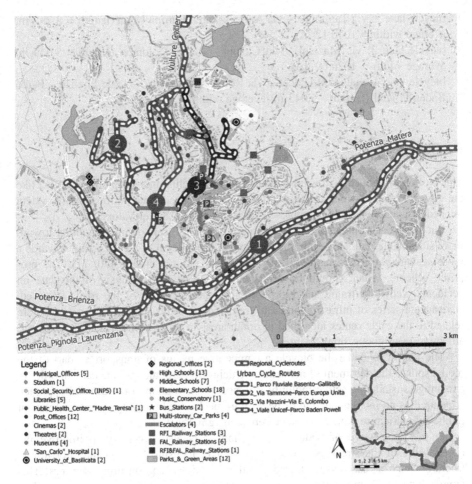

Fig. 7. Proposal for the development of urban cycling to integrate mechanized pedestrian mobility

The proposed intervention takes into account some Italian good practices. Among the main ones we report: 30 Zone in the "Piraghetto" district in Mestre [66], 30 Zone in the "Circoscrizione 2 Santa Rita - Mirafiori Nord" in Turin [67], urban redevelopment of "via E. Ospizio" in Reggio Emilia [68].

In this feasibility study, the construction of a bicycle route network requires the design of other incentive measures, such as restricted car use or traffic calming measures [69].

In the case of the city of Potenza it emerges that the four main routes to be nominated for an urban cycling project are:

- bicycle lane 1: Basento River Park – via del Gallitello (length = 10,288 m (of which Cycle Track: 4,657 m); average width = 956.38 m);

- bicycle lane 2: via Tammone – via Anzio – Parco Europa Unita (length = 3,792 m; average width = 1040.12 m);
- bicycle lane 3: via Mazzini – via Cavour – via E. Colombo (length = 3,049 m; average width = 1026.69 m);
- bicycle lane 4: viale dell'Unicef – via Roma – via Milano – viale Firenze – Parco Baden Powell (length = 5,043 m; average width = 1020.17 m).

5 Conclusions

This work highlights how it is possible to integrate cycling in a steep urban context like the city of Potenza, which can currently count on a consolidated infrastructure system for pedestrian/active mobility represented by escalators and elevators.

Such approach implies a radical shifting policy from cars oriented mobility toward more sustainable and active mobility schema at urban level, it means a shift towards a more sustainable urban management oriented on rational criteria [70, 71]. The proposed scheme, which should be deepened with a detailed analysis of the data on accidents, vehicular traffic and morphological characteristics of the roads involved, envisages a series of infrastructural and traffic calming measures. These measures are related to the cycle routes identified in urban areas in order to make them safe, linear, attractive, continuous, comfortable.

The aim is to make the bicycle a competitive means of transport as part of the modal split to the detriment of motorized vehicles (in particular private car). In order to encourage sustainable active mobility it is necessary to adopt a multimodal approach structured as an interconnection of pedestrian mechanized mobility system: a relèvant public infrastructure whose use is currently marginal in Potenza.

In the perspective of widespread cycling, it is also necessary to improve the accessibility of the street user travelling by bike, focusing both on mobility infrastructures (such as escalators, elevators, railway stations) and on urban services. This approach passes from a careful evaluation and from the project of dimensioning urban planning standards in favor of the bicycle transportation mode and in particular favoring the distribution of bicycle racks in the areas where the planned cycle routes are located. Moreover, inclusive and participation approach has to be consider in order to accompany infrastructural investments with soft actions oriented to facilitate users' behavioral change [72, 73]. Potenza has a long tradition about that, especially in informal and bottom up participatory approach [74–76].

References

1. European Parliament: Risoluzione sulla sicurezza stradale in Europa 2011–2020 (2010/2235 (INI)) (2011). http://www.europarl.europa.eu/sides/getDoc.do?pubRef=-//EP//TEXT+REPO RT+A7-2011-0264+0+DOC+XML+V0//IT. Accessed May 2019
2. United Nations: State of the World's Cities Report 2012/2013: Prosperity of Cities. United Nations Human Settlements Programme (2012)

3. Staricco, L.: Smart mobility: Opportunità e condizioni. TeMA J. Land Use Mob. Environ. **6**, 341–354 (2013)
4. European Strategy and Policy Analysis System. ESPAS: Global Trends to 2030: Can the EU Meet the Challenges Ahead? An inter-institutional EU project with the participation of the European Parliament, the Council of the European Union, the European Commission and the European External Action Service; European Strategy and Policy Analysis System: Brussels, Belgium, pp. 1–82 (2015). http://europa.eu/espas/pdf/espas-report-2015.pdf. Accessed 10 Dec 2018
5. European Commission: Together Towards Competitive and Resource-Efficient Urban Mobility. COM (2013) 913 Final; European Commission: Brussels, Belgium (2013)
6. European Commission: Green Paper: Towards a New Culture for Urban Mobility. COM (2007) 551 Final; European Commission: Brussels, Belgium (2007)
7. European Commission: Action Plan on Urban Mobility. COM (2009) 490 Final; European Commission: Brussels, Belgium (2009)
8. European Commission: White Paper: Roadmap to a Single European Transport Area— Towards a Competitive and Resource Efficient Transport System. COM (2011) 144 Final; European Commission: Brussels, Belgium (2011)
9. European Commission: A European Strategy for Low-Emission Mobility. COM (2016) 501; European Commission: Brussels, Belgium (2016a)
10. European Commission: European Political Strategy Center Strategic Notes towards Low-Emission Mobility—Driving the Modernisation of the EU Economy (2016b)
11. European Commission: Horizon 2020 Work Programme 2014–2015. 11. Smart, Green and Integrated Transport Revised. 10 December 2013 (2013a). http://ec.europa.eu/research/participants/data/ref/h2020/wp/2014_2015/main/h2020-wp1415-transport_en.pdf. Accessed 2 Dec 2018
12. Benevolo, C., Dameri, R.P., D'Auria, B.: Smart mobility in smart city. In: Torre, T., Braccini, A., Spinelli, R. (eds.) Empowering Organizations Enabling Platforms and Artefacts. LNISO, vol. 11, pp. 13–28. Springer, Cham (2016). https://doi.org/10.1007/978-3-319-23784-8_2
13. Pinna, F., Masala, F., Garau, C.: Urban policies and mobility trends in italian smart cities. Sustainability **9**, 494 (2017)
14. Lyons, G.: Getting smart about urban mobility – aligning the paradigms of smart and sustainable. Transp. Res. Part A **115**(2018), 4–14 (2016). https://doi.org/10.1016/j.tra.2016.12.001
15. Lam, D., Head, P.: Sustainable urban mobility. In: Inderwildi, O., King, S. (eds.) Energy, Transport, & The Environment. Springer, London (2012). https://doi.org/10.1007/978-1-4471-2717-8_19
16. Banister, D.: The sustainable mobility paradigm. Transp. Policy **15**, 73–80 (2008)
17. Curtis, C.: Planning for sustainable accessibility: the implementation challenge. Transp. Policy **15**, 104–112 (2008)
18. Lyons, G., Davidson, C.: Guidance for transport planning and policymaking in the face of an uncertain future. Transp. Res. Part A: Policy Pract. **88**, 104–116 (2016)
19. Cervero, R., Duncan, M.: Walking, bicycling, and urban landscapes: evidence from the San Francisco Bay Area. Am. J. Publ. Health **93**(9), 1478–1483 (2003)
20. Cervero, R., Kockelman, K.: Travel demand and the 3Ds: density, diversity, and design. Transp. Res. Part D: Transp. Environ. **2**(3), 199–219 (1997). https://doi.org/10.1016/s1361-9209(97)00009-6
21. Giles-Corti, B., Donovan, R.J.: Relative influences of individual, social environmental, and physical environmental correlates of walking. Am. J. Publ. Health **93**(9), 1583–1589 (2003)

22. Handy, S.L., Clifton, K.J.: Local shopping as a strategy for reducing automobile travel. Transportation **28**(4), 317–346 (2001). https://doi.org/10.1023/A:1011850618753
23. Elkins, T.H., Hofmeister, B.: Berlin – The Spatial Structure of a Divided City. USA: Methuen & Co. in Association with Methuen, Inc. (1988)
24. Bushell, M.: Design, policy, and bicycle ridership – a comparison between Berlin, Germany and Washington, DC. Master thesis, North Carolina: University of North Carolina (2010). http://dc.lib.unc.edu/cdm/ref/collection/spapers/id/1281
25. Meng, M., Koh, P.P., Wong, Y.D., Zhong, Y.H.: Influences of urban characteristics on cycling: experiences of four cities. Sustain. Cities Soc. **13**(2014), 78–88 (2014). https://doi.org/10.1016/j.scs.2014.05.001
26. Tira, M.: Safety of pedestrians and cyclists in Europe: the DUMAS approach. In: Sustainable Transport, pp. 339–350. Woodhead Publishing, Cambridge (2003)
27. Moccia, F.D.: Stazioni e città nella prospettiva ecologica. Inconsapevoli precursori. Urbanistica **145**, 64–76 (2011)
28. Marioli, L.: Mobilità sostenibile e trasporto intermodale. Rivista di diritto dell'economia, dei trasporti e dell'ambiente **11**, 19–39 (2013)
29. Ewing, R., Cervero, R.: Travel and the built environment. J. Am. Plan. Assoc. **76**, 265–294 (2010). https://doi.org/10.1080/01944361003766766
30. Kristianssen, A.-C., Andersson, R., Belinc, M.-A., Nilsene, P.: Swedish vision zero policies for safety – a comparative policy content analysis. Saf. Sci. **103**(2018), 260–269 (2018). https://doi.org/10.1016/j.ssci.2017.11.005
31. OECD/International Transport Forum (ITF): Zero Road Deaths and Serious Injuries: Leading a Paradigm Shift to a Safe System. OECD Publishing, Paris (2016). https://doi.org/10.1787/9789282108055-en
32. World Health Organization: Global status report on road safety 2018. World Health Organization, Geneva (2018). Licence: CC BYNC-SA 3.0 IGO
33. United Nations: Resolution A/RES/64/255. Improving Global Road Safety. Sixty-fourth session of the United Nations General Assembly, New York, 10 May 2010 (2010). http://www.who.int/violence_injury_prevention/publications/road_traffic/UN_GA_resolution-54-255-en.pdf?ua=1. Accessed 2 Dec 2018
34. Harris, M.A., et al.: Comparing the effects of infrastructure on bicycling injury at intersections and non-intersections using a case–crossover design. Inj. Prev. **19**, 303–310 (2013). injuryprev-2012-040561
35. Pedroso, F.E., Angriman, F., Bellows, A.L., Taylor, K.: Bicycle use and cyclist safety following Boston's bicycle infrastructure expansion, 2009–2012. Am. J. Publ. Health **106**, 2171–2177 (2016)
36. Poulos, R.G., et al.: An exposure based study of crash and injury rates in a cohort of transport and recreational cyclists in New South Wales, Australia. Accid. Anal. Prev. **78**, 29–38 (2015)
37. Pucher, J., Dill, J., Handy, S.: Infrastructure, programs, and policies to increase bicycling: an international review. Prev. Med. **50**, 106–125 (2010)
38. Thomas, B., DeRobertis, M.: The safety of urban cycle tracks: a review of the literature. Accid. Anal. Prev. **52**, 219–227 (2013)
39. Kondo, M.C., Morrison, C., Guerrad, E., Kaufmane, E.J., Wiebeb, D.J.: Where do bike lanes work best? A Bayesian spatial model of bicycle lanes and bicycle crashes. Saf. Sci. **103**(2018), 225–233 (2018). https://doi.org/10.1016/j.ssci.2017.12.002
40. Jacobsen, P.: Safety in numbers: more walkers and bicyclists, safer walking and bicycling. Inj. Prev. **9**, 205–209 (2003)

41. The Guardian: Superblocks to the rescue: Barcelona's plan to give streets back to residents (2016). https://www.theguardian.com/cities/2016/may/17/superblocks-rescue-barcelona-spai n-plan-give-streets-back-residents. Accessed 15 Oct 2018
42. Municipality of Barcelona: Urban Mobility Plan (2013–2018) (2013). https://ajuntament. barcelona.cat/ecologiaurbana/en/what-we-do-and-why/active-and-sustainable-mobility/ urban-mobility-plan. Accessed 11 Nov 2018
43. Zones 30: comment ça marche? (2018). www.paris.fr. Accessed 21 Mar 2018. https://www. paris.fr/actualites/zones-30-comment-ca-marche-5507. Accessed 3 Oct 2018
44. Le Parisien: Tout Paris à 30 km/h, c'est pour demain! 14 September 2017. http://www. leparisien.fr/paris-75005/tout-paris-a-30-km-h-c-est-pour-demain-14-09-2017-7261308.php. Accessed 3 Oct 2018
45. Municipality of Bilbao: Bilbao 30 (2018a). https://www.bilbao.eus/cs/Satellite?blobcol= urldata&blobheader=application%2Fpdf&blobheadername1=Content-disposition&blobheadername2=pragma&blobheadervalue1=attachment%3B+filename% 3DBilbao30.pdf&blobheadervalue2=public&blobkey=id&blobtable= MungoBlobs&blobwhere=1274207472664&ssbinary=true. Accessed 3 Dec 2018
46. Municipality of Bilbao: Plan de Movilidad Urbana Sostenible de Bilbao 2015–2030 (PMUS) (2018b). https://www.bilbao.eus/cs/Satellite?c=BIO_Noticia_FA&cid=1279179787848&lan guage=es&pageid=3012589425&pagename=Bilbaonet%2FBIO_Noticia_FA%2FBIO_Noti cia. Accessed 18 Nov 2018
47. Sgobbo, A., Basile, M.: Sharing sustainability. UPLanD – J. Urban Plan. Land. Environ. Des. 2(2), 255–297 (2017)
48. Basilicata Region: Regional Transport Plan 2016–2026, approved by the Regional Council on 21.12.2016 (2016). http://www.regione.basilicata.it/giunta/site/Giunta/detail.jsp?otype= 1101&id=3018870
49. Municipality of Potenza: City Plan, adopted in 31 March 2009 (2009), http://www.comune. potenza.it/?p=1681. Accessed 16 Dec 2018
50. Municipality of Potenza: Piano Urbano della Mobilità di Potenza (2008)
51. Basilicata Region, Municipality of Potenza: Documento Strategico ITI Sviluppo Urbano della città di Potenza (2017). http://www.comune.potenza.it/?p=23296. Accessed 23 Dec 2018
52. Ministry of Infrastructure and Transport: Italian Highway Code - Legislative Decree 295 of 30 April 1992 (1992). http://www.mit.gov.it/mit/site.php?p=normativa&o=vd&id=1&id_ cat=&id_dett=0. Accessed 15 Dec 2018
53. Aashto (American Association of State Highway and Transportation Officials): Aashto Guide for the Development of Bicycle Facilities. American Association of State Highway and Transportation Officials, Washington DC, USA (1999)
54. Las Casas, G., Murgante, B., Scorza, F.: Regional local development strategies benefiting from open data and open tools and an outlook on the renewable energy sources contribution. In: Papa, R., Fistola, R. (eds.) Smart Energy in the Smart City. GET, pp. 275–290. Springer, Cham (2016). https://doi.org/10.1007/978-3-319-31157-9_14
55. Carbone, R., et al.: Using open data and open tools in defining strategies for the enhancement of Basilicata region. In: Gervasi, O., et al. (eds.) ICCSA 2018. LNCS, vol. 10964, pp. 725–733. Springer, Cham (2018). https://doi.org/10.1007/978-3-319-95174-4_55
56. Sustrans: Sustrans Design Manual - Handbook for Cycle-Friendly Design. Sustrans, Bristol, April 2014
57. Institute of Transport Engineers (ITE): ITE traffic calming definition. ITE J. 67(7), 22–24 (1997)

58. Rahman, F., Takemoto, A., Sakamoto, K., Kubota, H.: Comparative study of design and planning process of traffic calming devices. In: Proceedings of the Eastern Asia Society for Transportation Studies, vol. 5, pp. 1322–1336. Saitama University, Saitama (2005)
59. Juhász, M., Koren, C.: Getting an insight into the effects of traffic calming measures on road safety. In: 6th Transport Research Arena 18–21 April 2016, Transportation Research Procedia, vol. 14, pp. 3811–3820 (2016) https://doi.org/10.1016/j.trpro.2016.05.466
60. Pardon, N., Average, C.: The effectiveness of traffic calming measures in reducing road carnage in Masvingo urban. Int. J. Sci. Knowl. 3(2), 2305–2493 (2013)
61. Taylor, M.C., Lynam, D.A., Baruya, A.: The effects of drivers' speed on the frequency of road accidents. TRL Report 421, Transport Research Laboratory, Crowthorne (2000)
62. Van Schagen, I. (ed.): Traffic calming schemes: opportunities and implementation strategies. SWOV Institute for Road Safety Research, Leidschendam, The Netherlands (2003)
63. National Association of City Transportation Officials (NACTO): Urban Bikeway Design Guide (2011)
64. European Transport Safety Council (ETSC): Briefing – Contraflow cycling, March 2018 (2018). https://etsc.eu/wp-content/uploads/Briefing-Contraflow-Cycling.pdf
65. Vandebulcke, G., Thomas, I., Int Panis, L.: Predicting cycling accident risk in Brussels: a spatial case-control approach. Accid. Anal. Prev. (2013). http://www.sciencedirect.com/science/article/pii/S0001457513002686
66. Di Bussolo, R.: Quartiere esteso a strade strette - Piraghetto – Mestre. In: Passigato, M. (eds.) La moderazione del traffico. Quaderno del Centro Studi FIAB Riccardo Gallimbeni, pp. 56–61 (2012). http://www.fiab-areatecnica.it/pubblicazioni/manuali-e-studi/fiab/434-la-moderazione-del-traffico.html
67. Manuetti, D.: Moderazione del Traffico a Mirafiori - Torino - Interventi e risultati. In: Passigato, M. (ed.) La moderazione del traffico. Quaderno del Centro Studi FIAB Riccardo Gallimbeni, pp. 67–70 (2012). http://www.fiab-areatecnica.it/pubblicazioni/manuali-e-studi/fiab/434-la-moderazione-del-traffico.html
68. Dondè, M.: Moderazione sugli assi urbani della viabilità principale - via Emilia Ospizio - Reggio Emilia. In: Passigato, M. (ed.) La moderazione del traffico. Quaderno del Centro Studi FIAB Riccardo Gallimbeni, pp. 75–76 (2012). http://www.fiab-areatecnica.it/pubblicazioni/manuali-e-studi/fiab/434-la-moderazione-del-traffico.html
69. Midgley, P.: Bicycle-sharing schemes: enhancing sustainable mobility in urban areas. Background Paper No. 8, CSD19/2011/BP8, Commission on Sustainable Development, United Nations (2011)
70. Las Casas, G., Scorza, F.: A renewed rational approach from liquid society towards anti-fragile planning. In: Gervasi, O., et al. (eds.) ICCSA 2017. LNCS, vol. 10409, pp. 517–526. Springer, Cham (2017). https://doi.org/10.1007/978-3-319-62407-5_36
71. Casas, G.L., Scorza, F.: Sustainable planning: a methodological toolkit. In: Gervasi, O., et al. (eds.) ICCSA 2016. LNCS, vol. 9786, pp. 627–635. Springer, Cham (2016). https://doi.org/10.1007/978-3-319-42085-1_53
72. Pontrandolfi, P., Scorza, F.: Sustainable urban regeneration policy making: inclusive participation practice. In: Gervasi, O., et al. (eds.) ICCSA 2016. LNCS, vol. 9788, pp. 552–560. Springer, Cham (2016). https://doi.org/10.1007/978-3-319-42111-7_44
73. Scorza, F., Pontrandolfi, P.: Citizen participation and technologies: the C.A.S.T. architecture. In: Gervasi, O., et al. (eds.) ICCSA 2015. LNCS, vol. 9156, pp. 747–755. Springer, Cham (2015). https://doi.org/10.1007/978-3-319-21407-8_53
74. Murgante, B., Botonico, G., Graziadei, A., Sassano, G., Amato, F., Scorza, F.: Innovation, technologies, participation: new paradigms towards a 2.0 citizenship. Int. J. Electron. Gov. 11(1), 62–88 (2019). https://doi.org/10.1504/IJEG.2019.098814

75. Saganeiti, L., Favale, A., Pilogallo, A., Scorza, F., Murgante, B.: Assessing urban fragmentation at regional scale using sprinkling indexes. Sustainability **10**(9), 3274 (2018). https://doi.org/10.3390/su10093274
76. Sassano, G., Graziadei, A., Amato, F., Murgante, B.: Involving citizens in the reuse and regeneration of urban peripheral spaces. In: Nunes, Silva C., Buček, J. (eds.) Local Government and Urban Governance in Europe. Urban Book Series, pp. 193–206. Springer, Cham (2017). https://doi.org/10.1007/978-3-319-43979-2_10

View Sheed Assessment for Urban Renovation Strategies: Landscape Values Perception Plays a Role for Urban Development

Arianna Mazzariello, Manuela Nardozza, and Francesco Scorza(✉)

Laboratory of Urban and Regional Systems Engineering, School of Engineering, University of Basilicata, 10, Viale dell'Ateneo Lucano, 85100 Potenza, Italy
ariannamazzariello@live.it, manuela47652@gmail.com,
francesco.scorza@unibas.it

Abstract. The starting position for this research is to consider "viewshed analysis" as a useful basis of the development of spatial planning practices aimed at the protection of the territorial landscape values. Considering the specific case study of the Potenza town, the scope of this work is to ensure landscape protection and to encourage design that look to the redevelopment of specific areas of the urban fabric actually classified as degraded. Together with the analytical approach based on view sheed analysis, local survey and classifications, and land suitability approach, a proposal had been developed in terms of strategic objectives to be included in a wider process of urban regeneration.

Keywords: Urban regeneration · Landscape · View sheed

1 Landscape Perception as a Driver for Urban Regeneration Policies

The focus on landscape comes from the observation that in the last fifty years, the Italian landscape was significantly changed from urban evolution, largely devoid of formal and functional qualities. The enormous development of automobile transport has led to a great dispersion of residential and production functions with huge land take, impairment of the most obvious landscape features, as well as loss of habitat and biodiversity, and energy expenditure [1–5].

The starting position for this research is to consider "viewshed analysis" as a useful basis of the development of spatial planning practices aimed at the protection of the territorial landscape values, which provides quantitative estimations for the major environmental interest areas, combining it with historical and cultural values in a specific urban context realizing a "place based" approach [6–9]. This plan aims at a high landscape quality as a key element in the sustainability and competitiveness of urban areas [10], therefore, is an attempt to optimize the quality of vision by carefully analyzing and reducing degradation of elements within it. The development of the area passes, first, by a heightened awareness of citizens [11–13], especially children because they will be the future key players and decision makers.

S. Misra et al. (Eds.): ICCSA 2019, LNCS 11624, pp. 308–317, 2019.
https://doi.org/10.1007/978-3-030-24311-1_22

The valuation of the potential of a place (and its value) was generally subjective assessment; otherwise based on special considerations, such as proximity to the city center and other services, and it make an assessment on the quality of the landscape, as linked to the perception of three key areas:

- Territorial environment: it gives value to the presence of natural elements on the territory: forests, rivers, areas subject to agricultural development, etc.;
- Cultural Identity: the presence on the territory of historical/cultural areas (e.g. the old villas, bridges, walls, historic monuments);
- Urban context: linked to build-up areas, the characteristics of buildings and the type of settlement system.

Results a complexity of the landscape domain, derived from its systemic character: *"a set of elements, a set of relationships and a set of meanings, meaning elements, relationships and meanings not only in material terms"* [14].

The scope of work is to ensure the landscape protection and encourage proposals that look to the redevelopment of specific areas of the urban fabric, to allow a local identity recovery Potenza's territory. Such ambitions in order to be effective has to consider the three basic principles of planning: *Equity*, Efficiency, Conservation of resources [12, 15, 16].

In a broader context that the New Urban Agenda [17] promote spatial assessment to define intervention priorities for urban regeneration through the implementation of 17 Sustainable Development Goals [18, 19]. Results an ambitious vision of the compact cities, developed along sustainable public transport axes and humanized by a poly-centric growth. Among the main points of the New Urban Agenda is the so-called right to city: "Cities are for people, not for profit" - a principle that drives governments to a schedule that favors the public over the private.

The NUA has the aim of exploiting the urban dynamism as an engine of sustainable development, but against the expansion invades and pollutes increasingly natural and precious resources, in fact natural ecosystems suffered fragmentation [20] and degra-dation. The NUA seeks to counter these phenomena while not providing practical guidance on the application of the principles on the financing of projects and the monitoring.

In the context of the right to the city is the methodological space of this research. In facts it analyze the relationship between people and their surroundings. The landscape is not only *landscape*, so as a vision of what the landscape is, but it is also *inscape*, that is what the landscape returns, as a result of the bond that exists between the place and the personality. For these reasons the landscape involves a number of dimensions which, although different from each other interpenetrate [21].

The perception of the landscape becomes a vehicle for the acquisition of scenic value for the individual and for the local authorities, as well stimulated the search for intervention strategies, appropriately selected in a program of development and urban regeneration. In accordance with the NUA regeneration must take place as a function of sustainability principles also looking to European environmental objectives and on the targeted choices to the preservation and enhancement of the territory, preserving the integrity of the protected areas and favoring a development that is proportional to the housing demand of reality under consideration.

2   Case Study Area: Town Power

The city of Potenza is located in Basilicata, one of the Italian regions. The territorial analysis developed to construct a proposal of intervention for the New Urban Agenda in the city, that considers the perception of the landscape as the selection criteria for projects and areas of intervention, is based on the following basic data:

- Digital Surface Model: with a resolution of 5 m and with the relative shares of the elements above the surface (buildings, trees, etc.) retrieved;
- Charter Land Use: classified in three levels of Corinne Land Cover present for Basilicata;
- Data on pasture or fallow: in shape file format;
- Data of the lots in the industrial valley of Basento river: in shape file format;
- Google Earth as open data useful for mapping urban and landscape degradation.

The viewshed Analysis [22] is a spatial analysis technique that uses algorithms of lines of sight in order to determine the visibility of areas from a certain point of observation of the territory. Viewshed is the area that can be seen from a certain location or from a line (a series of points) of observation. We get the display of the areas as a function of the morphology of the terrain and of the position (and possibly elevation on the ground) of the observation point.

Therefore, the factors that affect the scenic-perceptive analysis, or the identification of the visual relationships that make recognizable the landscape and its characteristic elements, are:

- amplitude of the field of view;
- effects of light and shadow;
- the physical properties of some landscape elements (landmarks);
- sighting dynamic (static or dynamic);
- atmospheric refraction.

In reference to the case study, the choice of the observation points is a characterizing element. In fact, we worry about the perception of the landscape where a citizen can enjoy moving within the major urban parks, squares selected as a meeting place and close to the architectural heritage in historical and cultural significance, and on routes that represent intangible assets related to the performance historical and tourist itineraries parades.

In order to fully represent the view within the urban parks, for each of them were considered to be three observation points in each main observation area. The following figure show the public spaces from which it was carried out the analysis of intervisibility (Fig. 1).

The Land Use Map, at the first level of Corine Land Cover, has been used to assign a criterion of landscape quality, recognizing the maximum value of quality to the wooded areas, both those subject to protection (ex L. 431/85 Galasso), and those who remain excluded; minimum and to urban areas. The remaining part of the data was used to produce a map of degraded areas. By degradation is meant the alteration of the character and landscape quality. The degradation is designed as a component of land

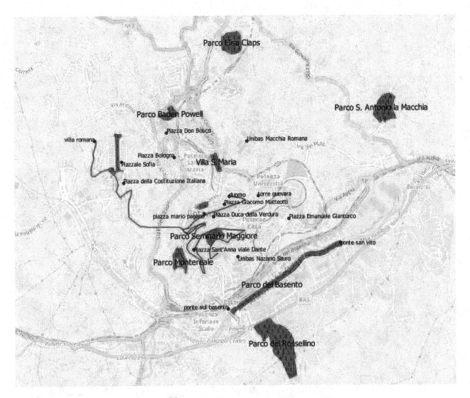

Fig. 1. Representation of OF1 points and routes.

transformation, often these degraded landscapes are mixed with the socio-economic processes deriving from de-industrialization. To identify an objective criterion in the definition of degradation, it is assumed everything within the urban fabric without a clear function representative of urban decay (Fig. 2).

The viewshed analysis, the reclassification of land use classes and the map of the degradation in the town of Potenza, are the criteria used to build a Land Suitability map. This is the base to assess the territorial specialization: analytical approach combining various layers of information for assess where it is strongest susceptibility intervention.

FAO looks to three degrees of suitability [23, 24]:

- S1 = plots that do not have significant limitations or have only minor limitations in order to support a particular type of soil use without a significant reduction in productivity or the benefits and not request further input in excess of an acceptable level;
- S2 = Land with limitations that, overall, are moderately severe for sustained application of the given type of land use; restrictions reduce productivity or benefits and increase the required input to the extent that the overall benefit you get from

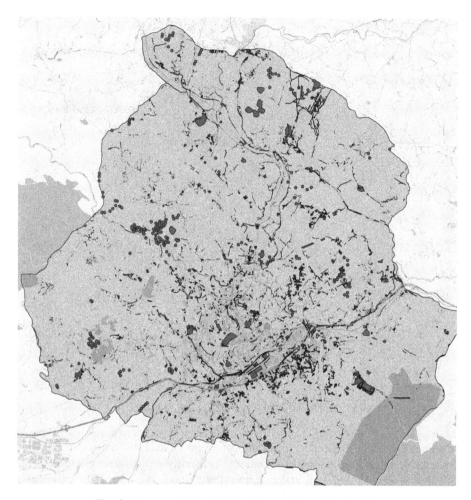

Fig. 2. Representation of urban decay areas and landscape.

use, although still attractive, it will be appreciated than that expected from the land of the S1 class.

- S3 = Land with limitations that, overall, are severe for the use prolonged application of soil data type and so reduce productivity or benefits, or increase the required inputs, that any expenditure will be only marginally justified.

As for the classification of GEODESIGN [25–28] however, they have identified these classes: feasible, suitable, capable, not appropriate, existing.

To obtain this classification different weights had been assigned to the three criteria (greatest weight to the degradation) and, in order to get a realistic scenario, the areas that are not visible had been classified as "not appropriate areas" for intervention since we can't make any consideration about them. Wooded areas with high visibility will be classified as "existing" since they are the areas to be protected without any interventions.

3   Results and Discussion

All areas visible from the observation points had been reclassified according to the visibility rate: from a single point (in white), up to the visibility from seven points (in green) (Fig. 3).

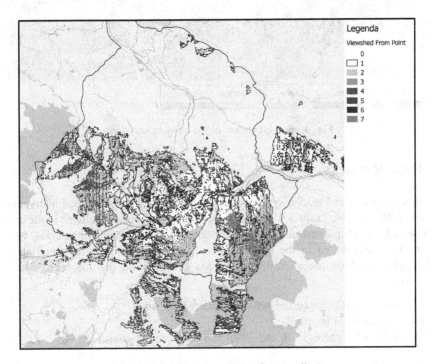

Fig. 3. Visibility rate. (Color figure online)

After that we included degradation analysis: urban-fabric vacant lots, abandoned buildings or in a bad state and maintenance state-suburban or peri – uncultivated, landfills, wind and solar plants. Such datasets represents those areas generating the landscape degradation. In terms of area extend in relation to the entire municipal area we obtained a 3.34%. This has allowed us to obtain the full map of lad suitability according with degradation degree (base-line approach) (Fig. 4).

On the right side of the image shows a zoom on the city center in scale 1: 50000, from which all degraded areas had been classified as "feasible".

In order to estimate intervention priorities threshold equal to 2.19 had been imposed in order to classify "feasible" territorial areas according with the expert perception of landscape degradation.

| Feasable | Suitable | Capable | Not Appropriate | Existing |

Fig. 4. Representation of the baseline scenario.

4 Final Remarks

In the map shown in Fig. 5 a synthetic representation of areas that need intervention (visible with "feasable" value) is available. Such category is more included in the urban area. It includes abandoned industrial lots or abandoned and uncultivated areas, which are mostly concentrated in the peri-urban and interurban fringe. The proposals for action on the whole municipality of Potenza is based on the following specific objectives:

- To preserve and enhance the heritage landscape exists;
- To reinforce local identity;
- To invest in the recovery of the urban and landscape degradation.

The proposed strategic framework for environmental protection will ensure the implementation of restrictions for new anthropic transformations avoiding territorial fragmentation and lad take. On the organizational point of view the protection of the existing landscape has to be monitored by an Observatory of the landscape, whose purpose is to be a meeting place between administrative levels of government, institutions, universities, professional sectors and the entire society operating in the field of landscape management. Other interventions regard the involvement and training in schools with activities already tested and promoted by "Legambiente" pointing at the education of a conscious and informed citizen [11–13, 29–31]. An example is represented by "Ecomuseums" project: a portion of the territory characterized by traditional living environments, natural and historical heritage art worthy of protection, restoration and enhancement.

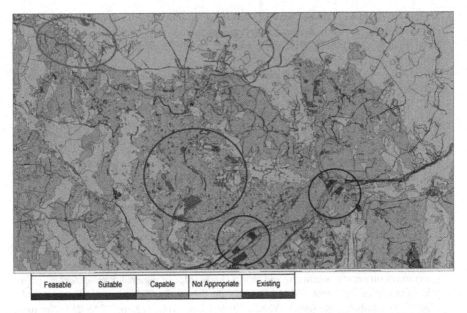

Fig. 5. Diversification of the scenario in relation to the second threshold value and identification of intervention priorities.

These proposals fit into a place based approach connected with several funding opportunities in order to concretely overcome landscape neglecting tradition in Pontenza planning.

A priority is represented by the need to recovery degraded urban areas starting from the redevelopment of vacant lots: in fact, the Land Suitability have been identified with the "feasable" value of the areas that fall mostly in the ASI area. The goal is to break down some sheds that flock to the state of decay (some with asbestos roofing, as shown in the Google Earth map) or abandonment (CIP ZOO) in order to clean up the surrounding area. It is necessary to redevelop the uncultivated areas identified in suburban area: all unused green areas are part of degradation, especially the urban ones, since areas with no functionality in the urban context.

Acknowledgement. This research was developed in the framework of the Territorial Engineering studios (AY 2018-2019) School of Engineering, University of Basilicata. The work reports main evidences from the analysis developed by students supervised by Francesco Scorza.

References

1. Ciabò, S.: The landscape value: interpretive categories, diagnostic techniques and management rules fast planning/ fast monitoring view project sprinkling model view project Serena Ciabò. Planum. J. Urban. **2** (2013)
2. Zoppi, C., Lai, S.: Land-taking processes: an interpretive study concerning an Italian region. Land Use Policy **36**, 369–380 (2014). https://doi.org/10.1016/j.landusepol.2013.09.011

3. Scorza, F., Pilogallo, A., Las Casas, G.: Investigating tourism attractiveness in inland areas: ecosystem services, open data and smart specializations. In: Calabrò, F., Della Spina, L., Bevilacqua, C. (eds.) ISHT 2018. SIST, vol. 100, pp. 30–38. Springer, Cham (2019). https://doi.org/10.1007/978-3-319-92099-3_4

4. Mazzariello, A., Pilogallo, A., Scorza, F., Murgante, B., Las Casas, G.: Carbon stock as an indicator for the estimation of anthropic pressure on territorial components. In: Gervasi, O., et al. (eds.) ICCSA 2018. LNCS, vol. 10964, pp. 697–711. Springer, Cham (2018). https://doi.org/10.1007/978-3-319-95174-4_53

5. Romano, B., Zullo, F.: Landscape fragmentation in Italy. Indices implementation to support territorial policies. In: Campagna, M., De Montis, A., Isola, F., Lai, S., Pira, C., Zoppi, C. (eds.) Planning Support Tools: Policy Analysis, Implementation and Evaluation, pp. 399–414. Franco Angeli, Milano (2012)

6. Barca, F.: An agenda for a reformed cohesion policy (2009)

7. Las Casas, G., Scorza, F.: Un approccio "context-based" e "valutazione integrata" per il futuro della programmazione operativa regionale in Europa. In: Bramanti, A., Salone, C. (eds.) Lo sviluppo territoriale nell'economia della conoscenza: teorie, attori strategie, Collana Scienze Regionali, pp. 253–269. Franco Angeli, Milano (2009)

8. Scorza, F., Casas, G.L., Murgante, B.: Overcoming interoperability weaknesses in e-government processes: organizing and sharing knowledge in regional development programs using ontologies. In: Lytras, M.D., Ordonez de Pablos, P., Ziderman, A., Roulstone, A., Maurer, H., Imber, J.B. (eds.) WSKS 2010. CCIS, vol. 112, pp. 243–253. Springer, Heidelberg (2010). https://doi.org/10.1007/978-3-642-16324-1_26

9. Murgante, B., Scorza, F.: Ontology and spatial planning. In: Murgante, B., Gervasi, O., Iglesias, A., Taniar, D., Apduhan, B.O. (eds.) ICCSA 2011. LNCS, vol. 6783, pp. 255–264. Springer, Heidelberg (2011). https://doi.org/10.1007/978-3-642-21887-3_20

10. European Commission: First Report on Economic and Social Cohesion (1996)

11. Murgante, B., Botonico, G., Graziadei, A., Sassano, G., Amato, F., Scorza, F.: Innovation, technologies, participation: new paradigms towards a 2.0 citizenship. Int. J. Electron. Gov. **11**, 62–88 (2019). https://doi.org/10.1504/IJEG.2019.098814

12. Las Casas, G., Scorza, F.: A renewed rational approach from liquid society towards anti-fragile planning. In: Gervasi, O., et al. (eds.) ICCSA 2017. LNCS, vol. 10409, pp. 517–526. Springer, Cham (2017). https://doi.org/10.1007/978-3-319-62407-5_36

13. Pontrandolfi, P., Scorza, F.: Making urban regeneration feasible: tools and procedures to integrate urban agenda and UE cohesion regional programs. In: Gervasi, O., et al. (eds.) ICCSA 2017. LNCS, vol. 10409, pp. 564–572. Springer, Cham (2017). https://doi.org/10.1007/978-3-319-62407-5_40

14. Castiglioni, B., Parascandolo, F., Tanca, M.: Landscape as Mediator, Landscape as Commons International Perspectives on Landscape Research, Padova (2015)

15. Casas, G.L., Scorza, F.: Sustainable planning: a methodological toolkit. In: Gervasi, O., et al. (eds.) ICCSA 2016. LNCS, vol. 9786, pp. 627–635. Springer, Cham (2016). https://doi.org/10.1007/978-3-319-42085-1_53

16. Las Casas, G., Scorza, F., Murgante, B.: New urban agenda and open challenges for urban and regional planning. In: Calabrò, F., Della Spina, L., Bevilacqua, C. (eds.) ISHT 2018. SIST, vol. 100, pp. 282–288. Springer, Cham (2019). https://doi.org/10.1007/978-3-319-92099-3_33

17. UN Habitat: New Urban Agenda, United Nations (2017)

18. Hák, T., Janoušková, S., Moldan, B.: Sustainable development goals: a need for relevant indicators. Ecol. Indic. **60**, 565–573 (2016). https://doi.org/10.1016/j.ecolind.2015.08.003

19. UN: Sustainable Development Goals (2014). http://www.igbp.net/download/18.62dc35801456272b46d51/1399290813740/NL82-SDGs.pdf. https://doi.org/10.1038/505587a

20. Saganeiti, L., Favale, A., Pilogallo, A., Scorza, F., Murgante, B.: Assessing urban fragmentation at regional scale using sprinkling indexes. Sustainability **10**, 3274 (2018). https://doi.org/10.3390/su10093274
21. Petrocelli, E.: Il Paesaggio: un tema transdisciplinare, Napoli (2019). https://doi.org/10.6093/978-88-6887-052-2
22. Joly, D., et al.: A quantitative approach to the visual evaluation of landscape. Ann. Assoc. Am. Geogr. **99**, 292–308 (2009). https://doi.org/10.1080/00045600802708473
23. Higgins, G.M., Kassam, A.H., Higgins Ah Kassam, G.M.: The FAO Agro-ecological zone approach to determination of land potentlal. Pedologie **XXXI**, 147–168 (1981)
24. Bydekerke, L., Van Ranst, E., Vanmechelen, L., Groenemans, R.: Land suitability assessment for cherimoya in southern Ecuador using expert knowledge and GIS. Agric. Ecosyst. Environ. **69**, 89–98 (1998). https://doi.org/10.1016/S0167-8809(98)00090-5
25. Steinitz, C.: A Frame Work for Geodesign. Changing Geography by Design (2012)
26. Campagna, M.: Geodesign from theory to practice: from metaplanning to 2nd generation of planning support systems. Tema - J. L. Use Mob. Environ. (2014). https://doi.org/10.6092/1970-9870/2516
27. Padula, A., Fiore, P., Pilogallo, A., Scorza, F.: Collaborative approach in strategic development planning for small municipalities. Applying geodesign methodology and tools for a new municipal strategy in Scanzano Jonico. In: Leone, A., Gargiulo, C. (eds.) Environmental and Territorial Modelling for Planning and Design, pp. 665–672. FedOApress (2018). https://doi.org/10.6093/978-88-6887-048-5
28. Fiore, P., Padula, A., Pilogallo, A., Scorza, F.: Facing urban regeneration issues through geodesign approach. The case of Gravina in Puglia. In: Leone, A., Gargiulo, C. (eds.) Environmental and Territorial Modelling for Planning and Design. FedOAPress (2018). https://doi.org/10.6093/978-88-6887-048-5
29. Scorza, F., Grecu, V.: Assessing sustainability: research directions and relevant issues. In: Gervasi, O., et al. (eds.) ICCSA 2016. LNCS, vol. 9786, pp. 642–647. Springer, Cham (2016). https://doi.org/10.1007/978-3-319-42085-1_55
30. Dvarioniene, J., Grecu, V., Lai, S., Scorza, F.: Four perspectives of applied sustainability: research implications and possible integrations. In: Gervasi, O., et al. (eds.) ICCSA 2017. LNCS, vol. 10409, pp. 554–563. Springer, Cham (2017). https://doi.org/10.1007/978-3-319-62407-5_39
31. Las Casas, G., Scorza, F., Murgante, B.: Conflicts and sustainable planning: peculiar instances coming from Val D'agri structural inter-municipal plan. In: Papa, R., Fistola, R., Gargiulo, C. (eds.) Smart Planning: Sustainability and Mobility in the Age of Change. GET, pp. 163–177. Springer, Cham (2018). https://doi.org/10.1007/978-3-319-77682-8_10

Land Suitability Analysis for New Urban Development Strategies Oriented to 'Active Mobility' and Walkability: Potenza Case

Giusy Brigante, Maria Carleo, and Francesco Scorza$^{(\boxtimes)}$

School of Engineering, Laboratory of Urban and Regional Systems Engineering,
University of Basilicata, 10, Viale Dell'Ateneo Lucano, 85100 Potenza, Italy
giusy.brigante92@gmail.com, carleo.maria@gmail.com,
francesco.scorza@unibas.it

Abstract. An urban characteristic directly connected with the principle of well-being and with sustainability concept is walkability. It influences the way people perceive and experience the city. The objective to increase pedestrian urban mobility in the city of Potenza represents the general purpose of this research. The analytical approach discussed in the paper carried out an assessment of the propensity to walkability of the city of Potenza, focusing on different attributes assigned to the roads and divided into three different groups: road characteristics, comfort and safety. The hypothesized interventions, in view of a strategic and integrated approach to urban planning, are aimed at completing the urban road network infrastructure for active mobility in Potenza and represent a precondition for citizens to implement modal shift from your own vehicle to more sustainable forms of travel in the city.

Keywords: Walkability · Urban development · Sustainability

1 Introduction

Sustainable mobility is an objective pursued of many countries, driven by the need to protect the planet, promote relevant welfare and improve the comprehensive development. 17 are the intentions/objectives of the United Nations gathered in Agenda 2030 [1, 2]. Of them, 4 fall within the sustainable mobility (Health and Wellness - Clean energy is available - Cities and sustainable communities - Climate action).

A key element is connected with the principle of well-being to that of sustainability is the concept of walkability. Wanting to provide a more comprehensive definition, but at the same time easy deduction say that walkability is the spatial quality and the ability to welcome and encourage pedestrian mobility in urban and along the roads (cfr [3–5].

It influences the way people perceive and experience the city. A key example it addresses global attention is inherent in the city of Stockholm. In virtuous northern metropolis and 'witnessed in recent years to a net reduction in accidents and a significant lowering the number of road victims as well as the emergence of greener cities, less polluted, free from the car, ready to welcome young people, workers, families and

© Springer Nature Switzerland AG 2019
S. Misra et al. (Eds.): ICCSA 2019, LNCS 11624, pp. 318–330, 2019.
https://doi.org/10.1007/978-3-030-24311-1_23

tourists. This objective and 'reached with an increase of the pedestrian internal mobility, on two wheels and electric.

We may affirm that to develop a 'sustainable' and walkable city represents an heavy challenge in conjunction with many factors including: the morphological characteristics, the climate but also the economic interests of the big oil multinationals.

Shrinking the scope on a small town 'of southern Italy: Potenza, it is possible to understand how and why 'morphological characteristics and climate penalize the spread of sustainable mobility, made even more' difficult by fragmentation the territory [6] which disadvantages optimal public service management and thus induces the public to the use of private vehicles.

In the next section, attention is focused on sustainable mobility from a global point of view, starting with an analysis of the objectives, and proceeding to the definition of the purposes referred to in the NUA.

In the paragraph 3 analyzes in-depth case-study of Potenza city also with the objective to proceed to a critical review of PUM, configured from a European guidelines in order to obtain a new PUMS.

With a 'geo-swot' analysis [7], all the territorial features have been outlined, taking into account, through brainstorming, the opinions and views of all the players in the game who may be affected or influenced in a more or less appreciated the process.

In the paragraph 4, and is' taken as a reference, the methodology of urban walkability assessment of the city of Alghero proposed by Blečić et al. [5], had been applied to *the case of Potenza municipality according to several specific adjustments.* Finally a land suitability had been achieved: it represents the observation of potential suitability of the area to be transformed considering the program structure of the LFM.

In the paragraph 5, taking into account the data acquired from the previous analysis preliminary assumptions on a strategic vision for the future of Potenza walkability were discussed.

2 NUA and Urban Sustainable Mobility in the Framework of EU New Cohesion Policy

The New Urban Agenda adopted by United Nations Conference on sustainable urban and development (Habitat III held in Quito, Ecuador, 17 to 20 October 2016) [1] represents a global reference framework for urban development. The objectives proposed by the New Urban Agenda are related general issues on which the agreement of sighing States identified a global commitment on: education for all, dignity at work, hunger, gender equality, the environment and urban living. They are interconnected and indivisible objectives and balance the three dimensions of sustainable development: economic, social and environmental [8, 9].

In reference to sustainable urban mobility there New Urban Agenda expresses a focused commitment to:

- *We are committed to promoting public spaces safe, inclusive, accessible, green and quality, including roads, cycle paths and sidewalks, plazas, promenades, gardens and parks, which are multifunctional areas for social interaction and inclusion, health and human well-being, economic exchange and expression and cultural dialogue among different people and cultures, and are designed and operated to ensure human development and build a peaceful, inclusive and participatory society, and to promote coexistence, connectivity and the inclusion social;*

- *We will support the delivery of well-designed network of roads safe, affordable, green, quality and other public spaces accessible to everyone and free from crime and violence (...) involving people in public spaces and promote walkability and cycling with ' aim to improve the health and well-being;*
- *We will take measures to improve road safety and integrate it into sustainable mobility and in the planning and design of transport infrastructure. Along with raising awareness, we will promote the security approach required in the Decade of Action for Road Safety, with special attention to the needs of all women and girls, as well as children and youth, the elderly and people with disabilities and people in vulnerable situations. We will work to adopt, implement and enforce policies and measures to actively protect and promote the safety of pedestrians and bicycle mobility (...) We will promote as a priority healthy and safe routes to school for each child;*
- *We will promote universal access to urban mobility, allowing a significant participation in social and economic activities in cities, integrating shippingrto and mobility plans in urban and regional plans and the promotion of a wide range of transportation and mobility options, in particular by supporting: a significant increase in accessible infrastructure, secure, efficient, affordable and sustainable public transport, as well as non-motorized options, such as walking and cycling, giving the above priority over the private motorized transport;*
- *We will encourage national and local governments to develop and expand financial - instruments that enable them to improve infrastructure and transport and mobility systems such as (...) walking and safe cycling infrastructure, sufficient and appropriate (...) to reduce congestion and pollution and improving efficiency, connectivity, accessibility, health and quality of life.*

3   Case Study Area: Potenza Town

The city of Potenza in Italy, with its 67,122 inhabitants, is the most populous city in Basilicata, with a demographic weight of around 12% on a regional basis and around 18% on a provincial basis. The population is distributed over an area of 175.43 km^2 with a density of 382.6 inhabitants per square kilometer. The morphology of the territory is purely mountainous, recording 1345 m s.l.m. as maximum quota and 605 m s.l.m. as a minimum quota; the maximum quota in urban areas is 819 m s.l.m. This is a highly vulnerable territory, both in terms of seismicity and hydrogeology. The city is characterized by the presence of various services: hospital, university, high schools, archiepiscopal see, prefecture, decentralized offices of the state administration, court, administrative offices of the Region and of the Province, centers of economic activities.

The town due to morphological reasons but also due to inadequate urban plans, has consolidated structural problems in urban mobility. The structure and functionality of the local public transport network is strongly conditioned by the morphology of the city and the characteristics of the road network, forcing tortuous routes with conventional means of modest capacity. To overcome the considerable height differences existing within the city, Potenza is crossed by a mechanized escalator infrastructure, the longest in Europe, which altogether extends over a distance of 1.3 km.

The city approved a Urban Mobility Plan (PUM) in 2008, which proposes a multimodal and multi-agency approach to urban mobility ensuring environmental, technical and economical sustainability. With the growing attention to the issues of sustainable mobility and the pursuit of urban development goals set by the European Union, it would be necessary to revise such mobility plan assuming new European guidelines (Sustainable Mobility Urban Plan (SMUP)).

This work considers as an assumption the strengthening of pedestrian mobility in the urban environment as an operational tool to structure a policy for sustainable urban development with consequent advantages in the field of transport and on public health, the economy and the environment. Walking is the most natural and spontaneous way of moving from one place to another and a way through which citizens become aware of the environment features around them. Individuals walking have the opportunity to establish a direct and non-mediated relationship with urban spaces, this helps to widen access to the opportunities offered by the city and make it easier, easier and more pleasant to use [10].

Due to the urban dispersion that has affected the city since the 1960s, pedestrian mobility has become an unusual option for citizens to move. Potenza has an urban dispersion index among the highest in Italy, equal to about 90% [11]. The phenomenon of urban dispersion manifests itself in the gradual abandonment of the historic center towards peripheries, complicating the management of infrastructures and services and making relations between the urban area and peripheral areas unsustainable.

The Integrated Territorial Investment of Urban Development in the city of Potenza [12] is the main strategic intervention program for the city financed with EU funds. It aims to strengthen the role of urban poles that supplies local services for regional basins: the city of Potenza has assumed such role over the years.

Within the ITI, the sustainable mobility strategy for the city is directed towards specific actions concerning: the infrastructure of new interchange areas, both rubber-rubber for the transfer from extra-urban buses to urban buses in order to reduce the overall bus traffic in the city, both rubber-installations to implement the use of mechanized systems linking with the historic center; the gradual decommissioning of the more obsolete TPL buses, to be replaced with Euro 6 and electric vehicles to achieve a reduction in polluting emissions and the development of an ITS infomobility project, to provide innovative services in the various modes of public transport and traffic management and urban mobility networks.

The pedestrian mobility of the urban environment and in particular of the road that includes the sidewalks and roadways, influence the way in which individuals perceive and use the city. What the concept of walkability allows to detect, in fact, is the quality of accessibility: how and how much the urban environment is able to encourage walking and to offer itself as a platform for a daily life based on pedestrian mobility [13, 14].

The classification of an urban area, in addition to the presence of opportunities, places of interest and services in space and in addition to their distances, it becomes relevant if they can also be reached on foot or by bicycle. Additionally If the pedestrian connection path is pleasant and spatially integrated with the environment surrounding, if it is rich in activity, if it is well maintained and perceived as safe, if it is not subservient to car traffic for design choices or for the prevailing social practices of use of space [15]. The research work was developed in the framework of the LFA methodology [7]. The SWOT analysis and the problem tree are shown below, from which emerges the picture of the critical issues identified regarding the general strategy to improve urban mobility according to environmental sustainability criteria (Table 1 and Fig. 1).

Table 1. SWOT analysis

Strengths:	Weaknesses
University city (30% of students living away from home on about 8000) Safe city compared to larger realities Presence of personnel to facilitate pedestrian crossing near to school Low pollution Presence of green areas Presence of pedestrian area in the historic centre Presence of places dedicated to culture, sport and leisure Presence of escalators and elevators Cultural and religious events	Weather and climate characteristics of the territory Morphology of the territory Demographic decline Bad rainwater runoff Low walkability (degradation, absence and inadequate size of sidewalks, poor lighting) Low maintenance of escalators Limited hours for the use of escalators and elevators Absence of information points Little control of isolated areas Fragmentation of the urban territory Peripheral shopping areas Cultural heritage not widespread and used Poor architectural, historical and urban quality High motorization rate (72 cars per 100 inhabitants)
Opportunities:	Threats:
Operational Programme - European Regional Development Fund (PO - ERDF) Urban Plans for Sustainable Mobility (UPSM) Bremen Declaration Amsterdam Pact European Urban Agenda 2014–2020 (5% of ERDF resources are allocated for sustainable urban development) Initiatives that promote sustainable mobility Administrative measures decided by public authorities for sustainable mobility development Natura 2000 Network Tourist, cultural and image effects thanks to Matera European Capital of Culture 2019 Rural Development Programs (RDP) - European Agricultural Fund for Rural Development (EAFRD)	Aging of the population (189,9 elderly people per 100 young people), depopulation and youth emigration Population profile Unsupervised pedestrians (security, stray dogs, prostitution, drugs, etc.)

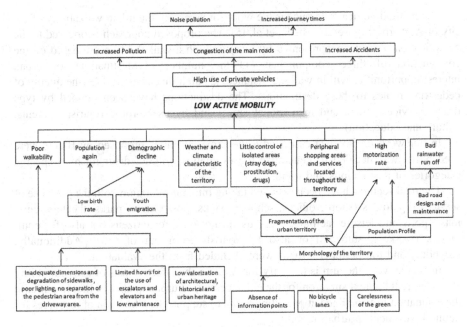

Fig. 1. Problem tree

4 Walkability Assessment: Criteria and Land Suitability

Walkability describes the characteristic of the urban environment to welcome and encourage walking and represents an indicator for assessing the liveability of places.

A substantial literature produced in recent years identifies walkability: the attribute of the physical environment to "be walked" as an important requirement of the quality of life in the city [16, 17]. In this context, walkability represents not only as an objective to be pursued in order to improve the citizens' quality of life, but also as a tool that urban planners and designers can use to re-develop methods of assessing the quality of life.

Providing a measure of walkability is a complex problem due to the multidimensional and multi-scalar nature that the concept implies. Therefore, measuring walkability levels can be interpreted by classifying the ability of a space to be traveled on foot; which translates into building a methodology that is able to synthetically express this quality of urban spaces. In recent decades, various methods and tools for measuring and assessing urban walkability have been proposed, which have allowed us to deepen our knowledge of the interdependent relationships between the organization of urban space and the spatial behavior of individuals.

Our approach is aimed at identifying the aspects that characterize the quality of the roads and that predispose the urban environment to encourage pedestrian mobility.

The assessment of walkability in Potenza was performed by associating to each arch of the road network, a specific set of attributes describing physical characteristics and qualitative aspects of roads. Each of these attributes has been assigned through in situ observations.

The methodological reference is the work for assessing the urban walkability of the city of Alghero proposed by Blečić et al. [5]. The proposed approach is oriented to the classification of routes (represented by arcs) through a walkability score based on the combination of three components: (1) the number of destinations of urban interest/opportunities within walking distance; (2) their distances; and (3) the quality of pedestrian routes to these destinations. The destinations have been divided by type (trade, services, green and recreational areas) and by user profile (tourists, parents, culture and education).

In our work on Potenza case study, the same attributes proposed by Blečić were used but it was decided to generalize the evaluation without distinguishing specific categories of destinations and users.

The road sections have been assessed taking into consideration both the presence of services typologies (shops, offices, schools, banks, post offices, parks, theaters, cinemas, sports and leisure facilities, etc.), useful not only for citizens but also for commuters (workers, students) or also for tourists from out of town. Additionally, secondary and too peripheral roads were excluded from the evaluation.

In Blečić work the aim is to verify for Alghero the effectiveness of active mobility on the current context situation for the enhancement of urban quality of life; in our case the evaluation is also aimed at providing a tool to support the allocation of resources for public investment in urban mobility.

Some of the attributes used represent requirements and characteristics of easily observable, recognizable and measurable roads such as: the presence of bicycle lanes, proximity to escalators and elevators, one-way streets, stops and parking along the road, the slope, the lighting, quality and level of maintenance of the flooring. Other attributes require a technical evaluation judgment. It is the case of "useful width of the pedestrian section" presenting values ranging from very wide sidewalks to the complete absence of space for pedestrians along road arcs. The separation of the pedestrian area from the driveway area is represented by the presence of horizontal and vertical physical elements (flower beds, trees, fences, walls, etc.) that increase the safety of pedestrian. Since the pleasantness of the walk is also given by the aesthetic aspect of the space surrounding the streets, they have been used as attributes: environmental interest and historical, architectural and urban interest, evaluating the presence and prevalence of pleasant elements or disturbing. The possibility of sheltering from sun, rain and wind, thanks to the presence of naturalistic and architectural elements, was assessed by the attribute of the shelter, a further factor of comfort for the pedestrian together with the possibility of parking and sitting, offered by the benches but also from staircases, walls and edges of the fountains. Another important attribute is the presence of activities and services, which not only constitute elements of attractiveness for pedestrians, but also increase the level of safety perceived along the roads thanks to the presence of other people and the increase in lighting. The attribute integration with the urban fabric serves to describe how the streets are integrated into the surrounding environment and finally the urban fabric attribute is evaluated based on the presence of squares, green spaces and parks (dense urban fabric) or based on in the presence of abandoned or non-built areas (low density urban fabric).

The attributes chosen for the assessment of the walkability of the streets of Potenza, have been divided into three groups: road characteristics, comfort and safety and each of them has been arbitrarily assigned a weight according to the degree of importance that has been given to each group (5, 3 and 1 respectively).

For each road section considered a walkability index was calculated, obtained as a linear combination of the judgments given to all the attributes considered for the evaluation, weighed with the values assigned to the groups to which they belong.

Below is the synoptic table of the attributes, divided into the three main groups, specifying the values assigned to each with reference to the descriptive meaning considered.

Table 2. Land suitability criteria.

Groups and weights	Attributes	Values
Road features Weight 5	**Width of sidewalk**	Wide (0.8) - Comfortable (0.7) - Minimum (0.5) - Inadequate (0.3) - Lacking (0.1)
	Cyclability	Exclusive lane (0.8) - Off-road lane (0.5) - On-road lane (0.3) - Not possible (0.1)
	Escalators	Directly connected (0.8) - Near (0.5) - Distant (0.1)
	Paving	Fine (0.8) - Cheap (0.5) - Bumpy(0.1)
	Path slope	Smooth (0.8) - Light (0.5) - Rise (0.1)
	Separation of pedestrian route from car roadway	Marked/Strong (0.8) - Weak (0.5) - Lacking (0.1)
Comfort Weight 3	**Lighting**	Excellent (0.8) - Good (0.6) - Inadequate (0.3) - Lacking (0.1)
	Sitting	Extended (0.8) - Thin (0.5) - Lacking (0.1)
	Shelter and shade (trees, cantilever roofs, porticos, balconies)	Strong (0.8) - Weak (0.5) - Lacking (0.1)
	Urban texture	Dense (0.8) - Park or green space (0.5) - Low density (0.3) - Undeveloped land (0.1)
	Frequency of services and activities	Abundant (0.8) - Somewhat (0.6) - Rare (0.3) - No services/activities (0.1)
	Transparency and permeability of the public-private space	Integrated (0.8) - Filtered (0.5) - Separated (0.1)
	Attractiveness from an environmental point of view	Preponderance of pleasant elements (0.8) - Presence of a few pleasant elements (0.6) - Lack of pleasant or disturbance elements (0.4) - Presence of few disturbance elements (0.2)
	Attractiveness from an architectural and urban viewpoint	Preponderance of pleasant elements (0.8) - Presence of a few pleasant elements (0.6) - Lack of pleasant or disturbance elements (0.4) - Presence of few disturbance elements (0.2)
Security Weight 1	**Width of the roadway**	Pedestrian way (0.8) - 1 car lane (0.6) - 2 car lanes (0.5) - 3 car lanes (0.3)
	One way street	Pedestrian way (0.8) - Yes (0.5) - No (0.1)
	On-street parking	Prohibited parking (0.8) - Permitted (0.5) - Illegal parking (0.1)

The walkability index, obtained for each road arc, allowed to construct synthesis maps in a GIS environment according to a land suitability approach [18]. Land suitability represents the degree of suitability of a land for a specific land use or for a specific transformation, and can be assessed for current conditions (suitability of the current land) or after an improvement action (suitability of the potential land). The suitability of real land is based on current soil conditions, without applying any input; information is based on physical environmental data obtained from soil surveys or from land resources. The potential suitability is the suitability that could be achieved after the land has been improved.

The methodology of GEODESIGN [19–22] foresees that the land suitability is represented through the following five classes: feasible, suitable, capable, not appropriate and existing; each class is symbolized by a different color: dark green, intermediate green, light green, yellow and red respectively.

The following maps represents the results obtained in terms of land suitability of main road network for walkability development policies in of Potenza (Figs. 2 and 3).

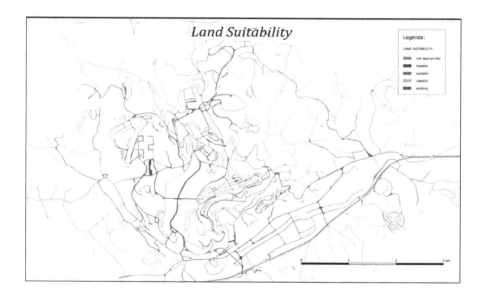

Description of the evaluation: increase and promote active mobility in the city of Potenza. The classification was carried out taking into consideration the physical characteristics of the roads (width of the pedestrian section, number of vehicle lanes, paving, slope of the route, lighting, etc.), their connection with the surrounding urban fabric, the presence of activities and services and elements with environmental, historical, architectural and urban interest

FEASIBLE	SUITABLE	CAPABLE	NOT APPROPRIATE	EXISTING
Roads that limit active mobility due to the absence of the characteristic elements of walkability in the most central areas of the city and in the areas where services, cultural and leisure	Roads that do not have overall characteristics that are favorable to pedestrian mobility, since most require interventions.	Roads suitable for walking but need some improvements to make active mobility optimal.	Areas that do not need intervention	Roads with high walkability: optimal lighting, possibility of parking and sitting, presence of activities and services,

Fig. 2. Land suitability (Color figure online)

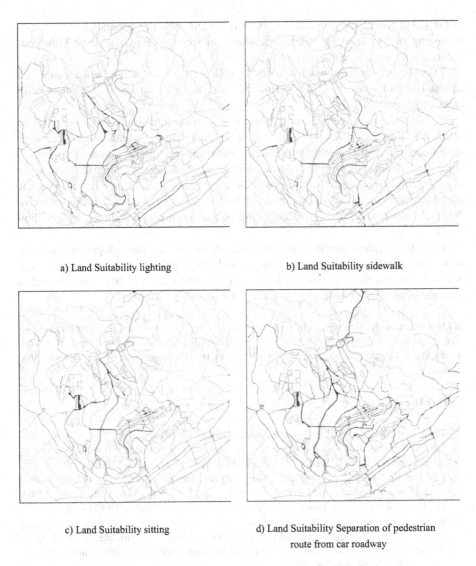

a) Land Suitability lighting   b) Land Suitability sidewalk

c) Land Suitability sitting   d) Land Suitability Separation of pedestrian
                                                route from car roadway

Fig. 3. Land suitability per attributes (Color figure online)

5 Strategic Vision and Conclusions

This study carried out an assessment of the propensity to walkability of the city of Potenza, focusing on different attributes assigned to the roads and divided into three different groups: road characteristics, comfort and safety.

Starting from the evidences discussed through the land suitability calculations described in the previous paragraph, a strategic proposal based on a program structure (objectives, results and actions) has been designed. The general objective is to enhance active mobility in the city. This is consistent with the pillars of the NUA [1], with the

SDGs [23]. The specific objectives, interconnected with the general objective, are: improving pedestrian areas, increasing safety in isolated areas and improving connections with peripheral areas.

These objectives refer to active mobility system in Potenza that have been analyzed through the attributes in Table 2. This critical description makes it easy to identify types of intervention.

The hypothesized interventions, in view of a strategic and integrated approach to urban planning [8, 9, 24–30], are aimed at completing the urban road network infrastructure for active mobility in Potenza and represent a precondition for citizens to implement modal shift from your own vehicle to more sustainable forms of travel in the city. A preliminary estimate of the cost of the interventions was also produced, which is useful to define the order of magnitude of the investment (which due to the nature of the works must be carried out mainly with public resources) amounting to 7 million euros.

Even in morphologically complex contexts, due to the high slopes or meteorological and climatic characteristics, with the right intervention and planning policies, it is possible to improve the conditions of the roads and make the city walkable with a consequent increasing pedestrian mobility of citizens.

Acknowledgement. This research was developed in the framework of the Territorial Engineering studios (AY 2018-2019) School of Engineering, University of Basilicata. The work reports main evidences from the analysis developed by students supervised by Francesco Scorza.

References

1. UN HABITAT: New Urban Agenda. United Nations (2017)
2. UN: Sustainable Development Goals (2014). https://doi.org/10.1038/505587a. http://www.igbp.net/download/18.62dc35801456272b46d51/1399290813740/NL82-SDGs.pdf
3. Carbone, R., Saganeiti, L., Scorza, F., Murgante, B.: Increasing the walkability level through a participation process. In: Gervasi, O., et al. (eds.) ICCSA 2018. LNCS, vol. 10964, pp. 113–124. Springer, Cham (2018). https://doi.org/10.1007/978-3-319-95174-4_9
4. Blecic, I., Cecchini, A., Congiu, T., Pazzola, M., Trunfio, G.A.: A design and planning support system for walkability and pedestrian accessibility. In: Murgante, B., et al. (eds.) ICCSA 2013. LNCS, vol. 7974, pp. 284–293. Springer, Heidelberg (2013). https://doi.org/10.1007/978-3-642-39649-6_20
5. Blečić, I., Cecchini, A., Congiu, T., Fancello, G., Trunfio, G.A.: Evaluating walkability: a capability-wise planning and design support system. Int. J. Geogr. Inf. Sci. **29**, 1350–1374 (2015). https://doi.org/10.1080/13658816.2015.1026824
6. Saganeiti, L., Favale, A., Pilogallo, A., Scorza, F., Murgante, B.: Assessing urban fragmentation at regional scale using sprinkling indexes. Sustainability **10**, 3274 (2018). https://doi.org/10.3390/su10093274
7. Casas, G.L., Scorza, F.: Sustainable planning: a methodological toolkit. In: Gervasi, O., et al. (eds.) ICCSA 2016. LNCS, vol. 9786, pp. 627–635. Springer, Cham (2016). https://doi.org/10.1007/978-3-319-42085-1_53

8. Dvarioniene, J., Grecu, V., Lai, S., Scorza, F.: Four perspectives of applied sustainability: research implications and possible integrations. In: Gervasi, O., et al. (eds.) ICCSA 2017. LNCS, vol. 10409, pp. 554–563. Springer, Cham (2017). https://doi.org/10.1007/978-3-319-62407-5_39

9. Scorza, F., Grecu, V.: Assessing sustainability: research directions and relevant issues. In: Gervasi, O., et al. (eds.) ICCSA 2016. LNCS, vol. 9786, pp. 642–647. Springer, Cham (2016). https://doi.org/10.1007/978-3-319-42085-1_55

10. Massimiliano, B.: Mobilità pedonale in città. In: ISPRA (ed.) XIII Rapporto "Qualità dell'ambiente urbano" (2017)

11. Consumo di suolo, dinamiche territoriali e servizi ecosistemici (2016)

12. Potenza Municipality: Investimento Territoriale Integrato (ITI) per lo Sviluppo Urbano Città di Potenza (2017). http://www.comune.potenza.it/wp-content/uploads/2017/09/Documento-Strategico_ITI-Sviluppo-Urbano-Potenza.pdf

13. Porta, S., Renne, J.L.: Linking urban design to sustainability: formal indicators of social urban sustainability field in Perth, Western Australia. Urban Des. Int. 10, 51–64 (2005)

14. Ewing, R., Handy, S.: Measuring the unmeasurable: urban design qualities related to walkability. J. Urban Des. 14, 65–84 (2009)

15. Blečić, I., Cecchini, A., Fancello, G., Talu, V., Trunfio, G.A.: Camminabilità e capacità urbane: valutazione e supporto alla decisione e alla pianificazione urbanistica. Territ. Ital. (2015). https://doi.org/10.14609/Ti_1_15_4i

16. Talen, E.: Pedestrian access as a measure of urban quality. Plan. Pract. Res. 17, 257–278 (2002)

17. Frank, L.D., et al.: The development of a walkability index: application to the neighborhood quality of life study. Br. J. Sports Med. 29, 1–38 (2009)

18. Collins, M.G., Steiner, F.R., Rushman, M.J.: Land-use suitability analysis in the United States: historical development and promising technological achievements. Environ. Manag. 28, 611–621 (2001). https://doi.org/10.1007/s002670010247

19. Campagna, M., De Montis, A., Isola, F., Lai, S., Pira, C., Zoppi, C.: Planning support tools: policy analysis, implementation and evaluation. In: Proceedings of the Seventh International Conference on Informatics and Urban and Regional Planning INPUT2012: Proceedings of the Seventh International Conference on Informatics and Ur (2012)

20. Campagna, M.: Metaplanning: about designing the geodesign process. Landsc. Urban Plan. 156, 118–128 (2016). https://doi.org/10.1016/J.LANDURBPLAN.2015.08.019

21. Campagna, M.: Geodesign from theory to practice: from metaplanning to 2nd generation of planning support systems. Tema - J. Land Use Mob. Environ (2014). https://doi.org/10.6092/1970-9870/2516

22. Batty, M.: Defining geodesign (= GIS + design?). Environ. Plan. B Plan. Des. 40, 1–2 (2013). https://doi.org/10.1068/b4001ed

23. Hák, T., Janoušková, S., Moldan, B.: Sustainable development goals: a need for relevant indicators. Ecol. Ind. 60, 565–573 (2016). https://doi.org/10.1016/j.ecolind.2015.08.003

24. Las Casas, G., Scorza, F., Murgante, B.: Conflicts and sustainable planning: peculiar instances coming from val d'agri structural inter-municipal plan. In: Papa, R., Fistola, R., Gargiulo, C. (eds.) Smart Planning: Sustainability and Mobility in the Age of Change. GET, pp. 163–177. Springer, Cham (2018). https://doi.org/10.1007/978-3-319-77682-8_10

25. Scorza, F., Las Casas, G.B., Murgante, B.: Spatializing open data for the assessment and the improvement of territorial and social cohesion. ISPRS Ann. Photogram. Remote Sens. Spat. Inf. Sci. 3 (2016)

26. Pontrandolfi, P., Scorza, F.: Sustainable urban regeneration policy making: inclusive participation practice. In: Gervasi, O., et al. (eds.) ICCSA 2016. LNCS, vol. 9788, pp. 552–560. Springer, Cham (2016). https://doi.org/10.1007/978-3-319-42111-7_44

27. Murgante, B., Botonico, G., Graziadei, A., Sassano, G., Amato, F., Scorza, F.: Innovation, technologies, participation: new paradigms towards a 2.0 citizenship. Int. J. Electron. Gov. **11**, 62–88 (2019). https://doi.org/10.1504/IJEG.2019.098814

28. Pontrandolfi, P., Scorza, F.: Making urban regeneration feasible: tools and procedures to integrate urban agenda and UE cohesion regional programs. In: Gervasi, O., et al. (eds.) ICCSA 2017. LNCS, vol. 10409, pp. 564–572. Springer, Cham (2017). https://doi.org/10. 1007/978-3-319-62407-5_40

29. Scorza, F., Pilogallo, A., Las Casas, G.: Investigating tourism attractiveness in inland areas: ecosystem services, open data and smart specializations. In: Calabrò, F., Della Spina, L., Bevilacqua, C. (eds.) ISHT 2018. SIST, vol. 100, pp. 30–38. Springer, Cham (2019). https:// doi.org/10.1007/978-3-319-92099-3_4

30. Scorza, F., Murgante, B., Las Casas, G., Fortino, Y., Pilogallo, A.: Investigating territorial specialization in tourism sector by ecosystem services approach. In: Stratigea, A., Kavroudakis, D. (eds.) Mediterranean Cities and Island Communities. PI, pp. 161–179. Springer, Cham (2019). https://doi.org/10.1007/978-3-319-99444-4_7

Integrated Public Transport Planning for Urban Sustainable Development in Potenza Town

Erika Di Pierro, Serena Serravallo, and Francesco Scorza(✉)

School of Engineering, Laboratory of Urban and Regional Systems Engineering,
University of Basilicata, 10, Viale dell'Ateneo Lucano, 85100 Potenza, Italy
erika.erikal10@tiscali.it, s.serravallo@gmail.com,
francesco.scorza@unibas.it

Abstract. Public transport represents a critical area of intervention for urban development. Assuming UN – HABITAT New Urban Agenda as a reference framework, the experimentation proposed in this work promotes an integrated approach for urban development policies. The main purpose it to implement measures, based on territorial specialization and to design place-based development strategies structured on sustainable mobility:

Main objects of the proposed approach are: the infrastructures of new interchange areas; phasing out the obsolete TPL buses to be replaced by Euro6 and electric vehicles for the reduction of polluting emissions; development of an ICT info-mobility project related to further and more incisive actions on mobility technological systems. The synthetical representation is based on land suitability approach delivered according with GEODESIGN methodological framework.

Keywords: Sustainable transport, sustainable urban development ·
Urban agenda

1 NUA and Urban Sustainable Mobility in the Framework of EU New Cohesion Policy

A city model looking at advanced criteria of sustainability, inclusiveness and equity [1–3] has to put in the agenda concrete efforts in facing both urban inequities of citizens and climate change issues. Public transport represents a critical area of intervention that we assumed as a stimulating background to perform a critical study for the sample context (the city of Potenza in Basilicata – Italy) assuming, in the design phase, UN – HABITAT New Urban Agenda [3] as a reference framework. According to the UN-HABITAT guidelines [4], it is possible to distinguish different levels of urban and territorial planning. At city and municipal level, both city development strategies and integrated development plans has to consider interactions between distant urban areas, looking for an optimal land use assets based on an effective organization of open urban spaces. On the other hand, at the neighborhood level, development projects for road

© Springer Nature Switzerland AG 2019
S. Misra et al. (Eds.): ICCSA 2019, LNCS 11624, pp. 331–346, 2019.
https://doi.org/10.1007/978-3-030-24311-1_24

and public space has the role to improve the urban quality, both social cohesion and inclusion and the protection of local resources. The urban and territorial planning will essentially promote more compact cities, through suitable road and interconnection schemes, which could reduce the urban mobility needs, as well as the costs of the services distribution. Therefore, the New Urban Agenda 2030, adopted during the United Nations Conference on urban and sustainable development (Habitat III held in Quito, Ecuador, from 17 to 20 October 2016), is clear and useful reference to improve the current planning system both at normative and methodological level.

Additionally, adopting the Agenda for Sustainable Development [5], all countries committed themselves to achieving the 17 Sustainable Development Goals (SDGs), through constant monitoring and regularly evaluating their progress [6, 7], in order to improve the performance of urban and territorial governance. In particular, the theme of urban mobility is addressed in the eleventh objective: "*sustainable cities and communities*". In fact, the goal for 2030 will be to provide access to safe, sustainable and affordable transportation systems for everyone, to improve road safety, in particular by expanding public transportation, with particular attention to women, children, people with disabilities and the elderly needs.

Improving the Local Public Transport (LPT) in terms of efficacy and efficiency means to removing some critical problems which are still present in the actual organization models of urban mobility. If we focus on the case study area, the main critical factors affecting Potenza urban mobility result from a lack of effective and integrated spatial planning policy, able to systematically deal with the dynamics of mobility at urban scale.

Potenza Municipality has adopted the Urban Mobility Plan (PUM) in 2008. This program proposes a multimodal and multi-action approaches to face the problems of urban mobility with the aim of ensuring a sustainable system on environmental, technical and economical point of view.

The experimentation proposed in this work is also based on OP FESR Basilicata 2014–2020 which promotes an integrated approach for urban development policies. The main purpose it to implement measures, based on territorial specialization and to design place-based development strategies [8–11]. Such integrated approach is realized through the Integrated Territorial Investment (ITI) [12] which is a programming instrument including negotiated development strategies on a specific area. In particular, integrated actions are initiated with the ITI of Potenza Municipality coherently with the thematic objectives defined in Regulation (EU) n. 1303/2013 [13]. The ITI program structured the sustainable mobility strategy of the city pointing out specific actions concerning:

- the infrastructures of new interchange areas for the transhipment from extra-urban buses to urban buses, with a view to reducing the overall traffic of buses in the city, and for promoting the use of automated systems;
- phasing out the most obsolete TPL buses to be replaced by Euro6 and electric vehicles for the reduction of polluting emissions;

- development of an ICT info-mobility project related to further and more incisive actions on mobility technological systems, providing innovative services through technological tools for the public transportation and the traffic management and urban mobility networks.

2 Case Study Area: Potenza Town

The City of Potenza is the capital of the Basilicata Region and with its 67168 inhabitants (ISTAT source) is the largest town of the region. The residents are distributed over an area of 175.42 km², with a density of 382.6 inh/km². Its area has mountainous characteristics, with a maximum altitude above sea level equal to 1345 m and a minimum of 605 m; the maximum altitude of the urban area is 819 m. The city is characterized by the presence of several services of local and regional interest (hospital, university, administrative offices of the Region and of the Province) and for this reason is therefore considered a functional pole for the whole regional community, namely a destination city for most of the journeys.

Hence the need for an urban mobility system able to respond to the increasing citizen's needs. The city has a very particular urban structure that places the historic center on the top of an hill and the remaining districts are settled at a lower altitudes. It is also known as the "City of the hundred stairs", due to its system of stairs, ancient and modern, which connect the various parts of the urban center.

The definition of an efficient and sustainable configuration of the urban mobility system for Potenza suffers from the morphological character of the city. We identified areas with a strong and concentration of activities and services compared with other neighborhoods developed as a result of a weak urban planning [14] and, consequently, a strong fragmentation of the settlement density [15–17]. Such urban configuration favored over decades exclusively the use of private vehicles of urban mobility.

Furthermore, from the analysis of transportation and mobility plan drawn up over the last few decades, we can highlight the substantially unchanged strategy. In fact not radical actions are promoted in order to shift from private cars mobility based system towards a more sustainable one.

Another weakness of the urban mobility management in Potenza town is connected with the usefulness undermined time scheduling of envisaged actions. Due to the excessive time span between the phase of planning/design and the operational implementation of actions, soft and hard measures, organizational schemes. Such delay makes ineffective the interventions due to the changes the settlement and functional context. Italy is one of the European countries with the highest motorization rate; in particular, Potenza ranks second among the regional capital cities, registering an increase in the motorization index of 3.4% from 2015 to 2017 (Fig. 1). At the same time, there was a decrease in LPT demand in the Municipality of Potenza at around 67% (Fig. 2).

The graph in Fig. 3 shows the modal imbalance deriving from the increasing use of individual transportation, which represents the main concern that persists in the urban mobility system.

Fig. 1. Motorization rate in the regional capitals

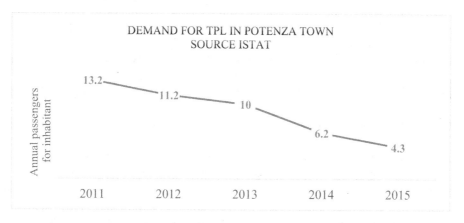

Fig. 2. TPL demand in the municipality of Potenza - Years 2011–2015

The few indicators discussed represent critical factors and, at the same time, unavoidable design constraints for any policy that pursues sustainability objectives. Therefore, it is necessary to structure integrated policies for the sustainable dimensioning of urban public transportation. However, the concept of 'mobility' must be regarded as inclusive as much as possible and it should meets the needs of every individual and citizen analyzed in a participatory way (cfr. [18–23] participation experiences in Potenza).

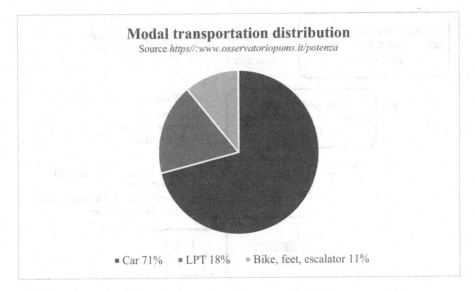

Fig. 3. Modal transportation distribution

The case study experimentation was carried out according with the Logical Framework Approach [24–26], which is a robust methodological framework based on the analysis of logical links between the activities included in a strategy or in a project and its objectives systems organized in a synthetic program structure. This methodology provides a structured and logical approach, which will establish priorities and determine the expected results. It includes the elaboration of four main outputs: SWOT Analysis, Problem Tree, Object Tree and Logical Framework Matrix.

A useful instrument to support the context analysis is the SWOT Analysis, from which an integrated view of the territorial context could be obtained. In the SWOT we summed up the salient aspects analyzed in internal Strengths and Weaknesses points, external Opportunities and Threats. In this way, it is possible to clearly and synthetically highlight the variables that can facilitate or hinder the project.

The analysis phase continues through the problems identification and the analysis of the objectives: the first one is realized with the development of the Problems' Tree, which lead to the identification of the cause-effect relationships existing between the negative issues. The second one is realized with the Objectives' Tree, which describes the future scenarios. Finally, in the synthesis phase the project idea is organized in operational parameters with the elaboration of the Logical Framework Matrix. It is a synthetic document that outlines how the project/strategy will guarantee the achievement of the selected objectives. Furthermore, it allows both the management and the evaluation of the efficiency and effectiveness of territorial transformation activities in terms of priorities and costs, through the use of indicators (Fig. 4).

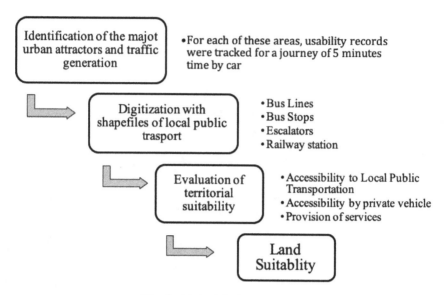

Fig. 4. Methodological flowchart

3   Methodology and Place Based Assessment

The analysis of the current situation were conducted using the open source software Q-GIS, through the identification of the major urban attractors and traffic generators (see Fig. 5):

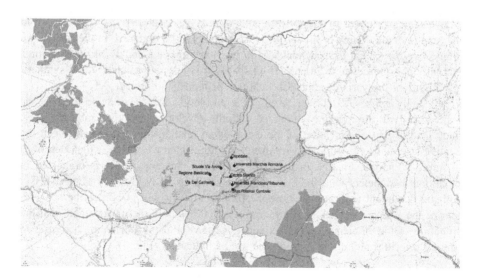

Fig. 5. Urban attractors and traffic generators

- the Historical Center which over time has gradually lost its function as a service center and is laboriously recovering the residential one and strengthening that of a center of quality trade and culture and leisure;
- the Francioso district with the presence of the historic headquarters of the University, the Court and the railway stations RFI and FAL;
- the Macchia Romana district, in continuous growth from the residential point of view and where the two largest territories of local services are concentrated: the Hospital and the University;
- the district of Poggio Tre Galli, characterized by a high residential load, several schools for upper-secondary education and the offices of the Basilicata Region;
- the Gallitello district where most of the commercial and working activities are concentrated.

For each of these areas, usability records were tracked for a journey of 5 min time by car, to evaluate the accessibility by private vehicle depending on their geographical location.

Regarding the structure of Local Public Transport service (Fig. 6), the system is served by 17 Urban Busses Lines and 10 School Busses Lines. The urban connection is integrated with the FAL rail service, which acts as an urban subway, connecting opposite parts of the city in a short time and at a reduced cost. As mentioned above, the city is famous for its escalators system that is divided into 4 different structures: Via Tammone - Santa Lucia (Ponte Attrezzato), Rione Mancusi - Via Due Torri, Viale Marconi - Centro Storico, Potenza Inferiore.

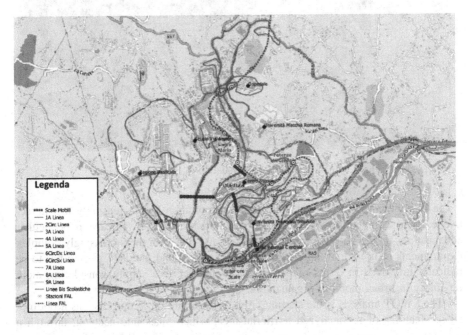

Fig. 6. Local Public Transport Service of the Municipality of Potenza

The system had been digitalized and data allowed to analyze and represent the actual situation. In particular, the study focused on the accessibility to main public services settled in the city through the Local Public Transport service. Although significant investments in the field of urban mobility (shelter renewal interventions as per *"Three-year Program of Public Works 2017/2019"*), the TPL sector continues to rest in inefficient conditions, severely affecting the users. Emblematic is the case of the *"ITS Infomobility Project - Intelligent Transportation Systems"*. Yet with the funds of the previous 2007–2013 programming cycle, a first project was carried out, which consisted in supplying of n. 80 poles with electronic information panel installed near the bus stops. This system, which was supposed to facilitate public buses tracking in real time, is currently not working. A further disadvantage of the urban mobility system is represented by the current abandonment and degradation state of mechanized facilities (Fig. 7); in addition to being poorly used and oversized compared with current demand for transportation, they lack of ordinary and extraordinary maintenance. Moreover, the service does not operate during night and some facilities are poorly integrated with road transportation due to the lack of parking areas.

Fig. 7. Abandonment and degradation of mechanized plants

In this view, it is clear that collective transportation has increasingly lost attractiveness and competitiveness compared with private cars. It appears to be neither adequate nor timely with the dynamics of land use and with the increasingly complex requirements of users mobility needs. To reverse this trend, the LPT system has to be radically improved in terms of performances and services supply considering more flexibility in urban mobility organization.

The SWOT analysis is the starting point of the entire design process, as it outlines all the features of the analyzed territorial area, which takes into account, through a

Table 1. SWOT analysis

Points of strength	Points of weakness
Widespread development of mechanized collective transport systems (elevators/escalators) that collocate the city in second place in the world Presence of the FAL line with the characteristics of a "light rail" with 7 city stops PICK ME APP ": service that allows you to book trips to Potenza on minibuses or cars at a reduced cost, with certain times of coverage and prices even for disabled users, tracked by a GPS detector to find out the position and arrival of a family member Arrangement of new shelters (In accordance with the three-year program of public works 2017/2019 with the intervention "stops and paths without barriers" - source of funding: FSC 2007/2013)	Poor quality levels of urban roads No info-mobility Overlap of urban and extra-urban vehicles Difficulty finding tickets for urban lines and mechanized systems Low frequencies of urban lines (40 min) and average travel time 1 h The urban service and the mechanized systems do not serve a night band (9.00 pm/10.00 pm) Elimination of single ticket for the urban service: 5-pass ticket € 5 Elimination of the single journey ticket for mechanized systems: 20 pass ticket € 5 State of abandonment of mechanized plants Overcrowding of the parking lots in the historic center
Opportunities	Threats
SMILE initiative Integrated territorial investment (ITI) for the urban development of the city of Potenza funded with resources from the OP FESR BASILICATA 2014/2020 operational plan Promote the development of an online app for urban mobility as experienced by the De Estudios Superiores De Monterrey Technological Institute (Moovit)	The citizen's tendency to want to prefer private transport to alternative means Disinterest of the citizen towards sustainable mobility

brainstorming, the opinions and points of view of all the involved subjects, who can endure the program or influence it in a more or less significantly way (Table 1).

Starting from Weakness and Strength identified with the SWOT analysis, we have selected issues related to an existing negative condition, leading to the Problems' Tree. By contrast, the objectives analysis consists in the definition of the consequent positively projection of the negative situation (Figs. 8 and 9).

The Land Suitability approach is a method of land classification which allows to evaluate the suitability of a territorial portion for a specific use considering the current situation and its possible improvement. Therefore, each area, obtained from the intersection of the accessibility isochrones, has been characterized on the basis of three criteria:

- Accessibility to Local Public Transportation
- Accessibility by private vehicle
- Services Endowment.

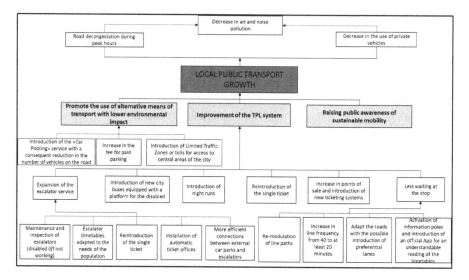

Fig. 8. Problems' Tree

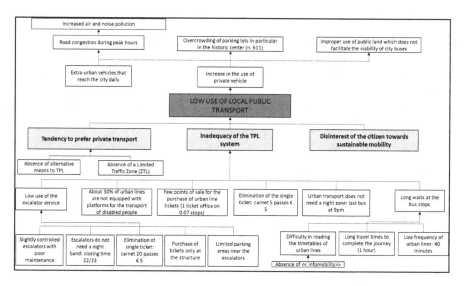

Fig. 9. Objectives' Tree

We select such criteria according with the overall objective to improve transportation modes, with the aim of balancing supply and demand, as well as integrating the services and transport infrastructures. The attributes included in the analysis represent requirements and characteristics that are easily observable, recognizable and measurable: the number of public busses lines that serves each area and, those equipped with platforms allowing the use of public transport vehicles by the disabled, the number of buss-stops, the number of public busses school lines, the functionality of transport information poles, the proximity to one or more escalators, the presence of parking lots and parking areas, the presence of services such as ticket offices, health points, schools and offices, commercial activities.

Each attribute has been weighted according to the importance it holds in our interpretation model. In order to pursue sustainable transportation mobility, as well as ensuring improved accessibility in urban area, we assigned higher weight to the attribute "accessibility to LPT". In the following Table 2 we present the list of attributes and corresponding weight for land suitability classification.

Table 2. Land Suitability criteria

Criteria	Attributes		Weights
Inhabitants	n. Inhabitants		10
TPL	n. lines that serve the area		10
Accessibility	n. lines with platform for the disabled for n. lines		10
	n. stops present		10
	n. of school lines Information posts at working stops	Presence (1) Absence (0)	10
	Frequency of lines		10
	Presence of escalators at 200mt	Presence (1) Absence (0)	7
	n. city subway stops		5
Car	n. poles reachable in 5 min by car		7
Accessibility	n. parking lots		5
	Parking areas	Presence (1) Absence (0)	7
Services	Ticket offices		10
	Education & Business		7
	Post offices		3
	Health		7
	Business		3
	Parks		5

In the following map the obtained land suitability is represented accompanied by the detailed definition of each classes according with Geodesign method [27–30] (Fig. 10, Table 3).

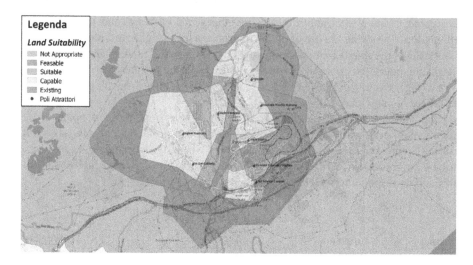

Fig. 10. Land suitability elaboration

Table 3. Land suitability classes

Description of the Evaluation map: Promote the increase of a sustainable mobility for the progressive reduction of the private car. The classification was made based on the uniformity and accessibility of the TPL, the supply of goods and services and the reachability by private means of the poles under study.

Feasible	Suitable	Capable	Not Appropriate	Existing
Areas where there is a non-existence or a strong lack of the TPL service (absence of stops and urban lines serving the area) and integrated transport services.	Areas served on average suitable for modest re-modulation of the lines and adjustment of services.	Area that has a good supply of TPL service, goods and services and reachability by private vehicle.	All the rest of the study area.	Areas with high accessibility to the TPL service and with a satisfactory endowment of services.

4 Strategic Vision

The choice of transport means to be used in a city defines a discriminating trait of the "mobility style" for the citizens and, at the same time, it determines the impact of the external costs that the community will have to shoulder (congestion costs, pollution, accidents, liveability of the public space). In the city of Potenza, the modal imbalance deriving from the increasing use of individual transport represents the main source of the problems. Therefore, this project aims to increase sustainable mobility in the city for the progressive reduction of the private car. The development of sustainable mobility requires the implementation of supply integration policies together with awareness-raising activities encouraging the use of alternatives to individual car. The proposed sustainable mobility strategy for Potenza town was directed towards specific interventions:

- re-modulation of lines and frequencies
- introduction of new ticketing systems
- increase in ticket sales points
- introduction of night lines
- extension of the urban lines timetable
- extension of the opening times of the escalators
- info-mobility system
- purchase of buses equipped with a platform for people with disabilities
- purchase of new urban buses with low polluting emissions
- introduction of the car-pooling service
- dissemination activities with initiatives such as "Mobility Days" and "downtown without cars".

These interventions categories can be realized by the financial means available in the OP-ERDF Basilicata 2014-2020. Therefore we refers to Axis IV (*"Energy and urban mobility"*) and Axis III (*"Competitiveness"*).

The Urban Mobility Plan proposes the development of ICT technologies for traffic monitoring and users' information, parking addressing, control and management of the LPT bus fleet and info-mobility. The total cost of the operation and financial coverage plan is € 1,000,000.00.

Axis III is instead addressed to the competitiveness of companies through the improvement of small and medium sized businesses (SME). The share of public funds for that is about € 2,500,000 in the framework of the call named "CreOpportunità", approved by D.G.R. n. 1223 of 26/10/2016.

5 Conclusions

Policies for promoting sustainable urban mobility require a deep integration between urban planning instruments, as well initiatives and programs aimed at the realization and adaptation of mobility infrastructures. Fundamental importance has to be payed to the capacity to promote an innovative mobility management of the overall urban mobility system that proposes a better use of existing infrastructures, favors the integration between the different modes of transport, guides the demand expressed by the users based on their direct involvement. It is necessary to stimulate the citizens to use the different public transport modes, which are already available in the city but currently under-utilized, in the perspective to overcome the chronic problem of Potenza town ranked in national statistics as one of the city with lowest use of public transport [31]. The correct project proposal is oriented to enhance quality factors for the supply system, namely:

- the density of the offer in terms of frequency and capillarity;
- average speed, punctuality and reliability;
- the cost to users;
- quality factors such as: accessibility, comfort and cleanliness, integrated travel information, easy interchange, easy to use and integrated ticketing.

Effective means/actions to reach such ambition are:

- to improve and expand the range of collective and semi-collective transport services, alternative to private cars (carpooling, call transport);
- to promote modes of transport with a lower energy and environmental impact by spreading electric or hybrid cars;
- to take the advantages deriving from the use of Intelligent Transportation System (ITS) technologies which with very limited investments can be used for different purposes: from information to users, to optimize their movements, to maximizing the existing urban network;
- to implement integrated actions and policies that attract and push users towards LPT and alternative methods to private cars;
- to promote awareness-raising activities towards sustainable mobility.

Acknowledgement. This research was developed in the framework of the Territorial Engineering studios (AA 2018-2019) School of Engineering, University of Basilicata. The work reports main evidences from the analysis developed by students supervised by Francesco Scorza.

References

1. Las Casas, G., Scorza, F., Murgante, B.: New urban agenda and open challenges for urban and regional planning. In: Calabrò, F., Della Spina, L., Bevilacqua, C. (eds.) ISHT 2018. SIST, vol. 100, pp. 282–288. Springer, Cham (2019). https://doi.org/10.1007/978-3-319-92099-3_33
2. Casas, G.L., Scorza, F.: From the UN new urban agenda to the local experiences of urban development: the case of Potenza. In: Gervasi, O., et al. (eds.) ICCSA 2018. LNCS, vol. 10964, pp. 734–743. Springer, Cham (2018). https://doi.org/10.1007/978-3-319-95174-4_56
3. UN HABITAT: New Urban Agenda. United Nations (2017)
4. UN HABITAT: International guidelines on urban and territorial planning. United Nations Publication, Nairobi GPO KENYA (2015)
5. UN: Sustainable Development Goals (2014). https://doi.org/10.1038/505587a. http://www.igbp.net/download/18.62dc35801456272b46d51/1399290813740/NL82-SDGs.pdf
6. Dvarioniene, J., Grecu, V., Lai, S., Scorza, F.: Four perspectives of applied sustainability: research implications and possible integrations. In: Gervasi, O., et al. (eds.) ICCSA 2017. LNCS, vol. 10409, pp. 554–563. Springer, Cham (2017). https://doi.org/10.1007/978-3-319-62407-5_39
7. Scorza, F., Grecu, V.: Assessing sustainability: research directions and relevant issues. In: Gervasi, O., et al. (eds.) ICCSA 2016. LNCS, vol. 9786, pp. 642–647. Springer, Cham (2016). https://doi.org/10.1007/978-3-319-42085-1_55
8. Barca, F.: An agenda for a reformed cohesion policy (2009)

9. Las Casas, G., Murgante, B., Scorza, F.: Regional local development strategies benefiting from open data and open tools and an outlook on the renewable energy sources contribution. In: Papa, R., Fistola, R. (eds.) Smart Energy in the Smart City. GET, pp. 275–290. Springer, Cham (2016). https://doi.org/10.1007/978-3-319-31157-9_14

10. Las Casas, G.B., Scorza, F.: I conflitti fra lo sviluppo economico e l'ambiente: strumenti di controllo. In: Atti della XIX Conferenza Nazionale SIU, Cambiamenti, responsabilità e strumenti per l'urbanistica a servizio del paese, pp. 1598–1606. Planum Publisher, Roma-Milano (2017)

11. Scorza, F.: Improving EU cohesion policy: the spatial distribution analysis of regional development investments funded by EU structural funds 2007/2013 in Italy. In: Murgante, B., et al. (eds.) ICCSA 2013. LNCS, vol. 7973, pp. 582–593. Springer, Heidelberg (2013). https://doi.org/10.1007/978-3-642-39646-5_42

12. Potenza Municipality: Investimento Territoriale Integrato (ITI) per lo Sviluppo Urbano Città di Potenza (2017). http://www.comune.potenza.it/wp-content/uploads/2017/09/Documento-Strategico_ITI-Sviluppo-Urbano-Potenza.pdf

13. European Parliament: Regulation (EU) No 1303/2013 (2013). https://eur-lex.europa.eu/legal-content/EN/TXT/PDF/?uri=CELEX:32013R1303&from=it

14. Scorza, F.: Quale città pubblica in un contesto di pianificazione debole. Evidenze dal dibattito urbanistico a Potenza. In: Giaimo, C. (ed.) Dopo 50 anni di standards urbanistici in Italia, pp. 182–186. INU Edizioni Srl, Roma (2019)

15. Saganeiti, L., Pilogallo, A., Scorza, F., Mussuto, G., Murgante, B.: Spatial indicators to evaluate urban fragmentation in basilicata region. In: Gervasi, O., et al. (eds.) ICCSA 2018. LNCS, vol. 10964, pp. 100–112. Springer, Cham (2018). https://doi.org/10.1007/978-3-319-95174-4_8

16. Amato, F., Maimone, B.A., Martellozzo, F., Nolè, G., Murgante, B.: The effects of urban policies on the development of urban areas. Sustainability. **8**, 297 (2016)

17. Saganeiti, L., Favale, A., Pilogallo, A., Scorza, F., Murgante, B.: Assessing urban fragmentation at regional scale using sprinkling indexes. Sustainability **10**, 3274 (2018). https://doi.org/10.3390/su10093274

18. Pontrandolfi, P., Scorza, F.: Sustainable urban regeneration policy making: inclusive participation practice. In: Gervasi, O., et al. (eds.) ICCSA 2016. LNCS, vol. 9788, pp. 552–560. Springer, Cham (2016). https://doi.org/10.1007/978-3-319-42111-7_44

19. Pontrandolfi, P., Scorza, F.: Making urban regeneration feasible: tools and procedures to integrate urban agenda and UE cohesion regional programs. In: Gervasi, O., et al. (eds.) ICCSA 2017. LNCS, vol. 10409, pp. 564–572. Springer, Cham (2017). https://doi.org/10.1007/978-3-319-62407-5_40

20. Pontrandolfi, P., Scorza, F.: Una sperimentazione di strumenti web-based per la partecipazione dei cittadini ai processi di rigenerazione urbana: l'infrastruttura ICT CAST e l'Urban Center Virtuale. In: Atti della XIX Conferenza Nazionale SIU, Cambiamenti, responsabilità e strumenti per l'urbanistica a servizio del paese, pp. 1069–1076. Planum Publisher, Roma-Milano (2017)

21. Pontrandolfi, P., Scorza, F.: Il progetto CAST: contenuti, finalità, partenariato, attività svolte. In: Rigenerazione Urbana e Cittadinanza Attiva. L'esperienza del progetto C.A.S.T, pp. 18–25. Librìa, Melfi (2017)

22. Murgante, B., Botonico, G., Graziadei, A., Sassano, G., Amato, F., Scorza, F.: Innovation, technologies, participation: new paradigms towards a 2.0 citizenship. Int. J. Electron. Gov. **11**, 62–88 (2019). https://doi.org/10.1504/IJEG.2019.098814

23. Amato, F., et al.: "Serpentone Reload" an experience of citizens involvement in regeneration of peripheral urban spaces. In: Gervasi, O., et al. (eds.) ICCSA 2015. LNCS, vol. 9156, pp. 698–713. Springer, Cham (2015). https://doi.org/10.1007/978-3-319-21407-8_50

24. Casas, G.L., Scorza, F.: Sustainable planning: a methodological toolkit. In: Gervasi, O., et al. (eds.) ICCSA 2016. LNCS, vol. 9786, pp. 627–635. Springer, Cham (2016). https://doi.org/10.1007/978-3-319-42085-1_53

25. Las Casas, G., Scorza, F., Murgante, B.: Conflicts and sustainable planning: peculiar instances coming from val d'agri structural inter-municipal plan. In: Papa, R., Fistola, R., Gargiulo, C. (eds.) Smart Planning: Sustainability and Mobility in the Age of Change. GET, pp. 163–177. Springer, Cham (2018). https://doi.org/10.1007/978-3-319-77682-8_10

26. Las Casas, G., Scorza, F.: A renewed rational approach from liquid society towards anti-fragile planning. In: Gervasi, O., et al. (eds.) ICCSA 2017. LNCS, vol. 10409, pp. 517–526. Springer, Cham (2017). https://doi.org/10.1007/978-3-319-62407-5_36

27. Padula, A., Fiore, P., Pilogallo, A., Scorza, F.: Collaborative approach in strategic development planning for small municipalities. Applying geodesign methodology and tools for a new municipal strategy in Scanzano Jonico. In: Leone, A., Gargiulo, C. (eds.) Environmental and Territorial Modelling for Planning and Design, pp. 665–672. FedOApress (2018). https://doi.org/10.6093/978-88-6887-048-5

28. Fiore, P., Padula, A., Pilogallo, A., Scorza, F.: Facing urban regeneration issues through geodesign approach. The case of Gravina in Puglia. In: Leone, A., Gargiulo, C. (eds.) Environmental and Territorial Modelling for Planning and Design. FedOAPress (2018). https://doi.org/10.6093/978-88-6887-048-5

29. Campagna, M.: Geodesign: dai contenuti metodologici all'innovazione nelle pratiche. In: Atti della XVII Conferenza Nazionale SIU. L'urbanistica italiana nel mondo, pp. 71–76 (2014)

30. Campagna, M., De Montis, A., Isola, F., Lai, S., Pira, C., Zoppi, C.: Planning support tools: policy analysis, implementation and evaluation. In: Proceedings of the Seventh International Conference on Informatics and Urban and Regional Planning INPUT2012: Proceedings of the Seventh International Conference on Informatics and Ur (2012)

31. Fiorillo, A., Laurenti, M., Bono, L.: Ecosistema urbano. Rapporto sulle performance ambientali delle città 2018 (2018)

Development Strategies of Agro-Food Sector in Basilicata Region (Italy): Evidence from INNOVAGRO Project

Lucia Saganeiti(✉), Angela Pilogallo, Carmen Izzo, Rosanna Piro,
Francesco Scorza, and Beniamino Murgante

Laboratory of Urban and Regional Systems Engineering (LISUT),
School of Engineering, University of Basilicata,
Viale dell'Ateneo Lucano 10, 85100 Potenza, Italy
{lucia.saganeiti,angela.pilogallo,carmen.izzo,
rosanna.piro,francesco.scorza,
beniamino.murgante}@unibas.it

Abstract. Agricultural production in Basilicata Region is strongly character-ized by a high degree of fragmentation, the large percentage of small family businesses and a generalized low propensity to entrepreneurship. Although there are productive realities that are suited to entrepreneurship, going beyond the local market dimensions. The low propensity of agricultural producers to associate in consortium or any other formal collaboration is also a factor to be reinforced in order to improve the competitiveness of the respective supply chains.

The project "Development of an innovative network for the promotion of extroversion of agro-food companies in Adriatic - Ionian Area" (INNOVAGRO) intents to capitalize existing experiences and to adopt innovative solutions in order to develop an intraregional approach combining innovative ICT tech-nologies, the establishment of a Transnational Innovative Agro-food Network and the promotion of environmentally- friendly farming practices.

This work illustrates a detailed context analysis aimed at addressing the general issues promoted by the INNOVAGRO project on specific features characterizing Basilicata Region in supporting new development strategies based on synergic relationships between the tourism sector and agro-food production.

Keywords: INNOVAGRO · Agro-food · Tourism · Sustainability · Basilicata region

1 The Implementation Context

Basilicata is a rural region, whose territory equal to about 10 000 km^2 is almost entirely mountainous or hilly with a few reliefs higher than 2000 m and only 8% lowland areas. Basilicata belongs to the less developed regions (lagging regions) identified by the EU as beneficiaries of ERDF and ESF funds as well as the Cohesion Fund for the period 2014–20.

© Springer Nature Switzerland AG 2019
S. Misra et al. (Eds.): ICCSA 2019, LNCS 11624, pp. 347–356, 2019.
https://doi.org/10.1007/978-3-030-24311-1_25

The territory is characterized by natural habitats and agricultural landscapes of great value. Agriculture occupies a key position in regional economy, contributing for €771 million in value added to the Basilicata economy in 2014 [1], increasing from 2010 both in absolute value and in percentage terms. The strong agricultural and rural character is also confirmed by the percentage of people employed in agriculture that up to 2010 reached almost 10%, more than double compared to Italian value [2].

The productive structure and territorial organization greatly influence rural development dynamics and agro-food chains growth, as evidenced by the recent emergence of Integrated Projects of Food Chain [3].

Although according to the classification adopted by the 2014–20 Partnership Agreement of September 2014, almost 75% of municipalities belongs "rural areas with development problems", agro-food sector is of strategic importance for the sustainable development thanks [4]. Spatial dislocation of farms and agro-food activities and the presence of food and wine products that constitute potential drivers of rural and natural tourism [5], make agro-economy a crucial issue for sustaining remote rural areas through the generation of income and jobs.

A detailed context analysis highlighted a lack of an entrepreneurial culture, causing rural out-migration, farm fragmentation and land abandonment, with all expected consequences in terms of land degradation [6]. However, some of the realities considered excellent for entrepreneurial skills as well as for sustainability, ability to penetrate trans-regional markets and transversality of services and products offered were identified and deeply analyzed.

The aim of "Development of an innovative network for the promotion of extroversion of agro-food companies in Adriatic - Ionian Area" (INNOVAGRO) project is indeed to take as an example existing virtuous models and develop innovative solutions to create a Transnational Innovative Agro-food Network. Expected result is a platform to combine ICT technologies and environmentally - friendly farming practices and to promote the exchange of positive experiences at a intraregional scale. This platform could support new development strategies based on synergic relationships between the tourism sector and agro-food production.

This work illustrates the main results of a SWOT analysis [7–9] that represent a preliminary context analysis from Basilicata region providing information about the relevance of the agro-food sector with the specific development characteristics.

2   Agro-Food Sector in the Study Area

Basilicata, in the South of Italy, is a sparsely populated region (about 56,7 inhabitants/Km^2 to 2018 [1]) with a constant negative population trend. Of relevance for the socio-economic implications are the presence of numerous small municipalities with less than 2,000 residents and the high fragmentation degree [10, 11] that characterizes the regional settlement environment.

Agricultural productivity accounts for about 49% of regional total amount registering a positive trend due to both an effective modernization and the development of activities related to tertiary sector. The rural development plan (RDP) has in fact promoted the diversification of agricultural sector, focusing on the establishment of activities related to receptivity (agritourism) and environmental education (educational farms) [12–14].

As regards the age structure of business owners, only 5% of all entrepreneurs are under 35 years and only 10% are younger than 40. This percentage furtherly drops to 3% if only female farmers are considered.

The Utilized Agricultural Area (UAA) is characterized by a prevalent use of arable land which, covering an extension of about 312 000 hectares, represents about 60% of regional UAA; permanent meadows and pastures represent a share of 30%, while agricultural woody cultivations represent only 10% of regional UAA.

Cereal cultivation is the most representative in terms of both UAA and number of farms involved, followed by legumes and vegetable crops.

Woody agricultural crops result classified among fruit trees (about 21% of UAA), citrus fruits (about 12% of UAA) and wine grape (about 11% of the UAA). Olive tree cultivation is the most representative woody cultivation representing more than 54% of regional woody UAA.

The most important cultivation areas are located in Metapontum region, in Ofanto-Bradano Valley and in Agri Valley; smaller but emerging areas are Mercure Valley, Sauro Valley and the periurban horticulture of S. Arcangelo and Senise municipalities. Metapontum area is the heart of fruit and vegetable production, representing three quarters of agricultural area and a recognized Quality Agro-food District [15].

2.1 Structure and Development Characteristics

The analysis of the regional context reveals a strong agricultural attitude of the Region that however suffers limited investments. Employment problems and difficulties in generational renewal induce low competitiveness. Entrepreneurs and workforce' aging and lack of specific skills and knowledge limit the spread of innovation. Difficulties of access to credit appear as a further factor strongly limiting investments.

For these reasons, the productive context of Basilicata region agriculture results strongly characterized by a high degree of fragmentation, by the large percentage of small family businesses and by low propensity to entrepreneurship.

Very low availability of agricultural producers to associate with each other is also a factor on which to influence in order to improve the supply chains' competitiveness [16] and gain larger market shares.

RDP funds and the interception of opportunities made available by the European Community, has allowed some production realities to emerge on larger markets and/or to network mobilizing larger more active partnerships [17].

That's the case, for example, of the Basilicata Regional strategy for research and innovation (also known as "Smart Specialization Strategy" or "S3") that gave innovative territorial leverage to support the emergence of new companies, new relationships and an improved programme from the alignment of and networking of actors.

This multi-actors, multi-disciplinaries approach allowed rural productive systems to create important inter-sectorial interconnections such as in the field of bioenergy (Fig. 1).

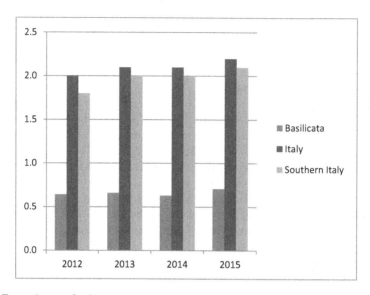

Fig. 1. Export in agro-food sector as percentage of GDP in Basilicata, Southern Italy and Italian contexts

Some companies, on the other hand, have exploited these opportunities to take advantage of a marketing network that has favored their export trend [18]. That's the case of Candonga Strawberry distributed by Club Candonga Consortium and traded at international events such as Fruit Logistica in Berlin (Germany).

3   Prospects and Trends of the Agro-Food Sector

In the last decade, the agricultural sector has been subject to structural changes in the productive systems of the farm, linked to different motivations, from adverse climatic conditions to frequent crises in the sector (inadequate market prices, high production costs, disaggregated supply). Recent calls for tenders for the establishment of new businesses have, on the one hand, favored the growth of the number of businesses managed by competent young people, but, on the other hand, favored the fragmentation of large farms into a number of businesses of a smaller size.

The growing trend of organic farming or the adoption of schemes aimed at greater sustainability of the sector, if it is to prove effective in the long term, must necessarily include training and integration within the context of specialized figures who support individual initiatives and know how to fully grasp the potential in terms of profitability and development of virtuous supply chains.

A positive trend is growing in relation to the corporatist approach that is becoming increasingly important, especially in production contexts related to the province of Matera. The establishment of Productive Organizations solves in part the problem of poor preparation of business leaders and, if well organized, contributes to the reduction of production costs and the implementation of marketing techniques that are inaccessible to individual producers and effective in penetrating some segments of the market.

A further perspective that suggests wide margins for growth is that of the integration between sustainable tourism and high quality products.

Since 2006, there has been an upward trend in the number of farms authorized to carry out agri-tourism activities, which account for almost all of the accommodation facilities in the entire region, and a greater territorial spread of activities connected with agriculture. Positive effects can in general be found in tourism sector, as shown by the increase in the number of both attendance and arrivals (see Fig. 2) that correspond to an increase in available bed supply all over the region.

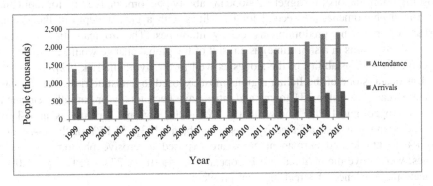

Fig. 2. Tourism flows in Basilicata region

The development of diversification activities, in addition to offering income opportunities in rural areas where agricultural production are less remunerative, meet the growing demand for goods and services of collective interest.

3.1 Sustainable Development Challenges

In addition to some intrinsic characteristics of the agricultural sector in Basilicata that over the years have become factors limiting the development of the entire sector (depopulation, lack of or delayed generational change, inadequate preparation of employees in the sector), a challenge for the development of the agricultural sector is certainly aimed at resolving the numerous environmental conflicts in the region.

The greatest of these is certainly the one relating to the Val d'Agri [19–21] where the emergence of excellent agricultural products and the penetration of markets on a larger scale must clash with the needs of conservation and protection related to the management of the National Park of the Apennines and, above all, with the coexisting oil industry and refining of extracted crude oil.

Another case of serious environmental conflict also occurs near the Ionian coast, where significant production in terms of economic weight as well as for the areas concerned, coexist with the Fuel Elements Treatment and Refabrication Plant (ITREC), a nuclear plant located in the Enea-Trisaia research center in Rotondella (MT) and used for the conservation and testing of the reprocessing of nuclear fuel derived from a thorium-uranium cycle.

In addition to the specific problems of the agricultural field, there are some that, although generalized, have important effects on the primary sector. Hydrogeological instability is for example a historical problem certainly inherent to its territory and its particular geological, geomorphological, hydrogeological and seismic characteristics, but worsened in the nineteenth century due to extensive deforestation, economic marginalization, depopulation, reduction of the garrison of the territory, adoption of inadequate cultivation practices, and cementification, this phenomenon also seems destined to a predictable, further exacerbation following the rapid evolution of climate change. Rainfall, whether short and intense or exceptional and prolonged, is one of the most important factors for triggering slope instability phenomena; the first for rapid and superficial phenomena, the second for landslides with a greater depth of the sliding surface or involving predominantly clayey lithotypes. The tropicalisation of rainy events (heavy rains in a short time) as a result of the global change would contribute to accentuating the instability of the slopes as well as the hydraulic risk [22].

Basilicata is one of the Italian regions most exposed to landslide risk. Over the last hundred years, 19 of the 131 towns and cities have been totally or partially relocated. The Hydrogeological Plan shows that 5.2% of the regional territory is at risk of landslides and it is also affected by erosive problems [23]: 34.19% of the UAA and 36.67% of arable and permanent crops are exposed to erosive phenomena. These values, well above the national and European average (Italy: 27.84%; Europe: 6.0%), indicate the existence of a real regional problem.

Although they affect a large part of the regional territory, the erosive phenomena are more widespread in the environment of the plio-pleistocene hills [24]. They have an average erosion value not tolerable by 61 municipalities, about 70% of the total, 31 of them are located in mountain area and 30 in hilly area.

The goal of protecting and promoting regional biodiversity is undoubtedly part of a sustainable development strategy that is effective in the long term but which immediately has an impact. There are several specific objectives to be pursued for its achievement: the reduction of the polluting impact of agricultural practices; the permanence of farms in mountainous and disadvantaged areas, the adoption of agricultural and forestry practices capable of reversing the phenomena of land degradation but also measures for the prevention of fires and the enhancement of forest resources.

Both the programming period ending in 2013 and the current programming period have provided for a number of measures (PDR 2007–2013: Measures 1, 2, 8, 10, 11 and 16) for the conservation of soil resources, such as reforestation, maintenance and implementation of agroforestry systems, as well as increasing the resilience and mitigation capacity of forest ecosystems.

4   Final Remarks and Perspectives of Project Implementation

The agricultural sector of Basilicata boasts products of excellence that could be further enhanced through appropriate interventions. The limited percentage of suitable agricultural area compared to a type of agriculture aimed at large distribution, does not allow Basilicata agricultural production to be competitive in large-scale retail trade. Nevertheless, our region is one of the most dynamic realities of the entire national sector, both in terms of numbers and specific production since fruit and vegetable chains are distinguished by quality and excellence. This happens for some horticultural and fruit species (brassica, fennel, apricot, strawberry, clementine), while for typical products, although the markets concerned are niche, both demand and sales prices are positive.

The sector, like other regions, is however affected by negative trend in consumption and a greater pressure of foreign competition, in addition to the low concentration of supply, the limited bargaining power of producers and the fragmentation of this sector. One solution to these problems is represented by NGOs that in Metapontum area, in particular, is represented by Producer Organizations that have been able to direct production and provide answers in terms of training and research.

The Integrated Supply Chain Design, synthesis of the effectiveness of the recent rural development policies, has allowed to plan investments in innovations to anticipate the competition on the markets and to extend its presence on them, to rationalize the production costs and improve their marketing. In order to further increase the potential of fruit and vegetable production, it is necessary to favor the diversification of supply, guarantee greater food safety, reduce production costs [25, 26] and achieve higher levels of efficiency in logistics systems.

Finally, a further evidence suggests that extra-agricultural activities and multi-functionality represent a possible strategy of income diversification both for farms and, in the future, for forestry companies. This could provide an incentive for small farms located in inland areas to overcome the lack of sufficient income from primary production and more extensive improvement of rural quality of life [27].

Former EU funded transnational cooperation projects allowed our research group to implement sectorial applications in sustainable development practices [28–32]. In the specific case of INNOVAGRO project, as comprehensive and long term expectations of project implementation, the contribution for the development of a rational and effective framework for territorial planning is expected [33, 34]. It goes in the direction of developing an integrated platform based on local specializations on which the operative programs are coherently organized in providing funding for public and private projects [35]. A critical component of such process is represented by monitoring systems (specialized on sustainability assessment [36, 37] that should reinforce decision making and citizens awareness on on-going processes and trends.

References

1. ISTAT. http://dati.istat.it/
2. Basilicata Region: Programma di Sviluppo Rurale Basilicata 2014–2020 (2015). www.basilicatapsr.it
3. Conto, F., La Sala, P., Papapietro, P.: Organization and structure of the chain in the Integrated Projects of Food Chain in Basilicata region: the effects on the new rural dynamics (2010). https://ageconsearch.umn.edu/record/95001/

4. Viccaro, M., Rocchi, B., Cozzi, M., Romano, S.: SAM multipliers and subsystems: structural analysis of the Basilicata's agri-food sector. Bio-based Appl. Econ. **7**, 19–38 (2018). https://doi.org/10.13128/bae-24046

5. Bencivenga, A., Vollaro, P.D., Forte, F., Giampietro, A.M., Percoco, A.: Food and wine tourism in Basilicata. Agric. Agric. Sci. Procedia **8**, 176–185 (2016). https://doi.org/10.1016/J.AASPRO.2016.02.091

6. Kelly, C., et al.: Community resilience and land degradation in forest and shrubland socioecological systems: evidence from Gorgoglione, Basilicata, Italy. Land Use Policy **46**, 11–20 (2015). https://doi.org/10.1016/J.LANDUSEPOL.2015.01.026

7. Helms, M.M., Nixon, J.: Exploring SWOT analysis – where are we now? J. Strateg. Manag. **3**, 215–251 (2010). https://doi.org/10.1108/17554251011064837

8. Pickton, D.W., Wright, S.: What's SWOT in strategic analysis? Strateg. Change **7**, 101–109 (1998). https://doi.org/10.1002/(SICI)1099-1697(199803/04)7:2%3c101:AID-JSC332%3e3.0.CO;2-6

9. Vaněk, M., Mikoláš, M., Žváková, K.: Evaluation methods of SWOT analysis/Metody Vyhodnocení SWOT Analýzy. Geosci. Eng. **58**, 23–31 (2012). https://doi.org/10.2478/gse-2014-0036

10. Saganeiti, L., et al.: Assessing urban fragmentation at regional scale using sprinkling indexes. Sustainability **10**, 3274 (2018). https://doi.org/10.3390/SU10093274

11. Saganeiti, L., Pilogallo, A., Scorza, F., Mussuto, G., Murgante, B.: Spatial Indicators to evaluate urban fragmentation in Basilicata region. In: Gervasi, O., et al. (eds.) ICCSA 2018. LNCS, vol. 10964, pp. 100–112. Springer, Cham (2018). https://doi.org/10.1007/978-3-319-95174-4_8

12. Scorza, F., Pilogallo, A., Las Casas, G.: Investigating tourism attractiveness in inland areas: ecosystem services, open data and smart specializations. In: Calabrò, F., Della Spina, L., Bevilacqua, C. (eds.) ISHT 2018. SIST, vol. 100, pp. 30–38. Springer, Cham (2019). https://doi.org/10.1007/978-3-319-92099-3_4

13. Scorza, F., Murgante, B., Las Casas, G., Fortino, Y., Pilogallo, A.: Investigating territorial specialization in tourism sector by ecosystem services approach. In: Stratigea, A., Kavroudakis, D. (eds.) Mediterranean Cities and Island Communities. PI, pp. 161–179. Springer, Cham (2019). https://doi.org/10.1007/978-3-319-99444-4_7

14. Pilogallo, A., Saganeiti, L., Scorza, F., Las Casas, G.: Tourism attractiveness: main components for a spacial appraisal of major destinations according with ecosystem services approach. In: Gervasi, O., et al. (eds.) ICCSA 2018. LNCS, vol. 10964, pp. 712–724. Springer, Cham (2018). https://doi.org/10.1007/978-3-319-95174-4_54

15. Contò, F., La Sala, P., Papapietro, P.: The metapontum agro-food district of quality. In: Agricultural and Environmental Informatics, Governance and Management, pp. 122–151. IGI Global. https://doi.org/10.4018/978-1-60960-621-3.ch007

16. INEA: Il settore agricolo e agroalimentare della Basilicata Analisi delle principali filiere agricole regionali

17. Notarnicola, B., Tassielli, G., Renzulli, Pietro A., Lo Giudice, A.: Life cycle assessment in the agri-food sector: an overview of its key aspects, international initiatives, certification, labelling schemesand methodological issues. In: Notarnicola, B., Salomone, R., Petti, L., Renzulli, P.A., Roma, R., Cerutti, A.K. (eds.) Life Cycle Assessment in the Agri-food Sector, pp. 1–56. Springer, Cham (2015). https://doi.org/10.1007/978-3-319-11940-3_1

18. Platania, M., Rapisarda, P., Rizzo, M.: Italian trade specialization: persistence and change in regional agri-food production. AGRIS On-line Pap. Econ. Inf. **7**, 101 (2015). ISSN 1804-1930

19. Las Casas, G., Scorza, F.: A renewed rational approach from liquid society towards anti-fragile planning. In: Gervasi, O., et al. (eds.) ICCSA 2017. LNCS, vol. 10409, pp. 517–526. Springer, Cham (2017). https://doi.org/10.1007/978-3-319-62407-5_36

20. Las Casas, G., Murgante, B., Scorza, F.: Regional local development strategies benefiting from open data and open tools and an outlook on the renewable energy sources contribution. In: Papa, R., Fistola, R. (eds.) Smart Energy in the Smart City. GET, pp. 275–290. Springer, Cham (2016). https://doi.org/10.1007/978-3-319-31157-9_14

21. Casas, G.L., Scorza, F.: Discrete spatial assessment of multi-parameter phenomena in low density region: the Val D'Agri case. In: Gervasi, O., et al. (eds.) ICCSA 2015. LNCS, vol. 9157, pp. 813–824. Springer, Cham (2015). https://doi.org/10.1007/978-3-319-21470-2_59

22. Coluzzi, R., et al.: Investigating climate variability and long-term vegetation activity across heterogeneous Basilicata agroecosystems. Geomat. Nat. Hazards Risk 10, 168–180 (2019). https://doi.org/10.1080/19475705.2018.1513872

23. Basso, B., et al.: Analysis of contributing factors to desertification and mitigation measures in Basilicata region. Ital. J. Agron. 5, 33 (2010). https://doi.org/10.4081/ija.2010.s3.33

24. Piccarreta, M., Capolongo, D., Boenzi, F., Bentivenga, M.: Implications of decadal changes in precipitation and land use policy to soil erosion in Basilicata, Italy. https://doi.org/10.1016/j.catena.2005.11.005

25. Nolè, G., Pilogallo, A., Lanorte, A., De Santic, F.: Remote sensing techniques in olive-growing: a review. Curr. Invest. Agric. Curr. Res. 2 (2018). https://doi.org/10.32474/CIACR.2018.02.000138

26. Lanorte, A., et al.: Agricultural plastic waste spatial estimation by Landsat 8 satellite images. Comput. Electron. Agric. 141, 35–45 (2017). https://doi.org/10.1016/J.COMPAG.2017.07.003

27. Soligno, R., Scorza, F., Amato, F., Casas, G.L., Murgante, B.: Citizens participation in improving rural communities quality of life. In: Gervasi, O., et al. (eds.) ICCSA 2015. LNCS, vol. 9156, pp. 731–746. Springer, Cham (2015). https://doi.org/10.1007/978-3-319-21407-8_52

28. Scorza, F., Attolico, A., Moretti, V., Smaldone, R., Donofrio, D., Laguardia, G.: Growing sustainable behaviors in local communities through smart monitoring systems for energy efficiency: RENERGY outcomes. In: Murgante, B., et al. (eds.) ICCSA 2014. LNCS, vol. 8580, pp. 787–793. Springer, Cham (2014). https://doi.org/10.1007/978-3-319-09129-7_57

29. Scorza, F., Attolico, A.: Innovations in promoting sustainable development: the local implementation plan designed by the province of Potenza. In: Gervasi, O., et al. (eds.) ICCSA 2015. LNCS, vol. 9156, pp. 756–766. Springer, Cham (2015). https://doi.org/10.1007/978-3-319-21407-8_54

30. Attolico, A., Scorza, F.: A transnational cooperation perspective for "low carbon economy". In: Gervasi, O., et al. (eds.) ICCSA 2016. LNCS, vol. 9786, pp. 636–641. Springer, Cham (2016). https://doi.org/10.1007/978-3-319-42085-1_54

31. Attolico, A., Smaldone, R., Scorza, F., De Marco, E., Pilogallo, A.: Investigating good practices for low carbon development perspectives in Basilicata. In: Gervasi, O., et al. (eds.) ICCSA 2018. LNCS, vol. 10964, pp. 763–775. Springer, Cham (2018). https://doi.org/10.1007/978-3-319-95174-4_58

32. Attolico, A., et al.: Engaged communities for low carbon development process. In: Gervasi, O., et al. (eds.) ICCSA 2017. LNCS, vol. 10409, pp. 573–584. Springer, Cham (2017). https://doi.org/10.1007/978-3-319-62407-5_41

33. Casas, G.L., Scorza, F.: Sustainable planning: a methodological toolkit. In: Gervasi, O., et al. (eds.) ICCSA 2016. LNCS, vol. 9786, pp. 627–635. Springer, Cham (2016). https://doi.org/10.1007/978-3-319-42085-1_53

34. Las Casas, G.B., Scorza, F., Murgante, B.: From the rules to the models and vice-versa for a new planning rationality. In: Leone, A., Gargiulo, C. (eds.) Environmental and Territorial Modelling for Planning and Design, pp. 499–508. FedOApress (2018). https://doi.org/10. 6093/978-88-6887-048-5

35. Scorza, F.: Improving EU cohesion policy: the spatial distribution analysis of regional development investments funded by EU structural funds 2007/2013 in Italy. In: Murgante, B., et al. (eds.) ICCSA 2013. LNCS, vol. 7973, pp. 582–593. Springer, Heidelberg (2013). https://doi.org/10.1007/978-3-642-39646-5_42

36. Dvarioniene, J., Grecu, V., Lai, S., Scorza, F.: Four perspectives of applied sustainability: research implications and possible integrations. In: Gervasi, O., et al. (eds.) ICCSA 2017. LNCS, vol. 10409, pp. 554–563. Springer, Cham (2017). https://doi.org/10.1007/978-3-319-62407-5_39

37. Scorza, F., Grecu, V.: Assessing sustainability: research directions and relevant issues. In: Gervasi, O., et al. (eds.) ICCSA 2016. LNCS, vol. 9786, pp. 642–647. Springer, Cham (2016). https://doi.org/10.1007/978-3-319-42085-1_55

Theoretical and Computational Chemistry and Its Applications (TCCMA 2019)

Cloud and Local Servers for a Federation of Molecular Science Learning Object Repositories

Sergio Tasso[1]([✉]), Simonetta Pallottelli[1], Osvaldo Gervasi[1],
Federico Sabbatini[1], Valentina Franzoni[1], and Antonio Laganà[2,3]

[1] Department of Mathematics and Computer Science, University of Perugia,
via Vanvitelli, 1, 06123 Perugia, Italy
{sergio.tasso,simonetta.pallottelli,osvaldo.gervasi}@unipg.it
federicosabbatini96@gmail.com
valentina.franzoni@dmi.unipg.it
[2] CNR ISTM, UOS Perugia, via Elce di sotto 8, 06123 Perugia, Italy
lagana05@gmail.com
[3] Master-UP s.r.l., Strada Sperandio, 15, 06125 Perugia, Italy

Abstract. The G-Lorep project of the European Chemistry Thematic
Network (ECTN), based on a federation of distributed repositories of
Molecular Science Learning Objects, leverages at present a "hybrid" cen-
tralized/distributed architecture in which the central node hosts a shared
database. The shared database deals only with the task of managing
metadata to the end of synchronizing the information made available to
the federation members at regular time intervals. In order to avoid missed
synchronization (in the case of the failure of the central node) a scheme
distributing the nodes, adopting a PaaS (Platform as a Service) strategy
and ensuring network security, is implemented and related performances
are evaluated. The efficiency of the developed new architecture of the
federation is measured for a set of Molecular Science Learning Objects
developed within some European distributed computing initiatives and
adopted for the Theoretical Chemistry and Computational Modeling
European Master and Doctoral joint courses. The evolution of the proposed Learning Objects is discussed also in view of the development of
the Molecular Simulator Enabled Cloud Services (MOSEX) pilot project.

Keywords: Chemical reactions · Cloud · Distributed systems ·
Learning objects · Molecular Science · PaaS · Repositories · Security ·
Synchronization

1 Introduction

G-Lorep is a technology aimed at facilitating [18] the sharing of *Learning Objects*
(LOs) among distributed repositories (whose typical scheme is illustrated in
Fig. 1). For this G-Lorep leverages the assembling of a federation of repositories

© Springer Nature Switzerland AG 2019
S. Misra et al. (Eds.): ICCSA 2019, LNCS 11624, pp. 359–373, 2019.
https://doi.org/10.1007/978-3-030-24311-1_26

among the members of a scientific community wishing to share their LOs and to offer them to other community members for further development. Each federate has a web server in its domain that resembles that of the other federates in order to make users feel, even visually, to be using the same environment even when they are operating on a different federate.

The network structure adopted by G-Lorep is hybrid. This permits each website to work stand-alone like (with no need to communicate with the other servers) and to use a central database to get information on the LOs made available on the network. Accordingly, each federate can contact autonomously the central node whose task is only the distribution of metadata so as to allow each member of the federation to update the information through a simple operation of synchronization occurring at regular time intervals. In particular, when an "update" request is received, the member refreshes its own database adding the new data received, creating an image of the LO equal to the original one and providing a link to the federate of origin.

In the G-Lorep initial implementation the central node was placed on a server physically located inside the University of Perugia. This, while guaranteeing a more direct control of the system, was reducing its fault tolerance in the case of Internet communication break-up causing miscommunication among the federates. An additional weakness of the initial implementation was the impossibility of guaranteeing that good practices of security (like the adoption of HTTPS, the automatic updating of Drupal and Linux, the configuring of SSH and Firewall) would be adopted.

Our choice to specialize G-Lorep on research driven Molecular Science (MS) applications [1–4] and, later, on Open MS Cloud [5,6] (see also VIRT& L-COMM.15.2018.4 in http://services.chm.unipg.it/ojs/index.php/virtlcomm/article/view/203) has further driven its evolution towards:

(a) an improvement of the technical quality of the service provided (like fault tolerance, availability, network survivability, etc.);
(b) the adoption of an evolutive policy in educational quality (integration of video and audio, easiness and traceability of the changes introduced, usability and evaluability of the product, etc.).

Accordingly, the paper focuses on the new architectural features of the G-Lorep federation obtained by moving the central node into the Cloud, using a PaaS approach, as discussed in Sect. 2 where the organization of G-Lorep in the cloud is described and Sect. 3 where the technique used to secure each G-Lorep server is detailed. In Sect. 4, then, the case study of the implementation of cooperative LOs related to the MS theoretical and computational foundations of the teaching course on Mechanisms and Dynamics of Chemical Reactions (MDCR) is analyzed in some detail. Finally, in Sect. 5, some conclusions are drawn and some directions of related future work are outlined.

2 G-Lorep in the Cloud

The new architecture of the G-Lorep federation with the central node moved into the Cloud according to a PaaS scheme is sketched in Fig. 1.

2.1 How G-Lorep Works

In the scheme of Fig. 1 each server runs a daemon called *server.php* whose task is to achieve the main architectural goal of the project: the synchronization of databases. Every N seconds *server.php* makes a query to sharedDB (a database accessible from the outside) asking the list of metadata about all *linkable objects* whose domain of origin differs from its own (*Delegated Objects*). Then it runs INSERT, UPDATE and DELETE on its own database for each *linkable object* whose received content differs from the one already present in its own *Delegated Objects* table.

After completion of synchronization, it elaborates its own *linkable objects* list (*Owned Objects*) and uploads relevant metadata to the database by running again INSERT, UPDATE and DELETE for each *linkable object* having the same origin domain and different content.

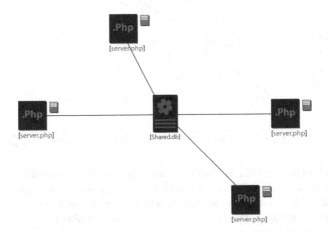

Fig. 1. The sharedBD based approach of typical federated repository of LOs.

2.2 The Shared Database

As already mentioned, sharedDB is a database accessible from the outside. It is a central node of a hybrid system acting like a meeting place where all federates can share their data sets. The shared database does not contain confidential information (like accounts or emails). It contains only meta-data of each repository (i.e. information like title, author, category, etc., which are all public information readable from a guest user that is visiting any federate website). It is important, though, to protect this database because an attacker could use the server to send malicious data to the federates and through it attack them too.

This approach bears advantages and disadvantages as pointed out below:

- **Advantages** - In the proposed hybrid scheme a federate does not need to send its metadata to all the other members of the federation and can update at the same time its local database with meta-data from all the members of the federation through synchronization. Using a central system, on the contrary, when shareddDB goes down, all websites are unable to read data from the database because no federate has a local database of *linkable objects* and this leads to a malfunction of the website.
- **Disadvantages** - The use of sharedDB (instead of a server like RESTFUL API), could incur both security and, if the central node goes down, federation synchronization problems.

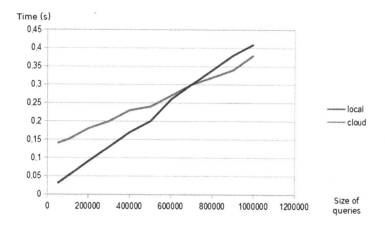

Fig. 2. Local (blue) and cloud (red) elaboration times for queries of different complexity (i.e. queries executed on tables with an increasing number of records) plotted as a function of size. The cloud elaboration is faster, but it requires a fixed time interval to send the output over the network (latency). (Color figure online)

In our approach security problems are, indeed, avoided by both using a firewall guaranteeing database access only to the IP addresses of the white-list of the federates and creating a user database for each member of the federation. If an account is violated, the data may become available only if the request is made by a G-Lorep member. In that case it is sufficient to create a new user database for that federate. In this way, the security is delegated to the database server, without the risk of creating new security exploits via either the RESTFUL API code or the daemon server hosting it.

Problems relevant to the central node fault tolerance, availability and network survivability are bypassed by inserting the node into the Cloud. In such case, using the PaaS (Platform as a Service) of a service provider, the above mentioned problems, including the security ones, are reconducted to the responsibility of the service provider. After all, the cost of the limited size of the involved database and of the small number of the involved queries is negligible with respect to the gained advantages (as shown in Fig. 2 in which both local and cloud elaboration times are plotted as a function of the number of records (size) of the queries).

2.3 Moving SharedDB into the Cloud

Choice of the Service Provider: As Cloud Service Provider we adopted Amazon whose AmazonRDS PaaS is specifically designed for databases (in the remainder of the paper we shall refer to it as DBaaS).

Creation of SharedDB and Data Import: Once created a dump of sharedDB into the old VPS located in the University of Perugia, it is migrated in a MariaDB instance created from the Amazon RDS Console. After completing the creation of the instance, a client can connect to the endpoint using an ad hoc created DB user. These information are provided to G-Lorep by a configuration file. The AmazonRDS has a security group configured to accept only connections taken from a white-list of IP addresses. In this way unauthorized connections are inhibited.

Performance Obtained: Advantages and disadvantages of using the Cloud for this purpose are:

- **Advantages**: the database is more secure and available, not only in the case of attacks, but also in cases of loss of data and machine malfunction. The AmazonRDS console permits to automatize various services like hardware provisioning, updates, backups while showing to the administrators all the information about CPU and memory usage, connections established, I/O performed, etc. Moreover there are increments of performance about speed of computation of big queries because the hardware and software used by Amazon is optimized for this purpose.
- **Disadvantages**: the database is located geographically away from the federation members and this could create latency problems. G-Lorep, however, is not latency sensitive and this is important because, actually, the federation may easily contain truly geographically dispersed servers.

3 Securing Each G-Lorep Server

Compromised federates could be extremely dangerous for the network, because they can send malicious data to sharedDB and make them to be downloaded onto the other members of the federation. In order to guarantee a high level of security the following measures have been adopted for each federate.

3.1   Security Policies

In order to increase internal safety, everybody must have a different account on the server. This will guarantee optimal logging and no need to password change and redistribution in case of troubles.

All users must have as a username a word that is not part of a dictionary and a secure password (as usual the password must contain uppercase, lowercase, number and symbol characters and not contain words). In order to enforce the adoption of these rules, the `libpam-cracklib` was installed.

Root user has been deactivated and **sudo** permission has been guaranteed only to a few users.

3.2   SSH Configurations

To the end of securing the *SSH* server, *SSHD* has been configured so as to accept only connections originating from trusted IP addresses, and has been activated only for few users belonging to a given particular group. The authentication is performed via a private key instead of using a password. The *root* login is totally forbidden.

Furthermore, the *SSHD* does not address itself to the default port (22) because it has been moved to a different one that is known only to a few authorized users.

3.3   Network Security

In each G-Lorep server various levels of network security are adopted.

The first level of security is provided by the network firewall, that is configured to guarantee only connections to ports 80 and 443 (*HTTP* and *HTTPS*, respectively). Connections to the *SSHD* port are negated too for those G-Lorep servers which have a *VPN* service that permits a connection via LAN or, as an alternative, connection is permitted only to a white-list of IP addresses. If a list of trusted IP addresses can not be prepared, the network firewall opens both the 22 and the true *SSHD* port and an ad hoc created daemon will listen to port 22. The task of this daemon is to add to the firewall a blacklist of all IP addresses that contact it. In this way a port scanning coming from a single machine (that is the first phase of an attack) is inhibited.

The second level of security is provided by the internal firewall of Linux, `iptables`, which is configured as the network firewall. In addition it has rules created to avoid spoofing. For certain chains, `iptables` changes its rules dynamically via two daemons: one daemon is used to get the list of TOR (from The Onion Project API) nodes and add all their IP addresses to the blacklist, the second daemon (Fail2Ban) provides a defense from brute force attacks. It reaches its task by scanning logs of various services (*SSHD*, Web server, etc.) and by adding the suspicious IP addresses to the chain. It sends also an email to the administrator with the *WHOIS* of the attacking server. In the end, some rules of `sysctl` permitting the forwarding and the redirection of packets (these are routing functions) have been deactivated.

3.4   Web Server and Database Protection

At present G-Lorep servers make use of HTTPS, instead of HTTP, by adopting *Certbot* (a software provided by the project **LetsEncrypt** of the **Linux Foundation**) that installs automatically a signed certificate for free.

In order to prevent dangerous actions from an attacker, the web server has both the `AllowOverride` (G-Lorep does not need `.htaccess` to work properly) and the `Indexes` options deactivated (with the latter one being motivated by the need of avoiding the analysis of the structure of the website).

PhpMyAdmin is the interface used for managing DB from the browser, without needing to login via SSH. It has been configured to permit connection only to a certain pool of IP addresses and for certain ad hoc created users. Furthermore, its directory has been hidden in order to prevent brute force attacks (like those provided by *DirBuster*). This is strengthened by the presence of Fail2Ban.

The website makes use of a database user differing from *root*. Such user can be accessed only via `root shell`. The database also has activated a logging of failed attempts of login.

Drupal is the CMS currently used inside G-Lorep. It has been upgraded to the latest version and an automatic upgrade has been activated for small updates.

3.5   Improve Security Monitoring Files and Logs

It is really important to monitor logs, installed software and related files in order to improve a better level of security.

In the server there is no software using daily `wget` or `curl`. Because of this these two softwares are configured to logging their executions and send an email to the administrators every time they are used. Furthermore, every time a root shell is created (for example with `sudo su`), an email is automatically sent with the logs to administrators.

In all servers software has been installed in order to provide protection against rootkits and other malware. Both Rkhunter and Chrootkit are installed to create a more complete protection against these category of attacks, and both send alerts to the administrator when problems arise.

Finally *Logcheck* has been installed for providing log analysis in a wide number of files with reports being sent via email.

3.6   Backups

A possible attacker can modify the website by adding PHP or JavaScript codes for installing mining software or creating a backdoor with a reverse shell. Into each G-Lorep server daily backup and upload actions have been also established to the end of facilitating disaster recovery. Furthermore, it is important to backup the logging files and the web site into a different space located into the Cloud in order to contrast the possible deletion by attackers that try to hide their actions.

4   Cooperative Learning Objects for Mechanisms and Dynamics of Chemical Reactions

As already mentioned, the Molecular Science application considered here is a set of LOs designed for the MDCR (Mechanisms and Dynamics of Chemical Reactions) course being developed as a collaborative endeavour among theoretical and computational chemists, theoretical and computational physicists, kinetics and molecular beam scattering experimentalists.

4.1   The Demand for Learning Objects to Support Chemistry e-Learning

The development of the Molecular science LOs discussed here was prompted by the activities of the European Chemistry Thematic Network (ECTN) and its Association. ECTN was started in the year 1996 as a result of the approval of the homonimous Life Long Learning project (ECTN later named ECTN-1). ECTN-1 gathered together over 130 Chemistry departments to define the European Core Chemistry and related practical skills. The ECTN members designed and developed for this purpose a solid de facto standard by harmonizing at European level Higher Education curricula in Organic Chemistry (OC), Physical Chemistry (PC), Inorganic Chemistry (IC), Analytical Chemistry (AC) together with Mathematics and Physics. In the years 2000/2003 the ECTN-2 project focused on e-learning and on the development of the EChemTest® appropriate e-test Libraries of Questions and Answers (Q&A)s for General Chemistry 1 and 2 (GC1 for Schools and GC2 for Universities), Biological Chemistry (BC3), AC3, IC3, OC3 and PC3 at Bachelor level with the technical support of the Perugia and Vienna Universities. In the years 2003/2009 the next funded ECTN-3 and ECTN-4 projects developed educational tools to support students' mobility and the activities of the Virtual Education Community (VEC) including the adoption of multimedia and networked ICT technologies [7].

During the 2009/2015 period, the EC2E2N-1 and EC2E2N-2 projects extended the work to the support material for the MDCR LOs considered in the present paper. The attempt to disseminate support materials for the MDCR LOs relies on the adoption of a collaborative user/producer model (that is often referred to as Prosumer) in science and education [5,6]). In the Prosumer model the activities of the members continuously feed new information into the system both as producers and as users improving continuously so far its quality in a tight interaction of the feedbacks obtained from the usage and the requirements of the assessment process. The main features of such collaborative scheme are: self-consistency, modularity, availability, reusability, interoperability with no locality and no (or extremely limited) ownership constraints of the knowledge as is typical of cloud services. These features are highly desirable as they give utmost thoroughness to information by prompting knowledge provision be flexibly aggregated and readily used (and re-used) thanks also to the association with metadata which allow to verify the existence and the properties of the information.

4.2   The Collaborative Science and Technology European Initiative for Molecular Science

In the case of the assembling of the MDRC LOs the Molecular Science community has leveraged in the last twenty years the COST (www.cost.eu/) activities aimed at gathering related collaborative efforts. The Action most directly correlated to this endeavour is D23 (METACHEM, www.cost.eu/COST_Actions/cmst/D23 launched by the University of Perugia in the year 2000). D23 initiated the development of tools connecting the activities of different Molecular Science research laboratories operating on a shared computing platform made of a geographically distributed cluster of heterogeneous computers connected on a network (LAN, MAN or WAN) through a software co-ordinating them as a single virtual parallel machine [8]. This established a network of the so called European Meta Laboratories fostering innovative solutions for chemical applications and a new paradigm for collaborative research. In the year 2006 a new COST Action (D37—Grid Computing in Chemistry: GRIDCHEM) was started to the end of developing collaborative distributed grid solutions and paradigms for molecular science research. GRIDCHEM leveraged the creation and use of distributed computing infrastructures ("Grids") and drove collaborative computer modelling and simulation in chemistry towards new frontiers in complexity and a new regime of time-to-solution [9] including molecular simulators of complex molecular reactive systems. This evolution line was then continued by the initiatives CMMST (virtual research environment), COMPCHEM (a Virtual Organization), GEMS (the Grid empowered molecular simulator) initiatives developed within the EGEE (Enabling Grids for E-sciencE) and the EGI (European Grid Infrastructure) European projects with its pilot MS computational applications [10] and [11] under the umbrella of the COMPCHEM Virtual Organization (VO) [12] and the computational frame of the Grid Empowered Molecular Simulator GEMS [13].

4.3   The Driving Force for Designing the LOs

In particular, the driving force for designing related LOs was provided by the wish to foster the development of competences in:

- selecting the compute resources based on quality parameters and a composition of higher level of complexity chained applications through the coordinated usage of distributed hardware and software,
- fostering the use of specialized web portals and workflows facilitating the production of data and know how in science and innovation, the direct reuse of the produced data and knowledge for education, training and further research
- producing and providing computational means designed for dealing with molecular and materials disciplines when carrying out multi-scale treatments necessary to reproduce the observables of realistic systems in the area of energy, environment, materials, pharmacology, chemistry, biology, biotechnologies, medicine, etc.

- developing state-of-the-art first principles electronic structure and nuclei dynamics methodologies,
- designing high level of accuracy multiscale complex molecular systems,
- knowledge managing for training in sciences and technologies,
- collecting the requirements,
- validating the developed procedures,
- disseminating the outcomes, user support and knowledge transfer tools,
- adopting existing scientific gateways, workflows, data management and commons.

which are the common scientific and technological background for modern MS.

4.4   The Support of the European Educational Initiatives

A significant impulse to such endeavour was given by the Theoretical Chemistry and Computational Modeling (TCCM) European Master and by the homonymous ITN European Doctorate (https://tccm.qui.uam.es/) both coordinated by the Universidad Autonoma of Madrid. Within these two initiatives, the mentioned LOs are being actively used to form a new generation of young researchers able to tackle the development of modern chemistry, biochemistry, chemical biology and material science applications using state-of-the-art first principles electronic structure and nuclei dynamics codes, implementing accurate multi-scale simulators of smart energy carriers in combustion, energy storage, space missions, bioinorganic chemistry, exploiting both ab initio and empirically parameterized kinetic data, designing materials and modelling supra-molecular phenomenology, handling extended information systems for the investigation of the structure and processes of complex molecular systems relevant to pharmacology, medicinal and biological systems, and managing distributed knowledge processes. A particularly systematic use of the mentioned LOs is made in parallel with the use of the book "Chemical Reactions: basic theory and computing" [14]. The mentioned LOs were used also for the School of Open Science Cloud, (SOSC) (see https://indico.cern.ch/event/605204/overview and http://services. chm.unipg.it/ojs/index.php/virtlcomm/issue/view/25 held in Perugia on June 2017 and for the sessions of the one month long Intensive Course (IC) of the last edition of the already mentioned TCCM Erasmus Mundus Master (Perugia September 2018).

4.5   The Proposed LOs

Within the above mentioned development environment the following tentative list of LOs was made [15]:

1. **From the phenomenology of chemical reactions to the study of two body collisions**
   LO 1.1 From Kinetics to Bimolecular Collisions (The phenomenological approach, Realistic kinetic models, The Transition State Theory approach, Towards detailed single collision studies)

LO 1.2 Classical mechanics of two particle collisions (Reference frame and elementary interactions, The equations of motion, The deflection angle)

LO 1.3 The computation of scattering properties (Trajectories integration (Hamilton equations), Numerical computation of the deflection angle, Other collisional properties, The cross section)

LO 1.4 Popular scattering model potentials (The rigid sphere model, The Repulsive Coulomb potential, Sutherland and Morse attractive-repulsive potentials, The scattering Lennard-Jones (6–12) potential)

2. **The quantum approach to the two-body problem**

LO 2.1 Quantum mechanics and bound states (The limits of the classical mechanics approach, The 3D quantum problem and its decomposition, The Harmonic Oscillator)

LO 2.2 Quantum elastic scattering (The Coulomb potentials and the hydrogen atom, The formulation of quantum elastic scattering, The quantum elastic scattering cross section)

LO 2.3 Realistic Models for scattering systems (Continuum solutions for hydrogen-like atoms at positive E values, The rigid sphere, The Morse potential)

LO 2.4 Numerical integration of the Schroedinger equation (Expectation values of the operators, Approximation to the Laplacian, Approximating the wave function, The approximation to the potential)

LO 2.5 Numerical applications (Systems of linear algebraic equations, The structure of the wavefunctions, The Time-Dependent method)

3. **Ab initio electronic structure for few-body systems**

LO 3.1 Structured Bodies (The one-electron wavefunction approach, Quantum Monte Carlo, Many electron wavefunctions, The electronic structure of molecules)

LO 3.2 Higher Level ab initio Methods (Beyond the Hartree-Fock method, The CI and MC-SCF methods, Perturbation methods)

LO 3.3 Towards extended applications (Computation of other molecular properties, Density Functional Theory methods, The valence electron method, Dropping multicenter integrals)

LO 3.4 Full range process potentials (The three body internuclear coordinates, Global formulation of the potential energy surface

4. **The treatment of few-and multi-body reactions**

LO 4.1 The combined dynamics of electrons and nuclei (The N body dynamical equations, A direct integration of the general equations, The Born-Oppenheimer approximation)

LO 4.2 Three atom systems (Three body orthogonal coordinates, Atom-diatom reactive scattering Jacobi method, Atom-diatom time independent APH method, The atom-diatom time-dependent APH method)

LO 4.3 Beyond full quantum calculations (Reduced dimensionality quantum treatments, Leveraging on classical mechanics, Semiclassical treatments)

LO 4.4 Basic features of atom-diatom reactions (Energy dependence of the detailed probabilities, Quantum effects, Experimental observables, Periodic orbits and statistical considerations, The last mile to the experiment)

LO 4.5 Towards more complex systems (Full range Ab initio PESs for many body systems, Fitting PESs for reactive and non reactive channels, Four atom Many Process Expansion, Four atom quantum and quantum-classical dynamics, Last mile calculations for crossed beam experiments).

Some examples of the MDCR LOs produced in collaboration with the Multimedia Centre of the University of Perugia are accessible at the G_Lorep address https://glorep.unipg.it. The abstract of the course is given in the upper part of Fig. 3 while the screenshot of the summary of the introductory LO00 (preliminary to the above mentioned Los) showing also the speakers is given in the lower box of the same Figure.

Fig. 3. Abstract of the MDCR course (upper part) and screenshot of the introductory slide of the initial LO (lower part).

4.6   The MOSEX Project

As mentioned in the programme of the OMSC (Open Molecular Science Cloud) workshop (see www.dcbb.unipg.it/euco2019) this effort is part of the plans for implementing MOSEX (MOlecular Simulator Enabled Cloud Services) as a European Open Science Cloud Pilot designed as a follow-up of the EGI COMPCHEM Virtual Organization (VO) activities. MOSEX aims to gather together and offer as a service on the cloud for the Molecular Science (as reported at the last meeting of the CTC Division Board of EuChemS at the end of August 2018 in Liverpool and will be planned in more detail during the last part of the mentioned OMSC workshop next September 5 and 6 at the "Accademia Nazionale delle Scienze (dei XL)" in Rome) by implementing the Prosumer Model for the following applications:

- Molecular electronic structure and dynamical properties programs like GEMS (small molecules chemical processes (including ab initio determination of analytical Potentials), their Quantum/Classical dynamics efficiency and properties obtainable from the analysis of the wavefunction, the Molecular Dynamics on excited states, VMS: (Virtual Spectrometer)
- Drug design programs and related cloud services (QSPR and 3D QSPR models)
- CHEMCONNECT (Distributed repository of molecular science data), IOCHEM (organization, publication and storage of molecular information on materials)
- Dissemination and evaluation of molecular knowledge like in MolSSI (Molecular science software tools development and training) and VIRT&L-COMM (e-magazine for virtual community activities dissemination).

5   Conclusion and Future Work

As discussed above, the organization of our G-Lorep federation of distributed repositories is suited to assemble MS Learning Objects in a cooperative way. This has been found to be extremely useful when dealing with LO materials implemented for supporting ECTN EChemTest Self evaluation assessment sessions. In the particular case discussed in the present paper, the LOs of the Mechanisms and Dynamics of Chemical Reactions course, one has to build on the expertise of theoretical and computational chemists, theoretical and computational physicists, kinetics and scattering experimentalists, to succeed in that one has keep the LO contents continuously updated and correct. The best products in fact can emerge only as a result of a continuous interaction between usage and production.

According to the high potentiality shown by G-Lorep in dealing with the LOs we plan also to consider in the near future the migration of G-Lorep from Drupal 7 to Drupal 8, the rewriting of part (if not all) of its modules using a PHP Framework and the abandoning of the use of a CMS to further improve security when needed. We are considering, as well, to create an image of Debian containing a version of G-Lorep pre-configured with the policy described in the present paper in order to simplify its installation and allow a better integration of new federates. This will imply the writing of a script that, once launched, customizes the system by changing all private information (like accounts and database credentials and related configuration file of the web server). It will make it easier to register as a member of the G-Lorep federation once that a new user database is provided to its server and is inserted into the white-list of the sharedDB node. A third future task of future work will be the creation of a general G-Lorep located in the Cloud where everyone can insert their own learning objects regardless of their institution of origin.

A further future improvement, being already experimented [16,17], is the introduction of the semantic metadata created by the G-Lorep Taxonomy Assistant in the standard format for use in the learning object exchange.

References

1. Tasso, S., Pallottelli, S., Bastianini, R., Lagana, A.: Federation of distributed and collaborative repositories and its application on science learning objects. In: Murgante, B., Gervasi, O., Iglesias, A., Taniar, D., Apduhan, B.O. (eds.) ICCSA 2011. LNCS, vol. 6784, pp. 466–478. Springer, Heidelberg (2011). https://doi.org/10. 1007/978-3-642-21931-3_36
2. Tasso, S., Pallottelli, S., Ferroni, M., Bastianini, R., Laganà, A.: Taxonomy management in a federation of distributed repositories: a chemistry use case. In: Murgante, B., et al. (eds.) ICCSA 2012. LNCS, vol. 7333, pp. 358–370. Springer, Heidelberg (2012). https://doi.org/10.1007/978-3-642-31125-3_28
3. Tasso, S., Pallottelli, S., Rui, M., Laganá, A.: Learning objects efficient handling in a federation of science distributed repositories. In: Murgante, B., et al. (eds.) ICCSA 2014. LNCS, vol. 8579, pp. 615–626. Springer, Cham (2014). https://doi. org/10.1007/978-3-319-09144-0_42
4. Pallottelli, S., Tasso, S., Rui, M., Laganà, A., Kozaris, I.: Exchange of learning objects between a learning management system and a federation of science distributed repositories. In: Gervasi, O., et al. (eds.) ICCSA 2015. LNCS, vol. 9156, pp. 371–383. Springer, Cham (2015). https://doi.org/10.1007/978-3-319-21407-8_27
5. Laganà, A., Gervasi, O., Tasso, S., Perri, D., Franciosa, F.: The ECTN virtual education community prosumer model for promoting and assessing chemical knowledge. In: Gervasi, O., et al. (eds.) ICCSA 2018. LNCS, vol. 10964, pp. 533–548. Springer, Cham (2018). https://doi.org/10.1007/978-3-319-95174-4_42
6. Laganà, A., Terstyanszky, G., Krüger, J.: Open molecular science for the open science cloud. In: Gervasi, O., et al. (eds.) ICCSA 2017. LNCS, vol. 10406, pp. 29–43. Springer, Cham (2017). https://doi.org/10.1007/978-3-319-62398-6_3
7. Laganà, A., et al.: From computer assisted to grid empowered teaching and learning activities in higher level chemistry education. In: Eilks, I., Byers, B. (eds.) Innovative Methods of Teaching and Learning Chemistry in Higher Education Royal Society of Chemistry (2009). ISBN 978-1-84755-958-6
8. Foster, I., Kesselman, C. (eds.): The Grid: Blueprint for a New Computing Infrastructure. Morgan Kaufmann Publishers, San Francisco (1999)
9. Foster, I., Kesselman, C., Tuecke, S.: The anatomy of the grid: enabling scalable virtual organisations. Int. J. Supercomput. Appl. 15(3), 200–222 (2001)
10. Storchi, L., Tarantelli, F., Laganà, A.: Computing molecular energy surfaces on a grid. In: Gavrilova, M., et al. (eds.) ICCSA 2006. LNCS, vol. 3980, pp. 675–683. Springer, Heidelberg (2006). https://doi.org/10.1007/11751540_71
11. Gervasi, O., Laganà, A.: SIMBEX: a portal for the a priori simulation of crossed beam experiments. Future Gener. Comput. Syst. 20(5), 703–716 (2004)
12. Laganà, A., Costantini, A., Gervasi, O., Faginas Lago, N., Manuali, C., Rampino, S.: COMPCHEM: progress towards GEMS a grid empowered molecular simulator and beyond. J. Grid Comput. 8(4), 571–586 (2010)

13. Rampino, S., Pirani, F., Laganà, A., Garcia, E.: A study of the impact of long range interactions on the N + N$_2$ reactivity using GEMS. Int. J. Web Grid Serv. **6**, 196–212 (2010)
14. Laganà, A., Parker, G.A.: Chemical Reactions Basic Theory and Computing. Springer, Heidelberg (2018). ISBN 978-3-319-62355-9
15. Moriconi, A., Pasqua, S., Squarta, G., Laganà, A.: Chemical reactions learning objects. VIRT&L-COMM.14.2018.4. http://services.chm.unipg.it/ojs/index.php/virtlcomm/article/view/191
16. Franzoni, V., Tasso, S., Pallottelli, S., Perri, D.: Sharing linkable learning objects between a content management system and a learning management system with the use of metadata and a taxonomy assistant for categorization. LNCS (in press)
17. Franzoni, V., Mencacci, M., Mengoni, P., Milani, A.: Semantic heuristic search in collaborative networks: measures and contexts. In: Proceedings - 2014 IEEE/WIC/ACM International Joint Conference on Web Intelligence and Intelligent Agent Technology - Workshops, WI-IAT 2014, vol. 1, pp. 187–217 (2014). https://doi.org/10.1109/WI-IAT.2014.27
18. Tasso, S., Gervasi, O., Locchi, A., Sabbatini, F.: Hahai: computational thinking in primary schools. In: Misra, S., et al. (eds.): ICCSA 2019, LNCS, vol. 11620, pp. 287–298 (2019, in press)

Molecular Simulations of $CO_2/N_2/H_2O$ Gaseous Mixture Separation in Graphtriyne Membrane

Noelia Faginas-Lago[1](✉)(iD), Yusuf Bramastya Apriliyanto[2](iD),
and Andrea Lombardi[1](iD)

[1] Dipartimento di Chimica, Biologia e Biotecnologie, Università di Perugia,
Perugia, Italy
noelia.faginaslago@unipg.it
[2] Department of Chemistry, Bogor Agricultural University,
Jl Tanjung Kampus IPB Dramaga, 16680 Bogor, Indonesia

Abstract. Graphynes are porous derivatives of graphene that can be considered as ideal 2D nanofilters. Here, we investigate by theoretical methods graphtriyne single layer, proposing them as membranes featuring pores of subnanometer size suitable for $CO_2/N_2/H_2O$ separation and CO_2 uptake. The potential energy surfaces, representing the intermolecular interactions within the $CO_2/N_2/H_2O$ gaseous mixtures and between the graphtriyne single layer and the molecules, have been formulated in an internally consistent way, by adopting potential models far more accurate than the traditional Lennard-Jones functions, routinely used to predict static and dynamical properties of matter.

Keywords: Molecular dynamics · Empirical potential energy surface ·
Gaseous separation · Graphtriyne membrane · DL_POLY

1 Introduction

CO_2 concentration in the atmosphere is in a high level and it keeps arising in recent decades due to economic growth reasons in most of countries [1]. Many problems arise from the excess of CO_2, for instance environmental pollution and climate change in connection to the global warming phenomenon [2]. Adsorption using porous materials is a promising way to capture CO_2 generated mostly by fossil fuels combustion, in order to mitigate greenhouse gas effects associated with excessive CO_2 emissions into the atmosphere [3–6]. This method is favoured in terms of its simplicity and low implementation costs than the traditional aqueous chemical absorption [7]. A range of porous materials such as nanoporous carbons [8–10], zeolites and zeolitic imidazolate framework (ZIFs) [11,12], metal-organic frameworks (MOFs) [13], porous polymer networks (PPNs) or also known as covalent organic frameworks/polymers (COFs/COPs) [14,15], and a slurry made of solid adsorbents in a liquid absorbent [16] have been exploited

© Springer Nature Switzerland AG 2019
S. Misra et al. (Eds.): ICCSA 2019, LNCS 11624, pp. 374–387, 2019.
https://doi.org/10.1007/978-3-030-24311-1_27

and reported for CO_2 capture in the past few years. An alternative to porous adsorbing materials is a nanoporous membrane that use a combination of surface adsorption and its intrinsic pores acting as molecular sieving to separate CO_2 from other gaseous mixtures [17].

However, due to the vast number of theoretically applicable materials, in practice it is very difficult or even an impossible task to experimentally synthesize, characterize and evaluate their performance for CO_2 capture and separation of all possible materials [18–20]. Up to this state, computer modelling and simulations play an important role in the material design and development, prior to the experimental stage [3]. A generic force fields like AMBER [21] and UFF [22] often does not have the appropriate parameters when we deal with a particular system, thus parts of the potential energy function have to be developed or refined on purpose, using available theoretical and experimental data. Although force fields parameterization is a delicate task, the development of force fields is an indispensable work. In the last years, various force fields have specifically been developed for evaluating gaseous adsorption in porous carbons, graphene and its derivatives [23–25] MOFs [26,27], zeolites [28] and other polymeric materials [29] to quantitatively describe molecular interactions providing realistic predictions of relevant adsorption dynamics and transport properties of gas under consideration. Recently, carbon-based membranes emerge as potential materials because of their exceptional properties (e.g. hydrophobic, chemically inert and thermally stable) are economically suitable and viable for post combustion CO_2 capture and separation [29,30]. MOFs and polymers for instance, although they exhibit good selectivity and permeability, they are susceptible to heat and water vapour which is a characteristic of post combustion flue gas. Permeability and selectivity are two main aspects to determine whether a membrane can be effective for gas separation. It is already known that permeability is inversely proportional to the thickness of the membrane. Therefore, single atom thick planar membrane may have great potential for gas separation [31]. γ-graphynes are single atomic layers belonging to the class of carbon allotropes where the carbon atoms are arranged as a function of the C-C triple bonds bridging two adjacent hexagons. γ-graphynes exhibit similar properties with graphene, but the pores are uniformly distributed and adjustable [32]. Moreover, γ-graphynes have lower dispersion forces that minimalize aggregates formation among graphyne molecules. Synthesis and characterization techniques of graphyne are actively being developed in the last years [33]. Force fields related to gas adsorption on γ-graphynes have also been developed and tested on accurate ab initio calculations in our previous works [34–37]. Therefore, in this report, extended molecular dynamics (MD) simulations were performed on a wide range of conditions of applied interest in post combustions; involving $CO_2/N_2/H_2O$ gaseous mixtures separation [38] in graphtriyne membrane (a form of γ-graphynes, in which each phenyl ring is connected through three acetylenic bonds placed as a bridge).

On an other hand, Molecular Dynamics (MD) simulations is a theoretical powerful tool to analyze extensively the structural rearrangement of pure solvents, solution mixtures and the combustion processes [39–45]. Combustion is a complex of chemical and physical nature of the process that leads to the conversion of chemical energy into heat energy stored in fuels. From a molecular point of view, the combustion is the result of numerous elementary processes, chemical reactions including mono-, bi- and ter-molecular and energy-transfer processes (which ensure the distribution of the energy released by the exothermic reactions to everything the system) [46–49].

The paper is organized as follows: in Sect. 2, we outline the methods and the construction of the potential energy function. We give in Sect. 3 the details of preliminary results and in Sect. 4 concluding remarks are given.

2   Methods

The MD simulations were performed in the simulation box of 72.210 Å × 62.523 Å× 280.0 Å. Each box consists of graphtriyne membrane with dimensions of 72.210 Å× 62.523 Å placed in the middle of the box. Four different temperatures (333, 353, 373 and 400 K) were employed for the simulations of $CO_2/N_2/H_2O$ gaseous mixture with equal composition of CO_2, N_2 and H_2O. The structures of graphtriyne membranes were taken from Ref. [50], where the structures had been optimized using periodic DFT calculations. A H_2O model reported in Ref. [51] was implemented with the charge distributions correspond to the dipole moment of water in gas phase (1.85 D) [52], while a three-charge-site N_2 model [53] and a five-charge-site CO_2 model [54] were adopted to account for the quadrupole moment (See Fig. 1).

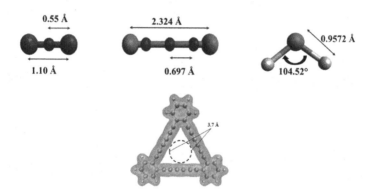

Fig. 1. The models used to represent nitrogen, carbon dioxide and water. Unit pore of graphtriyne represented by the electron density plot of its smallest molecular precursor. The dashed circle depicted inside the triangular pore correspond to its effective pore with a diameter of about 3.7 Å.

The intermolecular forces between the gas molecules, and between the gas molecules and the membranes were expressed using the Improved Lennard-Jones (ILJ) potential [55–59].

$$V_{ILJ}(r) = \varepsilon \left[\frac{m}{n(r) - m} \left(\frac{r_0}{r} \right)^{n(r)} - \frac{n(r)}{n(r) - m} \left(\frac{r_0}{r} \right)^{m} \right]$$ (1)

In Eq. 1, ε, r_0 and m are pair specific parameters and r is the distance between the positions of the two interacting centers placed on different molecules. The first term of the bracketed sum in Eq. 1 (the positive one) represents the size-repulsion contribution arising from each pair, while the second term (negative) represents the effective dispersion attraction contribution for the given pair of centers. The exponent $n(r)$ of the first term modulates the falloff of the repulsion and controls the strength of the attraction as a function of r as follows:

$$n(r) = \beta + 4.0 \left(\frac{r}{r_0} \right)^2$$ (2)

with β being an adjustable parameter able to modulate the hardness of the interaction [60,61]. The introduction of this modulating parameter (not present in the standard Lennard-Jones function (LJ)) provides ILJ with the possibility of indirectly taking into account some effects of the induction, charge transfer and atom clustering. The parameter β also corrects the dependence of the interaction on the internuclear distance, improving the LJ function in the asymptotic region. For a full account of the advantages of the ILJ function see Refs. [62–65] and references therein and also parallel studies for the construction of expansion basis sets for the quantum mechanical treatment of N-body problems of practical interest for intermolecular and intramolecular and reactive dynamics of polyatomic molecules and clusters [66–69]. In the interactions between neutral molecules m is set equal to 6.

All of the ILJ parameters used in this report was improved and tested in comparison with high level ab initio calculations Ref. [35,50]. The cutoff distance for the ILJ and electrostatic interactions is 15 Å, where the Ewald method was applied for the calculation of electrostatic interactions. All molecular dynamics simulation were performed using DL_POLY program [70] in the canonical (NVT) ensemble employing the Nose-Hoover thermostat with periodic boundary conditions in all directions. Each simulation was performed for 5.5 ns after 0.5 ns equilibration period with a fixed timestep of 1 fs, where the statistical data and trajectory were collected every 2 ps.

Seven different amounts of gas have been loaded into the simulation box for every system to investigate the influence of pressure in our simulations. The gas pressure was computed using the Peng-Robinson equation of state [71]. In order to mimic post-combustion conditions, the initial pressures were chosen at relatively low pressure, under 5.5 atm. The gas molecules were randomly distributed with equal amount into the two regions of box, thus there is no pressure gradient inside the box (Fig. 2). The membranes were considered as a frozen framework and the gas molecules were treated as rigid bodies. The gas molecules could cross the membrane multi times at both directions during the simulation. The number of permeation events was then monitored along with the z-density and radial distribution function profiles. All graphical representations of the molecular trajectories were processed using VMD package [72].

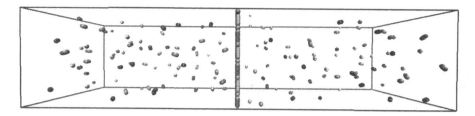

Fig. 2. The simulation box filled with gaseous mixture of CO_2, N_2 and H_2O. The cyan layer in the middle of the box is the graphtriyne single layer.

3   Results and Discussion

3.1   Gas Permeability

Production run of every simulation was initialized after the equilibration step. The number of permeation events occurred during the production run was counted and then plotted against the simulation time. The slope of this plot is an estimation of the gas permeation rate measured in a unit of molecules ps^{-1} (Fig. 3). Using this data, the gas permeance was then calculated by dividing the permeation rate with the corresponding pressure and area of the membrane. Gas permeances were reported in Fig. 4 using gas permeance unit (GPU), where 1 GPU is equal to 3.35×10^{-10} mol m^{-2} s^{-1} Pa^{-1}. Figure 4, left panel, shows that N_2 permeances are slightly affected by the pressures. Meanwhile, CO_2 and H_2O permeances are high at low pressure and relatively flat at higher pressures. However, for all gas molecules, their permeances do not vary much at pressures higher than 1 atm. Using this flat region, we calculated the average of gas permeance for each gas and plotted it as a function of temperature (Fig. 4, right panel).

Right panel of Fig. 4 shows that the average of gas permeance for all gas decreases with increasing of temperature. This phenomenon is related to the kinetic energy of molecules; the higher is the kinetic energy, the higher is the velocity of molecules to compete with attraction forces of the membrane. Therefore, high temperature decrease gas permeance by lowering attraction effect to steer molecules toward the membrane. The penetration process encounters energy barriers when CO_2 molecules approach membrane in parallel configurations [35]. This qualitatively explains why CO_2 molecules are more difficult to pass through the membrane even though the amounts of CO_2 molecules attracted and adsorbed by the membrane are larger than those of H_2O (can be seen in the z-density profiles, will be discussed later). Therefore, as can be seen in the Fig. 4, H_2O permeances are higher than those of CO_2 and N_2.

Furthermore, we calculated permeance selectivities as ratio between average of gas permeance and plotted the values as function of temperature (Fig. 5). Indeed the permeance selectivity depends on the temperature, but in general, the trend lines are relatively flat if we consider also the deviation error. Permeance selectivity of H_2O/N_2 is higher than CO_2/N_2 and H_2O/CO_2. Meanwhile,

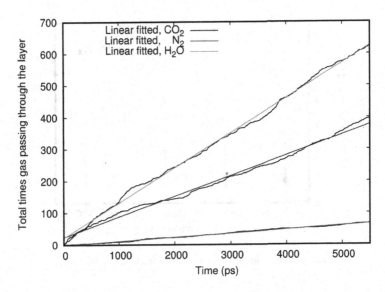

Fig. 3. The number of permeation events as a function of simulation time for single layer at 4.62 atm and 333 K.

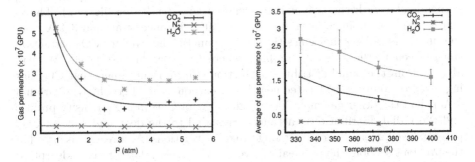

Fig. 4. Gas permeance of the single layer system at 333 K (left panel) and average of gas permeance of the single layer system as a function of temperature (right panel).

H_2O/CO_2 selectivity is around 2 which can be interpreted as the membrane is not selective enough for CO_2/H_2O separation. The CO_2 permeances (ranging from 1.0 to 2.0×10^{-7} GPU) are two order of magnitudes higher than those reported by Liu et al. [17] (2.8×10^{-5} GPU) for nanoporous graphene at 300 K and by Schrier [14] (3×10^{-5} GPU) for porous graphene (PG-ES1) at 325 K. However, the CO_2/N_2 permeance selectivities are lower than those reported by Liu et al. [17] and Schrier [14] (about 100 and 60 respectively).

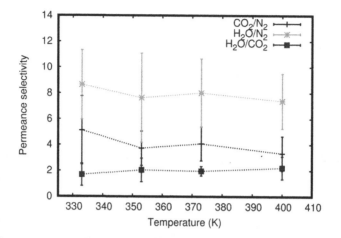

Fig. 5. Permeance selectivity for single layer system.

3.2   Gas Adsorption

The gas adsorption is reflected by the mean number of gas along the z-axis, perpendicular with the graphtriyne, denoted as z-density profiles $\rho(z)$. The z-density profiles of single layer system peak at a distance of around 3.4 Å from the surface for all gas molecules (Fig. 6, left panel). The stronger CO_2 attraction can be seen in the z-density profiles, where CO_2 has highest peaks. We can also see from the radial distribution function (Fig. 6, right panel) that CO_2 has highest probability to be located near to the carbon atom of graphtriyne (around 4 Å) than the other gas molecules. High peaks of CO_2 in the z-density profiles and the radial distribution functions correspond to the deep and wide of CO_2 potential well, meaning a strong long ranged attractions. As already discussed in the previous section, the permeation events are closely related to the adsorption of gas over the surfaces of membranes. The more molecules are adsorbed, the higher is their permeances. However, the stereodynamic requirements of CO_2 for crossing the membrane lead to lower permeances than those of H_2O.

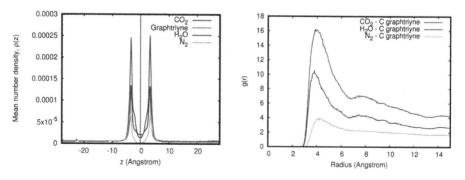

Fig. 6. z-Density profile (left panel) and radial distribution function (right panel) of the single layer system at 1 atm and 353 K.

We calculated the gas uptake by integrating the area under peaks of the z-density profiles. This area is considered as the adsorption region located in the range of ±6.9 Å with respect to the membrane position. Notice that, the z-density does not peak at the centre of the pore, place with the lowest potential energy. This feature of z-density had already been well-discussed in our previous report [35]. The gas uptakes for all applied pressures were presented in left panel of Fig. 7 as the adsorption isotherms. We can see that the gas uptake is linearly related to the initial pressure; the higher is the initial pressure applied, the higher is the gas uptake value. Therefore, using linear regression, we can estimate the adsorption coefficient from the slope of the linearly fitted isotherm adsorption. The adsorption coefficient for all gas molecules are reported in the right panel of Fig. 7 as a function of temperature. It can be seen from Fig. 7 that CO_2 has the highest gas uptakes and adsorption coefficients among gas molecules. On the other hand, despite H_2O has the highest permeance, its gas uptakes and adsorption coefficients are low, confirming weaker attraction forces than those of CO_2. Weak attraction of N_2 by the membrane is manifested by the fact that N_2 has the lowest adsorption coefficient (about 0.06 to 0.07 mmol g^{-1} atm^{-1}). Figure 7 (right panel) shows that in general, the adsorption coefficients decrease as the increasing of temperature. Obviously, higher temperature implies higher mobility of gas molecules inside the simulation box, thus gas physisorption is ineffective at relatively high temperature.

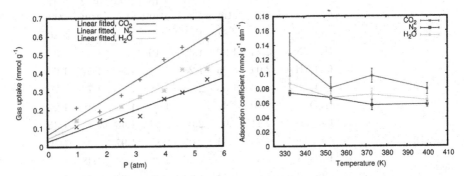

Fig. 7. Adsorption isotherm of the single layer system at 373 K (left panel) and adsorption coefficient plotted as a function of temperature for the single layer system (right panel).

The total adsorption selectivites were plotted in Fig. 8 and the full data are given in Table 1.

The CO_2/N_2 selectivities reported in Table 1 are higher than those reported in our previous report [35]. However, the gas uptake values and the corresponding adsorption coefficients are relatively lower than those obtained in the previous work. It is obvious that this difference comes from different kind of gaseous mixtures and conditions applied in the simulations. Therefore, with all advantages of carbon-based materials for postcombustion CO_2 capture and separation, graphtriyne layer is one of the most promising alternative of carbon-based membranes.

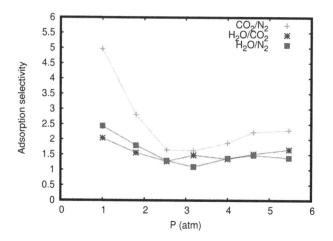

Fig. 8. Adsorption selectivity of gas at 333 K for the single layer system.

Table 1. Adsorption selectivity of $CO_2/N_2/H_2O$ gaseous mixture for single layer system.

Temperature (K)	Gas	Adsorption selectivity						
		1.00 atm	1.80 atm	2.54 atm	3.18 atm	4.00 atm	4.62 atm	5.47 atm
333	CO_2/N_2	4.97	2.81	1.65	1.63	1.88	2.24	2.30
	H_2O/N_2	2.44	1.80	1.30	1.10	1.38	1.48	1.39
	CO_2/H_2O	2.04	1.56	1.28	1.48	1.36	1.52	1.66
353	CO_2/N_2	4.43	1.53	2.43	1.78	1.63	1.73	1.70
	H_2O/N_2	2.10	1.40	1.21	1.13	1.11	1.19	1.25
	CO_2/H_2O	2.11	1.09	2.01	1.57	1.46	1.45	1.35
373	CO_2/N_2	2.30	1.34	2.07	2.37	1.97	1.98	1.70
	H_2O/N_2	1.38	0.95	1.56	1.70	1.20	1.48	1.17
	CO_2/H_2O	1.67	1.44	1.33	1.40	1.65	1.34	1.45
400	CO_2/N_2	2.66	2.23	1.71	1.96	1.83	1.53	1.69
	H_2O/N_2	1.05	1.72	0.98	1.39	1.25	1.17	1.13
	CO_2/H_2O	2.53	1.30	1.74	1.41	1.46	1.31	1.50

4   Conclusions

The performance of graphtriyne-based membranes for $CO_2/N_2/H_2O$ separation has been investigated by extensive MD simulations based on a new formulation of the force fields required to describe the interactions in gas phase and between the molecules and the layer. The model is a quantitative tool for the estimation of membrane properties, such as gas uptake, permeance, and selectivity in view of applications for postcombustion mixture separation and can be easily extended to carbon nanostructures interacting with a variety of different gaseous mixtures. Based on the molecular simulation results, we found that graphtriyne have a high permeance (and relatively good selectivity in comparation with other carbon-based separating membranes; the order of magnitude of 10^{-7}GPU). Despite single layer graphtriyne is not selective for CO_2-H_2O separation, it is relatively selective for CO_2-N_2 and H_2O-N_2 separation with permeance selectivity of 2.01 to 7.76 for CO_2/N_2; 5.26 to 11.33 for H_2O/N_2 (depending on the applied temperature). Permeation and adsorption depend on the applied temperature; high temperature decrease permeation and adsorption. These results suggest that graphtriyne exhibit good performance as an initial molecular sieve candidate for postcombustion CO_2 capture and separation achieved through combination of surface adsorption and its intrinsic pores.

Acknowledgement. The authors thank MIUR and Perugia University for financial support through the AMIS project ("Dipartimenti di Eccellenza-2018–2022"). AL thanks the Italian MIUR for funding through the program PRIN 2015 (contract 2015F59J3R 002). AL and NFL also thanks the Dipartimento di Chimica, Biologia e Biotecnologie for funding under the program Fondo Ricerca di Base 2017. AL and NFL also thank the OU Supercomputing Center for Education & Research (OSCER) at the University of Oklahoma (OU) for allocated computing time. YBA thanks to the LCPQ - Université de Toulouse III for allocated computing time.

References

1. (EPA), U.S. Environmental Protection Agency: Climate Change Indicators in the United States: Global Greenhouse Gas Emissions (2016)
2. (WRI), World Resources Institute: Climate Analysis Indicators Tool (CAIT) 2.0: WRI's Climate Data Explorer
3. Huck, J.M., et al.: Evaluating different classes of porous materials for carbon capture. Energy Environ. Sci. **7**, 4132–4146 (2014)
4. Bui, M., et al.: Carbon capture and storage (CCS): the way forward. Energy Environ. Sci. **11**, 1062–1176 (2018)
5. Li, J.R., et al.: Porous materials with pre-designed single-molecule traps for CO_2 selective adsorption. Nat. Commun. **4**, 1538 (2014)
6. Celiberto, R., et al.: Atomic and molecular data for spacecraft re-entry plasmas. Plasma Sour. Sci. Technol. **25**(3), 033004 (2016)
7. Smit, B.: Carbon capture and storage: introductory lecture. Faraday Discuss. **192**, 9–25 (2016)
8. Srinivas, G., Krungleviciute, V., Guo, Z.X., Yildirim, T.: Exceptional CO_2 capture in a hierarchically porous carbon with simultaneous high surface area and pore volume. Energy Environ. Sci. **7**, 335–342 (2014)
9. Ganesan, A., Shaijumon, M.: Activated graphene-derived porous carbon with exceptional gas adsorption properties. Microporous Mesoporous Mater. **220**, 21–27 (2015)
10. Ghosh, S., Sevilla, M., Fuertes, A.B., Andreoli, E., Ho, J., Barron, A.R.: Defining a performance map of porous carbon sorbents for high-pressure carbon dioxide uptake and carbon dioxide-methane selectivity. J. Mater. Chem. A **4**, 14739–14751 (2016)

11. Kim, J., Lin, L.C., Swisher, J.A., Haranczyk, M., Smit, B.: Predicting large CO_2 adsorption in aluminosilicate zeolites for postcombustion carbon dioxide capture. J. Am. Chem. Soc. **134**(46), 18940–18943 (2012)

12. Liu, B., Smit, B.: Molecular simulation studies of separation of CO_2/N_2, CO_2/CH_4, and CH_4/N_2 by ZIFs. J. Phys. Chem. C **114**(18), 8515–8522 (2010)

13. Lin, L.C., et al.: Understanding CO dynamics in metal-organic frameworks with open metal sites. Angew. Chem. Int. Ed. **52**(16), 4410–4413 (2013)

14. Schrier, J.: Carbon dioxide separation with a two-dimensional polymer membrane. ACS Appl. Mater. Interfaces **4**(7), 3745–3752 (2012)

15. Xiang, Z., et al.: Systematic tuning and multifunctionalization of covalent organic polymers for enhanced carbon capture. J. Am. Chem. Soc. **137**(41), 13301–13307 (2015)

16. Liu, H., et al.: A hybrid absorption–adsorption method to efficiently capture carbon. Nat. Commun. **5**, 5147 (2014)

17. Liu, H., Dai, S., Jiang, D.: Insights into CO_2/N_2 separation through nanoporous graphene from molecular dynamics. Nanoscale **5**, 9984–9987 (2013)

18. Lombardi, A., Lago, N.F., Laganà, A., Pirani, F., Falcinelli, S.: A bond-bond portable approach to intermolecular interactions: simulations for N-methylacetamide and carbon dioxide dimers. In: Murgante, B., et al. (eds.) ICCSA 2012. LNCS, vol. 7333, pp. 387–400. Springer, Heidelberg (2012). https://doi.org/10.1007/978-3-642-31125-3_30

19. Lombardi, A., Faginas-Lago, N., Pacifici, L., Costantini, A.: Modeling of energy transfer from vibrationally excited CO_2 molecules: cross sections and probabilities for Kinetic modeling of atmospheres, flows, and plasmas. J. Phys. Chem. A **117**(45), 11430–11440 (2013)

20. Falcinelli, S., et al.: Modeling the intermolecular interactions and characterization of the dynamics of collisional autoionization processes. In: Murgante, B., et al. (eds.) ICCSA 2013. LNCS, vol. 7971, pp. 69–83. Springer, Heidelberg (2013). https://doi.org/10.1007/978-3-642-39637-3_6

21. Pearlman, D., et al.: AMBER. A package of computer-programs for applying molecular mechanics, normal-mode analysis, molecular-dynamics and free-energy calculations to simulate the structural and energetic properties of molecules. Comput. Phys. Commun. **91**, 1–41 (1995)

22. Rappe, A.K., Casewit, C.J., Colwell, K.S., Goddard, W.A., Skiff, W.M.: UFF, a full periodic table force field for molecular mechanics and molecular dynamics simulations. J. Am. Chem. Soc. **114**(25), 10024–10035 (1992)

23. Vekeman, J., García Cuesta, I., Faginas-Lago, N., Wilson, J., Sánchez-Marín, J., Sánchez de Merás, A.: Potential models for the simulation of methane adsorption on graphene: development and CCSD(T) benchmarks. Phys. Chem. Chem. Phys. **20**(18), 25518–25530 (2018)

24. Lombardi, A., Faginas-Lago, N., Pacifici, L., Grossi, G.: Energy transfer upon collision of selectively excited CO_2 molecules: state-to-state cross sections and probabilities for modeling of atmospheres and gaseous flows. J. Chem. Phy. **143**(3), 034307 (2015)

25. Faginas-Lago, N., Albertí, M., Costantini, A., Laganà, A., Lombardi, A., Pacifici, L.: An innovative synergistic grid approach to the computational study of protein aggregation mechanisms. J. Mol. Model. **20**(7), 2226 (2014)

26. Boyd, P.G., Moosavi, S.M., Witman, M., Smit, B.: Force-field prediction of materials properties in metal-organic frameworks. J. Phys. Chem. Lett. **8**(2), 357–363 (2017)

27. Lin, L.C., Lee, K., Gagliardi, L., Neaton, J.B., Smit, B.: Force-field development from electronic structure calculations with periodic boundary conditions: applications to gaseous adsorption and transport in metal-organic frameworks. J. Chem. Theory Comput. **10**(4), 1477–1488 (2014)

28. Lim, J.R., Yang, C.T., Kim, J., Lin, L.C.: Transferability of CO_2 force fields for prediction of adsorption properties in all-silica zeolites. J. Phys. Chem. C **122**(20), 10892–10903 (2018)

29. DuBay, K.H., Hall, M.L., Hughes, T.F., Wu, C., Reichman, D.R., Friesner, R.A.: Accurate force field development for modeling conjugated polymers. J. Chem. Theory Comput. **8**(11), 4556–4569 (2012)

30. Bartolomei, M., Carmona-Novillo, E., Giorgi, G.: First principles investigation of hydrogen physical adsorption on graphynes' layers. Carbon **95**, 1076–1081 (2015)

31. Du, H., Li, J., Zhang, J., Su, G., Li, X., Zhao, Y.: Separation of hydrogen and nitrogen gases with porous graphene membrane. J. Phys. Chem. C **115**(47), 23261–23266 (2011)

32. James, A., et al.: Graphynes: indispensable nanoporous architectures in carbon flatland. RSC Adv. **8**, 22998–23018 (2018)

33. Gao, X., et al.: Ultrathin graphdiyne film on graphene through solution-phase van der Waals epitaxy. Sci. Adv. **4**(7), eaat6378 (2018)

34. Faginas, N., Huarte-Larrañaga, F., Laganà, A.: Full dimensional quantum versus semiclassical reactivity for thebent transition state reaction N + N_2. Chem. Phys. Lett. **464**(4–6), 249–255 (2008)

35. Apriliyanto, Y.B., et al.: Nanostructure selectivity for molecular adsorption and separation: the case of graphyne layers. J. Phys. Chem. C **122**(28), 16195–16208 (2018)

36. Faginas-Lago, N., Yeni, D., Huarte, F., Wang, Y., Alcamí, M., Martin, F.: Adsorption of hydrogen molecules on carbon nanotubes using quantum chemistry and molecular dynamics. J. Phys. Chem. A **120**(32), 6451–6458 (2016)

37. Yeamin, M.B., Faginas-Lago, N., Albertí, M., García Cuesta, I., Sánchez-Marín, J., Sánchez de Merás, A.: Multi-scale theoretical investigation of molecular hydrogen adsorption over graphene: coronene as a case study. RSC Adv. **4**, 54447–54453 (2014)

38. Barreto, P.R., et al.: Potential energy surfaces for interactions of H_2O with H_2, N_2 and O_2: a hyperspherical harmonics representation, and a minimal model for the H_2O-rare-gas-atom systems. Comput.Theor. Chem. **990**, 53–61 (2012)

39. Pallottelli, S., Tasso, S., Pannacci, N., Costantini, A., Lago, N.F.: Distributed and collaborative learning objects repositories on grid networks. In: Taniar, D., Gervasi, O., Murgante, B., Pardede, E., Apduhan, B.O. (eds.) ICCSA 2010. LNCS, vol. 6019, pp. 29–40. Springer, Heidelberg (2010). https://doi.org/10.1007/978-3-642-12189-0_3

40. Lago, N., Laganá, A., Gargano, R., Barreto, P.: On the semiclassical initial value calculation of thermal rate coefficients for the reaction N + N_2. J. Chem. Phys. **125**(11), 114311 (2006)

41. Laganà, A., Faginas Lago, N., Rampino, S., Huarte-Larrañaga, F., García, E.: Thermal rate coefficients in collinear versus bent transition state reactions: the N + N_2 case study. Phys. Scr. **78**(5), 058116 (2008)

42. Rampino, S., Faginas-Lago, N., Laganà, A., Huarte-Larrañaga, F.: An extension of the grid empowered molecular simulator to quantum reactive scattering. J. Comput. Chem. **33**, 708–714 (2012)

43. Laganà, A., Crocchianti, S., Faginas Lago, N., Pacifici, L., Ferraro, G.: A nonorthogonal coordinate approach to atom-diatom parallel reactive scattering calculations. Collect. Czech. Chem. Commun. **68**(2), 307–330 (2003)
44. Faginas Lago, N., Lombardi, A., Pacifici, L., Costantini, A.: Design and implementation of a grid application for direct calculations of reactive rates. Comput. Theor. Chem. **1022**, 103–107 (2013)
45. Lombardi, A., Faginas-Lago, N., Laganà, A.: Grid calculation tools for massive applications of collision dynamics simulations: carbon dioxide energy transfer. In: Murgante, B., et al. (eds.) ICCSA 2014. LNCS, vol. 8579, pp. 627–639. Springer, Cham (2014). https://doi.org/10.1007/978-3-319-09144-0_43
46. Skouteris, D., Balucani, N., Faginas-Lago, N., Falcinelli, S., Rosi, M.: Dimerization of methanimine and its charged species in the atmosphere of Titan and interstellar/cometary ice analogs. Astron. Astrophys. **584**, 8 (2015)
47. Rosi, M., et al.: Possible scenarios for SiS formation in the interstellar medium: electronic structure calculations of the potential energy surfaces for the reactions of the SiH radical with atomic sulphur and S_2. Chem. Phys. Lett. **695**, 87–93 (2018)
48. Podio, L., et al.: Silicon-bearing molecules in the shock L1157-B1: first detection of SiS around a Sun-like protostar. Mon. Not. Roy. Astron. Soc. Lett. **470**(1), 16–20 (2017)
49. Battaglia, S., Faginas-Lago, N., Andrae, D., Evangelisti, S., Leininger, T.: Increasing radical character of large [n]cyclacenes unveiled by wave function theory. J. Phys. Chem. A **121**(19), 3746–3756 (2017)
50. Bartolomei, M., Giorgi, G.: A novel nanoporous graphite based on graphynes: first-principles structure and carbon dioxide preferential physisorption. ACS Appl. Mater. Interfaces **8**(41), 27996–28003 (2016). PMID: 27667472
51. Albertí, M., Aguilar, A., Cappelletti, D., Laganà, A., Pirani, F.: On the development of an effective model potential to describe ater interaction in neutral and ionic clusters. Int. J. Mass Spec. **280**, 50–56 (2009)
52. Albertí, M., Pirani, F., Laganà, A.: Carbon dioxide clathrate hydrates: selective role of intermolecular interactions and action of the SDS catalyst. J. Phys. Chem. A **117**(32), 6991–7000 (2013)
53. Lombardi, A., Pirani, F., Laganà, A., Bartolomei, M.: Energy transfer dynamics and kinetics of elementary processes (promoted) by gas-phase CO_2-N_2 collisions: selectivity control by the anisotropy of the interaction. J. Comput. Chem. **37**(16), 1463–1475 (2016)
54. Bartolomei, M., Pirani, F., Laganà, A., Lombardi, A.: A full dimensional grid empowered simulation of the CO_2 + CO_2 processes. J. Comput. Chem. **33**(22), 1806–1819 (2012)
55. Pirani, P., Brizi, S., Roncaratti, L., Casavecchia, P., Cappelletti, D., Vecchiocattivi, F.: Beyond the Lennard-Jones model: a simple and accurate potential function probed by high resolution scattering data useful for molecular dynamics simulations. Phys. Chem. Chem. Phys. **10**, 5489 (2008)
56. Lombardi, A., Laganà, A., Pirani, F., Palazzetti, F., Lago, N.F.: Carbon oxides in gas flows and earth and planetary atmospheres: state-to-state simulations of energy transfer and dissociation reactions. In: Murgante, B., et al. (eds.) ICCSA 2013. LNCS, vol. 7972, pp. 17–31. Springer, Heidelberg (2013). https://doi.org/10.1007/978-3-642-39643-4_2
57. Lago, N.F., Albertí, M., Laganà, A., Lombardi, A., Pacifici, L., Costantini, A.: The molecular stirrer catalytic effect in methane ice formation. In: Murgante, B., et al. (eds.) ICCSA 2014. LNCS, vol. 8579, pp. 585–600. Springer, Cham (2014). https://doi.org/10.1007/978-3-319-09144-0_40

58. Faginas Lago, N., Albertí, M., Lombardi, A., Pirani, F.: A force field for acetone: the transition from small clusters to liquid phase investigated by molecular dynamics simulations. Theor. Chem. Acc. **135**(7), 161 (2016)

59. Faginas-Lago, N., Albertí, M., Laganà, A., Lombardi, A.: Ion-water cluster molecular dynamics using a semiempirical intermolecular potential. In: Gervasi, O., et al. (eds.) ICCSA 2015. LNCS, vol. 9156, pp. 355–370. Springer, Cham (2015). https:// doi.org/10.1007/978-3-319-21407-8_26

60. Pirani, F., Albertí, M., Castro, A., Moix Teixidor, M., Cappelletti, D.: Atombond pairwise additive representation for intermolecular potential energy surfaces. Chem. Phys. Lett. **394**(1–3), 37–44 (2004)

61. Pacifici, L., Verdicchio, M., Faginas-Lago, N.F., Lombardi, A., Costantini, A.: A high-level ab initio study of the $N_2 + N_2$ reaction channel. J. Comput. Chem. **34**(31), 2668–2676 (2013)

62. Faginas-Lago, N., Albertí, M., Laganà, A., Lombardi, A.: Water $(H_2O)_m$ or Benzene $(C_6H_6)_n$ aggregates to solvate the K_+? In: Murgante, B., et al. (eds.) ICCSA 2013. LNCS, vol. 7971, pp. 1–15. Springer, Heidelberg (2013). https://doi.org/10. 1007/978-3-642-39637-3_1

63. Faginas-Lago, N., Lombardi, A., Albertí, M., Grossi, G.: Accurate analytic intermolecular potential for the simulation of Na^+ and K^+ ion hydration in liquid water. J. Mol. Liq. **204**, 192–197 (2015)

64. Lombardi, A., Faginas-Lago, N., Gaia, G., Federico, P., Aquilanti, V.: Collisional energy exchange in CO_2–N_2 Gaseous mixtures. In: Gervasi, O., et al. (eds.) ICCSA 2016. LNCS, vol. 9786, pp. 246–257. Springer, Cham (2016). https://doi.org/10. 1007/978-3-319-42085-1_19

65. Albertí, M., Faginas-Lago, N.: Ion size influence on the Ar solvation shells of $M^+C_6F_6$ clusters (M = Na, K, Rb, Cs). J. Phys. Chem. A **116**(12), 3094–3102 (2012)

66. Aquilanti, V., Beddoni, A., Cavalli, S., Lombardi, A., Littlejohn, R.: Collective hyperspherical coordinates for polyatomic molecules and clusters. Mol. Phys. **98**(21), 1763–1770 (2000)

67. Aquilanti, V., Beddoni, A., Lombardi, A., Littlejohn, R.: Hyperspherical harmonics for polyatomic systems: basis set for Kinematic rotations. Int. J. Quantum Chem. **89**(4), 277–291 (2002)

68. Aquilanti, V., Lombardi, A., Littlejohn, R.: Hyperspherical harmonics for polyatomic systems: basis set for collective motions. Theoret. Chem. Acc. **111**(2–6), 400–406 (2004)

69. Sevryuk, M.B., Lombardi, A., Aquilanti, V.: Hyperangular momenta and energy partitions in multidimensional many-particle classical mechanics: the invariance approach to cluster dynamics. Phys. Rev. A **72**(3), 033201 (2005)

70. Smith, W., Yong, C., Rodger, P.: DL_POLY: application to molecular simulation. Mol. Simul. **28**(5), 385–471 (2002)

71. Elliott, J., Lira, C.T.: Introductory Chemical Engineering Thermodynamics. Prentice Hall, New Jersey (2012)

72. Humphrey, W., Dalke, A., Schulten, K.: VMD: visual molecular dynamics. J. Mol. Graph. **14**(1), 33–38 (1996)

Machine Learning of Potential-Energy Surfaces Within a Bond-Order Sampling Scheme

Daniele Licari, Sergio Rampino$^{(\boxtimes)}$ ⓘ, and Vincenzo Barone ⓘ

Scuola Normale Superiore, Piazza dei Cavalireri 7, 56126 Pisa, Italy
sergio.rampino@sns.it

Abstract. Predicting the values of the potential energy surface (PES) for a given chemical system is essential to running the associated dynamics and modeling its evolution in time. To the purpose of modeling chemical reactions involving few atoms, this task is usually accomplished by fitting or interpolating a set of energies computed at different nuclear geometries through accurate, though computationally demanding, quantum-chemical calculations. Among the several approaches for choosing an appropriate set of geometries and energies, a new scheme has been recently proposed (Rampino S, J Phys Chem A 120:4683–4692, 2016) which is based on a regular sampling in a space-reduced bond-order (SRBO) domain rather than in the more conventional bond-length (BL) domain. In this work we address the performances of four machine-learning (ML) models, as opposed to pure mathematical fitting or interpolation schemes, in predicting the PES of a three-atom system modeling an atom-diatom exchange reaction when coupled to the SRBO sampling scheme. The models (two ensemble-learning, an automated ML, and a deep-learning one), trained on both SRBO and BL datasets, are shown to perform better than popular fitting or interpolation schemes and to give the best results if coupled to SRBO data.

Keywords: Potential energy surface · Space reduced bond order · Atom diatom reactions · Machine learning · Deep learning · Neural networks

1 Introduction

Within the Born-Oppenheimer approximation, the dynamic modeling of a chemical system requires knowledge of the associated potential-energy surface (PES), i.e. the electronic energy (usually the ground-state one) as a function of the

The research leading to these results has received funding from Scuola Normale Superiore through project 'DIVE: Development of Immersive approaches for the analysis of chemical bonding through Virtual-reality Environments' (SNS18_B_RAMPINO) and program 'Finanziamento a supporto della ricerca di base' (SNS_RB_RAMPINO).

S. Misra et al. (Eds.): ICCSA 2019, LNCS 11624, pp. 388–400, 2019.
https://doi.org/10.1007/978-3-030-24311-1_28

nuclear coordinates. For a given a nuclear geometry, this can be accurately computed through high-level *ab initio* methods. However, performing such single-point calculations for all the geometries needed by the dynamics simulation may become computationally demanding and it is often convenient, if not mandatory, to be able to predict the PES on the basis of a limited set of computed energies. For chemical reactions involving three or four atoms, for which exact quantum-dynamics calculations are feasible, a number of methods have been proposed over the past decades based on mathematical fitting or interpolation schemes (see for instance Ref. [1] for a comprehensive review). More recently, the advent of machine learning (ML) has introduced a new class of powerful methods which have been successfully used also for modeling potential-energy surfaces [2–5] and have established as a robust alternative to pure mathematical fitting or interpolation methods.

When using either fitting/interpolation schemes or ML models, a central problem remains that of the choice of a minimal, most informative set of nuclear geometries at which the *ab initio* energies shall be computed. One of the authors recently faced this problem during the assembly of the grid-empowered molecular simulator GEMS [6–10] for the *a priori* modeling of elementary reactive processes [11–14], with a special focus on atom-diatom exchange reactions of the type

$$A + BC \rightarrow AB + C. \tag{1}$$

GEMS is articulated in a workflow combining electronic-structure, PES-fitting and quantum-dynamics calculations thanks to the definition of a common data format [15,16] for coordinated execution on the distributed platform of the European Grid Infrastructure (EGI) [17]. GEMS has been successfully used to study the dynamics and compute the reactive probabilities/cross sections and rate coefficients of atom-diatom reactions such as Li + FH [14], N + N_2 [18,19], O + O_2 [20,21], and C + CH^+ [22–24]. In this context, one of us has recently proposed an efficient scheme [25] that has built-in a metric based on the chemical concept of bond order and that is based on a regular sampling in a space-reduced bond-order (SRBO) domain rather than in the more conventional bond-length (BL) one. Using both a global fitting and a local interpolation scheme, the SRBO sampling proved to perform much better than the conventional BL one in converging the predicted PES values to the computed *ab initio* ones with increasing number of grid points.

On these grounds, and motivated by the growing success of ML in many branches of science, we decided to evaluate the performances of several ML techniques in predicting the PES for processes of the type of Reaction 1 when coupled to the SRBO sampling scheme. Accordingly, in this work we address the predictive accuracy of four ML models (two ensemble-learning, an automated ML, and a deep learning one) trained on both SRBO and BL datasets and compare it with that of both a global-fitting and a local-interpolation scheme. To this purpose, we choose the PES of a three-hydrogen system modeling the simplest atom-diatom chemical reaction, H + H_2 → H_2 + H. In Sect. 2, the SRBO sampling scheme is briefly reviewed. In Sect. 3, the considered ML models are described and their performances are discussed. In Sect. 4, some conclusions are given and future work is outlined.

2 Bond-Order Sampling and Computational Details

A suitable set of internal coordinates for modeling Reaction 1 is made of the bond-length (BL) variables r_1 and r_2 of the reactant (BC) and product (AB) diatomic, respectively, plus the angle ϕ formed by the two bonds. A simple and practiced recipe for building the above-mentioned set of energies, is to perform a regular sampling on a three-dimensional grid in r_1, r_2, and ϕ, once boundaries $r_{\min}$ and $r_{\max}$ have been defined for a given r in order to exclude the strongly repulsive (dynamically inaccessible) and the near-asymptotic regions (we shall refer to this sampling scheme as to the bond-length, BL, one). Based on the concept of 'bond order' introduced by Pauling more than sixty years ago [26] and revived in the context of PES fitting by Laganà and García [27–30], one of us has recently proposed an alternative sampling scheme that better accounts for the nature of the underlying chemical process governed by the PES under study [25]. The approach (so-called space-reduced bond-order, SRBO) is based on a space-reduced formulation of the so-called bond-order variables and shall be briefly reviewed in the following for the reader's convenience.

Bond-order (BO) variables are defined as the exponential of the weighed diatomic displacement

$$n = e^{-\beta(r-r_e)} \tag{2}$$

where β is a constant related to one or more diatomic force constants, r_e is the equilibrium distance and r is the internuclear distance, or BL variable, of the diatom. BO variables have the following appealing properties: (1) the BO space has origin at infinite internuclear distances and a finite limiting value of $e^{\beta r_e}$ corresponding to null internuclear distance (collapsed atoms) (2) the attractive and repulsive regions of the diatom configuration space are confined in the (0, 1) and (1, $e^{\beta r_e}$) range, respectively, with unity in BO space representing the equilibrium point. BO variables have been used in formulating polynomial representations of PESs [27,28] and rotating diatomic-like ones (like the rotating bond-order, ROBO, [29] and the largest-angle generalization of the rotating bond-order, LAGROBO [30]). In addition, BO variables have been used for producing relaxed, process-oriented PES representations [21] and developing the related quantum-reactive-scattering formalism [31,32].

A space-reduced formulation of the BO variables can be obtained by relaxing the condition that β is linked to spectroscopic properties, and allowing it to vary until a desired attractive over repulsive space ratio f is reached [25]:

$$f = \frac{1 - n_{\min}}{n_{\max} - 1} = \frac{1 - e^{-\beta(r_{\max}-r_e)}}{e^{-\beta(r_{\min}-r_e)} - 1} \, . \tag{3}$$

In so doing, once f has been fixed the same space relation between the attractive and repulsive region of configuration space will hold for any diatom, and f can be chosen to best suit the problem at hand. Test calculations reported in Ref. [25] show that an optimal value of f for the sampling of configuration space for a reactive processes is two (attractive region doubly represented with respect to the repulsive one). In Ref. [25], an automated way of setting r_{min} and r_{max} based on the energy-derivative at the equilibrium point is also suggested.

The SRBO sampling is obtained by taking regular grids in n_1, n_2, and ϕ rather than, as in the BL sampling, r_1, r_2, and ϕ. As clearly shown in Fig. 1, the advantage of a regular sampling in n (SRBO sampling) over that in r (BL sampling) is that, assuming an equal number of points, the SRBO points will distribute according to a 'force'-based metric thus better recovering the overall shape of the interaction potential.

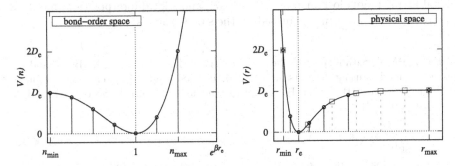

Fig. 1. Energies sampled by a 7-point SRBO ($f = 2$) grid in the bond-order space (left panel) and physical space (right panel). In the right panel, the points of a corresponding 7-point BL grid are also reported as gray squares.

3   Machine Learning of the H$_3$ Potential-Energy Surface

As already mentioned, we addressed the performances of four ML models in predicting the PES of the H$_3$ system when coupled to both the SRBO and BL sampling schemes using datasets of incresing size. The energy datasets considered in this work are the same as those of Ref. [25] (to which the reader is referred for a more detailed information), i.e. full configuration interaction (FCI) energies computed with a triple-ζ quality basis set with r_{min} and r_{max} set at 0.553 and 8.740 a_0, respectively, and are briefly summarized here. An angular grid of five values ranging from 180° (collinear configuration) to 60° in steps of 30° was set up for the ϕ variable. In the BL sampling, four uniform grids of different size (10, 13, 16, and 19 points) were set for both the r_1 and r_2 BL variables. In the SRBO sampling, analogous 10-, 13-, 16-, and 19-point grids were set in the corresponding n_1 and n_2 defined with $f = 2$. For each of the two sampling schemes (after removing redundant points due to the symmetry of the system and including the H_3 saddle point) this leads to four datasets of 276, 456, 681, and 951 points ('training sets' hereafter).

The performances of the considered predictive models were evaluated in terms of root-mean-square error (RMSE) of the predicted values with respect to a reference set of energies ('reference set' hereafter) computed on a finer grid of 2951 points obtained with a 25-points BL sampling for both r_1 and r_2 and an angular grid from 180° to 60° in steps of 15° for ϕ.

The four ML models considered herein are described and assessed in the following subsections. In particular, in Subsect. 3.1 we discuss two ensemble-learning models (referenced to as RF and XGB). In Subsect. 3.2 we discuss an automated ML and a deep learning model (referenced to as AS and DL). Our ML algorithms were implemented using the scikit-learn [33] (for RF and XGB), Autosklearn [34] (for AS) and Keras [35] (for DL) software. A complete summary of the results is given in Table 1, which also reports the performances of a global-fitting (Aguado-Paniagua, AP [36,37]) and a local-interpolation (modified Shepard, Sh [38]) scheme evaluated on the same grounds.

Table 1. RMSE with respect to the reference set of the AP, Sh, RF, XGB, AS and DL predictive models using datasets of $N = 276$, 456, 681, and 951 H_3 energies computed through both an SRBO and a BL sampling scheme as detailed in Sect. 2. AP and Sh data taken from Ref. [25].

| | RMSE /eV | | | | | | | | | | |
| | SRBO | | | | | | BL | | | | | |
N	AP	Sh	RF	XGB	AS	DL	AP	Sh	RF	XGB	AS	DL
276	0.029	0.123	0.021	0.027	0.019	0.018	1.455	11.636	0.121	0.121	0.088	0.049
456	0.026	0.060	0.010	0.017	0.020	0.011	0.264	3.636	0.029	0.028	0.029	0.036
681	0.027	0.021	0.009	0.016	0.009	0.013	0.144	2.982	0.023	0.024	0.023	0.018
951	0.025	0.016	0.008	0.015	0.008	0.012	0.077	2.407	0.020	0.024	0.015	0.021

3.1   Ensemble-Learning Methods

Ensemble learning methods are based on observation that the aggregate decision made by a group is often better than those of its individual members if specific conditions are satisfied (the wisdom-of-crowds theory [39]). The Random Forest (RF) [40] is an ensemble of decision trees [41] which operate on a random sample of the data outputting mean prediction of the individual trees. This randomness helps to make the model more robust than a single decision tree, and less likely to overfit on the training data. Instead, eXtreme Gradient Boosting (XGB) [42] builds an ensemble of trees by optimizing a differentiable loss function and uses a more regularized model formalization to control over-fitting. Basically, it helps to find a predictor which is a weighed average of all models used. XGB models dominate many data science competitions hosted at Kaggle (https://kaggle.com) as they work very well on conventional, also called tabular or structured, data (as those considered in this article).

Machine-learning models can require several input variables (called hyperparameters) that govern the training process itself. The choice of these parameters highly affects the performance of the models, thus hyperparameter tuning is a crucial task in the definition of a machine-learning model. The traditional way of performing hyperparameter optimization is a grid search which builds a model for each possible combination of all of the hyperparameter values provided and selects the one which produces the best results. This approach requires long execution time because it wastes time evaluating unpromising areas of parameter space. Instead, we used a Bayesian optimization method for hyperparameter tuning of RF and XGB models [43,44] evaluating on training sets.

This automatic approach, based on a probabilistic model for finding optimal hyperparameters, works by building a posterior distribution of functions (Gaussian process) that best describes the function we want to optimize (mean-squared-error, MSE, function). As the number of observations increases, the posterior distribution improves, and the algorithm becomes more confident of which regions of the parameter space are worth exploring and which are not. In our case, the target variable (the energy) to be optimized is measured as the average of MSEs from 5-fold cross-validation (CV) on the training set. A 5-fold CV would re-sample the training and validation sets in a non-overlapping fashion 5 times, such that all of the data is eventually used as training data. The CV error is then estimated by averaging the five resulting MSE estimates (CV is often used to estimate this generalization performance). The optimal hyperparameter values (herein obtained from the hyperparameter configuration space reported in Table 2) are those that have produced the lowest CV error.

As already mentioned, the performances of the RF and XGB models trained on the above defined training sets are reported in Table 1. Both ML models significantly improve the performance of fitting compared to AP and Sh. Predictive error of both methods are remarkably similar, with RF performing somewhat better than XGB. This may be because the RF has fewer parameters to set and therefore it is easier for a Bayesian optimizer to find the best hyperparameters.

Table 2. Configuration spaces of Random Forest and Extreme Gradient Boosting hyperparameters used into Bayesian optimization with 250 iterations.

Model	Hyperparameter name	Values
RF	n_estimators	[10, 2500]
	min_samples_split	[2, 25]
	max_features	[0.1, 0.999]
XGB	n_estimators	[100, 2500]
	learning_rate	[0.05, 0.3]
	max_depth	[3, 10]
	subsample	[2, 25]
	gamma	[0.01, 1.0]

3.2 Automatic Machine Learning and Deep Learning

Finding the best machine-learning algorithm and right data preprocessing steps for a specific dataset is a non-trivial and error-prone task for humans. Many more models are continuously being developed, hyper-parameter tuning is not an easy task, and preprocessing steps (such as data scaling, features selections and missing values) can be necessary to improve the performances. For this reason, automated ML (AutoML) has become a topic of considerable interest in recent years as they can automatically determine a well-performing ML pipeline for a specific dataset.

Existing state-of-the-art AutoML systems include auto-sklearn (AS) [34,45] which wraps 15 regressors/classifiers and 18 preprocessing methods, and exploits recent advances in Bayesian optimization, meta-learning and ensemble construction to search the right learning algorithm and optimize its hyperparameters. Bayesian optimization is used to optimize the hyperparameters of the best pipelines (preprocessing and models) resulting from the meta-learning process. Finally, auto-sklearn builds an ensemble of the 50 best models tested during the global optimization process to improve generalization.

Another ML approach that we tested is based on deep neural networks (NN), also referred to as deep learning (DL), which has raised broad interest due to its strong learning capacity for various problems in many scientific [46,47] and industrial [48] areas. Deep-learning [49] models are composed of multiple processing non-linear modules (called neurons) to lean representation of data with multiple levels of abstraction. Neurons are distributed in multiple layers (hidden layers) and each layer uses the output from the previous layer as input. It learns through an optimizer (e.g. Stochastic Gradient Descent or Adaptive Gradient Methods) which, during the training phase, minimizes an objective function that measures the error (MSE in our case) by computing its gradient vector and modifies the internal adjustable parameters to reduce this error.

Our feed-forward neural network (see a scheme in Fig. 2) takes the three internal coordinates as input, it is composed of 2 hidden layers (each layers contains 20 neurons) and its last node outputs the fitted energy. In general, neurons take several input numbers from the previous layer, apply an activation function to the weighed sum of inputs (weights are the fitting parameters of a NN) and yield the output. In biological processing the signal must exceed a certain threshold to be propagated, in NN this behaviour is simulated by the activation function. The non-linear functions used in our NN include the rectified linear unit (ReLU) $f(z) = \max(0, z)$, commonly used in recent years and Stochastic Gradient Descent as optimizer. Our NN was built with Keras [35] specifying the hyperparameters reported in Table 3 (we use default values for the remaining parameters, for which the reader is referred to the Keras documentation).

Table 3. Hyper-parameters of our neural network.

Name	Values
loss	MSE
optimizer	SGD
epochs	14000
batch_size	50
validation_split	0.2

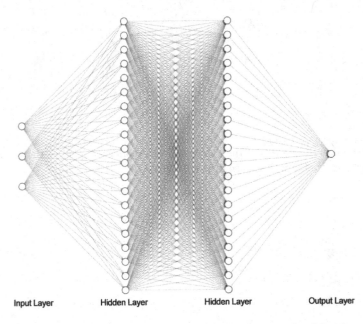

Input Layer   Hidden Layer   Hidden Layer   Output Layer

Fig. 2. Our neural-network topology is defined by 3 input nodes (the three internal coordinates), two hidden layers with 20 nodes per layer and one output node (E).

As previously done for the RF and XGB models, the predictive accuracy of the AS and DL models was evaluated in terms of RMSE of the predicted values with respect to the reference set and results are reported in Table 1. The results of these two models are quite similar. DL generalizes better than AS if one uses a training set of 256 points, on the contrary AS has better performances with training data of increasing size. Figure 3 and 4 show the overall performances of all the considered ML models trained with both SRBO (Fig. 3) and BL (Fig. 4) datasets, as compared to the performances of the AP fitting scheme. The SRBO sampling scheme provides great benefit on machine-learning algorithms considerably reducing the RMSE with respect to BL sampling. In addition, the performances of the ML models are considerably better than those of the AP fitting. Considering the performances, the simplicity of setting and the ease of parallelization, the RF on SRBO is the best algorithm for our case study.

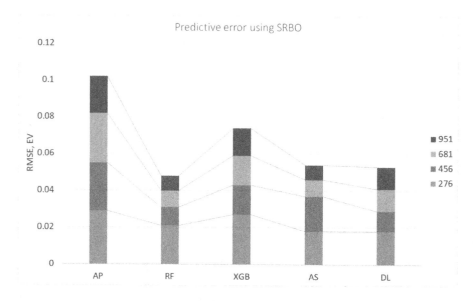

Fig. 3. Overall performances of the considered ML models coupled to the SRBO sampling scheme as compared to those of the AP fitting.

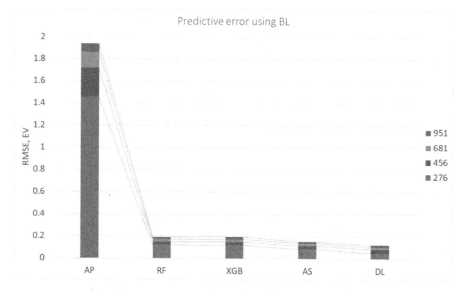

Fig. 4. Overall performances of the considered ML models coupled to the BL sampling scheme as compared to those of the AP fitting.

These results indicate that a combination of an SRBO sampling scheme with state-of-the-art ML methods offers the cheapest and most effective approach to PES fitting for the three-atom reactive systems herein considered.

4 Conclusions

In this paper we assess the performances of four machine-learning (ML) models in predicting the potential-energy surface (PES) of a three-atom chemical reactive process when coupled to the recently proposed space-reduced bond-order (SRBO) configuration sampling scheme, as opposed to the more conventional bond-length (BL) one. After training the ML models (two ensemble-learning, an automated ML, and a deep learning one) with SRBO and BL datasets of increasing size, their performances were evaluated by computing the root-mean-square error (RMSE) of the predicted energy with respect to a larger set of energies, and compared to those of established fitting/interpolation schemes.

Results indicate that for a training set of a given size ML techniques perform better than the considered global-fitting and local-interpolation schemes, and that better results are achieved if an SRBO sampling is adopted rather than a BL one. On the one hand, this confirms the SRBO sampling scheme as a reliable and efficient tool in PES-fitting problems of few-atom reactive systems. On the other hand, these results suggest that one-dimensional SRBO grids can be used as optimal building blocks for multi-dimensional grids in higher-dimensionality problems. Work is in progress in our laboratory to extend these computational approaches to larger systems and to exploit them for an efficient 3D-rendering for visualization purposes and immersive exploration of the PES through state-of-the-art virtual-reality technologies [50,51].

References

1. Jaquet, R.: Interpolation and fitting of potential energy surfaces: concepts, recipes and applications. In: Sax, A.F. (ed.) Potential Energy Surfaces. Lecture Notes in Chemistry, vol. 71, pp. 97–175. Springer, Berlin (1999). https://doi.org/10.1007/978-3-642-46879-7_3

2. Behler, J.: Neural network potential-energy surfaces for atomistic simulations. In: Chemical Modelling: Applications and Theory, vol. 7, pp. 1–41. The Royal Society of Chemistry, Cambridge (2010)

3. Handley, C.M., Popelier, P.L.A.: Potential energy surfaces fitted by artificial neural networks. The J. Phys. Chem. A 114(10), 3371–3383 (2010)

4. Hughes, Z.E., Thacker, J.C.R., Wilson, A.L., Popelier, P.L.A.: Description of potential energy surfaces of molecules using FFLUX machine learning models. J. Chem. Theor. Comput. 15(1), 116–126 (2019)

5. Raff, L., Komanduri, R., Hagan, M., Bukkapatnam, S.: Neural Networks in Chemical Reaction Dynamics. Oxford University Press, New York (2012)

6. Laganà, A., Costantini, A., Gervasi, O., Faginas Lago, N., Manuali, C., Rampino, S.: COMPCHEM: progress towards GEMS a grid empowered molecular simulator and beyond. J. Grid Comput. 8(4), 571–586 (2010)

7. Rampino, S.: Workflows and data models for atom diatom quantum reactive scattering calculations on the Grid. Ph.D. thesis, Università degli Studi di Perugia (2011)

8. Manuali, C., Laganà, A., Rampino, S.: GriF: a grid framework for a web service approach to reactive scattering. Comput. Phys. Commun. 181(7), 1179–1185 (2010)

9. Rampino, S., Faginas Lago, N., Laganà, A., Huarte-Larrañaga, F.: An extension of the grid empowered molecular simulator to quantum reactive scattering. J. Comput. Chem. **33**(6), 708–714 (2012)

10. Rampino, S., Storchi, L., Laganà, A.: Automated simulation of gas-phase reactions on distributed and cloud computing infrastructures. In: Gervasi, O., et al. (eds.) ICCSA 2017. LNCS, vol. 10406, pp. 60–73. Springer, Cham (2017). https://doi.org/10.1007/978-3-319-62398-6_5

11. Rampino, S., Skouteris, D., Laganà, A., Garcia, E.: A comparison of the isotope effect for the N + N$_2$ reaction calculated on two potential energy surfaces. In: Gervasi, O., Murgante, B., Laganà, A., Taniar, D., Mun, Y., Gavrilova, M.L. (eds.) Computational Science and Its Applications - ICCSA 2008. Lecture Notes in Computer Science, vol. 5072, pp. 1081–1093. Springer, Berlin Heidelberg (2008)

12. Laganà, A., Faginas Lago, N., Rampino, S., Huarte Larrañaga, F., García, E.: Thermal rate coefficients in collinear versus bent transition state reactions: the N+N$_2$ case study. Physica Scripta **78**(5), 058116 (2008)

13. Rampino, S., Pirani, F., Garcia, E., Laganà, A.: A study of the impact of long range interactions on the reactivity of N + N$_2$ using the Grid Empowered Molecular Simulator GEMS. Int. J. Web Grid Serv. **6**(2), 196–212 (2010)

14. Laganà, A., Rampino, S.: A grid empowered virtual versus real experiment for the barrierless Li + FH → LiF + H reaction. In: Murgante, B., et al. (eds.) ICCSA 2014. LNCS, vol. 8579, pp. 571–584. Springer, Cham (2014). https://doi.org/10.1007/978-3-319-09144-0_39

15. Rossi, E., et al.: Code interoperability and standard data formats in quantum chemistry and quantum dynamics: the Q5/D5Cost data model. J. Comput. Chem. **35**(8), 611–621 (2014)

16. Rampino, S., Monari, A., Rossi, E., Evangelisti, S., Laganà, A.: A priori modeling of chemical reactions on computational grid platforms: workflows and data models. Chem. Phys. **398**, 192–198 (2012)

17. EGI: The European grid infrastructure. http://www.egi.eu/. Accessed 27 Feb 2019

18. Rampino, S., Skouteris, D., Laganà, A., García, E., Saracibar, A.: A comparison of the quantum state-specific efficiency of N + N$_2$ reaction computed on different potential energy surfaces. Phys. Chem. Chem. Phys. **11**, 1752–1757 (2009)

19. Rampino, S., Garcia, E., Pirani, F., Laganà, A.: Accurate quantum dynamics on grid platforms: some effects of long range interactions on the reactivity of N + N$_2$. In: Taniar, D., Gervasi, O., Murgante, B., Pardede, E., Apduhan, B.O. (eds.) Computational Science and Its Applications - ICCSA 2010. Lecture Notes in Computer Science, vol. 6019, pp. 1–12. Springer, Berlin Heidelberg (2010). https://doi.org/10.1007/978-3-642-12189-0_1

20. Rampino, S., Skouteris, D., Laganà, A.: The O + O$_2$ reaction: quantum detailed probabilities and thermal rate coefficients. Theor. Chem. Acc.: Theor. Comput. Model. **123**(3/4), 249–256 (2009)

21. Rampino, S., Skouteris, D., Laganà, A.: Microscopic branching processes: the O + O$_2$ reaction and its relaxed potential representations. Int. J. Quantum Chem. **110**(2), 358–367 (2010)

22. Rampino, S., Pastore, M., Garcia, E., Pacifici, L., Laganà, A.: On the temperature dependence of the rate coefficient of formation of C$_2^+$ from C + CH$^+$. Monthly Not. Roy. Astron. Soc. **460**(3), 2368–2375 (2016)

23. Pacifici, L., Pastore, M., Garcia, E., Laganà, A., Rampino, S.: A dynamics investigation of the C + CH$^+$ → C$_2^+$ + H reaction on an *ab initio* bond-order like potential. J. Phys. Chem. A **120**(27), 5125–5135 (2016)

24. Rampino, S., Suleimanov, Y.V.: Thermal rate coefficients for the astrochemical process $C + CH^+ \rightarrow C_2^+ + H$ by ring polymer molecular dynamics. J. Phys. Chem. A **120**(50), 9887–9893 (2016)
25. Rampino, S.: Configuration-space sampling in potential energy surface fitting: a space-reduced bond-order grid approach. J. Phys. Chem. A **120**(27), 4683–4692 (2016)
26. Pauling, L.: Atomic radii and interatomic distances in metals. J. Am. Chem. Soc. **69**(3), 542–553 (1947)
27. Garcia, E., Laganà, A.: Diatomic potential functions for triatomic scattering. Mol. Phys. **56**(3), 621–627 (1985)
28. Garcia, E., Laganà, A.: A new bond-order functional form for triatomic molecules. Mol. Phys. **56**(3), 629–639 (1985)
29. Laganà, A.: A rotating bond order formulation of the atom diatom potential energy surface. J. Chem. Phys. **95**(3), 2216–2217 (1991)
30. Laganà, A., Ochoa de Aspuru, G., Garcia, E.: The largest angle generalization of the rotating bond order potential: three different atom reactions. J. Chem. Phys. **108**(10), 3886–3896 (1998)
31. Laganà, A., Crocchianti, S., Faginas Lago, N., Pacifici, L., Ferraro, G.: A nonorthogonal coordinate approach to atom-diatom parallel reactive scattering calculations. Collect. Czechoslovak Chem. Commun. **68**(2), 307–330 (2003)
32. Rampino, S., Laganà, A.: Bond order uniform grids for quantum reactive scattering. Int. J. Quantum Chem. **112**(7), 1818–1828 (2012)
33. Pedregosa, F., et al.: Scikit-learn: machine learning in Python. J. Mach. Learn. Res. **12**, 2825–2830 (2011)
34. Feurer, M., Klein, A., Eggensperger, K., Springenberg, J., Blum, M., Hutter, F.: Efficient and robust automated machine learning. In: Cortes, C., Lawrence, N.D., Lee, D.D., Sugiyama, M., Garnett, R. (eds.) Advances in Neural Information Processing Systems, vol. 28, pp. 2962–2970. Curran Associates, Inc. (2015)
35. Chollet, F.: Keras (2015). https://github.com/fchollet/keras. Accessed 27 Feb 2019
36. Aguado, A., Paniagua, M.: A new functional form to obtain analytical potentials of triatomic molecules. J. Chem. Phys. **96**(2), 1265–1275 (1992)
37. Aguado, A., Tablero, C., Paniagua, M.: Global fit of ab initio potential energy surfaces I. Triatomic systems. Comput. Phys. Commun. **108**(2–3), 259–266 (1998)
38. Shepard, D.: A two-dimensional interpolation function for irregularly-spaced data. In: Proceedings of the 1968 23rd ACM National Conference, ACM 1968, pp. 517–524. ACM, New York (1968)
39. Surowiecki, J.: The Wisdom of Crowds: Why the Many Are Smarter Than the Few and How Collective Wisdom Shapes Business, Economies, Societies, and Nations. Doubleday & Co, New York (2004)
40. Breiman, L.: Random forests. Mach. Learn. **45**(1), 5–32 (2001)
41. Quinlan, J.R.: Induction of decision trees. Mach. Learn. **1**(1), 81–106 (1986)
42. Chen, T., Guestrin, C.: XGBoost: a scalable tree boosting system. In: Proceedings of the 22nd ACM SIGKDD International Conference on Knowledge Discovery and Data Mining, KDD 2016, pp. 785–794. ACM, New York (2016)
43. Snoek, J., Larochelle, H., Adams, R.P.: Practical Bayesian optimization of machine learning algorithms. In: Proceedings of the 25th International Conference on Neural Information Processing Systems, NIPS 2012, vol. 2, pp. 2951–2959. Curran Associates Inc., USA (2012)
44. Brochu, E., Cora, V.M., de Freitas, N.: A tutorial on Bayesian optimization of expensive cost functions, with application to active user modeling and hierarchical reinforcement learning. eprint arXiv:1012.2599, arXiv.org, December 2010

45. Feurer, M., Eggensperger, K., Falkner, S., Lindauer, M., Hutter, F.: Practical automated machine learning for the AutoML challenge 2018. In: ICML 2018 AutoML Workshop (2018)

46. Esteva, A., et al.: A guide to deep learning in healthcare. Nat. Med. **25**(1), 24–29 (2019)

47. Zou, J., Huss, M., Abid, A., Mohammadi, P., Torkamani, A., Telenti, A.: A primer on deep learning in genomics. Nat. Genet. **51**(1), 12–18 (2019)

48. Nash, W., Drummond, T., Birbilis, N.: A review of deep learning in the study of materials degradation. npj Mater. Degrad. **2**(1), 37 (2018)

49. LeCun, Y., Bengio, Y., Hinton, G.: Deep learning. Nature **521**(7553), 436–444 (2015)

50. Salvadori, A., Fusè, M., Mancini, G., Rampino, S., Barone, V.: Diving into chemical bonding: an immersive analysis of the electron charge rearrangement through virtual reality. J. Comput. Chem. **39**(31), 2607–2617 (2018)

51. Salvadori, A., et al.: A walk through chemistry: exploring potential-energy surfaces with virtual reality (2019, in preparation)

A Modern-Fortran Program for Chemical Kinetics on Top of Anharmonic Vibrational Calculations

Surajit Nandi🆔, Danilo Calderini, Julien Bloino🆔, Sergio Rampino$^{(\boxtimes)}$🆔, and Vincenzo Barone🆔

Scuola Normale Superiore, Piazza dei Cavalieri 7, 56126 Pisa, Italy
sergio.rampino@sns.it

Abstract. We discuss the design and implementation of StarRate, a modern-Fortran program for the calculation of chemical kinetics coupled to anharmonic vibrational perturbative treatments. The program is written in the F language, a carefully crafted subset of Fortran 95, and is conceived in an object-based programming paradigm, i.e. the set of object-oriented programming features supported by Fortran 90/95. StarRate is made up of three main modules handling the involved molecular species, the elementary reaction steps, and the whole reaction scheme. Input data are accessed through an XML interface based on a cross-code hierarchical data format granting interoperability with popular electronic-structure packages and with the graphical interface of the Virtual Multifrequency Spectrometer developed in our group. Data parsing is performed through versatile Python scripts. Test calculations on the isomerization reaction of C-cyanomethanimine using anharmonic densities of states obtained with a development version of Gaussian are reported together with an account of ongoing developments.

Keywords: Object-based programming · Modern Fortran · Chemical kinetics · Anharmonic perturbative models · Reaction rates

1 Introduction

The concept of object-oriented programming (OOP), as opposed to procedural programming, originated as early as the Sixties [1] and has since influenced many programming languages. Nowadays, several flexible and powerful languages have emerged combining both the object-oriented and procedural

The research leading to these results has received funding from Scuola Normale Superiore through project "DIVE: Development of Immersive approaches for the analysis of chemical bonding through Virtual-reality Environments" (SNS18_B_RAMPINO) and program "Finanziamento a supporto della ricerca di base" (SNS_RB_RAMPINO). The authors are grateful to Dr. Daniele Licari (Scuola Normale Superiore) for fruitful discussions.

© Springer Nature Switzerland AG 2019
S. Misra et al. (Eds.): ICCSA 2019, LNCS 11624, pp. 401–412, 2019.
https://doi.org/10.1007/978-3-030-24311-1_29

programming paradigm, with Python and Ruby being the most popular languages among the scientific community, whereas Java is most widely used in commercial platforms.

Although these recent high-level, (semi-)interpreted programming languages are good at writing easy-readable codes, Fortran is the most widely adopted language in many branches of computational chemistry and physics. This is partly due to historical reasons (for instance, some of the first molecular electronic structure packages that are still universally used, such as the Gaussian package [2], were written and are actually developed in Fortran), partly to the availability of a large set of procedures related to mathematical operations which are quite fast in performance and thus make Fortran more suitable for computationally demanding problems. Whether to use the higher-level and system-independent languages or the lower-level, compiler-dependent languages is arguable and sometimes depends on the problem at hand. But as a matter of fact, especially among computational chemists, Fortran is still the most widely adopted programming language for intensive computing.

Despite the fact that Fortran is widely used in the scientific community and that the OOP concept is quite old, the use of the OOP paradigm with Fortran is quite rare in the scientific community. While many of the OOP features are included in Fortran 90/95 [3–5] thus making of it a so-called 'object-based'[1] language [7] with powerful capabilities (such as array syntax and built-in libraries) oriented to intensive computing, the procedural way of programming is still the prevailing one and Fortran software conceived in a OOP paradigm is very rare (see for instance Refs. [8–10] for some exceptions in the domain of computational chemistry and physics). Hence documenting on object-based implementations of Fortran computational-chemistry programs shall be beneficial for the computational-chemistry community.

In this article, we report on the development of an object-based Fortran program, StarRate, for the calculation of reaction kinetics coupled to anharmonic vibrational perturbative treatments. While doing so, we will discuss the software design and the related data structure in Sect. 2. In Sect. 3 an application is shown on the isomerization reaction of C-cyanomethanimine and the relevant computational details are given. Finally, conclusions and future work are outlined in Sect. 4.

2   Code Design and Data Structure

StarRate is an object-based Fortran program for the modeling of kinetics of multistep reactions such as those outlined, for the unimolecular case, in Fig. 1. It is written in the F language [11,12], a carefully crafted subset of Fortran 95, and is conceived in an OOP paradigm in terms of discrete objects incorporating data and behaviour through the use of Fortran derived datatypes and modules. Accordingly, StarRate is built around three core modules: molecules,

---

[1] Cardelli and Wegner identify using user-defined types for identity and classification without inheritance as object-based programming [6].

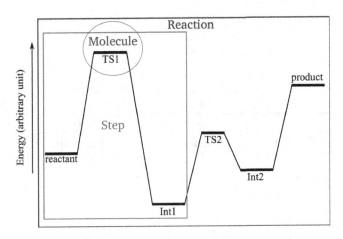

Fig. 1. Reaction scheme of a multistep unimolecular reaction involving two intermediates (Int1 and Int2) and two transition sates (TS1 and TS2).

steps, and reactions, naturally relating to the three components of the reaction scheme reported in Fig. 1: molecular species, reaction steps, and the whole reaction scheme. Three further modules, kinds, constants, and in_out, allow for handling the machine precision, the physical constants and the input/output operations, respectively.

A Unified Modeling Language (UML) diagram showing the code structure of StarRate focusing on the three core modules is shown in Fig. 2. The first module molecules contains the definition of a molecule datatype (including the relevant information for kinetics such as densities of states and sums of states, for which see Sect. 3) and the procedures to operate on a variable of the molecule type; the second module steps is in charge of handling single reaction steps (including the calculations of microcanonical and canonical rate coefficients); the third module reactions, which is currently under development, is in charge of combining the elementary reaction steps through a master-equation approach.

Input data are accessed by an interface, which is built on the XML format. At the beginning, the user will have to run a Python script which extracts data from the output files generated by quantum-chemistry calculations. Currently, Star-Rate supports output files from the Gaussian package (.log extension), though support for other popular electronic-structure programs is currently being pursued (see also Refs. [13,14] for the definition of a common data format for quantum chemistry). The interface is written in a simple script G2R.py with Python's xml.etree.ElementTree library. Python is chosen for data extraction from the .log files because of its versatility in file processing.

The structure of the XML interface to StarRate is built so as to be fully compatible with the Draw module of the Virtual Multifrequency Spectrometer (VMS-Draw) [15] developed in our laboratory. Accordingly, the whole XML document builds under a root element named escdata (electronic-structure

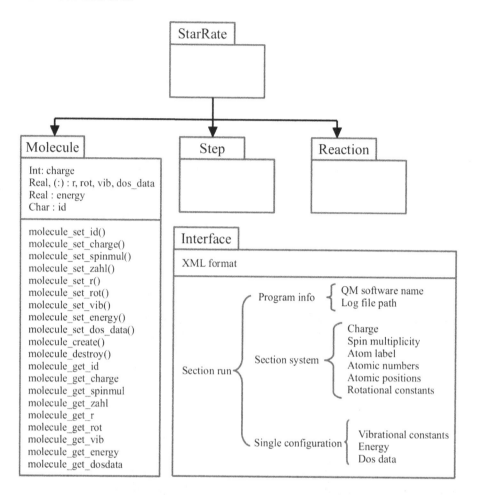

Fig. 2. A UML diagram representing the main module hierarchy of StarRate. Some details on the **molecules** module showing part of the related datatype and procedures are given for illustrative purposes.

calculation data). The `escdata` has one child element for each molecule named `section_run`. Then, `program_info`, `section_system`, and `system_single_configuration_calculation` are the siblings that fall under the `section_run` element. All the information regarding a molecule is handled by these three sibling nodes. The `program_info` node contains two subnodes which keep track of quantum chemical software name and .log file location. The `section_system` node contains basic information which does not require quantum chemical information (*viz.*, molecular charge, spin multiplicity, atom label, atomic numbers, rotational constants). The last sibling, `system_single_configuration_calculation` contains information which requires quantum chemical calculations (*viz.*, vibrational constants, SCF energy, density of state data).

Once the XML for a given reaction has been generated containing the information of all the involved molecular species, these data are read by StarRate through the FoX_DOM [16] library for XML parsing in Fortran.

3   Isomerization of C-Cyanomethanimine

C-cyanomethanimine is a complex organic molecule found in the interstellar medium (ISM) [17,18]. C-cyanomethanimine is essentially a dimer of HCN and a very important molecule in the context of prebiotic chemistry [19]. In fact, the oligomerization of HCN leads to the formation of nucleobases [20,21] via C-cyanomethanimine. Because of the importance of the molecule and availability of a number of works on its isomerization [22,23], we choose the simple yet important Z ⇌ E isomerization reaction of C-cyanomethanimine as a test case for a calculation with StarRate. The structures of the involved molecular species for this reaction together with the relevant data are summarized in Fig. 3.

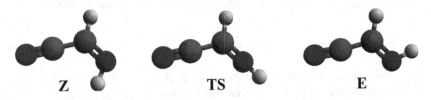

$$Z \qquad\qquad TS \qquad\qquad E$$

Fig. 3. Molecular species involved in the Z ⇌ E isomerization reaction. The computed anharmonic zero-point energies relative to the anharmonic zero-point energy of Z are 25.49 Kcal/mol for TS and 0.57 Kcal/mol for E.

A proper treatment of the time evolution of a chemical reaction should rely on the quantum modeling of the underlying nuclear dynamics. However, exact quantum-dynamics calculations are only feasible for systems with up to 3 or 4 atoms [24–27], and approximate quantum-dynamical methods are able to extend this limit only modestly. For the remaining systems, one has in practice to resort either to a (quasi-)classical treatment [28–30] or to more drastic approximations such as transition-state theory (TST) in one of its flavours, simply accounting for the energetic structure of a limited set of important points of the potential energy surface. Within the popular Rice-Ramsperger-Kassel-Marcus (RRKM) theory [31–33], the microcanonical rate coefficient for a unimolecular reaction, such as the above-mentioned one, is given by the equation [34]

$$k(E) = \frac{N^{\ddagger}(E)}{h\rho(E)} \qquad (1)$$

where h is Planck's constants, $N^{\ddagger}(E)$ is the sum of states of the TS (or a tunneling-corrected version of it) and $\rho(E)$ is the density of states (DOS) of the reactant molecule. A central quantity in this framework is thus the molecular rovibrational density of states $\rho(E) = \Delta N(E)/\Delta E$, i.e. the number $\Delta N(E)$ of rovibrational states per energy interval ΔE within the interval $[E, E + \Delta E]$, of the involved molecular species. The cumulative sum of states (SOS) up to energy E, $N(E)$, for a given species is in fact easily worked out from the related DOS:[2]

$$N(E) = \int_0^E \rho(E') \, \mathrm{d}E'. \tag{3}$$

The rotational motion and the vibrational motion of the molecule are usually assumed to be approximately separable from one another (in other words, the energy of the molecule, E, is approximately the sum of the rotational energy, E_r, and the vibrational energy, $E - E_r$). As a result, the rovibrational density of states can be written as a convolution of its rotational and vibrational counterparts [35]:

$$\rho(E) = \int_0^E \rho_r(E_r)\rho_v(E - E_r)dE_r.$$

While a classical expression can be used for the rotational DOS

$$\rho(E) = \frac{1}{\sigma}\sqrt{\frac{4E}{ABC}}, \tag{4}$$

with σ being the rotation symmetry number and A, B, and C the three rotational constants, a quantum anharmonic treatment is recommended for the vibrational motions. Within second-order anharmonic perturbative approaches [36,37], the vibrational energy E (expressed in cm^{-1}) in terms of the n quantum numbers $\{\nu_i\} \equiv (\nu_1, \dots, \nu_n)$ is given by

$$E = E_0 + \sum_{i=1}^n \nu_i\omega_i + \sum_{i,j=1}^n \chi_{ij}\left[\nu_i\nu_j + \frac{1}{2}\left(\nu_i + \nu_j\right)\right]. \tag{5}$$

In Eq. 5, E_0 is the zero-point vibrational energy, ω_i are the harmonic frequencies, and χ_{ij} are the elements of the anharmonic matrix (explicit function of cubic and semidiagonal quartic force constants, as well as Coriolis couplings).

While the density and sum of states of a molecule can be in principle computed by an exact state counting using the above expression (see for instance the Stein-Rabinovitch [38] adaptation of the Beyer-Swinehart [39] algorithm for uncopled anharmonic oscillators), this becomes rapidly unaffordable from a computational point of view with increasing system size. A viable alternative is represented by the Wang-Landau sampling method [40,41] as extended to

---

[2] The partition function $Q(T)$ can as well be computed from the density of states $\rho(E)$ by a Laplace transform:

$$Q(T) = \int_0^\infty \rho(E)e^{-\frac{E}{k_B T}}\mathrm{d}E \tag{2}$$

with k_B being the Boltzmann constant and T being the absolute temperature.

the quantum anharmonic vibrational problem by Basire et al. [42]. and further refined by Nguyen and Barker [43]. Within such scheme (the reader is referred to the original papers for more details) the DOS $\rho(E_j)$ is obtained iteratively for each j-th bin of an equally spaced energy grid in a given energy range by performing a random walk in the space of quantum numbers $\{\nu_i\}$.

The thermal rate coefficient can be easily computed from the microcanonical rate coefficients using the following equation:

$$k(T) = \frac{1}{Q(T)} \int_0^\infty k(E)\rho(E)e^{-E/k_\mathrm{B}T}\mathrm{d}E, \tag{6}$$

with $Q(T)$ being the partition function of the reactant species.

Calculations were performed with a locally modified version of the development version of Gaussian [44] using density-functional theory (DFT) at the B3LYP-D3BJ/SNSD level of theory (B3LYP exchange-correlation functional [45,46], semiempirical dispersion contributions by inclusion of the Grimme's D3BJ model [47], SNSD basis set [48]). Anharmonic calculations were performed with the GVPT2 model [36,49]. Cubic and semi-diagonal quartic force constant

Table 1. Cartesian coordinates in Å of the optimized structures for the Z, TS, and E species.

Z			
C	0.695181	0.486229	0.000000
H	0.894724	1.559531	0.000000
H	1.345237	−1.302417	0.000000
N	1.672019	−0.331592	0.000000
C	−0.702977	0.109125	0.000000
N	−1.821969	−0.199372	0.000000
TS			
C	−0.698654	0.482677	−0.000155
H	−0.831811	1.579112	−0.000380
H	−2.384044	−0.978647	0.000108
N	−1.627409	−0.333444	−0.000005
C	0.719560	0.085097	−0.000040
N	1.845003	−0.198736	0.000056
E			
C	0.687014	0.470848	0.000000
H	0.847507	1.554826	0.000000
H	2.525991	0.044966	0.000000
N	1.608625	−0.407966	0.000000
C	−0.703284	0.072983	0.000000
N	−1.836746	−0.173430	0.000000

were computed by numerical differentiation (with displacements of $0.01 \sqrt{amu}$ Å) of the analytical Hessian along each active normal coordinate. Optimized geometries for the Z, TS, and E species are reported in Table 1. The anharmonic vibrational densities of states for the three species were calculated by means of the Wang-Landau sampling method as refined in Ref. [43], which was directly implemented in a modified version of Gaussian. The DOS were computed on an energy grid from 10 to $50000\,\mathrm{cm}^{-1}$ with spacing $10\,\mathrm{cm}^{-1}$ using 1000 trials per

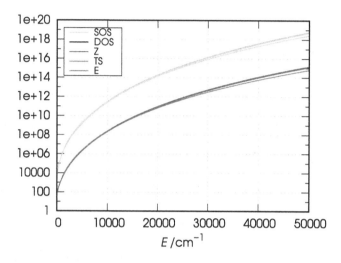

Fig. 4. Rovibrational DOS (full color) and SOS (light color) for the Z (red), TS (green), and E (blue) species. (Color figure online)

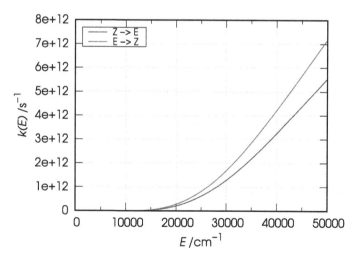

Fig. 5. Microcanonical rate constants for the Z → E (red line) and the E → Z (blue line) reactions. (Color figure online)

energy bin and a number of 21 iterations (the interested reader is referred to Ref. [43] for further details on these parameters). For the transition state, the density of states was computed by excluding the normal mode with an imaginary frequency.

The DOS and SOS of the three species Z, TS, and E are plotted in Fig. 4 as a function of the energy E on an energy scale having as zero the respective zero-point energy. Full-color curves represent the DOS (red for Z, green for TS, and blue for E), while light-color curves represent the DOS. Microcanonical rate coefficients for the Z $\rightarrow$ E (red line) and E $\rightarrow$ Z (blue line) isomerization reaction are reported in Fig. 5 as a function of the energy E on an energy scale having as zero the Z-isomer zero-point energy.

4 Conclusions

In this paper we describe the design and implementation of an object-based program written in the F subset of Fortran 95 for the modeling of chemical kinetics on top of anharmonic vibrational perturbative treatments. The program builds around three main modules relating to the entities that make up a reaction scheme: molecular species, elementary steps, and the whole reaction scheme. As an example, rate constants for the isomerization of C-cyanomethanimine computed within a density-functional theory framework and an anharmonic perturbative treatment are reported. Although test calculations are shown for the case of a unimolecular reaction, the program is being extended to the treatment of bimolecular reactions as well.

Specific care during the code design has been devoted to grant full interoperability with the Virtual Multifrequency Spectrometer (VMS) developed in our group, in order to provide our program with the powerful capabilities of the VMS graphical user interface, and with popular quantum-chemistry packages. This has been achieved through a specific XML interface between the program and the output files of quantum-chemical calculations fostered by dedicated libraries.

Current work is ongoing in our laboratory on the development of StarRate. On one hand the module handling elementary reaction steps is being enriched with a number of methods of different accuracy to compute the density of states, while the module handling the whole reaction scheme is being provided by a master-equation solver. On the other hand, we are developing a module of VMS providing a user-friendly graphical interface for calculating chemical kinetics using the StarRate program. While details on these aspects will be given in a forthcoming publication, the possibility of coupling chemical-kinetics calculations to three-dimensional representation and exploration of the potential-energy surface [50] by state-of-the-art immersive-virtual-reality technology [51] and to the analysis of detailed chemical-bonding features [52–54] is also being explored.

References

1. Ram, S.: Dr. Alan Kay on the meaning of Object-Oriented Programming (2003). http://www.purl.org/stefan_ram/pub/doc_kay_oop_en. Accessed 14 Mar 2019
2. Frisch, M.J., et al.: Gaussian 16 Revision B.01. Gaussian Inc., Wallingford CT (2016)
3. Cary, J.R., Shasharina, S.G., Cummings, J.C., Reynders, J.V., Hinker, P.J.: Comparison of C++ and Fortran 90 for object-oriented scientific programming. Comput. Phys. Commun. **105**(1), 20–36 (1997)
4. Decyk, V.K., Norton, C.D., Szymanski, B.K.: How to support inheritance and runtime polymorphism in Fortran 90. Comput. Phys. Commun. **115**(1), 9–17 (1998)
5. Gorelik, A.M.: Object-oriented programming in modern Fortran. Program. Comput. Softw. **30**(3), 173–179 (2004)
6. Cardelli, L., Wegner, P.: On understanding types, data abstraction and polymorphism. ACM Comput. Surv. **17**(4), 471–522 (1985)
7. Gray, M.G., Roberts, R.M., Dubois, P.F.: Object-based programming in Fortran 90. Comput. Phys. **11**(4), 355–361 (1997)
8. Kim, Y.H., Lee, I.H., Martin, R.M.: Object-oriented construction of a multigrid electronic-structure code with Fortran 90. Comput. Phys. Commun. **131**(1–2), 10–25 (2000)
9. Jayatilaka, D., Grimwood, D.J.: Tonto: a Fortran based object-oriented system for quantum chemistry and crystallography. In: Sloot, P.M.A., Abramson, D., Bogdanov, A.V., Gorbachev, Y.E., Dongarra, J.J., Zomaya, A.Y. (eds.) ICCS 2003. LNCS, vol. 2660, pp. 142–151. Springer, Heidelberg (2003). https://doi.org/10.1007/3-540-44864-0_15
10. Zaghi, S.: OFF, open source finite volume fluid dynamics code: a free, high-order solver based on parallel, modular, object-oriented Fortran API. Comput. Phys. Commun. **185**(7), 2151–2194 (2014)
11. Metcalf, M., Reid, J.: The F Programming Language. Oxford University Press Inc., New York (1996)
12. F Syntax Rules. http://www.fortran.com/F/F_bnf.html. Accessed 14 Mar 2019
13. Rossi, E., et al.: Code interoperability and standard data formats in quantum chemistry and quantum dynamics: the Q5/D5Cost data model. J. Comput. Chem. **35**(8), 611–621 (2014)
14. Rampino, S., Monari, A., Rossi, E., Evangelisti, S., Laganà, A.: A priori modeling of chemical reactions on computational grid platforms: workflows and data models. Chem. Phys. **398**, 192–198 (2012)
15. Licari, D., Baiardi, A., Biczysko, M., Egidi, F., Latouche, C., Barone, V.: Implementation of a graphical user interface for the Virtual Multifrequency Spectrometer: the VMS-draw tool. J. Comput. Chem. **36**(5), 321–334 (2015)
16. FoX in Fortran Wiki. http://fortranwiki.org/fortran/show/FoX. Accessed 14 Mar 2019
17. Zaleski, D.P., et al.: Detection of E-cyanomethanimine toward Sagittarius B2(N) in the Green Bank Telescope PRIMOS survey. Astrophys. J. **765**(1), L10 (2013)
18. Melosso, M., et al.: Laboratory measurements and astronomical search for cyanomethanimine. Astron. Astrophys. **609**, A121 (2018)
19. Nandi, S., Bhattacharyya, D., Anoop, A.: Prebiotic chemistry of HCN tetramerization by automated reaction search. Chem. Eur. J. **24**(19), 4885–4894 (2018)
20. Balucani, N.: Elementary reactions and their role in gas-phase prebiotic chemistry. Int. J. Mol. Sci. **10**(5), 2304–2335 (2009)

21. Chakrabarti, S., Chakrabarti, S.K.: Can DNA bases be produced during molecular cloud collapse? Astron. Astrophys. **354**, L6–L8 (2000)
22. Puzzarini, C.: Isomerism of cyanomethanimine: accurate structural, energetic, and spectroscopic characterization. J. Phys. Chem. A **119**(47), 11614–11622 (2015)
23. Vazart, F., Calderini, D., Skouteris, D., Latouche, C., Barone, V.: Reassessment of the thermodynamic, kinetic, and spectroscopic features of cyanomethanimine derivatives: a full anharmonic perturbative treatment. J. Chem. Theor. Comput. **11**(3), 1165–1171 (2015)
24. Rampino, S., Faginas Lago, N., Laganà, A., Huarte-Larrañaga, F.: An extension of the grid empowered molecular simulator to quantum reactive scattering. J. Comput. Chem. **33**(6), 708–714 (2012)
25. Rampino, S., Skouteris, D., Laganà, A.: Microscopic branching processes: the O + O_2 reaction and its relaxed potential representations. Int. J. Quantum Chem. **110**(2), 358–367 (2010)
26. Rampino, S., Skouteris, D., Laganà, A.: The O + O_2 reaction: quantum detailed probabilities and thermal rate coefficients. Theor. Chem. Acc. **123**(3/4), 249–256 (2009)
27. Laganà, A., Faginas Lago, N., Rampino, S., Huarte Larrañaga, F., García, E.: Thermal rate coefficients in collinear versus bent transition state reactions: the N + N_2 case study. Physica Scripta **78**(5), 058116 (2008)
28. Rampino, S., Pastore, M., Garcia, E., Pacifici, L., Laganà, A.: On the temperature dependence of the rate coefficient of formation of C_2^+ from C + CH^+. Monthly Not. Roy. Astron. Soc. **460**(3), 2368–2375 (2016)
29. Pacifici, L., Pastore, M., Garcia, E., Laganà, A., Rampino, S.: A dynamics investigation of the C + CH^+ → C_2^+ + H reaction on an *ab initio* bond-order like potential. J. Phys. Chem. A **120**(27), 5125–5135 (2016)
30. Rampino, S., Suleimanov, Y.V.: Thermal rate coefficients for the astrochemical process C + CH^+ → $C2^+$ + H by ring polymer molecular dynamics. J. Phys. Chem. A **120**(50), 9887–9893 (2016)
31. Rice, O.K., Ramsperger, H.C.: Theories of unimolecular gas reactions at low pressures. J. Am. Chem. Soc. **49**(7), 1617–1629 (1927)
32. Kassel, L.S.: Studies in homogeneous gas reactions. I. J. Phys. Chem. **32**(2), 225–242 (1927)
33. Marcus, R.A.: Unimolecular dissociations and free radical recombination reactions. J. Chem. Phys. **20**(3), 359–364 (1952)
34. Brouard, M.: Reaction Dynamics. Oxford Chemistry Primers. OUP Oxford (1998)
35. Green, N.J.B.: Chapter 1 - introduction. In: Green, N.J., (ed.) Unimolecular Kinetics. Volume 39 of Comprehensive Chemical Kinetics, pp. 1–53. Elsevier (2003)
36. Barone, V.: Anharmonic vibrational properties by a fully automated second-order perturbative approach. J. Chem. Phys. **122**(1), 014108 (2005)
37. Bloino, J., Biczysko, M., Barone, V.: General perturbative approach for spectroscopy, thermodynamics, and kinetics: methodological background and benchmark studies. J. Chem. Theor. Comput. **8**(3), 1015–1036 (2012)
38. Stein, S.E., Rabinovitch, B.S.: Accurate evaluation of internal energy level sums and densities including anharmonic oscillators and hindered rotors. J. Chem. Phys. **58**(6), 2438–2445 (1973)
39. Beyer, T., Swinehart, D.F.: Algorithm 448: number of multiply-restricted partitions. Commun. ACM **16**(6), 379 (1973)
40. Wang, F., Landau, D.P.: Efficient, multiple-range random walk algorithm to calculate the density of states. Phys. Rev. Lett. **86**(10), 2050–2053 (2001)

41. Zhou, C., Bhatt, R.N.: Understanding and improving the Wang-Landau algorithm. Phys. Rev. E **72**(2), 025701 (2005)
42. Basire, M., Parneix, P., Calvo, F.: Quantum anharmonic densities of states using the Wang-Landau method. J. Chem. Phys. **129**(8), 081101 (2008)
43. Nguyen, T.L., Barker, J.R.: Sums and densities of fully coupled anharmonic vibrational states: a comparison of three practical methods. J. Phys. Chem. A **114**(10), 3718–3730 (2010)
44. Frisch, M.J., et al.: Gaussian development version, revision i.13. Gaussian Inc., Wallingford CT (2018)
45. Lee, C., Yang, W., Parr, R.G.: Development of the Colle-Salvetti correlation-energy formula into a functional of the electron density. Phys. Rev. B **37**, 785–789 (1988)
46. Becke, A.D.: Density-functional thermochemistry. III. The role of exact exchange. J. Chem. Phys. **98**(7), 5648–5652 (1993)
47. Grimme, S., Ehrlich, S., Goerigk, L.: Effect of the damping function in dispersion corrected density functional theory. J. Comput. Chem. **32**(7), 1456–1465 (2011)
48. Double and triple-ζ basis sets of SNS families are available for download. http://smart.sns.it. Accessed 14 Mar 2019
49. Bloino, J., Barone, V.: A second-order perturbation theory route to vibrational averages and transition properties of molecules: general formulation and application to infrared and vibrational circular dichroism spectroscopies. J. Chem. Phys. **136**(12), 124108 (2012)
50. Rampino, S.: Configuration-space sampling in potential energy surface fitting: a space-reduced bond-order grid approach. J. Phys. Chem. A **120**(27), 4683–4692 (2016)
51. Salvadori, A., Fusè, M., Mancini, G., Rampino, S., Barone, V.: Diving into chemical bonding: an immersive analysis of the electron charge rearrangement through virtual reality. J. Comput. Chem. **39**(31), 2607–2617 (2018)
52. Bistoni, G., Rampino, S., Tarantelli, F., Belpassi, L.: Charge-displacement analysis via natural orbitals for chemical valence: charge transfer effects in coordination chemistry. J. Chem. Phys. **142**(8), 084112 (2015)
53. Fusè, M., Rimoldi, I., Cesarotti, E., Rampino, S., Barone, V.: On the relation between carbonyl stretching frequencies and the donor power of chelating diphosphines in nickel dicarbonyl complexes. Phys. Chem. Chem. Phys. **19**, 9028–9038 (2017)
54. Fusè, M., Rimoldi, I., Facchetti, G., Rampino, S., Barone, V.: Exploiting coordination geometry to selectively predict the σ-donor and π-acceptor abilities of ligands: a back-and-forth journey between electronic properties and spectroscopy. Chem. Commun. **54**, 2397–2400 (2018)

Molecular Dynamics of Chiral Molecules in Hyperspherical Coordinates

Andrea Lombardi[1,2(✉)], Federico Palazzetti[1], and Vincenzo Aquilanti[1]

[1] Dipartimento di Chimica, Biologia e Biotecnologie,
Università di Perugia, Perugia, Italy
ebiu2005@gmail.com, {federico.palazzetti,vincenzo.aquilanti}@unipg.it
[2] Consortium for Computational Molecular and Materials Sciences (CMS)[2],
Via Elce di Sotto, 8, 06123 Perugia, Italy
http://www.chm.unipg.it/gruppi?q=node/48

Abstract. The role of chirality in molecular collisions, in connection to chiral discrimination, lacks a striking experimental demonstration. This is due to difficulties in setting up apparatuses allowing for a strict control of the spatial distribution and alignment of the molecules and to lack of adequate theoretical and computational approaches to design experiments, anticipate results and interpret data. Here we illustrate a theoretical approach to the description of chiral effects in collisions to search for a stereo-directional origin of chiral discrimination.

Keywords: Molecular chirality · Chiral discrimination ·
Chiral recognition · Hyperspherical coordinates ·
Intermolecular interactions · Molecular collisions

1 Introduction

The quantum mechanical treatment of N-body problems is the theoretical background of quantum reactive scattering calculations. It can be formulated in terms of hyperspherical functions, an optimal choice for the expansion basis sets [1–4], and for the representation of intermolecular and intramolecular interactions. Hyperspherical and related techniques refer to a wide class of curvilinear coordinates for which the construction of relevant operators and functionals of interest in quantum and classical mechanics is relatively straightforward. Although the practical feasibility of full quantum treatments limits the use to three- or four-atom systems, one might go beyond this restriction by extending the hyperspherical approach to classical mechanics, so that applications to dynamics simulations of clusters and large molecules would become feasible, benefiting of the computational ease of classical trajectories. In the case of classical mechanics, the added value of the hyperspherical method is the separation of the degrees of freedom into homogeneous sets of variables corresponding to well defined kinetic energy terms, representing deformations, ordinary rotations and kinematic rotations [3,4].

© Springer Nature Switzerland AG 2019
S. Misra et al. (Eds.): ICCSA 2019, LNCS 11624, pp. 413–427, 2019.
https://doi.org/10.1007/978-3-030-24311-1_30

The hyperspherical formulation grounds on "classical" definitions of the hyperangular momenta and other dynamic quantities. The classical hyperspherical equation of motion can be consequently written, although terms dependent upon angular variables and singularities in the corresponding Hamilton function make it convenient integration in Cartesian coordinates. A proper matrix transformation permits the evaluation, as a function of time, of the terms appearing in the hyperspherical Hamilton function.

The peculiar feature of hyperspherical coordinates to be considered in this work is the definition of a chiral degree of freedom corresponding to the chiral sign of a given molecular system [5–7]. Such coordinates make the hyperspherical representation suited for studying chiral effects in collisions. To identify the microscopic mechanisms inducing chiral selection it is necessary to investigate how chiral molecules collide with atomic or molecular targets and their behaviour in gaseous environments. The transition to gas phase is crucial in order to single out the fundamental elementary molecular processes. Intriguing is the idea that the effects associated to the true chiral influence of roto-translational motions [8–10], proved for liquids phase, might occur also in gas phase. The sense of rotation of a vortex in gas phase could act selectively on the direction of a chiral molecule rotation. This affirmation is strengthened by the experimental observation that in supersonic beams of gaseous mixtures the component in excess induces directionality and orientation in dragging molecules [11], as amply discussed, for example in Ref. [12] and elsewhere. Molecular alignment is actually a powerful allied in the search for an experimental proof of chiral selection in collisions, being molecular rotations a source of averaging of orientation and stereodynamics effects, since in case of fast rotations the vector correlation of the specific polarization directions to the physically significant vector quantities in the body frame gets lost in the laboratory reference frame.

The aspects of collisions of molecules to put into relation to chirality are the intermolecular interactions driving molecular encounters and the stereodynamics of collisions involving different enantiomers. Although chiral effects are well known in the interaction of molecules with light (e.g. natural optical activity, dichroism), they are still nearly disregarded in the context of molecular collisions, since the molecular scattering theory has not been provided with an explicit description of chirality, for which the introduction of new parameters and methodologies is still required. In fact, the only efforts to set up reliable full quantum mechanical scattering calculations in the previous decades have been dedicated to the study of three-atom reactions, where chirality is not present (three atoms always lie on a plane), leaving aside more complex systems –mostly due to the exceedingly high computational costs– involving more than three atoms (or centers) for which chiral configurations exist [13–15].

In the following Sections, it will be given a description of the hyperspherical coordinates applied to chiral systems and of the related approach to the modeling of the interactions. Finally, a model system, prototype of chiral collisions, will be examined.

2   Theoretical Background

The tetrahedron is the simplest chiral polyhedron in the three-dimensional space, considering as distinguishable its four vertexes. Accordingly, tetratomic molecules are the simplest chiral systems. As a general consequence, chiral manifestations in elementary processes and interactions can in principle be reduced to four-center problems.

Quantum mechanical theory of molecular scattering, applied to four-atom systems, does not contain an explicit description of the effects of the chirality in collisions and it still requires the introduction of new parameters and methodologies. Indeed, when collision processes involve more than three atoms, simulations and related systematic computations cannot be efficiently grounded on quantum mechanics, since the feasibility of full quantum treatments is limited by the number of degrees of freedom. Because of this, related computations are usually carried out resorting to the so called quasi-classical trajectory calculations (QCT) (see e.g. [16] for a QCT program) or sometimes by combining quantum mechanics treatments (for selected bound degrees of freedom) with classical mechanics ones (for the remainder), the so-called quantum-classical methods (see e.g. [17]). A variety of semiclassical methods are also available [18–24]. Rarely, and almost exclusively for three atom systems, the calculation is performed using exact quantum full-dimensional treatments [25] and this excludes chirality.

To provide a theoretical background, we show how to identify a single chiral degree of freedom in four-center problems, within the hyperspherical coordinate framework, as a tool for molecular dynamics studies and structural recognition of chiral properties in dimers and clusters.

2.1   Coordinates for Chiral Molecules

Different enantiomers are commonly distinguished attributing them a sign, $+$ or $-$, accounting for the sense of rotation of the plane of polarization of light, in their optical activity. A chiral coordinate must be a variable that changes its sign according to the chiral sign of the enantiomer. An appropriate mathematical tool for the representation of four-center chiral systems is the *singular value decomposition* [26], a matrix decomposition theorem that can be applied to any given set of N atoms, after assigning to them a properly defined position matrix.

Given a system of $N \geq 2$ particles, let us denote by $m_1, \cdots, m_N$ the particle masses and by $\mathbf{r_1}, \cdots, \mathbf{r_N}$ the corresponding radii vectors in the center of mass reference system. A set of *mass scaled* radii vectors $\mathbf{q}_\alpha = (m_\alpha/M)^{1/2}\mathbf{r}_\alpha$ ($1 \leq \alpha \leq N$), can be constructed, where $M = \sum_\alpha^N m_\alpha$ is the total mass of the system.

The $3N$ components of the mass-scaled vectors are then arranged columnwise to form a $3 \times N$ position matrix as follows:

$$Z = \begin{pmatrix} q_{1,1} & q_{1,2} & \cdots & q_{1,N} \\ q_{2,1} & q_{2,2} & \cdots & q_{2,N} \\ q_{3,1} & q_{3,2} & \cdots & q_{3,N} \end{pmatrix}. \tag{1}$$

A matrix $Z' = R^t Z$ corresponds to the coordinate change occurring in passing to a rotated coordinate frame placed at the center of mass of the system, by the action of a rotation matrix R^t, transpose of a matrix $R \in O(3)$. A rotation of the coordinate frame can also be performed in the so called *kinematic space* [14, 15, 27], by action of an orthogonal matrix (right-multiplication) $K \in O(N)$ on the position matrix Z, $Z' = ZK$.

A reduced set of K matrices having the following form (see last column):

$$
K = \begin{pmatrix} k_{1,1} & k_{1,2} & \cdots & (m_1/M)^{1/2} \\ k_{2,1} & k_{2,2} & \cdots & (m_2/M)^{1/2} \\ \cdots & \cdots & \cdots & \cdots \\ k_{N,1} & k_{N,2} & \cdots & (m_N/M)^{1/2} \end{pmatrix}
\tag{2}
$$

generates a special subset of the possible Cartesian frames. Since the mass-scaled vectors sum to zero [27], $\sum_\alpha^N m_\alpha^{1/2} \mathbf{q}_\alpha = 0$, as a consequence of the rotation through K as in Eq. 2, the last column of Z' is invariably the zero-vector. In this special case, one only has to deal with a $3 \times (N-1)$ reduced Z matrix, meaning that the variables representing the motion of the center of mass have been separated. This smaller matrix Z is called *reduced position matrix*.

The set of (N-1) Jacobi vectors, adopted in the representation of molecular collision dynamics, forms a reduced matrix. The Jacobi vectors are obtained as a linear combinations of the N Cartesian particle position vectors, in which the coefficients are defined in terms of the particle masses [28, 29]. There is no unique set of such vectors, each of them corresponds to a different coupling scheme of the particles. The different sets are connected by kinematic rotations.

The *singular value decomposition* applied to the $3 \times n$ position matrix Z (where $n = N$ or $n = N - 1$) leads to the following product of three matrices:

$$
Z = R \Lambda K^t
\tag{3}
$$

where $R \in O(3)$ and $K \in O(n)$ are 3×3 and $3 \times n$ orthogonal matrices, respectively. The $3 \times n$ matrix Λ is such that its entries are zeroes, with the possible exception of the diagonal ones, $\Lambda_{11} = \lambda_1, \Lambda_{22} = \lambda_2, \Lambda_{33} = \lambda_3$, which are subjected to the inequality $\lambda_1 \geq \lambda_2 \geq \lambda_3 \geq 0$.

The values λ_i, $(i = 1, 2, 3)$ are called the *singular values* of the matrix Z and are uniquely determined, although the factors R and K in Eq. 3 are not. If $N \leq 3$ and Z is the full $3 \times N$ position matrix, then the smallest singular value λ_3 is necessarily zero. The λ's are invariant under both physical space and kinematic rotations [14, 27, 30, 31], a remarkable property, with possible applications to molecular collision dynamics [29, 32–35].

The case $n = 3$, corresponding to four particles or four centers, is peculiar, since R and K cannot be chosen to be *special orthogonal* matrices, $R \in SO(3)$ and $K \in SO(n)$, but must be orthogonal matrices. In this case, when the determinant of Z, denoted by $\det(Z)$ is lower than zero, its sign depends on the sign of $\det(\Lambda)$, see Eq. 3, meaning that one of the singular values must be negative: $\lambda_3 \leq 0$. This fact is directly connected to the mirror image of the system and relevant for chiral molecules.

Indeed, in a generic trajectory of a 4-atom system, the behaviour of the singular values is such that at a given time the λ_3 can approach the zero value and become negative (or positive), meaning the system has changed its chirality sign.

An alternative valid interpretation of the sign of λ_3 (namely the sign of $\det(Z)$) resorts to the volume in the physical space of the tetrahedron identified by the four centers. Considering the matrix Z^t, its determinant is equivalent to the scalar "triple" product of the three Jacobi vectors, say $\mathbf{Q}_1, \mathbf{Q}_2, \mathbf{Q}_3$, describing the system. Such a product, $\mathbf{Q} \cdot (\mathbf{Q}_2 \times \mathbf{Q}_3)$, is actually equivalent to the volume delimited by the tetrahedron defined by the same three vectors. By the way, the two "chiral" triple products are interconverted by space inversion (parity), but not by time reversal combined with any proper spatial rotation, so satisfying the Barron definition of true chirality, mentioned in Sect. 1, see Refs. [8–10].

2.2   The Characterization of the Interactions

Collision dynamics calculations require an accurate characterization of the inter-molecular interactions. In order to build up reliable Potential Energy Surfaces (PESs) it is necessary to match experimental information to calibrate *ab initio* techniques. To meet this target, one relies on a representation of the potentials in appropriate analytic forms, in which interaction parameters connected to collision observables can be directly incorporated [5].

The interaction occurring between a rare-gas atom and hydrogen peroxide and persulfide molecules, has been considered in previous works [36–38], motivated by the interesting problem of large amplitude motions–torsion motion around the O-O and S-S bonds–as a chirality inversion mechanism (note that these two molecules are chiral). In Fig. 2 a sketch of the coordinate system used to represent the corresponding intermolecular potential energy surface is shown. The distance r and the two polar angles α $(0 \leq \alpha \leq 2\pi)$ and β $(0 \leq \beta \leq \pi)$ are the variables which are used in the analytic representation of the potential energy surface and to which a further angle γ is to be added to describe low-frequency mode corresponding to the torsion around the middle O-O or S-S bond. A complete torsion connects the two chiral forms. In Fig. 3 the corresponding calculated potential energy profiles connecting the two enantiomeric forms are represented, as obtained by using different basis sets.

The expression of the potential energy of the H_2S_2 (or H_2O_2) is as follows:

$$V = V_{ext}(r; \alpha, \beta) + V_{int}(r; \gamma) \tag{4}$$

where the intermolecular potential V_{ext} is a function of the atom distance r and its position with respect to the molecule and the intramolecular energy V_{int} depends on the dihedral angle γ and has an expected mild dependence on the atomic distance r. It can be shown that the potential energy, so formulated, can be expressed in terms of combinations of real-valued hyperspherical harmonics [39–43], denoted by $R_{MM'}^{\mu}$, obtained by combination of complex-valued Wigner D-functions [44,45], as follows:

$$V(r; \alpha, \beta, \gamma) = \sum_{\mu, M, M'} v_{M,M'}^{\mu}(r) R_{MM'}^{\mu}(\alpha, \beta, \gamma) \tag{5}$$

where $\mu = 0, 1, 2, \cdots, M(M') = -\mu, -\mu+1, \cdots, 0, 1, \cdots, \mu$ and the radial coefficients $v_{MM'}^{\mu}(r)$ are the expansion moments. For additional details about hyperspherical harmonics see Refs. [14,27,30,31,46,47] and references therein. For a given geometry of the atom-molecule system and a given value of the torsion dihedral angle γ, the harmonic functions take a defined value, then, if the corresponding value of the $V(r; \alpha, \beta, \gamma)$ function is known over a range of the distance r, the only remaining unknown quantities are the radial coefficients. In practice, for any given atom-molecule mutual orientation, a system of linear equations can be set up and solved for the coefficients $v_{M,M'}^{\mu}$ as a function of r. This procedure allows to build up an analytic potential energy surface.

The number of harmonic functions in the above expansion is finite and limited by the number of the specific configurations. These are selected based on physical meaning to capture the essential of the problem to be studied. We remark that the torsion angle γ appearing in the analytic expression of the potential energy function is the chiral coordinate of the system.

The radial coefficients of the hyperspherical expansion in Eq. 5, describe the radial dependence of the different components of the intermolecular interaction, for example dispersion and induction forces, repulsion due to the overlap of the electron clouds, electrostatic contributions. The spherical average of the function in Eq. 5 defines the radial coefficient $v_{00}^{0}(r)$, which represent the isotropic contribution to the interaction (well representative of the van der Waals forces), directly connected to measurable features of the cross sections which are observed in the molecular beam collision experiments (see Ref. [5] and reference therein).

In general, a tentative set of energy profiles, needed to set up the system of linear equations from which a PES can be obtained, is provided by ab initio methods and further refined by comparison of the available experimental data with the corresponding quantities obtained by theoretical methods, using the PES. For example, the accuracy of the $v_{00}^{0}(r)$ coefficient, can be checked directly by comparison with molecular beam experiments.

The method described here for the modelling of the intermolecular interaction, can be extended to a variety of different cases involving more complex molecules [48–52], including interactions with ions and surfaces and in liquid phase [53–58]. For a representative set of the applications to practical cases of collision studies, see Refs. [48,49,58–70].

3   Dynamics Simulations of Collisions of Chiral Molecules

The hypothesis that alignment and orientation in gaseous streams could not only minimize averaging effects due to molecular rotations but crucially propitiate chiral effects in the differential scattering by oriented molecules (see Refs. [71,72] and references therein) has been assessed in previous work [5,73].

The simplest model of a chiral collision is given by a target chiral molecule well oriented or aligned with respect to an incoming stream of atoms. Accordingly, we make the hypothesis that a sample of chiral molecules in a collision chamber is under a controlled orientation distribution, achieved by one of the spatial control techniques illustrated in Ref. [5], and is the target of a beam of velocity selected atoms, coming along a specific direction.

The appropriate set of coordinates describing the orientation of the molecules with respect to the incoming atom directions is made up by a set of Euler angles, i.e. three angular variables denoted here by α, β, and Φ, ranging from 0 to 2π, π and 2π respectively. These angles actually set the orientation of the molecular frame with respect to a space fixed frame, whose z-axis coincides with the incoming molecule or atom propagation direction.

Euler angles varying within a narrow interval around some specific values describe a sharp molecular orientation distribution, so that the simulated processes can be thought of as "oriented collisions".

As a target chiral molecule, we choose the hydrogen persulfide, H_2S_2, for which the potential energy surface, describing the interaction with Rare-gas atoms, has been described in Sect. 2.2, and is available at Ref. [37].

The hydrogen peroxide, H_2O_2, also might have been chosen, at the price of a more complicated interpretation of the collision simulations, being fast interconversion expected as a consequence of a low torsion energy barrier (see Ref. [36]).

The coordinate system for the chiral collisions is shown in Fig. 4, where the molecular reference frame, the Euler orientation coordinates and the parameters of the collision are pictured. The orientation of the velocity vector of the Rg atom with respect to the molecule is given by a polar and an azimuthal angle, coinciding with the α and β angles previously mentioned. A further coordinate is represented by the azimuthal angle Φ (see the figure), accounting for rotations around the y-axis, determining the intersection point of the atom velocity direction line with a circle, of radius the impact parameter b, lying on the xz plane (see Fig. 1). Actually, the three angles, (α, β, Φ) parametrize the rotation needed to bring into coincidence the body frame of the molecule with the arrangement of Fig. 4, where the y-axis corresponds to the incoming atom direction in the laboratory frame.

The cross section of the collision depends on the collision energy E, the total angular momentum denoted by J, and the actual configuration of the molecule (dihedral angle between the two SH bonds and the central S–S bond, that we denoted as γ, see Sect. 2.2). The total angular momentum J can be expressed as the sum of the molecular angular momentum, here denoted by j, and the orbital angular momentum, associated to the rotation of the vector joining the centers of mass of the colliding bodies, during the collision. In classical mechanics the orbital angular momentum is given by the product $\mu v b$ of the reduced mass of the colliding particles μ, the collision velocity v and the impact parameter b (see Fig. 1). Except for the torsion around the central bond, the molecule is frozen (see Sect. 2.2), so that a quantum number formally associated to the torsion vibration mode, denoted as n, is sufficient to identify the quantum state of the molecule.

The scattering probability at an angle Θ can be defined as the fraction of collisions with impact parameter b that are deflected at Θ (see Fig. 1). Accordingly, we denote as $P_{\alpha,\beta}^{E,J,n}(\Phi,b,\Theta)$ the probability function. Note that all the relevant quantities illustrated above are contained in this expression, as variables or labels. Collisions correspond to a specific axial distribution of the molecules and therefore the collision observables are labelled by the orientation angles. So for example is the differential cross sections, which, as a function of the scattering angle Θ, is written as follows:

$$\sigma_{\alpha,\beta}^{E,J,n}(\Theta) = 2\pi \int_{b=0}^{b=b_{max}} \int_{0}^{2\pi} \int_{\gamma+}^{\gamma-} P_{\alpha,\beta}^{E,J,n}(\Phi,b,\Theta)b\,db\,d\gamma\,d\phi \qquad (6)$$

The values $\gamma+$ and $\gamma-$ are the classical turning points of the torsion coordinate γ.

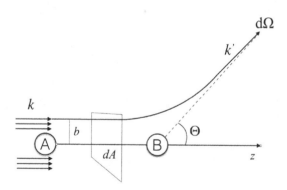

Fig. 1. Scheme of collision of structureless particles. k and k' are wavevectors before and after collision, b is the impact parameter, and $d\Omega$ is the differential solid angle receiving the scattered particles. dA is an area.

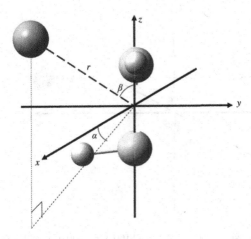

Fig. 2. Sketch of the coordinates parametrizing the interaction between a Rare-gas atom (pale blue particle) and the H_2S_2 (or H_2O_2) molecule. A vector **r** specifying the position of the atom with respect to the center of mass of the molecule (in its equilibrium geometry) is expressed in terms of its modulus r and polar angles α and β, with the axis z lying on the molecular axis. Reproduced with permission from Ref. [37]

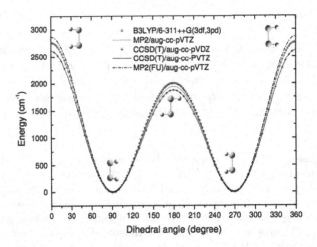

Fig. 3. Variation of the energy profile of the H_2S_2 molecule as a function of the dihedral angle γ for different theory levels and basis sets. The two different chiral forms are indicated corresponding to the two symmetric potential wells. The experimental barriers are of 2800(90) and 1990(15) cm^{-1} for cis and trans configurations, respectively [74]. Reproduced with permission from Ref. [37]

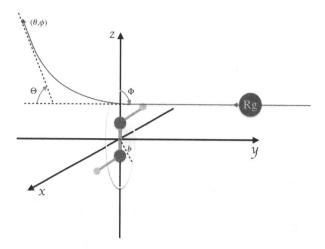

Fig. 4. Sketch of the geometry of an oriented collision involving a chiral molecule of type ABBA (e.g. H_2O_2 or H_2S_2) and a Rare-gas atom (Rg). The atom comes from the y direction, perpendicular to the xz plane. The orientation of the molecular O-O (or S-S) bond defines the z-axis. A circle in the xz plane of radius equal to the impact parameter b is shown along with a perpendicular line corresponding to the direction of motion of the incoming atom, intersecting the circle in a point defined by the azimuthal angle Φ. The scattering angle Θ between the initial and final velocities, and the recoil direction defined by the polar angles θ and ϕ, are indicated.

4   Conclusions

This account was dedicated to the theoretical study of the manifestations of chirality in molecular collisions, following the idea that chiral effects must occur in gaseous flows and streams. Systematic theoretical simulations are intended to inspire and address possible experimental efforts to reveal mechanisms of chiral generation and recognition, still a challenge in the field of molecular collision dynamics.

Acknowledgments. The authors acknowledge financial support from MIUR PRIN 2010-2011 (contract 2010ERFKXL_002) and from "Fondazione Cassa di Risparmio di Perugia (Codice Progetto: 2015.0331.021 Ricerca Scientifica e Tecnologica)". They also acknowledge the Italian Ministry for Education, University and Research, MIUR, for financial supporting through SIR 2014 "Scientific Independence for young Researchers" (RBSI14U3VF). Thanks are due to the Dipartimento di Chimica, Biologia e Biotecnologie dell'Università di Perugia (FRB, Fondo per la Ricerca di Base 2017) and to the MIUR and the University of Perugia for the financial support of the AMIS project through the program "Dipartimenti di Eccellenza". A. L. acknowledges financial support from MIUR PRIN 2015 (contract 2015F59J3R_002). A.L. thanks the OU Supercomputing Center for Education & Research (OSCER) at the University of Oklahoma, for allocated computing time.

References

1. Aquilanti, V., Beddoni, A., Cavalli, S., Lombardi, A., Littlejohn, R.: Collective hyperspherical coordinates for polyatomic molecules and clusters. Mol. Phys. **98**(21), 1763–1770 (2000)
2. Aquilanti, V., Beddoni, A., Lombardi, A., Littlejohn, R.: Hyperspherical harmonics for polyatomic systems: basis set for kinematic rotations. Int. J. Quantum Chem. **89**(4), 277–291 (2002)
3. Aquilanti, V., Lombardi, A., Littlejohn, R.: Hyperspherical harmonics for polyatomic systems: basis set for collective motions. Theoret. Chem. Acc. **111**(2–6), 400–406 (2004)
4. Sevryuk, M.B., Lombardi, A., Aquilanti, V.: Hyperangular momenta and energy partitions in multidimensional many-particle classical mechanics: the invariance approach to cluster dynamics. Phys. Rev. A **72**(3), 033201 (2005)
5. Lombardi, A., Palazzetti, F.: Chirality in molecular collision dynamics. J. Phys.: Condens. Matter **30**(6), 063003 (2018)
6. Lombardi, A., Palazzetti, F., Peroncelli, L., Grossi, G., Aquilanti, V., Sevryuk, M.: Few-body quantum and many-body classical hyperspherical approaches to reactions and to cluster dynamics. Theoret. Chem. Acc. **117**(5–6), 709–721 (2007)
7. Aquilanti, V., Lombardi, A., Yurtsever, E.: Global view of classical clusters: the hyperspherical approach to structure and dynamics. Phys. Chem. Chem. Phys. **4**(20), 5040–5051 (2002)
8. Barron, L.D.: True and false chirality and absolute asymmetric synthesis. J. Am. Chem. Soc. **108**, 5539–5542 (1986)
9. Barron, L.D.: True and false chirality and absolute enantioselection. Rend. Fis. Acc. Lincei **24**, 179–189 (2013)
10. Ribó, J.M., Crusatz, J., Sagués, F., Claret, J., Rubires, R.: Chiral sign induction by vortices during the formation of mesophases in stirred solutions. Science **292**, 2063–2066 (2001)
11. Aquilanti, V., Ascenzi, D., Cappelletti, D., Pirani, F.: Velocity dependence of collisional alignment of oxygen molecules in gaseous expansions. Nature **371**, 399–402 (1994)
12. Aquilanti, V., Grossi, G., Lombardi, A., Maciel, G.S., Palazzetti, F.: Aligned molecular collisions and a stereodynamical mechanism for selective chirality. Rend. Fis. Acc. Lincei **22**, 125–135 (2011)
13. Zhao, B., Guo, H.: State-to-state quantum reactive scattering in four-atom systems. WIREs Comput. Mol. Sci. **7**, e1301 (2017)
14. Aquilanti, V., Beddoni, A., Lombardi, A., Littlejohn, R.: Hyperspherical harmonics for polyatomic systems: basis set for kinematic rotations. Int. J. Quantum Chem. **89**, 277–291 (2002)
15. Aquilanti, V., Beddoni, A., Cavalli, S., Lombardi, A., Littlejohn, R.: Collective hyperspherical coordinates for polyatomic molecules and clusters. Mol. Phys. **98**, 1763–1770 (2000)
16. Hase, W., et al.: J. Quantum. Chem. Program Exch. Bull. **16**, 671 (1996)
17. Billing, G.: Comput. Phys. Rep. **1**, 239–296 (1984)
18. Laganà, A., Crocchianti, S., Faginas Lago, N., Pacifici, L., Ferraro, G.: A nonorthogonal coordinate approach to atom-diatom parallel reactive scattering calculations. Collect. Czech. Chem. Commun. **68**, 307–330 (2003)
19. Lago, N.F., Laganà, A., Garcia, E., Gimenez, X.: Thermal rate coefficients for the $N + N_2$ reaction: quasiclassical, semiclassical and quantum calculations. In: Gervasi, O., et al. (eds.) ICCSA 2005. LNCS, vol. 3480, pp. 1083–1092. Springer, Heidelberg (2005). https://doi.org/10.1007/11424758_113

20. Faginas-Lago, N., Laganá, A.: A comparison of semiclassical IVR and exact quantum collinear atom diatom transition probabilities for mixed reactive and non reactive regimes. In: AIP Conference Proceedings, vol. 762, p. 920 (2005)

21. Faginas-Lago, N., Laganà, A.: On the semiclassical initial value calculation of thermal rate coefficients for the N + N_2 reaction. J. Chem. Phys. **125**, 114311 (2006)

22. Faginas-Lago, N., Costantini, A., Huarte-Larrañaga, F.: Direct calculation of the rate coefficients on the grid: exact quantum versus semiclassical results for N+ N2. Int. J. Quantum Chem. **110**(2), 422–431 (2010)

23. Faginas, N., Huarte-Larranaga, F., Laganà, A.: Full dimensional quantum versus semiclassical reactivity for the bent transition state reaction N + N_2. Chem. Phys. Lett. **464**, 249–255 (2008)

24. Rampino, S., Faginas-Lago, N., Laganà, A., Huarte-Larrañaga, F.: An extension of the grid empowered molecular simulator to quantum reactive scattering. J. Comput. Chem. **33**, 708–714 (2012)

25. De Fazio, D.: The H + HeH^+ → He + H_2^++ reaction from the ultra-cold regime to the three-body breakup: exact quantum mechanical integral cross sections and rate constants. Phys. Chem. Chem. Phys. **16**, 11662–11672 (2014)

26. Horn, R.A., Johnson, C.R.: Matrix Analysis, 2nd edn. University Press, Cambridge (1990)

27. Sevryuk, M.B., Lombardi, A., Aquilanti, V.: Hyperangular momenta and energy partitions in multidimensional many-particle classical mechanics: the invariance approach to cluster dynamics. Phys. Rev. A **72**, 033201 (2005)

28. Gatti, F., Lung, C.: Vector parametrization of the n-atom problem in quantum mechanics. I. Jacobi vectors. J. Chem. Phys. **108**, 8804–8820 (1998)

29. Aquilanti, V., Lombardi, A., Yurtsever, E.: Global view of classical clusters: the hyperspherical approach to structure and dynamics. Phys. Chem. Chem. Phys. **4**, 5040–5051 (2002)

30. Aquilanti, V., Lombardi, A., Sevryuk, M.B.: Phase-space invariants for aggregates of particles: hyperangular momenta and partitions of the classical kinetic energy. J. Chem. Phys. **121**, 5579 (2004)

31. Aquilanti, V., Lombardi, A., Littlejohn, R.G.: Hyperspherical harmonics for polyatomic systems: basis set for collective motions. Theoret. Chem. Acc. **111**, 400–406 (2004)

32. Aquilanti, V., Carmona Novillo, E., Garcia, E., Lombardi, A., Sevryuk, M.B., Yurtsever, E.: Invariant energy partitions in chemical reactions and cluster dynamics simulations. Comput. Mater. Sci. **35**, 187–191 (2006)

33. Aquilanti, V., Lombardi, A., Sevryuk, M.B., Yurtsever, E.: Phase-space invariants as indicators of the critical behavior of nanoaggregates. Phys. Rev. Lett. **93**, 113402 (2004)

34. Calvo, F., Gadea, X., Lombardi, A., Aquilanti, V.: Isomerization dynamics and thermodynamics of ionic argon clusters. J. Chem. Phys. **125**, 114307 (2006)

35. Lombardi, A., Aquilanti, V., Yurtsever, E., Sevryuk, M.B.: Specific heats of clusters near a phase transition: energy partitions among internal modes. Chem. Phys. Lett. **30**, 424–428 (2006)

36. Barreto, P.R.P., Vilela, A.F.A., Lombardi, A., Maciel, G.S., Palazzetti, F., Aquilanti, V.: The hydrogen peroxide-rare gas systems: quantum chemical calculations and hyperspherical harmonic representation of the potential energy surface for atom-floppy molecule interactions. J. Phys. Chem. A **111**, 12754–12762 (2007)

37. Maciel, G.S., Barreto, P.R.P., Palazzetti, F., Lombardi, A., Aquilanti, V.: A quantum chemical study of h_2s_2: intramolecular torsional mode and intermolecular interactions with rare gases. J. Phys. Chem. A **129**, 164302 (2008)

38. Barreto, P.R.P., Palazzetti, F., Grossi, G., Lombardi, A., Maciel, G., Vilela, A.F.A.: Range and strength of intermolecular forces for van der Waals complexes of the type H_2X_n-Rg, with x = o, s and n = 1, 2. Int. J. Quantum Chem. **110**, 777–786 (2010)

39. Palazzetti, F., Munusamy, E., Lombardi, A., Grossi, G., Aquilanti, V.: Spherical and hyperspherical representation of potential energy surfaces for intermolecular interactions. Int. J. Quantum Chem. **111**, 318–332 (2011)

40. Aquilanti, V., Cavalli, S.: The quantum-mechanical Hamiltonian for tetraatomic systems in symmetric hyperspherical coordinates. J. Chem. Soc. Faraday Trans. **93**, 801–809 (1997)

41. Barreto, P.R.P., Albernaz, A.F., Palazzetti, F.: Potential energy surfaces for van der Waals complexes of rare gases with H_2S and H_2S_2: extension to xenon interactions and hyperspherical harmonics representation. Int. J. Quantum Chem. **112**, 834–847 (2012)

42. Lombardi, A., et al.: Spherical and hyperspherical harmonics representation of van der Waals aggregates. In: AIP Conference Proceedings, vol. 1790, p. 020005 (2016)

43. Aquilanti, V., Caglioti, C., Lombardi, A., Maciel, G.S., Palazzetti, F.: Screens for displaying chirality changing mechanisms of a series of peroxides and persulfides from conformational structures computed by quantum chemistry. In: Gervasi, O., et al. (eds.) ICCSA 2017. LNCS, vol. 10408, pp. 354–368. Springer, Cham (2017). https://doi.org/10.1007/978-3-319-62404-4_26

44. Aquilanti, V., Cavalli, S., Coletti, C., di Domenico, D., Grossi, G.: Int. Rev. Phys. Chem. **20**, 673 (2001)

45. Varshalovich, D.A.: Quantum Theory of Angular Momentum. World Scientific, Singapore (1958)

46. Castro-Palacio, J.C., Velasquez Abad, L., Lombardi, A., Aquilanti, V.: Normal and hyperspherical mode analysis of NO-doped Kr crystals upon Rydberg excitation of the impurity. J. Chem. Phys. **126**, 174701 (2007)

47. Castro Palacio, J.C., Rubayo-Soneira, J., Lombardi, A., Aquilanti, V.: Molecular dynamics simulations and hyperspherical mode analysis of NO in Kr crystals with the use of ab initio potential energy surfaces for the Kr-NO complex. Int. J. Quantum Chem. **108**, 1821–1830 (2008)

48. Lombardi, A., Lago, N.F., Laganà, A., Pirani, F., Falcinelli, S.: A bond-bond portable approach to intermolecular interactions: simulations for N-methylacetamide and carbon dioxide dimers. In: Murgante, B., et al. (eds.) ICCSA 2012. LNCS, vol. 7333, pp. 387–400. Springer, Heidelberg (2012). https://doi.org/10.1007/978-3-642-31125-3_30

49. Lombardi, A., Laganà, A., Pirani, F., Palazzetti, F., Lago, N.F.: Carbon oxides in gas flows and earth and planetary atmospheres: state-to-state simulations of energy transfer and dissociation reactions. In: Murgante, B., et al. (eds.) ICCSA 2013. LNCS, vol. 7972, pp. 17–31. Springer, Heidelberg (2013). https://doi.org/10.1007/978-3-642-39643-4_2

50. Lago, N.F., Albertí, M., Laganà, A., Lombardi, A.: Water $(H_2O)m$ or Benzene $(C_6H_6)n$ aggregates to solvate the K^+? In: Murgante, B., et al. (eds.) ICCSA 2013. LNCS, vol. 7971, pp. 1–15. Springer, Heidelberg (2013). https://doi.org/10.1007/978-3-642-39637-3_1

51. Faginas-Lago, N., Albertí, M., Costantini, A., Laganá, A., Lombardi, A., Pacifici, L.: An innovative synergistic grid approach to the computational study of protein aggregation mechanisms. J. Mol. Model. **20**(7), 2226 (2014)

52. Faginas-Lago, N., Yeni, D., Huarte, F., Alcamì, M., Martin, F.: Adsorption of hydrogen molecules on carbon nanotubes using quantum chemistry and molecular dynamics. J. Phys. Chem. A **120**, 6451–6458 (2016)
53. Faginas-Lago, N., Lombardi, A., Albertí, M., Grossi, G.: Accurate analytic intermolecular potential for the simulation of Na+ and K$^+$ ion hydration in liquid water. J. Mol. Liq. **204**, 192–197 (2015)
54. Albertí, M., Faginas Lago, N.: Competitive solvation of k$^+$ by C_6H_6 and H_2O in the k$^+$−$(C_6h_6)_n$−$(H_2O)_m$ ($n = 1 - 4; m = 1 - 6$) aggregates. Eur. Phys. J. D **67**, 73 (2013)
55. Albertí, M., Faginas Lago, N.: Ion size influence on the ar solvation shells of M$^+$-C_6F_6 clusters (m = na, k, rb, cs). J. Phys. Chem. A **116**, 3094–3102 (2012)
56. Albertí, M., Faginas Lago, N., Pirani, F.: Ar solvation shells in K$^+$-HFBz: from cluster rearrangement to solvation dynamics. J. Phys. Chem. A **115**, 10871–10879 (2011)
57. Lago, N.F., Albertí, M., Laganà, A., Lombardi, A., Pacifici, L., Costantini, A.: The molecular stirrer catalytic effect in methane ice formation. In: Murgante, B., et al. (eds.) ICCSA 2014. LNCS, vol. 8579, pp. 585–600. Springer, Cham (2014). https://doi.org/10.1007/978-3-319-09144-0_40
58. Faginas-Lago, N., Huarte Larrañaga, F., Albertí, M.: On the suitability of the ILJ function to match different formulations of the electrostatic potential for water-water interactions. Eur. Phys. J. D **55**(1), 75 (2009)
59. Bartolomei, M., Pirani, F., Laganà, A., Lombardi, A.: J. Comput. Chem. **33**, 1806 (2012)
60. Albertí, M., Faginas-Lago, N., Laganà, A., Pirani, F.: A portable intermolecular potential for molecular dynamics studies of NMA-NMA and NMA-H_2O aggregates. Phys. Chem. Chem. Phys. **13**(18), 8422–8432 (2011)
61. Albertí, M., Faginas-Lago, N., Pirani, F.: J. Phys. Chem. A **115**(40), 10871–10879 (2011)
62. Albertí, M., Faginas-Lago, N.: Eur. Phys. J. D **67**, 73 (2013)
63. Albertí, M., Faginas-Lago, N., Pirani, F.: Chem. Phys. **399**, 232 (2012)
64. Falcinelli, S., et al.: Modeling the intermolecular interactions and characterization of the dynamics of collisional autoionization processes. In: Murgante, B., et al. (eds.) ICCSA 2013. LNCS, vol. 7971, pp. 69–83. Springer, Heidelberg (2013). https://doi.org/10.1007/978-3-642-39637-3_6
65. Lombardi, A., Faginas-Lago, N., Pacifici, L., Costantini, A.: Modeling of energy transfer from vibrationally excited CO_2 molecules: cross sections and probabilities for kinetic modeling of atmospheres, flows, and plasmas. J. Phys. Chem. A **117**(45), 11430–11440 (2013)
66. Lombardi, A., Pirani, F., Laganà, A., Bartolomei, M.: Energy transfer dynamics and kinetics of elementary processes (promoted) by gas-phase CO_2-N_2 collisions: selectivity control by the anisotropy of the interaction. J. Comput. Chem. **37**, 1463–1475 (2016)
67. Pacifici, L., Verdicchio, M., Faginas-Lago, N., Lombardi, A., Costantini, A.: A high-level ab initio study of the $N_2 + N_2$ reaction channel. J. Comput. Chem. **34**(31), 2668–2676 (2013)
68. Lombardi, A., Faginas-Lago, N., Pacifici, L., Grossi, G.: Energy transfer upon collision of selectively excited CO_2 molecules: state-to-state cross sections and probabilities for modeling of atmospheres and gaseous flows. J. Chem. Phys. **143**, 034307 (2015)

69. Lombardi, A., Faginas-Lago, N., Pacifici, L., Costantini, A.: Modeling of energy transfer from vibrationally excited CO_2 molecules: cross sections and probabilities for kinetic modeling of atmospheres, flows, and plasmas. J. Phys. Chem. A **117**, 11430–11440 (2013)
70. Celiberto, R., et al.: Atomic and molecular data for spacecraft re-entry plasmas. Plasma Sources Sci. Technol. **25**, 033004 (2016)
71. Musigmann, M., Busalla, A., Blum, K., Thompson, D.G.: Enantio-selective collisions between unpolarized electrons and chiral molecules. J. Phys. Chem. B **34**, L79–L85 (2001)
72. Aquilanti, V., Grossi, G., Lombardi, A., Maciel, G.S., Palazzetti, F.: The origin of chiral discrimination: supersonic molecular beam experiments and molecular dynamics simulations of collisional mechanisms. Phys. Scr. **78**, 058119 (2008)
73. Lombardi, A., Palazzetti, F., Maciel, G.S., Aquilanti, V., Sevryuk, M.B.: Simulation of oriented collision dynamics of simple chiral molecules. Int. J. Quantum Chem. **111**, 1651–1658 (2011)
74. Herbst, E., DeFrees, D.J., McLean, A.D.: Ab initio determination of mode coupling in HSSH: the torsional splitting in the first excited S-S stretching state. J. Chem. Phys. **91**, 5905 (1989)

The Invariance Approach to Structure and Dynamics: Classical Hyperspherical Coordinates

Andrea Lombardi[1,2]([envelope]), Noelia Faginas-Lago[1,2], and Vincenzo Aquilanti[1]

[1] Dipartimento di Chimica, Biologia e Biotecnologie,
Università di Perugia, Perugia, Italy
ebiu2005@gmail.com, {noelia.faginaslago,vincenzo.aquilanti}@unipg.it
[2] Consortium for Computational Molecular and Materials Sciences (CMS)[2],
Via Elce di Sotto, 8, 06123 Perugia, Italy
http://www.chm.unipg.it/gruppi?q=node/48

Abstract. The hyperspherical coordinate systems have been extensively adopted in the study of few-body scattering problems of nuclear and molecular physics, for example in the practical implementation of demanding quantum calculations typical of chemical reactions. Hyperangular momenta are the dynamical quantities used in this representation and the hyperspherical harmonics are the corresponding basis functions. The use of such formalism is limited to the treatment of three- or four-center problems, due to the exceedingly high computational cost of quantum dynamics calculations. To circumvent this restriction, an hyperspherical formulation has been developed in a series of works during the last decades, suitable for the simulation of cluster and large molecular system dynamics. Such a hyperspherical formulation is based on classical definitions of the hyperangular momenta and on the search of invariant dynamical quantities. Exploiting invariance of hyperspherical shape coordinates with respect to rotations and kinematic rotations, we consider the use of the classical hyperspherical representation as a tool for the static analysis of geometry and minimum energy structures of atomic and molecular structures, showing some applications to relatively simple systems.

Keywords: Hyperspherical coordinates · Intermolecular interactions · Atomic clusters · Global minimum · Isomers · Shape coordinates

1 Introduction

The hyperspherical approach to molecular dynamics has been widely exploited in the field quantum reactive scattering calculations during the last decades, with significant progress in the theory and implementation of methods based on hyperspherical functions [1–3]. Full dimension calculations for three-body systems are now feasible, while much work has been done on hyperspherical

© Springer Nature Switzerland AG 2019
S. Misra et al. (Eds.): ICCSA 2019, LNCS 11624, pp. 428–438, 2019.
https://doi.org/10.1007/978-3-030-24311-1_31

harmonics basis sets for four-body systems (see e.g [4–9]). These approaches are more suited to represent multi-channel reactive collision processes, due to the invariance of the quantum Hamiltonian with respect to the possible product arrangements. In this sense, the hyperspherical one is largely preferable with respect to other approaches (see e.g. semiclassical [10–17]).

Besides their use as quantum scattering basis sets, hyperspherical functions are suitable to be applied to the representation of intermolecular and intramolecular interactions in collision studies [18–45].

So far the practical feasibility of full quantum calculations in hyperspherical coordinates has been limited to three- or at most four-atom systems. This restriction can be in part bypassed, extending the hyperspherical methods to classical dynamics, by which medium size and large molecules and atomic and molecular clusters can be simulated, taking advantage of the lower computational cost of classical trajectories (see e.g. [46]). As a consequence of expressing the classical Hamilton function in terms of hyperspherical coordinates, the degrees of freedom get separated into homogeneous sets of variables corresponding to well defined kinetic energy contributions, accounting for shape deformation, ordinary rotations and kinematic rotations [6, 47–49]. The hyperangular momenta appearing in the Hamilton function and the other relevant dynamic quantities are given "classical" definitions, so that classical hyperspherical equations of motion could in principle be obtained, although integration in Cartesian coordinates is certainly preferable, provided a specific matrix transformation that permits the evaluation, as a function of time, of the energy terms appearing in the Hyperspherical Hamilton function.

As a last remarkable aspect, it is noticeable that the hyperspherical scheme splits the degrees of freedom into two different sets of rotational coordinates (ordinary rotations and rotations in the kinematic space), so that the remaining three degrees of freedom turn out to be invariant with respect to both kinds of rotation action and solely depend on the global shape of the aggregates of particles. This "invariance'" approach to structure and dynamics has been validated in a series of applications [47, 50–52].

In this paper, we want to review the use of invariant hyperspherical deformation indexes for the study and classification of local and global minimum energy structures of atomic and molecular clusters. In the following Sections, it will be given a description of the hyperspherical coordinates applied to generic N-particle systems and of the related approach to structural aspects of clusters of atoms and molecules. Finally, some applications will be illustrated.

2   Theoretical Background

The representation of N-particle systems in hyperspherical coordinates can be obtained introducing a set of $N - 1$ Jacobi vectors $\mathbf{Q}_\alpha$, with $\alpha = 1, \cdots, N - 1$, made up by proper combinations of the radial vectors of the particles in the center of mass reference frame, the latter denoted by $\mathbf{r}_\alpha$ [47]. A "canonical" sequence of such vectors can be built by taking the vector which connects particles 1 and

2, then the one connecting the center of mass of the pair to the third particles, and so on, up to the $(N-1)$th vector, which connects the center of mass of the first $N-1$ particles to the Nth particle. The vectors have to be combined being multiplied by proper coefficients which depends on the particle masses, see Sect. 2.1 for details. The next step consists in the definition of an hyperradius ρ as the modulus of a vector of dimension $3N-3$, spanning the configuration space of the system. The Cartesian components of the hyperradial vector, given by the ordered sequence of the Jacobi vector components, can be parametrized by means of the hyperradius and $3N-4$ "hyperangles", which define the hyperspherical coordinate system. The angular parametrization is not unique. Among the various alternatives, for our purposes we select the one corresponding to the so called Symmetric hyperspherical representation, which is a result of a matrix transformation, the *singular value decomposition*, acting on a properly constructed position matrix. In the next sections we will detail the procedure to generate hyperspherical coordinates, outlining some important features.

2.1 Hyperspherical Coordinates for Atomic and Molecular Aggregates

An appropriate mathematical tool for the representation of N-center systems is the *singular value decomposition* [53], a matrix decomposition theorem that can be applied to any given set of N atoms, after assigning to them a properly defined position matrix.

Let us suppose we have a collection of $N \geq 2$ particles with masses $m_1, \cdots, m_N$ and positions identified by a set of radii vectors in the center of mass reference frame, $\mathbf{r_1}, \cdots, \mathbf{r_N}$. Mass *scaled* radii vectors $\mathbf{q}_\alpha = (m_\alpha/M)^{1/2}\mathbf{r}_\alpha$ $(1 \leq \alpha \leq N)$, can be obtained, where $M = \sum_\alpha^N m_\alpha$ is the total mass of the system.

A $3 \times N$ position matrix denoted by Z containing column-wise the components of the mass scaled vectors, can be generated, as follows:

$$Z = \begin{pmatrix} q_{1,1} & q_{1,2} & \cdots & q_{1,N} \\ q_{2,1} & q_{2,2} & \cdots & q_{2,N} \\ q_{3,1} & q_{3,2} & \cdots & q_{3,N} \end{pmatrix}. \tag{1}$$

The coordinate frame can be rotated, acting (left-multiplication) on the position matrix by an orthogonal matrix R^t, transpose of a matrix $R \in O(3)$. A rotation of the coordinate frame can also be performed in the so called *kinematic space* [5,48], by action of an orthogonal matrix (right-multiplication) $K \in O(N)$ on the position matrix Z, $Z' = ZK$.

It is possible to identify a subset of K matrices having the following form (see last column):

$$K = \begin{pmatrix} k_{1,1} & k_{1,2} & \cdots & (m_1/M)^{1/2} \\ k_{2,1} & k_{2,2} & \cdots & (m_2/M)^{1/2} \\ \cdots & \cdots & \cdots & \cdots \\ k_{N,1} & k_{N,2} & \cdots & (m_N/M)^{1/2} \end{pmatrix} \tag{2}$$

and its application to the Z matrix generates a subset of all the possible Cartesian frames. Note that the elements of the last column of such rotated Z matrices are always zero, due to the relation $\sum_\alpha^N m_\alpha^{1/2} \mathbf{q}_\alpha = 0$, valid for the mass scaled vectors. In such special cases, one only has to deal with a $3 \times (N-1)$ "reduced" Z matrix. The physical meaning of such a condition is that one separates the motion of the center of mass. This smaller matrix Z is called *reduced position matrix*.

The sets of $(N-1)$ Jacobi and related vectors form reduced matrices. The Jacobi vectors are defined as a linear combinations of the N Cartesian particle position vectors, with coefficients being a function of the particle masses [54,55]. Kinematic rotations connect different Jacobi vector sets corresponding to the different coupling schemes and reactive channels of the system.

The *singular value decomposition* theorem applied to the $3 \times n$ position matrix Z (where $n = N$ or $n = N-1$) leads to the following product of three matrices:

$$Z = R\Xi K^t \tag{3}$$

where $R \in O(3)$ and $K \in O(n)$ are 3×3 and $3 \times n$ orthogonal matrices, respectively. The elements of the $3 \times n$ matrix Ξ are zeroes, with the possible exception of the diagonal entries, $\Xi_{11} = \xi_1, \Xi_{22} = \xi_2, \Xi_{33} = \xi_3$, which are subjected to the inequality $\xi_1 \geq \xi_2 \geq \xi_3 \geq 0$.

The values ξ_i, $(i = 1, 2, 3)$ are called the *singular values* of the matrix Z and are uniquely determined, although the factors R and K in Eq. 3 are not. If $N \leq 3$ and Z is the full $3 \times N$ position matrix, then the smallest singular value ξ_3 is necessarily zero. An important relation can be easily obtained [47,48]:

$$\xi_1^2 + \xi_2^2 + \xi_3^2 = \rho^2. \tag{4}$$

The ξ's are invariant under both ordinary rotations in the physical space and kinematic rotations [5,6,48,56], a remarkable property, with possible applications to molecular dynamics [47,57–60] and properties of the minimum energy structures of N-particle aggregates.

The symmetric case $n = N - 1 = 3$, corresponding to four particles or four center systems, is special, since the two matrices R and K cannot be chosen to be *special orthogonal* ($R \in SO(3)$ and $K \in SO(n)$), but are required to be just orthogonal matrices ($O(3)$). In this case, if the determinant of Z is lower than zero, its sign depends on the sign of the product of the ξ's, and so one has $\xi_3 \leq 0$. This fact is directly connected to the mirror image and chirality sign of the system [50,61,62].

As a result of the matrix transformation described above, we can group the $3N - 3$ degrees of freedom of a system of N particles into three distinct sets of coordinates: three angles, parametrizing the rotation matrix R and accounting for spatial rotations, $3N - 9$ angles, parametrizing the rotation matrix K, accounting for rotations in the kinematic space, and 3 ξ's, which are related to the hyperradius, being the only quantities with length units.

2.2   Hyperradius and Invariant Deformation Indexes

The singular values (ξ_1, ξ_2, ξ_3) are considered to be "kinematic invariants" [63], for the reason that they are independent from spatial and kinematic rotations, see Sect. 2.1. They are also directly related to the moments of inertia of the system, through the following relations:

$$\frac{I_1}{M} = \xi_2^2 + \xi_3^2$$
$$\frac{I_2}{M} = \xi_1^2 + \xi_3^2 \tag{5}$$
$$\frac{I_3}{M} = \xi_1^2 + \xi_2^2$$

where I_1, I_2 and I_3 are the moments of inertia in the principal axis reference frame. From Eq. 4 one obtains:

$$I_1 + I_2 + I_3 = 2M\rho^2. \tag{6}$$

Due to the previous relations, the ξ's can be used to classify the rotational properties of the system, in terms of asymmetric, symmetric and spherical rotors. One has a spherical top configurations for $\xi_1 = \xi_2 = \xi_3$, a prolate top for $\xi_3 = \xi_2 < \xi_1$ and an oblate top for $\xi_1 = \xi_2 > \xi_3$.

In order to complete the angular parametrization the invariant ξ's can be expressed by a canonical set of spherical coordinates, ρ, θ and ϕ as follows:

$$\xi_1 = \rho \sin \theta \cos \phi$$
$$\xi_2 = \rho \sin \theta \sin \phi \tag{7}$$
$$\xi_2 = \rho \cos \theta$$

This connection of the singular values with the distribution of the inertia associated to the N- particle system, has suggested to define a measure of the deviation from the spherical top shape, by two *deformation indexes* [47]:

$$\xi_+ = \frac{\xi_2^2 - \xi_3^2}{\rho^2}, \quad \xi_+ \geq 0 \tag{8}$$

which is zero for prolate top configurations, and

$$\xi_- = \frac{\xi_2^2 - \xi_1^2}{\rho^2}, \quad \xi_+ \leq 0 \tag{9}$$

which is zero for oblate top configurations. From the above definitions follows that when both the indexes are zero, the cluster is a spherical top.

2.3   Deformation Indexes of Atomic and Molecular Clusters

To show a perspective use of deformation indexes for the search of trends, symmetries and regularities in the global an local minimum energy structures of clusters of increasing size, we consider the deformation indexes and the hyper-radius of a number of sets of atomic clusters bound by different potentials. To determine the value of the indexes, namely of the invariant ξ's of each cluster configuration, one can simply observe that from Eq. 3 the following relation can be obtained:

$$ZZ^t = R\Xi\Xi^t R^t \tag{10}$$

where the product $\Xi\Xi^t$ is 3×3 square diagonal matrix, whose entries are the squares of the ξ's. The diagonal entries are just the eigenvalues of the matrix product ZZ^t involving the position matrix. Therefore, for any given configuration, one can construct the Z matrix, using the Cartesian components of the atomic position vectors (see Sect. 2.1), calculate the ZZ^t matrix and diagonalize it, numerically, or by using the well known Cardano's formula for the characteristic equation [47].

Here we consider a series of cluster minima structures, freely available from the Cambridge Cluster Database [64]. In particular, we consider Lennard-Jones (LJ) clusters, with N ranging from 310 to 561 and metal clusters bound by a Sutton-Chen potential 12-6 (see Ref. [65]) In Fig. 1, the deformation indexes of Sect. 2.2 for the LJ clusters are reported for the minimum energy configurations, as a function of the atom number N. The trend shows marked oscillations, interrupted by the occurrence of spherical top configurations. In Fig. 2 the same plot is shown for Sutton-Chen clusters. Such structures are of smaller dimensions, N up to 78, and exhibit strong deviations from the spherical symmetry.

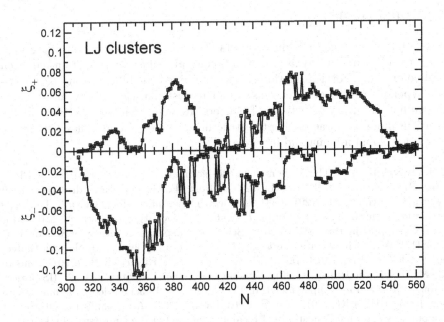

Fig. 1. Plot of the ξ_+ and ξ_+ deformation indexes for the minimum energy structures of Lennard-Jones (LJ) 12-6 clusters for N from 310 to 561. Smaller LJ clusters have been analyzed in Ref. [47]. Structures have been obtained from the database [64]

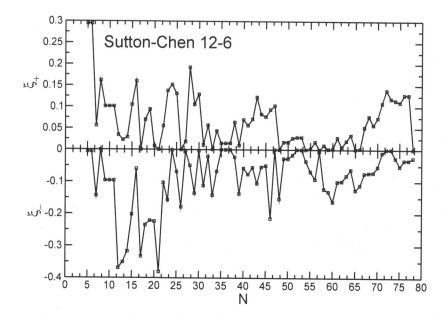

Fig. 2. Plot of the ξ_+ and ξ_+ for the minimum energy structures of atom clusters bound by a Sutton-Chen potential 12-6, for N from 5 to 78.

3   Conclusions

In this paper we reviewed some aspects of the hyperspherical coordinate approach to structure and dynamics of molecules and clusters. Attention has been focused on the use of deformation indexes, obtained combining rotational invariant hyperspherical coordinates, as a tool to systematically study and classify the minimum energy structures of clusters. Regular trends or patterns in the invariant indexes characterizing the structures, wherever found, may help in the search for global minima and in similarity studies.

Acknowledgments. The authors acknowledge financial support from MIUR PRIN 2010-2011 (contract 2010ERFKXL_002) and from "Fondazione Cassa di Risparmio di Perugia (Codice Progetto: 2015.0331.021 Ricerca Scientifica e Tecnologica)". They also acknowledge the Italian Ministry for Education, University and Research, MIUR, for financial supporting through SIR 2014 "Scientific Independence for young Researchers" (RBSI14U3VF). Thanks are due to the Dipartimento di Chimica, Biologia e Biotecnologie dell'Università di Perugia (FRB, Fondo per la Ricerca di Base 2017) and to the MIUR and the University of Perugia for the financial support of the AMIS project through the program "Dipartimenti di Eccellenza". A. L. acknowledges financial support from MIUR PRIN 2015 (contract 2015F59J3R_002). A.L. thanks the OU Supercomputing Center for Education & Research (OSCER) at the University of Oklahoma, for allocated computing time.

References

1. Zhao, B., Guo, H.: State-to-state quantum reactive scattering in four-atom systems. WIREs Comput. Mol. Sci. **7**, e1301 (2017)
2. Skouteris, D., Castillo, J., Manolopoulos, D.E.: ABC: a quantum reactive scattering program. Comp. Phys. Comm. **133**, 128–135 (2000)
3. Lepetit, B., Launay, J.M.: Quantum mechanical study of the reaction $He+H^+_2 \to HeH^+ + H$ with hyperspherical coordinates. J. Chem. Phys. **97**, 5159–5168 (1991)
4. Aquilanti, V., Beddoni, A., Cavalli, S., Lombardi, A., Littlejohn, R.: Collective hyperspherical coordinates for polyatomic molecules and clusters. Mol. Phys. **98**(21), 1763–1770 (2000)
5. Aquilanti, V., Beddoni, A., Lombardi, A., Littlejohn, R.: Hyperspherical harmonics for polyatomic systems: basis set for kinematic rotations. Int. J. Quantum Chem. **89**(4), 277–291 (2002)
6. Aquilanti, V., Lombardi, A., Littlejohn, R.: Hyperspherical harmonics for polyatomic systems: basis set for collective motions. Theoret. Chem. Acc. **111**(2–6), 400–406 (2004)
7. Kuppermann, A.: Quantum reaction dynamics and hyperspherical harmonics. Isr. J. Chem. **43**, 229 (2003)
8. De Fazio, D., Cavalli, S., Aquilanti, V.: Benchmark quantum mechanical calculations of vibrationally resolved cross sections and rate constants on ab initio potential energy surfaces for the F + HD reaction: Comparisons with experiments. J. Phys. Chem. A **120**, 5288–5299 (2016)
9. Aquilanti, V., Cavalli, S.: The quantum-mechanical hamiltonian for tetraatomic systems insymmetric hyperspherical coordinates. J. Chem. Soc. Faraday Trans. **93**, 801–809 (1997)
10. Laganà, A., Crocchianti, S., Faginas Lago, N., Pacifici, L., Ferraro, G.: A nonorthogonal coordinate approach to atom-diatom parallel reactive scattering calculations. Collect. Czech. Chem. Commun. **68**, 307–330 (2003)
11. Lago, N.F., Laganà, A., Garcia, E., Gimenez, X.: Thermal rate coefficients for the $N + N_2$ reaction: quasiclassical, semiclassical and quantum calculations. In: Gervasi, O., et al. (eds.) ICCSA 2005. LNCS, vol. 3480, pp. 1083–1092. Springer, Heidelberg (2005). https://doi.org/10.1007/11424758_113
12. Faginas-Lago, N., Laganá, A.: A comparison of semiclassical IVR and exact quantum collinear atom diatom transition probabilities for mixed reactive and non reactive regimes. In: AIP Conference Proceedings, vol. 762, p. 920 (2005)
13. Faginas-Lago, N., Laganà, A.: On the semiclassical initial value calculation of thermal rate coefficients for the N + N_2 reaction. J. Chem. Phys. **125**, 114311 (2006)
14. Faginas-Lago, N., Costantini, A., Huarte-Larrañaga, F.: Direct calculation of the rate coefficients on the grid: exact quantum versus semiclassical results for $N+ N_2$. Int. J. Quantum Chem. **110**(2), 422–431 (2010)
15. Faginas, N., Huarte-Larranaga, F., Laganà, A.: Full dimensional quantum versus semiclassical reactivity for the bent transition state reaction N + N_2. Chem. Phys. Lett. **464**, 249–255 (2008)
16. Rampino, S., Faginas-Lago, N., Laganà, A., Huarte-Larrañaga, F.: An extension of the grid empowered molecular simulator to quantum reactive scattering. J. Comput. Chem. **33**, 708–714 (2012)
17. Laganà, A., Faginas-Lago, N., Rampino, S., Huarte-Larrañaga, F., García, E.: Thermal rate coefficients in collinear versus bent transition state reactions: the N + N_2 case study. Phys. Scr. **78**(5), 058116 (2008)

18. Lombardi, A., Lago, N.F., Laganà, A., Pirani, F., Falcinelli, S.: A bond-bond portable approach to intermolecular interactions: simulations for N-methylacetamide and carbon dioxide dimers. In: Murgante, B., et al. (eds.) ICCSA 2012. LNCS, vol. 7333, pp. 387–400. Springer, Heidelberg (2012). https://doi.org/10.1007/978-3-642-31125-3_30

19. Lombardi, A., Laganà, A., Pirani, F., Palazzetti, F., Lago, N.F.: Carbon oxides in gas flows and earth and planetary atmospheres: state-to-state simulations of energy transfer and dissociation reactions. In: Murgante, B., et al. (eds.) ICCSA 2013. LNCS, vol. 7972, pp. 17–31. Springer, Heidelberg (2013). https://doi.org/10.1007/978-3-642-39643-4_2

20. Lago, N.F., Albertí, M., Laganà, A., Lombardi, A.: Water $(H_2O)m$ or benzene $(C_6H_6)n$ aggregates to solvate the K^+? In: Murgante, B., et al. (eds.) ICCSA 2013. LNCS, vol. 7971, pp. 1–15. Springer, Heidelberg (2013). https://doi.org/10.1007/978-3-642-39637-3_1

21. Faginas-Lago, N., Albertí, M., Costantini, A., Laganá, A., Lombardi, A., Pacifici, L.: An innovative synergistic grid approach to the computational study of protein aggregation mechanisms. J. Mol. Model. **20**(7), 2226 (2014)

22. Faginas-Lago, N., Yeni, D., Huarte, F., Alcamì, M., Martin, F.: Adsorption of hydrogen molecules on carbon nanotubes using quantum chemistry and molecular dynamics. J. Phys. Chem. A **120**, 6451–6458 (2016)

23. Faginas-Lago, N., Lombardi, A., Albertí, M., Grossi, G.: Accurate analytic inter-molecular potential for the simulation of Na+ and K^+ ion hydration in liquid water. J. Mol. Liq. **204**, 192–197 (2015)

24. Albertí, M., Faginas Lago, N.: Competitive solvation of k^+ by C_6H_6 and H_2O in the $k^+-(C_6H_6)_n-(H_2O)_m$ $(n = 1 - 4; m = 1 - 6)$ aggregates. Eur. Phys. J. D **67**, 73 (2013)

25. Albertí, M., Faginas Lago, N.: Ion size influence on the ar solvation shells of M^+-C_6F_6 clusters (m = na, k, rb, cs). J. Phys. Chem. A **116**, 3094–3102 (2012)

26. Albertí, M., Faginas Lago, N., Pirani, F.: Ar solvation shells in K^+-HFBz: from cluster rearrangement to solvation dynamics. J. Phys. Chem. A **115**, 10871–10879 (2011)

27. Lago, N.F., Albertí, M., Laganà, A., Lombardi, A., Pacifici, L., Costantini, A.: The molecular stirrer catalytic effect in methane ice formation. In: Murgante, B., et al. (eds.) ICCSA 2014. LNCS, vol. 8579, pp. 585–600. Springer, Cham (2014). https://doi.org/10.1007/978-3-319-09144-0_40

28. Faginas-Lago, N., Huarte Larrañaga, F., Albertí, M.: On the suitability of the ILJ function to match different formulations of the electrostatic potential for water-water interactions. Eur. Phys. J. D **55**(1), 75 (2009)

29. Bartolomei, M., Pirani, F., Laganà, A., Lombardi, A.: J. Comput. Chem. **33**, 1806 (2012)

30. Albertí, M., Faginas-Lago, N., Laganà, A., Pirani, F.: A portable intermolecular potential for molecular dynamics studies of NMA-NMA and NMA-H_2O aggregates. Phys. Chem. Chem. Phys. **13**(18), 8422–8432 (2011)

31. Albertí, M., Faginas-Lago, N., Pirani, F.: J. Phys. Chem. A **115**(40), 10871–10879 (2011)

32. Albertí, M., Faginas-Lago, N.: Eur. Phys. J. D **67**, 73 (2013)

33. Albertí, M., Faginas-Lago, N., Pirani, F.: Chem. Phys. **399**, 232 (2012)

34. Falcinelli, S., et al.: Modeling the intermolecular interactions and characterization of the dynamics of collisional autoionization processes. In: Murgante, B., et al. (eds.) ICCSA 2013. LNCS, vol. 7971, pp. 69–83. Springer, Heidelberg (2013). https://doi.org/10.1007/978-3-642-39637-3_6

35. Lombardi, A., Faginas-Lago, N., Pacifici, L., Costantini, A.: Modeling of energy transfer from vibrationally excited CO_2 molecules: cross sections and probabilities for kinetic modeling of atmospheres, flows, and plasmas. J. Phys. Chem. A **117**(45), 11430–11440 (2013)

36. Lombardi, A., Pirani, F., Laganà, A., Bartolomei, M.: Energy transfer dynamics and kinetics of elementary processes (promoted) by gas-phase CO_2-N_2 collisions: selectivity control by the anisotropy of the interaction. J. Comput. Chem. **37**, 1463–1475 (2016)

37. Pacifici, L., Verdicchio, M., Faginas-Lago, N., Lombardi, A., Costantini, A.: A high-level ab initio study of the $N_2 + N_2$ reaction channel. J. Comput. Chem. **34**(31), 2668–2676 (2013)

38. Lombardi, A., Faginas-Lago, N., Pacifici, L., Grossi, G.: Energy transfer upon collision of selectively excited CO_2 molecules: state-to-state cross sections and probabilities for modeling of atmospheres and gaseous flows. J. Chem. Phys. **143**, 034307 (2015)

39. Lombardi, A., Faginas-Lago, N., Pacifici, L., Costantini, A.: Modeling of energy transfer from vibrationally excited CO_2 molecules: cross sections and probabilities for kinetic modeling of atmospheres, flows, and plasmas. J. Phys. Chem. A **117**, 11430–11440 (2013)

40. Celiberto, R., et al.: Atomic and molecular data for spacecraft re-entry plasmas. Plasma Sources Sci. Technol. **25**(3), 033004 (2016)

41. Faginas-Lago, N., Lombardi, A., Albertí, M.: Aqueous n-methylacetamide: new analytic potentials and a molecular dynamics study. J. Mol. Liq. **224**, 792–800 (2016)

42. Palazzetti, F., Munusamy, E., Lombardi, A., Grossi, G., Aquilanti, V.: Spherical and hyperspherical representation of potential energy surfaces for intermolecular interactions. Int. J. Quantum Chem. **111**(2), 318–332 (2011)

43. Lombardi, A., Palazzetti, F.: A comparison of interatomic potentials for rare gas nanoaggregates. J. Mol. Struct. (Thoechem) **852**(1–3), 22–29 (2008)

44. Barreto, P.R., Albernaz, A.F., Palazzetti, F., Lombardi, A., Grossi, G., Aquilanti, V.: Hyperspherical representation of potential energy surfaces: intermolecular interactions in tetra-atomic and penta-atomic systems. Phys. Scr. **84**(2), 028111 (2011)

45. Barreto, P.R., et al.: Potential energy surfaces for interactions of H_2O with H_2, N_2 and O_2: a hyperspherical harmonics representation, and a minimal model for the H_2O-rare-gas-atom systems. Comput. Theoret. Chem. **990**, 53–61 (2012)

46. Nakamura, M., et al.: Dynamical, spectroscopic and computational imaging of bond breaking in photodissociation: roaming and role of conical intersections. Faraday Discuss. **177**, 77–98 (2015)

47. Aquilanti, V., Lombardi, A., Yurtsever, E.: Global view of classical clusters: the hyperspherical approach to structure and dynamics. Phys. Chem. Chem. Phys. **4**(20), 5040–5051 (2002)

48. Sevryuk, M.B., Lombardi, A., Aquilanti, V.: Hyperangular momenta and energy partitions in multidimensional many-particle classical mechanics: the invariance approach to cluster dynamics. Phys. Rev. A **72**(3), 033201 (2005)

49. Castro Palacio, J., Velazquez Abad, L., Lombardi, A., Aquilanti, V., Rubayo Soneira, J.: Normal and hyperspherical mode analysis of NO-doped Kr crystals upon Rydberg excitation of the impurity. J. Chem. Phys. **126**(17), 174701 (2007)

50. Lombardi, A., Palazzetti, F.: Chirality in molecular collision dynamics. J. Phys.: Condens. Matter **30**(6), 063003 (2018)

51. Lombardi, A., Palazzetti, F., Peroncelli, L., Grossi, G., Aquilanti, V., Sevryuk, M.: Few-body quantum and many-body classical hyperspherical approaches to reactions and to cluster dynamics. Theoret. Chem. Acc. **117**(5–6), 709–721 (2007)
52. Aquilanti, V., Grossi, G., Lombardi, A., Maciel, G.S., Palazzetti, F.: Aligned molecular collisions and a stereodynamical mechanism for selective chirality. Rend. Fis. Acc. Lincei **22**, 125–135 (2011)
53. Horn, R.A., Johnson, C.R.: Matrix Analysis, 2nd edn. University Press, Cambridge (1990)
54. Gatti, F., Lung, C.: Vector parametrization of the n-atom problem in quantum mechanics. I. Jacobi vectors. J. Chem. Phys. **108**, 8804–8820 (1998)
55. Aquilanti, V., Lombardi, A., Yurtsever, E.: Global view of classical clusters: the hyperspherical approach to structure and dynamics. Phys. Chem. Chem. Phys. **4**, 5040–5051 (2002)
56. Aquilanti, V., Lombardi, A., Sevryuk, M.B.: Phase-space invariants for aggregates of particles: hyperangular momenta and partitions of the classical kinetic energy. J. Chem. Phys. **121**, 5579 (2004)
57. Aquilanti, V., Carmona Novillo, E., Garcia, E., Lombardi, A., Sevryuk, M.B., Yurtsever, E.: Invariant energy partitions in chemical reactions and cluster dynamics simulations. Comput. Mater. Sci. **35**, 187–191 (2006)
58. Aquilanti, V., Lombardi, A., Sevryuk, M.B., Yurtsever, E.: Phase-space invariants as indicators of the critical behavior of nanoaggregates. Phys. Rev. Lett. **93**, 113402 (2004)
59. Calvo, F., Gadea, X., Lombardi, A., Aquilanti, V.: Isomerization dynamics and thermodynamics of ionic argon clusters. J. Chem. Phys. **125**, 114307 (2006)
60. Lombardi, A., Aquilanti, V., Yurtsever, E., Sevryuk, M.B.: Specific heats of clusters near a phase transition: energy partitions among internal modes. Chem. Phys. Lett. **30**, 424–428 (2006)
61. Lombardi, A., Maciel, G.S., Palazzetti, F., Grossi, G., Aquilanti, V.: Alignment and chirality in gaseous flows. J. Vac. Soc. Jpn. **53**(11), 645–653 (2010)
62. Palazzetti, F., et al.: Aligned molecules: chirality discrimination in photodissociation and in molecular dynamics. Rend. Lincei **24**(3), 299–308 (2013)
63. Littlejohn, R.G., Mitchell, A., Aquilanti, V.: Quantum dynamics of kinematic invariants in tetra-and polyatomic systems. Phys. Chem. Chem. Phys. **1**, 1259–1264 (1999)
64. Wales, D.J., Doye, J.P.K., Dullweber, A., Hodges, M.P., Naumkin, F.Y., Calvo, F., Hernández-Rojas, J., Middleton, T.F.: The Cambridge Cluster Database. http://www-wales.ch.cam.ac.uk/CCD.html
65. Doye, J.P.K., Wales, D.J.: Global minima for transition metal clusters described by Sutton-Chen potentials. New J. Chem. **22**, 733–744 (1998)

Screens Displaying Structural Properties of Aminoacids in Polypeptide Chains: Alanine as a Case Study

Concetta Caglioti[1], Robenilson Ferreira Dos Santos[2,3],
Andrea Lombardi[1], Federico Palazzetti[1(✉)],
and Vincenzo Aquilanti[1,4]

[1] Dipartimento di Chimica, Biologia e Biotecnologie,
Università di Perugia, via Elce di Sotto 8, 06123 Perugia, Italy
federico.palazzetti@unipg.it
[2] Instituto de Fìsica, Universidade Federal da Bahia,
Campus Universitario de Ondina, Salvador, BA 40210-340, Brazil
[3] Instituto Federal de Alagoas-Campus Piranhas,
Piranhas, AL 57460-000, Brazil
[4] Istituto di Struttura della Materia-Consiglio Nazionale delle Ricerche,
00016 Rome, Italy

Abstract. Large sets of data need to be compacted for classification and extraction of information regarding structural changes of aminoacid units in specific sequences of proteins. The screen is constructed by opposite sides of the virtual tetrahedron built by the six distances between four centers and provides coordinates for a two-dimensional square plot. As alternative *e.g.* to Ramachandran diagrams based on angles, it may offer greater accuracy and sensitivity. The screen was initially employed to peroxides and persulfides, to monitor the distances relevant to chirality changing processes and successively to show some electric and kinetic properties. The smallest chiral aminoacid, alanine, was therefore chosen for the basic illustration presented here. A virtual tetrahedron is built by the six distances between four centers of the aminoacid skeleton: they do not necessarily coincide with bonds, so a computer program permits their calculation from tabulations of experimental and theoretical data. Here, the screen is applied to treat significant geometrical features of alanine as affected by adjacent aminoacids in peptide chains, as available on protein databases. In this exemplary presentation applications of screen plots are limited to biochemistry: elsewhere have been shown useful in other areas, such as spin networks and the kinematics of a four-bar mechanism.

Keywords: Four-center processes · Aminoacid ·
Quantum angular momentum theory · Protein · Database

© Springer Nature Switzerland AG 2019
S. Misra et al. (Eds.): ICCSA 2019, LNCS 11624, pp. 439–449, 2019.
https://doi.org/10.1007/978-3-030-24311-1_32

1 Introduction

The peptide bond is at the basis of biological chemistry: it constitutes the link between two aminoacids, the building blocks of proteins. It is directly connected to sequences of aminoacids in the protein chain, which forms the primary structure. Experimental information on structure of proteins now includes myriads of compounds inspired by their involvement in areas that span from pharmaceutical and medical chemistry, to biochemistry and biophysics, until astrochemistry and astrobiology [1, 2]. More recent is the explosion of considerable interest by the numerous communities of theoretical and computational chemists (see for example [3]).

This wealth of data is not always homogeneous: accuracies vary and need assessment; also, it may be necessary to fill gaps among data accumulated sparsely on vast but poorly interconnected areas.

To focus on a prototypical study, our choice is to present here the example of the simplest chiral aminoacid, alanine. One of the most debated topics concerns the origin of the homochirality in nature: all aminoacids in proteins are levorotatory, on the contrary sugars involved in biological processes are rigorously dextrorotatory. Many hypotheses have been proposed in the course of the years without reaching unanimous consensus: statistical fluctuations and following amplification that determine the prevalence of one enantiomer; lower energy of one of the two enantiomers due to weak nuclear forces; a possible role played by stereoselectivity in molecular encounters [4–17].

In this paper, we sketch basic theoretical and computational tools for building a representation frame, the "screen", that permits to classify and compact the enormous variety of data on proteins essentially based on information on interatomic distances (this is to be contrasted for example to the Ramachandran plots [18], that report the permitted steric conformations of aminoacids by plotting a pair of dihedral angles typical of the aminoacid unit). The method can be extended to visualize other physico-chemical properties.

The screen representation relies on six distances between four position of atoms in the aminoacids and the diagram is obtained by plotting a pair of "diagonals", according to the classification given for the (not necessarily planar) quadrilaterals that can be individuated in three ways out of any tetrahedron. The screen representation was applied for the first time to a chemical problem specifically for peroxides [19–21] and persulfides [22] to monitor the distances related to chirality changing properties [23] and successively to visualize physico-chemical properties [24]. Here, we report case studies on alanine geometrical features as affected by the aminoacids directly connected, to it in about fifty proteins, whose structural parameters were extracted from Protein Data Bank [25].

The screen representation is not only specifically useful for molecular structure and dynamics: it was initially introduced in quantum angular momentum theory to classify the range of permitted geometries of the tetrahedra related to the vector recoupling and to study spin networks in the semiclassical limit [26]. Lately, it was employed to provide connections between the classical four-bar linkage problem and the theory of $6j$ symbols of quantum mechanical angular momentum theory [27].

The paper is structured as follows: in Sect. 2, we review some fundamental properties of tetrahedra (and lower dimensional projections such as quadrilaterals and quadrangles). The formalism and the basic equations have been adapted from the theory developed for studies of the Wigner-Racah $6j$ symbols; in Sect. 3, we survey applications to the cases of peroxides and persulfides and introduce the variants needed to the specific case of aminoacids; in Sect. 4, final remarks conclude the paper.

2 The Square Screen Representation of the Six Four-Center Distances

2.1 Elementary Properties of Quadrilaterals, Quadrangles and Tetrahedra

The construction of the screen relies on the geometrical properties of figures with four vertices (quadrilaterals, quadrangles and tetrahedra). A quadrilateral is defined, according to the planar Euclidean geometry, as a polygon with four sides and four angles. The sum of the four inner angles is 360°, a property no longer valid if we admit a three dimensional structure. The lines joining the opposite vertices of quadrilaterals are called diagonals. Their classification relies on the position of the diagonals inside or outside the quadrilateral: a quadrilateral formed by two inner diagonals is convex; it is concave if an inner and an outer diagonal are present; it is called biconcave, if both diagonals are external (the butterfly). In projective and affine geometries, diagonals are considered as further sides, and a complete quadrilateral is formed by four points and six lines.

A complete quadrangle, under most aspects is the same thing but formally is characterized by having four lines incident in six points. In projective geometry, duality permits exchange of role of points and lines, thus the two complete figures are identical, while from an affine viewpoint they are considered different. Extension to three dimension is the usual way that permits to define a tetrahedron, composed by four vertices and six edges on four triangular faces. Considering a tetrahedron of zero volume, or a similar figure obtained by projection on a plane is a way to obtain complete quadrangles, formed by four points and the six joining segments as mentioned above.

There are three ways of choosing couples of diagonals from the six sides of the complete quadrangles and it is possible to define three four-sided figures. The edges a, b, c, d are labelled as follows (according to the "canonical ordering" defined in [26]): a is identified as the shortest side and c is opposite to a, the d side is the longest between the two remaining ones. The two diagonals, x and y, are assigned as follows: x is the one joining the meeting point of a and b with that of c and d, and y is the other one. In conclusion, in a complete quadrilateral one can single out four "sides" (the parameters a, b, c, d) and two "diagonals" (the variables x and y) that represent the abscissa and ordinate of the screen. We also define the minimum values of x and y, respectively x_{min} and y_{min}, and their maximum values, x_{max} e y_{max}, keeping fixed the length of the sides. Their variation range is given by the following relations:

$$
\begin{aligned}
x_{min} &= b - a \\
x_{max} &= b + a \\
y_{min} &= d - a \\
y_{max} &= d + a
\end{aligned}
\tag{1}
$$

These properties are *e.g.* detailed in [26], see also next section, and show that the screen is confined into a square with sides $x_{max} - x_{min}$ and $y_{max} - y_{min}$, or in the (0–1) range if the sides are properly scaled. In this latter case, the lengths related to the shorter and the longer diagonal must be shortened by $b - a$ or $d - a$ and normalized by $b + a$ or $d + a$, respectively.

2.2   The *Screen* Applied to 6*j*-Symbols

The screen representation was originally developed for and applied to 6*j* symbols, whose entries are designated $j_1, j_2, j_3, j_4, j_{12}, j_{23}$, to represent the allowed range of existence of the tetrahedron [28, 29] obtained by alternative vector couplings of the four "spins" j_1, j_2, j_3, j_4 through plots of the discrete variables, j_{12} and j_{23} that are intermediate coupling spins (see [29–33]). The six-distance system discussed in Sect. 2.1, in the original representations of the 6*j* symbols of Wigner-Racah coefficients, was introduced to visualize matrix elements between different coupling schemes of quantum mechanical angular momenta (for the applications to 6*j* symbols, see for example [26, 34]). A geometrical interpretation of these elements was given by Wigner and Racah, who associated the lengths of the edges of a generally irregular tetrahedron to the six entries of the 6*j* symbols. Ponzano and Regge [35] investigated the functional dependence of the 6*j* symbol on their entries, arguing that geometrical properties of the tetrahedron, such as volume and dihedral angles, played a role in the amplitude and phase of a semiclassical approximated wave-function. Rigorous derivations, based on earlier work by Neville [36] and Schulten and Gordon [37, 38], and the definitions and the introduction of efficient computational procedures, were developed in [32–34, 39, 40].

2.3   Features of the Screen

Inspired by to the application to the 6*j* symbols, a model of six distances is proposed and employed to plot the tetrahedron associated to a class of molecules, in a 2-dimensional *x-y* plane (*x* and *y* are continuous variables in this case): the square "screen" has allowed ranges x_{min}, x_{max}, and y_{min}, y_{max} given in Eq. (1). Here we define some features of the screen. Let *V* be the volume of the tetrahedron (formulas resumed in [32–34]). The caustic line is the curve corresponding to $V = 0$ (a tetrahedron of zero-volume), while the area within the caustic is related to that of a finite volume tetrahedron. The caustic touches the sides of the screen in four points called North, South, East and West gates (N, S, E, W). N is the value of *x* corresponding to the maximum of *y*; on the opposite side, S is the value of *x* for which *y* is the minimum; E is the value of *y* corresponding to the maximum of *x*; finally, W is the value of *y* for which *x* is the minimum. The shape of the caustic, approximately an ovaloid, and the locations of the gates, are typical of the geometry of each examined system assimilated to a tetrahedron.

Ridges are curves that mark configurations of the associated tetrahedron when two specific pairs of triangular faces are orthogonal [26]. Formulas to calculate the location of the gates, the equations of the caustic and the ridges, and the volume of the associated tetrahedron are given in [27] and references therein.

2.4 Screen Representations of Peroxides and Persulfides

Screen representations of peroxides and persulfides have been discussed in Refs. [23]. Molecules of this class are schematically represented by the formula R1 – O1 – O2 – R2 for peroxides, and R1 – S1 – S2 – R2 for persulfides, where O1 – O2 are the oxygens forming the peroxidic bond (or S1 – S2 the sulfurs of the persulfidic bond), and R1 and R2 are the atoms or groups connected to O1 and O2 (or S1 and S2), respectively.

One can individuate three distances corresponding to the bond lengths between the atom (or group) R1 and the O1 atom, between the atoms O1 and O2, and between the atom O2 and the atom (or group) R2, these distances lie along the three bonds that identify the stereogenic units of peroxides (see Fig. 1 of Ref. [23]). Three additional distances are given by R1 – O2, R2 – O1, and R1 – R2. This 6-distance system defines a tetrahedron that, when confined or projected in the plane results in a "quadrangle", whose joints are precisely the elements of the stereogenic unit. As mentioned previously, in principle all three pairs of distances can be plotted, however in this case R1 – R2 is the most suitable one to monitor the chirality changing processes. Thus, R1 – O1, R1 – O2, R2 – O1, R2 – O2 are selected as the sides of the "quadrilateral", while the distances O1 – O2 and R1 – R2 are diagonals of the quadrilateral, i.e. the variables. It must be noted, see Ref. [23], that ridges connect the geometries of persulfides or peroxides, (cis, equilibrium and trans).

3   Screen Representation of Peptides

Screens are now shown to display structural properties of proteins taken from Protein Data Bank [25]. Here, we list those proteins included in the screen, all involving alanine. For each protein chosen given in order of complexity from small to longer ones, we report the four-character code, the name of the peptide, the organism from which it was isolated, and in parenthesis the number of the aminoacid residues:

5aht Isomerase *H. Sapiens* (43), 5jpx Metal binding protein *H. Sapiens* (45), 1hgv Coat protein filamentous bacteriophage (46), 1hgz Coat protein filamentous bacteriophage (46), 1hh0 Coat protein filamentous bacteriophage (46), 1nh4 Coat protein filamentous bacteriophage (50), 2n8t Ligase *R. norvegicus* (53), 1new Cytochrome (electron transport) *D. acetoxidans* (68), 5lg7 Ligase *H. Sapiens* (69), 2ltf Viral protein (Tail protein) *Escherichia phage P2* (71), 2cqj RNA binding protein *H. Sapiens* (71), 6axd Transferase *H. Sapiens* (72), 2lze Ligase *E. coli* (87), 1x4q RNA binding protein *H. Sapiens* (92), 1e1g Human prion protein (104), 1e1j Human prion protein (104), 1e1p Human prion protein (104), 1e1s Human prion protein (104), 1e1u Human prion protein (104), 1e1w Human prion protein (104), 1hjm Human prion protein (104), 1hjn Human prion protein (104), 2l9q Heat shock protein *S. cerevisiae* (109), 1xyk Canine prion protein (111), 1xyj Cat prion protein (111), 1xyw Elk prion protein (111), 2ku4 Horse prion protein (113), 6gt7 Transferase *S. islandicus* (115), 1lwb Hydrolase *S. violaceoruber* (122), 1k8h RNA binding protein *A. aeolicus* (133), 5v7z Signaling protein *H. Sapiens* (132), 6do6 Lipid binding protein *H. Sapiens* (135), 2fe0 Protein transport (membrane protein) *L. major* (136), 6do7 Lipid binding protein *H. Sapiens* (142), 5w4s Transferase *R. norvegicus* (151), 2lu5 Oxidoreductase *H. Sapiens* (153),

2i83 Cell adhesion *H. Sapiens* (160), 1qlx Human prion protein (210), 1qlz Human prion protein (210), 6f2x Transferase *M. tuberculosis* (216), 5lg0 Ligase *H. Sapiens* (223), 2h35 Oxygen storage/transport *H. Sapiens* (574), 2m6z Oxygen transport *H. Sapiens* (574), 5kk3 Protein fibril *H. Sapiens* (756), 4gdi Neuraminidase Influenza A virus (2238).

Here, we discuss structural features plotting significant distances related to the peptidic bond, no attention being payed to caustics and ridges. See [23] of relevance for dynamics (*e.g.* changes of chirality) to be considered in future work.

In Fig. 1, we report an example of the virtual tetrahedron built in an aminoacid unit, specifically alanine. The four vertices are the atoms directly bounded to the asymmetric carbon atom denoted by C_A, the nitrogen atom N, one of the hydrogen atoms H_A, the carboxylic carbon C and the carbon of the alanine C_B. The six distances that form the edges of the virtual tetrahedron are N-H_A, N-C_B, N-C, H_A-C_B, H_A-C, C-C_B. The screen is a plot having as coordinate a couple of two opposite distances, that can be chosen in three ways: N-H_A and C-C_B, N-C_B and H_A-C; N-C and H_A-C_B. The caustic curve, described in the previous section but not presented here, would delimit the field of existence of the tetrahedron of zero volume, that corresponds to a planar quadrangle, *i.e.* with the four vertices that lie on the same plane. Being the arrangement of the four atoms in general vertices of a tetrahedron of non zero volume, the points are placed internally to the caustic.

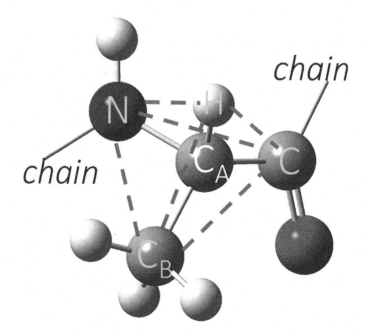

Fig. 1. In the virtual tetrahedron built in the aminoacid unit (alanine), dashed red lines are the six edges joining the four vertices that are: the nitrogen denoted by N (in blue), the carbon atom of the lateral chain CH_3 denoted by C_B (in grey), the hydrogen connected to the central α-carbon H_A (in white), the carboxylic carbon atom C (in grey). Note that the central α-carbon, C_A (in grey) is not a vertex: it is located at the center of the tetrahedron and in grey we indicate the four chemical bonds. (Color figure online)

In Fig. 2, we report the screen of the distances $H_A - C_B$ and $N - C$ of alanine. The red dot at $H_A - C_B$ 2.16 Å and $N - C$ 2.47 Å corresponds to the geometry of the most stable conformer of isolated alanine [41]. Adding substituents in the N side of the unit or in the C side unit, the $H_A - C_B$ length (y) may shrink from *ca.* 2.15 to *ca.* 2.0, while the $N - C$ length (x) varies from 2.45 Å to the range 2.3 – 2.6 Å. The points can be classified into two main regions: the first one with the $H_A - CB$ distance lower than 2.1 Å and concentrated in the range of distances $N - C$ between 2.35 Å and 2.5 Å. The second one is located at values of the $H_A - C_B$ distance higher than 2.1 Å and span a wider range of $N - C$ distances, between 2.25 Å and 2.6 Å. Future work should distinguish shortening and lengthening according to the nature of connected aminoacids.

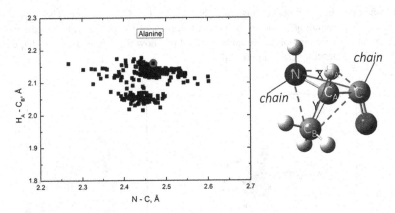

Fig. 2. Screen of the distances (in angstrom) $H_A - C_B$ *vs.* $N - C$ in alanine. The red dot shows the distances corresponding to the most stable conformer of isolated alanine. On the right, the tetrahedron built on the aminoacid, continuous red lines showing the diagonals X ($N - C$ distance) and Y ($H_A - C_B$ distance). (Color figure online)

In Fig. 3, we report the screen of the distances $N - H_A$ and $C - C_B$ of alanine. The red dot at $N - H_A$ 2.15 Å and $C - C_B$ 2.51 Å corresponds to the geometry of the most stable conformer of isolated alanine [41]. Adding substituents in the N side of the unit or in the C side unit, the $N - H_A$ length (y) may shrink from *ca.* 2.1 to *ca.* 1.95 Å, while the $C - C_B$ length (x) varies from 2.5 Å to 2.35 – 2.6 Å.

In Fig. 4, we report the screen of the distances $N - C_B$ and $H_A - C$ of alanine. The red dot at $H_A - C$ 2.13 Å and $N - C_B$ 2.48 Å [41] corresponds to the geometry of the most stable conformer of isolated alanine [41]. Adding substituents in the N side of the unit or in the C side unit, the $N - C_B$ length (y) may vary from 2.48 Å to *ca.* 2.35 – 2.55 Å, while the $H_A - C$ length (x) varies from 2.13 Å to *ca.* 2.05 – 2.2 Å. The points are distributed between two main regions: the first one at values of the $H_A - C$ distance lower than 2.1 Å and the second one with values of the $H_A - C$ distance included between 2.1 and 2.2 Å.

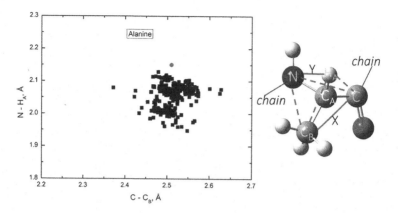

Fig. 3. Screen of the distances (in angstrom) N – H$_A$ *vs.* C – C$_B$ in alanine. The red dot shows the distances corresponding to the most stable conformer of isolated alanine. On the right, the tetrahedron built on the aminoacid, continuous red lines show the diagonals X (C – C$_B$ distance) and Y (N – H$_A$ distance). (Color figure online)

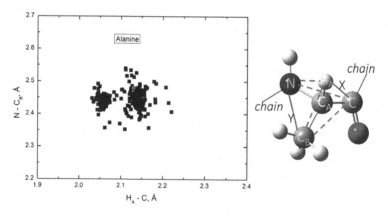

Fig. 4. Screen of the distances (in angstrom) N – C$_B$ *vs.* H$_A$ – C in alanine. The red dot shows the distances corresponding to the most stable conformer of isolated alanine. On the right, the tetrahedron built on the aminoacid, continuous red lines showing the diagonals X (H$_A$ – C distance) and Y (N – C$_B$ distance). (Color figure online)

4   Final Remarks

The square screen serves to display molecular properties by properly plotting significant distances among not necessarily bonded atoms. Here, it has been applied to the structural properties related to alanine in peptides.

It is important to point out that among the choices of distances that can be in principle done, most representative are those between atoms present in all the aminoacids, *i.e.* those atoms directly connected to the central α-carbon. The variation of distances are expected to be related to the structure of the protein under the action of the peptide chain environment.

The choice of distances in our plot is arguably showing a better alternative perspective with respect to that of dihedral angles, because they can be extracted directly from the most common and employed databases. Also shortening or lengthening of bonds can be intuitively correlated to increasing or decreasing binding energies. It has been shown that this approach is suitable to treat systems not exclusively related to these classes of molecules, and in general the algorithms will allow to deal with extensive inputs from databases much wider than considered here.

In future applications, moving from structure to dynamics, the caustics and ridges can be profitably calculated and exhibited on screens, both to represent the field of existence of the intra- and inter-aminoacid unit distances, and to monitor the dynamical processes related for example to change of chirality.

Acknowledgements. The authors acknowledge the Italian Ministry for Education, University and Research, MIUR, for financial supporting through SIR 2014 Scientific Independence for young Researchers (RBSI14U3VF).

Bibliography

1. Palazzetti, F., Maciel, G.S., Lombardi, A., Grossi, G., Aquilanti, V.: The astrochemical observatory: molecules in the laboratory and in the cosmos. J. Chin. Chem. Soc. **59** (2012). https://doi.org/10.1002/jccs.201200242

2. Gianturco, F.A., et al.: Exploring a chemical route for the formation of stable anions of polyynes [Cn H−(n = 2, 4)] in molecular clouds. Astrophys. J. **830**, 2 (2016). https://doi.org/10.3847/0004-637X/830/1/2

3. Wang, X., Li, Y., Yang, Z., Lu, C., Zhu, T.: A quantum mechanical computational method for modeling electrostatic and solvation effects of protein. Sci. Rep. **8**, 5475 (2018)

4. Lombardi, A., Palazzetti, F., Aquilanti, V., Pirani, F., Casavecchia, P.: The astrochemical observatory: experimental and computational focus on the chiral molecule propylene oxide as a case study. In: Gervasi, O., et al. (eds.) ICCSA 2017. LNCS, vol. 10408, pp. 267–280. Springer, Cham (2017). https://doi.org/10.1007/978-3-319-62404-4_20

5. Palazzetti, F., et al.: Stereodirectional photodynamics: experimental and theoretical perspectives. In: AIP Conference Proceedings, vol. 1790, p. 020020 (2016). https://doi.org/10.1063/1.4968646

6. Kasai, T., et al.: Directions of chemical change: experimental characterization of the stereodynamics of photodissociation and reactive processes. Phys. Chem. Chem. Phys. **16**, 9776–9790 (2014). https://doi.org/10.1039/c4cp00464g

7. Barreto, P.R.P., et al.: Potential energy surface for the interaction of helium with the chiral molecule propylene oxide. In: Gervasi, O., et al. (eds.) ICCSA 2018. LNCS, vol. 10964, pp. 593–604. Springer, Cham (2018). https://doi.org/10.1007/978-3-319-95174-4_46

8. Su, T.-M., Palazzetti, F., Lombardi, A., Grossi, G., Aquilanti, V.: Molecular alignment and chirality in gaseous streams and vortices. Rend. Lincei **24**, 291–297 (2013). https://doi.org/10.1007/s12210-013-0249-x

9. Che, D.-C., Kanda, K., Palazzetti, F., Aquilanti, V., Kasai, T.: Electrostatic hexapole state-selection of the asymmetric-top molecule propylene oxide: rotational and orientational distributions. Chem. Phys. **399**, 180–192 (2012). https://doi.org/10.1016/j.chemphys.2011.11.020

10. Lombardi, A., Maciel, G.S., Palazzetti, F., Grossi, G., Aquilanti, V.: Alignment and chirality in gaseous flows. J. Vac. Soc. Jpn. **53**, 645–653 (2010). https://doi.org/10.3131/jvsj2.53.645

11. Albernaz, A.F., Barreto, P.R.P., Aquilanti, V., Lombardi, A., Palazzetti, F., Pirani, F.: The astrochemical observatory: the interaction between helium and the chiral molecule propylene oxide. In: AIP Conference Proceedings, vol. 2040, p. 020018 (2018). https://doi.org/10.1063/1.5079060

12. Lin, K.-C., et al.: Angular distribution of bromine atomic photofragment in oriented 2-bromobutane via hexapole state selector. In: AIP Conference Proceedings, p. 020001 (2017). https://doi.org/10.1063/1.5012287

13. Nakamura, M., et al.: Stereodirectional images of molecules oriented by a variable-voltage hexapolar field: fragmentation channels of 2-bromobutane electronically excited at two photolysis wavelengths. J. Chem. Phys. **147** (2017). https://doi.org/10.1063/1.4981025

14. Falcinelli, S., et al.: Double photoionization of propylene oxide: a coincidence study of the ejection of a pair of valence-shell electrons. J. Chem. Phys. **148**, 114302 (2018). https://doi.org/10.1063/1.5024408

15. Lombardi, A., Palazzetti, F., Aquilanti, V., Grossi, G.: Chirality in molecular collisions. In: AIP Conference Proceedings, vol. 1906, p. 030012 (2017). https://doi.org/10.1063/1.5012291

16. Aquilanti, V., et al.: The astrochemical observatory: computational and theoretical focus on molecular chirality changing torsions around O–O and S–S bonds. In: AIP Conference Proceedings, vol. 1906, p. 030010 (2017). https://doi.org/10.1063/1.5012289

17. Che, D.-C., Palazzetti, F., Okuno, Y., Aquilanti, V., Kasai, T.: Electrostatic hexapole state-selection of the asymmetric-top molecule propylene oxide. J. Phys. Chem. A **114**, 3280–3286 (2010). https://doi.org/10.1021/jp909553t

18. Carrascoza, F., Zaric, S., Silaghi-Dumitrescu, R.: Computational study of protein secondary structure elements: Ramachandran plots revisited. J. Mol. Graph. Model. **50**, 125–133 (2014)

19. Lombardi, A., Palazzetti, F., Maciel, G.S., Aquilanti, V., Sevryuk, M.B.: Simulation of oriented collision dynamics of simple chiral molecules. Int. J. Quantum Chem. **111**, 1651–1658 (2011). https://doi.org/10.1002/qua.22816

20. Barreto, P.R.P., Palazzetti, F., Grossi, G., Lombardi, A., Maciel, G.S., Vilela, A.F.A.: Range and strength of intermolecular forces for van der Waals complexes of the type H2Xn-Rg, with X = O, S and n = 1, 2. Int. J. Quantum Chem. **110**, 777–786 (2010). https://doi.org/10.1002/qua.22127

21. Barreto, P.R.P., Vilela, A.F.A., Lombardi, A., Maciel, G.S., Palazzetti, F., Aquilanti, V.: The hydrogen peroxide-rare gas systems: quantum chemical calculations and hyperspherical harmonic representation of the potential energy surface for atom-floppy molecule interactions. J. Phys. Chem. A **111**, 12754–12762 (2007). https://doi.org/10.1021/jp076268v

22. Maciel, G.S., Barreto, P.R.P., Palazzetti, F., Lombardi, A., Aquilanti, V.: A quantum chemical study of H2S2: intramolecular torsional mode and intermolecular interactions with rare gases. J. Chem. Phys. **129**, 164302 (2008). https://doi.org/10.1063/1.2994732

23. Aquilanti, V., Caglioti, C., Lombardi, A., Maciel, G.S., Palazzetti, F.: Screens for displaying chirality changing mechanisms of a series of peroxides and persulfides from conformational structures computed by quantum chemistry. In: Gervasi, O., et al. (eds.) ICCSA 2017. LNCS, vol. 10408, pp. 354–368. Springer, Cham (2017). https://doi.org/10.1007/978-3-319-62404-4_26

24. Caglioti, C., Santos, R.F.D., Aquilanti, V., Lombardi, A., Palazzetti, F.: Screen mapping of structural and electric properties, chirality changing rates and racemization times of chiral peroxides and persulfides. In: AIP Conference Proceedings, vol. 2040, p. 020021 (2018). https://doi.org/10.1063/1.5079063

25. Protein Data Bank, PDB. https://www.rcsb.org/

26. Bitencourt, A.C.P., Ragni, M., Littlejohn, R.G., Anderson, R., Aquilanti, V.: The screen representation of vector coupling coefficients or Wigner $3j$ symbols: exact computation and illustration of the asymptotic behavior. In: Murgante, B., et al. (eds.) ICCSA 2014. LNCS, vol. 8579, pp. 468–481. Springer, Cham (2014). https://doi.org/10.1007/978-3-319-09144-0_32

27. Aquilanti, V., et al.: Quadrilaterals on the square screen of their diagonals: Regge symmetries of quantum mechanical spin networks and Grashof classical mechanisms of four-bar linkages. Rend. Lincei 30, 67–81 (2019). https://doi.org/10.1007/s12210-019-00776-x

28. Littlejohn, R.G., Yu, L.: Uniform semiclassical approximation for the Wigner 6j-symbol in terms of rotation matrices. J. Phys. Chem. A 113, 14904–14922 (2009)

29. Aquilanti, V., Haggard, H.M., Hedeman, A., Jeevangee, N., Littlejohn, R., Yu, L.: Semiclassical mechanics of the Wigner 6j-symbol. J. Phys. A. 45, 065209 (2012)

30. Aquilanti, V., Capecchi, G.: Harmonic analysis and discrete polynomials from semiclassical angular momentum theory to the hyperquantization algorithm. Theoret. Chem. Acc. 104, 183–188 (2000)

31. De Fazio, D., Cavalli, S., Aquilanti, V.: Orthogonal polynomials of a discrete variable as expansion basis sets in quantum mechanics the hyperquantization algorithm. Int. J. Quantum Chem. 93, 91–111 (2003)

32. Aquilanti, V., Cavalli, S., De Fazio, D.: Angular and hyperangular momentum coupling coefficients as hahn polynomials. J. Phys. Chem. 99, 15694–15698 (1995)

33. Bitencourt, A.C.P., Marzuoli, A., Ragni, M., Anderson, R.W., Aquilanti, V.: Exact and asymptotic computations of elementary spin networks: classification of the quantum–classical boundaries. In: Murgante, B., et al. (eds.) ICCSA 2012. LNCS, vol. 7333, pp. 723–737. Springer, Heidelberg (2012). https://doi.org/10.1007/978-3-642-31125-3_54

34. Aquilanti, V., Bitencourt, A.C.P., da S. Ferreira, C., Marzuoli, A., Ragni, M.: Combinatorics of angular momentum recoupling theory: spin networks, their asymptotics and applications. Theoret. Chem. Acc. 123, 237 (2009)

35. Ponzano, G., Regge, T.: Semiclassical limit of Racah coefficients. In: Spectroscopic and Group Theoretical Methods in Physics. North-Holland, Amsterdam (1968)

36. Neville, D.: A technique for solving recurrence relations approximately and its application to the 3j and 6j symbols. J. Math. Phys. 12, 2438 (1971)

37. Schulten, K., Gordon, R.: Semiclassical approximations to 3j- and 6j-coefficients for quantum-mechanical coupling of angular momenta. J. Math. Phys. 16, 1971–1988 (1975)

38. Schulten, K., Gordon, R.: Exact recursive evaluation of 3j- and 6j-coefficients for quantum mechanical coupling of angular momenta. J. Math. Phys. 16, 1961–1970 (1975)

39. Ragni, M., Bitencourt, A.C.P., Aquilanti, V., Anderson, R.W., Littlejohn, R.G.: Exact computation and asymptotic approximations of 6j symbols: illustration of their semiclassical limits. Int. J. Quantum Chem. 110, 731–742 (2010)

40. Aquilanti, V., Cavalli, S., Coletti, C.: Angular and hyperangular momentum recoupling, harmonic superposition and Racah polynomials: a recursive algorithm. Chem. Phys. Lett. 344, 587–600 (2001)

41. Berlin ab-initio amino acid DB. http://aminoaciddb.rz-berlin.mpg.de/

The Increase of the Reactivity of Molecular Hydrogen with Hydroxyl Radical from the Gas Phase versus an Aqueous Environment: Quantum Chemistry and Transition State-Theory Calculations

Valter H. Carvalho-Silva[1(✉)], Eduardo C. Vaz[1,2],
Nayara D. Coutinho[2], Hikaru Kobayashi[3], Yuki Kobayashi[3],
Toshio Kasai[3,4], Federico Palazzetti[2], Andrea Lombardi[2],
and Vincenzo Aquilanti[2,5]

[1] Grupo de Química Teórica e Estrutural de Anápolis,
Ciências Exatas e Tecnológicas, Universidade Estadual de Goiás,
CP 459, Anápolis, GO 75001-970, Brazil
fatioleg@gmail.com
[2] Dipartimento di Chimica, Biologia e Biotecnologie, Università di Perugia,
Via Elce di Sotto 8, 06123 Perugia, Italy
[3] The Institute of Scientific and Industrial Research, Osaka University,
8-1 Mihogaoka, Osaka, Ibaraki 567-0047, Japan
[4] Department of Chemistry, National Taiwan University, Taipei 10617, Taiwan
[5] Istituto di Struttura della Materia, Consiglio Nazionale delle Ricerche,
00185 Rome, Italy

Abstract. One of the simplest elementary reactions, that between H_2 and OH, is of great theoretical interest in chemical kinetics. Surprisingly it turned out recently to be of importance in medical and biological environments, in search of role of hydrogen as radical scavenger participating in the human body: water is supposed to be of possible influence in this reaction. However, there are no theoretical studies considering solvent effects in the title reaction which in the gas phase is slow. Here, we aim to analyze the H_2 + OH reaction with a blend of electronic structure calculations and the *deformed* Transition-State Theory (*d*-TST) approach. Inclusion of the continuum solvation model density (SMD) was applied for mimicking the role of the aqueous phase. Preliminary results demonstrate an enormous increase in the reactivity between H_2 and OH molecules in water environment, approximately 150- and 138-fold at 25 °C and 36.5 °C, respectively. We expect that these results can help to shed new light on the understanding of the H_2 + OH reaction in aqueous phase, paving the way to research for medical and technological applications.

1 Introduction

The reaction between H_2 and OH molecules is being demonstrated to be of great importance in biological and medical [1] environments, in spite of the simplicity of the molecules participating in the process. The H_2 molecule is the smallest gas molecule

© Springer Nature Switzerland AG 2019
S. Misra et al. (Eds.): ICCSA 2019, LNCS 11624, pp. 450–459, 2019.
https://doi.org/10.1007/978-3-030-24311-1_33

composed of two protons and two electrons, forming a very stable compound that reacts with the oxide radical ion (O^-) [2]. There are several documentations regarding the antioxidant performance of the H_2 molecule. Studies of selectivity of H_2 molecule in cells inducing oxidative stress and reducing cytotoxicity reactive of oxygenated species, $i.e.$, hydroxyl radical [2–4]. Due to the applicability on the human body, water is supposed to be of great influence in this reaction, however, there are scarce studies from a theoretical viewpoint [5].

The four-body reaction investigation has been propitiated a deep understanding of the mechanism and reactivity of chemical reactions in the gas phase [6–9]. Recently, the prototypical H_2 + OH reaction has been highlighted due to the publication of a paper by Ohsawa et al. [4], which presented results with a significant reduction of cerebral infarction in rats when exposed to of 2% to 4% v/v of molecular hydrogen mixtures. Later works [2, 3, 5, 10–16] obtained promising results in the treatment of 63 types of diseases with the administration of H_2 in several medical areas. The efficacy of the hydrogen molecule was suggested due to neutralization of OH radical [17], in a few cases prejudicial to a living organism, which H_2 has reactive specificity [4]. Concomitantly, this reaction came out to be important in other applications, such as the control of free radicals in the atmosphere [18], gas- and condensed phase reactions [19–21] and photosensitive materials [22]. On another context, the H_2 + OH reaction has been mainly exploited to redirect H_2 gases from nuclear power plants to be reformed. Molecular hydrogen (H_2) has been playing a key role in nuclear power plants since water is used in the refrigeration of reactors with consequent high concentration H_2 and hydrogen peroxide (H_2O_2) formation due water radiolysis – interaction with alpha, beta and gamma radiation [23–25]. The high concentration of these generated gases is a concern to avoid explosive conditions since the water radiolysis under extreme conditions is not fully understood due to the rich and inherent complexity of chemical activity [26].

There is extensive experimental and theoretical rate constant investigation of the title reaction [5] and, due to its importance, many potential energy surfaces (PES) have been proposed to estimate theoretically thermodynamic and kinetic parameters. Chen et al. [27] proposed recently a global PES using neural networks method based on approximately 17,000 ab $initio$ energies calculated via UCCSD(T)-F12a/AVTZ. Additionally, quantum-classical (QC) investigations reported the connection of the reactivity of H_2 with vibrational excitation energy exchange while OH radicals are not affected [28]. Recently, Kastner et al. [20] obtained theoretical reaction rate constant, in the range of the 150 K to 1000 K, with excellent agreement with experimental data. Talukdar et al. [29] and Bhattacharya et al. [6] demonstrated the presence of an isotopic effect in the reaction involving molecular hydrogen - especially in low-temperature conditions – a classical signature of quantum tunneling effect [6, 29].

Here, the H_2 + OH reaction in the gas-phase and in the aqueous environments (due relevance in living organism previously described) has been investigated with a blend of electronic structure calculations - Quadratic Configuration Interaction involving single, double and triple substitutions excitations QCISD(T), with the *deformed*

Transition-State Theory (d-TST) to account for the tunneling effect. A similar approach was previously developed and illustrated by our group in various cases of four-body reactions, with promising results suggesting a significant role of stereodynamics, roaming and quantum effects in influencing the rates of reactive [18, 20, 30–32], so qualifying our theoretical tools to cope with this reaction.

2 Computational Procedures

2.1 Stationary Electronic Structure Calculations

The electronic structure properties of the reactants, the products, and the transition state were calculated employing the Møller-Plesset [33], Configuration Interaction [34], in combination with 6-311++G(3df,3pd) and aug-cc-pVDZ basis set. The specific level of calculation was selected to perform analyses and comparison with experimental data: CISD(T)/aug-cc-pVDZ//MP2/6-311+G(3df,2pd). The stationary points were characterized by analytic harmonic frequency calculations. The absence or existence of one imaginary frequency for crossing the barrier characterizes the optimized structures as local minimum or transition state, respectively. The zero-point vibrational energy contributions were considered in the calculation of the barrier. To account for the solvent effect the continuum solvation model density was applied to mimicking the water ambiance (SMD) [35].

2.2 Reaction Rate Theories

The reaction rate constants (k) were calculated by deformed-transition state theory (d-TST). This phenomenological formulation covers cases of concave deviation from Arrhenius law against the reciprocal of temperatures for elementary chemical reactions, exhibiting *sub*-Arrhenius behavior. In general, this behavior is a signature of quantum tunneling. To account the quantum tunneling in chemical reactions in the *deformed* formulation, d parameter is introduced from transitivity concept γ [36, 37] namely the inverse of activation energy ($1/E_a$) with reciprocal of the temperature (β) truncated at an order higher than one:

$$\gamma \equiv \frac{1}{E_a} = \frac{1}{\varepsilon^{\ddagger}} - d\beta \tag{1}$$

where $\varepsilon^{\ddagger}$ is a constant and represents an energetic obstacle to the reaction at high temperatures and $\beta = 1/k_B T$, where k_B is Boltzmann's constant and T is the absolute temperature. In Ref. [38], an explicit procedure for calculation of d was developed as inversely proportional to the square of the barrier ($\varepsilon^{\ddagger}$) and directly proportional to the square of the frequency for crossing the barrier $(v^\ddagger)$ at maximum in the minimum energy path on the potential energy surface,

$$d = -\frac{1}{3}\left(\frac{hv^\ddagger}{2\varepsilon^\ddagger}\right)^2 \tag{2}$$

where h is Planck's constant.

The tunneling corrected averaged by Boltzmann factor from TST formulation was replaced by the deformed exponential function, yielding the d-TST formulation [39]

$$k(\beta) = \frac{1}{h\beta}\frac{Q^\ddagger}{Q_{Reac}}\left(1 - d\varepsilon^\ddagger\beta\right)^{1/d} \tag{3}$$

where Q_{Reac} and $Q^\ddagger$ are the partition function (translational, vibrational, rotational and electronic contributions) of the reactants and of the activated complex, respectively. Equation (4) recovers the TST rate constant when d tends to zero, due to the Euler limit, $\lim\limits_{d\to 0}\left(1 - d\varepsilon^\ddagger\beta\right)^{1/d} = e^{-\varepsilon^\ddagger\beta}$.

The tunneling regime can be characterized considering the crossover temperature parameter $T_c = hv^\ddagger/2\pi k_B$[40, 41], conventionally establishing (within some arbitrariness) the ranges of the regimes for a specific imaginary frequency at the top of the barrier point, $v^\ddagger$: negligible $(4T_c > T > 2T_c)$, moderate $(2T_c > T > T_c)$ and deep $(T_c > T)$ regimes.

A phenomenological representation for the temperature dependence of obtained rate constants to cover the regimes, except at deep tunneling, can be obtained by Aquilanti-Mundim deformed Arrhenius formula (AM) [42]

$$k(\beta) = A(1 - \bar{d}E_0\beta)^{1/\bar{d}} \tag{4}$$

A and $\bar{d}$ are the pre-exponential factor and the deformed parameter, respectively. [Note a change in the notation here, needed in order to avoid ambiguities: in terms of the fitted equation, we defined $\bar{d}$ which is different from d and E_0 which is different from $\varepsilon^\ddagger$.

All kinetic and associated parameters were calculated with the Transitivity Code-version 1.0.0: details of the computational program can be found on the www. vhcsgroup.com/transitivity web page.

3   Results and Discussion

Table 1 shows theoretical imaginary vibrational frequency (cm^{-1}), crossover temperature and relative energies (in $kcal\,mol^{-1}$) of the stationary points along the $H_2 + OH \rightarrow H_2O + H$ reaction coordinate at carefully chosen different levels of theory. The transition state in gas-phase presents an imaginary vibrational frequency of $1531i$ at MP2/6-311++G(3df,3pd), clearly different from the result obtained by Meisner and Kastner ($1199i$) at CCSD(T)-F12/cc-pVDZ-F12. Consequently, a difference around 100 K is observed for crossover temperature. This difference suggests an improvement in our calculation, which was performed only in energy at CISD(T)/aug-cc-pVDZ//MP2/6-311+G(3df,2pd) level.

Table 1. Imaginary vibrational frequencies $\left(v^{\ddagger} \right)$ in cm^{-1}, cross over temperature (T_c) in Kelvin, the barrier height $\left(\varepsilon^{\ddagger} \right)$ and exothermicity-type energies in kcal.mol^{-1} for OH + H$_2$ reaction both gas- and aqueous-phase. Theoretical data are also presented for comparison.

	$v^{\ddagger}$	T_c	$\varepsilon^{\ddagger}$	ΔE
Gas-phase [MP2]	$1531i$	350	8.05	−22.97
Gas-phase [CISD(T)//MP2]	–		6.63	−14.30
Aqueous-phase [CISD(T)//MP2]	–		6.27	−16.71
Meisner and Kastner (Gas phase) [20]	$1199i$	270	5.38	−16.27

Table 1 also present barrier height calculated at MP2 level of theory in gas-phase, around 8 kcal.mol^{-1}, different from Meisner and Kastner obtained with coupled cluster level of calculation. However, our calculation yields a significant decrease in barrier energy and in exothermicity values at CISD(T)/aug-cc-pVDZ//MP2/6-311+G(3df,2pd) level with a reasonable agreement with Meisner and Kastner [20]. To account for the solvent effect, the continuum solvation model density was applied for mimicking the aqueous-phase (SMD) at CISD(T)/aug-cc-pVDZ//MP2/6-311+G(3df,2pd) level of calculation. Comparison between gas- and aqueous-phase presents a slight decrease in the barrier height at the similar level of calculation.

We calculate the kinetic rate constant using deformed-Transition State Theory (d-TST) in a realistic range of temperature (250–350 K) at CISD(T)/aug-cc-pVDZ//MP2/6-311+G(3df,2pd) level of calculation for the title reaction in gas- and aqueous-phase. Figure 1 shows the comparison of the d-TST rate constant with previous theoretical [20, 43] and experimental [29, 30, 44–47] results for H$_2$ + OH $\rightarrow$ + H$_2$O + H reaction: it is observed a slight difference with the literature in reaction rate constants in gas-phase, and an improvement in the reactivity with the inclusion of solvent effect. Here, we show experimental data of the reaction rate constants in aqueous-phase [48–50], and our preliminary calculations yield a reasonable qualitative agreement.

In this work, we use the AM formula, Eq. (4), to fit the temperature dependence of the reaction rate constants in gas- and aqueous-phase. AM formula has been successfully applied to a variety of chemical processes [42, 51–56]. The temperature dependence of the reaction rate constants can be expressed as

$$k_{Gas}(T) = 2.94 \times 10^{-10} \left(1 + \frac{459.40}{T} \right)^{-12.32}, \tag{5}$$

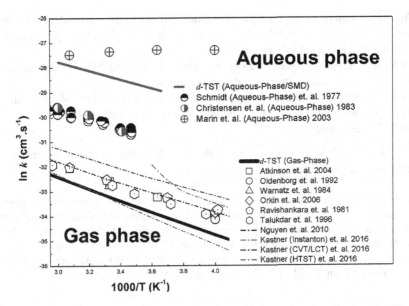

Fig. 1. Comparison of the d-TST rate constant with previous theoretical [20, 43] and experimental [29, 30, 44–47] results for $H_2 + OH \rightarrow + H_2O + H$ reaction.

and

$$k_{Aqueous}(T) = 1.64 \times 10^{-9} \left(1 + \frac{479.95}{T}\right)^{-8.55}.$$

(6)

The water environment produced a significant effect in the reactivity of the molecular hydrogen with hydroxyl radical as observed in Fig. 1. The reaction rate constants in aqueous-phase increase approximately 150- and 138-fold at 25 °C and 36.5 °C, respectively, see Eq. (7). The former temperature is conventionally used as the referential temperature in chemical reactions and the last mimics the human corporal temperature.

$$\frac{k_{Aqueous}(25\,°C)}{k_{Gas}(25\,°C)} \approx 150; \quad \frac{k_{Aqueous}(36.5\,°C)}{k_{Gas}(36.5\,°C)} \approx 138$$

(7)

4   Conclusion

In summary, in this work we established the role of the aqueous environment for the OH + H_2 reaction based on high-level *deformed* Transition-State Theory. The following key findings emerged from our investigation and support the assumptions presented in this work:

- All the stationary points with the energetics and geometric parameters involved in the reaction were accurately characterized at the CISD(T)/aug-cc-pVDZ//MP2/6-311+G(3df,2pd) level of calculation.
- *Deformed* Transition-State Theory is shown to be suitable for describing the reaction rate constants in gas- and aqueous-phases.
- Water ambiance produced a significant effect in the reactivity of the molecular hydrogen with hydroxyl radical, approximately 150- and 138-fold at 25 °C and 36.5 °C, respectively.

We expect that these results will pave the way to future studies for medical and technological applications.

Acknowledgments. VHCS thanks Brazilian agency CNPq for the research funding programs [Universal 01/2016 - Faixa A - 406063/2016-8] and Organizzazione Internazionale Italo-Latino Americana (IILA) for Biotechnology Sector-2019 scholarship. VA, FP, AL acknowledge the Italian Ministry for Education, University and Research, MIUR, for financial support: SIR 2014 "Scientific Independence for young Researchers" (RBSI14U3VF). AL acknowledges the financial support from MIUR PRIN 2015 (contract 2015F59J3R 002).

References

1. Che, D.C., Shimouchi, A., Mizukami, T., Nose, K., Seiyama, A., Kasai, T.: Emanation of hydroxyl radicals from human skin. IEEE Sens. J. **13**, 1223–1227 (2013). https://doi.org/10.1109/JSEN.2012.2228016
2. Ohno, K., Ito, M., Ichihara, M., Ito, M.: Molecular hydrogen as an emerging therapeutic medical gas for neurodegenerative and other diseases. Oxid. Med. Cell. Longev. **2012** (2012). https://doi.org/10.1155/2012/353152
3. Hayashida, K., et al.: Inhalation of hydrogen gas reduces infarct size in the rat model of myocardial ischemia-reperfusion injury. Biochem. Biophys. Res. Commun. **373**, 30–35 (2008). https://doi.org/10.1016/j.bbrc.2008.05.165
4. Ohsawa, I., et al.: Hydrogen acts as a therapeutic antioxidant by selectively reducing cytotoxic oxygen radicals. Nat. Med. **13**, 688–694 (2007). https://doi.org/10.1038/nm1577
5. Ichihara, M., Sobue, S., Ito, M., Ito, M., Hirayama, M., Ohno, K.: Beneficial biological effects and the underlying mechanisms of molecular hydrogen - comprehensive review of 321 original articles. Med. Gas Res., 1–21 (2015). https://doi.org/10.1186/s13618-015-0035-1
6. Bhattacharya, S., Panda, A.N., Meyer, H.D.: Multiconfiguration time-dependent Hartree approach to study the OH + H_2 reaction. J. Chem. Phys. **132**, 0–8 (2010). https://doi.org/10.1063/1.3429609
7. Coutinho, N.D., Aquilanti, V., Sanches-Neto, F.O., Vaz, E.C., Carvalho-Silva, V.H.: *First-principles* molecular dynamics and computed rate constants for the series of OH-HX reactions (X = H or the halogens): *non*-arrhenius kinetics, stereodynamics and quantum tunnel. In: Gervasi, O., et al. (eds.) ICCSA 2018. LNCS, vol. 10964, pp. 605–623. Springer, Cham (2018). https://doi.org/10.1007/978-3-319-95174-4_47
8. Coutinho, N.D., Aquilanti, V., Silva, V.H.C., Camargo, A.J., Mundim, K.C., De Oliveira, H. C.B.: Stereodirectional origin of anti-arrhenius kinetics for a tetraatomic hydrogen exchange reaction: born-oppenheimer molecular dynamics for OH + HBr. J. Phys. Chem. A **120**, 5408–5417 (2016). https://doi.org/10.1021/acs.jpca.6b03958

9. Panarese, A., Longo, S.: Monte Carlo calculation of the translational relaxation of superthermal H atoms in thermal H_2 gas. Astrophys. J. (2012). https://doi.org/10.1088/0004-637X/749/1/23

10. Nakayama, M., et al.: Novel haemodialysis (HD) treatment employing molecular hydrogen (H_2)-enriched dialysis solution improves prognosis of chronic dialysis patients: a prospective observational study. Sci. Rep. **8**, 1–10 (2018). https://doi.org/10.1038/s41598-017-18537-x

11. Nakashima-Kamimura, N., Mori, T., Ohsawa, I., Asoh, S., Ohta, S.: Molecular hydrogen alleviates nephrotoxicity induced by an anti-cancer drug cisplatin without compromising anti-tumor activity in mice. Cancer Chemother. Pharmacol. **64**, 753–761 (2009). https://doi.org/10.1007/s00280-008-0924-2

12. Dole, M., Wilson, F.R., Fife, W.P.: Hyperbaric hydrogen therapy: a possible treatment for cancer. Science **190**, 152–154 (1975). https://doi.org/10.1126/SCIENCE.1166304

13. Iuchi, K., et al.: Molecular hydrogen regulates gene expression by modifying the free radical chain reaction-dependent generation of oxidized phospholipid mediators. Sci. Rep. **6**, 1–12 (2016). https://doi.org/10.1038/srep18971

14. Sobue, S., et al.: Simultaneous oral and inhalational intake of molecular hydrogen additively suppresses signaling pathways in rodents. Mol. Cell. Biochem. **403**, 231–241 (2015). https://doi.org/10.1007/s11010-015-2353-y

15. Ostojic, S.M.: Molecular hydrogen: an inert gas turns clinically effective. Ann. Med. **47**, 301–304 (2015). https://doi.org/10.3109/07853890.2015.1034765

16. Huang, C.S., Kawamura, T., Toyoda, Y., Nakao, A.: Recent advances in hydrogen research as a therapeutic medical gas. Free Radical Res. **44**, 971–982 (2010). https://doi.org/10.3109/10715762.2010.500328

17. Imamura, K., Kimura, K., Fujie, S., Kobayashi, H.: Hydrogen generation from water using Si nanopowder fabricated from swarf. J. Nanopart. Res. **18**, 1–7 (2016). https://doi.org/10.1007/s11051-016-3418-x

18. Lam, K.Y., Davidson, D.F., Hanson, R.K.: A shock tube study of $H_2 + OH \rightarrow H_2O + H$ using OH laser absorption. Int. J. Chem. Kinet. **45**, 363–373 (2013). https://doi.org/10.1002/kin.20771

19. Nguyen, T.L., Stanton, J.F., Barker, J.R.: Ab initio reaction rate constants computed using semiclassical transition-state theory: $HO + H_2 \rightarrow H_2O + H$ and isotopologues. J. Phys. Chem. A **115**, 5118–5126 (2011). https://doi.org/10.1021/jp2022743

20. Meisner, J., Kästner, J.: Reaction rates and kinetic isotope effects of $H_2 + OH \rightarrow H_2O + H$. J. Chem. Phys. **144** (2016). https://doi.org/10.1063/1.4948319

21. Brito, B.G.A., Cândido, L., Teixeira Rabelo, J.N., Hai, G.Q.: Thermodynamic properties of solid molecular hydrogen by path integral Monte Carlo simulations. Chem. Phys. Lett. **691**, 330–335 (2018). https://doi.org/10.1016/j.cplett.2017.11.043

22. Liu, Q., Liu, B., Zhang, Q., Gao, J., Ma, J.: A low-cost, high-efficiency and durable homogeneous system for molecular hydrogen. Mater. Lett. **221**, 46–50 (2018). https://doi.org/10.1016/j.matlet.2018.03.072

23. Scholes, G.: The radiation chemistry of aqueous solutions of nucleic acids and nucleoproteins. Prog. Biophys. Mol. Biol. **13**, 59–104 (2006). https://doi.org/10.1016/s0079-6107(63)80014-0

24. Spotheim-Maurizot, M., Mostafavi, M., Douki, T., Belloni, J.: Radiation Chemistry: From Basics to Applications in Material and Life Science. EDP Sciences, Les Ulis Cedex (2008)

25. Olivera, G.H., Galassi, M.E., Rivarola, R.D., Gervais, B., Beuve, M.: Production of HO_2 and O_2 by multiple ionization in water radiolysis by swift carbon ions. Chem. Phys. Lett. **410**, 330–334 (2005). https://doi.org/10.1016/j.cplett.2005.05.057

26. Gérard, B., Bernard, H.: Water radiolysis under extreme conditions. Application to nuclear industry. In: Radiation Chemistry: From Basics to Applications in Material and Life Sciences, pp. 53–64 (2008)

27. Chen, J., Xu, X., Zhang, D.H.: A global potential energy surface for the H_2 + OH $\leftrightarrow$ H_2O + H reaction using neural networks. J. Chem. Phys. **138** (2013). https://doi.org/10.1063/1.4801658

28. Martí, C., Pacifici, L., Laganà, A., Coletti, C.: A quantum-classical study of the OH + H_2 reactive and inelastic collisions. Chem. Phys. Lett. **674**, 103–108 (2017). https://doi.org/10.1016/j.cplett.2017.02.040

29. Talukdar, R.K., Gierczak, T., Goldfarb, L., Rudich, Y., Madhava Rao, B.S., Ravishankara, A.R.: Kinetics of hydroxyl radical reactions with isotopically labeled hydrogen. J. Phys. Chem. **100**, 3037–3043 (1996). https://doi.org/10.1021/jp9518724

30. Orkin, V.L., Kozlov, S.N., Poskrebyshev, G.A., Kurylo, M.J.: Rate constant for the reaction of OH with H_2 between 200 and 480K. J. Phys. Chem. A **110**, 6978–6985 (2006). https://doi.org/10.1021/jp057035b

31. Kaufman, F., Del Greco, F.P.: Fast reactions of oh radicals. In: Symposium Combustion, vol. 9, pp. 659–668 (1963). https://doi.org/10.1016/S0082-0784(63)80074-0

32. Coutinho, N.D., Sanches-Neto, F.O., Carvalho-Silva, V.H., de Oliveira, H.C.B., Ribeiro, L. A., Aquilanti, V.: Kinetics of the OH + HCl → H_2O + Cl reaction: rate determining roles of stereodynamics and roaming, and of quantum tunnelling. J. Comput. Chem. **39**, 2508–2516 (2018). https://doi.org/10.1002/jcc.25597

33. Head-Gordon, M., Head-Gordon, T.: Analytic MP2 frequencies without fifth-order storage Theory and application to bifurcated hydrogen bonds in the water hexamer. Chem. Phys. Lett. **220**, 122–128 (1994). https://doi.org/10.1016/0009-2614(94)00116-2

34. Head-Gordon, M., Maurice, D., Oumi, M.: A perturbative correction to restricted open shell configuration interaction with single substitutions for excited states of radicals. Chem. Phys. Lett. **246**, 114–121 (1995). https://doi.org/10.1016/0009-2614(95)01111-L

35. Marenich, A.V., Cramer, C.J., Truhlar, D.G.: Universal solvation model based on solute electron density and on a continuum model of the solvent defined by the bulk dielectric constant and atomic surface tensions. J. Phys. Chem. B. **113**, 6378–6396 (2009)

36. Aquilanti, V., Coutinho, N.D., Carvalho-Silva, V.H.: Kinetics of low-temperature transitions and reaction rate theory from non-equilibrium distributions. Philos. Trans. R. Soc. London A **375**, 20160204 (2017). https://doi.org/10.1098/rsta.2016.0201

37. Aquilanti, V., Borges, E.P., Coutinho, N.D., Mundim, K.C., Carvalho-Silva, V.H.: From statistical thermodynamics to molecular kinetics: the change, the chance and the choice. Rend. Lincei Sci. Fis. e Nat. **28**, 787–802 (2018). https://doi.org/10.1007/s12210-018-0749-9

38. Silva, V.H.C., Aquilanti, V., De Oliveira, H.C.B., Mundim, K.C.: Uniform description of non-Arrhenius temperature dependence of reaction rates, and a heuristic criterion for quantum tunneling vs classical non-extensive distribution. Chem. Phys. Lett. **590**, 201–207 (2013). https://doi.org/10.1016/j.cplett.2013.10.051

39. Carvalho-Silva, V.H., Aquilanti, V., de Oliveira, H.C.B., Mundim, K.C.: Deformed transition-state theory: deviation from Arrhenius behavior and application to bimolecular hydrogen transfer reaction rates in the tunneling regime. J. Comput. Chem. **38**, 178–188 (2017)

40. Christov, S.G.: The characteristic (crossover) temperature in the theory of thermally activated tunneling processes. Mol. Eng. **7**, 109–147 (1997). https://doi.org/10.1023/A:1008274213168

41. Bell, R.P.: The Tunnel Effect in Chemistry. Champman and Hall, London (1980)

42. Aquilanti, V., Mundim, K.C., Elango, M., Kleijn, S., Kasai, T.: Temperature dependence of chemical and biophysical rate processes: phenomenological approach to deviations from Arrhenius law. Chem. Phys. Lett. **498**, 209–213 (2010). https://doi.org/10.1016/j.cplett. 2010.08.035

43. Nguyen, T.L., Stanton, J.F., Barker, J.R.: A practical implementation of semi-classical transition state theory for polyatomics. Chem. Phys. Lett. **499**, 9–15 (2010). https://doi.org/ 10.1016/j.cplett.2010.09.015

44. Atkinson, R., et al.: Evaluated kinetic and photochemical data for atmospheric chemistry: volume I - gas phase reactions of Ox, HOx, NOx and SOx species. Atmos. Chem. Phys. **4**, 1461–1738 (2004). https://doi.org/10.5194/acp-4-1461-2004

45. Oldenborg, B.C., Loge, G.W., Harradine, D.M., Winn, K.R.: Kinetic study of the OH + H_2 reaction from 800 to 1550 K. J. Phys. Chem. **96**, 8426 (1992)

46. Gardiner, W.C. (ed.): Combustion Chemistry. Springer-Verlag NY Inc. (1984). https://doi. org/10.1007/978-1-4684-0186-8

47. Ravishankara, A.R., Nicovich, J.M., Thompson, R.L., Tully, F.P.: Kinetic study of the reaction of OH with H2 and D2 from 250 to 1050K. J. Phys. Chem. **85**, 2498–2503 (1981)

48. Marin, T.W., Jonah, C.D., Bartels, D.M.: Reaction of OH* radicals with H_2 in sub-critical water. Chem. Phys. Lett. **371**, 144–149 (2003). https://doi.org/10.1016/S0009-2614(03) 00064-2

49. Christensen, H., Sehested, K.: Reaction of hydroxyl radicals with hydrogen at elevated temperatures. Determination of the activation energy. J. Phys. Chem. **87**, 118–120 (1983). https://doi.org/10.1021/j100224a027

50. Schmidt, K.H.: Measurement of the activation energy for the reaction of the hydroxyl radical with hydrogen in aqueous solution. J. Phys. Chem. **81**, 1257–1263 (1977). https://doi.org/10. 1021/j100528a008

51. Santin, L.G., Toledo, E.M., Carvalho-Silva, V.H., Camargo, A.J., Gargano, R., Oliveira, S. S.: Methanol solvation effect on the proton rearrangement of curcumin's enol forms: an ab initio molecular dynamics and electronic structure viewpoint. J. Phys. Chem. C **120**, 19923–19931 (2016). https://doi.org/10.1021/acs.jpcc.6b02393

52. Machado, D.F.S., et al.: Fully relativistic rovibrational energies and spectroscopic constants of the lowest X:(1)0+g, A':(1)2u, A:(1)1 u, B':(1)0-u and B:(1)0+u states of molecular chlorine. J. Mol. Model. **18**, 4343–4348 (2012). https://doi.org/10.1007/s00894-012-1429-9

53. Carvalho-Silva, V.H., Coutinho, N.D., Aquilanti, V.: Description of deviations from Arrhenius behavior in chemical kinetics and materials science. In: AIP Conference Proceedings, p. 20006. AIP Publishing (2016). https://doi.org/10.1063/1.4968632

54. Agreda, N.J.L.: Aquilanti-Mundim deformed Arrhenius model in solid-state reactions: theoretical evaluation using DSC experimental data. J. Therm. Anal. Calorim. **126**, 1175–1184 (2016). https://doi.org/10.1007/s10973-016-5566-8

55. Romagnoli, É.S., Borsato, D., Silva, L.R.C., Chendynski, L.T., Angilelli, K.G., Canesin, E.A.: Kinetic parameters of the oxidation reaction of commercial biodiesel with natural antioxidant additives. Ind. Crops Prod. (2018). https://doi.org/10.1016/j.indcrop.2018.08. 077

56. Carvalho-Silva, V.H., Coutinho, N.D., Aquilanti, V.: Temperature dependence of rate processes beyond arrhenius and eyring: activation and transitivity. Front. Chem. **7**, 380 (2019). https://doi.org/10.3389/fchem.2019.00380

Hypergeometric Polynomials, Hyperharmonic Discrete and Continuous Expansions: Evaluations, Interconnections, Extensions

Cecilia Coletti[1], Federico Palazzetti[2]([⊠]), Roger W. Anderson[3],
Vincenzo Aquilanti[2,4], Noelia Faginas-Lago[2], and Andrea Lombardi[2]

[1] Dipartimento di Farmacia, Università "G. D'Annunzio"
Chieti-Pescara, Chieti, Italy
[2] Dipartimento di Chimica, Biologia e Biotecnologie, Università di Perugia,
via Elce di Sotto 8, 06123 Perugia, Italy
{federico.palazzetti,noelia.faginaslago,
andrea.lombardi}@unipg.it
[3] Department of Chemistry, University of California,
Santa Cruz, CA 95064, USA
[4] Istituto di Struttura della Materia-Consiglio Nazionale delle Ricerche,
00016 Rome, Italy

Abstract. The important mathematical subject of special functions and orthogonal polynomials found in the last decades a systematization regarding those of hypergeometric type. The growth of these developments are due to interconnections with quantum angular momentum theory which is basic to that of spin-networks, of recent relevance in various branches of physics. Here we consider their power as providing expansion basis sets such as specifically are needed in chemistry to represents potential energy surfaces, the achievements being discussed and illustrated. A novel visualization of key members of the polynomial sets attributes a central role to the Kravchuk polynomials: its relationship with Wigner's rotation matrix elements are here emphasized and taken as exemplary for computational and analytical features. The sets are considered regarding progress on the formulation of a discretization technique, the hyperquantization, which allows to efficiently deal with physical problems where quantum mechanical operators act on continuous manifolds, to yield discrete grids suitable for computation of matrix elements without need of multidimensional integration.

Keywords: Quantum angular momentum · Spin networks · Hyperquantization

1 Introduction

A survey has been recently presented [1] on the connection between atomic and molecular orbitals to be used as basis sets in applied quantum chemistry and those advances in the mathematics of special functions and orthogonal polynomials, not commonly explicitly related in the numerous expositions of the quantum theory of angular momentum.

The original version of this chapter was revised: two authors have been added. The correction to this chapter is available at https://doi.org/10.1007/978-3-030-24311-1_41

S. Misra et al. (Eds.): ICCSA 2019, LNCS 11624, pp. 460–476, 2019.
https://doi.org/10.1007/978-3-030-24311-1_34

We restricted the list to nine functions, some defined on discrete grids and others spanning ranges of continuous variables. In discrete cases, the Sturm-Liouville theory of differential equations, to which Schrödinger equations belong, has its counterpart in the theory of difference equations, of recurrence relationships, of Jacobi (tridiagonal and symmetric) matrices.

Here we focus on features of these sets of orthogonal polynomials, as expansion basis sets. When properly normalized, they constitute archetypal complete sets for expanding, for example as far quantum chemistry is concerned, atomic orbitals, or in case of molecules, in terms of orthogonal polynomials centered in different space points: in general, even for molecular systems under the effect of fields where the possibility of expanding the fields themselves in the same sets of orthogonal polynomials at the end makes analytical the calculations of all the involved integrals turns out analytically advantageous and eventually also computationally.

The main mathematical ideas actually were developed also in connection with one of the pillars of theoretical physics: the quantum theory of angular momentum. In the quantum theory of angular momentum, the group theoretical aspects led to discrete sets of orthogonal objects, differently called vector coupling or recoupling coefficients, or, in equivalent language, $3j$, $6j$, ..., $3nj$ symbols of quantum angular momentum theory.

The connection between the two areas became clear in the Thirties when the one-century old Jacobi theory of orthogonal polynomials reached its maturity (see [1] and references therein). At that point it was clear that Jacobi polynomials were playing a leading role and all the rest of orthogonal polynomials, depending on a smaller number of parameters, could be arranged in a way that one could in essence solve all the problems in second order ordinary differential equations, which could be reconducted to the Gaussian hypergeometric series. Wigner established the connection between Jacobi polynomials and his reduced rotation matrix elements, so the road was open to discover discrete polynomials, such as the Meixner and in particular the Kravchuk set as simple connected by explicit duality operations.

In Fig. 1, we report the 3×3 matrix partial representation of the Askey scheme with duality relations and the asymptotic connection from discrete to continuous representations. Figure 2 gives visually an impression of the content of the paper. The double arrow shows the connection of the Kravchuk polynomials with Jacobi and Meixner that proceed toward continuous type polynomials toward Laguerre and Charlier polynomials, leading to the analytical solution of the Schrödinger equation for the hydrogen atom and on the other side discrete representations, toward the Hahn and Racah polynomials, related to the theory of angular momentum to $3j$ and $6j$ respectively.

Next section gives exemplary computational illustrations for the key Kravchuk polynomials and their discrete representations [2–11]. They are functions of two variables and span a square manifold, the screen: this two-dimensional approach gives interesting insights, being a natural extension to exhibit the role of these discrete functions as matrix elements. The screen has demonstrated to be versatile and applicable to various fields that go from the theory of angular momentum to the geometrical features of molecules and the four-bar linkage mechanism in kinematics.

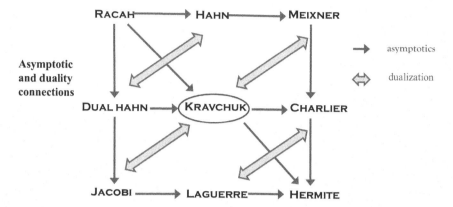

Fig. 1. The nine polynomial sets in the 3 × 3 matrix representation, adapted from [1], as a modification of a portion of the Askey scheme, emphasizing that dualization, namely exchange of role of polynomial degree and variable, appears as a reflection with respect to the main diagonal; asymptotic connections physically correspond to semiclassical limits.

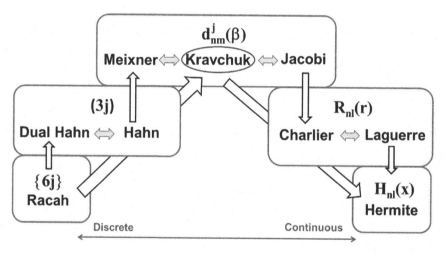

Fig. 2. The stepping stones of Fig. 1 consolidated as a bridge, where arrangement was given as a staircase, to be contrasted to the corresponding Fig. 1 in [1]. Details on the connections and emphasis of central role for the Kravchuk polynomial given in the text.

Section 3 summarizes the ingredients developed for quantum chemistry, hyperspherical harmonics [12–19] and Sturmian orbitals [20–29], applied to the methods of theoretical chemistry (see also [1]), and present conclusions.

In an Appendix we deal with use of expansions, both in continuous and in discrete sets: the sets of orthogonal polynomials [30–32] described in [1] are connected with the theory of angular momentum, specifically with the spin networks [3–5, 29, 33–45]. The hyperquantization algorithm [46–55], has been introduced to solve the reactive scattering Schrödinger equation. It employs a symmetric version of hyperspherical coordinates, and a discretization procedure based on the special properties of the Hahn orthogonal polynomials [56]. Connections to stereodynamics [57–59] and alignment are also reported [60–68]. Spherical and hyperspherical harmonics have been employed to expand analytical expressions of potential energy surfaces of systems. The method, initially applied to treat the case of atom (p orbital) – atom (s orbital), has been extended to systems of increasing complexity including singlet-states atoms and molecules such as atom – diatom, diatom – diatom, water – atom, water – diatom, and floppy-molecule – atom [69–84].

2 Kravchuk Polynomials: Features, Computational, Caustics, Asymptotics

Section 2 of this paper presents the quantitative connections between the Kravchuk polynomials ($d^j_{mm'}(\beta)$ functions) with the Dual Hahn polynomials (Wigner 3j symbols) and the Racah polynomials (Wigner 6j symbols). The qualitative relationships are shown on the left side of Fig. 2, and the resulting screens are naturally on a square grid. This section illustrates the exemplary case of Kravchuk polynomials (the equations in this first paragraph are taken from [85]); the orthogonality relation is

$$\sum_{x=0}^{N} \binom{N}{x} p^x (1-p)^{N-x} K_m(x;p,N) K_n(x;p,N) = \binom{N}{n}^{-1} \left(\frac{1-p}{p}\right)^n \delta_{mn}, \quad 0 \le p \le 1$$

The transformation [85]

$$U_{pN}(x,n) = \sqrt{\frac{p^x(1-p)^{N-x}}{x!(N-x)!}} K_n(x;p,N)$$

leads to the symmetric three-term recurrence relation

$$\varsigma r_+(x) U_{pN}(x+1,n) + \varsigma_0 r_0(x,N) U_{pN}(x,n) + \varsigma r_-(x) U_{pN}(x-1,n) = \varsigma_0 \lambda(n) U_{pN}(x,n)$$

where

$$r_-(x) = \sqrt{x(N-x+1)}, \quad r_+(x) = r_-(x+1) = \sqrt{(x+1)(N-x)}$$
$$r_0(x) = x(2p-1) - pN, \quad \lambda(n) = -n.$$

We solve the eigenvalue/eigenvector equation using double precision arithmetic. To assure the correct number of nodes and eigenvalue order we choose $\varsigma = \varsigma_0 = -1$. Figure 3 shows the screen for $|U_{pN}(x,n)|$, where $N = 201$ and $p = 0.25$.

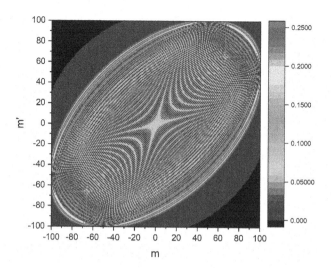

Fig. 3. Screen for Kravchuk polynomial, $U_{pN}(x, n)$, $j = 100$ and $p = 0.25$. The axes are labeled with m and m', but an alternative uses x and n with ranges 0 to N.

Nikiforov *et al.* [86] states in Eq. 5.1.27a (p. 236) that:

$$d_{mm'}^{j}(\beta) = (-1)^{\varphi} \frac{\sqrt{\rho(x)}}{d_n} K_n(x; p, N) = (-1)^{\varphi} U_{pN}(x, n)$$

with $\sin^2 \beta/2 = p$, $j = N/2$, $m = x - N/2$, and $m' = n - N/2$. The identity $\cos \beta = 1 - 2p$ is also useful. The equation indicates that $d_{mm'}^{j}(\beta)$ and $U_{pN}(x, n)$ are identical apart from a phase factor. We have independently calculated $d_{mm'}^{j}(\beta)$ for $j = 100$ and $\cos \beta = 0.5$ with multi-precision arithmetic, and the values of $|d_{mm'}^{j}(\beta)|$ and $|U_{pN}(x, n)|$ are identical with an absolute error less than 5×10^{-14}. With $\varsigma = \varsigma_0 = -1$ and a requirement that $K_n(x; p, N)$ is positive for $x = N$, all of the phases for $d_{mm'}^{j}(\beta)$ and $U_{pN}(x, n)$ are correct. We find that diagonalization of the tridiagonal matrix for $U_{pN}(x, n)$ is an accurate, fast method for calculation of many $d_{mm'}^{j}(\beta)$. For the computer used in this work the diagonalization method is thousands of times faster than the multiple arithmetic method. The caustics of $d_{mm'}^{j}(\beta)$ are determined by an ellipse given in [87] $j^2 \sin^2 \beta - m^2 - m'^2 + 2mm' \cos \beta = 0$. The ellipse touches the left boundary of the square at the point $(m, m') = (-j, -j \cos \beta)$. The right, bottom, and top boundaries are $(j, j\cos \beta)(-j\cos \beta, -j)(j\cos \beta, j)$. The caustics for $U_{pN}(x, n)$ are given by the same ellipse with the equivalencies for p, N, x, and n given above.

2.1   Representation of $d^j_{mm'}(\beta)$ with $6j$ Symbols. Caustics for $6j$ Symbols: $\begin{Bmatrix} a & b & x \\ c & d & y \end{Bmatrix}$

Setting $A = a + \frac{1}{2}$, $B = b + \frac{1}{2}$, $C = c + \frac{1}{2}$, $D = d + \frac{1}{2}$, $X = x + \frac{1}{2}$, $Y = y + 1/2$, we can calculate the ridges:

$$X^{*2} = \frac{\left[(B^2 - C^2)(D^2 - A^2) + J_t^2 Y^2 - Y^4\right]}{2Y^2},$$

$$Y^{*2} = \frac{\left[(A^2 - B^2)(C^2 - D^2) + J_t^2 X^2 - X^4\right]}{2X^2}$$

and $J_t^2 = A^2 + B^2 + C^2 + D^2$.

The maximum tetrahedron volume along the X* and Y* curves:

$$V_{max,X^*} = 2F(A,D,Y)F(B,C,Y)/3Y, \qquad V_{max,Y^*} = 2F(A,B,X)F(D,C,X)/3X$$

Then   the   caustic   becomes
$X_z^2 = X^{*2} \pm 12V_{max,X^*}/Y$ and $Y_z^2 = Y^{*2} \pm 12V_{max,Y^*}/X$.

To have $6j$ coefficients in Canonical order there must be some restrains on a, b, c and d. Then $N = 2a + 1$ and k, m, and n are non-negative integers.

$$\begin{Bmatrix} a & b & x \\ c & d & y \end{Bmatrix} = \begin{Bmatrix} a & a + \frac{n}{2} & x \\ a + \frac{|m-n|}{2} + k & a + \frac{m}{2} & y \end{Bmatrix} \quad 0 \le k \le m + n - |m - n|,$$

$$n/2 \le x \le 2a + n/2, \; m/2 \le y \le 2a + m/2$$

We find the $6j$ symbols that correspond to $d^j_{mm'}$ functions by investigating the caustic curves for both $6j$ and $d^j_{mm'}$. For the $6j$ caustics we have:

Consider $Y^{*2} = \left[(A^2 - B^2)(C^2 - D^2) + J_t^2 X^2 - X^4\right]/2X^2$ which becomes for $B = D$: $Y^{*2} = \left[(A^2 - B^2)(C^2 - B^2) + J_t^2 X^2 - X^4\right]/2X^2$. We have $X = B - A$ the bottom of the screen, so $Y^{*2} = [A^2 B - AB^2 - B^3 + AC^2]/[A - B]$.

The location of the gate on the west side corresponding to $X = B - A$ is given by $y = \sqrt{[A^2 B - AB^2 - B^3 + AC^2]/[A - B]} - (B - A)$. We put this expression into a more tractable form by introducing: $r = A/B$. Since A will be much smaller than B, r is much less than unity. Keeping terms of first order in r we have: $Y^* \approx 2A(1 - C^2/4B^2)$ and from the limitations for Canonical form we have $a \le c \le 2(b - a)$. Comparing the gate position for $d^j_{mm'}$, we see that the parameter, p, in the Kravchuk polynomials is $p = 1 - \frac{C^2}{4B^2}$, $\sin^2 \frac{\beta}{2} = 1 - \frac{C^2}{4B^2}$, $\cos \frac{\beta}{2} = \frac{C}{2B}$. Figure 4a shows the caustic curves for $c = \sqrt{3} \times 10^8$, and $b = 10^8$. Fig. 4b and c show caustics for $c = 1000000$ and $c = 99000000$.

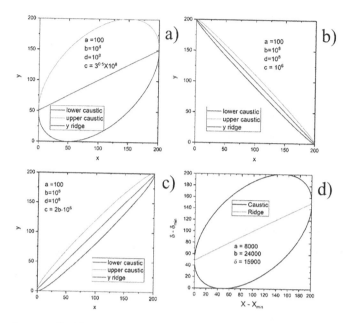

Fig. 4. Caustic curves for (a) $p = 0.25$; (b) $p = 0.999975$; (c) $p = 0.009975$; (d) $3j$ approximation to d function with $p = 0.25$

2.2   Representation of $d^j_{mm'}(\beta)$ with 3j Symbols 3j Caustics

$$\text{for } \begin{pmatrix} a & b & x \\ \sigma+\delta & \sigma-\delta & -2\sigma \end{pmatrix}$$

Now we consider correspondence between $3j$ symbols and d functions. Neglecting the difference between A, B, X and a, b, x; where $A = a + \frac{1}{2}$, $B = b + \frac{1}{2}$, and $X = x + \frac{1}{2}$ we have:

Ridges:

$$\delta^*(x) = \frac{\sigma(a^2 - b^2)}{x^2}, \qquad x^*(\delta) = \sqrt{a^2 + b^2 + 2(\sigma^2 - \delta^2)}$$

$$max(|a - b|, |2\sigma|) \leq x \leq a+b,$$

$$\max(-a - \sigma, -b+\sigma) \leq \delta \leq \min(a - \sigma, b+\sigma)$$

$$\delta = (\alpha - \beta)/2, \qquad \sigma = -\gamma/2 = (\alpha + \beta)/2$$

Upper and lower caustics are given by

$$\delta_\pm(x) = \delta^*(x) \pm \frac{2F(a,b,x)\sqrt{x^2 - 4\sigma^2}}{x^2},$$

Where

$$F(a,b,x) = \sqrt{(a+b+x)(-a+b+x)(a-b+x)(a+b-x)}/4$$

In our analysis, we will have large values for a, b, x and σ. We note that on the right $x_{max} = a + b$ and on the left side of the screen that $x_{min} = |2\sigma|$. Hence the number of intervals, n, is given by $n = x_{max} - x_{min} = a + b - |2\sigma|$, or $|\sigma| = (a+b-n)/2$. We see that n is much smaller than a, b, x, and σ. We also assume that b is greater than a, or that $b = ay$ where $y \geq 1$.

To proceed further we must consider whether σ is positive or negative. When s is positive, the bottom of the screen corresponds to $\delta_{min} = -b + \sigma$ and the top of the screen corresponds to $\delta_{max} = a - \sigma$. (Note that $n = \delta_{max} - \delta_{min}$, so the screen is square.). Now we relate y and p, and we see on the right side of the screen that:

$$\delta^*(x_{max}) - \delta_{min} = \sigma(a^2 - b^2)/(a+b)^2 + b - \sigma = (1-p)n$$
$$= \sigma(1-y)/(1+y) + ay - \sigma = (1-p)n$$

After substitution with $|\sigma| = (a+b-n)/2$, we can easily find that $y = \frac{1-p}{p}$ for $0 \leq p \leq 1/2$. Now we can calculate

$$\delta^*(x_{min}) - \delta_{min} = \sigma(a^2 - b^2)/(2\sigma)^2 + b - \sigma = p'n$$
$$= a^2(1-y^2)/(2\sigma) + ay - \sigma = p'n$$

We can now prove that $p' \to p$ for large a. Solving the last equation for p', we find that $p' = \frac{(2a-n)p}{2n-2np} \approx p(1 + \frac{n}{2a} + \cdots)$. For large a, $p' \to p$.

Figure 4d shows a *3j* approximation to d for $p = \frac{1}{4}$. The figure is drawn with calculations based on A, B, and X. Hence the small difference with expected results from the simplified theory in this paper.

To obtain *3j* approximations to d functions with $1/2 < p \leq 1$, we must consider negative σ. Now $\delta_{min} = -a - \sigma$, and $\delta_{max} = b + \sigma$. Repeating the above derivation, we find that $y = p/(1-p)$ and $p' \to p$.

3 Summarizing and Concluding Remarks

In a recent paper [1] we provided an overview from an orthogonal polynomial set perspective on the quantum mechanics of hydrogen-like atom, augmented by the Fock's projection (1935) initiating use of hyperspherical harmonics as orbitals for the solution of atomic and molecular structure problems. Only recently the search started on exploiting unique properties and computational advantages leading to the development of Sturmian basis sets (see also [22]) which are essentially orthogonal polynomials of the classical series, and also to highlight how the orbitals in the reciprocal (momentum) space are hyperspherical harmonics. Not only they are continuous sets of hypergeometric polynomials, but also the connections between different representations (or of different systems of separable coordinates) can be all written as orthogonal polynomials of discrete type, of the Hahn and Racah series. To complete picture, we found it useful to generalize to the multidimensional hydrogenic Coulomb orbitals in dimensions higher than physical. They are also useful in quantum cosmology, quantum field theory, quantum information science, not to mention that the dimensional dependence of the entropic properties for the stationary states of the multidimensional quantum systems is extensively studied for the large content in quantum information not available from the standard representation [33–36].

Sturmian basis sets in configuration space can be obtained as a product of Laguerre polynomials (one of our nine players) and a multidimensional hyperspherical harmonic, or, according to the chosen coordinate system, as the product of two Laguerre polynomials (as in parabolic coordinates) and a lower dimensional hyperspherical harmonic. These hyperspherical harmonics can, in turn, in the most general case, be written as the set of Jacobi polynomials (another player in our scheme), and, in case of special values of the parameters down to Gegenbauer, or further to Legendre, polynomials, or even to the Wigner d - matrix (*e.g.* occurring in the four dimensional symmetric harmonics on the sphere S^3).

When we move to the momentum space perspective, Coulomb Sturmian basis sets can be Fourier transformed to hyperspherical harmonics (or Jacobi polynomials), for which it is easy to explicitly work out the superposition coefficients allowing the passage from one coordinate system to another (or, alternatively, from one spatial quantization scheme to a different one, *i.e.* to different sets of quantum numbers). Indeed, such coefficients are multidimensional integrals over a product of continuous orthogonal polynomials, which, in the most general case, corresponds to discrete Racah polynomials (the upper level of our scheme), or generalized $6j$ coefficients. Again, upon simplification down to lower dimensionality, these coefficients asymptotically reduce to either Hahn (or dual Hahn) discrete polynomial sets, that are essentially Clebsch-Gordan or $3j$ coefficients, or to the Wigner d rotation matrices starting as our cornerstone in the conceptual scheme that we have come to describe as the bridge of Fig. 2.

Our survey of current advances in quantum chemistry, especially as far as the expansion of atomic and molecular orbitals is concerned as a function of mathematically and physically motivated basis sets, involved combined observations of relationships of this area with other related ones. In particular, from the mathematical point of view, it is expedient to present the important connections as far as concerning the widely investigated area of recent mathematics: they involve special functions and orthogonal polynomials, in turn related to the theory of representation of groups, specifically continuous groups, and therefore the Lie theory.

In our current work and in this paper, we have tried to provide a picture of what is our appreciation of this aspect. The presentation started with an adaptation of the current general scheme for orthogonal polynomials of hypergeometrical type as a ladder that goes from Hermite up to Racah polynomials, immediately bringing inside further connections with the theory of angular momentum: in turn, this feature has been more and more intimately connected to the area of investigation of spin-networks. Individuating the main characters of the play were restricted to nine orthogonal polynomial sets of discrete variable and arranging them as a matrix is a compact way of putting the pieces of the mosaic into a unified scheme.

What we analyzed in this paper is limited to some aspects, essentially focused on the leading role of the polynomial of Kravchuk type and its equivalent in quantum mechanical language, the d-matrix.

A further survey will also consider well known important features: however still needing compactness. For instance, the explicit expression of the objects as truncated converging terminating series, needing some care for computation, are put into reference within the theory of hypergeometric generalized series. Regarding computation, the direct sums often present calculation difficulties, often dealt with, in modern research, by using the property that all these functions, being orthogonal polynomials, obey recurrence relationships. These relationships offer an important computational tool: they are seen to be also in connection with the fact that they are always in the scheme associated by duality with difference equation, or, in the case of the lower steps of the ladder, with differential equations of Schrödinger type, the fundamental tool in quantum theory.

The concept of special duality that involves the underlying theory is often usefully represented as a bidimensional plot, that we define as the screen that has been illustrated elsewhere for the crucial member of the set, the Kravchuk polynomials. The centrality of this function was the theme of the paper and it involved as mirror modification of the sequences in the Askey scheme, interchanging position with the Jacobi polynomial.

On the other hand the scheme has extremely important amplifications when including passage from spherical to elliptic or parabolic manifolds. The literature on q-hypergeometrical polynomials is a subject of wide interest in modern mathematics, but they are less developed as tools for expansion basis sets in quantum mechanics. Some steps were undertaken recently [4].

Appendix: Discrete and Continuous Harmonic Expansions of Intermolecular Interaction

Experiments carried out by the Stern-Gerlach magnet in the early 1990s, shown that under supersonic conditions seeded O_2 would undergo variation in speed and redistribution of the internal states (for the case of oxygen rotational and vibrational cooling), producing as additional effect the molecular alignment, *i.e.* the possibility of forcing the molecule to rotate in a preferential plane. Alignment was initially induced to various diatomic molecules and linear hydrocarbons, then extended to disk-shaped molecules like benzene. Current developments are attempting to exploit the helicoidal motion of chiral molecules. The technique determined significant advances in the area of the molecular beam scattering, especially for what concerns the phenomenology of anisotropies related to van der Waals interactions.

A conceptually important advance of the asymptotic (semiclassical) discretization of continuous function exemplified in this work lead to hyperquantization algorithms.

They are based on the observation that discrete analogues of hyperspherical harmonics can be defined by means of the 3nj symbols. The method was initially employed to solve the Schrödinger equation for the prototypical reaction F + H$_2$ and generalized to include other triatomic systems and various quantum effects. Exact representations have been also employed to describe steric effects in quantum mechanics, such as the interpretation of reactive scattering resonances. Tools refined for the quantum mechanical treatment of few body systems have been employed to give a reformulation of the classical mechanics protocol, to be applied in many-body problems characterizing atomic and molecular clusters.

More conventionally, spherical and hyperspherical harmonics are implemented in quantum chemical calculations to compute energy as a function of a properly defined distance and of one or more angles, according to the complexity of the system. This approach is inspired by the open-shell – closed-shell atom–atom interactions, where the angle θ defines a minimal model for collinear ($\theta = 0$) and perpendicular ($\theta = \pi/2$) configurations and had been initially to the atom – diatom case [60, 69, 88]. The method consists in an exact transformation of quantum chemical (or experimental) input data related to a minimum set of configurations, the "leading configurations", whose choice relies upon geometrical and physical characteristics of the system, by a multipolar expansion [89].

Extension of the simplest case, the abovementioned triatomic system, have been done for four- and five- body problems. For example, systems formed by two diatomic molecules can be described by two Jacobi vectors lying along the chemical bonds and a third vector which joins the centers-of-mass of the two molecules. Hyperspherical harmonics have also been applied to describe interactions of floppy molecules, characterized by having an active torsional motion, as a prototype of enantiomeric change in chiral molecules [71, 73].

References

1. Coletti, C., Aquilanti, V., Palazzetti, F.: Hypergeometric orthogonal polynomials as expansion basis sets for atomic and molecular orbitals: the Jacobi ladder. Adv. Quantum Chem. https://doi.org/10.1016/bs.aiq.2019.05.002
2. Anderson, R.W., Aquilanti, V., Cavalli, S., Grossi, G.: Stereodirected discrete bases in hindered rotor problems: atom-diatom and pendular states. J. Phys. Chem. **97**, 2443–2452 (1993). https://doi.org/10.1021/j100112a053
3. Anderson, R.W., Aquilanti, V.: The discrete representation correspondence between quantum and classical spatial distributions of angular momentum vectors. J. Chem. Phys. **124**, 214104 (9 p.) (2006)
4. Anderson, R.W., Aquilanti, V., da S. Ferreira, C.: Exact computation and large angular momentum asymptotics of 3nj symbols: semiclassical disentangling of spin networks. J. Chem. Phys. **129**, 161101 (5 p.) (2008)
5. Anderson, R.W., Aquilanti, V., Marzuoli, A.: 3nj morphogenesis and semiclassical disentangling. J. Phys. Chem. A **113**, 15106–15117 (2009). https://doi.org/10.1021/jp905212a

6. Aquilanti, V., Caglioti, C., Lombardi, A., Maciel, Glauciete S., Palazzetti, F.: Screens for displaying chirality changing mechanisms of a series of peroxides and persulfides from conformational structures computed by quantum chemistry. In: Gervasi, O., et al. (eds.) ICCSA 2017. LNCS, vol. 10408, pp. 354–368. Springer, Cham (2017). https://doi.org/10.1007/978-3-319-62404-4_26

7. Caglioti, C., Santos, R.F.D., Aquilanti, V., Lombardi, A., Palazzetti, F.: Screen mapping of structural and electric properties, chirality changing rates and racemization times of chiral peroxides and persulfides. In: AIP Conference Proceedings, vol. 2040, p. 020021 (2018). https://doi.org/10.1063/1.5079063

8. Aquilanti, V., et al.: Quadrilaterals on the square screen of their diagonals: Regge symmetries of quantum mechanical spin networks and Grashof classical mechanisms of four-bar linkages. Rend. Lincei 30, 67–81 (2019). https://doi.org/10.1007/s12210-019-00776-x

9. Anderson, R.W., Aquilanti, V., Bitencourt, A.C.P., Marinelli, D., Ragni, M.: The screen representation of spin networks: 2D recurrence, eigenvalue equation for 6j symbols, geometric interpretation and Hamiltonian dynamics. In: Murgante, B., et al. (eds.) ICCSA 2013. LNCS, vol. 7972, pp. 46–59. Springer, Heidelberg (2013). https://doi.org/10.1007/978-3-642-39643-4_4

10. Bitencourt, A.C.P., Ragni, M., Littlejohn, R.G., Anderson, R., Aquilanti, V.: The screen representation of vector coupling coefficients or Wigner 3j symbols: exact computation and illustration of the asymptotic behavior. In: Murgante, B., et al. (eds.) ICCSA 2014. LNCS, vol. 8579, pp. 468–481. Springer, Cham (2014). https://doi.org/10.1007/978-3-319-09144-0_32

11. Aquilanti, V., et al.: The astrochemical observatory: computational and theoretical focus on molecular chirality changing torsions around O - O and S - S bonds. In: AIP Conference Proceedings, vol. 1906, p. 030010 (2017). https://doi.org/10.1063/1.5012289

12. Aquilanti, V., Cavalli, S.: Coordinates for molecular dynamics: orthogonal local systems. J. Chem. Phys. 85, 1355–1361 (1986). https://doi.org/10.1063/1.451223

13. Aquilanti, V., Cavalli, S., Grossi, G.: Hyperspherical coordinates for molecular dynamics by the method of trees and the mapping of potential energy surfaces for triatomic systems. J. Chem. Phys. 85, 1362–1375 (1986). https://doi.org/10.1063/1.451224

14. Aquilanti, V., Capecchi, G., Cavalli, S.: Hyperspherical coordinates for chemical reaction dynamics. Adv. Quantum Chem. 36, 341–363 (2000). https://doi.org/10.1016/S0065-3276(08)60491-8

15. Aquilanti, V., Tonzani, S.: Three-body problem in quantum mechanics: hyperspherical elliptic coordinates and harmonic basis sets. J. Chem. Phys. 120, 4066–4073 (2004). https://doi.org/10.1063/1.1644098

16. Aquilanti, V., Ascenzi, D., Fedeli, R., Pirani, F., Cappelletti, D.: Molecular beam scattering of nitrogen molecules in supersonic seeded beams: a probe of rotational alignment. J. Phys. Chem. A 101, 7648–7656 (2002). https://doi.org/10.1021/jp971237t

17. Aquilanti, V., Lombardi, A., Littlejohn, R.G.: Hyperspherical harmonics for polyatomic systems: basis set for collective motions. Theoret. Chem. Acc. 111, 400–406 (2004). https://doi.org/10.1007/s00214-003-0526-3

18. Aquilanti, V., Lombardi, A., Sevryuk, M.B.: Phase-space invariants for aggregates of particles: hyperangular momenta and partitions of the classical kinetic energy. J. Chem. Phys. 121, 5579 (2004). https://doi.org/10.1063/1.1785785

19. Sevryuk, M.B., Lombardi, A., Aquilanti, V.: Hyperangular momenta and energy partitions in multidimensional many-particle classical mechanics: the invariance approach to cluster dynamics. Phys. Rev. A - At. Mol. Opt. Phys. 72, 033201 (2005). https://doi.org/10.1103/PhysRevA.72.033201

20. Aquilanti, V., Cavalli, S., Coletti, C., Grossi, G.: Alternative Sturmian bases and momentum space orbitals: an application to the hydrogen molecular ion. Chem. Phys. **209**, 405–419 (1996). https://doi.org/10.1016/0301-0104(96)00162-0

21. Aquilanti, V., Cavalli, S., Coletti, C.: The d-dimensional hydrogen atom: hyperspherical harmonics as momentum space orbitals and alternative Sturmian basis sets. Chem. Phys. **214**, 1–13 (1997). https://doi.org/10.1016/S0301-0104(96)00310-2

22. Aquilanti, V., Capecchi, G.: Regular article Harmonic analysis and discrete polynomials. From semiclassical angular momentum theory to the hyperquantization algorithm. Theoret. Chem. Acc. **104**, 183–188 (2000). https://doi.org/10.1007/s002140000148

23. Aquilanti, V., Cavalli, S., Coletti, C., Di Domenico, D., Grossi, G.: Hyperspherical harmonics as Sturmian orbitals in momentum space: a systematic approach to the few-body Coulomb problem. Int. Rev. Phys. Chem. **20**, 673–709 (2010). https://doi.org/10.1080/01442350110075926

24. Aquilanti, V., Caligiana, A., Cavalli, S.: Hydrogenic elliptic orbitals. Coulomb Sturmian sets, and recoupling coefficients among alternative bases. Int. J. Quantum Chem. **92**, 99–117 (2003)

25. Aquilanti, V., Caligiana, A.: Sturmian approach to one-electron many-center system: integrals and iteration schemes. Chem. Phys. Lett. **366**, 157–164 (2002)

26. Aquilanti, V., Caligiana, A., Cavalli, S., Coletti, C.: Hydrogen orbitals in momentum space and hyperspherical harmonics: elliptic Sturmian basis sets. Int. J. Quantum Chem. **92**, 212–228 (2003)

27. Calderini, D., Cavalli, S., Coletti, C., Grossi, G., Aquilanti, V.: Hydrogenoid orbitals revisited: from Slater orbitals to Coulomb Sturmians. J. Chem. Sci. **124**, 187–192 (2012). https://doi.org/10.1007/s12039-012-0215-7

28. Coletti, C., Calderini, D., Aquilanti, V.: D-dimensional Kepler-Coulomb Sturmians and hyperspherical harmonics as complete orthonormal atomic and molecular orbitals. Adv. Quantum Chem. **67**, 73–127 (2013). https://doi.org/10.1016/B978-0-12-411544-6.00005-4

29. Calderini, D., Coletti, C., Grossi, G., Aquilanti, V.: Continuous and discrete algorithms in quantum chemistry: polynomial sets, spin networks and Sturmian orbitals. In: Murgante, B., et al. (eds.) ICCSA 2013. LNCS, vol. 7972, pp. 32–45. Springer, Heidelberg (2013). https://doi.org/10.1007/978-3-642-39643-4_3

30. Aquilanti, V., Cavalli, S., Coletti, C.: Angular and hyperangular momentum recoupling, harmonic superposition and Racah polynomials: a recursive algorithm. Chem. Phys. Lett. **344**, 587–600 (2001)

31. Aquilanti, V., Coletti, C.: 3nj-symbols and harmonic superposition coefficients: an icosahedral abacus. Chem. Phys. Lett. **344**, 601–611 (2001). https://doi.org/10.1016/S0009-2614(01)00757-6

32. De Fazio, D., Cavalli, S., Aquilanti, V.: Orthogonal polynomials of a discrete variable as expansion basis sets in quantum mechanics the hyperquantization algorithm. Int. J. Quantum Chem. **93**, 91–111 (2003)

33. Aquilanti, V., Marinelli, D., Marzuoli, A.: Symmetric coupling of angular momenta, quadratic algebras and discrete polynomials. J. Phys: Conf. Ser. **482**, 012001 (2014). https://doi.org/10.1088/1742-6596/482/1/012001

34. Dos Santos, R.F., et al.: Couplings and recouplings of four angular momenta: alternative 9j symbols and spin addition diagrams. J. Mol. Model. **23**, 147 (2017). https://doi.org/10.1007/s00894-017-3320-1

35. Arruda, M.S., Santos, R.F., Marinelli, D., Aquilanti, V.: Spin-coupling diagrams and incidence geometry: a note on combinatorial and quantum-computational aspects. In: Gervasi, O., et al. (eds.) ICCSA 2016. LNCS, vol. 9786, pp. 431–442. Springer, Cham (2016). https://doi.org/10.1007/978-3-319-42085-1_33

36. Dos Santos, R.F., et al.: Quantum angular momentum, projective geometry and the networks of seven and ten spins: Fano, Desargues and alternative incidence configurations. J. Mol. Spectrosc. **337**, 153–162 (2017). https://doi.org/10.1016/j.jms.2017.05.005

37. Aquilanti, V., Marzuoli, A.: Projective Ponzano-Regge spin networks and their symmetries. J. Phys: Conf. Ser. **965**, 012005 (2018). https://doi.org/10.1088/1742-6596/965/1/012005

38. Coletti, C., Dos Santos, R.F., Arruda, M.S., Bitencourt, A.C.P., Ragni, M., Aquilanti, V.: Spin networks and Sturmian orbitals: orthogonal complete polynomial sets in molecular quantum mechanics. In: AIP Conference Proceedings, vol. 1906, p. 030013 (2017). https://doi.org/10.1063/1.5012292

39. Anderson, R.W., Aquilanti, V.: Spherical and hyperbolic spin networks: the q-extensions of Wigner-Racah $6j$ coefficients and general orthogonal discrete basis sets in applied quantum mechanics. In: Gervasi, O., et al. (eds.) ICCSA 2017. LNCS, vol. 10408, pp. 338–353. Springer, Cham (2017). https://doi.org/10.1007/978-3-319-62404-4_25

40. Aquilanti, V., Haggard, H.M., Littlejohn, R.G., Yu, L.: Semiclassical analysis of Wigner 3 j-symbol. J. Phys. A **40**, 5637–5674 (2007)

41. Aquilanti, V., Bitencourt, A.C.P., da S. Ferreira, C., Marzuoli, A., Ragni, M.: Quantum and semiclassical spin networks: from atomic and molecular physics to quantum computing and gravity. Phys. Scr. **78**, 058103 (2008)

42. Aquilanti, V., Bitencourt, A.C.P., da S. Ferreira, C., Marzuoli, A., Ragni, M.: Combinatorics of angular momentum recoupling theory: spin networks, their asymptotics and applications. Theoret. Chem. Acc. **123**, 237 (2009)

43. Aquilanti, V., Haggard, H.M., Hedeman, A., Jeevangee, N., Littlejohn, R., Yu, L.: Semiclassical mechanics of the Wigner 6j-symbol. J. Phys. A **45**, 065209 (2012)

44. Bitencourt, A.C.P., Marzuoli, A., Ragni, M., Anderson, R.W., Aquilanti, V.: Exact and asymptotic computations of elementary spin networks: classification of the quantum–classical boundaries. In: Murgante, B., et al. (eds.) ICCSA 2012. LNCS, vol. 7333, pp. 723–737. Springer, Heidelberg (2012). https://doi.org/10.1007/978-3-642-31125-3_54

45. Aquilanti, V., Marinelli, D., Marzuoli, A.: Hamiltonian dynamics of a quantum of space: hidden symmetries and spectrum of the volume operator, and discrete orthogonal polynomials. J. Phys. A Math. Theor. **46** (2013). https://doi.org/10.1088/1751-8113/46/17/175303

46. Aquilanti, V., Grossi, G.: Discrete representations by artificial quantization in the quantum mechanics of anisotropic interactions. Lett. Al Nuovo Cimento Ser. 2(42), 157–162 (1985). https://doi.org/10.1007/BF02739563

47. Aquilanti, V., Cavalli, S., Grossi, G.: Discrete analogs of spherical harmonics and their use in quantum mechanics: the hyperquantization algorithm. Theoret. Chim. Acta **79**, 283–296 (1991). https://doi.org/10.1007/BF01113697

48. Aquilanti, V., Cavalli, S., De Fazio, D.: Hyperquantization algorithm. I. Theory for triatomic systems. J. Chem. Phys. **109**, 3792–3804 (1998)

49. Aquilanti, V., et al.: Hyperquantization algorithm. II. Implementation for the F + H_2 reaction dynamics including open-shell and spin-orbit interactions. J. Chem. Phys. **109**, 3805–3818 (1998). https://doi.org/10.1063/1.476980

50. Aquilanti, V., Cavalli, S., De Fazio, D., Volpi, A., Aguilar, A.: Probabilities for the F + H = HF + H reaction by the hyperquantization algorithm: alternative sequential diagonalization schemes. The Hamiltonian matrix. Phys. Chem. Chem. Phys. **1**, 1091–1098 (1999)

51. Aquilanti, V., et al.: Exact reaction dynamics by the hyperquantization algorithm: integral and differential cross sections for F + H_2, including long-range and spin – orbit effects. **4**, 401–415 (2002). https://doi.org/10.1039/b107239k

52. Aquilanti, V., Cavalli, S., De Fazio, D., Volpi, A., Aguilar, A., Lucas, J.M.: Benchmark rate constants by the hyperquantization algorithm. The F + H$_2$ reaction for various potential energy surfaces: features of the entrance channel and of the transition state, and low temperature reactivity. Chem. Phys. **308**, 237–253 (2005). https://doi.org/10.1016/j.chemphys.2004.03.027

53. Aquilanti, V., Cavalli, S., De Fazio, D., Simone, A., Tscherbul, T.V.: Direct evaluation of the lifetime matrix by the hyperquantization algorithm: narrow resonances in the reaction dynamics and their splitting for nonzero angular momentum. J. Chem. Phys. **123**, 054314 (2005). https://doi.org/10.1063/1.1988311

54. Aquilanti, V., Cavalli, S., Simoni, A., Aguilar, A., Lucas, J.M., De Fazio, D.: Lifetime of reactive scattering resonances: Q-matrix analysis and angular momentum dependence for the F + H$_2$ reaction by the hyperquantization algorithm. J. Chem. Phys. **121**, 11675–11690 (2004). https://doi.org/10.1063/1.1814096

55. Aquilanti, V., Cavalli, S., De Fazio, D., Volpi, A.: Theory of electronically nonadiabatic reactions: rotational, coriolis, spin – orbit couplings and the hyperquantization algorithm. Int. J. Quantum Chem. **85**, 368–381 (2001)

56. Aquilanti, V., Cavalli, S., De Fazio, D.: Angular and hyperangular momentum coupling coefficients as Hahn polynomials. J. Phys. Chem. **99**, 15694–15698 (1995)

57. Littlejohn, R.G., Mitchell, K.A., Reinsch, M., Aquilanti, V., Cavalli, S.: Internal spaces, kinematic rotations, and body frames for four-atom systems. Phys. Rev. A - At. Mol. Opt. Phys. **58**, 3718–3738 (1998). https://doi.org/10.1103/PhysRevA.58.3718

58. Alvarino, J.M.M., et al.: Stereodynamics from the stereodirected representation of the exact quantum S matrix: the Li + HF = LiF + H reaction. J. Phys. Chem. A **102**, 9638–9644 (1998)

59. Aldegunde, J., Alvariño, J.M., De Fazio, D., Cavalli, S., Grossi, G., Aquilanti, V.: Quantum stereodynamics of the F + H$_2$ → HF + H reaction by the stereodirected S-matrix approach. Chem. Phys. **301**, 251–259 (2004). https://doi.org/10.1016/j.chemphys.2004.02.002

60. Aquilanti, V., Liuti, G., Pirani, F., Vecchiocattivi, F.: Orientational and spin-orbital dependence of interatomic forces. J. Chem. Soc. Faraday Trans. 2 Mol. Chem. Phys. **85**, 955–964 (1989). https://doi.org/10.1039/F29898500955

61. Kasai, T., et al.: Directions of chemical change: experimental characterization of the stereodynamics of photodissociation and reactive processes. Phys. Chem. Chem. Phys. **16**, 9776–9790 (2014). https://doi.org/10.1039/c4cp00464g

62. Lombardi, A., Palazzetti, F., Aquilanti, V., Grossi, G.: Collisions of chiral molecules theoretical aspects and experiments. In: AIP Conference Proceedings, vol. 2040, p. 020020 (2018). https://doi.org/10.1063/1.5079062

63. Lombardi, A., Palazzetti, F.: Chirality in molecular collision dynamics. J. Phys.: Condens. Matter **30**, 063003 (2018). https://doi.org/10.1088/1361-648X/aaa1c8

64. Albernaz, A.F., Barreto, P.R.P., Aquilanti, V., Lombardi, A., Palazzetti, F., Pirani, F.: The astrochemical observatory: the interaction between helium and the chiral molecule propylene oxide. In: AIP Conference Proceedings, vol. 2040, p. 020018 (2018). https://doi.org/10.1063/1.5079060

65. Lombardi, A., Palazzetti, F., Aquilanti, V., Pirani, F., Casavecchia, P.: The astrochemical observatory: experimental and computational focus on the chiral molecule propylene oxide as a case study. In: Gervasi, O., et al. (eds.) ICCSA 2017. LNCS, vol. 10408, pp. 267–280. Springer, Cham (2017). https://doi.org/10.1007/978-3-319-62404-4_20

66. Palazzetti, F., Maciel, G.S., Lombardi, A., Grossi, G., Aquilanti, V.: The astrochemical observatory: molecules in the laboratory and in the cosmos. J. Chin. Chem. Soc. **59** (2012). https://doi.org/10.1002/jccs.201200242

67. Che, D.-C., Kanda, K., Palazzetti, F., Aquilanti, V., Kasai, T.: Electrostatic hexapole state-selection of the asymmetric-top molecule propylene oxide: rotational and orientational distributions. Chem. Phys. **399**, 180–192 (2012). https://doi.org/10.1016/j.chemphys.2011.11.020

68. Che, D.-C., Palazzetti, F., Okuno, Y., Aquilanti, V., Kasai, T.: Electrostatic hexapole state-selection of the asymmetric-top molecule propylene oxide. J. Phys. Chem. A **114**, 3280–3286 (2010). https://doi.org/10.1021/jp909553t

69. Aquilanti, V., Beneventi, L., Grossi, G., Vecchiocattivi, F.: Coupling schemes for atom-diatom interactions and an adiabatic decoupling treatment of rotational temperature effects on glory scattering. J. Chem. Phys. **89**, 751–761 (1988). https://doi.org/10.1063/1.455198

70. Barreto, P.R.P., Albernaz, A.F., Palazzetti, F., Lombardi, A., Grossi, G., Aquilanti, V.: Hyperspherical representation of potential energy surfaces: intermolecular interactions in tetra-atomic and penta-atomic systems. Phys. Scr. **84**, 28111 (2011). https://doi.org/10.1088/0031-8949/84/02/028111

71. Barreto, P.R.P., Vilela, A.F.A., Lombardi, A., Maciel, G.S., Palazzetti, F., Aquilanti, V.: The hydrogen peroxide-rare gas systems: quantum chemical calculations and hyperspherical harmonic representation of the potential energy surface for atom-floppy molecule interactions. J. Phys. Chem. A **111**, 12754–12762 (2007). https://doi.org/10.1021/jp076268v

72. Maciel, G.S., Barreto, P.R.P., Palazzetti, F., Lombardi, A., Aquilanti, V.: A quantum chemical study of H_2S_2: intramolecular torsional mode and intermolecular interactions with rare gases. J. Chem. Phys. **129**, 164302 (2008). https://doi.org/10.1063/1.2994732

73. Barreto, P.R.P., Palazzetti, F., Grossi, G., Lombardi, A., Maciel, G.S., Vilela, A.F.A.: Range and strength of intermolecular forces for van der Waals complexes of the type H_2X_n-Rg, with X = O, S and n = 1, 2. Int. J. Quantum Chem. **110**, 777–786 (2010). https://doi.org/10.1002/qua.22127

74. Lombardi, A., Palazzetti, F., Maciel, G.S., Aquilanti, V., Sevryuk, M.B.: Simulation of oriented collision dynamics of simple chiral molecules. Int. J. Quantum Chem. **111**, 1651–1658 (2011). https://doi.org/10.1002/qua.22816

75. Lombardi, A., Palazzetti, F., Peroncelli, L., Grossi, G., Aquilanti, V., Sevryuk, M.B.: Few-body quantum and many-body classical hyperspherical approaches to reactions and to cluster dynamics. Theoret. Chem. Acc **117**, 709–721 (2007). https://doi.org/10.1007/s00214-006-0195-0

76. Lombardi, A., Palazzetti, F., Grossi, G., Aquilanti, V., Castro Palacio, J.C., Rubayo Soneira, J.: Hyperspherical and related views of the dynamics of nanoclusters. Phys. Scr. **80**, 048103 (2009). https://doi.org/10.1088/0031-8949/80/04/048103

77. Lombardi, A., et al.: Spherical and hyperspherical harmonics representation of van der Waals aggregates. In: AIP Conference Proceedings, vol. 1790, pp. 020005 (2016). https://doi.org/10.1063/1.4968631

78. Aquilanti, V., Bartolomei, M., Cappelletti, D., Carmona-Novillo, E., Pirani, F.: The N_2–N_2 system: an experimental potential energy surface and calculated rotovibrational levels of the molecular nitrogen dimer. J. Chem. Phys. **117**, 615 (2002)

79. Aquilanti, V., et al.: Molecular beam scattering of aligned oxygen molecules. The nature of the bond in the O_2-O_2 dimer. J. Am. Chem. Soc. **121**, 10794–10802 (1999). https://doi.org/10.1021/ja9917215

80. Aquilanti, V., Bartolomei, M., Carmona-Novillo, E., Pirani, F.: The asymmetric dimer N_2–O_2: characterization of the potential energy surface and quantum mechanical calculation of rotovibrational levels. J. Chem. Phys. **118**, 2214 (2003)

81. Barreto, P.R.P., et al.: The spherical-harmonics representation for the interaction between diatomic molecules: the general case and applications to CO–CO and CO–HF. J. Mol. Spectrosc. **337**, 163–177 (2017). https://doi.org/10.1016/j.jms.2017.05.009

82. Barreto, P.R.P., Ribas, V.W., Palazzetti, F.: Potential energy surface for the H_2O-H_2 system. J. Phys. Chem. A **113**, 15047–15054 (2009). https://doi.org/10.1021/jp9051819

83. Barreto, P.R.B., et al.: Potential energy surfaces for interactions of H_2O with H_2, N_2 and O_2: a hyperspherical harmonics representation, and a minimal model for the H_2O-rare-gas-atom systems. Comput. Theoret. Chem. **990**, 53–61 (2012). https://doi.org/10.1016/j.comptc.2011.12.024

84. Barreto, P.R.P., Albernaz, A.F., Palazzetti, F.: Potential energy surfaces for van der Waals complexes of rare gases with H_2S and H_2S_2: extension to xenon interactions and hyperspherical harmonics representation. Int. J. Quantum Chem. **112**, 834–847 (2012). https://doi.org/10.1002/qua.23073

85. Anderson, R.: Discrete orthogonal transformations corresponding to the discrete polynomials of the Askey scheme. In: Murgante, B., et al. (eds.) ICCSA 2014. LNCS, vol. 8579, pp. 490–507. Springer, Cham (2014). https://doi.org/10.1007/978-3-319-09144-0_34

86. Nikiforov, A.F., Suslov, S.K., Uvarov, V.B.: Classical Orthogonal Polynomials of a Discrete Variable. Springer, Berlin (1991). https://doi.org/10.1007/978-3-642-74748-9_2

87. Braun, P.A., Gewinski, F., Haake, H., Schomerus, H.: Semiclassics of rotation and torsion. Z. Phys. B **100**, 115–127 (1996)

88. Aquilanti, V., Grossi, G.: Angular momentum coupling schemes in the quantum mechanical treatment of P-state atom collisions. J. Chem. Phys. **73**, 1165–1172 (1980). https://doi.org/10.1063/1.440270

89. Palazzetti, F., Munusamy, E., Lombardi, A., Grossi, G., Aquilanti, V.: Spherical and hyperspherical representation of potential energy surfaces for intermolecular interactions. Int. J. Quantum Chem. **111**, 318–332 (2011). https://doi.org/10.1002/qua.22688

Virtual Reality and Applications (VRA 2019)

A Mathematica Package for Visualizing Objects Inmersed in $\mathbb{R}^4$

Ricardo Velezmoro[1]🆔, Robert Ipanaqué[1(✉)]🆔, and Josel A. Mechato[2]🆔

[1] Universidad Nacional de Piura, Urb. Miraflores s/n, Castilla, Piura, Peru
{rvelezmorol,ripanaquec}@unp.edu.pe
[2] Universidad Privada Antenor Orrego,
Av. Los Tallanes Zona Los Ejidos s/n, Piura, Peru
jmechatod1@upao.edu.pe

Abstract. Visualizing objects in a space of a certain dimension is quite useful to facilitate the understanding of the mathematical concepts linked to such objects, through the geometric interpretation of them. This paper describes a new Mathematica package, 4DSketches, for visualizing objects immersed in $\mathbb{R}^4$ (points, lines, arrows, curves, surfaces, solids and complex surfaces) using 3D models as an extension of the 2D models, already established, for visualizing objects immersed in $\mathbb{R}^3$. To simulate the change of views in $\mathbb{R}^4$ rotational matrices are used. In addition, our outputs are consistent with Mathematica's notation. To show the performance of the package, several illustrative and interesting examples are described.

Keywords: 3D models to viewing objects in $\mathbb{R}^4$ · Plot surfaces in $\mathbb{R}^4$ · Plot solids in $\mathbb{R}^4$ · Plot complex surfaces

1 Introduction

The visualization of hiper-objects in spaces of dimension greater than three was proposed by Noll [8]. Then we find the works of Hoffman and Zhou [6,15] in which the visualization of surfaces in four-dimensional space is described, as well as some applications are provided. Subsequently, several articles related to the visualization of objects immersed in four-dimensional space have been written [2,3,5,11–13].

3D models to visualize objects immersed in the four-dimensional Euclidean space can be considered as an extension of the 2D models to visualize objects immersed in the three-dimensional Euclidean space. These models can be defined by the origin of $\mathbb{R}^3$, an apocryphal basis and a submersion from $\mathbb{R}^4$ in $\mathbb{R}^3$. Mathematica can be used to perform the various calculations [14]. In addition, since we do not have a "spatial" screen, we only have a flat screen (the computer screen), we can take advantage of Mathematica's capabilities to simulate the graphs in $\mathbb{R}^3$. To simulate different points of view in $\mathbb{R}^4$ we can use rotation matrices, similar to how they are used in $\mathbb{R}^3$ [6,8,15].

© Springer Nature Switzerland AG 2019
S. Misra et al. (Eds.): ICCSA 2019, LNCS 11624, pp. 479–493, 2019.
https://doi.org/10.1007/978-3-030-24311-1_35

This paper presents a new Mathematica package, 4DSketches, which incorporates commands for visualizing points, lines, arrows, curves, surfaces and solids inmersed in $\mathbb{R}^4$. In addition, commands have been incorporated for visualizing graphs of complex functions, of complex variables, defined in explicit parametric and polar forms. The commands provides the user with a highly intuitive, mathematical-looking output consistent with Mathematica's notation and syntax [7].

The structure of this paper is as follows: Sect. 2 introduce some mathematical definitions about the submersion, apocryphal basis and an m-dimensional model for visualizing objects inmersed in $\mathbb{R}^{m+1}$. For the sake of illustration, some 2D and 3D models are also briefly described in this section. Then, Sect. 3 introduces the new Mathematica package, 4DSketches, and describes the commands implemented within. The performance of the package is also discussed in this section by using some illustrative examples to plot points, lines, arrows, curves, surfaces, solids and complex surfaces. Finally, Sect. 4 closes with the main conclusions of this paper.

2   Mathematical Preliminaries

Definition 1. A mapping is called an *submersion* if it has the same local type as a canonical projection of Euclidean spaces [9].

Definition 2. An *apocryphal basis* $\hat{\mathcal{B}}$ of $\mathbb{R}^m$ consists of a set of $m+1$ tangent vectors to $\mathbb{R}^m$ such tha rank $\left(\hat{\mathcal{B}}\right) = m$.

Definition 3. An *m-dimensional model* for visualizing objects inmersed in $\mathbb{R}^{m+1}$ consists of a triad $\{O, \hat{\mathcal{B}}, \varphi\}$; where O is the origin of $\mathbb{R}^m$, $\hat{\mathcal{B}}$ is an apocryphal basis of $\mathbb{R}^m$, and φ is a submersion from $\mathbb{R}^{m+1}$ to $\mathbb{R}^m$.

Previous definitions will be considered only for values $m = 2$ and $m = 3$.

2.1   2D Models to Visualize Objects in $\mathbb{R}^3$

In practice, to chance, we use two-dimensional models for visualizing objects immersed in $\mathbb{R}^3$. In effect, in general, we have

$$O = \{0,0\}, \quad \hat{\mathcal{B}} = \{\mathbf{e}_1, \mathbf{e}_2, \mathbf{e}_3\} \quad \text{and} \quad \varphi(\mathbf{p}) = \begin{pmatrix} p_1 & p_2 & p_3 \end{pmatrix} \begin{pmatrix} e_{11} & e_{12} \\ e_{21} & e_{22} \\ e_{31} & e_{32} \end{pmatrix}.$$

To plot a point in $\mathbb{R}^3$ the submersion φ must be applied and then proceed to plot the point. For example, for the point $\mathbf{p} = (p_1, p_2, p_3)$ in $\mathbb{R}^3$ we will graph

$$\mathbf{q} = \varphi(\mathbf{p}) = (e_{11}p_1 + e_{21}p_2 + e_{31}p_3, \ e_{12}p_1 + e_{22}p_2 + e_{32}p_3)$$

in $\mathbb{R}^2$. And so for any triad. In particular, we could fixing the model

$$O = \{0,0\}, \quad \hat{\mathcal{B}} = \left\{ \frac{3}{5\sqrt{2}}(-1,-1), (1,0), (0,1) \right\} \quad \text{and}$$

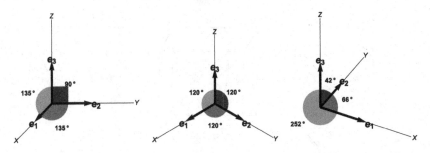

Fig. 1. 2D models to visualize objects in $\mathbb{R}^3$. Dimmetric (left), symmetric (center) and trimmetric (right).

$$\varphi(\mathbf{p}) = \left(p_2 - \frac{3p_1}{5\sqrt{2}},\ p_3 - \frac{3p_1}{5\sqrt{2}} \right).$$

that will lead us to the preferred model by a large majority of authors of mathematical texts. This model is known as the *dimmetric model* (Fig. 1).

We can also choose $\hat{\mathcal{B}} = \left\{ \frac{1}{2}\left(-\sqrt{3},-1\right), \frac{1}{2}\left(\sqrt{3},-1\right), (0,1) \right\}$ (*symmetric model*) or the apocryphal basis that allows simulating the *Mathematica* default view point

$$\hat{\mathcal{B}} = \left\{ \frac{11}{10}\left(\cos(18^\circ),-\sin(18^\circ)\right), \frac{3}{4}\left(\sin(42^\circ),\cos(42^\circ)\right), (0,1) \right\},$$

this set gives rise to the *trimmetric model* (Fig. 1). For example, Fig. 2 show the graphs of some objects immersed in $\mathbb{R}^3$ obtained by means of the dimmetric model.

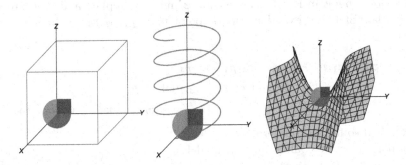

Fig. 2. Visualization of some objects immersed in $\mathbb{R}^3$ with a 2D dimmetric model. Cube (left), curve (center) and surface (right).

The graphs obtained by any model lack movements in $\mathbb{R}^3$, only admit movements in $\mathbb{R}^2$. To simulate movements in $\mathbb{R}^3$ it is necessary to use rotation matrices. For example, the product

$$R = R_z(\gamma)\, R_y(\beta)\, R_x(\alpha),$$

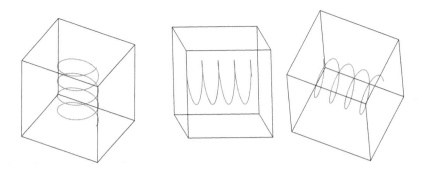

Fig. 3. Simulation of 3D rotations of a curve in $\mathbb{R}^3$.

serves to represent a rotation about axes z, y and x. In this way, starting from any model (which initially only allows movements in $\mathbb{R}^2$), we could simulate interactive movement in $\mathbb{R}^3$. Figure 3 was obtained after applying rotations to the coordinate functions of the curve starting from the trimmetric model.

2.2   3D Models to Visualize Objects in $\mathbb{R}^4$

In general, a 3D model for visualizing objects immersed in the $\mathbb{R}^4$ is given by

$$O = \{0,0,0\}, \quad \hat{\mathcal{B}} = \{\mathbf{e}_1, \mathbf{e}_2, \mathbf{e}_3, \mathbf{e}_4\} \quad \text{and} \quad \varphi(\mathbf{p}) = \begin{pmatrix} p_1\ p_2\ p_3\ p_4 \end{pmatrix} \begin{pmatrix} e_{11}\ e_{12}\ e_{13} \\ e_{21}\ e_{22}\ e_{23} \\ e_{31}\ e_{32}\ e_{33} \\ e_{41}\ e_{42}\ e_{43} \end{pmatrix}.$$

To plot a point in $\mathbb{R}^4$ the submersion φ must be applied and then proceed to plot the point. For example, for the point $\mathbf{p} = (p_1, p_2, p_3, p_4)$ in $\mathbb{R}^4$ we will graph

$$\begin{aligned} \mathbf{q} = \varphi(\mathbf{p}) = (&e_{11}p_1 + e_{21}p_2 + e_{31}p_3 + e_{41}p_4, \\ &e_{12}p_1 + e_{22}p_2 + e_{32}p_3 + e_{42}p_4, \\ &e_{13}p_1 + e_{23}p_2 + e_{33}p_3 + e_{43}p_4) \end{aligned}$$

in $\mathbb{R}^3$. And so for any quatern.

In particular, we could fixing the model

$$O = \{0,0,0\}, \quad \hat{\mathcal{B}} = \left\{ \tfrac{3}{5\sqrt{3}}(-1,-1,-1), (1,0,0), (0,1,0), (0,0,1) \right\} \quad \text{and}$$

$$\varphi(\mathbf{p}) = \left(p_2 - \frac{3p_1}{5\sqrt{3}}, \ p_3 - \frac{3p_1}{5\sqrt{3}}, \ p_4 - \frac{3p_1}{5\sqrt{3}} \right).$$

We will call to this model the *trimmetric-trimmetric model* (Fig. 4).

We can also choose

$$\hat{\mathcal{B}} = \left\{ \left(-\tfrac{\sqrt{2}}{3}, -\sqrt{\tfrac{2}{3}}, -\tfrac{1}{3}\right), \left(-\tfrac{\sqrt{2}}{3}, \sqrt{\tfrac{2}{3}}, -\tfrac{1}{3}\right), \left(\tfrac{2\sqrt{2}}{3}, 0, -\tfrac{1}{3}\right), (0,0,1) \right\}.$$

We will call the model obtained from these set the *symmetric model* (Fig. 5).
Or, we could also choose

$$\hat{\mathcal{B}} = \left\{ \tfrac{1}{\sqrt{26}} \left(5, 0, -1\right), \tfrac{1}{5\sqrt{17}} \left(0, 16, -4\right), \tfrac{7}{10\sqrt{22}} \left(3, 3, 2\right), \left(0, 0, 1\right) \right\}.$$

We will call the model obtained from these set the *asymmetric model* (Fig. 6).
For example, Figs. 7 and 8 show the graphs of some objects immersed in $\mathbb{R}^4$
obtained using the trimmetric-trimmetric model.

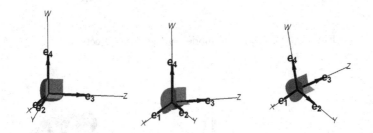

Fig. 4. 3D trimmetric-trimmetric model to visualize objects in $\mathbb{R}^4$.

Fig. 5. 3D symmetric model to visualize objects in $\mathbb{R}^4$.

The graphs obtained by any model lack movements in $\mathbb{R}^4$, only admit movements in $\mathbb{R}^3$. To simulate movements in $\mathbb{R}^4$ it is necessary to use rotation matrices. For example, the product

$$R = R_{zw}\left(\psi\right) R_{yw}\left(\phi\right) R_{yz}\left(\delta\right) R_{xw}\left(\gamma\right) R_{xz}\left(\beta\right) R_{xy}\left(\alpha\right),$$

serves to represent an rotation in the planes zw, yw, yz, xw, xz and xy. In
this way, starting from any model (which initially only allows movements in
$\mathbb{R}^3$), we could simulate interactive movement in $\mathbb{R}^4$. Figure 9 was obtained after
applying rotations to the coordinate functions of the surface starting from the
trimmetric-trimmetic model.

3D models to visualize geometric objects of $\mathbb{R}^4$ require a "spatial" screen,
that is, a parallelepiped box in which three perpendicular axes can be located

Fig. 6. 3D asymmetric model to visualize objects in $\mathbb{R}^4$.

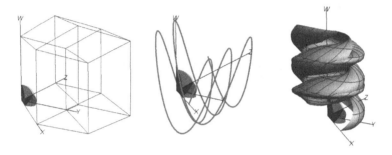

Fig. 7. Visualization of tesseract (left), curve (center) and surface (right) with a 3D asymmetric model.

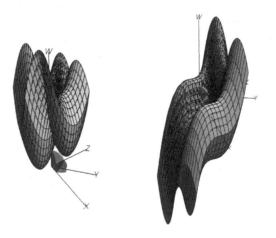

Fig. 8. Visualization of solids with a 3D asymmetric model.

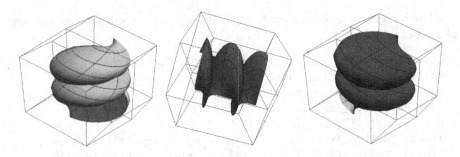

Fig. 9. Simulation of 4D rotations of the surface $S(u,v) = (\cos(u)\cos(v), \sin(u)\cos(v), \sin(v), \frac{u+v}{8})$.

[10], for example, one another and another axis on the extension of the diagonal of the cube, whose sides measures 1, located in the first octant (similar to the most common of the 2D models). Figure 10 clarifies this idea. Since we do not have these types of screens, we will use *Mathematica* since this system of computational algebra has wide graphic capabilities, so that the observer has the clear idea of seeing in $\mathbb{R}^3$ the graphics obtained the standard built-in commands, but in reality they are seen on a 2D screen (computer's flat screen).

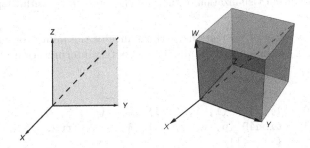

Fig. 10. The most common 2D model (left) and a simile 3D model (right).

3   The Package 4DSketches: Some Illustrative Examples

This section describes some examples of the application of this package. Firstly, we load the package:

```
<<4DSketches.m
```

The commands incorporated in this package are:

```
Graphics4D, Plot4D, ParametricPlot4D, ComplexPlot,
     ComplexParametricPlot, ComplexPolarPlot
```

Here we show a mini program to calculate the vector resulting from the sum of a set of vectors in $\mathbb{R}^4$.

```
Addition4D[v : {{_, _, _, _} ..}, p_: {0, 0, 0, 0}] :=
  Module[{n = Length[v], aux, vs, res},
   aux = FoldList[Plus, p, v];
   vs = Partition[aux, 2, 1];
   res = {aux[[1]], aux[[n + 1]]};
   {{Red, Tooltip[Arrow[Tube[#]], Last[#] - First[#]] & /@ vs},
    {Blue, Tooltip[Arrow[Tube[res]], Last[res] - First[res]]},
    {AbsolutePointSize[5], Tooltip[Point[p], p]}}]
```

Fig. 11. Graphical visualization of the sum of vectors in $\mathbb{R}^4$ with `Graphics4D`.

In the following way we test the performance of the mini program and with the `Graphics4D` command we obtain the geometric interpretation of the sum of vectors in $\mathbb{R}^4$.

```
p = {-1, -1, 0, 0};
u = {1, 1, 0, -1}; v = {1, 1, 1, 1}; w = {-2, 3, 0, -1};
Graphics4D[Addition4D[{u, v, w}, p], Axes -> True,
  AxesLength -> {-1, 4}]
```
See Fig. 11.

With the `Plot4D` command it is possible to visualize the graph of the solid $M : w = x^2 + y^2 + z^2$ and the two solids together $M : w = x^2 + y^2 + z^2$ and $N : w = x^2 + y^2 - z^2$.

```
Plot4D[x^2 + y^2 + z^2, {x, -1, 1}, {y, -1, 1}, {z, -1, 1},
  AxesLength -> {-1, 2}]
```
See Fig. 12 (left).

```
Plot4D[{x^2 + y^2 + z^2, x^2 + y^2 - z^2}, {x, -1, 1}, {y, -1, 1},
  {z, -1, 1}, AxesLength -> {-2, 2.5}, PlotStyle -> {Directive[Red,
  Opacity[0.6]], Directive[Blue, Opacity[0.6]]}]
```
See Fig. 12 (right).

Fig. 12. Graphical visualization of solids in $\mathbb{R}^4$ with `Plot4D`.

Below are the sentences to obtain the graphs of a single curve and two curves together in $\mathbb{R}^4$ using the `ParametricPlot4D` command.

```
ParametricPlot4D[{Cos[u/Sqrt[5]], Sin[u/Sqrt[5]],
   Cos[2 u/Sqrt[5]], Sin[2 u/Sqrt[5]]}, {u, 0, 5 Pi},
   AxesLength -> {-1, 2}]
```

See Fig. 13 (left).

```
ParametricPlot4D[{{Cos[u/Sqrt[5]], Sin[u/Sqrt[5]],
   Cos[2 u/Sqrt[5]], Sin[2 u/Sqrt[5]]},
   {Cos[u/Sqrt[5]], Sin[u/Sqrt[5]],
   Cos[2 u/Sqrt[5]], -Sin[2 u/Sqrt[5]]}}, {u, 0, 5 Pi},
   AxesLength -> {-1, 2}]
```

See Fig. 13 (right).

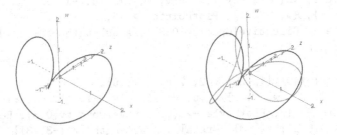

Fig. 13. Graphical visualization of curves in $\mathbb{R}^4$ with `ParametricPlot4D`.

Using the following sentences it is possible to obtain the graphs of a single surface and two surfaces together in $\mathbb{R}^4$ by means of the `ParametricPlot4D` command.

```
ParametricPlot4D[{u, v, u^2 + v^2, -2 u v}, {u, -1, 1},
  {v, -1, 1}, AxesLength -> {-2, 3}]
```

See Fig. 14 (left).

```
ParametricPlot4D[{{u, v, u^2 + v^2, -2 u v},
  {u^2 + v^2, v, -2 u v, u}},
 {u, -1, 1}, {v, -1, 1}, AxesLength -> {-2, 3}]
```

See Fig. 14 (right).

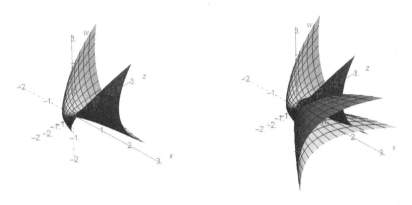

Fig. 14. Graphical visualization of surfaces in $\mathbb{R}^4$ with `ParametricPlot4D`.

The following sentences make it possible to obtain the graphs of a single solid and of two solids together in $\mathbb{R}^4$ using the `ParametricPlot4D` command.

```
ParametricPlot4D[{u^2 - v^2, 2 u v, w, u}, {u, -1, 1},
  {v, -1, 1}, {w, -1, 1}, PlotPoints -> 15,
 PlotStyle -> Directive[Opacity[0.8]], AxesLength -> {-3, 3}]
```

See Fig. 15 (left).

```
ParametricPlot4D[ {{u^2 - v^2, 2 u v, w, u},
 {u^2 - w^2, 2 u w, v, w}}, {u, -1, 1}, {v, -1, 1}, {w, -1, 1},
 PlotPoints -> 15, PlotStyle -> {Directive[Opacity[0.8], Red],
  Directive[Opacity[0.8], Green]}, AxesLength -> {-3, 3}]
```

See Fig. 15 (right).

Since the graph of a complex function $F : \mathbb{C} \to \mathbb{C}$ is a surface that supports a local parameterization by means of a Monge patch of the form

$$S(x, y) = (\Re(z), \Im(z), \Re(F(z)), \Im(F(z))),$$

where $z = x + iy$, then it is possible to use the proposed models to obtain the graphs of such functions. In the case that the function is given in parametric

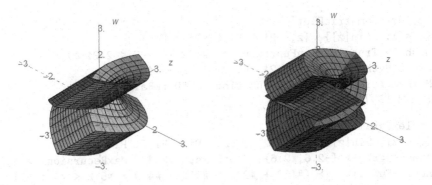

Fig. 15. Graphical visualization of solids with `ParametricPlot4D`.

form, ie $\alpha : \mathbb{C} \to \mathbb{C}^2$ such that $\alpha(z) = (\alpha_1(z), \alpha_2(z))$, then we express it in the form

$$S(x,y) = (\Re(\alpha_1(z)), \Im(\alpha_1(z)), \Re(\alpha_2(z)), \Im(\alpha_2(z)))$$

where $z = x + iy$, to be able to use the proposed models in the graphic representation of them.

Below are the sentences to obtain the graphs of a single complex surface and two complex surfaces together in $\mathbb{R}^4$ using the `ComplexPlot` command.

```
ComplexPlot[z^2, {z, -1 - I, 1 + I}, AxesLength -> {-2, 2}]
```
See Fig. 16 (left).

```
ComplexPlot[
  {z^2, z^3}, {z, -1 - I, 1 + I}, AxesLength -> {-2, 2}]
```
See Fig. 16 (right).

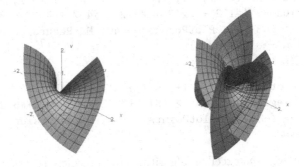

Fig. 16. Graphical visualization of complex surfaces in $\mathbb{R}^4$ with `ComplexPlot`.

The following sentences make it possible to obtain the graphs of a single complex surface and of two complex surfaces together in $\mathbb{R}^4$ using the `ParametricComplexPlot` command.

```
ComplexParametricPlot[
{Cos[z], Sin[z]}, {z, -Pi - Pi I, Pi + Pi I},
Mesh -> True, RegionFunction -> (#1^2 + #2^2 < 2 Pi &),
AxesLength -> {-3.2, 3.2}, PlotPoints -> 40,
MaxRecursion -> 8, ColorFunction -> "DarkRainbow"]
```
See Fig. 17 (left).

```
ComplexParametricPlot[
{{Cos[z], Sin[z]}, {z, z^2}}, {z, -Pi - Pi I, Pi + Pi I},
AxesLength -> {-2.6, 2.6}, PlotPoints -> 40, MaxRecursion -> 8,
RegionFunction -> (#1^2 + #2^2 + #3^2 + #4^2 + #5^2 < 7 Pi &)]
```
See Fig. 17 (right).

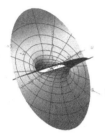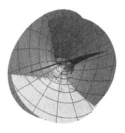

Fig. 17. Graphical visualization of complex surfaces in $\mathbb{R}^4$ with `ComplexParametric-Plot`.

Finally, we can see the graphs of a single surface and two surfaces together in $\mathbb{R}^4$ using the `ComplexPolarPlot` command.

```
ComplexPolarPlot[Sin[2 T], {T, -Pi-Pi I/2, Pi+Pi I/2}, Mesh->True,
RegionFunction -> (#1^2 + #2^2 + #3^2 + #4^2 + #5^2 < 8 &),
AxesLength -> {-3, 3}, PlotPoints -> 40, MaxRecursion -> 8,
ColorFunction -> "Rainbow"]
```
See Fig. 18 (left).

```
ComplexPolarPlot[{Sin[2 T], 1+Cos[T]}, {T, -Pi-Pi I/2, Pi+Pi I/2},
Mesh->True, RegionFunction -> (#1^2+#2^2+#3^2+#4^2+#5^2 < 8 &),
AxesLength -> {-3, 3}, PlotPoints -> 40, MaxRecursion -> 8]
```
See Fig. 18 (right).

3D models have been excellent algorithms to implement several commands in *Mathematica* to visualize geometric objects immersed in $\mathbb{R}^4$. These commands will help explore several aspects of various geometric objects immersed in $\mathbb{R}^4$. For example, given a function $f : \mathbb{R} \to \mathbb{R}$, geometrically, its derivative gives us the value of the slope of the tangent line to the graph of f at a given point in its domain. In such a way that it is easy to find the equation of the tangent line to the graph of any differentiable function in an arbitrary point of its domain.

Fig. 18. Graphical visualization of complex surfaces in $\mathbb{R}^4$ with `ComplexPolarPlot`.

It is amazing to verify, geometrically, that this result is also true for complex functions $F : \mathbb{C} \to \mathbb{C}$.

Next we define the function $F(z) = z^2$ and the point $(z_0, w_0) = (0.75 + 0.5i, F(0.75 + 0.5i))$, then we plot the function, its tangent plane at the given point and the point of tangency. For this, the standard `Show` command is used together with the new `ComplexPlot` and `Graphics4D` commands.

```
F[z_] := z^2;
z0 = .75 + .35 I;
w0 = F[z0];
Show[ ComplexPlot[{F[z], w0 + F'[z0] (z - z0)}, {z, 0, 1 + I}],
  Graphics4D[{AbsolutePointSize[10], Point[{Re[z0], Im[z0],
  Re[w0], Im[w0]}]}] ]
```
See Fig. 19.

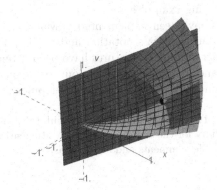

Fig. 19. Geometric interpretation of the derivative of a complex function, at a point in its domain, with `ComplexPlot` and `Graphics4D`.

The authors are aware that there is still a need to investigate hidden faces, lighting, shading, etc. in $\mathbb{R}^4$ to have a real perception of geometric objects [1,4]. An idea of this is appreciated in Fig. 20; in which two graphs are compared, one obtained in rudimentary form (using a 2D model and *Mathematica* commands that are not for $\mathbb{R}^3$) and the other obtained with the `ContourPlot3D` command. However, we get satisfactory sketches for now.

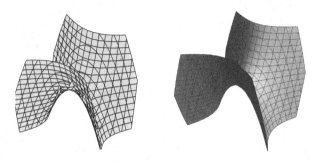

Fig. 20. The same surface generated rudimentarily (left) and generated with `ContourPlot3D` (right).

4 Conclusions

In this paper, a new Mathematica package for visualizing points, lines, arrows, curves, surfaces, solids and complex surfaces inmersed in $\mathbb{R}^4$ is introduced. The incoporated commands in this package will help explore several aspects of various geometric objects immersed in $\mathbb{R}^4$. The algorithms for these commands are based on 3D models built as an extension of the 2D models used to visualize objects immersed in $\mathbb{R}^3$. The performance of the package is discussed by means of some illustrative and interesting examples.

All the commands have been implemented in Mathematica version 11.0 and are consistent with Mathematica's notation and results. The powerful Mathematica functional programming [7] features have been extensively used to make the program shorter and more efficient. From our experience, Mathematica provides an excellent framework for this kind of developments.

Acknowledgements. The authors would like to thank to the authorities of the Universidad Nacional de Piura for the acquisition of the Mathematica 11.0 license and the reviewers for their valuable comments and suggestions.

References

1. Agoston, M.K.: Computer Graphics and Geometric Modelling. Springer, London (2005). https://doi.org/10.1007/b138805
2. Ohori, A., et al.: Visualising higher-dimensional space-time and space-scale objects as projections to $\mathbb{R}^3$. PeerJ Comput. Sci. **3**, e123 (2017). https://doi.org/10.7717/peerj-cs.123

3. Banchoff, T.F.: Beyond the Third Dimension: Geometry, Computer Graphics, and Higher Dimensions. Scientific American Library Series. W. H. Freeman & Company, New York (1990)
4. Buss, S.R.: 3D Computer Graphics: A Mathematical Introduction with OpenGL. Cambridge University Press, Cambridge (2003)
5. Brandel, S.: 4D objects for animation: immersion on virtual reality. In: 9th Virtual Reality International Conference, Laval, France, pp. 1–5 (2007)
6. Hoffmann, C.M., Zhou, J.: Visualization of surfaces in four-dimensional space. Computer Science Technical Reports, Paper 814 (1990)
7. Maeder, R.: Programming in Mathematica, 2nd edn. Addison-Wesley, Redwood City (1991)
8. Noll, M.: A computer technique for displaying n-dimensional hyperobjects. Commun. ACM **10**(8), 469–473 (1967). https://doi.org/10.1145/363534.363544
9. Pham, F.: Some notions of local differential topology. In: Ramakrishnan, A. (ed.) Symposia on Theoretical Physics and Mathematics, pp. 65–100. Springer, Boston (1968). https://doi.org/10.1007/978-1-4684-7727-6_3
10. Sakai, Y., Hashimoto, S.: Interactive four-dimensional space visualization using five-dimensional homogeneous processing for intuitive understanding. J. Inst. Image Inf. Telev. Eng. **60**(10), 1630–1647 (2006). https://doi.org/10.3169/itej.60.1630
11. Séquin, C.H.: 3D visualization models of the regular polytopes in four and higher dimensions. In: Bridges 2002, Towson, Maryland, USA, pp. 37–48 (2002)
12. Volkert, K.: On models for visualizing four-dimensional figures. Math. Intelligencer **39**, 27–35 (2017). https://doi.org/10.1007/s00283-016-9699-1
13. Wang, W.M., et al.: Interactive exploration of 4D geometry with volumetric halos. The Eurographics Association (2013)
14. Wolfram, S.: The Mathematica Book, 4th edn. Wolfram Media, Cambridge University Press, Champaign, Cambridge (1999)
15. Zhou, J.: Visualization of four dimensional space and its applications. D. Phil. thesis, Department of Computer Science Technical Reports, Paper 922 (1991)

Posture Classification Based on a Spine Shape Monitoring System

Icxa Khandelwal[1]([✉]), Katharina Stollenwerk[2], Björn Krüger[3],
and Andreas Weber[1]

[1] University of Bonn, Bonn, Germany
icxakhandelwal04@gmail.com
[2] Hochschule Bonn-Rhein Sieg, Sankt Augustin, Germany
[3] Gokhale Method Institute, Stanford, CA, USA

Abstract. Lower back pain is one of the leading causes for musculoskeletal disability throughout the world. A large percentage of the population suffers from lower back pain at some point in their life. One non-invasive approach to reduce back pain is postural modification which can be learned through training. In this context, wearables are becoming more and more prominent since they are capable of providing feedback about the user's posture in real-time. Optimal, healthy posture depends on the position (sitting, standing, hinging) the user is in. Meaningful feedback needs to adapt to the current position and, in the best case, identify the position automatically to minimize necessary interactions from the user. In this work, we present results of classifying the positions of users based on the readings of the *Gokhale SpineTracker™* device. We computed various features and evaluated the performance of K-Nearest Neighbors, Extra Trees, Artificial Neural Networks and AdaBoost for global inter-subject classification as well as for personalized subject-specific classification.

1 Introduction

Before diving into the matter, we need to fix some terminology. While generally used interchangeably in everyday language, throughout this paper we will differentiate between *position* and *posture*. *Position* will refer to the (static) state a human body is in, e.g., sit, stand, bend, hinge. *Posture* describes how a position is realized by a person. Thus, a position resembles a passive state description whereas posture becomes a multi-factor dynamic process. Factors therein include bone or, more general, skeletal alignment as well as muscle activation.

According to the Global Burden of Diseases, Injuries, and Risk Factors Study 2016 [1], lower back pain is one of the leading causes for years lived with disability throughout the world. It was reported that two major causes of musculoskeletal disability are lower back pain and neck pain. Due to the sedentary lifestyle and long sitting hours at work, a large number of people are at a high risk of developing spine related issues. The low back pain fact sheet [2] explains that people who are not physically fit have weak back and abdominal muscles.

S. Misra et al. (Eds.): ICCSA 2019, LNCS 11624, pp. 494–509, 2019.
https://doi.org/10.1007/978-3-030-24311-1_36

Fig. 1. Placement of the SpineTracker sensors on a subject's back. Posture training with real-time feedback of the spine shape. Screenshots of the iPhone app: Spine curve and Spine simulation.

Consequently, these muscles cannot properly support the spine and thereby cause pain in the long run. If, in addition, such individuals are obese, more stress is put on the muscles, bones, and discs at the back which also leads to pain.

Gokhale Method Enterprise Inc.[1] is a Silicon Valley-based company specialized in posture training. According to this company's philosophy, the key to a healthy spine is healthy lifestyle and correct posture. Hence it provides various training classes to interested customers so that they can improve their posture. Gokhale Method has developed several posture supportive products, one of them being the *Gokhale SpineTracker™* to support posture training in classes. This device comprises of five wearable sensors equipped with three-axis accelerometers. It is attached along the spine of the user to provide a reasonable approximation of user's spine shape. The data obtained through this device can be visualized in real-time via an iPhone application [3]. See Fig. 1 for some examples.

Since healthy spine shape strongly depends on the current position, an automatic detection of the position would be highly beneficial. In this work, we use data of the *Gokhale SpineTracker™* to automatically detect the position the user assumed. We have done so by using supervised machine learning techniques for the classification of a user's posture into different classes (positions), i.e., sitting, standing, and hinging. These positions are especially challenging to be classified from accelerometer readings as they are mostly static. Thus, there are only slight changes in the sensor readings over time. In particular, this makes the distinction between sitting and standing very hard. This problem is further increased by the variability of postures between subjects.

The remainder of this paper is organized as follows: We give an overview on related work in Sect. 2. Section 3 briefly describes the datasets (Sect. 3.1) this work is based on and covers feature computation (Sect. 3.2). An overview on used classification techniques is given in Sect. 4. The different classification experiments performed in this work are described in Sect. 5. We present the classification results in Sect. 6 and conclude the paper in Sect. 7.

---

[1] https://gokhalemethod.com/.

2   Related Work

Motion Capturing Techniques. Capturing and recording of human motion data has become a standard technique in may domains, such as computer animation, sport sciences [4], biology [5], and rehabilitation [6]. Optical motion capture with passive markers and a large array of cameras has become the gold standard of capturing motions due to its high temporal and spatial resolution and accuracy [7]. However, optical motion capture is limited in the capture volume and its general usability. The user has to wear a motion capture suit and undergo a complex calibration process which is not suited for everyone. Thus, alternative techniques based on inertial sensors, especially with few accelerometers only, were developed to capture full body motions [8–11]. While full body motion capture based on few sensors gives a good overview of the general motion, it is not yet possible to capture all body parts in high spatial resolution. Specialized systems were developed to more accurately capture specific body parts, such as faces [12,13], arms [14], legs [15], hands [16–18], and the spine [19,20].

Supervised machine learning techniques have proven to be especially useful in the field of computer vision-based human motion capture. Examples hereof include capturing of motions from video [21,22] and retrieval of single poses from one image [23,24]. Machine learning has also been successfully applied for reconstruction of motions from other sensor modalities [8–10]. An application beyond the capturing of motions is the classification of motions. Here, identifying certain actions [25,26] was done as well as the detection of biometric parameters [27].

Spine Shape Reconstruction and Motion Classification. A vast variety of systems and technologies have evolved around the capture the shape of the spine for posture monitoring. Such technologies range from ribbon-shaped fibre-optic sensors [19], over strips of strain-gauge elements [28], accelerometers [20,29] to various inertial sensor-based systems [30–33]. Many of the aforementioned systems use posture or activity classification as field of application.

StraightenUp+ [33] is a vest with three inertial sensors vertically mounted to the vest's back. Using the sensor data of 30 participants, the authors use decision trees in order to identify physical activities such as sitting and walking from a fixed sequence of eight activities. Wong and Wong [30] developed a smart garment with three inertial sensors for posture training. Their system defines posture change as change in inclination between pairs of neighboring sensors. In a small posture-feedback study, this information is used as an indicator for the straightness of the spine and hence an indirectly indicator for, e.g., slouching. In a larger study (429 participants) Consmüller et al. [28] used the Epidonis SPINE system to record five repetitions of a choreographed sequence of back movements consisting of rotations in the sagittal, frontal, and transverse plane. Using linear discriminant analysis they successfully classify the resulting back motions. Fathi and Curran [32] place three inertial sensors on cervical, thoracic, and lower lumbar spine to record and classify two positions (hunch, slouch) using template-string matching. Distributing five 3D accelerometers equidistantly over the spine, Jeyhani et al. [29] differentiate sitting positions (straight, hunch, arch) based on trends in the per-sensor mean inclination.

There are generally few works for posture classification that use real-world data and consist of a large amount of data from a wide range of users. This is especially true for classification of spine shapes (postures) using wearables. This paper contributes to filling this gap by providing an evaluation of different classification techniques for both inter-subject and subject-specific posture classification of postures in three different positions that are meaningful for posture training in a database of almost 4,200 spine movements from over 100 subjects.

3   Data Processing

This section provides a general overview of the data and data processing steps used in this work. It includes details on different datasets and a description of features derived from the raw data.

3.1   Datasets

The dataset is obtained from the sensors via the iPhone application for *Gokhale SpineTracker™*. The sensors' data are stored in a binary file, which is uploaded to one central server. Per default, data are captured with a sampling frequency f of 50 Hz. Each file contains the following relevant information:

Position refers to the position the user assumed. In this work, we focus on *standing*, *sitting*, and *hinging* as these are part of the standard posture training. Other positions are ignored also because we do not have sufficient samples for learning approaches.

Event describes the event occurring at the end of each motion sequence. User interactions trigger events in the iPhone application (closed application, connection aborted, or switched posture for instance). In this work, we are interested only in sequences that are ended by the event *snapshot*. This event signifies that the user took a snapshot of his pose and confirmed the position he has taken the snapshot from. Therefore, the position label is reliable in this case. In other events the user might have switched to another pose, without changing the position in the application. Thus, there would be many mislabeled data for other events, which is not suitable for supervised learning approaches.

Readings contains a table with timestamps and the raw sensor data.

From the data uploaded by the application, a set of data was extracted for this work. This raw dataset ($\mathcal{DB}_{\mathrm{raw}}$) contained 15,873 files, belonging to 150 subjects. Preprocessing, included removal of files corresponding to the wrong event type, removal of corrupt files, and removal of files with less than one second of data. The complete dataset ($\mathcal{DB}_{\mathrm{full}}$) we continued to work with contained 4,178 files from 106 subjects, finally. For some experiments we separated a partial dataset ($\mathcal{DB}_{\mathrm{partial}}$) consisting of 1,457 files covering 37 subjects.

3.2   Feature Computation

We computed various types of features based on the sensors' accelerometer data. Each of the five sensors captures acceleration values in three axes resulting in a 15-dimensional multivariate time series of raw accelerations. Features were computed on windows of fixed temporal length s ($s \in [1,10]$ s), varying the time before a snapshot event occurred. Based on these fixed-length segments, we compute different feature types as listed below:

Raw features Here, the original, raw data obtained from the sensors are taken as feature. This results in a $(15 \cdot f \cdot s)$-dimensional feature vector.

Statistical features: For each of the 15 time series, we computed eight basic statistical measures: length, mean, standard deviation, minimum value, maximum value, median, 25% quantile, and 75% quantile. This results in a 120-dimensional feature vector.

Fourier features The absolute Fourier transform of the data was considered for this feature type. For each of the 15 time series, their discrete Fourier transform was computed using the `numpy.fft.fft()` function of Python's scipy library [34]. The result is $(15 \cdot f \cdot s)$-dimensional feature vector.

Angular features This feature type stores the *forward tilt* τ_{acc} of each sensor. For static poses, it can be assumed that the sensor is not displaced from its position. As a consequence, that sensor will only measure acceleration due to gravity pointing downwards, and we can compute its *forward tilt* as

$$\tau_{\mathrm{acc}} = \arctan 2\,(a_z, -a_y), \qquad (1)$$

where a_z and a_y denote the acceleration of the sensor measured in its local z-axis and y-axis respectively [20]. For each frame, we obtain five forward tilts, one from each sensor. Additionally, the difference of forward tilt between two consecutive sensors was computed (four values for each frame). Hence the dimensionality of this feature set is $((5+4) \cdot f \cdot s)$.

3.3   Principal Component Analysis

Principal Component Analysis (PCA) is one of the most common linear dimensionality reduction techniques. In a first step, a linear mapping of the feature space is computed, where dimensions are sorted by variance in the data. Dimensions in this space are called Principal Components (PCs). In a second step, one can truncate PCs representing small variance in the data. This allows for the reducing the dimensionality, while maintaining control over the degree of data loss in the compressed space.

4   Supervised Machine Learning Techniques

We provide a short introduction to the supervised machine learning (SML) techniques used for posture classification in this section. All of the described techniques have a specific set of parameters. The concrete parameter values we used are listed and described in Table 1. Machine learning techniques generally require the dataset to be split into two independent datasets, one for training the classifier (training dataset) and one for assessing its performance (validation dataset). After training, the classifier can be used for making predictions on the unknown dataset (test dataset).

Table 1. List of classifiers, parameters, their short description, and values used in this work for classification. The parameter n specifies the number of samples in the training set. A detailed description of the parameters can be found at scikit-learn [34].

Classifier (model)	Parameter	Description (values used)
KNN	k	Number of nearest neighbors ($k = n/d$, $d \in \{10, 20, \ldots, 100\}$)
	w	Weighing of neighbors ($w \in \{$uniform (U), distance-based (D)$\}$)
Extra-Trees	e	Number of decision trees ($e \in \{10, 100, 250, 500\}$)
	f_{sq}	Function to measure the quality of a split ($f_{sq} \in \{$Gini impurity (G), entropy (E)$\}$)
ANN	h_i	Number of neurons per hidden layer
	f_{act}	Hidden layer activation function ($f_{act} \in \{$identity (i), logistic sigmoid (l), tanh (t), rectified linear unit (r)$\}$)
	f_{opt}	Weight optimization function ($f_{opt} \in \{$ family of quasi-Newton methods (l), stochastic gradient descent (s), specific stochastic gradient-based (a)$\}$)
	l	Type of learning rate ($l \in \{$const. (c), invscaling (i), adaptive (a)$\}$)
AdaBoost	e	Number of decision trees ($e \in \{10, 100, 250, 500\}$)
	c	Classifier used (all possible combination of Extra-Trees)

4.1 *K*-Nearest Neighbor Models

K-Nearest Neighbor (KNN) [35] classifiers store features of the training dataset as vectors. For classifying a test instance, the distance between that test element and all elements in the training dataset is computed. Distance metric used most commonly for this purpose is the Euclidean distance. For a pre-defined number K of closest elements of the training set, a majority vote is performed. The class belonging to most of the K neighbors is assigned to the test sample. It has been observed that this classifier is successful for datasets in which the decision boundary is very irregular [36].

Bhatia et al. [37] describe the strengths and weaknesses of KNN. Advantages of this classifier are that it trains very fast, is robust to noisy training data and is effective on large training datasets. One of its biggest limitation is that the optimal value of K needs to be determined. Additionally, it is not clear which distance metrics and attributes shall be used to obtain best possible results. Weighted KNN [37] technique can be used to overcome the inherent limitation of KNN to assign equal weights to K nearest neighbors. In this technique, weights are assigned to the neighbors based on their distance from the test instance. In this work, KNN models are created using the function `KNeighborsClassifier()` of scikit-learn library of Python [34] and the weights parameter is varied as either uniform or distance based weights.

4.2 Extremely Randomized Trees (Extra-Trees) Models

In a decision tree [38], leaf nodes represent classes and internal nodes represent different tests on a set of features. The branches depict the flow in the tree based on logical conjunctions of nodes considered until now. The aim is to develop a model which can predict the class of a test dataset element based on a selected set of features. It employs top-down divide and conquer by considering the information entropy of different features. The complete process [35] consists of three steps: 1. Determine feature and threshold to partition the training set at each internal node. 2. At each node check whether to continue splitting or to make it a leaf node. 3. Assign class labels to leaf nodes with minimum estimated error rate.

According to Ho [39], one of the biggest advantages of decision trees is that they are easily to interpret. They perform well on large datasets, but might learn highly irregular patterns from the data if the trees are very deep. Thus the resulting model will highly fit the training data but may perform poorly on test data (overfitting). To overcome this limitation, meta estimators of decision trees such as Extra-Trees (ET) [40] are used. Extra-Trees combine multiple decision trees which are trained on different sub-samples of the dataset. The overall performance is determined by calculating the average of performance of all decision trees. In this work, we used the extra trees model implemented in `ExtraTreesClassifier()` function of scikit-learn library of Python [34].

4.3 Artificial Neural Network Models

Artificial Neural Network models (ANN) simulate the functioning of neurons in the brain. The most common ANN model used is a multi-layer perceptron with backpropagation [38]. Its architecture [35] consists of three types of layers: 1. The *input layer* feeds the feature vector of the training set to the first hidden layer. 2. One or more *hidden layers* weight all prior outputs differently and add a bias term. 3. The *output layer* processes the output of the final hidden layer. It contains a unit representing each class.

ANN [41] are capable of detecting complex non-linear relationships between classes and the features associated with the training data. Using ANN it is possible to detect all possible interactions between the features. But these networks exhibit black box behavior, i.e., it is not possible to identify the exact causal relationship between the variables which lead to a particular outcome. In this work, ANN models are created using `MLPClassifier()` function of the scikit-learn library [34].

4.4 Adaptive Boosting Models

Adaptive boosting (AdaBoost) is a meta estimator. It constructs a strong classifier using weak classifiers which can be any other supervised machine learning algorithm with low accuracy on the given data [42]. From the list of classifiers used in this work and considering the implementation of AdaBoost in scikit-learn library of Python, we decided to use the Extra-Trees classifier as a weak classifier for running AdaBoost. This algorithm will first fit the Extra-Trees model on the original dataset and then fit the additional copies of the classifier in such a way that the these classifiers focus more on the incorrectly classified instances [43]. The function used here is `AdaBoostClassifier()`.

4.5 Validation Schemes

Validation schemes are used to determine how accurate the predictions made by the models are. We used two different cross validation (CV) schemes:

n-fold Cross Validation: In this strategy, the given dataset is partitioned into n equal subsets. Each subset is once used as a validation dataset and remaining $n-1$ subsets form a training dataset. This process is repeated n times and the overall performance is calculated by computing the average over all n runs. In this work, we have used three-fold CV for model selection and ten-fold CV for assessing performance of the models.

Leave One Subject Out Cross Validation (LOSOCV): LOSOCV is similar to n-fold cross validation. Instead of splitting the data arbitrarily into n subsets, the data are grouped by p subjects. This strategy helps identifying how well the data from $p-1$ different subjects are capable of classifying the data of the singled out subject.

5 Evaluation Approach

The general classification approach, we follow in this work, consists of the following steps: First, a feature set is computed. Feature sets can consist of any combination of the features described in Sect. 3.2. Second, a feature selection step is carried out. Third, we select the best performing models for each feature type based on the outcome of a three-fold CV on $\mathcal{DB}_{partial}$. Using this information we perform classification on $\mathcal{DB}_{full}$. There are small differences between the global classification approach and the personalized classification approach, which are explained in this section. Figure 2 outlines the overall approach.

5.1 Global Classifiers

In this strategy, feature computation and selection are performed separately for $\mathcal{DB}_{partial}$ and $\mathcal{DB}_{full}$. Model selection is performed on $\mathcal{DB}_{partial}$ and the information obtained from this step is used for classification of $\mathcal{DB}_{full}$. The steps are explained in detail below:

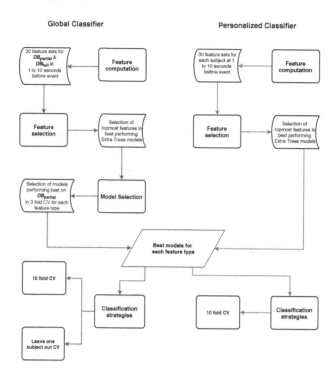

Fig. 2. Flowchart of the complete classification approach. Blue arrows mark the flow for global classifiers, red arrows represent the personalized classifiers. (Color figure online)

Feature Computation: Raw, statistical, Fourier, and angular features are computed for all specified segment lengths. Additionally, we generate more feature types by considering all possible combinations of the four features mentioned above. For each of these feature sets, we compute the PC projection and use them as another feature set. Hence there are 30 feature sets for each segment length.

Feature Selection: This step is based on the Extra-Trees classifier. For each feature set, we perform a ten-fold CV on all possible combinations of parameters for Extra-Trees models. In each validation step, we store each model's performance (accuracy) and feature importances. Feature importance reflects a feature's relevance in the classification. Based on each model's highest average accuracy, we select the best models. From these we compute the union of the previously saved topmost features. These features are used in our subsequent analysis.

SML Models: The feature sets used in this step are the ones that have been obtained after feature selection step.

1. Model Selection - Since there are a wide variety of possible models it is better to start with the $\mathcal{DB}_{\mathrm{partial}}$ for identifying the best models for each feature set. For each feature set, we perform three-fold CV with all possible models. We compute performance measures for assessing the performance of classifiers.

We then determine the best models by considering the best values for each performance measure keeping seconds, features constant. We generate a list of models that have been identified as best with specific feature sets and save them in **SelectedModels**.

2. For $\mathcal{DB}_{full}$, we perform ten-fold CV using the information in **SelectedModels**. We compute performance measures and determine the highest accuracy for each feature set. We also perform LOSOCV for each subject in $\mathcal{DB}_{full}$.

Validation of Model Selection: To validate our model selection step, we compared the average ratio of misclassified samples during three-fold CV for $\mathcal{DB}_{partial}$ with the average ratio when performing ten-fold CV on $\mathcal{DB}_{full}$. It turned out, that performance is comparable (e.g., 0.24 for three-fold CV on $\mathcal{DB}_{partial}$ and 0.25 for ten-fold CV on $\mathcal{DB}_{full}$). Hence, it is reasonable to infer model and feature combination that would work the best for the $\mathcal{DB}_{full}$ dataset by using information from $\mathcal{DB}_{partial}$.

5.2   Personalized Classifiers

In this strategy, classification is performed separately for each subject which has at least ten samples and further contains at least three samples of each, hinging, standing, and sitting. The complete workflow is shown in Fig. 2. There are small differences in this approach compared to the global classifier approach. Here, in **feature computation**, the 30 feature sets are computed for each subject separately instead of computing feature sets for all samples in the dataset together. **Feature selection** is performed in a similar manner as in Sect. 5.1. Model and feature combination is determined from **SelectedModels** which had been generated in Sect. 5.1. This information is used to perform classification using **ten-fold CV** on feature sets obtained after feature selection.

6   Results

In this section, we present the main results obtained through global and personalized classifier approaches.

6.1   Global Classification Results

In global classification, ten-fold CV on $\mathcal{DB}_{full}$ resulted in highest average classification accuracy values between 0.61 and 0.80 depending on the feature sets. The highest average classification accuracy was achieved using PC of statistical feature set, while the lowest average classification accuracy was obtained with PC of angular feature set. Various feature sets performed well with an average classification accuracy of 0.79.

For PC of statistical feature set, the highest average classification accuracy of 0.80 was achieved by using eight specific AdaBoost models and two specific Extra-Trees models at a window size of $s = 1$ s before the event. Table 3 (a) shows values of the respective confusion matrix. Figure 3 shows the average classification accuracy and standard deviation of several specific models for window sizes ranging from $s = 1\,\mathrm{s}$ to $s = 10\,\mathrm{s}$ for ten-fold CV on $\mathcal{DB}_{\mathrm{full}}$. We found that all models performed best at a window size of one second. Considering longer motion sequences did not improve classification results in this scenario.

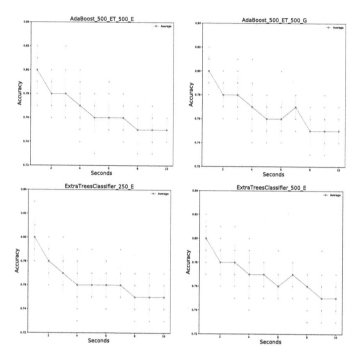

Fig. 3. Average classification accuracy of ten-fold CV for $\mathcal{DB}_{\mathrm{full}}$ (blue dots and lines) with standard deviation (vertical cyan lines) using PC of Statistical feature set generated at $s = 1, 2, \ldots, 10\,\mathrm{s}$ before the event. Grey dots mark the accuracy value in each fold of the ten-fold CV. The title of each plot contains the classifier and the values of the parameters used to train that model. (Color figure online)

In ten-fold CV, samples for training and validation are taken randomly. Thus, we cannot derive concrete conclusions how well the classification works for a new, unknown user. To this end, we performed LOSOCV. In this scenario, all subjects have highest classification accuracy greater than 0.50 i.e. with different feature sets and model combinations it is possible to classify each subject with accuracy at least more than 0.50. 65% and 46% of the total number of subjects have highest classification accuracy of over 0.80 and 0.90 respectively. 37% of the total number of subjects reached a classification accuracy of 1. Figure 4 shows a plot representing the percentage of subjects which have accuracy x or more where $x = 0.0, 0.1, \ldots, 1.0$. Table 3 (b) shows the confusion matrix at a window size of $s = 1\,\mathrm{s}$. This quality was achieved which for 32% of the subjects.

6.2 Personalized Classification

Samples belonging to 41 different subjects in the $\mathcal{DB}_{\mathrm{full}}$ dataset satisfied the requirements for personalized analysis described in Sect. 5.2. Hence, they have

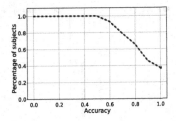

Fig. 4. Percentage of subjects with an average classification accuracy of x or more for $x = 0.0, 0.1, ..., 1.0$ in $\mathcal{DB}_{\text{full}}$. On the vertical axis 1.0 represents 100%.

Table 2. List of features and classifiers including used parameter values which performed best in the classification.

Feature	Classifier	Value of parameter
Angular	AdaBoost	$e = 500$ & $c =$ Extra Trees with $e = 500$ & Entropy
Raw	ANN	$h_i = 900, f_{\text{act}} = l, f_{\text{opt}} = s$ & $l = a$
PC of statistical	ANN	$h_i = 600, f_{\text{act}} = l, f_{\text{opt}} = s$ & $l = a$
Raw & angular	ANN	$h_i = 800, f_{\text{act}} = l, f_{\text{opt}} = s$ & $l = a$
PC of statistical & angular	ANN	$h_i = 300, f_{\text{act}} = l, f_{\text{opt}} = s$ & $l = a$
PC of statistical & angular & raw	ANN	$h_i = 300, f_{\text{act}} = l, f_{\text{opt}} = s$ & $l = a$
PC of statistical & angular & Fourier	ANN	$h_i = 600, f_{\text{act}} = l, f_{\text{opt}} = a$ & $l = i$

Table 3. Confusion matrix values for global and personalized classification approaches. HI abbreviate hinging, SI sitting, and ST standing. Sub-tables (a) and (b) contain results from the global classifier. In (a), ten-fold CV was used, in (b) LOSCOV. Sub-table (c) and (d) show two exemplary results from the personalized classifier.

True & Predicted	(a)			(b)			(c)			(d)		
	HI	SI	ST	HI	SI	ST	HI	SI	ST	HI	SI	ST
HI	0.93	0.02	0.01	1	0	0	0.99	0.00	0.01	1.00	0.00	0.00
SI	0.04	0.73	0.21	0	1	0	0.00	0.72	0.18	0.00	1.00	0.03
ST	0.03	0.25	0.78	0	0	1	0.01	0.28	0.81	0.00	0.00	0.97

been considered for further per subject analysis. We performed ten-fold CV for each of these subjects and calculated the average accuracy for each subject. From these average accuracies the models with highest average accuracies were identified keeping model category, feature sets, segment length and subject constant. The obtained models were further reduced by selecting the models having highest average accuracies at all segment lengths for a given subject and feature set. A detailed specification of these models is given in Table 2. The average accuracy over subjects for the models in Table 2 lies between 0.70 and 0.85. Figure 5 shows average accuracy and standard deviation plots of four such models. Tables 3 (c) and (d) show the confusion matrix obtained for a subject with

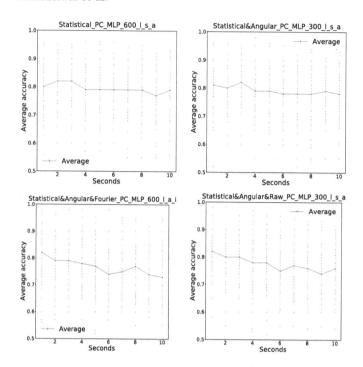

Fig. 5. Average classification accuracy of the four best performing ANN models for all subjects and at all time ranges on $\mathcal{DB}_{full}$.

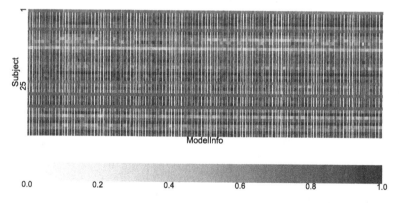

Fig. 6. Heatmap of the average accuracy for $\mathcal{DB}_{full}$. Subjects are on the y-axis and feasible combinations of PC feature, time range and model on the x-axis.

average classification accuracy of 84% and 98% respectively. By using a certain set of features and models it is possible to classify the postures of 15 subjects with 100% average classification accuracy resulting in an ideal confusion matrix. To get an overall idea of the performance of different models and features for the 41 subjects, Fig. 6 shows a heatmap of average classification accuracies. Each cell in the heatmap denotes the average accuracy obtained for a given subject on the

y-axis and model as well as feature combination on the x-axis. The horizontal view of the heatmap shows that there are certain subjects which have accuracies of over 50% in almost all possible model and feature combinations. The vertical view shows that certain model and feature combinations fail to accurately classify any subject.

7 Conclusion and Future Work

In this work, we presented a series of approaches for classification of a user's position, based on posture readings of a wearable device. We tested various feature sets and classifiers using global and personalized classification approaches.

It turned out that a personalized classification approach can better predict the position than a global approach if sufficient data is available for training of such personalized models. We found that 65% of the subjects have an average accuracy of larger than 0.8 for global classification. In our case, it was feasible to perform personalized analysis on 38% of total number of subjects. We observed that 97% of these subjects reached an average accuracy of over 0.8 and for 68% the average accuracy climbed to over 0.9. Hence, it is possible to come up with personalized posture classification based on the *Gokhale SpineTracker*^{TM} readings, even if only few samples are given per subject and position.

This classification can be further extended to differentiate between good and bad postures so as to notify the user whenever they are in the wrong posture for a particular task. Additionally, allowing a user to train custom positions and adding these into classification is of interest and challenging when only few data points are present. Further extension is also possible by modifying the sensors to improve the performance of the automated system. The accelerometer sensors can be further developed into inertial sensors by extending them with a gyroscope. This would provide more information and potentially improve the classification of postures.

References

1. Vos, T., Abajobir, A.A., Abate, K.H., Abbafati, C., Abbas, K.M., et al.: Global, regional, and national incidence, prevalence, and years lived with disability for 328 diseases and injuries for 195 countries, 1990–2016: a systematic analysis for the global burden of disease study 2016. The Lancet **390**(10100), 1211–1259 (2017)
2. NINDS: Low back pain fact sheet (2017). https://www.ninds.nih.gov/Disorders/Patient-Caregiver-Education/Fact-Sheets/Low-Back-Pain-Fact-Sheet/. Accessed 16 May 2018
3. Enterprises, G.M.: Gokhale spinetracker. https://gokhalemethod.com/. Accessed 23 July 2018
4. Noiumkar, S., Tirakoat, S.: Use of optical motion capture in sports science: a case study of golf swing. In: 2013 International Conference on Informatics and Creative Multimedia, pp. 310–313. IEEE (2013)
5. MacIver, M., Sharabash, N., Nelson, M.: Prey-capture behavior in gymnotid electric fish: motion analysis and effects of water conductivity. J. Exp. Biol. **204**(3), 543–557 (2001)

6. Culhane, K.M., O'Connor, M., Lyons, D., Lyons, G.M.: Accelerometers in rehabilitation medicine for older adults. Age Ageing **34**(6), 556–560 (2005)
7. Merriaux, P., Dupuis, Y., Boutteau, R., Vasseur, P., Savatier, X.: A study of vicon system positioning performance. Sensors **17**(7), 1591 (2017)
8. Riaz, Q., Guanhong, T., Krüger, B., Weber, A.: Motion reconstruction using very few accelerometers and ground contacts. Graph. Models **79**, 23–38 (2015)
9. Slyper, R., Hodgins, J.K.: Action capture with accelerometers. In: Proceedings of the 2008 ACM SIGGRAPH/Eurographics Symposium on Computer Animation. SCA 2008, pp. 193–199. Eurographics Association (2008)
10. Vlasic, D., et al.: Practical motion capture in everyday surroundings. ACM Trans. Graph. **26**(3), 35 (2007)
11. Farella, E., Benini, L., Riccò, B., Acquaviva, A.: MOCA: a low-power, low-cost motion capture system based on integrated accelerometers. Adv. Multimedia **2007**(1), 1 (2007)
12. Weise, T., Bouaziz, S., Li, H., Pauly, M.: Realtime performance-based facial animation. ACM Trans. Graph. **30**(4), 77:1–77:10 (2011)
13. Cao, C., Bradley, D., Zhou, K., Beeler, T.: Real-time high-fidelity facial performance capture. ACM Trans. Graph. **34**(4), 46:1–46:9 (2015)
14. Hoffmann, J., Brüggemann, B., Krüger, B.: Automatic calibration of a motion capture system based on inertial sensors for tele-manipulation. In: 7th International Conference on Informatics in Control, Automation and Robotics, June (2010)
15. Ma, C.Z.H., Ling, Y.T., Shea, Q.T.K., Wang, L.K., Wang, X.Y., Zheng, Y.P.: Towards wearable comprehensive capture and analysis of skeletal muscle activity during human locomotion. Sensors **19**(1), 195 (2019)
16. Zhao, W., Chai, J., Xu, Y.Q.: Combining marker-based mocap and RGB-D camera for acquiring high-fidelity hand motion data. In: Proceedings of ACM SCA, pp. 33–42 (2012)
17. Stollenwerk, K., Vögele, A., Krüger, B., Hinkenjann, A., Klein, R.: Automatic temporal segmentation of articulated hand motion. In: Gervasi, O., et al. (eds.) ICCSA 2016. LNCS, vol. 9787, pp. 433–449. Springer, Cham (2016). https://doi.org/10.1007/978-3-319-42108-7_33
18. Wan, C., Probst, T., Van Gool, L., Yao, A.: Dense 3D regression for hand pose estimation. In: Proceedings of the IEEE Conference on Computer Vision and Pattern Recognition, pp. 5147–5156 (2018)
19. Williams, J.M., Haq, I., Lee, R.Y.: Dynamic measurement of lumbar curvature using fibre-optic sensors. Med. Eng. Phys. **32**(9), 1043–1049 (2010)
20. Stollenwerk, K., Müllers, J., Müller, J., Hinkenjann, A., Krüger, B.: Evaluating an accelerometer-based system for spine shape monitoring. In: Gervasi, O., et al. (eds.) ICCSA 2018. LNCS, vol. 10963, pp. 740–756. Springer, Cham (2018). https://doi.org/10.1007/978-3-319-95171-3_58
21. Xu, W., et al.: MonoPerfCap: human performance capture from monocular video. ACM Trans. Graph. **37**(2), 27:1–27:15 (2018)
22. Alldieck, T., Magnor, M., Xu, W., Theobalt, C., Pons-Moll, G.: Detailed human avatars from monocular video. In: International Conference on 3D Vision, pp. 98–109. IEEE (2018)
23. Iqbal, U., Doering, A., Yasin, H., Krüger, B., Weber, A., Gall, J.: A dual-source approach for 3D human pose estimation from single images. Comput. Vis. Image Underst. **172**, 37–49 (2018)
24. Dabral, R., Mundhada, A., Kusupati, U., Afaque, S., Sharma, A., Jain, A.: Learning 3D human pose from structure and motion. In: Ferrari, V., Hebert, M., Sminchisescu, C., Weiss, Y. (eds.) ECCV 2018. LNCS, vol. 11213, pp. 679–696. Springer, Cham (2018). https://doi.org/10.1007/978-3-030-01240-3_41

25. Bernard, J., Dobermann, E., Vögele, A., Krüger, B., Kohlhammer, J., Fellner, D.: Visual-interactive semi-supervised labeling of human motion capture data. In: Visualization and Data Analysis, January (2017)
26. Baumann, J., Wessel, R., Krüger, B., Weber, A.: Action graph: a versatile data structure for action recognition. In: GRAPP 2014 - International Conference on Computer Graphics Theory and Applications, SCITEPRESS, January (2014)
27. Riaz, Q., Vögele, A., Krüger, B., Weber, A.: One small step for a man: estimation of gender, age, and height from recordings of one step by a single inertial sensor. Sensors **15**(12), 31999–32019 (2015)
28. Consmüller, T., et al.: Automatic distinction of upper body motions in the main anatomical planes. Med. Eng. Phys. **36**(4), 516–521 (2014)
29. Jeyhani, V., Mahdiani, S., Viik, J., Oksala, N., Vehkaoja, A.: A novel technique for analysis of postural information with wearable devices. In: IEEE 15th International Conference on Wearable and Implantable Body Sensor Networks, March, 30–33 (2018)
30. Wong, W.Y., Wong, M.S.: Trunk posture monitoring with inertial sensors. Eur. Spine J. **17**(5), 743–753 (2008)
31. Voinea, G.D., Butnariu, S., Mogan, G.: Measurement and geometric modelling of human spine posture for medical rehabilitation purposes using a wearable monitoring system based on inertial sensors. Sensors **17**(1), 3 (2017)
32. Fathi, A., Curran, K.: Detection of spine curvature using wireless sensors. J. King Saud Univ.-Sci. **29**(4), 553–560 (2017)
33. Cajamarca, G., Rodríguez, I., Herskovic, V., Campos, M., Riofrío, J.C.: StraightenUp+: monitoring of posture during daily activities for older persons using wearable sensors. Sensors **18**(10), 3409 (2018)
34. Pedregosa, F., Varoquaux, G., Gramfort, A., Michel, V., Thirion, B., Grisel, O., et al.: Scikit-learn: machine learning in Python. J. Mach. Learn. Res. **12**, 2825–2830 (2011)
35. Tarca, A.L., Carey, V.J., Chen, X., Romero, R., Drăghici, S.: Machine learning and its applications to biology. PLoS Comput. Biol. **3**(6), e116 (2007)
36. Scikitlearn: Nearest neighbors. http://scikit-learn.org/stable/modules/neighbors.html. Accessed 19 Sept 2018
37. Bhatia, N.: Vandana: Survey of nearest neighbor techniques. CoRR abs/1007.0085 (2010)
38. Lan, K., Wang, D.T., Fong, S., Liu, L.S., Wong, K.K., Dey, N.: A survey of data mining and deep learning in bioinformatics. J. Med. Syst. **42**(8), 139:1–139:20 (2018)
39. Ho, T.K.: Random decision forests. In: Third International Conference on Document Analysis and Recognition, vol. 1, pp. 278–282 (1995)
40. Geurts, P., Ernst, D., Wehenkel, L.: Extremely randomized trees. Mach. Learn. **63**(1), 3–42 (2006)
41. Tu, J.V.: Advantages and disadvantages of using artificial neural networks versus logistic regression for predicting medical outcomes. J. Clin. Epidemiol. **49**(11), 1225–1231 (1996)
42. Freund, Y., Schapire, R.E.: A decision-theoretic generalization of on-line learning and an application to boosting. J. Comput. Syst. Sci. **55**(1), 119–139 (1997)
43. Hastie, T., Rosset, S., Zhu, J., Zou, H.: Multi-class adaboost. Stat. Interface **2**(3), 349–360 (2009)

Collective, Massive and Evolutionary Systems (WCES 2019)

Set Semantic Similarity for Image Prosthetic Knowledge Exchange

Valentina Franzoni[1,2]($\boxtimes$), Yuanxi Li[3], and Alfredo Milani[1]

[1] Department of Mathematics and Computer Science, University of Perugia,
via Vanvitelli, 1, 06123 Perugia, Italy
valentina.franzoni@dmi.unipg.it
[2] Department of Computer, Control, and Management Engineering
"Antonio Ruberti", Sapienza University of Rome, via Ariosto, 25,
00185 Rome, Italy
[3] Department of Computer Science, Hong Kong Baptist University,
Kowloon, Hong Kong, China
csxyli@comp.hkbu.edu.hk

Abstract. Concept information can be expressed by text, images or general objects which semantic meaning is clear to a human in a specific cultural context. For a computer, when available, text with its semantics (e.g., metadata, comments, captions) can convey more precise meaning than images or general objects with low-level features (e.g., color distribution, shapes, sound peaks) to extract the concept underlying the object. Among semantic measures, web-based proximity measures e.g., confidence, PMING, NGD, Jaccard, Dice, are particularly useful for concept evaluation, exploiting statistical data provided by search engines on terms and expressions provided in texts associated with the object.

Where Artificial Intelligence can be a support for impaired individuals, e.g., having disabilities related to vision and hearing, understanding the concept underlying an object can be critical for an intelligent artificial assistant. In this work we propose to use the set semantic distance, already used in literature for semantic similarity measurement of web objects, as a tool for artificial assistants to support knowledge extraction; in other words, as prosthetic knowledge.

Keywords: Information retrieval · Artificial Intelligence · Assistants ·
Semantic proximity · Group distance

1 Introduction

With the persistent diffusion of digital social interactions, the investigation of the information conventional by human-machine interactions became a critical research problem, as an increasing quantity of economic, personal and physical connections is digitally intermediated, stored and tracked, and can be used to predict and influence the way people or entities interact, vote, work, and behave [1, 2]. The snowballing amount of information daily produced using mobile devices, e.g., images, videos, music, with explicit (e.g., tags, hashtags, and keywords) or implicit (e.g., captions or metadata) content, can augment the information value of the document. Such informative content

© Springer Nature Switzerland AG 2019
S. Misra et al. (Eds.): ICCSA 2019, LNCS 11624, pp. 513–525, 2019.
https://doi.org/10.1007/978-3-030-24311-1_37

can be called Prosthetic Knowledge (PK), as the evidence that a user does not know can be accessed using technology.

When such information is not retrievable with high usability, an average user is informatively-impaired, even if without having physical or psychic disabilities. On the other hand, when the information is available in proper media, even a physical or psychic impaired user can become fully able to benefit from it.

In this environment, PK is the latent knowledge underlying augmented information in augmented documents, generated and eventually shared by users using technologies in high-tech devices and that, stored in structure or semi-structured form, can be used by intelligent assistants to enhance the information retrieval capabilities of the device, thus of the user [3–5].

In the following sections, the use of a set semantic similarity scheme is proposed for prosthetic knowledge. In Sect. 2, Concept-based Image Retrieval is presented with its pros and cons. In Sect. 3, related works on set semantic image similarity are summarized. In Sect. 4, experiments on the efficacy of the set proximity scheme for image similarity calculation is proposed as an example of the application of prosthetic knowledge. In Sect. 5, conclusions are drawn.

2   Concept-Based and Content-Based Image Retrieval

In *Content-based* Image Retrieval, proximity measures of low-level features [6] guide the process of retrieval. Content-based Image Retrieval aims to involve the proximity from a perceptual point of view, and deep-semantic relations among images cannot be discovered, because they require to integrate Content-based similarity with the broader notion of *Concept-based* Image similarity, [7] more useful for retrieval aims, as shown in Fig. 1.

Opening with the reflexion that the textual information related to images, such as captions, labels, tags, and comments, convey more concept-related than content-based information, we can concentrate on the textual context e.g., metadata and social networks links among objects, media and users themselves.

The features of big networks of concepts, built collaboratively by a collaboration of users, provide numerous advantages, among which:

1. *Information sharing and explanation direction*: context knowledge is annotated and filtered manually, with the unambiguous purpose of knowledge sharing, e.g., the hyperlink structure of Wikipedia.
2. *Open end and dynamic update*: collaborative networks of concepts are nonstop updated by a crowd of users, enhancing the temporal and qualitative value of the information, where new knowledge is timely added to the network as soon as such information arises. Semantic ontologies, such as WordNet, [8] tend on the other hand to be more stationary and to reflect the cultural or personal biases of their authors, due to the smaller number of contributors, even if experts.
3. *Heterogeneousness*: collaborative and social networks contain information about several different objects, users and relations as sources to deduce semantic

Fig. 1. Different similarity connotations between human and computer.

knowledge; the objects/documents in the network are included in a relevant semantic context.

Such features are useful for some applications, including:

- *Query expansion*, where the notion of the original term in the query can be extended with a set of suitable keywords in order to retrieve related objects. Our method exploits the textual information of entities, relying on outward web-based knowledge bases. Measuring the proximity of objects by scheming the similarity of their related annotations can be productive using similarity/distance measures. Such way exploits basic web-based semantic proximity between two objects (i.e., among their textual annotations), and our proposed method delivers a new class of measures for group/set distance and context extraction, composing concept similarity measures.
- *Prediction* of annotation of images using prosthetic knowledge, [9, 10] and the suggestion of explicit annotations with image sub-structures, to predict their similarity.

3   Semantic Similarity Measures

We propose to use for prosthetic knowledge a set distance built on web-based proximity measures. Such a distance is a combination of selected values obtained by the calculation of several web-based proximity measures, some of which presented in detail in the following sub-paragraphs: first, related works are presented, then our set distance is exposed. Statistic-based measures can be straightforwardly calculated from search engine statistical results, while ontology-based measures require to navigate static ontologies (e.g., Wordnet) or dynamic ontologies (e.g., Wikipedia). It is worth to note that in both cases of statistics on search engines and dynamic ontologies, the measures can reflect the dynamic information underlying the knowledge of the users uploading data.

3.1   Ontology-Based Semantic Similarity

A. WordNet Distance [8, 11, 12]

The *WordNet Distance* (WD) defines the similarity between two concepts x and y in WordNet, exploiting the information about the concepts that subsume the given concepts in the ontology:

$$D_{wnet}(x, y) = \frac{2 \times \log P(lso(x, y))}{\log P(x) + \log P(y)} \tag{1}$$

where *lso(x, y)* is the lowest super-ordinate (i.e., most specific common subsumer) of concepts x and y, i.e., the closest common ancestor in the ontology, and *P(z)* is the probability of hitting a *synset* (i.e., synonyms set, the fundamental entity in WordNet) z, using a Shannon measure of the information content [13].

B. Wikipedia Distances

In Wikipedia, the hyperlinks among articles build a semantic explanation network among the pages.

The *WikiRelate* model [14] has the achievement to be the first model to compute semantic proximity measures using Wikipedia relationships. This approach uses techniques previously applied to WordNet and modifies them for Wikipedia's links category hierarchy.

Second, among the first models to use Wikipedia, the *Wikipedia Link Vector Model* [15, 16] uses the hyperlink structure of Wikipedia to provide a structured knowledge base without considering the categories anymore. The probability of the D_{wiki} distance in the Wikipedia Link Vector Model is defined as the fraction of the number of links to a target page on the total number of pages. Thus, if t is the total number of articles within Wikipedia, then the weighted value for the link $x \to y$ is:

$$D_{wiki}(x \to y) = |x \to y| \times \log(\sum_{i=1}^{t} \frac{t}{|i \to y|}) \tag{2}$$

where x and y denote the two articles about terms x and y.

To be mentioned, the set of the *Heuristic Semantic Search* (HSW) [17] measures, calculating the semantic distance in Wikipedia through a random walk guided by a web-based measure. This model is the first hybrid model to use web-based semantic proximity in Wikipedia and offers the benefit to provide several publications tracking the advancement and application of the model [18–23]. Moreover, the HSW model can be used and enhanced with any suitable proximity measure.

C. Flickr Distance

Flickr distance (FD) [24] is a model to measure the relationship between semantic concepts in a visual domain like Flickr.

The FD between two concepts x and y are measured by the average square root of the Jensen-Shannon divergence between the corresponding latent topic-based visual language model.

The major drawback of the Flickr distance is that it has not been validated with other datasets.

$$D_{flickr}(x, y) = \sqrt{\frac{\sum_{i=1}^{K} \sum_{j=1}^{K} D_{JS}(P_{z_i}x \| P_{z_j}y)}{K^2}} \tag{3}$$

where

$$D_{JS}(P_{z_j}x \| P_{z_j}x) = \frac{1}{2} D_{KL}((P_{z_i}x \| M) + \frac{1}{2} D_{KL}(P_{z_j}x \| M)). \tag{4}$$

The Kullback-Leibler divergence, expressed by:

$$D_{KL}(Q \| R) = \sum_i Q(i) \log \frac{Q(i)}{R(i)}, \tag{5}$$

is a standard measurement of the difference between two probability distributions Q and R. in the Flickr context, it can be seen as a measurement of the mutual entropy between two visual language models.

Moreover, computing the distance requires a computationally demanding process on the images content to calculate the probability distributions, which is hardly applicable to large and dynamical domains.

D. Structural Distances for Proximity Prediction

Link Prediction (LP) [25] is a method to establish the strength of ties in a graph: the more the strength, the more robust the ties among potential collaborators, e.g., co-authors in a bibliometric network [26]. The structural, i.e., the topological, similarity is a suitable candidate method for link prediction.

Common Neighbours-based (CN) rankings (e.g., Jaccard, Adamic-Adar [27]) represent a class of similarity measures for link prediction, which efficiently evaluate the likelihood of a new link based on the neighbors frontier of the already existing nodes. The CN proximity measures are more efficient than others (e.g., preferential attachment, path-based distances), but they have the weakness of returning a large 0-tail: [19, 20] a zero-rank value is given to all the links of pair of nodes, which have no common neighbors. Even if the rating is equal to 0, such links may be potentially suitable for link prediction.

Recent approaches for link prediction [28, 29] use topological (e.g., Adamic, Common Neighbours) and semantic similarity (e.g., Confidence, [30–32] PMI [33] and PMING [34–36]) together [37] or similarly, [9] to predict future links or infer existing unknown links from a social network or graph-based database [26]. Using the proper metrics, this approach allows shortening the 0-tail [10, 38–40].

Other approaches use a 2-steps or 3-steps traversal in order to navigate the network in short paths by different directions, in order to enhance the probability to find candidates for prediction.

3.2 Web-Based Semantic Similarity

The class of Web-Based Proximity Measures (WBPM) [3, 4, 41–43] is characterized by the probabilities of events used in their definitions, which can be approximated by frequencies drawn from popular web engines. Search engines are a accepted source of evidence about semantic affinity. The general idea is to use a search engine S as a black box to submit queries on a term or a set of terms.

In the following, we will use the term similarity and proximity as synonymous while, in other cases, when we will refer to distances. Simple arithmetic and normalization are used to transform a distance into proximity and vice-versa. We observe that WBPM can be equivalently based on probabilities or frequencies.

If the frequency $f(x) = |S(x)|$ denotes the cardinality of the results of a query to S based the search term x, and N is the total number of objects indexed by the S, $P(x) = f(x)/N$.

Different similarity measures have been experimented to assess the effectiveness of WBPM.

In the following, the WBPMs considered in our set-distance experiments are detailed.

A. Confidence and Mutual Confidence

Confidence (Conf) is a statistical measure applied in rule mining.

Given a rule $x \rightarrow y$, given the number of transactions that contain x, confidence calculates the percentage of transactions that also contain y:

$$Conf(x \rightarrow y) = \frac{P(x \wedge y)}{P(x)} = \frac{f(x \wedge y)}{f(x)} \tag{6}$$

Confidence cannot be used in a group distance, because it is not symmetric. Therefore, Mutual Confidence [22–24] is defined with the idea is to calculate the confidence of a term pair in both directions:

$$MC(x \leftrightarrow y) = \frac{1}{2} \frac{P(x)P(x \wedge y) + P(y)P(x \wedge y)}{P(x)P(y)} \tag{7}$$

B. Jaccard Similarity Measure

Jaccard similarity [19, 31, 32] is defined as a similarity ratio:

$$Jaccard = \frac{a}{a+b+c} \tag{8}$$

where a, b, and c represent the documents frequency of two terms w_1 and w_2 in a search:

$$a = w_1 \wedge w_2 \quad b = w_1 \wedge \neg w_2 \quad c = w_2 \wedge \neg w_1$$

C. Dice Similarity Measure

Dice similarity measure, [44] i.e. *Czekanowski* or *Sorenson*, gives more emphasis to the presence of common interactions between the compared sets, with respect to Jaccard:

$$Dice = \frac{2a}{2a + b + c} \tag{9}$$

where a, b, and c are defined as in the Jaccard measure.

3.3   Set Semantic Similarity

Our web-based set similarity [45–47] is defined on the elements extracted with a simple pre-processing from the context of a pair of images I_i and I_j. The set similarity scheme composes the elementary web-based similarities (or distances) d of the elements in the first and second sets of concepts.

$G_i = \{T_i1, T_i2, ..., T_im\}$ and $G_j = \{T_j1, T_j2, ..., T_jm\}$ is the group of concept elements (e.g. terms, hashtags, categories) associated to the images I_i and I_j.

The *Document Concept Set* (DCS) distance, measuring the mutual similarity of images I_i and I_j., is then defined by:

$$Dcs(I_i, I_j) = AVG_2\{AVG_1\{SEL \bigcup_{\substack{r\in 1,n \\ k\in 1,m}} d(T_{i_k}, T_{j_r})\}, AVG_1\{SEL \bigcup_{\substack{k\in 1,n \\ r\in 1,n}} d(T_{j_r}, T_{i_k})\}\} \tag{10}$$

where $SEL \in \{MAX, AVG, MIN\}$ and d is the web-based proximity or the composition of more web-based proximities. In our experiments, $d \in \{MC, Jaccard, Dice\}$.

As previously noticed, the DCS scheme defines a new class of semantic proximity measures, [26] where several elementary distances and a different composition operator generate a single semantic similarity function of the class.

4   Experiments

In our experiments, we demonstrated the applicability of the set distance for prosthetic knowledge on images in the Flickr repository, and then we designed a project to apply it to the exchange of learning objects between e-learning systems through an Artificial Intelligence-based assistant.

4.1   Image Set Similarity Experiments on Flickr Images

The Set Image Similarity model has been evaluated by experiments on a data set including 520 pairs of images from Flickr using our DCS [48].

The image tags annotated by Flickr users have been used as groups of concepts representing the knowledge associated with the image. Nine different instances of the DCS have been calculated varying SEL, with $SEL \in \{MAX, AVG, MIN\}$ and $d \in \{MC, Jaccard, Dice\}$.

Table 1. A subset of the experiment results

image1	image2	HSE user score	D_{CS} MC	D_{CS} Jaccard	D_{CS} dice
1	2	0.4783	0.3980	0.5241	0.6309
3	4	0.5304	0.3372	0.4208	0.8384
5	4	0.3739	0.2956	0.1653	0.3431
6	4	0.4174	0.2885	0.8518	0.1335
2	7	0.3217	0.2779	0.5383	0.8821
8	9	0.2957	0.2593	0.4587	0.5877
1	10	0.4348	0.2493	0.7110	0.5320
11	6	0.7565	0.2374	0.2803	0.4891
12	13	0.3130	0.2288	0.4917	0.5219
4	14	0.1304	0.2266	0.6247	0.6996
4	15	0.1652	0.2105	0.3844	0.8873

A human similarity evaluation (HSE) of each pair of images has been gained as ground truth for evaluation, gathering the votes of 120 students of the Hong Kong Baptist University, who contributed to the tests on 100 casually mined pairs for each contributor. Each dyad of images has been evaluated giving a ranking score from *0* (=very different) to *5* (=very similar), based on subjective decision. The students' ranking scores have been averaged to acquire the HSE for each image dyad.

The DCS occurrences have been calculated using the statistics gave back from the search engines *Google* and *Bing*, and the search interface of *Wikipedia*. In order to assess the performance of the rank of image dyads formed by the different occurrences of DCS and HSE, we have calculated the Pearson's correlation between them. Table 1 shows a pre-normalization HSE, i.e., the contributor's average score for some image dyad of the tests before normalization; MC ranks the results.

The systematic evaluation of the experimental results shows that the composition scheme where SEL = MAX and d = Dice is the most effective among the class, compared to human evaluation. The best values of Pearson's correlation score for MAX-Dice is 0.732, while MAX-MC is 0.726. The other grouping of measures attained lower scores on this specific task, without noteworthy variances regarding the different search engines.

4.2   Searching e-Learning Objects with an AI-Based Assistant

Recently, Artificial Intelligence (AI) has been introduced to e-learning systems [5]. In our environment, the exchange of Linkable Learning Objects (LLO) [49, 50] can be used for a dialogue between Learning Systems to obtain information, especially with the use of semantic or structural similarity measures to enhance the classification.

Learning open-source platforms, e.g., GLOREP and Moodle, are particularly suitable to be enhanced with AI-based tools, e.g., an intelligent assistant to support information exchange. A feasible solution is to develop an assistant based on existing devices, e.g. Google Home, Amazon Alexia, Microsoft Cortana, which offer a set of API for voice control. The module *moodledata* can be used to manage the information exchange between learning systems, both in GLOREP and in Moodle.

In such a web-based environment, web-based similarity measures, which rely on search engines (e.g., Google, Bing) to obtain frequency values used for semantic proximity calculation, can be easily integrated into an AI to obtain a set of LLO to exchange among learning systems.

Figure 2 depicts the scheme of our AI-based LLO search system, showing the exchange of LLOs between Moodle and a human. The first set of terms is the expression pronounced by the human via the voice control system of the AI-assistant, and the second set of terms is each set of metadata included in the learning system database.

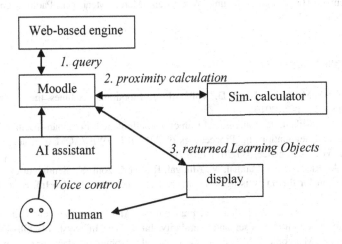

Fig. 2. AI-based LLO exchange

5   Conclusions and Future Work

Concept information can be expressed by text, images or general objects which semantic meaning is clear to a human in a specific cultural context. For a computer, when available, text with its semantics (e.g., metadata, comments, captions) can convey more precise meaning than images or general objects with low-level features (e.g., color distribution, shapes, sound peaks) to extract the concept underlying the object. We have shown how web-based proximity measures are sufficient for concept evaluation, exploiting statistical data provided by search engines on terms and expressions provided in texts associated with the object. We experimented the set image on the web-based distances Mutual Confidence, Dice and Jaccard with a selection scheme using Average, Maximum and Minimum on the Wikipedia search, Google and Bing. Experiments indicate that the best composition scheme is the one using Dice and MAX, compared to human evaluation on both the search engines compared to the Wikipedia search.

Furthermore, where Artificial Intelligence can be a support for impaired individuals, e.g., having disabilities related to vision and hearing, understanding the concept underlying an object can be critical for an intelligent artificial assistant. Also, for people neither mentally nor physically impaired, knowledge can be prosthetic in the sense of augmenting the knowledge through a device.

In this work we proposed to use the set semantic distance, already used in literature for semantic similarity measurement of web objects, as a tool for artificial assistants to support knowledge extraction; in other words, as prosthetic knowledge. As an example application, we designed a learning object selector, capable of selecting in a learning system the object that best suits a search made via an AI assistant.

Acknowledgments. The authors thank the students involved in the experiments, and the authors of previous works of the image set similarity project, cited in this paper, in particular Alfredo Milani, Clement H.C. Leung, Sheung Wai Chan, Marco Mencacci, Paolo Mengoni, and Simonetta Pallottelli.

References

1. Franzoni, V., Milani, A., Nardi, D., Vallverdú, J.: Emotional machines: the next revolution. Web Intell. **17**, 1–7 (2019)
2. Franzoni, V., Milani, A., Vallverdú, J.: Emotional affordances in human-machine interactive planning and negotiation. In: Proceedings of 2017 IEEE/WIC/ACM International Conference on Web Intelligence, WI 2017 (2017)
3. Milani, A., Rajdeep, N., Mangal, N., Mudgal, R.K., Franzoni, V.: Sentiment extraction and classification for the analysis of users' interest in tweets. Int. J. Web Inf. Syst. **14**, 29–40 (2018)
4. Mudgal, R.K., Niyogi, R., Milani, A., Franzoni, V.: Analysis of tweets to find the basis of popularity based on events semantic similarity. Int. J. Web Inf. Syst. **14**, 438–452 (2018)
5. Franzoni, V., Mengoni, P., Milani, A.: Dimensional morphing interface for dynamic learning evaluation. In: Information Visualisation - Biomedical Visualization, Visualisation on Built and Rural Environments and Geometric Modelling and Imaging, IV 2018 (2018)
6. Gervasi, O., Franzoni, V., Riganelli, M., Tasso, S.: Automating facial emotion recognition. Web Intell. **17**, 17–27 (2019)
7. Zhang, L., Ma, W.-Y., Li, X., Lin, F., Chen, L.: Image annotation by large-scale content-based image retrieval (2007)
8. Budanitsky, A., Hirst, G.: Evaluating WordNet-based measures of lexical semantic relatedness. Comput. Linguist. **32**, 13–47 (2006)

9. Milani, A., Franzoni, V., Biondi, G., Li, Y.: Integrating binary similarity measures in the link prediction task (2019)
10. Franzoni, V., Chiancone, A., Milani, A.: A multistrain bacterial diffusion model for link prediction. Int. J. Pattern Recognit Artif Intell. **31**, 1759024 (2017)
11. Budanitsky, A., Hirst, G.: Semantic distance in WordNet : an experimental, application-oriented evaluation of five measures. In: Workshop on WordNet and Other Lexical Resources, vol. 2 (2001)
12. Pedersen, T., Patwardhan, S., Michelizzi, J.: WordNet:: similarity: measuring the relatedness of concepts. In: Demonstration Papers at HLT-NAACL 2004 (2004)
13. Lin, J.: Divergence measures based on the shannon entropy. IEEE Trans. Inf. Theory **37**, 145–151 (1991)
14. Strube, M., Ponzetto, S.P.: WikiRelate! Computing semantic relatedness using Wikipedia. Am. Assoc. Artif. Intell. **6**, 1419–1424 (2006)
15. Gabrilovich, E., Markovitch, S.: Computing semantic relatedness using wikipedia-based explicit semantic analysis. In: IJCAI International Joint Conference on Artificial Intelligence (2007)
16. Milne, D.: Computing semantic relatedness using Wikipedia link structure. In: Work (2007)
17. Franzoni, V., Milani, A.: Heuristic semantic walk: browsing a collaborative network with a search engine-based heuristic (2013)
18. Franzoni, V., Milani, A.: A pheromone-like model for semantic context extraction from collaborative networks. In: Proceedings of 2015 IEEE/WIC/ACM International Joint Conference on Web Intelligence and Intelligent Agent Technology, WI-IAT 2015 (2016)
19. Franzoni, V., Mencacci, M., Mengoni, P., Milani, A.: Semantic heuristic search in collaborative networks: measures and contexts. In: Proceedings of 2014 IEEE/WIC/ACM International Joint Conference on Web Intelligence and Intelligent Agent Technology - Workshops, WI-IAT 2014 (2014)
20. Franzoni, V., Milani, A.: Heuristic semantic walk for concept chaining in collaborative networks. Int. J. Web Inf. Syst. **10**, 85–103 (2014)
21. Franzoni, V., Mencacci, M., Mengoni, P., Milani, A.: Heuristics for semantic path search in Wikipedia (2014)
22. Franzoni, V., Milani, A.: Semantic context extraction from collaborative networks. In: Proceedings of the 2015 IEEE 19th International Conference on Computer Supported Cooperative Work in Design, CSCWD 2015 (2015)
23. Pallottelli, S., Franzoni, V., Milani, A.: Multi-path traces in semantic graphs for latent knowledge elicitation. In: Proceedings of the International Conference on Natural Computation (2016)
24. Wu, L., Hua, X.-S., Yu, N., Ma, W.-Y., Li, S.: Flickr distance: a relationship measure for visual concepts. IEEE Trans. Pattern Anal. Mach. Intell. **34**, 863–875 (2012)
25. Liben-Nowell, D., Kleinberg, J.M.: The link-prediction problem for social networks. JASIST **58**, 1019–1031 (2007)
26. Franzoni, V., Lepri, M., Li, Y., Milani, A.: Efficient graph-based author disambiguation by topological similarity in DBLP. In: Proceedings of 2018 1st IEEE International Conference on Artificial Intelligence and Knowledge Engineering, AIKE 2018 (2018)
27. Adamic, L.A., Lento, T.M., Adar, E., Ng, P.C.: Information evolution in social networks. In: WSDM, pp. 473–482. ACM (2016)
28. Hoffman, M., Steinley, D., Brusco, M.J.: A note on using the adjusted Rand index for link prediction in networks. Soc. Netw. **42**, 72–79 (2015)
29. Han, S., Xu, Y.: Link prediction in microblog network using supervised learning with multiple features. JCP **11**, 72–82 (2016)

30. Biondi, G., Franzoni, V., Li, Y., Milani, A.: SEMO: a semantic model for emotion recognition in web objects. In: ICCSA. Springer, Heidelberg (2017)
31. Franzoni, V., Biondi, G., Milani, A.: A web-based system for emotion vector extraction. In: Gervasi, O., et al. (eds.) ICCSA 2017. LNCS, vol. 10406, pp. 653–668. Springer, Cham (2017). https://doi.org/10.1007/978-3-319-62398-6_46
32. Huang, A.H., Yen, D.C., Zhang, X.: Exploring the potential effects of emoticons. Inf. Manag. **45**, 466–473 (2008)
33. Turney, P.D.: Mining the web for synonyms: {PMI-IR} versus {LSA} on {TOEFL}. CoRR. cs.LG/0212 (2002)
34. Franzoni, V., Milani, A.: PMING distance: a collaborative semantic proximity measure. In: Proceedings of 2012 IEEE/WIC/ACM International Conference on Intelligent Agent Technology, IAT 2012 (2012)
35. Biondi, G., Franzoni, V., Li, Y., Milani, A.: Web-based similarity for emotion recognition in web objects. In: Proceedings of 9th IEEE/ACM International Conference on Utility and Cloud Computing, UCC 2016 (2016)
36. Franzoni, V., Milani, A., Biondi, G.: SEMO: a semantic model for emotion recognition in web objects. In: Proceedings of 2017 IEEE/WIC/ACM International Conference on Web Intelligence, WI 2017 (2017)
37. Franzoni, V., Milani, A.: Structural and semantic proximity in information networks. In: Gervasi, O., et al. (eds.) ICCSA 2017. LNCS, vol. 10404, pp. 651–666. Springer, Cham (2017). https://doi.org/10.1007/978-3-319-62392-4_47
38. Chiancone, A., Franzoni, V., Li, Y., Markov, K., Milani, A.: Leveraging zero tail in neighbourhood for link prediction. In: Proceedings of 2015 IEEE/WIC/ACM International Joint Conference on Web Intelligence and Intelligent Agent Technology, WI-IAT 2015 (2016)
39. Chiancone, A., Milani, A., Poggioni, V., Pallottelli, S., Madotto, A., Franzoni, V.: A multistrain bacterial model for link prediction. In: Proceedings of International Conference on Natural Computation (2016)
40. Chiancone, A., Franzoni, V., Niyogi, R., Milani, A.: Improving link ranking quality by quasi-common neighbourhood. In: Proceedings of 15th International Conference on Computational Science and Its Applications, ICCSA 2015 (2015)
41. Franzoni, V., Milani, A.: A semantic comparison of clustering algorithms for the evaluation of web-based similarity measures. In: Gervasi, O., et al. (eds.) ICCSA 2016. LNCS, vol. 9790, pp. 438–452. Springer, Cham (2016). https://doi.org/10.1007/978-3-319-42092-9_34
42. Franzoni, V., Li, Y., Mengoni, P.: A path-based model for emotion abstraction on facebook using sentiment analysis and taxonomy knowledge. In: Proceedings of 2017 IEEE/WIC/ACM International Conference on Web Intelligence, WI 2017 (2017)
43. Leung, C.H.C., Li, Y., Milani, A., Franzoni, V.: Collective evolutionary concept distance based query expansion for effective web document retrieval. In: Murgante, B., et al. (eds.) ICCSA 2013. LNCS, vol. 7974, pp. 657–672. Springer, Heidelberg (2013). https://doi.org/10.1007/978-3-642-39649-6_47
44. Brown, A., Randall, S., Ferrante, A., Boyd, J.: Partial Agreements in Probabilistic Linkages. Int. J. Popul. Data Sci. **3**, 293 (2018)
45. Franzoni, V., Leung, C.H.C., Li, Y., Mengoni, P., Milani, A.: Set similarity measures for images based on collective knowledge. In: Gervasi, O., et al. (eds.) ICCSA 2015. LNCS, vol. 9155, pp. 408–417. Springer, Cham (2015). https://doi.org/10.1007/978-3-319-21404-7_30
46. Zhang, J., Zhou, Q., Zhuo, L., Geng, W., Wang, S.: A CBIR system for hyperspectral remote sensing images using endmember extraction. IJWPRAI **31**(4) (2016)

47. Franzoni, V., Milani, A., Pallottelli, S., Leung, C.H.C., Li, Y.: Context-based image semantic similarity. In: 2015 12th International Conference on Fuzzy Systems and Knowledge Discovery, FSKD 2015 (2016)
48. Chan, S.W., Franzoni, V., Mengoni, P., Milani, A.: Context-based image semantic similarity for prosthetic knowledge. In: Proceedings of 2018 1st IEEE International Conference on Artificial Intelligence and Knowledge Engineering, AIKE 2018 (2018)
49. Franzoni, V., Tasso, S., Pallottelli, S.: Sharing linkable learning objects between a content management system and a learning management system with the use of metadata and a taxonomy assistant for categorization. In: LNCS, ICCSA 2019 (2019)
50. Tasso, S., Pallottelli, S., Gervasi, O., Sabbatini, F., Franzoni, V.: Cloud and local servers into a federation of learning object repositories. In: ICCSA 2019, LNCS. Springer, Heidelberg (2019)

Neural Network Based Approach for Learning Planning Action Models

Alfredo Milani[1], Rajdeep Niyogi[2], and Giulio Biondi[3(✉)]

[1] Department of Mathematics and Computer Science, University of Perugia,
Perugia, Italy
milani@unipg.it
[2] Department of Computer Science and Engineering,
Indian Institute of Technology Roorkee, Roorkee 247667, India
rajdpfec@iitr.ac.in
[3] Department of Mathematics and Computer Science, University of Florence,
Florence, Italy
giulio.biondi@unifi.it

Abstract. Artificial Intelligence (AI) planning technology represents one of the most efficient solutions to guide goal driven agents in domain problems which are mostly characterized by problem solving features. The current proliferation of physical and virtual autonomous agents have therefore triggered a growing interest in the automatic acquisition of action models, which can take advantage of the observation capabilities of agents, which sense world states through their sensors. In this work we present a Neural Network (NN) based approach for learning AI planning action models by observation in noisy environments. The system learns by observing a set of execution patterns of the same action in different contexts. The perceptions of both pre/post action execution states are used to train the NN learning component and are assumed to be affected by noise, which could be due to inaccurate reading or malfunctioning of the sensors. Preliminary experiments shows that the proposed NN learning module seems to be more resilient to unforeseen situations with respect to traditional propositional-based approaches to action model learning.

Keywords: Planning · Neural Networks

1 Introduction

Artificial Intelligence (AI) planning and scheduling has been one the first research area of AI [6] and has obtained many relevant successful results [1]. In recent years the ubiquitous successful application of Neural Networks (NN) based machine learning approaches has given a great contribution to a large number of different AI fields such as visions, speech recognition and synthesis including learning agents behaviour [23]. The successful application of deep NN for learning agent behaviours, such as driving a car or playing a video game console, cannot

© Springer Nature Switzerland AG 2019
S. Misra et al. (Eds.): ICCSA 2019, LNCS 11624, pp. 526–537, 2019.
https://doi.org/10.1007/978-3-030-24311-1_38

be replicated for goal oriented agents, whose utility function is characterized by efficient problem solving features. For instance, a good video-game playing agent is characterized by obtaining a certain utility by a policy for reactive actions, e.g. points [15], while a problem solving agent is primarily characterized by exactly solving a goal, e.g. executing the right plan of sequence of actions to disassemble an engine to reach and substitute a faulty component, rather than doing it partially; in this situation, "nearly reaching the faulty piece" is totally useless. In such cases having a preconditions/effects model of the world to which to apply an AI planning solution is much more efficient and effective, especially in domains where replanning is not allowed or irreversible states exists. In those "problem solving characterized" domains, action knowledge and explicit action reasoning can develop a plan reaching a goal which can change from problem to problem [20], whereas a behavioural agent is basically characterized by the same goal to reach in different context, e.g.deciding an action reactively given a state [16], in order to maximize a smooth utility function.

The current proliferation of physical and virtual autonomous agents has triggered a growing interest in the automatic acquisition of action models, thus allowing rapid adaptation to new agents and avoiding any bias that an expert domain modeller, usual a human, could introduce [21]. The idea is being able to rapidly training a domain learning component by observations [2].

Several approached have been proposed in the planning literature for the problem of learning planning domain by observations [24]; most of the proposed solutions focus on a totally logic based reasoning approach and assume a deterministic and totally observable domain. The typical input of those learners is represented by a sequence of actions [5,19], or perfect state descriptions [13], which is quite unlikely in a real situation. Real world is dynamical, sometimes unpredictable and full of noise, given by the inaccuracy of sensors information.

To be able to do domain learning based on the state actually perceived by an agent would allow to take advantage of the real observation capabilities of agents, which sense the external world through their sensors and build a world state representation upon them [3,22], even if sensors are faulty [27] or perceive unpredictable situations. Possible applications range from supervised-learn applications, where an agent is trained by repeatedly showing real examples of single actions [17,18,25], similarly to teaching a small child to properly manage a spoon, to *self-learn applications*, where an agent in unknown environments observes other agents executing unknown actions, trying to augment the similarity [7,9] between the agent view of the world and the state transition semantic [10,11] embedded in action representation.

Our focus was on developing the ability to predicting the relevant world states changes before and after an action execution, thus allowing the reuse of the learned actions in a planning context. The basic idea to implement this solution to use the pre/post action execution states perceived by the agent to train a NN based learning component where the perceptions can be affected by noise, which could be due to inaccurate reading or malfunctioning of the sensors. The objective is that the trained NN component will be able to predict the state following the action execution in a given input state, i.e. the *state transition* in search space terms [4,8,14]. The trained NN component can then be used by a planner, e.g. a forward planner [12], as the actual action representation on which planning reasoning can take place. In the next Sect. 2 some basic notions of planning theory are recalled and the main motivations and features of the NN-based learning action model are described; experiments design, evaluation metrics and results are presented and discussed in Sect. 3, together with details of the noise model used. Conclusions are finally drawn in Sect. 4.

2   Learning Planning Action Model

2.1   Planning: States, Actions, Domains

The planning problem, according to well known and classical definitions [6,26], can be characterized as the problem of finding a plan, i.e. a sequence of actions, that, if executed in an *initial state* I will produce a final goal state F, i.e. a state which verifies a certain goal G. More formally in propositional or predicative planning, given a set P of boolean symbols, i.e. propositional symbols or ground predicates, a *state* s is a function $s : P- > \{T, F\}$, which defines a truth assignment for each symbol $p \in P$. An action a is defined by two sets of predicates symbols $pre(a)$ and $post(a)$ respectively called *preconditions* and *postconditions* or *effects* of a, where symbols are assigned either T, *positive* conditions, or F *negative* conditions. An actions a is executable in a state s if all the predicates $pre(a)$ are assigned in state s the truth values that they have in $pre(a)$. Assuming that, in a given planning domain, S is the set of all possible states defined over P and A is the set of all possible ground actions in the domain, then the function $execution : S \times A- > S$, defines the state s_2 resulting from executing $a \in A$ in state $s_1 \in S$, if a is not executable in s_1 then $s_2 = s_1$, i.e. the action does not produce any effect; if a is executable in s_1 then s_2 is obtained by assigning all the symbols in $pre(a)$ according to their assignment in a's postconditions, and leaving all the other symbols assignments unchanged. It is straightforward to see that any action a can be seen as a function which tranforms states into states. The planning problem can then be stated as, given a tuple (P, I, G, A), where P is a set of predicate symbols, I is an *initial state* and G a *goal state* defined on P, A is a set of actions with pre/post conditions on P, the problem of finding a sequence of actions $[a_1, ..., a_n]$, $a_i \in A$ such that a_1 is executable in I, for *in* a_i is executable in $execute(a_{i-1}, execute(a_{i-2}, ..., execute(a_1, I)))$ and $execute(a_n, execute(a_{n-1}, ..., execute(a_1, I))) = G$, i.e. if the sequence of actions transforms the initial state I into a goal state G.

2.2   The Neural Networks Based Action Learning Model

The basic idea of the NN based *action learning model* is to design an agent doing supervised learning by observations, based on the agent's internal boolean predicates state representation. The supervising process is making the learning agent aware that a particular action a has been executed by labeling a the observed transition of the world state. In other words, the objective is to devise a system which is able to learn by example the transition function for a. Each submitted training example can be modeled by a triple $(s1, s2, a)$, where s_1 represents the state perceived before, and s represents the state perceived after the execution of action a.

It is straightforward to think to apply *Neural Networks* techniques to a complete representation of state predicates, where each pre or post state can be seen as a vector of length $|P|$ of binary bits representing the truth values of the corresponding predicate. If we assume to promote the vector binary components to real numbers (namely 1.0 and 0.0), the problem can therefore be modeled as a *regression task* solved by a NN, where the predicted output state vector is required to be as close as possible to the real expected one after actions execution. A typical way to achieve this goal is using Mean Squared Error (MSE) as loss function during the NN training phase. The network structure will consist of an initial layer with size $=|P|$ and sigmoid activation function, followed by a variable number of hidden layers, i.e. 5, 7 or 10, of size $2 * |P|$ and ReLU activation function, and a final output layer with the same size as the input one.

In the test phase for a triple (s_1, s_2, a), the execution of a given action a in a given state s_1, i.e. submitting a state s_1 to the trained network $NN_t rained$, will produce a predicted state vector $s_p redicted = NN_t rained(s_1)$ consisting of real numbers values, within $[0,1]$, for each predicate. A more useful *boolean assignment* $s_p red$ can be obtained by applying to it a *thresholding operation*, with a typical a threshold value $\alpha = 0.5$. After thresholding a bit-by-bit comparison of $s_p red$ with the real expected output state s_2 is performed.

In order to illustrate the concept, let consider the *blocksworld* domain. The state of the world at a given time is usually described by a set of predicates associated to their truth values, i.e. True or False; such a set completely defines the actual state. In particular, in the problem analyzed, three predicates are defined:

- $(ON \ BLOCK_i \ BLOCK_j)$, indicating that $BLOCK_i$ is on top of $BLOCK_j$
- $(TABLE \ BLOCK_i)$, indicating that $BLOCK_i$ sits on the table
- $(CLEAR \ BLOCK_i)$, indicating that there is no other $BLOCK_j$ on top of $BLOCK_i$.

Let N be the number of blocks in the world; the set P of all the possible predicates is composed of a ON predicate for each pair in the cartesian product of the set of blocks (excluding self-pairs, i.e. $(ON \ BLOCK_i \ BLOCK_i)$), plus a $(TABLE \ BLOCK_i)$ and a $(CLEAR \ BLOCK_i)$ for each block in the world. The cardinality of P is then $|P| = N \cdot (N - 1) + N + N$. If a total ordering on the blocks is given, it is possible to build an ordered vector ctx containing the truth values, 1 or 0, for each of the possible predicates. An action $(PUTON \ BLOCK_i \ BLOCK_j)$, with $BLOCK_i$ on top of $BLOCK_k$, changes the state producing as effects $(ON \ BLOCK_i \ BLOCK_j)$ and $(CLEAR \ BLOCK_k)$, and conversely negating the previously true predicates $(ON\ BLOCK_i\ BLOCK_k)$ and $(CLEAR\ BLOCK_k)$. A visual sample of such move is provided in Fig. 1; in this example $N = 10$ and $P = 110$.

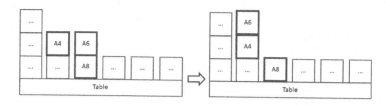

Fig. 1. A sample of pre and post state for the action (PUTON A6 A4)

In Fig. 2 the architecture and the workflow of the proposed action learning system is shown.

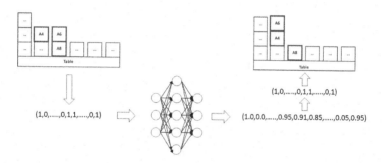

Fig. 2. The learning planning action model workflow

3   Experiments Design and Results

Experiments have been designed in order to vary the amount of noise introduced during the training and test phase; the same amount of noise is applied both to the training and to the test sets. The ground truth used to compute the accuracy of prediction is represented by the perfect no-noise states.

The data set samples used in the experiments are represented by triples $(s1, s2, a)$, where s_1/s_2 represents the perceived pre/post action a states, and have been generated by a particular technique of *random consistency*.

The NN implementation used in the experiments is based on the Keras Python Framework with Tensorflow background was used to build the neural network model.

3.1 Noise Model

The *noise model* we have used assumes that some sensors can be faulty or inaccurate, or the interpretation of sensors data into true/false predicates can be inaccurate. Whatever the reason, the noise will produce in the agent's perceived state model a wrong value for certain predicates, i.e. a certain bit in the bit-vector representing the state will be flipped from true/false or vice-versa. In order to tune and control the noise we used two parameters: p_{states} establishing the percentage of noisy states samples to be altered and p_{state} which determine the percentage of the predicates of each single noisy state sample which will be randomly modified. For instance, let $N = 200000$, $|P| = 110$, $p_{states} = 0.9$ and $p_{state} = 0.01$; ≈ 180000 sample states records will be altered, and for each sample state $110 * 0.01 = \approx 1$ bit will be flipped. The alteration is uniformly distributed among the sample states and inside each sample state, so that at the end of the alteration phase each predicate truth value will have been inverted approximately the same number of times. Since each sample defines a pair of states *pre/post* execution, any noise alteration induced in a predicate of the *pre* state is operated in the state after execution too.

3.2 Evaluation Metrics

Accuracy of the state predicted by the trained NN was chosen as the evaluation metric. The expected output vector and the predicted vector are compared bit-by-bit; only those which completely match are counted as correct.

3.3 The Random Consistent States Generator

In order to generate the dataset for training and testing, a *random consistent states* generator was developed for the *blocksworld* domain. The sample states are randomly generated as variations of the *blocksworld* using the three predicates previously described (i.e. *table*, *on* and *clear*) with the characteristic of being consistent with the usual constraints: single block stacking and blocks gravity (one block can be directly on one block only, a tower of blocks has the lower block on the table etc,); the post state is generated from the pre state just applying the semantic of the considered action a. The random consistent states generator is characterized by the following parameters:

- The *number of samples* N to be generated
- The *number of blocks* in the world, named sequentially using the "A*" style, e.g. A1, A2, A3...
- The *number of towers*, i.e. the number of available locations on the table; note that some locations could be empty after the generation.
- The three blocks subject of the move, e.g. "A1", "A2" and "A3", which represent the action (PUTON,A1,A3), with the pre-condition ON(A1,A2).
- The maximum height *maxheight* of a tower, i.e. the maximum number of blocks that can be stacked.
- The type of samples to be generated

The sample generator outputs N tuples of the form (preVector, postVector, move, maxHeight, sampleType), each representing an instance of the move in a different, but consistent, scenario. preVector and postVector are one-hot encoding vectors that associate each of the possible predicates in the domain with its truth state, i.e. 0 if the predicate is false, 1 otherwise; sampleType can be either *positive*, meaning that the move should be executable in the generated state, or *negative*, for states in which the action is not allowed. In the latter case, the post state is equal to the pre state, i.e. trying to execute the action when it is not possible leads to observing no changes in the environment.

3.4   The Data Sets

For the experiments, two data sets were produced with the generator described in Sect. 3.3; the sample state triple represent instances of the move (PUTON,A6,A4), with the precondition (ON A6,A8). Note that, for the move to be executable, in positive samples two other predicates must hold: (CLEAR A6) and (CLEAR A4). The first data set, POS, contains 200000 positive records; the second, POS/NEG, includes the records in POS as well as 200000 negative records, for a total of 400000 records equally balanced between the two types.

3.5   Test Series 1: Tuning the NN

The purpose of the first series of test was both to tune the neural network structure in terms of hidden layers, to assess the action model learning capabilities and to establish a performance upper bound of the model in absence of noise. The performance of the network have been tested on a clean data set, i.e. without noise. The training process was repeated for both the POS and POS/NEG data sets, in order to choose the best settings combination for the network.; for test series 1, as well as test series 2 and 3, performances were evaluated using a ten-fold cross-validation. Results are reported in table in Fig. 3. The best performances for both data sets has been obtained by including seven hidden layers and training for 100 epochs. In such configuration settings the system reaches nearly optimal performance with no overfitting; the settings thus determined were applied for the subsequent experiments using a noisy environment.

3.6   Test Series 2: Positive only Training Samples

In this test series, the network was fed with positive samples, i.e. showing the agent only perceived pre/post states of correct execution and the action under training. Random noise was applied in different percentages to the data sets; in the selected training samples, both the pre and post state were perturbed together, i.e. the same bits were flipped, whereas in the test records only the pre states were affected by noise, and the predicted states were compared against the perfect clean, not noisy post states.

Results for Test 2 are reported in table in Fig. 4. With only a quarter of the training samples altered, the performances of the model are stable, showing an

Dataset	Training Epochs	Hidden Layers	Avg Accuracy	Variance
POS	50	5	0.888195	0.001286
POS	100	5	0.880915	0.000827
POS	50	7	0.939730	0.000434
POS	**100**	**7**	**0.963085**	**0.000243**
POS	150	10	0.893290	0.000956
POS	200	10	0.901670	0.001315
POS/NEG	50	5	0.855028	0.001616
POS/NEG	100	5	0.888728	0.000654
POS/NEG	50	7	0.843653	0.000957
POS/NEG	**100**	**7**	**0.903338**	**0.000352**
POS/NEG	150	10	0.737005	0.004638
POS/NEG	200	10	0.763370	0.002550

Fig. 3. Results of test 1. Values are averaged over 10 folds.

% of Noisy Records	% Noise per record	Avg Accuracy	Variance
25	1	0.814800	0.000413
25	5	0.752745	0.000136
25	10	0.730915	0.002585
25	20	0.745075	0.000008
50	1	0.686275	0.000116
50	5	0.560100	0.000252
50	10	0.491115	0.000185
50	20	0.488590	0.000053
75	1	0.579250	0.000112
75	5	0.377300	0.000140
75	10	0.247105	0.000045
75	20	0.231825	0.000018

Fig. 4. Results of test 2. Values are averaged over 10 folds.

appreciable ability of the system to resist to the increase in noise. However, with higher percentages, such resistance is much lower.

3.7 Test Series 3: Positive and Negative Training Samples

In the third test series, the neural network has been fed with the POS/NEG training state samples. As mentioned before negative examples correspond to cases where, notwithstanding the action is not executable, i.e. at least one action precondition is not verified, the tentative of executing the action does not produce appreciable changes in the post state, i.e. the action is not executed. In the table in Fig. 5 the results of the test are reported; figures are on average lower or on par with the corresponding network in test 2. In the table in Fig. 6 the number of correctly and wrongly predicted samples in test 3 are reported, for both positive and negative samples and at various levels of noise; figures are averaged over 10 folds. It can be observed that, regardless of the amount of noise applied to the data, positive samples are easier to predict, i.e. more positive samples are correctly predicted than negative ones. In Fig. 8 the percentage of correctly predicted records in test 3 for the two types of records, positive and negative, is shown, grouped by the noise percentages. It can be seen that the gap between the two types, initially negligble, increases with the amount of noise. This could mean that a higher percentage of noise in the negative samples effectively hides that there should be no changes between the pre and post state. On the contrary, the network is able to better understand and learn the fixed changes in truth values of the predicates that occur in the positive samples. A further comparison between the results of test 2 and 3 in Fig. 7 shows that the accuracy score is similar for the networks trained and tested on the two different data sets; however, when the amount of noise per record becomes grows to 20%, the network predicting positive samples only delivers better performances. This is consistent with the results in Fig. 8.

% of Noisy Records	% Noise per record	Avg Accuracy	Variance
25	1	0.785740	0.000379
25	5	0.724420	0.000610
25	10	0.727368	0.000141
25	20	0.701115	0.000084
50	1	0.685510	0.000408
50	5	0.590473	0.000221
50	10	0.499955	0.000172
50	20	0.433398	0.000172
75	1	0.585430	0.004902
75	5	0.462773	0.000212
75	10	0.261468	0.000405
75	20	0.144035	0.000118

Fig. 5. Results of test 3. Values are averaged over 10 folds.

% of altered records	% of alt. bits	Correct Positive	Correct Negative	Wrong Positive	Wrong Negative
25	1	16331	15098	3669	4902
25	5	14924	14053	5077	5947
25	10	14945	14150	5055	5850
25	20	14826	13219	5174	6782
50	1	14362	13058	5638	6942
50	5	12405	11214	7595	8786
50	10	10624	9375	9376	10626
50	20	9704	7632	10296	12368
75	1	12513	10904	7487	9096
75	5	9887	8624	10113	11376
75	10	6027	4432	13973	15568
75	20	4598	1164	15402	18836

Fig. 6. Number of correctly and wrongly predicted samples

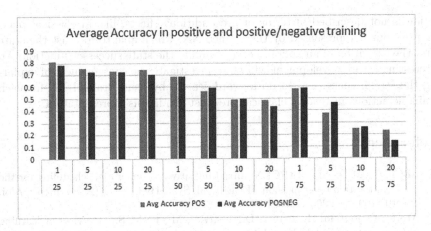

Fig. 7. Comparison of performance with positive only and positive and negative samples

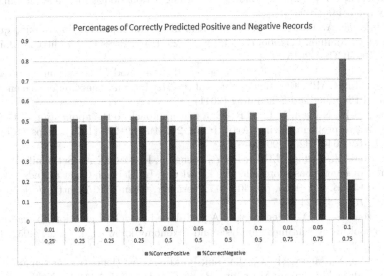

Fig. 8. Percentages of correctly predicted positive and negative records

4   Conclusions

We have introduced an original neural network-based architecture to learn planning action models by observations. Experiments show that the accuracy obtained is quite promising and the proposed model is able to be resilient with respect to noise, which is indeed a quite realistic hypothesis for learning agents situated in the real world. To the best of our knowledge this is the first planning action learning model based on NN, which is able to cope with noise affected perceptions. Moreover another innovative contribution of this work is the intro-duction of a new concept of action representation, where the resulting learned action is not described in terms of preconditions effects, like in classical planning [6], but is represented by the trained NN, which able to forecast the state after the execution of an action, i.e. to compute the state successor function. An interesting future development will be to investigate the consequences of exploring the search space, e.g. to do forward search, by using trained NN for each available actions instead of classical pre/post conditions representation.

References

1. Ai-Chang, M., et al.: MAPGEN: mixed-initiative planning and scheduling for the mars exploration rover mission. IEEE Intell. Syst. **19**(1), 8–12 (2004). https://doi.org/10.1109/MIS.2004.1265878
2. Arora, A., Fiorino, H., Pellier, D., Métivier, M., Pesty, S.: A review of learning planning action models. Knowl. Eng. Rev. **33**, e20 (2018). https://doi.org/10.1017/S0269888918000188
3. Balac, N., Gaines, D.M., Fisher, D.: Learning action models for navigation in noisy environments (2000)
4. Chiancone, A., Franzoni, V., Niyogi, R., Milani, A.: Improving link ranking quality by quasi-common neighbourhood, pp. 21–26. IEEE Press (2015). https://doi.org/10.1109/ICCSA.2015.19
5. Cresswell, S., Gregory, P.: Generalised domain model acquisition from action traces. In: ICAPS 2011 - Proceedings of the 21st International Conference on Automated Planning and Scheduling (2011)
6. Fikes, R.E., Nilsson, N.J.: STRIPS: a new approach to the application of theorem proving to problem solving. Artif. Intell. **2**(3–4), 189–208 (1971). https://doi.org/10.1016/0004-3702(71)90010-5
7. Franzoni, V., Leung, C.H.C., Li, Y., Mengoni, P., Milani, A.: Set similarity measures for images based on collective knowledge. In: Gervasi, O., et al. (eds.) ICCSA 2015. LNCS, vol. 9155, pp. 408–417. Springer, Cham (2015). https://doi.org/10.1007/978-3-319-21404-7_30
8. Franzoni, V., Li, Y., Mengoni, P.: A path-based model for emotion abstraction on Facebook using sentiment analysis and taxonomy knowledge, pp. 947–952. IEEE Press (2017)
9. Franzoni, V., Mencacci, M., Mengoni, P., Milani, A.: Heuristics for semantic path search in Wikipedia. In: Murgante, B., et al. (eds.) ICCSA 2014. LNCS, vol. 8584, pp. 327–340. Springer, Cham (2014). https://doi.org/10.1007/978-3-319-09153-2_25
10. Franzoni, V., Milani, A.: PMING distance: a collaborative semantic proximity measure, vol. 2, pp. 442–449. IEEE Press (2012). https://doi.org/10.1109/WI-IAT.2012.226
11. Franzoni, V., Milani, A., Pallottelli, S., Leung, C., Li, Y.: Context-based image semantic similarity, pp. 1280–1284. IEEE Press (2016). https://doi.org/10.1109/FSKD.2015.7382127
12. Hoffmann, J.: FF: the fast-forward planning system. AI Mag. **22**, 57 (2001)
13. Jiménez, S., De La Rosa, T., Fernández, S., Fernández, F., Borrajo, D.: A review of machine learning for automated planning. Knowl. Eng. Rev. **27**(4), 433–467 (2012). https://doi.org/10.1017/S026988891200001X

14. Leung, C.H.C., Li, Y., Milani, A., Franzoni, V.: Collective evolutionary concept distance based query expansion for effective web document retrieval. In: Murgante, B., et al. (eds.) ICCSA 2013. LNCS, vol. 7974, pp. 657–672. Springer, Heidelberg (2013). https://doi.org/10.1007/978-3-642-39649-6_47

15. Mnih, V., et al.: Human-level control through deep reinforcement learning. Nature **518**, 529 (2015). https://doi.org/10.1038/nature14236

16. Molineaux, M., Aha, D.W.: Learning unknown event models. In: Proceedings of the Twenty-Eighth AAAI Conference on Artificial Intelligence, AAAI 2014, pp. 395–401. AAAI Press (2014)

17. Mourao, K.: Learning probabilistic planning operators from noisy observations. In: 31st Workshop of the UK Planning & Scheduling Special Interest Group (PlanSIG 2013) (2014)

18. Mourao, K., Zettlemoyer, L.S., Petrick, R.P.A., Steedman, M.: Learning STRIPS operators from noisy and incomplete observations, October 2012

19. Newton, M.A.H., Levine, J.: Implicit learning of compiled macro-actions for planning. Front. Artif. Intell. Appl. **215**, 323–328 (2010)

20. Safaei, J., Ghassem-Sani, G.: Incremental learning of planning operators in stochastic domains. In: van Leeuwen, J., Italiano, G.F., van der Hoek, W., Meinel, C., Sack, H., Plášil, F. (eds.) SOFSEM 2007. LNCS, vol. 4362, pp. 644–655. Springer, Heidelberg (2007). https://doi.org/10.1007/978-3-540-69507-3_56

21. Shah, M., et al.: Knowledge engineering tools in planning: state-of-the-art and future challenges. Knowl. Eng. Plann. Sched. **53**, 53 (2013)

22. Shen, W.M.: Discovery as autonomous learning from the environment. Mach. Learn. **12**(1), 143–165 (1993). https://doi.org/10.1023/A:1022827618816

23. Silver, D., et al.: Mastering the game of Go with deep neural networks and tree search. Nature **529**, 484 (2016)

24. Wang, X.: Learning by observation and practice: an incremental approach for planning operator acquisition. In: Machine Learning Proceedings 1995, January, pp. 549–557 (1995). https://doi.org/10.1016/B978-1-55860-377-6.50074-8

25. Weber, B.G., Mateas, M., Jhala, A.: Learning from demonstration for goal-driven autonomy. In: Proceedings of the Twenty-Sixth AAAI Conference on Artificial Intelligence, AAAI 2012, pp. 1176–1182. AAAI Press (2012)

26. Winograd, T.: Understanding Natural Language. Academic Press Inc., Orlando (1972)

27. Zhuo, H.H., Kambhampati, S.: Action-model acquisition from noisy plan traces. In: Proceedings of the Twenty-Third International Joint Conference on Artificial Intelligence, IJCAI 2013, pp. 2444–2450. AAAI Press (2013)

Parallel and Distributed Data Mining (WPDM 2019)

The Distributed p-Median Problem
in Computer Networks

Anas AlDabbagh[1], Giuseppe Di Fatta[2]([✉])(iD), and Antonio Liotta[3]

[1] Department of Computer Science, University of Mosul, Mosul, Iraq
mnc_computer@hotmail.com
[2] Department of Computer Science, University of Reading, Reading, UK
G.DiFatta@reading.ac.uk
[3] Department of Electronics, Computing and Mathematics, University of Derby,
Derby, UK
a.liotta@derby.ac.uk

Abstract. Many distributed services in computer networks rely on a set of active facilities that are selected among a potentially large number of candidates. The active facilities then contribute and cooperate to deliver a specific service to the users of the distributed system. In this scenario graph partitioning or clustering is often adopted to determine the most efficient locations of the facilities. The identification of the optimal set of facility locations is known as the p-median problem in networks, is NP-hard and is typically solved by using heuristic methods. The goal is to select p locations among all candidate network nodes such that some cost function is minimised. A typical example of such a function is the overall communication cost to deliver the service to the users of the distributed system. Locating facilities in near-optimal locations has been extensively studied for different application domains. Most of these studies have investigated sequential algorithms and centralised approaches. However, centralised approaches are practically infeasible in large-scale and dynamic networks, where the problem is inherently distributed or because of the large communication overhead and memory requirements for gathering complete information about the network topology and the users. In this work distributed approaches to the p-median problem are investigated. Two solutions are proposed for addressing the facility locations problem in a fully distributed environment. Two different iterative heuristic approaches are applied to gradually improve a random initial solution and to converge to a final solution with a local minimum of the overall cost. While the first approach adopts a fine granularity by identifying a single change to improve the solution at each iteration, the second approach applies changes to every component of the solution at each iteration. An experimental comparative analysis based on simulations has shown that the approach with a finer granularity is able to deliver a better optimisation of the overall cost with longer convergence time. Both approaches have excellent scalability and provide an effective tool to optimise the facility locations from within the network. No prior knowledge of the system is required, no data needs to be gathered in a centralised server and the same process is used to identify and to deploy the facility locations solution in the network since the process is fully decentralised.

ⓒ Springer Nature Switzerland AG 2019
S. Misra et al. (Eds.): ICCSA 2019, LNCS 11624, pp. 541–556, 2019.
https://doi.org/10.1007/978-3-030-24311-1_39

Keywords: p-median problem · Graph partitioning ·
Graph clustering · Distributed systems · Computer networks

1   Introduction

Locating facilities in near-optimal locations to deliver some service to users has received a significant interest [1–3]. A facility is an object or node (such as server or a network device) that provides services such as a distributed memory cache, while users are the network nodes that benefit from the service offered by these facilities. A facility can be either in an open or closed state: an open facility means it can serve connected clients to it, while a closed one is a candidate location where a facility can be opened if required. To provide a more efficient service to the users the topological location of an open facility should be close to many user nodes. The p-median problem, in particular, aims to identify the set of the open facilities (medians) among all the candidate locations such that the overall cost of the solution is minimized according to an objective function [3–5]. In many scenarios the cost of the solution is associated to the communication overhead, e.g. the total number of hops in the shortest paths that connect each user node to its closest open facility. This formulation is very similar to the classic partitional clustering problem in data mining, best represented by algorithms such as k-means and k-medoids, where the goal is to find the ideal locations of k centres that minimise the sum of the squared distances from each item to its closest centre.

The main motivation for this work is that previous works on the p-median problem have used a centralised approach based on heuristic methods for finding near-optimal solutions. In that case the required information needs to be collected in order to apply a sequential algorithm to find a solution. A centralised approach is infeasible in large-scale networks due to the time and space complexity of the sequential algorithms as well as the large communication cost and latency to aggregate the global information [6–8]. Therefore, this work investigates distributed algorithms to solve the p-median problem directly within distributed environments.

In this paper, two new approaches for solving the p-median problem in a distributed environment are proposed. Both are designed to be executed without any centralised collection of the data in a single node. They apply an iterative heuristic approach to improve a random initial solution and to converge to a final solution with a local minimum of the cost.

The first approach builds a global view of the system and improves a current solution by replacing a single facility at each iteration. The second approach, is designed on the logic of the k-medoids clustering algorithm. At each iteration, a local view of each cluster is generated and all facilities can be updated to optimise the solution.

Both approaches were implemented in *PeerSim*, a Java-based network simulator, for investigating the performance in large-scale systems with several tests with different parameters such as the network size, the number of facilities to be located, the total number of candidate facilities and different initial states. The results have shown that the first protocol is more accurate at selecting the locations of the facilities, since it converges to a lower total cost of the solution than the second protocol. However, the second one has shown a better convergence time in optimising the solution.

The rest of the paper is organised as follows. Section 2 introduces the problem, the notation and discusses some related work. Sections 3 and 4 describe the two proposed methods. Section 5 presents the simulations and the comparative experimental results. Finally, Sect. 6 provides conclusive remarks.

2   The p-Median Problem Definition, Formulation and Related Work

The p-median problem intends to find p locations of active (open) facilities among several candidate locations in a way that the total distance (cost) from the user nodes to the open facility nodes is minimised according to an objective function [9–11]. As most location problems, the p-median problem is classified as NP-hard and solved using heuristic methods [12].

The p-median problem formulation [3,4] is formally defined as follows. Let us consider a graph $G = (V, E)$, where V is the set of nodes and E the set of links between nodes, the set $F = \{f_1, f_2, ..., f_m\}$ of m facilities, the set $U = \{u_1, u_2, ..., u_n\}$ of n users, where $V = F \cup U$, an integer number $p < m$, which is the target number of open facilities, and a distance function $d : U * F \to \mathbb{N}$ of the number of hops between users and facilities. A greedy optimisation procedure is applied to build a solution from an initial set of p randomly selected facilities from F. The procedure seeks to identify a better neighbour solution to the current one. A neighbour solution is a minimal alteration of the current solution that improves the cost.

A vertex substitution procedure developed by Teitz and Bart [4] is one of the standard algorithms for solving the p-median problem [13,14]. In vertex substitution, p candidate facilities from F are arbitrarily selected (opened) to start the algorithm. The algorithm reallocates (swap) an open facility with one of the candidate (closed) facilities whenever the swap improves the solution. The algorithm then iterates from the existing solution looking for another pair of facilities to be swapped to improve the solution until the best solution is reached. The algorithm is then terminated with a local optimum solution.

Building up on the vertex substitution algorithm, the *fast interchange heuristics* algorithm is proposed by Whitaker [15]. It implements a swap once a profitable facilities pair is found. The removed facility is deleted from F and never comes back to the solution [3].

Another study has been done by Hansen and Mladennovic, who used the *best improvement strategy* in which all possible swaps are evaluated, then the most profitable one is executed. In addition, the way to finding the best facility to open, which is used in the previous method, is evaluated to be less complicated [16].

Based on the above studies, another method to solve the p-median problem was suggested by Resende and Werneck [3]. In their study, all possible swaps were evaluated according to Eq. 1 and the most profitable pair was chosen for the swap.

$$profit(f_i, f_r) = gain(f_i) - loss(f_r) + extra(f_i, f_r) \tag{1}$$

As noticed from Eq. 1, the first component *gain* is associated with the candidate facility f_i to be inserted in the solution. The *gain* value is the amount of distance saved by reallocating some user nodes to f_i, for which f_i is closer than their current closest facility. The functions $d_1(u)$ and $d_2(u)$ are used to indicate the distance from the user node u and, respectively, the closest and second closest open facilities $\phi_1(u)$ and $\phi_2(u)$. The *gain* value is computed for all candidates f_i according to the Eq. 2, so that it results in a vector of size $m - p$.

$$gain(f_i) = \sum_{u \in U} \max\left(0, d_1(u) - d(u, f_i)\right) \tag{2}$$

As a consequence of removing the open facility f_r from the solution, users assigned to it must be reassigned to their second closest open facility ϕ_2, which is further away than f_r by definition. This leads to an additional cost that is identified by a *loss* function and is computed according to the Eq. 3.

$$loss(f_r) = \sum_{u \in U : \phi_1(u) = f_r} [d_2(u) - d_1(u)] \tag{3}$$

However, some of the user nodes, which were assigned to the removed facility f_r, are in fact assigned to f_i rather than their second closest facility, leading to an additional saving in the total cost. This affects the total cost of the solution and a correction factor called *extra* profit has to be included for these cases. The *extra* value is computed as in Eq. 4.

$$extra(f_i, f_r) = \sum_{u \in U : [\phi_1(u) = f_r] \wedge [d(u, f_i) < d_2(u)]} [d_2(u) - \max\left(d(u, f_i), d_1(u)\right)] \tag{4}$$

In a distributed environment the information about the network topology, the users and the facilities needs first to be collected in a server in order to compute a solution with a centralised approach. Moreover, once the solution is computed, it will have to be distributed among the nodes in the network for its deployment. This process will then repeat every time there is need to update the solution. In the remainder, two novel distributed protocols, DPM and KM, are presented to solve the p-median problem directly in a distributed environment without prior knowledge about the network topology. No data needs to be gathered in a centralised server and the same process is used to identify and to deploy a p-median solution in the network since the process is intrinsically distributed.

3   The Distributed p-Median (DPM) Protocol

As shown in Fig. 1, the DPM protocol design is based on three main phases to overcome the synchronisation problems of the distributed environment. It is assumed that an initial solution is available, e.g. an initial random solution of p open facilities. The protocol is started with phase 1 by sending BROADCAST messages from all facilities to all nodes in the network. The user nodes are gradually building a view of facilities in the network and determine the closest open facility. Each user node joins its closest open facility via a JOIN message. From the JOIN messages each open facility builds a view of the user nodes assigned to it.

Thereafter, the facility nodes transit to phase 2. In this phase, the open facilities exchange the required information to build a distributed global view about the network and determine the best pair of facilities to swap in the current solution.

In phase 3, the open facilities implement the swap. Both of phases 2 and 3 are repeatedly executed to improve the solution until convergence.

The following subsections describe the details of each phase of the protocol.

3.1   Phase 1: Initialisation and Information Collection

In Phase 1 all the candidate (open and closed) facilities disseminate a BROADCAST message to advertise their presence and to facilitate the computation of the shortest paths. This message holds specific information about the facility: ID, status and the distance to reach the facility in number of hops. As described in Algorithm 1, from the broadcast messages each user node builds a view about the facilities in the network, which is used to select the closest open facility to join, as further explained in the subsections below.

Build a User Partial View. At the start of this phase, the user nodes are kept waiting until receipt of the facility broadcast messages. As soon as a user node receives a new broadcast message, it creates a corresponding *local user record* by extracting the information from the broadcast message payload, such as the ID of the facility that sends the message, the shortest distance to the facility, the status of the facility and some routing information (e.g., the next hop to reach the facility).

Due to the randomness of the flooding approach for the broadcast messages, the user node may receive a broadcast message from the same facility several times via different paths. If the message comes from a shorter path, the user node updates its *local user record*, increments the distance field, and forward the message to all its neighbours except the source.

Join the Closest Open Facility. While there are no more new messages, the user node computes its loss value, gain and extra vectors. It then sends them to the closest open facility which is determined from its *local user record*.

When the facility receives the join message from a user node, it updates its local record by adding the user's loss value to the local facility value and the user's gain and extra vector values to their corresponding values in the local facility record, as shown in Fig. (2). When all join messages are received, the open facilities can transit to phase 2.

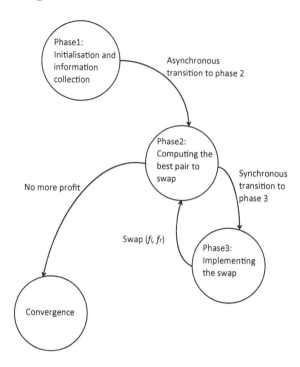

Fig. 1. The DPM protocol consists of three main phases. In phase 1 facility information is disseminated over the network and user nodes join their closest open facilities. In phase 2 the open facilities find the best swap of facilities $<f_i, f_r>$ to minimise the cost. In phase 3 the facilities implement the swap.

3.2   Phase 2: Exchange the Necessary Information and Find the Best Pair to Swap

Each open facility f_r is associated to a subset (a cluster) of user nodes, which have identified f_r as the closest open facility from which to receive the service.

At the transition to phase 2, an open facility f_r has determined its local value of $loss(f_r)$ and the two vectors $gain(f_i)$ and $extra(f_i, f_r)$ for the local cluster. In this phase, the open facilities need to exchange and aggregate these local values and vectors to build a global view of the network and of the current p-median solution. Figure 3 shows the collective communication operations (gather and sum), for the aggregation of local information into global information by means of facility *exchange* messages.

The global loss, gain and extra are initialised with the local values and vectors. When an open facility receives an exchange message containing the remote contribution to the global information, it aggregates the loss of the message into a global loss, adds the $gain(f_i)$ to the global gain vector and collects the $extra(f_i, f_r)$ to build a global $extra(f_i, f_r)$.

As shown in Algorithm 2, when an open facility receives $p - 1$ number of exchange messages, it computes the profit values according to the Eq. 1 for all possible pairs $<f_i, f_r>$, where f_i is a closed facility to be inserted in the solution

Algorithm 1. Phase 1 - initialisation and information collection, all the facilities send BROADCAST messages $<FID, distance, status>$ to all nodes, where FID is a unique facility ID and the binary *status* indicates if the facility is open or closed in the current solution. The user nodes build summarised view about the facilities in the network.

```
1  forall the open and closed facilities do
2  |  Send a facility broadcast message m = <FID, 1, status> to all neighbours
```

```
3  At event: a facility broadcast message is received at a user node:
4  if the m.FID is not in the user local table then
5  |  Add the message payload to the user local table
6  |  m.distance++
7  |  Forward the message to all neighbours except the source
8  else if the m.distance field < the current matching record.distance then
9  |  Update the local table
10 |  m.distance++
11 |  Forward the message to all neighbours except the source
12 else
13 |  Drop the message /* The FID message is coming from a longer path */
```

```
14 At event: a facility broadcast message is received at a facility node:
15 if the m.FID != the local facility ID then
16 |  m.distance++
17 |  Forward the message to all neighbours except the source
18 else
19 |  Drop the message /* message of the same facility */
```

and f_r is an open facility to be removed from the solution. The pair of facilities that provides the greatest profit is chosen for the swap. Based on the shared global view all the open facilities take the same decision by deterministically choosing the same pair of facilities $<f_i^*, f_r^*>$ for the swap and thus transiting to phase 3 to implement the swap.

3.3   Phase 3: Swap Implementation

As shown in Algorithm 3, in this phase the candidate f_r^* sends a CHANGE_STATUS message to f_i^* asking to change its status to open and to accept join messages from user nodes. The f_r^* also send a SWAP $<f_i^*, f_r^*>$ message to its user nodes (local cluster). If the user node u is closer to the inserted facility f_i^* than to its second closest open facility $\phi_2(u)$, then u sends a *join* message to f_i^*, otherwise it sends it to $\phi_2(u)$.

The current open facilities in the system inform the user nodes in their clusters about the swap by sending an UPDATE_SOLUTION $<f_i^*, f_r^*>$ message. If a user node u is closer to f_i^* than to its current open facility $\phi_1(u)$, then u leaves its current cluster and sends a join message to f_i^*.

The solution at this stage is reconfigured. Accordingly, the weight values of the clusters are changed. This may lead to find another pair of facilities to swap in the next iteration to improve the solution further. The process is repeated from phase 2 and the total cost keeps improving until reaching the best (local minimum) configuration for the locations of the candidate facilities, given the initial solution.

3.4   Convergence

The convergence status is the final state of the solution, since no more swaps can improve the solution.

4   The k-Medoids (KM) Protocol

The second proposed approach is the k-medoids (KM) protocol. This is inspired by the classic Partitioning Around Medoids (PAM), or k-medoids, clustering algorithm [17]. The main idea of the KM protocol is to partition the network around the open facilities, then to iteratively carry out facility swaps with a similar heuristic method used by the k-medoids clustering algorithm. The KM protocol is organised in three main phases, as explained in the following sections.

Algorithm 2. Phase 2 - The open facilities exchange the local information and build the same global view. The best pair of candidate facilities $<f_i^*, f_r^*>$ are selected for a swap.

---

1   Initialise the global table with the local facility record
2   Set counter to one
3   max_profit = 0
4   f_r^* = null
5   f_i^* = null
6   **forall the** *open facilities excluding itself* **do**
7   $\quad$ send a facility *exchange* message with the local information records to a remote open facility

---

8   **At event: receiving a facility *exchange* message**
9   Add the message payload to the global table
10   counter++
11   **if** *(counter == p)* **then**
12   $\quad$ **for** *all f_i in the global table* **do**
13   $\quad\quad$ **for** *all f_r in the global table* **do**
14   $\quad\quad\quad$ compute $profit(f_i, f_r)$
15   $\quad\quad\quad$ **if** $profit(f_i, f_r) > max\_profit$ **then**
16   $\quad\quad\quad\quad$ $f_r^* = f_r$
17   $\quad\quad\quad\quad$ $f_i^* = f_i$

Algorithm 3. Phase 3 - Implementing the swap $<f_i^*, f_r^*>$

---

1 **if** *this node is an open facility* **then**
2   **if** *this node is f_r^** **then**
3   this.status = closed
4   send message CHANGE_STATUS to f_i^*
5   **forall the** *users in the local cluster* **do**
6   Send a swap $<f_i^*, f_r^*>$ message to user

---

7 **At event: received message change_status:**
8 this.status = open

---

9 **At event: received a swap $<f_i^*, f_r^*>$ message:**
10 Update the local user record
11 **if** $\phi_1 == f_r^*$ **then**
12   **if** *f_i^* closer than ϕ_2* **then**
13   send join message to f_i^*
14   **else**
15   send join message to ϕ_2
16 **else if** *f_i^* closer than ϕ_1* **then**
17   send leave message to ϕ_1
18   send join message to f_i^*

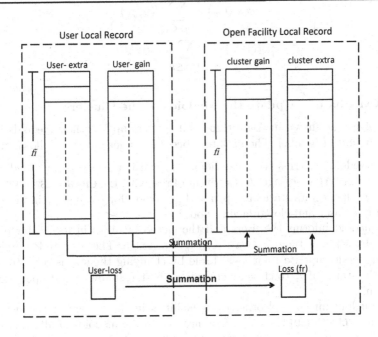

Fig. 2. The open facility builds a within-cluster knowledge from the JOIN messages of the user nodes

4.1 KM Phase 1: Information Dissemination and Clusters Configuration

Phase 1 is started by the announcement of the facilities about their locations with broadcast messages similarly to the DPM protocol. Nodes gradually build a summarised view of the available open facilities in the network. They build a local view of facilities, including ID, distance and status. Finally user nodes join the closest open facility forming p clusters. A cluster C_k is the set of user nodes associated to the open facility f_k, such that the distance $d(u, f_k)$ is minimal in the current solution, i.e. $\phi_1(u) = f_k$.

During this phase, each open facility (medoid) builds a local table of the closed facilities (candidate medoid) and their associated cost before moving to Phase 2, as shown in Algorithm 4.

4.2 KM Phase 2: Find the Best f_i to Swap

As shown in Algorithm 5, each medoid f_k computes the cost of its cluster C_k as the sum of the contributed cost values of the users in the cluster ($u \in C_k$), as per Eq. (5). Then it evaluates all the candidate facilities that could be opened within its cluster by computing the cost of these closed facilities as if they would be swapped with the current medoid. The total cost of the solution is given in Eq. (6). If the cost of one of the candidate facility f_i is lower than the cost of the medoid f_k, then the solution is updated in phase 3.

$$cost(C_k) = \sum_{u \in C_k} d(u, f_k) \tag{5}$$

$$cost(\{C_k\}) = \sum_{0 < k \leq p} cost(C_k) \tag{6}$$

4.3 KM Phase 3: Update the Medoids of the Clusters

In this phase, as shown in Algorithm 6, all clusters update their medoids independently and in parallel. The update process is implemented as following:

1. The medoid informs the candidate f_i with the swap by sending a CHANGE_STATUS message. At the event of receiving the CHANGE_STATUS message; f_i changes its status to open and get ready for receiving join messages from both user and closed facility nodes.
2. The medoid informs the users and the closed facilities in its cluster of the swap by sending them a SWAP $<f_i, f_r>$ message. The user and the closed facility nodes update their local table by changing the status of f_i to open and the status of f_r to closed, determine a better, if any, closest open facility to join.
3. The medoid informs all other open facilities in the system of the swap by sending CLUSTER_UPDATE$<f_i, f_r>$ message to the medoids of all other clusters. At the event of receiving CLUSTER_UPDATE$<f_i, f_r>$ message, the medoid informs the user and closed facilities nodes in its clusters about the swap.

Algorithm 4. KM Phase 1 - The information about all facilities is disseminated in the network. The user nodes and the closed facilities build a summarised view about the available open facilities in the network.

---

1 **forall the** *open and closed facilities* **do**
2 | Send a facility broadcast message $m = \ <FID, distance = 1, status>$ to all neighbours

---

3 **At event: receiving a facility broadcast message at user node:**
4 **if** *the m.FID is not in the user local table* **then**
5 | Add the message payload <FID, distance, status> to the user local table record
6 | m.distance++
7 | Forward the message m to all neighbours except the source

8 **else if** *the m.distance < the current FID.distance* **then**
9 | Update the local table
10 | m.distance++
11 | Forward the message to all neighbours except the source

12 **else**
13 | Drop the message /* The same message has been received from a longer path*/

---

14 **At event: receiving a broadcast message at an open facility node**
15 m.distance++
16 Forward the message to all neighbours except the source

---

17 **At event: receiving a broadcast message at a closed facility node:**
18 **if** *m.FID is not in the local facility record* **then**
19 | Add the message payload <FID, distance, status> to the user local table record
20 | m.distance++
21 | Forward the message to all neighbours except the source

22 **else if** *the m.distance < the current FID.distance* **then**
23 | Update the local table
24 | m.distance++
25 | Forward the message to all neighbours except the source

26 **else**
27 | Drop the message /* The same message has been received from a longer path*/

4.4 Convergence State

Phases 2 and 3 are repeatedly executed and the clusters medoids are updated continuously until no more update messages are received: in this case the facilities make a transition into the convergence state and the algorithm is terminated in a solution with a locally optimal cost.

Algorithm 5. KM Phase 2 - Find the best f_i to swap

---

1 Initialise The new medoid of the cluster = null
2 **if** *This is an open facility* **then**
3 $\quad$ **forall the** *Users in the cluster* **do**
4 $\quad\quad$ The cost of the cluster += user.cost
5 $\quad\quad$ **forall the** *Closed facilities in the cluster* **do**
6 $\quad\quad\quad$ The cost of the f_i += $user.f_i.cost$
7 $\quad$ **forall the** *Closed facilities in the cluster* **do**
8 $\quad\quad$ **if** *current cluster cost* $< f_i.cost$ **then**
9 $\quad\quad\quad$ The new medoid of the cluster is f_i
10 $\quad$ **if** *The new medoid of the cluster == null* **then**
11 $\quad\quad$ There is no swap

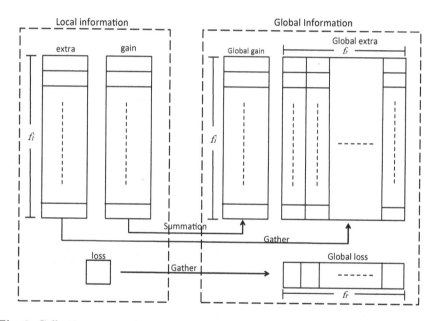

Fig. 3. Collective communication operations (gather and sum) among the open facilities for the aggregation of local information to build a global view

5 Simulation and Experimental Results

A Java-based discrete-event P2P simulation tool called PeerSim [18] is used to simulate the proposed protocols. PeerSim allows simulating large networks with different configurations. In addition to its ability to observe the internal state of nodes in the simulated topology, it allows to keep track of the messages between the facilities and the user nodes. This aids in the performance analysis of the protocols.

Algorithm 6. KM Phase 3 - Update the solution, the current medoid is closed and the determined f_i is opened. All the user nodes in the cluster are informed about the swap as well as all the other medoids in the solution.

1	**if** *This is facility* $== fr$ **then**
2	facility.status = closed
3	send CHANGE-STATUS message to the fi
4	send SWAP $<f_i,f_r>$ message to the join users and the closed facilities to inform them about the close decision
5	send CLUSTER-UPDATE$<f_i,f_r>$ message to the other open facilities in the solution

6 **At event: receiving a swap$<f_i,f_r>$ message**
7 update the user local table
8 determine the closest medoid
9 join the new closest medoid

10 **At event: receiving a change-status message**
11 facility.status = open

12 **At event: receiving facility cluster-update**
13 update the facility local table
14 inform the user nodes about the update

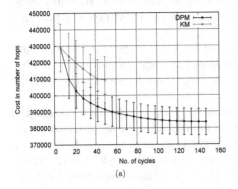
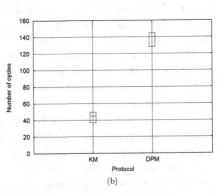

Fig. 4. Convergence analysis: mean and standard deviation over 10 trials (N = 100K, m = 100, p = 25)

The DPM and KM protocols are extensively tested over a range of the network size (up to $500K$ nodes) of artificial and real network topologies.

Figure 4(a) shows the run of both protocols until convergence: the mean and the standard deviation over 10 trials with different randomly chosen initial solutions are shown. The results demonstrate a reduction on the overall cost of the solution at each iteration (swap) until convergence for both protocols. However, KM protocol shows a higher cost of the solution during all cycles. This

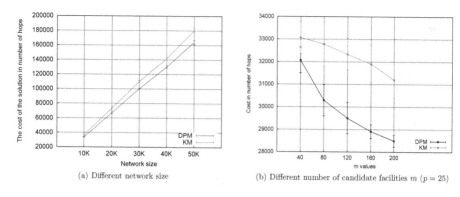

(a) Different network size   (b) Different number of candidate facilities m ($p = 25$)

Fig. 5. Cost (mean and standard deviation) of the solution at convergence

confirms that the DPM protocol based on global knowledge is more effective in improving the solution cost than the KM protocol, which improves the location of the facilities based on local cluster information.

As shown in Fig. 4(b), the KM protocol converges faster than the DPM protocol. However, the DPM protocol is found to be capable to identify better final locations for the facilities.

For testing the DPM and KM on different graphs, many trials were carried out on different network sizes (Fig. 5(a)): the mean cost and the standard deviation of these trials showed for all graph sizes that the DPM protocol provides a lower cost than the KM protocol.

Both protocols are also tested on a varying number (m) of the available candidate locations for the facilities on the same topology. As shown in Fig. 5(b), DPM takes better advantage than KM of the larger search space for the solution of the p-median problem.

Since both the DPM and KM protocols depend on network messages for addressing the p-median problem, the communication overhead in terms of the number of messages is analysed for the different types of messages. As shown in Fig. 6, the most significant number of messages among the nodes is the facility BROADCAST messages. These messages flood the network to propagate information from all facilities to all user nodes.

Practically, each facility is meant to serve nodes in its cluster, typically a local part of the topology. Further investigation has shown that it is unnecessary to forward the broadcast messages to the whole network since it causes a heavy load on the network and an unnecessary delay. Instead, the outreach of the broadcast messages can be restricted to a maximum number of hops (limited time-to-live). This restriction is not affecting the performance of the protocols, while it is significantly reducing the communication cost, as shown in Fig. 6.

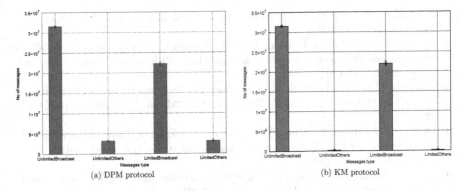

(a) DPM protocol   (b) KM protocol

Fig. 6. Comparison of communication overhead for broadcast and other types of messages, and for unlimited and limited (maximum time-to-live) message propagation (N = 50K, m = 100, p = 25)

6 Conclusions

This paper has presented two novel distributed approaches for the p-median problem in networks. The proposed methods are executed without a prior knowledge of the network topology. Network information, such as the topology and the set of candidate facilities and users, do not need to be gathered for a centralised execution of a sequential algorithm. The computation in the proposed protocols is intrinsically distributed in the network nodes.

A comparative analysis over many simulations has revealed that addressing the location problem for facilities based on a global view of the network (as in DPM) leads to more accurate optimisation of the cost than clustering the network and optimising each facility location based on the local view of each cluster separately (as in KM). However, the former solution takes more cycles to converge.

The simulations have also shown that when more candidate facilities are available, both protocols can find a better solution in terms of cost. Also in this case DPM has confirmed to have better performance in taking advantage of more locations. However, when more locations are available both protocols require additional time to reach convergence.

References

1. Alcaraz, J., Landete, M., Monge, J.F.: Design and analysis of hybrid metaheuristics for the reliability p-median problem. Eur. J. Oper. Res. **222**(1), 54–64 (2012)
2. Melo, M.T., Nickel, S., Saldanha-Da-Gama, F.: Facility location and supply chain management-a review. Eur. J. Oper. Res. **196**(2), 401–412 (2009)
3. Resende, M.G., Werneck, R.F.: A fast swap-based local search procedure for location problems. Ann. Oper. Res. **150**(1), 205–230 (2007)
4. Teitz, M.B., Bart, P.: Heuristic methods for estimating the generalized vertex median of a weighted graph. Oper. Res. **16**(5), 955–961 (1968)

5. Hale, T.S., Moberg, C.R.: Location science research: a review. Ann. Oper. Res. **123**(1-4), 21–35 (2003)
6. Mashayekhi, H., Habibi, J., Khalafbeigi, T., Voulgaris, S., Van Steen, M.: GDCluster: a general decentralized clustering algorithm. IEEE Trans. Knowl. Data Eng. **27**(7), 1892–1905 (2015)
7. Di Fatta, G., Blasa, F., Cafiero, S., Fortino, G.: Epidemic K-means clustering. In: 2011 IEEE 11th International Conference on Data Mining Workshops, pp. 151–158 (2011)
8. Di Fatta, G., Blasa, F., Cafiero, S., Fortino, G.: Fault tolerant decentralised K-means clustering for asynchronous large-scale networks. J. Parallel Distrib. Comput. **73**(3), 317–329 (2013)
9. Alp, O., Erkut, E., Drezner, Z.: An efficient genetic algorithm for the p-median problem. Ann. Oper. Res. **122**(1–4), 21–42 (2003)
10. Labbé, M., Ponce, D., Puerto, J.: A comparative study of formulations and solution methods for the discrete ordered p-median problem. Comput. Oper. Res. **78**, 230–242 (2017)
11. Karatas, M., Razi, N., Tozan, H.: A comparison of p-median and maximal coverage location models with Q-coverage requirement. Procedia Eng. **149**, 169–176 (2016)
12. Marianov, V., Serra, D.: Median problems in networks. In: Eiselt, H., Marianov, V. (eds.) Foundations of Location Analysis, pp. 39–59. Springer, Boston (2011). https://doi.org/10.1007/978-1-4419-7572-0_3
13. Mahmutogullari, A.I., Kara, B.Y.: Hub location under competition. Eur. J. Oper. Res. **250**(1), 214–225 (2016)
14. Hodgson, M.J., Shmulevitz, F., Körkel, M.: Aggregation error effects on the discrete-space p-median model: the case of Edmonton, Canada. Can. Geographer/Le Géographe canadien **41**(4), 415–428 (1997)
15. Whitaker, R.: A fast algorithm for the greedy interchange for large-scale clustering and median location problems. INFOR: Inf. Syst. Oper. Res. **21**(2), 95–108 (1983)
16. Mladenović, N., Brimberg, J., Hansen, P., Moreno-Pérez, J.A.: The p-median problem: a survey of metaheuristic approaches. Eur. J. Oper. Res. **179**(3), 927–939 (2007)
17. Kaufman, L., Rousseeuw, P.: Clustering by means of Medoids. In: Statistical Data Analysis Based on the L_1-Norm and Related Methods, pp. 405–416 (1987)
18. Montresor, A., Jelasity, M.: PeerSim: a scalable P2P simulator. In: IEEE Ninth International Conference on Peer-to-Peer Computing. P2P 2009, pp. 99–100. IEEE (2009)

Clustering Data in Secured, Distributed Datasets

Sayantan Dey$^{(\boxtimes)}$, Lee A. Carraher, Anindya Moitra, and Philip A. Wilsey ⓘ

Department of EECS, University of Cincinnati, Cincinnati, OH 45221, USA
deysn@mail.uc.edu, leecarraher@gmail.com, wilseypa@gmail.com

Abstract. The massive growth in data generation and collection has brought to the forefront the necessity to develop mechanized methods to analyze and extract information from them. Data clustering is one of the fundamental modes to discover new insights from data. However, high dimensional data has its own challenges where many conventional clustering algorithms fails either in accuracy or scalability. To further complicate the issue, distinct subsets of sensitive data may reside in geographically separated locations with the sensitive nature of the data preventing (or inhibiting) its access for mechanized analysis. Thus, methods to discover information from the collective whole of these secured, distributed data sets that also preserves the integrity of the data must be found. In this paper we develop and assess a distributed algorithm that can cluster geographically separated data while simultaneously preserving the strict privacy requirements of non sharing of protected high dimensional data. We implement our algorithm on the distributed map-reduce based platform Spark and demonstrate its performance by comparing it to the standard data clustering algorithms.

Keywords: Data clustering · Data mining · Privacy preserving · Spark · Distributed · Map-reduce

1 Introduction

Many traditional data mining algorithms do not scale well with increases in the sample size or high dimensionality of modern data collection activities. Furthermore, the extreme scaling sizes of the expanding collections of data aggravates an issue in clustering known as *the curse of dimensionality* (or COD) [9]. The COD hinders clustering as the traditional distance matrices that are used for similarity measures can end up rendered meaningless. Another phenomenon in high dimensional big data is that they are sometimes distributed across multiple locations. When these large datasets are geographically distributed they cannot always be easily moved to a central location. Furthermore, in the cases of secure data stored in multiple locations (such as patient medical data), the

Support for this work was provided in part by the National Science Foundation under grant ACI–1440420.

S. Misra et al. (Eds.): ICCSA 2019, LNCS 11624, pp. 557–572, 2019.
https://doi.org/10.1007/978-3-030-24311-1_40

ability to exchange or share the data for analysis may be impossible; even if its common analysis would be significantly beneficial to understanding and identifying important membership classes (clusters) distributed collectively throughout the data sets. This has now become a well known research area by itself and is called *Privacy Preserving Data Mining* [2].

This paper presents a scalable distributed data clustering algorithm that can process very large high-dimensional distributed datasets *without sharing the collective data stored in the secured location.* The algorithm, called RPHash, combines *random projection* with *locality sensitive hashing* (LSH) to provide a scalable solution for clustering high-dimensional distributed datasets. The RPHash algorithm can be embedded in a map-reduce style distributed computing framework and operates without sharing or exchanging the data stored in the distributed locations. Essentially, RPHash distributes common seeds for the algorithms deployed to the remote sites. The local node algorithm uses random projection and LSH to compute candidate centroids and frequency counts for the candidate centroids. The candidate centroids and frequency counts are then combined and reduced at a central site to select specific global candidate centroids as the cluster centers. These selected cluster centers are then retransmitted back to the remote locations where the final steps of the algorithm can associate each local record to its centroid. This algorithm utilizes random projection as a destructive operation and exchanges only probable approximate centroids in the projected dimensional vector space. Thus, information on the specific nature of the original data is obfuscated such that its un-retrievable [11].

This work extends earlier designs of RPHash [12,17] to deliver higher performance, more accurate distributed clustering performance. We apply the concepts of dimensionality reduction, locality sensitive hashing, discrete subspace quantizer lattices and tree based clustering to achieve this capability. Our results demonstrate that our algorithms is fast, accurate and stable. Its accuracy is comparable to other well known standard clustering algorithms such as k-means [18], Kmeans++ [8], SOTA [19], and Ward's Hierarchical agglomerative [27], while being much faster in general. The RPHash software is released under an open source license and is publicically available from git repositories at https://github.com/wilseypa/rphash-java.

This paper is organized as follows. Section 2 summarizes some of the related work done in the area of privacy preserving data mining. Section 3 presents some background information. Section 4 introduces the RPHash algorithm. Section 5 explains the datasets used, experiments performed and comparison of results to standard algorithms. Finally, Sect. 6 contains some concluding remarks.

2   Related Work

The need for distributed Privacy Preserving Data Mining is surveyed in [2]. Most work in this area is based on the application of cryptographic encryption that are basically secure sub-protocols through which the data is exchanged. Two algorithms described in [23] and [22] address distributed clustering. In [23] the authors approximate each feature vector so as to minimize data transmission between nodes and thereby compromising on the accuracy of the result. There is a trade-off between the accuracy and percentage of approximation as seen from their results. They rely on transmitting only the approximation vectors. Jagannathan *et al.* [22] develop an algorithm called K-clustering which is based on the K-Means algorithm. Their algorithm preserves privacy as they do not reveal the intermediate candidate cluster centers.

3 Background

The RPHash algorithms uses *random projection* and *locality sensitive hashing* to improve performance and obfuscate secured data to facilitate privacy preserving data mining. The projection step relies on the bounded error results from the Johnson-Lindenstrauss Lemma (JL-Lemma) [34] and the DB-Friendly projection studies [1] (both projection methods are implemented in the system, but only one is used for any given run). Locality Sensitivity Hashing (LSH) is a family of hashing methods that tend to hash higher-dimensional data to buckets with the goal of mostly placing similar items into the same bucket. For RPHash, the (LSH) function is employed, as a probabilistic representation of vector locality to improve the prohibitive limits of the subspace embedding dimensionality requirements of the JL-Lemma. Stated more formally, an LSH function is any hash function with the property that hashed records with more similar components are more likely to be hashed to the same bucket than records with fewer similarities. That is:

Definition 1 (Locality Sensitive Hash Function [13]). A hash function $h \in \mathbb{H} = \{h : S \to U\}$ is $(r_1, r_2, p_1, p_2) -$ sensitive if for any $u, v \in S$

$$\text{if } d(u,v) \leq r_1 \text{ then } Pr_{\mathbb{H}}[h(u) = h(v)] \geq p_1$$
$$\text{if } d(u,v) > r_2 \text{ then } Pr_{\mathbb{H}}[h(u) = h(v)] \leq p_2$$

Informally, this states that exists a family of hash functions (LSH functions) $\mathbb{H}$. When a vector is hashed by a hash function selected uniformly at random from $\mathbb{H}$, it will hash vectors u and v into the same bucket with a high probability p_1 if their distance is bounded by r_1 and with low probability p_2 if the distance exceeds r_2. While considerable work has gone into finding better and near optimal [6] functions for optimizing the signal to noise ratio for LSH functions, the best solutions often require multiple passes over the data to build data aware functions.

Map-Reduce [15] is a paradigm where an algorithm is written so that it can be efficiently deployed for distributed execution. The distributed computing machines may be locally connected or geographically distributed to form a cluster. The map-reduce framework helps enable the processing of very large datasets in reasonable time. This is achieved by decomposing an algorithm into a map function and a reduce function. The input data is converted into tuples of key-value pairs and segmented into parts. The map function operates on these segmented files of tuples on compute nodes where each segment is assigned. The result of key-value pairs are stored and sorted by the keys. The reducers task takes in all the results from the mappers in parallel sorting them and producing a new combined key, value pair grouped by the same key. The reduce function then applies a user defined function to process this to produce the final results.

Hadoop [36] and Spark [37] are two frameworks or engines for implementing the distributed processing of MapReduce. Spark which was released later than Hadoop also has its streaming API which allows for processing data streams. Spark has more functionalities than Hadoop and is a hundred times faster than Hadoop when computation is in memory and ten times when done on disk.

4   The **RPHash** Algorithms

RPHash [11] is a data clustering algorithm. It can be used for dense region and microcluster identification. This algorithm requires two map-reduce phases for its distributed version implementation. RPHash-TWRP is a version of RPHash that varies its LSH function with the usage and construction of a tree to identify clusters while requiring only one map and reduce phase.

The degenerative cases for LSH k-nearest neighbor search is used for identifying candidate cluster centers in RPHash. In the (RPHash) algorithm, both approximate and randomized techniques are employed to provide a stochastic element to this clustering algorithm. To combat the curse of dimensionality, RPHash performs multi-probe, random projection of high dimensional vectors to the unique partitions of the Leech Lattice (Λ_{24}) [5] or hypersphere surface [30]. Then clustering region assignments are performed by decoding vector points into partitions of the Lattice.

The sequential implementation of the RPHash algorithm relies on the efficient Leech lattice decoder of Vardy, Sun, Be'ery, and Amrani [3,4,29,33] as a discrete space quantizer. The 24 dimensional subspace partitioned by the Leech Lattice is small enough to exhibit the spherical clustering benefit of random projection. Low distortion random embeddings are also feasible for very large dataset objects while avoiding the occultation problem [31]. Projected clustering of representative cluster centroids will not in general be correlated with other projections of data into projected cluster centroids. To recover data from the projection step, we must map projected vectors back to their original un-projected data space counterparts. The original data space vectors is then used to compute centroids corresponding to the clusters in the projected space.

The Distributed version of the RPHash is shown in Algorithms 1 and 2. We assume n nodes are there. x_k is the data vector of a partial dataset X. P denotes the set of projection matrices. H is a LSH function. C is the set of set of bucket collision counts. m and d original and projected dimensions. This approach is inspired from the works of [32] and [10].

In contrast to the original RPHash method that only updates LSH buckets, the RPHash-TWRP method combines bucket updation with a counter that increments the counts of all sub-hashes as well. This bares a slight resemblance

Algorithm 1. 2-Pass RPHash

Data: n: number of compute nodes used

MapPhase 1

forall the *nodes n* **do**
    forall the $x_k \in X$ **do**
        forall the $p_i \in \mathbb{P}$ **do**
            $\tilde{x}_k \leftarrow \sqrt{\frac{m}{d}} p_i^\intercal x_k$
            $t = \mathbb{H}(\tilde{x}_k)$
            $L[k][i] = t$
            $C.\text{add}(t)$

ReducePhase 1

forall the $C_i \in n$ **do**
    get C_i from n nodes
$C = merge(C_i)$

MapPhase 2

forall the *nodes n* **do**
    forall the $x_k \in X$ **do**
        forall the $c_i \in C.top(K)$ **do**
            if $L[k] \cap M[i][0] \neq 0$ **then**
                $\Delta = M[k] - x_k$
                $M[k] = M[k] + \Delta/count$
                $L[k].\text{add}(M[i][0])$
    Result: M_i

ReducePhase 2

forall the $M_i \in n$ **do**
    get M_i from n nodes
$M = merge(M_i)$
Result: M

to Liu *et al.* [24] while adapting their algorithm to work in distributed setting and without using any supervised learning. RPHash-TWRP can use a variety of metrics for the tree splitting condition. Unlike Liu *et al.* RPHash-TWRP does not concern itself with the more complicated to compute C4.5 entropy method, or the possibility of splitting clusters with random hyperplanes. RPHash-TWRP, avoids the latter restriction by virtue of its application to high dimensional data sets and the probability of splitting a cluster going to zero as the dimensionality grows. The theorem below is a consequence of the curse of dimensionality.

Theorem 1 (Hyperrectangle Splitting). *The probability of splitting a hyperrectangular region into two equal mass clusters where subsequent dimensional cuts contain the smaller of the two induced regions region approaches 0 exponentially in d.*

Algorithm 2. Adaptive LSH

$i = 1$

$ct, ct\_prev = C(\mathbb{H}^{i+1}(x)), C(\mathbb{H}^i(x))$

while $i < n$ **and** $2ct > ct\_prev$ **do**

$\quad \lfloor\; ct\_prev, i = ct, i + 1$

$\qquad ct = C(\mathbb{H}^i(x))$

Result: $\mathbb{H}^i(x)$

$$\lim_{d \to \infty} \frac{Vol(R) - Vol_{removed}(R)}{Vol(R)} = 0, \; R \; Rectangle \; \in \mathbb{R}^d. \tag{1}$$

Proof.

Let X s.t. $x_j = [0...c...0] \in \mathbb{R}^d$ is orthogonal, $c \in [0, 1)$,

$\sum\limits_i^n x_i = \mathbb{P}$, is a plane in $\mathbb{R}^d$,

R is a unit hyper-rectangle in $\mathbb{R}^d$ with $Vol(R) = 1$.

Let: $S_1(p)$ be the volume of the projection of R on x_p

If we restrict $S_1(p) + \tilde{S}_1(p) = 1$, $S_1(p) \leq \tilde{S}_1(p)$ for all p we obtain a dimension-wise construction for the volume of the smaller region of a hyhper-rectangle split by a hyperplane.

Next consider the volume of such a hyper-rectangular region $V(R_{s(X)})$

$$V(R_{s(X)}) = \prod_p^n S_1(p) \text{ where } S_1(p) \in U[0, \tfrac{1}{2}).$$

$V(R_{s(X)}) \leq 2^{-n}$ for all n

$\lim\limits_{n \to \infty} 2^{-n} = 0$

$\Rightarrow V(R_{S(X)}) + V(\tilde{R}_{S(X)}) = V(s)$

$V(\tilde{R}_{S(X)}) = V(s)$ as $d \to \infty$ ∎

Algorithms 3 and 4 together constitutes the RPHash-TWRP algorithm, where x denotes a single vector belonging to the dataset X, n is the number of compute nodes, m and d are the projected and original number of feature dimensions, $p \in P$ is the projection matrix, h is the hashed vector obtained by hashing with the hash function H, and C is the set of centroids and hash ids. In the off-line Algorithm 4 we output a overestimate of our centroids denoted by L. We can then use any algorithms such as k-means or Hierarchical Agglomerative to reduce the centroids to the desired number. The algorithm is linear in the input vector size X. For each vector RPHash-TWRP must compute the projection, and update the counter (Algorithm 3). This algorithm introduces two new operations the $+$ to mean population weighted addition, and $\gg$ for the bit shift operation.

Algorithm 3. Tree Generation

$MapPhase$
forall the *nodes* n **do**
    forall the $x \in X$ **do**
        $\tilde{x} = \sqrt{\frac{m}{d}} p^\mathsf{T} x$ `// Projection`
        $h := \mathbb{H}(\tilde{x})$ `// LSH Hashing`
        while $h > 0$ **do**
            $h = h \gg 1$
            $x' = C[h] + x$
            $C.\text{add}(h, x')$

$ReducePhase$
forall the $C_i \in n$ **do**
    get C_i from n nodes
$C = merge(C_i)$
Result: C

Projection using the db friendly approach of Achlioptas [1] can be performed in $dm/3$ operations where d is the original dimensionality, m is the projection sub-dimension. The off-line step consists of exploring and updating the count records (as shown in Algorithm 4). In general it follows a depth first search traversal for candidate clusters with a worse case complexity of exploring all non-leaf nodes, $\theta(2^{m-1})$.

Algorithm 4. Off-line Tree Search

---

forall the $H \in sort(C.ids)$ **do**
    if $2C[H] < C[H \gg 1]$ **then**
        $C[H \gg 1] = 0$
$L = []$
forall the $h \in sort(C.counts)$ **do**
    $L \leftarrow \text{medoid}(C[H])$
return L

4.1 Distributed **RPHash-TWRP** on Spark

The RPHash-TWRP algorithm was implemented on Apache Spark as shown in Fig. 1. It is important to note that the Spark framework was used to suit our need of a framework on which the distributed version can be run. Generally the dataset is maintained on a shared drive and then Spark distributes it to the nodes for use. In our case the data is composed of multiple secured datasets located at the compute site. Thus to make use of the Spark infrastructure, a null RDD (Resilient Distributed Dataset) is created and distributed to satisfy the requirement of Spark. The input to the driver node is the JAVA JAR (Java

ARchive) file containing the code to be run, the file locations, and the number of cluster centers (K) to find. The code generates a seed which it distributes to the worker nodes along with the K parameter and the null RDD created. The JAR is kept at a shared location. The input JAR file had the code that would perform local computations. The driver node or master node distributed the JAR file along with the seed, location of the local files, and the number of clusters. Then the worker nodes run the Map-Phase shown in Algorithm 3 to create the partial tree. These partial trees are then sent back to the driver node. In the reduce phase the driver node merges the received partial trees to form the complete tree. After merging, the driver node executes Algorithm 4 to return the centroids. Thus, for this RPHash-TWRP algorithm only a single Map-Reduce step is required to locate the cluster centroids.

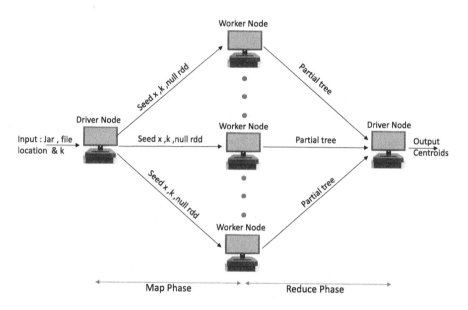

Fig. 1. RPHash-TWRP Map-Reduce implementation architecture on Apache Spark

4.2 Data Security

The important aspect of data security was kept in mind while implementing the algorithms. The algorithms do not transmit any of the original data vectors to remote sites, thereby nullifying any attempts of the attacker who might steal information from the communication channel. It can also be observed from [11] that the probability of getting back the original vector from the projected vector is insignificant. The transferred centroids are just approximations of several data vectors and are not accurate sensitive information that are in the actual data files. This is beneficial for different organizations that do not want to share their own data but get a collective result of the collective data. For example, this algorithm would preserve the HIPPA [20] privacy rules as no patient information would need to be shared and yet provide, for example, the ability to locate common/frequent behaviors/responses to specific trials across multiple hospitals.

5 Experimental Assessment

The experimental assessment of the RPHash-TWRP algorithm consists of both synthetic (with and without noise) and real world test data. Synthetic test data of 10,000 vectors from dimensions 100 to 7,000 were generated. Each data set has 10 Gaussian clusters with labels recorded for all points. We also generated data sets with varying amount of noise. We chose the dimensionality of 1000 and then injected noise varying from 5 to 40% in increments of 5. To generate them we first generated a dataset with no noise and then we replaced the specified percentage of vectors with randomly generated vectors but preserving the original label. Four datasets of 1,000 dimensions having 300,000, 600,000, 900,000 and 1,200,000 vectors with 5% noise and 20 clusters each were also generated.

We also used five real world datasets to test the performance of RPHash-TWRP. These data sets are all available at the UCI machine learning repository.

1. The *Human Activity Recognition Using Smartphones (HAR)* dataset taken from [7] consists of 10,299 vectors containing 561 features comprising of 6 clusters.
2. The *Smartphone Dataset for Human Activity Recognition (HAR) in Ambient Assisted Living (HARAAL)* dataset [14] has 5,744 vectors and 561 features. It has 6 clusters.
3. The *gene expression cancer RNA-Seq Data Set (RNASEQ)* dataset is taken from [16]. It has 801 vectors and 20,531 features and 4 clusters.
4. The *Smartphone-Based Recognition of Human Activities and Postural Transitions Data Set (HAPT)* dataset taken from [28] has 10,929 vectors and 561 features. This data has 12 clusters.
5. The *Gas Sensor Array Drift (GSAD)* dataset [35] has 13910 vectors and 128 features. It is composed of 6 clusters.

5.1 Algorithms Used for Comparison

We compared the performance our RPHash-TWRP against seven standard well known algorithms.

- *K-Means*: This algorithm of Hartigan and Wong [18] is implemented with the function k-means in R [25].
- Four methods of *Agglomerative Hierarchical clustering*, namely: Single Linkage, Complete Linkage, Average Linkage and Ward's algorithm of minimum variance method [27]. We have used the function hclust in R for implementing these algorithms.

- *Self-organizing Tree Algorithm* (SOTA): This algorithm is based on neural network. It is implemented using the 'sota' (Package 'clValid') in R [25].
- The parallel Spark implementation of *K-Means++* available in Spark *MLlib* for the distributed datasets.

These algorithms are selected due of their importance, popularity and availability in R statistical computing framework. These algorithms use FORTRAN, C and C++ subroutines from R to make them run faster. The implementation language of RPHash is Java.

5.2   Hardware Platforms

We captured the run times (in secs) for the scalability study on the synthetic and the real world datasets. They were run on a 16 core Intel(R) Xeon(R) E5-2670 @ 2.6 GHz with 64 GB RAM. For the Spark compute platform, we created the cluster with three machines. Two identical machines composed of an Intel Core(TM)i7-4770 CPU with 4 cores @ 3.40 GHz and having 32 GB memory. The third machine composed of an Intel Core(TM)W3550 CPU with 4 cores @ 3.07 GHz with 16 GB memory.

5.3   Experiment Methodology

Each of the configurations of RPHash-TWRP is tested on all the synthetically generated labeled data sets. The combination of parameters that produces the most consistent and best clustering accuracy on the data set is chosen as the optimal configuration for them for that synthetic dataset. We then chose the most common configuration for the noise test, where we ran RPHash-TWRP on the synthetically generated noise datasets. Finally, We also tested the algorithms on the real world datasets.

This configuration having projected dimension of 16, and offline cluster of Agglomerative clustering for RPHash-TWRP was implemented for the distributed version on spark platform and tested on the same datasets. The datasets were split into approximately three equal parts and kept in the three machines. These partial datasets were local to each machines. Spark was setup in the standalone mode.

5.4   Experimental Results

The clustering accuracy of RPHash is evaluated using 2 external clustering validation measures: Adjusted Rand Index (ARI) and Cluster Purity. We also use the internal measure, WCSS for evaluation. ARI [21] measures the extent to which points from the same ground-truth partition appear in the same cluster, and the extent to which points from different ground-truth partitions are grouped in different clusters. Cluster purity [26] measures how many data points were correctly assigned to its original cluster. WCSS (also called WCSSE or SSE) is the within cluster sum of squared error. A lower value of WCSS indicates better clustering performance. It is basically the objective function that k-means algorithm tries to minimize in order to find suitable clusters.

Because of the stochastic nature of RPHash-TWRP, we run every configuration of the algorithm 6 times on all data sets and compute the mean and standard deviation of the measures. Similarly, K-means is also run 6 times and means and standard deviation are recorded. The other algorithms are run once as they are deterministic.

The measured ARI, PURITY and WCSS for the synthetic datasets are plotted in Fig. 2. We observed, that, RPHash-TWRP has the value of 1 for ARI and PURITY for all these datasets, indicating perfect clustering. RPHash-TWRP's WCSS also matches the baseline WCSS (*i.e.*, the actual WCSS for a dataset) for these synthetic data.

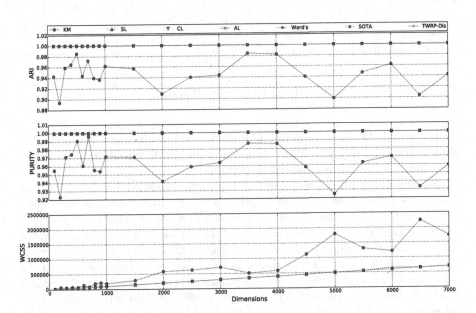

Fig. 2. ARI, Purity and WCSS Plotted Against Increasing dimension. The legend abbreviations for this and all plots are: KM: k-means (Hartigan and Wong), SL: Single Linkage Agglomerative, CL: Complete Linkage Agglomerative, AL: Average Linkage Agglomerative, Wards's: Ward's algorithm, and TWRP-Dis: RPHash-TWRP distributed

For the noise injected data, ARI, and WCSS are plotted in Fig. 3. The WCSS of RPHash-TWRP is lower than single, average and complete linkage and SOTA algorithms. RPHash-TWRP also performs comparably to the other clustering algorithms in terms of ARI. As the noise grows to 40% (when the signal itself is poor) all the algorithms tend to perform poorly.

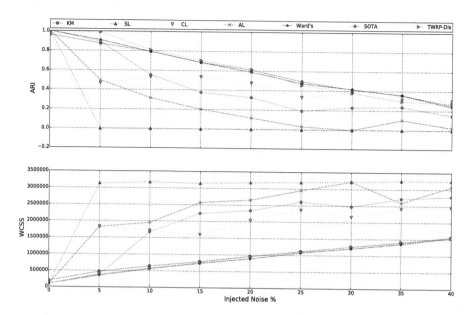

Fig. 3. ARI and WCSS plotted against noise

The results for the real world HAR dataset are summarized in Fig. 4. The results show that RPHash-TWRP, K-means, and Wards algorithm have similar performances. In contrast, single link performs poorly.

The scalability results are shown in Table 1 for the synthetic data sets from dimensions 100 to 7,000. RPHash-TWRP shows very little growth as the dimension increases. The same cannot be said of the other algorithms as we know that their time complexity depends on the data dimensionality. We also tested the run time of our algorithms as we increased the number of vectors keeping the dimension fixed at 1,000 as shown in Fig. 5. We see a linear growth in the run time of RPHash-TWRP and it is more than 10 times faster than the Sparks default K-Means++. Interestingly, in all cases, RPHash-TWRP has higher external measure accuracy than distributed K-Means++.

Table 1. Scalability with respect to dimension.(Run time in secs)

Dim.	100	500	1K	2K	3K	4K	5K	6K	7K
Time	7.54	7.87	8.51	10.73	13.39	13.78	15.14	17.24	19.8

Dataset	Measures	ARI	Purity	WCSS	Time
HAR	k-means	0.4610	0.6002	182 169	66.33
	SL	0.0000	0.1890	556 519	493.95
	CL	0.3270	0.3770	222 044	494.47
	AL	0.3321	0.3588	236 143	494.21
	Ward's	0.4909	0.6597	191 441	494.64
	SOTA	0.3143	0.3966	210 490	23.63
	RPHash-TWRP-Dis	0.4788	0.6407	189 817	7.69
HAPT	k-means	0.3988	0.6498	2 498 381	182.90
	SL	0.0003	0.1821	6 023 519	601.98
	CL	0.0488	0.2505	4 584 352	602.42
	AL	0.0055	0.2046	5 491 388	602.04
	Ward's	0.4033	0.6624	2 617 769	602.68
	SOTA	0.3026	0.3848	2 990 195	31.13
	RPHash-TWRP-Dis	0.3698	0.6119	2 780 331	8.06
HARAAL	k-means	0.2461	0.4240	1 618 089	23.55
	SL	0.0000	0.1964	3 166 056	148.43
	CL	0.0003	0.2002	3 043 579	148.53
	AL	0.0001	0.1972	3 097 976	148.45
	Ward's	0.2764	0.3929	1 653 179	148.58
	SOTA	0.2370	0.3785	1 814 593	12.30
	RPHash-TWRP-Dis	0.2953	0.3887	1 913 092	7.41
Gas-Sensor	k-means	0.1539	0.4427	27 714 236 160 297	9.05
	SL	0.0000	0.2165	192 076 751 899 323	42.61
	CL	0.0380	0.3474	47 050 045 285 192	42.57
	AL	0.0037	0.2865	75 622 509 139 114	42.45
	Ward's	0.2007	0.4378	31 162 058 051 998	42.87
	SOTA	0.0281	0.3435	46 727 103 818 336	11.93
	RPHash-TWRP-Dis	0.1759	0.4426	55 266 567 437 976	6.11
RNASEQ	k-means	0.6438	0.8402	12 834 131	180.32
	SL	0.0007	0.3783	16 007 266	97.10
	CL	−0.0124	0.3758	15 692 260	97.10
	AL	0.0007	0.3783	16 007 266	97.08
	Ward's	0.5955	0.8202	12 916 461	97.09
	SOTA	0.3205	0.6317	13 632 923	87.72
	RPHash-TWRP-Dis	0.4770	0.7416	21 363 363	10.7

Fig. 4. Performance for real data sets

Data Size	Algorithm	ARI	Purity	Time
300K	k-means++parallel spark	0.8134	0.8247	655.0
	RPHash-TWRP	0.997	0.999	58.5
600K	k-means++parallel spark	0.8533	0.8750	1265
	RPHash-TWRP	0.997	0.998	111.0
900K	k-means++parallel spark	0.8809	0.9136	1905
	RPHash-TWRP	0.998	0.999	162.0
1.2M	k-means++parallel spark	0.8496	0.8728	2808
	RPHash-TWRP	0.998	0.999	212.0

Fig. 5. Scalability and measures with respect to size of dataset (seconds)

6 Conclusions

In this work we introduced the distributed version of the Tree-Walk addition to the RPHash algorithm (RPHash-TWRP) for clustering large datasets with log-linear processing complexity. We implemented RPHash-TWRP on the distributed platform Spark using Map-Reduce framework and evaluated it using real world datasets, synthetic data, and synthetic data with variable noise percentage. The results show that RPHash-TWRP performs comparable to various other common standard clustering methods. In tests with synthetic data with noise, we find that our method outperforms other standard implementation of K-Means++ from the spark library MLlib in both run time and accuracy. RPHash-TWRP exhibited more stability when compared to k-Means.

The complexity measures of our method shows that it scales well both in time and space complexity, with very little loss in clustering performance accuracy. The overall scalability is predictable and does not hide large constants. RPHash-TWRP is designed to process very large high dimensional distributed clustering problems while preserving privacy. The results shows that RPHash-TWRP achieves this goal by means of its running time, scalability and accuracy.

References

1. Achlioptas, D.: Database-friendly random projections. In: Proceedings of the 20th Symposium on Principles of Database Systems, pp. 274–281 (2001)
2. Aggarwal, C.C., Yu, P.S. (eds.): Privacy-Preserving Data Mining: Models and Algorithms. Springer, Boston (2008). https://doi.org/10.1007/978-0-387-70992-5
3. Amrani, O., Be'ery, Y.: Efficient bounded-distance decoding of the hexacode and associated decoders for the Leech lattice and the Golay code. IEEE Trans. Commun. **44**(5), 534–537 (1996)
4. Amrani, O., Be'ery, Y., Vardy, A., Sun, F.W., van Tilborg, H.C.A.: The Leech lattice and the Golay code: bounded-distance decoding and multilevel constructions. IEEE Trans. Inf. Theory **40**(4), 1030–1043 (1994)
5. Andoni, A.: Nearest neighbor search: the old, the new, and the impossible. Ph.D. thesis, Massachusetts Institute of Technology, September (2009)
6. Andoni, A., Indyk, P.: Near-optimal hashing algorithms for approximate nearest neighbor in high dimensions. In: 47th Annual IEEE Symposium on Foundations of Computer Science. FOCS 2006, pp. 459–468 (2006)
7. Anguita, D., Ghio, A., Oneto, L., Parra, X., Reyes-Ortiz, J.L.: UCI machine learning repository (2012). https://archive.ics.uci.edu/ml/datasets/Human+Activity+Recognition+Using+Smartphones
8. Arthur, D., Vassilvitskii, S.: K-means++: the advantages of careful seeding. In: Proceedings of the Eighteenth Annual ACM-SIAM Symposium on Discrete Algorithms, SODA 2007, pp. 1027–1035. Society for Industrial and Applied Mathematics, Philadelphia, PA, USA (2007), http://dl.acm.org/citation.cfm?id=1283383.1283494
9. Bellman, R.E. (ed.): Adaptive Control Processes: A Guided Tour. Princeton University Press, Princeton (1961)
10. Cafaro, M., Tempesta, P.: Finding frequent items in parallel. Concurr. Comput.: Pract. Exper. **23**(15), 1774–1788 (2011). https://doi.org/10.1002/cpe.1761

11. Carraher, L.A., Wilsey, P.A., Moitra, A., Dey, S.: Multi-probe random projection clustering to secure very large distributed datasets. In: 2nd International Workshop on Privacy and Security of Big Data, October (2015)

12. Carraher, L.A., Wilsey, P.A., Moitra, A., Dey, S.: Random projection clustering on streaming data. In: IEEE 16th International Conference on Data Mining Workshops (ICDMW), December, pp. 708–715 (2016)

13. Datar, M., Immorlica, N., Indyk, P., Mirrokni, V.S.: Locality-sensitive hashing scheme based on p-stable distributions. In: Proceedings of the twentieth annual symposium on Computational geometry, SCG 2004, pp. 253–262. ACM, New York (2004). https://doi.org/10.1145/997817.997857

14. Davis, K.A., Owusu, E.B.: UCI machine learning repository (2016). https://arch ive.ics.uci.edu/ml/datasets/Smartphone+Dataset+for+Human+Activity+Recogn ition+%28HAR%29+in+Ambient+Assisted+Living+%28AAL%29

15. Dean, J., Ghemawat, S.: MapReduce: simplified data processing on large clusters. Commun. ACM 51(1), 107–113 (2008)

16. Fiorini, S.: UCI machine learning repository (2016). https://archive.ics.uci.edu/ ml/datasets/gene+expression+cancer+RNA-Seq

17. Franklin, J., Wenke, S., Quasem, S., Carraher, L.A., Wilsey, P.A.: streamingR-PHash: random projection clustering of high-dimensional data in a mapreduce framework. In: IEEE Cluster 2016, September (2016). (poster)

18. Hartigan, J.A., Wong, M.A.: A k-means clustering algorithm. JSTOR: Appl. Stat. 28(1), 100–108 (1979)

19. Herrero, J., Valencia, A., Dopazo, J.: A hierarchical unsupervised growing neural network for clustering gene expression patterns (2001)

20. Health insurance portability and accountability act (2004). http://www.hhs.gov/ ocr/hipaa/

21. Hubert, L., Arabie, P.: Comparing partitions. J. Classif. 2(1), 193–218 (1985)

22. Jagannathan, G., Pillaipakkamnatt, K., Wright, R.N.: A new privacy-preserving distributed k-clustering algorithm. In: Proceedings of the 2006 SIAM International Conference on Data Mining, pp. 494–498 (2006). https://doi.org/10.1137/ 1.9781611972764.47

23. Kriegel, H.-P., Kunath, P., Pfeifle, M., Renz, M.: Approximated clustering of distributed high-dimensional data. In: Ho, T.B., Cheung, D., Liu, H. (eds.) PAKDD 2005. LNCS (LNAI), vol. 3518, pp. 432–441. Springer, Heidelberg (2005). https:// doi.org/10.1007/11430919_51

24. Liu, B., Xia, Y., Yu, P.S.: Clustering through decision tree construction. In: Proceedings of the Ninth International Conference on Information and Knowledge Management, CIKM 2000, pp. 20–29. ACM, New York (2000). https://doi.org/10. 1145/354756.354775

25. Maechler, M., Rousseeuw, P., Struyf, A., Hubert, M., Hornik, K.: cluster: Cluster Analysis Basics and Extensions (2013). (r package version 1.14.4)

26. Manning, C.D., Raghavan, P., Schütze, H.: Introduction to Information Retrieval. Cambridge University Press, Cambridge (2008)

27. Murtagh, F., Legendre, P.: Ward's hierarchical agglomerative clustering method: which algorithms implement Ward's criterion? J. Classif. 31(3), 274–295 (2014). https://doi.org/10.1007/s00357-014-9161-z

28. Reyes-Ortiz, J.L., Oneto, L., Sam, A., Parra, X., Anguita, D.: UCI machine learning repository (2015). https://archive.ics.uci.edu/ml/datasets/Smartphone-Based+Recognition+of+Human+Activities+and+Postural+Transitions

29. Sun, F.W., van Tilborg, H.C.A.: The Leech lattice, the octacode, and decoding algorithms. IEEE Trans. Inf. Theory 41(4), 1097–1106 (1995)

30. Terasawa, K., Tanaka, Y.: Spherical LSH for approximate nearest neighbor search on unit hypersphere. In: WADS, pp. 27–38 (2007)
31. Urruty, T., Djeraba, C., Simovici, D.A.: Clustering by random projections. In: Perner, P. (ed.) ICDM 2007. LNCS (LNAI), vol. 4597, pp. 107–119. Springer, Heidelberg (2007). https://doi.org/10.1007/978-3-540-73435-2_9
32. Vaidya, J., Clifton, C.: Privacy preserving association rule mining in vertically partitioned data. In: Proceedings of the Eighth ACM SIGKDD International Conference on Knowledge Discovery and Data Mining, KDD 2002, pp. 639–644. ACM, New York (2002). https://doi.org/10.1145/775047.775142
33. Vardy, A.: Even more efficient bounded-distance decoding of the hexacode, the Golay code, and the Leech lattice. IEEE Trans. Inf. Theory **41**(5), 1495–1499 (1995)
34. Vempala, S.S.: The Random Projection Method. DIMACS Series. American Mathematical Society, Providence (2004)
35. Vergara, A., Fonollosa, J., Rodriguez-Lujan, I., Huerta, R.: UCI machine learning repository (2013). https://archive.ics.uci.edu/ml/datasets/Gas+Sensor+Array+Drift+Dataset+at+Different+Concentrations
36. White, T.: Hadoop: The Definitive Guide. O'Reilly Media Inc., Sebastopol (2009)
37. Zaharia, M., et al.: Apache spark: a unified engine for big data processing. Commun. ACM **59**(11), 56–65 (2016). https://doi.org/10.1145/2934664

Correction to: Hypergeometric Polynomials, Hyperharmonic Discrete and Continuous Expansions: Evaluations, Interconnections, Extensions

Cecilia Coletti, Federico Palazzetti, Roger W. Anderson,
Vincenzo Aquilanti, Noelia Faginas-Lago, and Andrea Lombardi

Correction to:
Chapter "Hypergeometric Polynomials, Hyperharmonic
Discrete and Continuous Expansions: Evaluations,
Interconnections, Extensions" in: S. Misra et al. (Eds.):
Computational Science and Its Applications – ICCSA 2019,
LNCS 11624, https://doi.org/10.1007/978-3-030-24311-1_34

The original version of this chapter was inadvertently published without two authors who contributed to the chapter also. The missing authors were Noelia Faginas-Lago and Andrea Lombardi. Their names and affiliations have now been added and the correct sequence of the authors is: Cecilia Coletti, Federico Palazzetti, Roger W. Anderson, Vincenzo Aquilanti, Noelia Faginas-Lago and Andrea Lombardi.

The updated version of this chapter can be found at
https://doi.org/10.1007/978-3-030-24311-1_34

© Springer Nature Switzerland AG 2021
S. Misra et al. (Eds.): ICCSA 2019, LNCS 11624, p. C1, 2021.
https://doi.org/10.1007/978-3-030-24311-1_41

Author Index

Printed in the United States
By Bookmasters